American vision

The films of Frank Capra

Translating words into moving pictures and visions into vision: Frank Capra in 1934, at the time he made *It Happened One Night*.

American vision

The films of Frank Capra

RAYMOND CARNEY
Stanford Humanities Center

The right of the
University of Cambridge
to print and sell
all manner of books
was granted by
Henry VIII in 1534.
The University has printed
and published continuously
since 1584.

CAMBRIDGE UNIVERSITY PRESS

CAMBRIDGE

LONDON   NEW YORK   NEW ROCHELLE

MELBOURNE   SYDNEY

Published by the Press Syndicate of the University of Cambridge
The Pitt Building, Trumpington Street, Cambridge CB2 1RP
32 East 57th Street, New York, NY 10022, USA
10 Stamford Road, Oakleigh, Melbourne 3166, Australia

First published 1986

Printed in the United States of America

Library of Congress Cataloging-in-Publication Data
Carney, Raymond.
American vision.
Filmography: p.
Bibliography: p.
Includes index.
1. Capra, Frank, 1897–   – Criticism and interpretation.
I. Title.
PN1998.A3C26145   1987   791.43′0233′0924   86–14800

British Library Cataloguing in Publication Data
Carney, Raymond
American vision : the films of Frank Capra.
1. Capra, Frank – Criticism and interpretation
I. Title
791.43′0233′0924   PN1998.A3C26

ISBN 0 521 32619 2

To my dear friend William Harris

An American dreamer in the tradition
of Frank Capra and John Cassavetes

Contents

I'm a rebel against control of any kind. I'm a bad organization man. I like to be my own man and I don't like somebody else to tell me what to do. It was just the natural rebel in me that I couldn't take orders.

– Frank Capra, Interview with Richard Glatzer

There sits the old master, over in Europe. Like a parent. Somewhere deep in every American heart lies a rebellion against the old parenthood of Europe ... America has never been easy, and is not easy today. Americans have always been at a certain tension. Their liberty is a thing of sheer will, sheer tension ... Men are free when they belong to a living, organic, *believing* community, active in fulfilling some unfulfilled, perhaps unrealized purpose. Not when they are escaping to some wild west. The most unfree souls go west, and shout of freedom. Men are freest when they are most unconscious of freedom. The shout is always a rattling of chains, always was.

– D. H. Lawrence, Studies in Classic American Literature

Preface: American modernism and the movies

> The furthest frenzies of French modernism or futurism have not yet reached the pitch of extreme consciousness that Poe, Melville, Hawthorne, and Whitman reached. The European moderns are all *trying* to be extreme. The great Americans I mention just were it.
>
> – D. H. Lawrence, *Studies in Classic American Literature*

Frank Capra made thirty-six feature films between 1926 and 1961. There are few filmgoers who have not at some time been deeply affected by one or more of them. The maker of *It's a Wonderful Life, Mr. Smith Goes to Washington, Meet John Doe, Lost Horizon, It Happened One Night, Mr. Deeds Goes to Town, Pocketful of Miracles,* and twenty-nine other movies is probably America's best-known and most beloved filmmaker. This book is, in the first place, an homage to that achievement and an expression of gratitude for what these films have taught us about ourselves and our world.

Capra's work has had a profound emotional and psychological effect on more than three generations of American audiences. One naturally wonders why these particular films have spoken so powerfully to so many different viewers over so many years. How is it that a Sicilian immigrant, working for a minor, "poverty row" Hollywood studio,* and expressing himself in the most relentlessly compromised of art forms – popular film – could have made so many things that still matter to us? The attempt to answer that question is the second subject of this book. What makes these films so appealing and emotionally arresting? What allows them to speak so compellingly to so many of us even today?

I believe the power of Capra's work, especially for American audiences, is a result of the fact that he was – unconsciously, no doubt – making films that explore certain prototypical imaginative situations that are deeply ingrained in the American experience. In his personal struggles with the institutional

---

* Capra made twenty-five films at Columbia Pictures, which he almost singlehandedly transformed into a major studio in the process of making his movies there.

bureaucracies of the studio system and his artistic struggles with the formal constraints of Hollywood feature filmmaking, Capra transformed himself into what Emerson would have called a representative man of his culture, in all of the expressive glory and frustration of that situation. The films can be read as his spiritual autobiography, his ongoing reflections on the predicament in which he found himself as he made them and in which so many other Americans find themselves in their daily lives in the imaginative force field of American society.

To talk about Capra's life and work as in some way representative of a general American expressive predicament requires locating the films within a larger tradition of post-Romantic expression, particularly with respect to specific works of nineteenth- and twentieth-century American literature, drama, art, philosophy, and history. Capra's work must be considered alongside the work of Hawthorne, Emerson, Homer, Whitman, Eakins, James, Sargent, and Hopper, to name only the most obvious examples. I want to emphasize that in making comparisons between the work of Capra and these other artists I am not trying to equate their respective achievements or to dignify Capra with a fancy intellectual pedigree. Above all, I am not suggesting any direct influence on Capra's films and would, in fact, be quite surprised if Capra could be shown even to have heard of the work of most of these artists. My purpose is rather to map a common imaginative territory that all these American artists inhabit and of which their individual works are the most detailed surviving surveys. My attempt, though I have no illusions about its definitiveness, is to chart some sort of rough geography of the imaginative world that Capra, his audiences, and these other American artists share and that they are mutually engaged in trying to understand and explore.

I would call this territory and tradition (there are other, coexisting traditions and ways of feeling and seeing within the culture that are not considered here) the realm of American modernism, but what is meant by such a term is far from obvious. Most of our notions of modernism and post-Romantic expression have been imported from abroad as descriptions of artistic movements that originated on the other side of the Atlantic and of artists working in what are inevitably somewhat alien expressive traditions. There are thus two general problems with which to contend: The first is that since there is no generally accepted concept of American modernism (or American Romanticism) upon which to draw, a considerable portion of my argument will have to be devoted to offering some speculations on this fairly elusive subject. The second obstacle is that since our prevailing notions of modernism have been taken chiefly from European models, my argument will often need to differentiate between the two traditions in order to establish the *distinctive* character of American modernism.★

★ The question as to why this "European bias" should exist in the first place is an interesting one, which there is unfortunately not sufficient space to go into here and now. Suffice it to say that it is a result of diverse factors, ranging from the kinds of critical training and attitudes present in American universities, to the general resistance of most American art and artists to critical

The argument of this book is that the American figures I have named, and others, do define a coherent – if diverse and complex – modernist sensibility that unconsciously informs the work of Capra,★ helps us to understand it, and gives it its power over us. It is a modernism that deviates at several points from the forms of modernism in the works of the major European artists roughly contemporaneous with that of the Americans I have named, at the same time as it admittedly also has many qualities in common with the modernist agenda of such artists as Flaubert, Proust, Joyce, Beckett, Antonioni, and Fellini.

There are many reasons why, to eyes trained in the European traditions, the works of the Americans I have named, and the works of Capra above all, just do not look "modern." The American texts do not appear to be as sophisticated or "advanced" as I would argue they actually are. The very essence of the American position is its antitheoretical, practical, and pragmatic qualities. It avoids many of the world-forsaking tendencies, the aesthetic elitism, the cultivation of the isolated artistic sensibility, and the cult of the artist as sage and visionary of the European positions. It is socially engaged in ways that make the European traditions seem at times comparatively escapist or hermetic. That is why, until quite recently, Eakins has patronizingly been regarded as a "realist," Sargent as a "society portraitist," and Homer more or less as a "primitive," just as Capra has been patronized as a "populist." It is not surprising that the examples of American modernism that *are* recognized and admitted for study are those like John Cage, Maya Deren, Robert Wilson, or Nam June Paik (to name as wide a range of artistic accomplishments as possible), whose art, I would argue, is generally European-derived or -influenced and more or less outside of the particular tradition that I am describing as defining a great native American tradition.

All of this will take a good deal more specification in order to be clear, and a book on the American tradition in nineteenth- and early twentieth-century painting will follow this one to continue and refine the argument conducted here. Briefly put, my goal in the following pages is a double one: to describe Capra both as a kindred artistic spirit working in the tradition of Emerson, James, Eakins, and Hopper and as a filmmaker whose movies were instantly and naively recognized by the American filmgoing public of the 1930s and 1940s, most of whom had never heard of these other American artists and who simply laughed or cried in the dark without any awareness of this artistic tradition. American modernism is not something Capra or Capra's audiences had to study or learn, then or now. It is what they lived and breathed and dreamed about, and unconsciously accepted or fought against as the expressive reality of their lives. It is what we are born into in this culture, whether we

theorizing of any sort – which then leaves them and their works victims by default of other cultures' critical theorizing, to what can only, even at this late date in American studies, be called a continuing artistic inferiority complex on this side of the Atlantic.

★ As well as informing the work of John Cassavetes and other more recent filmmakers, as I argue in a companion volume: *American Dreaming: The Films of John Cassavetes and the American Experience* (Berkeley: University of California Press, 1985).

want to be or not. It is a quality of consciousness and expressiveness that no one who lives in the society of the American dream and nightmare can entirely avoid, and, as we shall see, it is something that is speakable even in America's most compromised and commercialized art. Perhaps, it is supremely speakable in such an emphatically impure form of artistic expression as a Hollywood movie.

Acknowledgments

I am profoundly indebted to Jeanine Basinger, curator of the Frank Capra Archives at Wesleyan University, for her tireless assistance and unfailing encouragement of this project. Charles Wolfe generously read the entire manuscript and offered many corrections and suggestions. Kit Parker, the president of Kit Parker Films, provided prints of many of Capra's early films for viewing.

Douglas Sprigg of the Department of Theater at Middlebury College discussed twentieth-century acting strategies with me, and Christopher Wilson of the Department of Art directed my reading on American painting. Charles Silver at the Museum of Modern Art made screening facilities available on short notice, as did Barbara Humphrys at the Library of Congress.

For illustrative materials, I am grateful to a number of individuals: to Mary Corliss at the Museum of Modern Art for film stills from Capra's work; to Robert B. Ray of the University of Florida for frame enlargements from *It's a Wonderful Life*; to John Wilmerding of the National Gallery, Paul Mellon, Jim Hanelius, and James Thomson, all of whom personally extended themselves in various ways to help me obtain material.

My typists, Edith Illick and Mary Longey, performed above and beyond the call of duty in helping to prepare the manuscript, and the individuals at Cambridge University Press with whom I worked in the production of this project – Elizabeth Maguire, Jeanne Burke, Michael Gnat, and Christie Lerch – have been consistently helpful and supportive. I thank them all.

R. C.
Middlebury, Vermont

PART I

A preview and an overview

That Certain Thing, 1928
The Way of the Strong, 1928
The Younger Generation, 1929
Lady for a Day, 1933
Meet John Doe, 1941
The Name above the Title, 1971

1

Frank Capra and American Romanticism

What is I believe called Idealism seems to me to suggest ... the course of inquiry and desert of favor for our New World metaphysics, their foundation of and in literature, giving hue to all. The elevating and etherealizing ideas of the unknown and of unreality must be brought forward with authority, as they are the legitimate heirs of the known, and of reality, and at least as great as their parents. Fearless of scoffing ... let us take our stand, our ground, and never desert it, to confront the growing excess and arrogance of realism. To the cry, now victorious – the cry of sense, science, flesh, income, farms, merchandise, logic, intellect, demonstrations, solid perpetuities, buildings of brick and iron ... fear not, my brethren, my sisters, to sound out with equally determined voice ... illusions! apparitions! figments all! True, we must not condemn the show, neither absolutely deny it, for the indispensability of its meanings; but how clearly we see that, migrate in soul to what we can already conceive of superior and spiritual points of view, and palpable as it seems under present relations, it all and several might, nay certainly would, fall apart and vanish.

— Walt Whitman, *Democratic Vistas*

It is useful and only a slight simplification, to make a fundamental distinction between two alternative traditions of mainstream American feature film-making in order to suggest an essential difference between Frank Capra's work, which emanates out of the one, and that of most other major Hollywood directors of the thirties and forties, which emanates out of the other. If one calls them the complementary lines of "idealistic" and "pragmatic" filmmaking, it is to suggest that they parallel a split in the American artistic and popular consciousness that can be traced back at least as far as the eighteenth century, in, say, the difference between the writing of Jonathan Edwards on the one hand and that of Benjamin Franklin or William Byrd on the other, a difference that is repeated in a finer tone in the early twentieth century in the difference between the work of Henry James and that of Edith Wharton. What Edwards and James represent (along with Hawthorne, Emerson, Whitman, William James, Faulkner, Mailer, and Capra), notwithstanding all of the other differences that distinguish these artists, is a visionary, idealistic, romantic strain within our culture. In contrast, Franklin, Byrd, and Wharton (along with Dreiser, Dos Passos, and filmmaking contemporaries of

3

Capra such as Hawks, Cukor, Lubitsch, Stevens, Wellman, and Wyler, and, more recently, Ritt, Pakula, Kramer, and Pollack) represent an opposite sensibility – a commitment to the authority of practical and realistic forms and forces that exclude or resist the individual imagination or severely limit its power and range of expression.

To some extent this distinction is not absolute, since the strongest work of each type to some degree includes the feelings of the other. Dreiser, Henry James, and Emerson are only the most obvious examples of artists whose work is, at times, almost torn apart by the antinomies it holds in suspension. However, it is important to insist on the essential difference in emphasis of the two tendencies, since if, as I will subsequently argue, Capra's work itself contains both tendencies, expressing the energies of both imaginative idealism and social practicality, it is his extreme idealism that makes his work most distinctive and that separates it from the vast body of other American film, both contemporaneous with it and subsequent to it.

The work of "idealistic" filmmakers like Capra (though Chaplin, Ford, Von Sternberg, McCarey, Curtiz, Ray, John Cassavetes, and several others might also be used as examples) differs from that of "pragmatic" filmmakers like Hawks, Lubitsch, Cukor, Wyler, and Sturges (or from the whole group of postwar "realistic" filmmakers) in the different valuation it gives to the claims of the energies of individual imagination and desire and the counterpointed forces of society, space, time, and history. It is not that either tradition of filmmaking simply eliminates the forces central to the other but that each weighs differently the competing pulls of the pressure of individual imagination and desires on the one hand, and the responsibilities of social expression and interaction on the other. To compare Capra only with the two filmmakers who were the greatest contemporaneous practitioners of the other sort of filmmaking, Hawks and Sturges, they more often than not corrode and interrogate romantic ideals in the course of their films and gradually replace them with flexible, unillusioned, practical social arrangements among the characters, whereas Capra does the opposite. At the beginning of his films his characters may be embedded in elaborate and highly articulated societies (and indeed in the course of the films they are never allowed to completely remove themselves from these groups), but as the films go on, the societies they constitute and the network of personal relationships they define are progressively criticized. At their most radical and most successful, Capra's films gradually make imaginative space for energies of idealism and feeling that potentially bring into question all mere political, social, and practical arrangements (even the social arrangements by means of which their happy endings are invariably achieved). The net result is that one emerges from a Capra (or Chaplin, Von Sternberg, McCarey, Ray, Cassavetes, or May) film with almost the opposite set of feelings as from a Hawks, Wyler, Lubitsch, Cukor, or Sturges film. Capra, Chaplin, and other idealistic filmmakers ask one to embrace a realm of feeling and imagination at times almost detached from, and always more important than, social events or practical consequences in their work. Hawks,

Sturges, and other pragmatic filmmakers suggest, on the contrary, that no abstract ideals, emotions, or values of this sort have any overwhelming authority. In place of such things they argue for the preeminent importance of resourceful social arrangements.

It is, of course, possible to take sides about this difference, and critics who automatically denigrate all of Capra's, Chaplin's, or McCarey's work because it is "sentimental" or axiomatically praise Lubitsch's, Sturges's, or Hawks's work because it is "tough-minded" and "unillusioned" are implicitly elevating one tradition at the expense of the other. Rather than rejecting one kind of expression in the interest of approving the other, it is more useful, I think, to understand the difference between these two traditions of American film-making as embodying a long-standing division of allegiance in the American artistic consciousness, a division that can be traced through our literature, philosophy, painting, and drama for more than two hundred years. Not-withstanding all of the realistic political and social trappings of his films, Capra's work continues the trajectory of the High Romantic tradition in twentieth-century American art, whereas Hawks's or Sturges's work embodies an equally venerable and durable reaction against that tradition, frequently expressed in the corrosiveness of explicitly antiromantic satire, farce, and parody. (I leave for another day the consideration of whether one does not pay as much homage to the power of an ideal in attempting to satirize it as in straightforwardly affirming it.)

In short, I would urge that we understand the difference between the two kinds of Hollywood filmmaking as more or less analogous to the difference between, say, the work of Carl Dreyer (which in its retardation of pace and its suppression of actions attempts to open to view a state of pure feeling and imagination similar to that in a Capra film) and the work of Jean Renoir (a filmmaker who is as uncannily close to Hawks in sensibility, both in his uses of farce and in the neoclassical qualities of his serious dramas, as he is different from Capra). No one would ever confuse a Dreyer film with a Renoir film, but the mistake would be to attempt to judge the one by the standards of the other, and not to understand the enormous difference in expressive intention between the two. A work of High Romantic art, with its lyricism, Gothicism, melodrama, and imaginative exorbitance, simply cannot be judged in the terms one reserves for neoclassical works, with their interest in decorum, poise, and complexly nuanced personal relations. It would be like judging Henry James's writing in the terms one reserves for Jane Austen's, Italian opera in the terms one reserves for French opera, or Wordsworth as if he were Pope.

This is what has happened to Capra's films, however. Their surface realism is deceiving. Critics are quick to recognize (though not always extremely helpful in analyzing) the special imaginative claims made by two kinds of idealistic films: the narratively stylized or visually expressionistic, like those of Dreyer or Von Sternberg, and the blatantly melodramatic or sentimental, like those of Chaplin or DeSica. In the case of an apparently realistic filmmaker like

Capra, whose films are populated with "realistic" characters, dialogue, sets, props, and actions, confusion unfortunately sets in. The manifest political and social content of his work makes Capra appear to be a filmmaker who offers particular, practical, social and political structurings of experience in his films, when in fact, more often than not, his films are engaged in criticizing and exploring the limitations of such understandings and arrangements. He appears to be a populist, when actually he would more accurately be described as a transcendentalist. That is why, as has frequently been noticed, for all their explicit political content, Capra's films are so politically unclassifiable and ideologically elusive. It is impossible to say whether the political philosophy of *Mr. Deeds Goes to Town*, *Mr. Smith Goes to Washington*, or *Meet John Doe* is fundamentally Republican or Democratic, New Deal or anti–New Deal, populist or elitist. That is not because the films are muddled ideologically but because they are engaged in an analysis of human experience deeper than that described by ideology, an analysis that is fundamentally antiideological. The fervid, one wants to say operatic, emotionalism of Capra's films implicitly criticizes all ideological and social structurings of experience.

More than being about states of political or social affairs, as they are usually taken to be, Capra's films are more correctly described as being explorations of states of feeling that cut beneath all abstract or intellectual ways of understanding life. The films are, in the great American Romantic tradition, about movements of mind and awareness, not about populist, political movements. They are explorations of possibilities of transcendence of the very sorts of social categories they are usually said to serve.

I do not mean to suggest that Capra's work has been deliberately singled out for mistreatment by critics. Any work of art exploring extreme states of consciousness or moments of vision or intense emotion is notoriously difficult for criticism to deal with. Most modern criticism of art, literature, and film is implicitly neoclassical or realistic in its interests. It is attuned to the description of social events and interactions among characters. It is good at analyzing psychology and motivations. It is, in brief, really quite adept at describing and understanding who said what to whom, why he or she said it, and what the consequences in the plot plausibly should or should not be. Such an approach works admirably with the work of Hawks, Lubitsch, or Cukor, but the difficulty with works in the tradition I am describing is simply that frequently nothing that matters is "happening" in those ways. As Dreyer's *Gertrud* so well exemplifies, nothing may be going on socially, verbally, or interpersonally that is very important. The only "event" taking place at a given moment may be a derangement in the style or in the tone (in literature); the occurrence of an expressive close-up of a figure's face (in a film); or the brightness and quality of light falling on the wall of a room (in a painting). These may be "actions" or "events" potentially as momentous as those in the other sort of work of art, but they are obviously not analyzable in terms of psychology, dialogue, or social interaction.

The American work of art participating in this tradition of expression has always presented a special problem for criticism, especially any criticism that places a high value on the presentation of unexaggeratedly "realistic" political or social events, enacted by characters defined by plausibly "realistic" forms of behavior and dialogue. The problem is that Hawthorne, Melville, Von Sternberg, Hopper, James, Poe, Homer, Capra, Ray, and Mailer simply are rather uninterested in such forms of so-called reality. The reality to which they pay allegiance, in fact, is a reality that positively offers itself as an alternative to manners, social standing, and political categories as definitions of the individual or as indexes of his or her capacities of performance. They are interested in precisely the moments in which a character or a dramatic situation escapes from being understood in such terms. They are interested in moments when social or political definitions break down or when an individual is released into another, less limiting relationship to his or her surroundings.

The reality that they are engaged in depicting in their works is a state of imagination and desire that may have little or no social form of expression. Thus it becomes incumbent on anyone who would understand this tradition of expression in American art – and Capra's films in particular – to pay special attention to kinds of moments that are generally ignored by critics who focus on populism or politics. These are the sorts of moments or scenes that descriptions of the characters or summaries of the plot of the movie leave out. They are scenes or fleeting moments within scenes in which perhaps nothing is happening socially – moments, for instance, when characters simply sit still and are silent; when they look at each other but do not speak; when music swells on the sound track, or the rhythm of the editing changes, or a special lighting effect is employed, even though nothing is apparently happening in terms of the advancement of the plot or the dialogue spoken. Such moments, when the social situations of the characters or the lines they speak *cease* to express the meaning of a scene, are frequently the most important ones in Capra's movies: They are the moments when the film is laboring to express feelings or visions that are too intense or private to be expressed in terms of ordinary social manners and forms.

Not only do American artists working in the idealistic tradition leave out of their works most of what realistic criticism defines as reality, but they tend to violate realistic standards of representation for what they do present. It becomes easier to dismiss the melodramatic heightenings, the metaphysical insistences, the performative extravagances, and the emotional intensifications – all the actual, undeniable, blatant distortions of reality in Nicholas Ray's, Elaine May's, or John Cassavetes's films, Norman Mailer's novels, or Sam Shepard's plays – as evidence of mere shrillness, hysteria, or artistic incompetence than it is to understand that these artists are attempting to legitimize imaginative realities alternative to the reality defined by manners, dialogue, and social interactions. These artists are (admittedly, sometimes incoherently) attempting to register a pressure of individual imagination and desire that can free the individual from what they feel to be the limitations and constraints of social, political, or critical categories.

I am, I feel, only stating the obvious about a central tradition of American artistic expression and would dispense with it entirely if it were not for the fact that recurring confusions, not only about Capra's and Cassavetes's work but about much of the most important American painting and literature of the last two centuries, require some reply. In discussions of American painting of the period from around 1860 to 1940 – specifically the work of Homer, Eakins, Sargent, and Hopper, the four major figures in American art since the Civil War – a mistaken conception of them as psychological or social realists has arisen, exactly parallel to the mistaken conception of Capra as a realistic film-maker. It is a confusion that probably has its origins in the writing of De Tocqueville, who was the first and the most enduringly influential of the expounders of "American realism." What De Tocqueville left out of his account, however, was simply everything represented by Emerson, which is why the American is a far more useful guide to the geography of the American imagination than the Frenchman.

The persistence of the idea of American realism as an explanatory thesis is in itself a significant fact, however, and those who would define the American artistic tradition in terms of practicality, physicality, and bourgeois realism are partly right. Romantic art in the American tradition I am defining is truly different from most forms of European Romanticism in that even in its most idealistic or visionary forms, American Romanticism never turns its back on the forms and structures of ordinary, waking, socially defined reality (unlike European surrealism, for example). Like the writing of Emerson himself, which attempts to express the most exalted visionary impulses in the very social styles and verbal tones that might be thought to be anathema to them, the greatest works of American art tensely inject vision *into* society, rather than treating it as an alternative to society. That, most rudimentarily, is what separates *Moby-Dick*, *Huckleberry Finn*, and *The Golden Bowl* from *The Remembrance of Things Past*, *A Portrait of the Artist as a Young Man*, and *Molloy*. That is also why conventional narrative exposition (in fiction and film) and "realistic" portraiture (in painting) can be, in American art, at the same time the most radical, experimental forms of expression. It is radical and daring that the three American works I have just named – though profound imaginative transformations of reality – present themselves as simple stories with characters and realistic events. It is radical and daring that Homer, Eakins, Sargent, and Hopper did not abandon the laws of optical perspective or the realistic presentation of the human figure. In the realm of film, Chaplin, Ray, and Cassavetes are not doing what Dali and Buñuel, Antonioni, and Rivette do. The essential fact about Capra, romantic as he may be, is that he did not choose to become a lyric poet or an avant-garde filmmaker but instead chose to make movies in Hollywood, movies with ostensibly realistic plots and characters.

For James, Eakins, Twain, Hopper, and Capra, states of dreaming, vision, and reverie are not imaginative openings out of the ordinary world, escapes from daily life, but potential enrichments of everyday reality. To twist a phrase of Lionel Trilling's, the American position takes modernism out of the museums and libraries and works of art and puts modernism in the streets. Eakins, Homer, Hopper, and Capra are misperceived as realists because, in a distinctively American way, they attempt to suggest that visionaries need not retreat to a Coriolanian "world elsewhere" but undergo their imaginative experiences in their daily lives. Hopper's sun worshipers, his lighthouses reaching up into brightness, his store fronts bathed in sunrise, Eakins's meditative doctors, inventors, and worldly men of affairs, like Homer's figures staring into the distance or at the horizon, offer possibilities of enriching, cleansing, stimulating vision not as a dream state or a cultivated artistic achievement, but as something experienced in the world of apartment dwellers and working people.

It is this faith that it is possible for the everyman on the street to entertain a new relationship with the universe that to my mind makes the American vision even more audacious and challenging than the European. This is a Romanticism that is not artistically elitist and aristocratic but truly democratic, as perhaps only Americans could dare to believe possible. The American artists I have named believe that not only mystics, poets, artists, or social outcasts but ordinary people can break free of the limitations of history, society, past roles, and identities, and express themselves and their consciousnesses anew in the world.

In Capra's films, the grand dream is imagined to be experienced by the Smiths, Does, and Baileys of the world. It is significant that this state of transcendence, this sublime American dream experienced by the ordinary Joes of Capra's films does not manifest itself as an abstruse state of aesthetic emotion, a world-forsaking condition of personal beatitude or anomie, or as an incommunicable vision but expresses itself in the eminently practical forms of falling in love, singing a song, giving a patriotic speech, or performing a self-sacrificing act of kindness. It is the sheer worldliness and practicality of this grand, exalted American dreaming that is its most radical quality, as well as what makes it so easy to confuse with mere practicality. That is why, for an observer whose eye has been trained by exposure to European forms of Romanticism, the American variety appears not to be Romanticism at all. (Eakins and Sargent have been the most notable victims of this misunderstanding.) Capra's central figures can only be appreciated once it is understood that notwithstanding their dogged realism, they are Emersonian transcendentalists. Just as in the grand Emersonian project, though, they do not cut themselves off from society but attempt to express their infinities of imagination and desire in ordinary life. That the wild, exotic dream of Romantic poetry could be lived in the real world of prose was, after all, the initial American dream.

A brief examination of a series of paintings may help to define the Romantic tradition to which Capra's work belongs and to illustrate how such art is misunderstood when too much stress is placed on its realistic aspects. There almost always is a social, realistic aspect to these artists' work, but they can be at the same time as visionary, contemplative, or romantic as the most advanced twentieth-century European modernists. It is possible to discuss Eakins's or Sargent's portraits as realistic social and psychological studies of particular sitters. It is possible to discuss Hopper's paintings as social and psychological studies of personal loneliness, failures of communication, or the bleakness of the modern urban environment. It is possible to discuss groups of Homer's paintings (his series of schoolmarm and schoolwork paintings, for example) in similar terms. Such glosses are not wrong, as far as they go; they just do not go far enough, for the visionary side of the work of these same painters offers releases from the very categories of understanding with which these realistic analyses begin and end. To describe these works in conventional social and psychological terms is to fail to appreciate what is most radical about them, which is that the imaginative energies they release are unplaceable within their own realistic structures of representation. They generate intensities of emotion and imagination that will not be repackaged within tidy narrative bundles of character and motivation. On the other hand, the imaginative effect does not have to be gaudy and large to be disruptive of realistic categories of understanding. Especially in Hopper, Homer, and Eakins, and frequently in Capra, it is sometimes a figure's sheer mysterious inwardness or quietness that makes it most unsettling and elusive of a realistic description.

The theatrical lighting and coloring in Hopper's *Second Story Sunlight*, *Morning Sun*, and *Early Sunday Morning*, for example, are meant to offer a potential visionary transformation of the material impoverishment of the realistic details in the paintings. The sun worshipers in the first two scenes are meant to be as fully liberated from the occasional physical squalor or simplicity of their surroundings as is a viewer of the painting. To take another example, Eakins's portrait work, though beginning with and grounding itself in psychological and social insights about his sitters, is an exploration of states of awareness that ultimately render such descriptions of his characters beside the point. Consider his portrait of Amelia C. van Buren. The most recent exhibition catalog analyzes the painting in the following terms:

> The chair in which she sits was one of Eakins' favorite studio props, an ornate Renaissance Revival armchair probably dating from the 1850s. The chair was old-fashioned by this time, and had bulky, masculine proportions, yet Eakins used it repeatedly for portraits of women, and it almost always dwarfed the sitter and underscored the frailty of both her person and her psyche.... The youthfulness and gaiety of her dress seem to have been deliberately chosen by Eakins to contrast with his sitter's melancholy expression; she wears the clothes of a young woman and holds a fan, a coquettish accessory; yet her hair, the lines around her mouth and at her brow, and her tense, bony hands describe a woman of middle age, a spinster whose charms have passed unnoticed.*

---

* Carol Troyen, in *A New World: Masterpieces of American Painting, 1760–1910*, ed. Theodore Stebbins, Carol Troyen, and Trevor Fairbrother (Boston: Museum of Fine Arts, 1983), p. 328.

Thomas Eakins, *Miss van Buren* (portrait of Miss Amelia C. van Buren). The Phillips Collection, Washington; acquired from Miss van Buren.

The critic reads the presence of the fan, the sitter's costume, the chair, and her face and hands as providing a series of discrete psychological or social glosses on the meaning of the portrait. This is what I have been calling the reading of American art entirely within realistic conventions of expression. Again, this reading is not wrong, but it seems to me that this painting, and indeed almost all of Eakins's work, if it has any claim on our attention at all, is interesting precisely for the ways in which it moves away from such realistic, social analyses. It attempts to capture states of consciousness that realistic, social portraits exclude.

The ornate but shabby chair, the wrinkled costume (which, in its slight disarray, calls all the more attention to itself as a costume), the stock artistic prop of the fan are there to remind us that we are not simply eavesdropping on a spinster at home. We are looking into an artist's studio at a someone sitting for a portrait. Furthermore, the fact that the costume is at this moment slightly rumpled, the fan is resting forgotten in the sitter's lap, and she is leaning pensively, distractedly to one side of the chair tells us that we are seeing her not as she is posed during a sitting but at a moment of abstraction between sittings. (We can imagine that Eakins has briefly stepped out of the studio and told his sitter to relax. While he is out, she slumps down in the chair and looks abstractedly out of the window in front of which he has placed her.) In short, Eakins is deliberately focusing on the sort of moment *left out of* realistic portraiture. It is a moment of private, personal, unarranged contemplation, when fans, chairs, and costumes, because they are revealed as artistic props, *cease* to signify, cease to express what is going on in reverie, dream, or meditation.

What the realistic reading of the painting ignores is that the painting is Eakins's expression of a state of awareness that the social text cannot express. In this painting, as in many others by him (one thinks immediately of the great portraits of Dr. John H. Brinton, Brinton's wife, and Maud Cook, and the oil called *The Concert Singer*), a powerful meditative or spiritual subtext is communicated in the turn of the sitter's body away from public scrutiny, in the shadows placed on his or her face, and in the position of the hands. This subtext is opposed to anything expressible within the public, social text read by the critic, who treated the painting as if it were an American Van Dyke or Holbein when in fact it is the deconstruction of such a mode of expression.

American Romantic texts of this type deliberately resist realistic treatment, since they attempt to move their viewers or the characters within them beyond limiting social, sexual, and psychological definitions. Eakins asks us to move beyond the kind of notions invoked by the critic I quoted – notions of coquettishness or spinsterdom, youth and age, and frailty and charm – or rather to realize that there is a realm of visionary attainments in comparison with which such categories are reduced to unimportance.

Another literal misreading is often made of Homer's *A Summer Night* (originally titled *Buffalo Gals*). Since the principal figures in the painting are two women dancing together, it is not uncommon for critics writing about it to allude to an unspecified sexual failure in Homer's work and his inability or reluctance to depict a healthy, robust heterosexual relationship in his major

Thomas Eakins, *Dr. John H. Brinton*. The National Gallery of Art, Washington, D.C. Lent by the Medical Museum of the Armed Forces Institute of Pathology.

paintings, as if the paired males or females in his work represented a general deficiency. Is it not possible, though, that Homer was attempting to communicate a kind of relationship that was potentially richer and more stimulating than a sexual relationship? What if the two women were transformed into a man and a woman? What if this Homer painting itself were transformed

Winslow Homer, *A Summer Night* (*A Moonlit Sea* or *Buffalo Gals*). Giraudon/Art Resource, New York.

into Renoir's *Le Déjeuner des Canotiers* or Monet's *Terrace at the Seaside near Le Havre?* Would there not be as much of a loss as a gain? Homer's work imagines the possibility of a spiritual relationship of person to person, of person to landscape, and of person to music larger than any sexual or social pairing can communicate. In this enchanted, moonlit scene, he attempts to transport the viewer in the same way that the two women themselves are transported: beyond anything definable in sexual or social terms. The mystery and unspecified imaginative excitement of the moment are the interest of it. The viewer is carried along with the two central figures in an appreciation of the sublimity of the effects of the light on the water. The viewer is carried outward, literally and metaphorically, outside of the walls of the beach hotel and beyond social groupings, as much as in a painting by Lane, Gifford, or Church, to the imaginative claim of the horizon. Social definitions of behavior and relationships have been replaced by a state of heightened imagination and feeling and an appreciation of romance, mystery, and excitement that are not amenable to social or sexual analysis.*

This painting is, along with his *Promenade on the Beach* (1880), one of Homer's most Monet-like works, but a comparison with a painting by Monet or any of the other contemporary French impressionists only reveals the radical differences between the French and the American sensibilities and helps to define the distinctive Romantic qualities in the American work. Seurat, Monet, Renoir, and Degas, whatever the differences among them, live in the realm of the senses; Homer, Hopper, Eakins – and Capra – breathe the brisker, more bracing air of the American sublime.

Perhaps the most striking illustration of this radical difference in intention is visible in Winslow Homer's transformation of Charles Nègre's photograph, "Henry le Secq at Nôtre Dame Cathedral" into the painting *Gargoyles of Nôtre Dame.* Homer wittily reverses the roles and postures of the man and the gargoyles. In Nègre's photograph, the gargoyle muses and the man looks; in Homer's painting, the man muses and the gargoyle looks. Whereas in Nègre's photograph Henry le Secq is a dandy, a poised, confident man of the world, Homer's man is cut of another cloth. Like one of the gargoyles staring out of the facade of a cathedral at the march of centuries, he stands above the world and muses speculatively, looking outward but apparently really seeing inward, caught in a moment of reverie. If, as James Hanelius speculates, the figure is actually a self-portrait, it brilliantly expresses Homer's own medita-

---

* The equivalent to this miscategorization in the realm of literature would be the critical debates, especially subsequent to the work of Leslie Fiedler, that have arisen over the sexual content (or lack of sexual content) in the writing of Cooper, Twain, and James. To a realist like Fiedler and many of his followers, the male bonding and lack of heterosexual relationships in their work suggest homoerotic tendencies. The only way to answer that is to notice that the very effort of these works is an attempt to liberate themselves from all sexual categories of understanding, especially those of the sort imposed by such critics. A critic who faults James or Lambert Strether for Strether's failure to enter into a sexual relationship with Maria Gostrey is missing the point that the imaginative stimulations and consummations Strether experiences are meant to make merely sexual stimulations and social consummations comparatively unimportant.

Winslow Homer, *Gargoyles of Nôtre Dame*. Collection of James Thomson; photograph by Jim Hanelius.

Charles Nègre, *Henry le Secq at Nôtre Dame Cathedral*. Collection of André Jammes; photograph by National Gallery of Canada, Ottawa.

tive relationship to his surroundings in contrast to le Secq's social stance.*

When John Sloan dismissed French Impressionist work in toto as "eyesight painting," his remark went to the heart of the difference between the two traditions. Homer, and the painters within the tradition with which Sloan sought to affiliate himself, are engaged in a deliberate attempt to move beyond the perceptions of the social, sexual, and physical eye – to open another eye in our being altogether: an eye not of sight (though it must be rendered in terms of sight), but of insight – the mind's eye that registers our dreams, fears, and desires. Whereas the French Impressionists regale us with the seductive pleasures of the body and the life of the senses, Homer, Eakins, and Hopper, in an Emersonian way, practice a transcendental painting that attempts to make bodies transparently responsive to universal currents of feeling.

Notwithstanding their superficial similarity of subject matter, that is why there is all the difference in the world between Degas's bathers drying themselves alone in a room and Hopper's naked women standing alone at sunrise or sunset in their bedrooms. Whereas Degas's figures are withdrawn into a pure, physical awareness of their own bodies – he aptly compared them to cats washing themselves – Hopper's gesture in the opposite direction – imaginatively outward, beyond the frame of the painting, out of the physical space in which they stand, to a state of imaginative heightening. Hopper's women, without sacrificing their physicality, bathed in sunlight, have a luminist spirituality and ineffability. If Degas's figures represent the possibilities of the pure life of the senses, Hopper's women, like Homer's, always hold out the possibility of the life of the mind, the soul, and the imagination. Though we cannot see the window through which the woman is looking in *A Woman in the Sun*, our eye is carried out through the window to her left to the line of hills outside of her room, as a visionary release from the physical confinements of the room and the shallow perspectival space of the painting itself. The lovely roundness and greenness of those hills (in contrast to the sharp, gray, rectilinearity of the boxlike room) is something this woman participates in, Hopper shows us in two different ways: not only by making their curves echo the curves of her breasts, buttocks, and thighs, but additionally by making the patch of floor she stands on take on the same green hues as the outdoor scene. If one wanted further confirmation of the figure's imaginative participation in the pastoral world beyond the walls of the room in which she stands, it is given by the evidence of the breeze that bathes her body (apparent in the blowing of the curtain she faces). Just as in his *Evening Wind* etched forty years earlier, Hopper uses the presence of the breeze, as it is represented by the movement of the curtains, to draw the mind of the viewer and the imagination of the work's figure outward, outside of her physical confinements. (This is a use of the wind in a painting that Hopper very likely learned from Homer, who does much the same thing by representing the way the breeze blows the clothing of many of his figures.)

At the same time, the American Romantic position needs to be distinguished

* Also, compare Homer's painting with Hopper's *New York Movie* (p. 494).

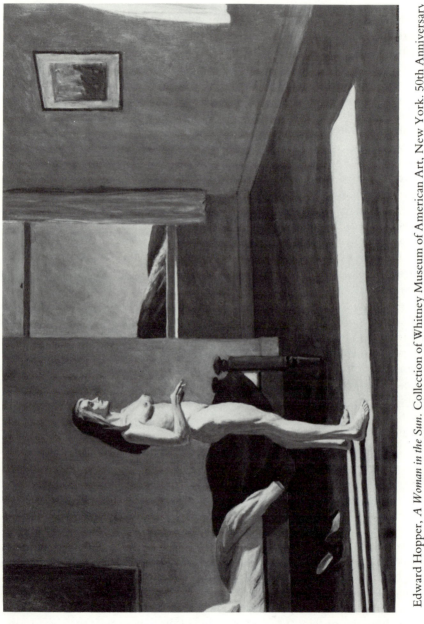

Edward Hopper, *A Woman in the Sun*. Collection of Whitney Museum of American Art, New York. 50th Anniversary Gift of Mr. and Mrs. Albert Hackett in honor of Edith and Lloyd Goodrich.

from the languid, nostalgic, world-renouncing impulses of pre-Raphaelite and Edwardian art and criticism, which focus on states of reverie, spirituality, and aesthetic emotion. This is not the time or place for a critical history of this tradition, which would have to begin with the poetry and prose of Keats and Shelley; consider the poetry of Tennyson, Swinburne, Moore, and Yeats; include the drawings of Beardsley, the essays of Pater, the novels of Meredith and the Brontës, and social/aesthetic phenomena like *The Yellow Book*; and look ahead to lingering reverberations in the criticism of Fry, Reade, Clive Bell, and the fiction of Joyce and Woolf. Suffice it to say that Homer and Eakins were contemporaries of Rossetti, Hunt, Burne-Jones, and Millais, just as Hawthorne and James were roughly contemporaries of Tennyson and Pater, and that both the pre-Raphaelite position and the fin de siècle Aesthetic Movement appealed powerfully to American artists insofar as both American and British artists shared the aspiration to break away from the historical traditions of the past and the social encumbrances of the present in order to achieve fresher, more spiritual possibilities of relationship.

The differences between the two positions are at least as important as their similarities, however. Those in the British tradition believed that a deliberate distancing of oneself from the felt-to-be compromising forms and forces of social expression and interaction was a necessary precondition to free personal or artistic expression. Pre-Raphaelite and Edwardian artists typically retreated from the ethical and social confusion of contemporary life into a mythical past, and into the work of art itself as a self-contained universe of autonomous meaning. They aspired to escape into a land of romance and imagination. For the American artist in the tradition I am describing, though, romance represented not an escape from the world but (as Hawthorne wrote in the introduction to *The Scarlet Letter*) a "neutral territory between the real world and fairyland, where the Actual and the Imaginary may meet." Though Hawthorne calls it neutral territory, in most American work it is in fact the opposite of neutral. It is a place where the rival claims of "the Actual and the Imaginary" are put into competition and conflict, usually to outright war. In any case, for these American artists the Imaginary and the Actual are not alternatives as the pre-Raphaelites conceived of them. In American imagination is thought to be, with however complex or painful consequences, potentially expressible in the real world. In the greatest American art, imagination is never "pure"; it is savingly impure, since it is forced to be mediated in practical, social forms of expression.

Consider Homer's *A Fair Wind* (also known as *Breezing Up*). His voyagers are embarked on an imaginative voyage as much as a seagoing one, but the crucial point to notice, in this painting about balance, is how Homer himself maintains the delicate balance between the counterpointed tugs of the two realms – the claims of the imagination and those of the world. Let me consider the figures as imaginative voyagers first. Notice that there is little or no sense of physical strain in their positions. Their bodies are relaxed, and they are released from the physical rigors of sailing a small boat in a high wind, almost

Winslow Homer, *Breezing Up* (*A Fair Wind*). National Gallery of Art, Washington, D.C. Gift of W. L. and May T. Mellon Foundation.

as if they were transformed in fact, as well as in figure of speech, into Emersonian "transparent eyeballs." Unlike the figures in pre-Raphaelite works, however (and this is usually overlooked in discussions of the painting), not only are they embedded in the actual world: Their most salient aspect is that they are not individual, isolated visionaries but members of a small, tightly knit community. They may be rapt in their own states of contemplation, but Homer insists that, in the richest sense of the phrase, they are "all in the same boat." They are engaged in a complexly interrelated series of practical tasks: one holding the tiller, another holding the mainsheet, and the two others counterbalancing the craft. Each one's performance is necessary to keep the small vessel tacking smartly in the strong wind.

Though discussions of the painting invariably refer to the figures' staring at the horizon, it seems clear to me that Homer has further emphasized the task-oriented interdependency of their practical performances by having none of them look at the horizon. The three younger figures are watching the luff of the sail and balancing the boat, and the older figure is paying attention to the roll of the boat and the course along which they are tacking. In short, rather than being a revelry in mere vision, the painting might be taken to be an allegory of America itself, as it was thought of by these artists: It is about the harnessing of individual visions to a complex, interrelated, practical group effort. Homer was guided by a belief that the life of the imagination could be lived not in contradiction to but in consonance with the most prosaic practical tasks. One notes the fish in the bottom of the boat. This visionary voyage has served to nourish more than vision.

To oversimplify only slightly, the American idealist position (as descended from Emerson, through Homer, Eakins, and Sargent, to Capra, Ray, and Cassavetes) may be said to locate itself somewhere between the physicalism of Degas, Renoir, and Monet, on the one hand, and the supernaturalism of the British late Romantic tradition on the other. The distinctive differences between these three lines of modernism can be suggested, a trifle schematically, by comparing a pre-Raphaelite painting by Burne-Jones, *Le Chant D'Amour*; a painting by Homer, *The Amateur Musicians*; and one by Degas, *The Artist's Father Listening to Pagans Playing the Guitar*, all on the subject of music. The Burne-Jones is an exercise in spiritual incense burning. It is necrophilic perfume making, entirely dissociated from the actual smells of the real world. The Degas, in contrast, is a realistic psychological and social study of youth and age, action and meditation, artist and audience. The interest of the Homer painting is its ability, in effect, to marry the spiritually of the Burne-Jones with the tangibility of the Degas. As in the Degas, there are a pair of realistically presented modern figures (unlike the pseudomedieval ones in the Burne-Jones); however, Homer deliberately defends against the particularization of character, age, and relationship that gives Degas's work its strictly practical social and psychological meanings. Homer's figures avoid these physical and social significations in order to take on a more abstract, spiritual signification. (In many of his other paintings he does this – the equivalent to Capra's

Burne-Jones, Sir Edward Coley, *The Love Song* (*Le Chant d'Amour*). The Metropolitan Museum of Art. Alfred N. Punnett Endowment Fund.

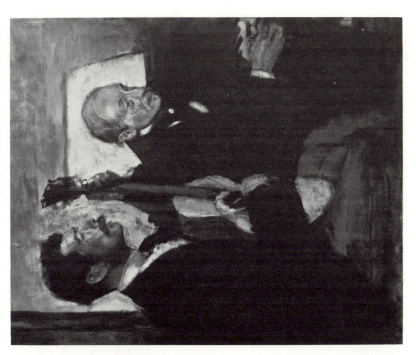

Edgar Degas, *The Artist's Father Listening to Pagans Playing the Guitar.* Courtesy of the Museum of Fine Arts, Boston; bequest of John T. Spaulding.

Winslow Homer, *The Amateur Musicians.* The Metropolitan Museum of Art, Samuel D. Lee Fund.

peopling his films with Smiths and Does and having them played by actors who embody "blankness" more than "character" – by deliberately angling the face of his figure away from the viewer in order to hide it, and by extension to universalize it.) A window, out of sight, above and behind the figures provides just the slightest nimbus of light around the heads of Homer's musicians to make their spirituality visible. (Capra used a key light on the hair of his actresses for the same effect.) In an earlier version of this painting, Homer put a Gothic window behind his cello player to suggest the degree to which this is a visionary painting, a painting about a spiritual opening out of an otherwise quite confining visual and social space (an imaginative opening out of social and psychological readings of the painting that Degas probably could not even entertain). Even in this medievalized version, it is significant, however, that Homer, unlike Burne-Jones, does not imagine his musicians passing out of the world of actuality through that window. He provides an imaginative window into a medieval courtyard, but life must be lived on this side of the window.

These three paintings might be said to summarize the parting of the ways in early twentieth-century American art. Childe Hassam and Frank Benson elected to follow the path of Degas, Renoir, and Monet and adopt the methods of French Impressionism; Thomas Wilmer Dewing, Edmund Tarbell, and Arthur B. Davies went the route of the pre-Raphaelites into reverie, romance, and fantasy. It is my contention that Homer, Eakins, Hopper, and the other American Romantics whose work is the strongest managed to marry the energies of both traditions, the energies of imagination expressed in the world.

Perhaps this makes American Romanticism sound too happy and naive, but in almost every work of art by these artists it is the failure or pain of this audacious attempt to live the dream in the world that is documented. (European artists would not feel this failure at all, since they would not have believed in the possibility of expressing their visions in the form of the world in the first place.) My individual discussions of Capra's films will, I hope, amply document the difficulty that this effort created for him and his characters. One can enthuse over the "visionary communities" created within *A Summer Night*, *A Fair Wind*, and *The Amateur Musicians*, but it is important to realize that it is principally the absence of such visionary communities or the loneliness and difficulty of living in one that Homer's, Eakins's, Hopper's, James's, or Capra's work usually documents. There is inevitably a darker, at times nightmarish, side to the American dream that involves a recognition of the hazards of the attempt to live the life of the imagination outside of the support and sanction of social organizations of behavior. There is an appreciation of the potential bewilderment and estrangement of the visionary in all of these artists' work. The American meditators in Hopper's work cannot escape from the drabness of their lives and the tenements they inhabit. Eakins's marvellously stimulating sitters – the meditative doctors, artists, inventors, and women he paints – are also lonely and weary. The American sublime is a chilly home for the social figure.

If the particular energies liberated by Homer, Hopper, Eakins, and other painters in the American Romantic tradition can be most clearly defined by noticing how their work contrasts with contemporaneous European painting, perhaps the best way to clarify the uniqueness of Capra's distinctively romantic form of filmmaking is to compare it with the work of contemporaneous Hollywood directors, beginning with Howard Hawks, arguably the greatest of Capra's contemporaries. The nearest Hawks comes to acknowledging the energies of imagination and feeling that interest Capra is in the wildest and most anarchic of his comedies – *Bringing up Baby*, *Monkey Business*, and *His Girl Friday*. In those films, just as in the best work of the Marx Brothers, the comedy takes place just this side of an alluded to, and occasionally glanced at, chaos of feeling and imagination that cannot be controlled or ordered in the patterned exchanges of the dialogue and the formal symmetries of the narrative. The manic, frantic pace, the frenzied characters and zany situations of Hawks's best comedies are indeed evidence of energies in excess of normative psychological categories and unplaceable in the forms of well-made, realistic drama. Hawks's films occasionally provide explicit openings into that frightening yet enticing darkness, the most extraordinary of which is Molly's astonishing plunge out the window in *His Girl Friday*. It is significant, however, that for Hawks the alternative to the well-lighted world of social convention is an opening into darkness, anarchy, madness, or wildness. (In *Monkey Business* the escape from the staidness and repressiveness of adult social forms is a regression to childishness, cruelty, impulsiveness, and animality.) In his comedies Hawks can briefly glance or gesture into a darkness where the forces of unorganized feeling and desire disrupt social forms, but the released energies of the id in his work provide no basis upon which new identities and relationships can be established for the characters (as the energies of imaginative idealism do in Capra's work). That is why, in film after film, after glancing into the darkness, Hawks and his characters must ultimately retreat from it. Insofar as they provide only holiday flirtations with wildness, his films are engines first of escapism and then, inevitably, of repression (which is always the flip side of escapism). Hawks always eventually withdraws his camera and his narrative capital from the world of wildness and excitement. In *His Girl Friday*, he has no desire to follow Molly out of that opening or for any of his other characters to emulate her. That way, for Hawks, and for his characters, only death or madness lies. Hawks in effect has to shove Molly out of the window in order to save appearances in his social comedy. Her jump is his confession that he cannot make a place for her fevered imagination in the social drama he has chosen to create.

This marks a fundamental difference between Hawks and Capra. To continue the metaphor of *His Girl Friday*, for Capra and his characters, windows and balconies are openings into the a world beyond social forms, but they are openings not into atavism and madness but into possibilities of imaginative stimulation and creation. There are many characters in Capra's films who look out of windows (and a few who contemplate jumping out of them – many characters who move away from crowds of people, out onto balconies, bridges, or parapets – but they are doing the opposite of what Molly is doing in *His Girl Friday*. Rather than ending their lives with such movements, they are truly beginning them for the first time. For Capra – as for Homer, Sargent, Eakins, and Hopper in painting, or for Hawthorne, Melville, Thoreau, Whitman, and James in literature – such a meditative movement off to one side of society, such an imaginative plunge off the deep end may be frightening or disorienting, but it represents the possibility of a stimulating enlargement of consciousness. That haunting territory that Hawks, for whatever complex social and psychological reasons, kept glancing into but ultimately cordoned off from the well-lighted world of his films and repressed and expunged from his narratives, Capra and his characters move in to inhabit and explore. Whereas Hawks, in his best comedies, imagines only a brief escape from the repressiveness of social arrangements in an id-energized, and usually frightening, drop beneath social conventions, Capra imagines the possibility of a complete, enduring transformation of all social relationships through the power of the imagination.

For Capra, the individual is not forced either to accept the surrounding social forms or to flee from them into varieties of escapism, primitivism, or childishness; rather, he or she is endowed with the power to make new systems of meaning, fresh ways of understanding and expression and to reanimate old. This faith in the essential power of the human imagination to transform existing social forms and structures is Capra's deepest and most stirring connection with Emerson, who wrote in "The Divinity School Address" of the power of the soul to revivify even systems as ancient as those of the church:

> All attempts to contrive a new system are as cold as the new worship introduced by the French to the goddess of Reason – today pasteboard and filigree and ending tomorrow in madness and murder. Rather let the breath of new life be breathed by you through the forms already existing. For, if once you are alive, you shall find they become plastic and new. The remedy of their deformity is first, soul, and second, soul, and evermore, soul. A whole popedom of forms, one pulsation of virtue can uplift and vivify.

(It would be hard to find a more succinct description of what Jefferson Smith undertakes in *Mr. Smith Goes to Washington*.) "Faith makes its own forms," as Emerson says elsewhere in the same essay, and by faith and soul he means something very much like what I have been describing in terms of the power of the imagination. Emerson never despaired of this ideal, which animates his own work from the early lecture "The American Scholar" to the late essay "Fate," where he writes:

> Every solid in the universe is ready to become fluid on the approach of the mind, and the power to flux it is the measure of the mind. If the wall remain adamant, it accuses the want of thought. To a subtle force it will stream into new forms, expressive of the character of the mind.

Capra's buoyantly Emersonian faith in the power of the human spirit to re-form social structures and ways of understanding and not merely to be forced either to come into slavish congruence with them or to leave them behind should suggest the limitations of Andrew Bergman's analysis of thirties screwball comedy of the sort that Capra makes:

> The comic technique of these comedies became a means of unifying what had been splintered and divided. Their "wackiness" cemented social classes and broken marriages; personal relations were smoothed and social discontent quieted. If early thirties comedy was explosive, screwball comedy was implosive: it worked to pull things together.*

The problem is that Bergman is defining the function of comedy exclusively in terms of what I have called pragmatic filmmaking. His formula works perfectly well for Howard Hawks's work, as well as for the work of the vast majority of Hollywood filmmakers, because they make pragmatic films that create social disturbances in order to offer social solutions that reweave the temporarily unraveled fabric of society around the characters all the more tightly at the end of the film. In the realm of screwball comedy, most films do conform to this pattern. *It's a Wonderful World*, *Design for Living*, and the comedies of Hawks, to name otherwise unrelated movies, all fit the formula. Capra's movies do not, because they are concerned with deeper realms than social disturbances and social resolutions. They ask where the individual imagination finds personal expression in the social matrix. They ask whether society and social harmonizations are themselves potentially repressive of our finest, freest impulses and feelings. That is why the social integration or harmonization taken for granted by Bergman as a desirable end in itself is inherently problematic in Capra's work. Capra's work is never automatically repressive of the impulses of the individual in this way, and Bergman's sense of film is just too conservative and too tame to describe Capra's wildly passionate and crazily idealistic work.

Capra's work is doing something quite different from what Bergman describes. In the first place, it creates states of imaginative energy that potentially bring all conventional social structures and ways of understanding into question. In the second, it attempts (with extremely complex and far from unequivocal results) to encourage these energies to transform the preexisting social system the film and character began with. Much of the following argument will be devoted to tracing the very complex results of that process and the difficulties Capra encounters in this effort. I have called Capra Emersonian in his optimism about the possibility of reforming social arrangements and structures under the pressure of the imagination, but as much as Emerson, Capra – though never abandoning this ideal – saw the real complexities involved in such an attempt. Much of his work is unblinkingly about the failures and frustrations resulting from the effort. As do essays like

---

* Andrew Bergman, *We're in the Money: Depression America and Its Films* (New York: Harper & Row, 1971), pp. 133–4.

"Fate," Capra's finest films relentlessly acknowledge all of the arguments on the other side of the question from his own and make the sheer difficulty of the expression of the imagination in the world their explicit subject, without quite abandoning faith in the attempt itself.

In these extreme cases, Capra's films seem designed to create moments of crisis, emotionality, or confusion in which all socially accepted understandings of reality break down or prove inadequate. They seem to exist in order to validate private intensities of feeling that force a shift or reorganization of all accepted values. And, frequently, in these problematic films, it seems that there is no adjustment of the social system that can accommodate the intensities of energy released by the work. The emotionality (some would call it the melodrama or sentimentality) of the film or specific scene is so great that it will not be translated into a social form of expression. Capra's work at these times takes its place alongside comparable expressions of the American sublime, from the writing of Hawthorne to the painting of the abstract expressionists, in which what is being expressed is an energy or vision that cannot be organized socially or "spoken" more publicly or interpersonally.

The frivolous wackiness that Bergman points out is at the heart of Hawks's or Sturges's work is not really present at all in Capra's. His movies expose the viewer to potential bewilderments of imagination and personal identity that are too serious and profound to be called wackiness. They are too threatening to social structures to be dismissed as momentary lapses of good sense or to be written off at the film's end as mere jokes. Capra's characters are moved to states of idealism, contemplation, reverie, or vision that make them, at least potentially, outsiders forevermore to the rules and unexamined expressive forms of society. They, like the viewer, are moved to a meditative position forever half inside and half outside of the social and political forms of the films. To adopt Bergman's metaphor, far from being "implosive," the meditative course along which Capra propels his characters is closer to being "explosive" of all social or narrative forms that would contain it.

Perhaps calling them "explosive" helps to suggest what is wrong with the fashionable dismissal of many of Capra's films as "fantasies of goodwill." (The clear implication is that because many of his films do not deal with "hard" social issues in a gritty way and may have token happy endings, he played the old game of escapism and irresponsibility that Hollywood is still playing today.) I would argue, though, that the socially and politically unassimilable and potentially disruptive states of idealism and feeling that Capra admits into his work serve as more radical and searching critiques of the failures and repressions of the American social system than *Juarez*, *Fury*, *Dead End*, and *The Grapes of Wrath* combined, in the same way that Hawthorne is a far more radical novelist (in the political sense) than Harriet Beecher Stowe and Emerson a much more profoundly subversive speaker than Daniel Webster. The writing of the American Romantics and the writing of American romances has never been an evasion of reality but an exploration of the space remaining for the expression of the imagination in a world that everywhere thwarts and represses it. Capra's movies measure the distance between ordinary life and the moments of vision or idealism within them.

It is not at all accidental that even Capra's lightest and most comic works like *Lady for a Day* or *It Happened One Night* deal with intense romantic love and powerful imaginative states of personal idealism, altruism, or patriotism, as the films of Hawks, Sturges, and other social or pragmatic filmmakers almost never do. Their nominally romantic films are about the codes and rituals of sexual relationships, about verbal and physical jockeying for position between men and women, about courtship and marriage insofar as such things are defined in social dimensions, but they are not about love and romance (or other human passions and dreams) in the absolute, idealistic form in which Capra presents them.

Compare the relationship between Carole Lombard and John Barrymore in *Twentieth Century*, Barbara Stanwyck and Gary Cooper in *Ball of Fire*, and Ginger Rogers and Cary Grant in *Monkey Business* with the relationship between Robert Williams and Jean Harlow in *Platinum Blonde*, Claudette Colbert and Clark Gable in *It Happened One Night*, and Jean Arthur and Gary Cooper in *Mr. Deeds Goes to Town*. There are witty sexual battles and complex dramatizations of sexual politics and manipulativeness in both Hawks's work and Capra's – but is there anything in Hawks corresponding to the romance or love that Capra presents? One has to ask why Hawks repeatedly backs away from the states of intense emotion and fevered imagination that Capra positively courts, or why, when love does rear its ugly head in the Hawks film, it is almost invariably equated with infatuation, infantilism, and atavism (especially if it is depicted in a man), a series of metaphors that *Monkey Business* effectively literalizes. Hawks backs away from the very imaginative and passional territory that Capra moves in to explore.

I have confined most of my examples to the different comedic methods of Hawks and Capra, but the visionary element in Capra's serious dramas make them as different from the serious work of Hawks and other filmmakers as his comedies are from theirs. Capra was equally fluent in expressing his idealistic interests in comedy and serious drama – a rare achievement. Both Chaplin and McCarey, for example, though brilliant directors of comedy in the idealistic tradition, were embarrassingly unable to express their idealism in serious dramatic forms. Chaplin's *Limelight* and *The Great Dictator*, and virtually all of McCarey's attempts at serious drama, fall into bathos and sentimentality. Sternberg, on the other hand, is a maker of serious idealistic dramas who would never have been able to make a comedy. His serious films are already too precariously close to absurdity and hysteria to withstand even the slightest comic confession that there might be something funny going on in them. Sternberg has to maintain the sternest of straight faces in order to prevent the whole project from degenerating into high camp (for which it is still some-times mistaken) at the slightest sign of a knowing directorial wink or a smile.

It is true that almost all of the directors I am calling pragmatic made patriotic war films dealing with the same ostensibly idealistic themes as Capra's. *Mrs. Miniver*, *To Be or Not to Be*, and *Sergeant York*, to name works from three different directors, all apparently engage themselves with noble feelings and grandly stirring themes of the sort I am attributing distinctively to Capra. Are they really, though, in praise of anything more than the same sort of plucky pragmatism in their characters and the deft negotiation of social orders that Bergman accurately describes as being the function of prewar screwball comedy? Compare *Sergeant York*, apparently the most idealistic of all of Hawks's films (arguably to the point of jingoism and sentimentality) with Capra's *Meet John Doe*. The two movies were released the same year, coincidentally star the same two actors in the male leads – Walter Brennan and Gary Cooper – and even resemble each other in plot: A character interested in minding his own business, in keeping pretty much to himself, and in looking out only for himself is converted into an idealist and a patriot in the course of the film. Within those general parameters, however, the differences between Hawks's and Capra's treatments of imagination and desire are telling.

Notwithstanding the fact that Hawks based his film on the real life story of Alvin York, potentially the most idealistic and high-minded character in all of his work, he manages to strip his character of virtually any shred of idealism, romance, or even abstract patriotism. He turns him into a down-to-earth, practical-minded, shrewd country boy. York's religious convictions (which, in the novel on which Hawks based the film, were mystical) and his wartime heroics are transformed into common sense, practicality, and levelheadedness. The novel's idealism, mysticism, and commitment to abstract principles are replaced, in Hawks's character, by prudence, cleverness, and native wit.

Hawks exorcizes York's abstract devotion to impractical principles and his religious conviction (or criticizes such attitudes) because of his own commitment to the values of social practicality and reasonableness. When York's religious adviser in the movie, Parson Pyle (played by Walter Brennan), tells him, "You've got the using kind of religion, not the meetinghouse kind," it is clear that not only does Hawks unequivocally endorse the remark but that he and his film are unable even to conceive of the value of a religion that is not useful in such a way.

York's conversion experience on the mountaintop at the climax of the film is especially revealing. At a moment of doubt about whether to become a conscientious objector, York goes off alone with a Bible under one arm and a history book under the other to sit and think. Torn between the claims of God and country, he, in effect, decides in favor of country and against God's moral law with Hawks's complete endorsement of his decision. York is, after all, only narratively enacting the decision Hawks artistically enacts in the film he is in: at every opportunity to substitute secular values in place of abstract ones; to replace impractical moral stands with practical ethical and social commitments; to render the things of God as if they were seen through the eyes of Caesar (to paraphrase the verse from Matthew 22:21 that York uses to justify his rejection of pacifism in the film).

It is of a piece with the rest of the film that Hawks denies York even any real "heroism" in his wartime activity. World War I becomes only the world's largest turkey shoot: a matter of clever hunting tactics, skillful aim, and humorous mannerisms (like York's "gobbling" and his wetting his gunsight prior to murdering an enemy soldier). Issues of heroism, courage, or patriotism are as irrelevant as they would be in a hunting party. The equation of modern warfare and down-home turkey shooting is an example of that famous Hawks wit, but surely to be capable of being witty in such ways and about such things is to change the nature of the experience one is describing. Nothing is sacred in this film, not even religion or human life. All of life has been transformed into a matter of cunning, moral opportunism, and social improvisation. War may not be man's favorite sport, according to Hawks, but it is nonetheless morally (that is to say, cinematically) only another sport or game. Killing men is not all that different from shooting a flock of turkeys, just as taking prisoners is not fundamentally different from packing the subway at rush hour.

It is not at all surprising that explicit religious and churchgoing experience is similarly transformed. The midnight meditations, anguished soul-searchings, and private revelations and epiphanies of the book more or less disappear in Hawks's film to be replaced by a sense of religion as a public, social occasion. Squarely in the tradition of twentieth-century American Protestantism, the church is turned into a kind of meetinghouse where the consumption of baked-bean-and-hot-dog suppers is much more central to the experience than the eating of the body and the blood of Christ, and colorful country conversation is more important than mystical communion. (It seems not irrelevant at this point to remember the entirely different religious and spiritual background from which Capra, the Sicilian immigrant, emerged.) Hawks cannot expunge York's flash of revelation in which he decides to become a pacifist entirely from the film since it is essential to his story, but in the scene of York's late-night conversion, it is interesting to watch the rapidity with which Hawks moves away from this glimpse of York's personal, private experience to transform it into a social event. York is immediately made to talk about his conversion in a nearby meetinghouse. With that narrative device, Hawks has again transformed a potentially private, mystical experience into a public, social one. During the meeting Hawks lavishes attention on York's folksy speech and on the faces of his listeners. York then goes around making friends with his previous antagonists, and it is, significantly, the country comedy of manners that interests Hawks, not any deeper moral or psychological issues. It would, in short, be difficult to imagine a sense of the possibilities of experience farther from that of filmmakers like Ford, McCarey, or Capra.

If there were sufficient space it would be interesting to contrast Hawks's *Twentieth Century* and *Ball of Fire*, and Sturges's *Sullivan's Travels*, *The Palm Beach Story*, and *Hail the Conquering Hero*, on the one hand, with Capra's *Ladies of Leisure*, *Forbidden*, *It Happened One Night*, *Mr. Deeds Goes to Town*, and *Meet John Doe* on the other. In every pairing of these alternative kinds of film-making one can see that whereas Capra is interested in depictions of spiritual, psychological, and visionary depths, Hawks and Sturges confine their explorations to social, theatrical, and verbal surfaces.

An extreme form of the contrast between the two modes of understanding experience could be revealed by contrasting, in particular, Capra's *The Miracle Woman* or *Ladies of Leisure* with Sturges's *The Lady Eve*. In both the Sturges and the Capra films, Barbara Stanwyck (in strikingly similar roles) is a dazzling mistress of performative polymorphism, a chameleon of quick changes and mercurial masquerades. What differs is the attitude of each director to that state of affairs. Sturges and his heroine revel in behavior that Capra and his heroine ultimately repudiate. For Sturges there is nothing more exciting and interesting than such theatrical or social capacities of performance, whereas Capra, who is chiefly interested in exploring the spiritual condition of the self underneath the social surfaces, always finds something suspicious or off-putting about performative virtuosity. Sturges regards his characters' performative capacities as desirable ends in themselves. Performance is unproblematic, painless, and has no troubling psychological or emotional side effects for the performer. Capra, on the other hand, sees a hollowness at the center of all role playing. That is why Capra's performers in general, and, in *Ladies of Leisure* and *The Miracle Woman*, the characters played by Barbara Stanwyck, eventually break down in their efforts to keep endlessly on the move. Their self-proliferations threaten them ultimately with self-destruction. For Sturges and his Lady Eve there is nothing but the joyous proliferation of the self in a never-ending series of public performances; for Capra there must always be something beneath such social stances, and indeed the drama of these two films is the depiction of the identity crises of characters who attempt to turn their lives into endless performances, who attempt to deny their own deeper emotional and spiritual integrity.

The difference I am describing goes far beyond Capra's differences from Sturges and Hawks, or the differences between Capra's comedy and other comedy of the thirties and forties. William Wyler and Capra were contemporaries, the closest of friends (ultimately joining together in a postwar filmmaking partnership with George Stevens to found their own independent company, Liberty Films), and they had the highest respect for each other's work, yet the differences between Capra and Wyler echo those that separate Capra from Hawks and Sturges. Compare Capra's *It's a Wonderful Life* with Wyler's *The Best Years of Our Lives*. The superficial resemblances of the two films run farther than the similarity of their titles. Both were their directors' first postwar films. They were released in the same year, 1946, and competed with each other for Academy Awards in several categories. (At the final tallying, Wyler's beat Capra's hands down in every matchup.) Not surprisingly, they both deal with similar postwar subjects – the difficulty of life in small-town America for an individual who feels psychologically and socially displaced, wounded, or crippled (a metaphor that Wyler literalizes by making one of his characters an amputee).

With these similarities of theme and situation the resemblance between the two directors' work ends. *The Best Years of Our Lives* (along with Wyler's earlier *Mrs. Miniver*) could be taken to define the very opposite sensibility to Capra's. In its narrative, photography, and editing, Wyler's film is an effort to neutralize desire, to normalize behavior, and to integrate the individual into the larger society, whereas Capra's goal is the opposite. His is an argument on behalf of the power of individual imagination against the social forces working to repress it, in favor of the absolute individuality of the particular character, and the unnormalizable energy and eccentricity of his feelings. *The Best Years of Our Lives* labors to exorcize the private frustrations and anxieties that *It's a Wonderful Life* is devoted to discovering at the heart of the American way of life. Whereas Wyler's film works to endorse the grinding down of its three returning servicemen in the all-powerful mill of society, to harmonize their behavior with that of their families and friends, and to sublimate their excesses of feeling into safe, sane marriages with safe, sane women, Capra's text of desire cries out about all that is lost in the incorporation of the individual into such cozy domesticity. In an ominous early scene in Wyler's film, Al Stephenson and his son have a brief conversation about the lessons of the last war and the prospect of another war now that the atomic bomb has been invented, which concludes with the son and father agreeing that "we have reached a point where the whole human race has either got to find a way to live together . . . or else," all too perfectly summarizing the subtext of social repression in the film as a whole.

The style of Wyler's mise-en-scène and photography epitomize all that is implicit in his narrative project itself. André Bazin praised Wyler's and Gregg Toland's long takes and compositions in depth for their ability to convey a complex reality presented seamlessly in an extended space and time, but I would argue on the contrary, that rather than communicating the clutter, complexity, and mess of a life seen whole, Wyler's style (like that of Orson Welles, George Stevens, Alfred Hitchcock, Robert Altman, and Brian De Palma) represents a radical simplification of experience. As Bazin points out, Wyler (like these other filmmakers) frequently has more than one action going on in a shot or more than one group of characters performing in front of the camera at the same time. Bazin fails to recognize, however, that this device is usually employed (especially by a filmmaker like Altman or De Palma) as a heavy-handed form of editorial tendentiousness, with events in the foreground and background of a scene commenting on each other ironically, sentimentally, or sardonically in the most banal ways. Even when it is done with more delicacy or intelligence, and less sententiousness, such a mutual commentary almost inevitably simplifies rather than complicates our perception of either of the terms involved in the counterpointed or doubled relationship. Instead of being drawn into one event or action, which, if it were presented alone, could be developed more complexly or mysteriously, a viewer of two such ongoing simultaneous events is provided with a moral tag line or social point with which to understand both of them and thereby is discouraged from complex response to either of them. That state of abstraction, and not of intimate involvement, is what Wyler's compositions in depth encourage in the viewer.

Perhaps one could ignore these editorializing or ironically "touching" juxtapositions of Wyler's if it were not for the deeper, more ominous stylistic message they communicate. His characters are so oppressively embedded in groups (photographically, editorially, narratively, and socially) that an attempt to hold onto an identity or a stance independent of the institutions and relationships continuously in place around them becomes futile, or is made to look mistaken. Wyler's use of extended temporal, spatial, and social groupings of characters in *The Best Years of Our Lives*, and perhaps even more emphatically in *Mrs. Miniver*, is itself a powerful form of repression. In *Mrs. Miniver* the photography, like the narrative, encloses the characters in networks of British history and home and family traditions; in the later movie they are framed and enclosed and their movements are circumscribed by the normative demands of wives, families, and occupations. When Wyler arranges and photographs Al Stephenson's reunion with his wife at home, Al and Millie embrace in the background of the shot, while their son and daughter form another couple watching in the foreground. Wyler then cuts from close-ups of the parents' faces to close-ups of the children's. This foreground – background pairing, the tight-figured two- and three-shots, the intercutting from one group of characters to another all serve the same purpose. There can be no valid freedom or independence for the individual here. Everyone must sublimate his or her energies into the smooth functioning of the modern corporate family – which is why the smug, clever women in this film and in *Mrs. Miniver* are so terrifying. Wyler leads the way to the ritual male humiliations and emasculations of television in the Eisenhower years. (Nor, looking backward, has Myrna Loy's general narrative function changed all that much from her pairings with William Powell in the *Thin Man* series.)

The narrative, not surprisingly, tells the viewer the same thing that the mise-en-scène, photography, and editing do. Give a guy a decent job; marry him off to a woman who can "understand" him (in the most harrowing sense of the word); provide for his physical needs with shelter, clothing, sex, and money; tolerate his occasional regrettable lapses from rectitude (there has to be some occasional escape hatch built into such a relentlessly confining world) – and everything is solved. In the best Hollywood tradition, the profound emotional disturbances of the first half of the film – the disturbances and worries felt by the wounded, confused, displaced men as they return home from the war – are opened to view only to be repressed by the inexorable progress of the plot.

The ending of the film summarizes it all. All the imaginative and emotional ghosts have been exorcized; all male wildness has been domesticated into the mildness of the costumes, rituals, and social arrangements of a wedding ceremony for Homer and Wilma. A newly reasonable and responsible Al is present as a guest with his wife. A newly reasonable and responsible Fred is present as a guest, exchanging romantic glances with Peggy Stephenson.

Everyone is about to be knotted up in a newly reasonable and responsible system of relationships. Everyone finally has been "placed" physically, socially, familially, and photographically in the extended group compositions of Wyler's staging of the scene, and none of this enforced harmonization, homogenization, and blandness is apparently felt as a loss by any of them or their director. No psychological loose ends, personal eccentricities of feeling or behavior, or emotional intensities remain that cannot be tied up in the tidy bundle of the modern American corporate family.

Capra, too, is a filmmaker of families and larger groups, of individual relationships to fathers, mothers, siblings, friends, and others, needless to say, but the differences from Wyler are great. In Capra's work the family or the group or society around a figure is not something to be reclined into or something with which one brings oneself into conformity. It is not something that absorbs individuals, erasing their individualism or damping their unique imaginative energies. Rather it is closer to a field of combat or of healthy, desirable sport. Not only do individuals have to struggle continuously and energetically within the family to maintain their identity and margin for free movement, but it is in such a struggle that they are tested and, if successful, grow, mature, and forge an identity. They are always in a dynamic, and frequently unstable, relationship to the group around them, never (if they interest Capra) in mere conformity with its standards or easy congruity with its behavior.

That is why all of Capra's work can be said to be about conditions of leadership and the hazards of followership. In his radically individualistic work, unlike Wyler's, it is the individual who, in effect, makes the group matter – by leading it, by inspiring it, by giving it new values to live for – and not the group that validates the meaning and value of the individual life. The group usually threatens the individual in Capra, whereas it validates his worth in both Wyler films. The things Wyler esteems – to be smoothly integrated into group activities, to function harmoniously within society, to be psychologically normalized and behaviorally merged with the group – represent the ultimate loss of one's identity for Capra. This is not to say that individuals are cut loose from the group, the family, or society in Capra's work. The contrary is true. Individuals are never allowed to be imaginative solipsists. Imagination and desire are relentlessly forced to negotiate the obstacles and snares of group activity, but their energy, volatility, and mobility are never neutralized or compromised in the process. They are, for Capra, what Henry James would call "values intrinsic." In Capra and Wyler we are dealing with a difference almost as great as that between an Elizabethan and an Augustan sensibility (and there is something decidedly Elizabethan about the power granted to the imagination in Capra's work). In the chapter that follows I will consider some of the specific ways in which the individual in one of Capra's films attempts to forge his (or her) own identity and to establish a creative relationship to the social group of which he is a member.

2

Self-made men and women

The Name above the Title
Meet John Doe
The Younger Generation

For pluralistic pragmatism, truth grows up inside all the finite experiences. They lean on each other, but the whole of them, if such a whole there be, leans on nothing... Nothing outside the flux secures the issue of it. It can hope salvation only from its own intrinsic promises and potencies...

To rationalists this describes a tramp and vagrant world, adrift in space, with neither elephant nor tortoise to plant the sole of its foot upon.... The authority of "the State," and that of an absolute "moral law," have resolved themselves into expediencies, and holy church has resolved itself into "meeting-houses." Not so as yet within the philosophic classrooms. A universe with such as *us* contributing to create its truth, a world delivered to *our* opportunisms and private judgement! Home rule for Ireland would be a millennium in comparison. We're no more fit for such a part than the Filipinos are "fit for self-government."...

What then would tighten this loose universe, according to the professors? Something to support the finite many, to tie it to, to unify and anchor it. Something unexposed to accident, something eternal and unalterable.

– William James, "Pragmatism and Humanism"

In 1971, at the age of seventy-four, Frank Capra published his autobiography, *The Name above the Title*. The reviewer in the *Hollywood Reporter* summarized the general reaction to the book, describing it as a "traditional American success story, real and inspirational" – though certainly he meant a traditional Hollywood success story. We all know life is not like that. Capra indeed does make the story of his life sound at times as much like a fairy tale as the plots of his films have been accused of being. In the course of the narrative, he single-handedly slays the dragons of the studio-system bureaucracies, vanquishes or intimidates evil sorcerers – like Harry Cohn, the head of Columbia Pictures – who dare to oppose him, and eventually triumphs over the entire Academy Award establishment, to win the golden grail of Oscars from the powers that be.

It makes for a rousing, inspiring narrative in an autobiography or a Hollywood movie, but surely no life was ever lived this way. The David-beats-Goliath story is an upbeat, affirmative, and optimistic form for a career or a work of art, but it is also a simplistic, superficial, and inadequate description of the complexities of life as it is actually lived. Careers are just not that simple – even David's career after he slays Goliath. Confrontations are not that clearly drawn, and resolutions are not that definitive. If Capra's personal life, Hollywood career, and films were what such an account suggests they were, they would not be worth the bother of investigating today.

In one part of his mind Capra obviously needed to believe such a myth of personal independence, self-reliance, and self-sufficiency, but read between the lines, in one local moment after another, *The Name above the Title* fortunately tells another, entirely different story that makes it worth reading. Underneath all of the Capra-corny comic anecdotes with invariably happy endings, the bright bon mots and witty exchanges Capra recounts from his conversations with studio executives, and the audacity of his Sicilian chutzpah as he struggles up the studio-system and Academy Awards ladder is a much darker subtext that Capra plays down but cannot entirely cover up. It is a subtext of Capra's recurrent fear of inadequacy, doubts about his accomplishments, and feelings of shame. He almost succeeds in hiding his fears behind his smart-aleck cuteness and self-deprecating wittiness (in his life as well as in his narrative), but it is impossible for an astute reader to miss the undercurrent of feelings of powerlessness, victimization, and humiliation that runs just below the narration of even his moments of greatest public success. The official, optimistic party line of the book, in this light, is a kind of desperate whistling in the dark to cover up the profound crises of confidence and identity of a man who could never adequately convince himself of the ultimate value of his life and his work.

This is a man who was so insecure about his chosen profession that he maintained (up until the time of *It Happened One Night*) that he was only doing it so that he could put aside enough money to return to college and get a Ph.D. in physics, his alleged true interest. This is a man who, while claiming to be above the petty commercial compromises of the studio system, previewed and reprieved each of his films in front of numerous audiences; recorded their live responses scene by scene; and, after studying them, reedited his films in accordance with them before he felt confident enough to release final prints.★ This is a man who, although pretending to be indifferent to awards and ceremonies, was driven on an almost insatiable quest for social and critical approval (especially in the tangible form of Academy Awards), a man who, no matter how high he climbed, apparently needed endless, repeated validation of his accomplishments and place, and who never ceased to feel like an outsider to the real community of Hollywood. Capra eventually became a self-made millionaire, and his was one of a small number of authentic American success stories, but never was the vulnerability of the spunkily improvised American identity more apparent than in his life.

★ In the late 1930s, Capra's insecurity took the baroque form of shooting as many as five different endings for his films and testing the audience's reaction to each of them before he felt confident enough to release a final print of the film. (The much-revised texts of *Lost Horizon*, *Smith*, and *Doe* are the most notorious examples of this practice.)

As a result, Capra's texts (both filmic and autobiographical) reveal profound ambivalences and anxieties about the situation of the individual struggling to create his or her own identity and to express him- or herself within the inevitably repressive bureaucracies of contemporary life and the technologies of Hollywood film. His work is riddled with implicit contradictions of feeling and occasionally almost torn apart by allegiances to contradictory value systems. Consequently, it is at times forced to perform its own complex acts of narrative repression and selection, to keep itself from coming apart at the seams. In the final analysis, however, far from being a defect, that is what makes Capra's autobiography and his films so profoundly interesting. It is the flaws, the fissures, and the expressive ambivalences in his work that make it so humanly engaging.

In its expressive confusions and doubts, Capra's work embodies inconsistencies built into the American experience that appear repeatedly in our most profound works of art and in our major institutions and cultural systems of value. The autobiography and the films indeed take the American success story and the assertion of ideals and the power of the individual against the repressiveness of the expressive systems within which he functions as their subject, only implicitly to raise the most profound questions about the whole effort of self-creation and expressive self-reliance that they dramatize. Far from being uncritical celebrations of the power of the "little guy," as simple plot summaries of them might suggest, the autobiography and the films are documents of Capra's and his characters' repeated crises of identity and failures of faith and confidence in the power of the individual.

It is these seams and fault lines, the discrepancies between the ostensible texts of the autobiography and the films and their secret subtexts that I shall focus on, not for what they can tell us about the specific outlines of Capra's life but for what they can tell us about the general contours of the American experience. I want, in short, to consider Frank Capra, and the central characters in his films (almost all of whom are alter egos for their director), as exemplary American figures in exemplary American predicaments. He and they are "representative men" of our culture, and embody many of the central imaginative strains and conflicts of the American experience.

It is not entirely accidental that Capra should be the filmmaker to do this. As the immigrant son of an immigrant father, rising to prominence as a director in the darkest depths of the depression, and making his way as a temperamental maverick almost alone, and always overpowered, against the studio bureaucracies and the Hollywood establishment (yet, at the same time, paradoxically, vying for their approval), Capra was in a position to become highly sensitized to the contradictions and counterpulls of the American imaginative predicament. He lived and experienced what Emerson wrote about: the conflict between imaginative self-reliance and the rival claims of social and institutional responsibility; the gap between our dreams and the forms of expression available to us in art, language, and society; the difference between the two lives, that of the understanding and that of the soul.

Capra's true spiritual autobiography, however, is written not in his book but in his films. Perhaps precisely because of their fictional guise, Capra was able to explore confusions of selfhood much more candidly and fully in the movies than he could in his autobiography. His own exemplary crises of identity in the brave new world of Hollywood became transformed in his films into the stuff of his protagonists' struggles with themselves and those around them. Capra was too vulnerable and personal an artist to succeed in keeping his anxieties out of his films, even if he intended to. The films are troubled meditations concerning the very project upon which Capra himself was anxiously embarked – the great American project of fashioning a self and finding a place for it in the world that can live up to the claims that the imagination places upon it. Much more than the work of Hawks, more even than the work of Welles or Wilder – three other cinematic explorers of this imaginative territory – Capra's films are about the dangerous adventure of putting together a self from the ground up and encouraging it to attempt to enact its dreams in the world.

The psychological, social, and artistic entrepreneurs in the films are as uncertain of their identities as Capra himself was, and as reluctant to admit it. The way in which Capra's films mirror his own self-doubts and anxieties in the figures of his protagonists, even while trying to conceal the fact, are what make them the most profound questioning of the whole idealistic mythology of success and the creation of the free and independent self in all of Hollywood filmmaking. They are films about idealists and individualists (as Capra was) who attempt to live the most extreme forms of the American dream of free self-expression (as Capra did), and who (as Capra did) get into profound emotional, psychological, and social trouble because of their efforts. It is not the central characters' invariably ambiguous or partial victories at the ends of these films that are most moving but the crises of confidence and identity into which such bootstrap operations of creating a self invariably plunge them.

Although the films are more revealing autobiographical documents than the autobiography itself, two related autobiographical facts from Capra's life can enrich our understanding of the films. The first was his situation as a Sicilian immigrant in early twentieth-century America and in Hollywood. The second was the death of his father at a crucial time in Capra's life.

The very essence of Capra's situation, and the recurring awareness that informs almost every episode in the autobiography, is his consciousness of himself as an outsider. As a refugee from the Sicilian ghetto of Los Angeles (who came to this country at the age of six and was, moreover, too short and swarthy to blend into the woodwork in a Hollywood of WASP – or WASPish looking – writers and actors), Capra was conspicuously an outsider in most of the groups within which he functioned. As his entire career illustrates, however, alienation is not necessarily a negative condition, especially if it is a state of moderate alienation like that experienced by Capra. The result can be the granting of a creative critical perspective on the systems of power and social organization unavailable to either a more embedded or a more dismissive stance. The practical consequence for the greatest American artists who have been, like Capra, caught betwixt and between has been an imaginatively invigorating and stimulating allegiance to both the claims of the larger society and the free movements of individual imagination. Within the tradition that I am describing, the American artist – Walt Whitman, Henry James, Frank Capra, Elaine May, John Cassavetes – attempts to have it both ways. He or she ambivalently straddles the claims of the individual and the society. It is an ambivalence that is critical to the American tradition.★

One may be moderately alienated from the system of which one is a part, but the attainment of a critical distance is a step toward potential creativity on its margins. To function on the margins of a system of discourse is potentially to gain imaginative leverage within it and to have possibilities of imaginative movement that are otherwise unavailable. It seems hardly accidental that the American filmmakers whose work is most closely allied imaginatively with Capra's – Chaplin, Cassavetes, Elaine May, Barbara Loden, Robert Kramer, and Paul Morrissey – were themselves, almost without exception, in the same imaginatively and socially marginal position as he was. This condition of marginality repeats or reinforces the Romantic stance I described in the preceding chapter. To be alienated as Capra was is, of necessity, to be placed at a distance from the structures of society, to feel that one is not spoken by them or that one cannot express oneself entirely comfortably within them. It is a truism to observe that the Romantic poets and the post-Romantic American artists who followed them adopted this condition of social and ideological marginality as their chosen artistic stance.

The death of Capra's father is the second circumstance that clearly had a profound effect on his films. When Capra was in his junior year of college, his life was suddenly and radically changed by his father's violent death in an accident on the family farm. In his autobiography Capra passes fairly quickly over the event, probably as much because of his reluctance to relive it as out of respect for the memory of his father, but its impact on his life was immediate and permanent. Prior to that day, Capra's future as a soon-to-be graduate of California Institute of Technology with a degree in chemical engineering had seemed comfortably assured; after it, everything in his life and future was jeopardized.

Before his father's death, Capra was part of an immigrant family attempting to attain financial and social success in the New World. The father had mortgaged his life and soul to buy a farm outside of Los Angeles where they could all work together to lift themselves out of poverty. After his death, the dream of success through hard work came falling down around their ears. The family income was wiped out by creditors. Some of the children were forced to leave home. The farm was lost, and Capra's mother and sister moved back

★ One could attempt to trace such an ambivalence to specific historical events in American culture, such as the socially alienating effect of the Civil War on writers like James and Whitman or the comparable effect of the Great Depression on an artist like Capra, but it seems at least as likely to me that the feeling of moderate alienation creates the attitude to the event, and to that extent creates the event itself, rather than the other way around.

in defeat to the Sicilian ghetto of Los Angeles. Young Capra managed to finish college and simultaneously contribute to the support of the two women by holding a variety of part-time jobs around the clock, but he was on his own, financially, socially, and psychologically, as he had never been before. It was utterly devastating to the young Capra. For years afterward, he seemed to have lost the point and purpose of his life. He wandered from job to job, from one period of unemployment to another, apparently unable to find his bearings or to decide what he wanted to make of himself. In short, though it is dealt with quite briefly in the autobiography, the death of Capra's father and the profound bewilderment Capra felt as a result of it is arguably the single most important happening in the book. It is an event that summarizes and objectifies all of the son's feelings of marginality, aimlessness, and uncertainty about his identity that run through the rest of the autobiography.

What is most telling is that the same sequence of events reappears in film after film in almost the identical form it takes in the autobiography: a sudden, disastrous personal loss precipitates a profound crisis of vocation, identity, or self-confidence, resulting in an enduring sense of desperation and confusion. The initiating event that generates the principal drama in almost all of Capra's greatest films is explicitly imagined to be the literal or metaphoric death of the central character's father or of some other authority figure in his or her life.

Sometimes the literal death of the central character's father is the precipitating event. In the opening scene of *The Miracle Woman*, Florence Fallon comes directly from the arms of her dead father to confront the church congregation that he served as a minister and whose unreasonable demands she believes killed him. In *It's a Wonderful Life*, the death of George Bailey's father early in the film abruptly changes the course of his life. Sometimes the death of a character's father is only alluded to as a determinant of his or her behavior – as in a scene early in *Mr. Smith Goes to Washington*, when Jefferson Smith describes the death of his father twenty years earlier and "adopts" Senator Joseph Paine as his foster father in the Senate.

More frequently, however, it is not the actual life or death of a real father that matters so much in these films but the imaginative presence or absence of a symbolic father. *For the Love of Mike, The Younger Generation, Ladies of Leisure, The Miracle Woman, The Bitter Tea of General Yen, Lady for a Day, It Happened One Night, Mister Deeds Goes to Town, Mr. Smith Goes to Washington, Meet John Doe*, and *It's a Wonderful Life*, each in its different way, takes as its initial dramatic event the symbolic death, abdication, or removal of an authority figure whose absence throws the central character into confusing, unpredictable, or potentially uncontrollable situations.

As writers from D. H. Lawrence to Michael Rogin and Bryan Jay Wolf have argued, the symbolic presence or absence of the father is of great imaginative importance in the American consciousness.* Max Lerner has written that to

* See D. H. Lawrence, *Studies in Classic American Literature* (New York: Penguin Books, 1971); Bryan J. Wolf, *Romantic Re-Vision: Culture and Consciousness in Nineteenth-Century American Painting and Literature* (Chicago: University of Chicago, 1983); Michael Paul Rogin, *Subversive Geneology: The Politics and Art of Herman Melville* (New York: Knopf, 1983).

live in America is to live essentially in a state of moral interregnum, and the determining event both in Capra's films and in much of American art is the opening of a moral, psychological, and familial interregnum of values and authority that is symbolized by the literal or metaphoric displacement of the father within the works. America is prototypically the land of kinglessness, masterlessness, and fatherlessness, the land of a people who have been denied or deny themselves any absolute authority for their positions and movements. The displacement of the father that initiates most of Capra's important films represents the sudden unhinging of stable, inheritable, traditional values, an unhinging upon which this country was predicated. Personal roles, relationships, and identities are frighteningly available for rearrangement. To have a father (or a family) is to be imaginatively at home in the world; not to have one is to be imaginatively unmoored, at sea, and without any easily inheritable identity or sense of one's self and purpose in life. The imaginative importance of the death of the father in these films is that characters are wrenched out of the old world of traditional, patriarchal values and left to wander in the moral confusion of a new world in which the old authorities no longer rule. The parallels with the young Capra's situation are obvious. Like the young immigrant drifter who wandered from job to job before he ended up working on films almost by accident, the central characters are suddenly unmoored and set adrift in a social and psychological sea, without a chart by which to navigate. They are stranded in a moral and social wilderness of uncharted possibilities.

An imaginative doubleness results from the loss of the father. If the father represents a point of fixity or a source of authority, his loss represents an opportunity for creative improvisation, as well as a potential fall into chaos and confusion. His absence or death can occasion both a feeling of estrangement or bewilderment and one of stimulating improvisatory possibility to make new meanings. One is freed for both the harrowing crises of values and identity and the unfettered entrepreneurial opportunities that the films explore.

One of the most pointed recognitions in American painting of this doubleness is Winslow Homer's *Waiting for Dad*. This painting is a work about physical, familial, social, and metaphysical disconnectedness that has striking affinities with Capra's films. Its subject is precisely the decentering of values from received historical, social, and artistic authorities that I have been suggesting is so important to Capra's work. "Dad" is gone; but obviously much more than that is absent from the painting, which uncannily anticipates twentieth-century European surrealism in the forms of practical nineteenth-century American experience – European surrealism not as a dream state or artistic stance but brought back into the waking world and lived in the broad daylight. The painting shows us a deliberately decentered family group, denied the obvious center of their existences they all need and want. The father who would unify them and organize their lives is missing, and the result of making him absent from the painting (even as his ghost is powerfully present

Winslow Homer, *Waiting for Dad (Dad's Coming)*. Collection of Mr. and Mrs. Paul Mellon, Upperville, Virginia.

in their desires to reinstate him into the group) is to unmoor them in a profoundly disturbing way.

Waiting for Dad speaks visually and compositionally at least as compellingly as it speaks thematically. The formal elements of the work represent a daring visual representation of the profound epistemological and personal decentering that takes place in Capra's life and work. There is simply no center to the painting – socially, visually, or metaphysically. Its figures are turned inward or outward meditatively, just as they are turned out of ordinary life and expression. The angling of the figures' bodies with respect to each other; the failure of eye contact between them, or between them and a viewer; the absence of any hierarchical visual organization (the elevation of the two children to the same eye level as the mother, for example, is a brilliant way of preventing the creation of a Renaissance pyramid that would stabilize the composition); the vagueness or inscrutability of the figures' expressions; and the visionary passivity of their stances tell us how far traditional organizing centers – social, philosophical, psychological or aesthetic – have been left behind. (It is not surprising that Homer's editor at *Harper's* changed the name of the work to *Dad's Coming* when it was included as an engraving in the magazine. He was not blind to the upsetting energy of the work and was attempting to suggest the possibility of the return of the center that is so powerfully absent.)

The work is a nightmarish hallucination about a world in which literal or metaphoric fathers are not available. By placing the young boy in the boat, Homer even denies us (and the mother figure) the possibility of imagining that this boy will step in to organize this family and their life ashore in the future. He is all too obviously en route to going the way of his own father – in a boat, out to sea, to leave another family gropingly waiting for him in his turn.

Yet this is to put it too negatively. The lesson of the painting, and its relevance to an understanding of Capra's films, is that the release to potential madness and despair is also a potential release to vision and imagination. *Waiting for Dad* is a painting about disorientation and bewilderment, but it is also about the stimulation of a richer (if potentially disturbing) consciousness and imagination than would be present in a harmoniously integrated familial or social group. *Waiting for Dad* stimulates the viewer's imaginings, though it also shows that the energies are potentially those of nightmare. That visionary doubleness defines the American Romantic predicament and is, I would argue, the point of both Capra's autobiography and of most of his films. Frank Capra and his characters could never have been freed for the daring imaginative performances they stage without having first been uprooted in this way from the traditional familial hierarchies and social centers of value; and yet, in this freedom, and in this liberation of energies of imagination and possibilities of personal performance, is also a potential hysteria and anxiety, a sense of homelessness and aimlessness that is summarized in Homer's painting. Such a movement of his characters or his narrative outside the boundaries of life described by social intercourse and the structures of family life is, for Capra, almost always an act of creative engagement with energies that established social structures in life and film necessarily frustrate or repress.

Capra takes the standard "catastrophe beginning" of early thirties films, but instead of employing it merely to get the audience's attention, he elevates it into a metaphysical statement about life. It was a beginning thoroughly familiar to film audiences of the time. In the first seconds of the movie a speeding car hurtles off a cliff, an airplane or train crashes, a montage of telephone conversations, telegraph messages, or newspaper headlines announces the death of a prominent public figure or a pillar of the community.

In Capra's work, however, the catastrophe beginning is used to create an opening to social and filmic discourse. A social and metaphysical gap is created that must be filled – socially by a repositioning of all of the characters who follow, and imaginatively by ad hoc assertions of human values. Capra never abandons the cataclysmic opening (*Deeds* begins with a shot of a millionaire-playboy's car plunging off a cliff and *State of the Union* with the suicide of a political power broker), but he always uses it to create the sense of functioning in the wake of a radical decentering of all life and value. The breakages and the disruptions of all of the old social orders and authorities with which the films begin launch the characters on social and imaginative voyages in which they attempt to fill the gap initially created with their own bootstrap creations of values.

The opening scenes of one of Capra's greatest films, *Meet John Doe*, can stand as an apt summary both of the metaphysical and social decentering that precipitates the drama in most of his work, and of some of the possible responses of the characters to that decentering as its ramifications ripple throughout the film. The two principal characters are "Long John" Willoughby (played by Gary Cooper) and Anne Mitchell (played by Barbara Stanwyck). A common misreading of the film begins by typing each of them, Willoughby as an unsophisticated country bumpkin, Mitchell as a tough, smart, cynical newspaper reporter. However, neither has such a fixed identity: Both violate their apparent "types." Each is functioning in the moral and psychological interregnum that I have described: There is a vagueness and plasticity to their identities and beliefs that becomes the subject of the film. Rather than filling in the background or sketching the roots of either of the two main characters, the opening moments of *Doe* (like the opening moments of almost all of Capra's films) deliberately cut off both Willoughby and Mitchell from any support system of moral, social, or familial connections and social responsibility. Rather than being established within a system of fixed relationships, each of them is forcibly torn away from the networks of meaning constituted by a stable past, home, family, or occupation. Far from being stereotypes, they are almost anonymous. They are virtually characterless – characters in quest of a character. Each is a figure incomplete in the process of self-figuration. A character's achievement of an identity (or his or her failure to achieve an identity) becomes one of the principal subjects of the film itself. An apt literary analogy would be with a story like Hawthorne's "My Kinsman, Major

Molineux," where it is just this initial lack of character in a central character (or the character's discovery that he cannot depend on inheriting a character and must instead fashion one for himself) that is the dramatic premise of the work.

The metaphysical and social breakage of old forms, roles, and structures of experience, the radical decentering of values that *Doe* takes as its dramatic premise, is summarized in its first two scenes. In the opening shot the screen is filled with a close-up of a jackhammer chiseling away the name and motto of a corporation from the front of a building. It is an extraordinarily violent opening for a film, one that rather than establishing things in the opening shots, as is usual Hollywood practice, disestablishes everything. The scene's purpose is perversely and purely a negative and assaultive one. It functions – like the suicides or deaths of characters in the opening minutes of some of the other films, or like the noisy, violent jackhammer itself – strictly as an act of erasure, wiping out, in the first ten seconds or so, the facade of a building, the existence of an institution, and a way of life that can never be restored.

While the jackhammer continues its publicly disruptive work on the street level of the building's facade, Capra, who is always more interested in the personal psychological consequences of an event than in its merely institutional dimensions, cuts to the upper floors to focus on the personal disruptions of roles, values, and identities that parallel the public, institutional ruptures. The offices of the *New Bulletin – A Streamlined Paper for a Streamlined World*, the streamlined institution that has replaced the "old" *Bulletin*, are a scene of turmoil and confusion. In particular, Anne Mitchell, one of the columnists on the old paper, has just been fired, cut loose from the institution to which she has devoted her life.

Capra sees much more in Anne's situation than merely the fact of her losing her job. She has been cut loose from the old *Bulletin* and prevented from joining the *New Bulletin*, but in that very instant of being alienated from both systems of institutional relationships she gains something that membership within any one system could not give her. In becoming alienated from either system she is able to possess each of them in a way she never did before; she has gained in imaginative mobility and fluidity of identity at least as much as she has lost in institutional definition and security.

I am tempted to digress at this point and compare her with earlier American imaginative exiles, expatriates, and fugitives from social affiliation like Emerson, Hawthorne, Whitman, or William or Henry James who at the same time chose to express themselves in eminently social styles and tones. But perhaps the most revealing analogy that presents itself is between her situation and that of another much earlier unsuccessful job applicant named Iago whose initial and subsequent dramatic status is strikingly similar to Anne's. As Shakespeare's conspicuously unemployed and underemployed character is only the first to demonstrate, to be cut loose from an official system of tasks, relationships, and values is, if one is talented and imaginative enough, to be all the more free to play imaginatively with and within the system in exciting and creative ways. That is to say, it is by being bumped outside of the reigning value system (as in both cases, when one loses or does not get a job) that one becomes capable, perhaps for the first time, of seeing it, and of playing with it and within it, *as a system*. What makes Iago the first postmodern character is precisely this recognition and his capacity to follow up on it as a performer. Rather than being disoriented or bewildered by his unmooring (though Shakespeare may have had one in mind, I intend no pun), Iago gains leverage over the system, a capacity of imaginative performance, that he couldn't have had as a semiotic function within it. All of which is to argue that, as much as in Shakespeare's plays, the ruptures, erasures, deaths, and evictions that initiate Capra's films are far from being merely negative events. They open possibilities of discourse; they release performative possibilities that would not have existed otherwise.

Anne Mitchell is out of a job, but at that very moment of being levered out of the system in which she was previously embedded, she gains imaginative leverage within it. She has for the first time seen it as a system and has consequently become able freely to use the system to express herself as she never could have as a regular columnist for the newspaper. To put it more abstractly, it is only in seeing the "structurality of structure," and in that act asserting one's ability to use that structure or to move outside of it, that the possibility of being a creative artist is born. For her farewell column Anne vents her spleen by composing a fictional letter from a made-up "John Doe," expressing his intention to commit suicide on Christmas Eve by jumping from the roof of City Hall to protest the state of the world. Once a mere journalist, a slave to wages and facts, Anne has now become a creative writer.

In that creative act, she has liberated herself once and for all from the journalistic worlds of both the old and the new *Bulletins*. To drive home the point, Capra has Anne perform a powerfully physical and personal act of breakage and erasure of her own on the *New Bulletin* that is strictly parallel to the jackhammer's activity on the old *Bulletin*. Even as the jackhammer is still working down below, erasing her past life, chiseling away her previous institutional affiliation with the old *Bulletin*, she cuts herself off irrevocably from any possibility of affiliating herself with the *New Bulletin* by throwing a paperweight through the glass in her editor's office door. Anne has been cut loose from the semiotic system of the old *Bulletin* by her firing and by the scene of the jackhammer breaking up the letters of the word, and she now deliberately and violently cuts herself loose from the new system by herself shattering the letters that spell out *New Bulletin* on the glass. From this moment on she functions in the film visually, socially, and metaphysically suspended excitingly between these two ruptures. Hers is the archetypal situation of the central characters in these films and can stand as Capra's basic definition of the initial condition of the strange, perilous, exhilarating American predicament: the individual cut loose from an old system, yet unable to join a new one.

In the events that take place between these two breakages in the first five minutes of *Doe* Capra brilliantly summarizes the release of imaginative and social energy in which her betwixt-and-between position has resulted. It is, however, an energy that typically can find no humane or socially constructive form of expression. As the film demonstrates, there is no real John Doe who can live up to Anne's impassioned imagination of him, and nothing humanly valuable is accomplished by her destruction of the glass in her editor's door. She represents the liberation of imaginative energies that can find no place in the world of journalistic facts and events. The attempt to find a place for them is the implicit drama of the rest of this film and of many of Capra's others. This energy – call it antinomianism, desire, idealism, or simply imagination, since it takes each of these forms in American culture and keeps changing from one moment to another – is released in the opening scene of each of the films, and each of them spends the better part of the rest of the narrative attempting to express and control it without merely channeling it into yet another new or old repressive system.

Capra is well aware of the systematizing and repressive forces at work in all culture and art. After the liberation of the energies at the beginning of the film, all of the forces of language and society mobilize almost immediately to repress or to channel them into a new system. The ghost of the father is as hard to exorcise as in *Hamlet*. In the temporary absence or abdication of one father, there is always another father figure instantly ready to step into his empty shoes and to assert his authority in place of the absent one. Anne, in fact, is no sooner free from her old newspaper and the patronizing tyranny of her new editor than she is haunted by the specter of her own dead father, whose diaries she pillages for moral absolutes to underpin the costume-party masquerade she stages with "John Doe." And later on in the film, even more threateningly, the sinister father figure of D. B. Norton steps in to play an even more domineering father to her, in order to further his own self-serving purposes. He is a protofascist financier who "adopts" Anne, arranges her courtship (as a dutiful father would), and works to control the John Doe movement that springs up around Willoughby. He is one in a long line of figures in Capra's work who abhor moral or social vacuums of any kind and instantly step in to recenter things – recentering the decentered world around his own desires and his own self-serving hierarchy of values, of course.

With both bureaucratic and sexual resonances, Norton offers Mitchell the social and political authority that she, as a mere female reporter, lacks and badly wants to have. He offers her (and her creation, John Doe) the bribe of a stable identity and a dependable part to play in their otherwise potentially bewildering games of improvised acting and ad lib ventriloquizing. He is a type who thrives in the American moral interregnum because he provides the possibility of grounding unmoored values and of converting doubts to certainties. Since he has bureaucratically fixed and institutionalized them, he never has any of the doubts or confusions about his role and his identity that John Doe and Anne Mitchell do. His singlemindedness of purpose and moral authoritarianism, Capra suggested long before postwar studies of Hitler's Germany and Mussolini's Italy came to the same conclusion, are almost irresistibly tempting responses to institutional disenfranchisement, social disorientation, and the loss of conventional moral values.

In each of Capra's films, surrogate father figures offer the enticing if illusory prospect of recentering the decentered universe. Like the McCarthyite witch-hunters, the religious fanatics, and intellectual fascists of all stripes who prosper in our culture for the same reasons, they would paper over the metaphysical void with their particular brand of moral absolutism. Like William James's "rationalists" and "professors," referred to in the epigraph to this chapter, they would remove the mess, chanciness, and chaos from a universe of potential confusion and doubt. They offer the almost irresistible bribe of providing clear-cut goals for otherwise destinationless desire. D. B. Norton in *Doe*, Jim Taylor in *Smith*, Potter in *It's a Wonderful Life*, and Hornsby in *The Miracle Woman*, to name only the most obvious examples, go into action to fill the empty throne opened up by the moral interregnum.

Capra's analysis goes one step further than James's in the epigraph to this chapter, however. He suggests that there is a third possible response to the uncertainties of the American experience that is more threatening than Norton's moral absolutism. He criticizes and places the Nortons and other moral absolutists and authoritarians in his work so definitively that there is never really any danger of a viewer's being taken in by them, but it is much harder for him to sort out his relationship to another group of figures who are at the opposite pole from the authoritarians – figures representing escapism, opportunism, and moral disengagement. They are people who, discovering that the universe has been decentered, have decided to renounce all moral commitments and human responsibilities, even self-serving ones. They resemble the Yankee peddlers and con men who strut so vividly through our folk literature, for whom there are no values greater than shrewdness and opportunism.

Whereas the moral authoritarians take virtually the same form throughout Capra's work, appearing as big, fat, sedentary, cigar-chomping heads of large bureaucracies (often with an uncanny physical resemblance to Harry Cohn, Capra's sometimes tyrannical boss at Columbia Pictures), these small, flexible figures of moral anarchy, fugitiveness, and opportunism are significantly polymorphous. They keep changing their weasely shapes and functions according to the demands of the moment. In the earliest films they are usually figured as dissolute party girls and playboys with no aspirations but to seize the sexual and social opportunities of the day. In many of the middle films they are disillusioned reporters, secretaries, editors, and small-time politicians who may have begun their careers with high hopes and exalted ideals but have been wised up by life into embracing a rootless, unprincipled pragmatism.* In the

---

* This, to be sure, is the threat Capra saw in the reporters who figure prominently in so many of the major films. They are not evil schemers like the Taylors or Nortons but something perhaps even more insidious and dangerous – clear-eyed figures of amorality who have moved beyond all ethical stands, beyond good or evil. They have moved into a realm of unillusioned knowing-ness and petty moral and social expediency.

later films they frequently are figured as homeless wanderers, tramps, or travellers always just about to set off for somewhere else. All of them survive by making exploitation of the possibilities of the moment the only principles of their lives. Abandoning all enduring human values, they are emotional drifters and moral scavengers.

Is it unfair to associate these figures with events and occupations in Capra's own life? Before he got into filmmaking he made a living as a general-purpose vagabond, cathouse guitar player, poker hustler, and door-to-door salesman of Heartsook Photographs, Elbert Hubbard self-improvement books, and worthless mining stocks, who kept one step ahead of his bilked customers only by constantly moving on to a new town. In the late twenties and early thirties, after being divorced from his first wife and before marrying his second, by his own account and that of several others, he played the part of a Malibu playboy par excellence. By the middle and late thirties, in an effort to escape the clutches of Harry Cohn and seize control of his own career, he made himself into a kind of small-time political and social promoter of his own reputation and an opportunistic Hollywood power broker of sorts.

Between these two poles – the moral absolutists and the amoral nihilists – is created the force field that surrounds the principal characters in a Capra film. Separated from their old values and thrust into a new world in which few of their previous values seem to apply, they are torn between the temptation to be irresponsible and to run away from commitments or to embrace a new absolutist moral order. It is, significantly, not a question of simply choosing one alternative or the other. The films do not document a simple alternative but the continuous push and pull of opposing forces. The central figures are never allowed to stop moving and adjusting their positions. As a result, the effect on a character is more like being suspended in a Calder mobile than like being projected along the fixed trajectory of choice and resolution in a traditional melodramatic crisis film.

Through these characters Capra explores the process of attaining an identity in a world in which traditional identities and roles are no longer available. One is always on the brink of losing one's identity – either by absorption or by erasure (either by being conscripted into someone else's scheme of moral and social absolutism or by simply giving up one's identity to moral and social irresponsibility and vagabondage). This is, needless to say, the opposite of the usual appreciation of Capra's work in which his central characters are said to be stock stereotypical figures of unearned identity – the country mouse, the common man, the idealistic leader.* Rather than accepting and endorsing unearned identities, like that of the "little man," or prefabricated, predictable destinies, like the triumph of "a messianic innocent" over the "forces of

---

* Certain characters in each of the films do have fixed, stereotypical identities – for example, most of the villains – but the stock figures are used, as they are in every literary or dramatic work, to contribute to creating a network of dramatic pressures on the central characters, not as being deeply interesting in themselves.

entrenched greed," to quote one of Capra's best-known critics,* Capra's films use these fixed characters and dramatic conflicts to generate complex social and psychological crises in his films' undefined "free" figures, to explore how their identities and destinies are created, manipulated, changed, maintained, or lost.

This is a radical departure from most other Hollywood characterization. Whereas even the most challenging and interesting Hollywood films offer dramas based essentially on the conflict of various fixed character types, Capra's films take the creation of free character itself as their subject. The process of shaping a free identity for themselves is the task of the central figures.

One might speculate that that is the reason Capra found Jimmy Stewart, Gary Cooper, and Barbara Stanwyck of such use in his films. Each of them brought to a role almost the opposite of the "star quality" that a Greta Garbo, Bette Davis, or Clark Gable would have brought with them. They represent a vacancy, blankness, or indefiniteness that, though it is frequently exasperating in their work with other directors, is exactly right for Capra's investigations of the achievement of identity. Their personal qualities are very different, Stewart's strongest quality being a boyish clumsiness and dreamy idealism, Cooper's a blank stoicism and wooden impassivity, and Stanwyck's a breathless, vague emotionality, often bordering on hysteria, looking for an adequate form of expression. Capra uses them in different ways, but each of them brings something entirely different from what the usual character actor or star brings to a role. They are figures of desire or inarticulate idealism searching for a cause to follow, a leader to embrace, or a satisfactory form of personal expression. Like Robin in "My Kinsman, Major Molineux," they are figures of undefined idealism and imagination potentially victimized by their quest for a fixed, inheritable social or moral identity. In their search for a father or authority to whom to attach themselves, they become easily manipulated by the false fathers around them and continuously run the danger of turning themselves into dummies ventriloquized by others, actors mouthing someone else's lines.

Thus the achievement of identity cannot be a matter of merely embracing or rejecting a particular stereotypical role. It becomes a uniquely American power of performance, a capacity to navigate a course between both the imaginative imperialists and the Yankee peddlers in life. Few films put a greater performative burden on the individual or the individual actor, since in few films is the self forced to become more responsive to outside influences, even as it is more fragile and vulnerable, because utterly unable to recline into a prefabricated role.

Yet for all that, few filmmakers have a more optimistically American belief that, as William James put it, "The inmost nature of reality is congenial to

* Richard Griffith in R. Griffith and P. Rotha, *The Film Till Now* (Middlesex: Hamlyn, 1960), p. 452; the treatment of Capra's work is reprinted in Richard Griffith, *Frank Capra* (London: British Film Institute, 1951).

powers which you possess."* Capra is directly in the line of Emerson and William James in his conviction that the individual is the only legitimate author of value in the universe and that he is fully adequate to the task of authorship before him. Although other – say, Marxist or Hegelian – analyses would "de-author" systems and define human values in terms of institutional structures, Capra is most American in his practical insistence that it is the individual who shapes the system, and not the other way around. In an understanding of events completely opposed to that of Michel Foucault, in Capra's work power is almost always defined as the direct extension or emanation of personality, and the correction of abuses of power is almost always within the capability of individual performers.†

Capra is often thought to be a maker of patriotic abstractions, but it should be noted that patriotism in the abstract sense is almost absent from his work. Patriotism exists in his films not as the depersonalized mass reverence for one's country and its institutions, as it does, say, in the contemporary work of Leni Riefenstahl, but as the individual, personal love of particular people in its history. History is, as in the Emersonian project, only biography writ large, and patriotism is not an instance of mob psychology but a direct personal expression of individual imagination. The patriotic impulse has been returned to its root significance as the search for an imaginative father. Grant, Lincoln, and Jefferson are referred to in the later films in their capacities as pragmatic individual performers, as the fathers of their country, in the entirely practical sense of the word. It is their individuality that Capra's heroes admire and emulate, not their institutional abstractness.

A character must learn to shape his or her unique identity and personal performance within the larger system of some sort of family and within the mutually interdependent roles of father or mother, husband or wife, brother or sister. The family is a microcosm of the force field of relations in which a character learns to function without a father, to combat a false father, or to father him- or herself. The families in Capra's films are riddled with father – son conflicts, with fathers who directly or indirectly frustrate or limit their sons, fathers who represent nearly impossible ideals for sons or daughters to live up to, fathers who burden their children with the responsibilities of past commitments. Most insidiously of all, as has already been mentioned, the films are also full of surrogate fathers who offer to "adopt" the son or daughter and replace a dead or missing father but turn out to be false fathers who betray their trust in major or minor ways.

In the largest sense, in these films every son must learn to become his own

---

* William James, "The Sentiment of Rationality", in *The Writings of William James: A Comprehensive Edition*, ed. John J. McDermott (Chicago: University of Chicago Press, 1977), p. 331.

† To the extent that power is systematic and depersonalized in Capra's work, as it is in his late films – *Smith*, *Doe*, the *Why We Fight* series, *It's a Wonderful Life*, and *State of the Union* – it all the more requires the intervention of the individual agent to repersonalize it and attempt to correct its distortions of values.

father and to make his own family. No one else can father him, and no one else's family can adopt him. He must move from a situation of dependency, bereavement, or irresponsibility (as a son) to one of self-reliance, responsibility, maturity, and mastery (as a father). The boyish Boy Ranger, Jefferson Smith, comes to Washington and wants Senator Paine to be his father/guide/authority in the wilderness. Paine "adopts" Smith metaphorically (actually calling him "son" at several points) and becomes his mentor. The point of the film though, is that it is impossible to escape from responsibility by remaining a boy and embracing a father in this way. Smith discovers that he must not only father himself but become a kind of spiritual father to others – to his secretary Saunders, the page boys in the Senate, his constituents back home, and finally even to Paine himself.

For Capra, selfhood cannot be inherited or reclined into but must be forged out of one's own self-reliant energies of performance. One's powers of performance and the family system one creates around oneself are responses to the flux of values within which one exists. Watching this process in the films it is impossible not to think of Capra himself, looking for a place, a role, and an identity in the stylistic jungle of Los Angeles in the 1920s. Max Lerner has movingly characterized the strange, confusing situation of the immigrants who came to this country at the turn of the century:

> For years, perhaps for the rest of their lives, many of these immigrants were to remain ... alienated men – alienated from the culture they had left and from the one that had not yet wholly welcomed them and that they did not understand, and alienated finally from themselves. The old patterned ways of the village community, however galling, formed a path of stability, where a man knew what was expected of him. The new ways of the ... American cities and the quickly growing farm villages were bewildering. The immigrant became an object, caught within forces over which he had no mastery.*

It is not surprising that this immigrant drifter in quest of an identity should become the great historian of the American quest for identity.

Capra's final silent film, *The Younger Generation*, takes the process of the creation of an individual identity within an unstable, fluid society as its explicit subject. It focuses on the intermeshed stories of a brother and a sister in an impoverished immigrant family. The young man ruthlessly fights his way up in the world, repudiating his family and his past in the process; the daughter stays closer to her parents and never succeeds as significantly as the son. In the end the son has reconstituted his entire identity, moving out of the ghetto, turning his back on his ethnic background and his former friends and family, changing his name, and becoming a member of high society. The daughter, on the other hand, marries happily but modestly and stays close to her parents and friends in the ghetto. The climactic scene involves the death of the father of the family and the final disposition of the children, momentarily brought together around his deathbed. The daughter mourns as part of the tight-knit ethnic

___

* Max Lerner, *America as a Civilization* (New York: Simon & Schuster, 1957), p. 87.

family group and goes off to live with her mother and husband; the son remains alone and bereft in his palatial mansion. It is hard not to view the film as veiled autobiography, and it is telling that Capra's deepest emotional involvement in his story is strikingly not with the loyal, "good" daughter who chooses to stay home and recline into an automatic and easily inherited familial identity but, strangely enough, with the "evil" son who tries to make his identity ex nihilo and loses everything in the process. The daughter represents values that Capra officially endorses in the film, but the son is obviously much closer to him psychologically and socially. The paradox with which *The Younger Generation* ends is that if the American dream of perfect personal freedom and independence (as represented by the career of the son) is a potential nightmare of alienation and loneliness, the alternative (represented by the daughter) is even more bleak: to remain smothered within the bosom of the nuclear family and never to be able to move beyond it, or beyond one's past.

All of Capra's subsequent films are caught on the horns of the dilemma of *The Younger Generation*, attempting to affirm both the conservative values of familial continuity and responsibility represented by the daughter, and yet simultaneously attracted to the radical individualism and independence of the maverick son in his attempt to make himself over in his own image of himself. They ask whether one can have things both ways – whether there can be a home and family in the world for the individual committed to the free exercise of his or her imagination in creating a self ab ovo. They are films of individual quests for independence and social success, and documents of their perhaps unsustainable psychological cost. They are films of boys and girls trying to become their own fathers, reconstitute their identities, and make values in a valueless world, and paying the sometimes exorbitant price of such declarations of independence. They are, like *The Younger Generation*, films of self-division, puzzlement, and doubt rather than of programmatic solutions. They raise profound questions about the American belief that personal identities can be made to order, or willed into existence, and they document the endless anxieties of a character on his or her own, outside of the support systems of family and friends.

The fact that in *The Younger Generation* Capra worked so hard to hide this division of his own allegiances and apparently intended a viewer simply to condemn the son and admire the daughter alerts us to be on the lookout in his subsequent work for such complexities of feeling. Capra repeatedly attempted to repress his own most troubling insights about the relationship between the individual imagination and society. More than forty-two years later, in *The Name above the Title*, one feels the same divisions and uncertainties, although Capra does his best to make his narrative read as much like a Horatio Alger novel as possible. His narration is riddled with doubts and fears about the project of self-creation on which he is launched. Capra's emotional vulnerability, his sense of social alienation, and his doubts about his ability to perform within the studio-system bureaucracy reveal something he felt about the darker side of the archetypal American dream of exceptionalism and individualism that comes out even more frighteningly in his films. The films tell us something that even Whitman and Thoreau left out of their sometimes too euphoric and untroubled accounts of self-creation, something about the fears and vulnerabilities of the "simple naked self," something about the endless anxiety of the individual who attempts to function outside of established institutional supports.

In Capra's films, as in the essays of Emerson or the novels of Henry James, there is an appreciation of character not as a fixity but as a series of imaginative possibilities or impulses in exhilarating and frequently frightening flux. These characters make us aware of how much larger they are than any single identity or role they play. In short, as one finds them in the writing of Whitman and James and the films of Cassavetes, these characters are too imaginatively mobile and energetic to be reduced to dramatic "characters." These are characters simultaneously in search of and in flight from any one "character."

Capra's films expose the viewer to selves like those in Copley's or Sargent's portraits. The American selves, unlike those in portraits by Van Dyke, Gainsborough, Raeburn, Romney, or Lawrence are visibly fashioning their own loosely fitting identities out of whatever scraps of roles, and props and costumes, come to hand. The upwardly aspiring, even bourgeois quality of both American painters' figures, which many critics deplore, is really the source of their imaginative daring. They reveal the self-made fragility and vulnerability – as well as the imaginative audacity – of the achieved, or sometimes not achieved, identities they depict. Copley and Sargent (the latter with special success) present selves that are almost always posing. They are selves that reveal their imaginative insecurity by their very effort to create and maintain their identities, which must be forged (often in both senses of the word) into existence. (We will encounter both senses of posing and forging explicitly in Capra's *That Certain Thing, Ladies of Leisure, The Miracle Woman, Bitter Tea, Lady for a Day, Doe,* and *Pocketful of Miracles.*) This is the edge of anxiety and willed theatricality that Sargent's portraiture (so similar in its depiction of characters on the make to Henry James's early novels) captures. His characters, like Capra's, must theatrically invent themselves as they go along and precariously maintain themselves in the parts in which they have cast themselves. They are, to change the metaphor, entrepreneurs of their own identities.★ The fundamental question explored by all four American artists – Copley, James, Sargent, and Capra – is the adequacy or inadequacy of social, verbal, and artistic systems to represent the energies of the imagination in publicly visible and enactable forms of expression and behavior. It is the central inquiry of American Romanticism.

In Sargent especially, posing becomes a means of self-composition. *Madame X,* his portrait of Madame Gautreau, tells us with every aspect of her theatricality – the turn of her head, the studied placement of her right hand on

---

★ Copley specializes in the economic entrepreneur in the Chamber of Commerce sense of the word; Sargent in the social entrepreneur of the nouveau riche class, but both focus on individuals who handcraft their own identities, whether Paul Revere or Dr. Pozzi.

John Singer Sargent, *Madame X* (*Mme. Gautreau*). The Metropolitan Museum of Art, Arthur H. Hearn Fund.

the "prop" of the table next to her, the slight angling of her upper body, the daring décolletage of her stunning "costume" – that she is creating a deliberately calculated effect. One thinks of the colloquy between Isabel Archer and Madame Merle, in *The Portrait of a Lady*, about the importance (or unimportance) of costume and props to the expression of the self:

> "When you've lived as long as I you'll see that every human being has his shell and that you must take the shell into account. By the shell I mean the whole envelope of circumstances. There's no such thing as an isolated man or woman; we're each made up of some cluster of appurtenances. What shall we call our 'self'? Where does it begin? Where does it end? It overflows into everything that belongs to us – and then it flows back again. I know a large part of myself is in the clothes I choose to wear. I've a great respect for *things*! One's self – for other people – is one's expression of one's self; and one's house, one's furniture, one's garments, the books one reads, the company one keeps – these things are all expressive."
>
> This was very metaphysical; not more so, however than several observations Madame Merle had already made. Isabel was fond of metaphysics, but was unable to accompany her friend into this bold analysis of human personality. "I don't agree with you. I think it is just the other way. I don't know whether I succeed in expressing myself, but I know that nothing else expresses me. Nothing that belongs to me is any measure of me; everything's on the contrary a limit, a barrier, and a perfectly arbitrary one. Certainly the clothes which, as you say, I choose to wear, don't express me; and heaven forbid they should!"
>
> "You dress very well," Madame Merle lightly interposed.
>
> "Possibly; but I don't care to be judged by that. My clothes may express the dressmaker, but they don't express me. To begin with it's not my own choice that I wear them; they're imposed upon me by society."
>
> "Should you prefer to go without them?" Madame Merle enquired in a tone which virtually terminated the discussion.★

There is no question but that Madame Gautreau would side with Madame Merle in this dispute, and probably be just as dismissive of Isabel's commitment to the existence of a naked self outside of social definitions and beyond forms of expression. To complete the artistic parallel, if Madame Merle is a figure out of Sargent, Isabel is a figure out of Eakins, a figure who reminds us how separate she is from any costume she happens to wear at the moment and how costumes do not, cannot contain or express her. Yet Sargent's Madame Gautreau and James's Madame Merle, in an alternative way, also express a notion of the transcendental self. Insofar as they *stage* their effects and self-expressions and are not merely identical with them or unselfconsciously defined by them, we are aware of a self beyond the costume, behind the gesture, underneath the role, a self not completely represented by the part it plays. This is a crucial (and commonly misunderstood) point, and it helps one to see why theatrical impulses and transcendental aspirations are not opposed concepts (and why Madame Merle and Isabel Archer are therefore not

★ Henry James, *The Portrait of a Lady*, Chapter 19.

entirely opposed characters, as one might naively conclude). They are rather alternative responses on the part of the self to the same condition of having too much imagination for expression in ordinary, received social roles and functions. While Isabel Archer quests after a disencumbered state of freedom, Madame Merle (like Eugenia of *The Europeans* and many of James's other heroines) transforms herself into a flambuoyant actress of her own life. It is in this sense that Sargent and Eakins, though apparently so entirely opposed in their art, actually reflect a common cultural background and a shared set of assumptions about self-expression. As we shall see in the early films, Barbara Stanwyck will be an actress who will stimulate Capra to entertain both conceptions of the self. In some scenes and films she will play a visionary questing for a release from worldly categories and definitions similar to Isabel Archer. In others she will play a consummate actress of her own life in a dazzling display of a mastery of alternative tones, styles, and costumes. The two kinds of characters are really only the same character imagined in two different forms of self-expression.*

If we did not already know this, one of Sargent's great double portraits would have helped us to see it. I have in mind *Mrs. Fiske Warren and Her Daughter Rachel*. In the figures of the portrait Sargent embodies the two alternatives for the self I am describing. The daughter is Isabel Archer – all vague, undeveloped, uncostumed dreaming; the mother is Madame Merle – poised, proper, posed, social presence of mind. We can read the two tightly intertwined and enjambed figures (and the two heads in particular) in several different ways: as the private self and the public manner; as figures of the past and the future; of innocent possibility and experienced realization; but however we gloss them, it is clear that in the unfocused, indirect gaze into the distance of the daughter Sargent is giving us a view of a state of reverie or imagination that necessarily will be, he suggests, sooner or later expressed socially in the fixed, direct look into our eyes of the mother. The figures are really one figure viewed twice, he tells us.

Of course, the painting also raises the implicit question of whether there is more of a loss or of a gain in this process of the mother's socialization or theatricalization of the daughter's incoherent reverie or vision but then, James's novels and Capra's films repeatedly ask the same question. In all three artists' work, a character's alluring theatricality (in the case of the first Sargent painting) or social polish and poise (in the case of the second) represent the

---

* Compare my discussion of *Shadows* in *American Dreaming: The Films of John Cassavetes and the American Experience* (Berkeley: University of California Press, 1985) and the cross-references to "scene making" in the work of Henry James for a somewhat fuller consideration of how theatricality, posing, and scene making are related, and not opposed to transcendental and visionary aspirations. The American self – half within, half outside of, social roles and definitions – expresses itself both in visionary flights from society and in theatrical play within it (and, in fact, the one thing is at times almost indistinguishable from the other). The passage from James's *Autobiography* that I quote farther on in my discussion (on the scene making of his cousin Marie and his own imaginative appreciation of her activity and of the moment) makes the connection between theatricality and transcendence explicit.

John Singer Sargent, *Mrs. Fiske Warren (Gretchen Osgood) and Her Daughter Rachel*. Courtesy of the Museum of Fine Arts, Boston; gift of Rachel Warren Barton and the Emily L. Ainsley Fund.

working off of unplaceable imaginative energies in stylistic flair. Yet, at the same time, they are also evidence of the anxiety, fragility, and vulnerability of the achieved self. Sargent's sitters are never relaxed or at ease. There is a tension, a willfulness to their creations of themselves which Sargent brings out in his figures that entirely distinguishes his portraits from those one finds in the English country-house portrait tradition (with which his work is often unfortunately lumped). In that tradition, stable identities can be taken for granted, can be reclined into amid the silks, the setters, and the grand, green pastoral settings. That lack of ease in James's, Sargent's, and Capra's work results in the sense of anxiety and vulnerability that one feels in their most ambitious figures, even as it is also the source of their creativity and the stimulus to the dangerously daring performances these figures launch themselves on, which are absent from the English tradition.

Capra's films explore the dangers and difficulties as well as the stimulations and incentives available to these precariously poised American selves. They ask the questions that are central to understanding our culture. How is the bootstrap project of creating a self and a place for the self in the world to be accomplished? What kinds of personal performances are possible in a decentered universe? Is there an alternative to moral authoritarianism that is not moral nihilism? Can values ever be recentered in the old way, or can personal performances find a new source of values beyond the superseded moral, social, and paternal centers? What is the destiny of the weak and vulnerable self that breaks free from institutional supports and imagines itself an exception to all preordained social forms? Can it ever find expression for its imagination in the real world of space and time, within the repressive structures of social organization and language, or is it doomed to perpetual imaginative homelessness? In the terms of *The Younger Generation*, can one avoid the destiny of the home-bound daughter without being doomed to the alienation and homelessness of the social-climbing son? For even provisional answers to these questions, one must turn to the films.

3

The dream and the world

That Certain Thing
Lady for a Day

> The actually possible in this world is vastly narrower than all that is demanded; and there is always a *pinch* between the ideal and the actual which can only be got through by leaving part of the ideal behind.
>
> – William James, "The Moral Philosopher and the Moral Life"

> Between the idealist and the pragmatist lies the truth, and they are often rubbing against each other.
>
> – Frank Capra, Interview with James Childs

If Capra's work can be viewed as an extended meditation on the imaginative relationship of fathers and sons and on the attempt of sons to become fathers, there is a daughter–husband metaphor that parallels the father–son metaphor. It is the Cinderella story, and it figures directly or indirectly in virtually all of Capra's films. Molly Kelly in *That Certain Thing*, Stew Smith in *Platinum Blonde*, Longfellow Deeds in *Mr. Deeds Goes to Town*, Peter Warne in *It Happened One Night*, Jefferson Smith in *Mr. Smith Goes to Washington*, and Emalee Jones in *Here Comes the Groom* are all, at one point or another in their films, referred to as "Cinderella" men or women. As is usually the case in instances of literary indebtedness, however, the presence of a myth can be felt even more powerfully when it is literally absent. *The Bitter Tea of General Yen*, *Lady for a Day*, *The Miracle Woman*, and *Pocketful of Miracles* do not refer to the Cinderella story in any explicit way, because they do not have to. Each is so clearly a Cinderella story that an explicit reference would be redundant.

What does the Cinderella story represent in Capra's imagination? Like any other moderately complex piece of cultural mythology, it resonates with many kinds of meanings. It is clear that when the newspapers call Longfellow Deeds or Jefferson Smith a "Cinderella man," they are using the allusion in a simply pejorative way. "Cinderella man" is journalistic shorthand for a man who has progressed from rags to riches without earning his way. Horatio Alger's heroes were respected because they made their way against adversity, but Cinderella prospers in an eminently un-American way – as a result of family connections (what else is a fairy godmother?) and by marrying money. Cinderella as the journalists interpret the story, represents not only an un-American but an unmanly way to get ahead, and that is why Deeds and Smith are livid at the comparison.

As befits the character of the newspapermen who pen it, this is a cynical interpretation of the Cinderella story. There is an alternative way of reading it as a distinctly American fantasy of upward mobility. If a poor boy can allegedly become President, then there is nothing un-American in a char girl's becoming a princess. The Cinderella story, according to this interpretation, is a fairy-tale version of the American dream of rising as high up on the social ladder as one's imagination carries one.

There are characters in Capra's films who represent both of these readings, but the interesting thing is how different Capra's understanding of Cinderella is from either of these interpretations. Both the un-American and the all-American readings understand the story almost entirely in economic and social terms. For Capra, though, it is not a parable of unearned, undeserved preferment nor of wholesome upward mobility but of something only tenuously connected with material gain. It is a myth about possible imaginative transformations of identity and about the potential crises of selfhood precipitated by such metamorphoses – a fable about not financial, but imaginative enrichments and about not social movements, but movements of desire.

The first film over which Capra had full artistic control – by his own account writing, directing, and editing it himself – was his initial film for Columbia, a silent picture called *That Certain Thing*, and it is, not surprisingly, a direct retelling of the Cinderella story. Capra gives a thumbnail synopsis of the plot in his autobiography, but, interestingly enough, he misremembers it, transforming its Cinderella story into a prototypical father–son conflict, suggesting how closely allied the two fables were in his mind. In Capra's synopsis, the film goes as follows. A wealthy businessman-father, A. B. Charles, Sr., has made his fortune running a chain of restaurants. When his son Andy Charles, Jr., marries Molly Kelly, a girl from the wrong side of the tracks, without his permission he disinherits him. Molly and Andy eventually triumph by founding their own box-lunch company, which takes business from the father's restaurant chain, earning his respect and his eventual approval of their marriage.

Since most of Capra's films are in an essential respect father–son stories, this summary is not entirely false to the film. What it leaves out is that the central character is neither A. B. Charles, Sr., nor Andy Charles, Jr., but Molly Kelly. In the first half of the film the two male characters, in fact, make only cameo appearances, and the first two-thirds of the movie come as close to being a version of the Cinderella story as anything Capra ever filmed. Capra even begins the film, as it were, on the hearthstone where the traditional Cinderella story commences. The first scene starts with a shot of Molly's mother slaving away at lighting a fire and doing the day's chores in a run-down cold water walk-up, and follows with a shot of Molly in the dilapidated bathroom, giving her two younger brothers a bath. Molly Kelly will go from rags to riches and back again in the next forty minutes of the film, just as Cinderella does, but Capra's version of the Cinderella story is always only incidentally about social transformation and economic enrichment. His real subject is imaginative transformation and the enrichments of life that consciousness can create. Even in this first scene in the shabby apartment, it is the richness of Molly's consciousness and not the impoverishment of her surroundings to which Capra draws a viewer's attention.

In a shorthand equation that he employs frequently in his subsequent work, Molly's special consciousness is immediately suggested by the fact that while her mother is immersed in the drudgery of housework, she transcends the prosaicness of her own task by turning it into an occasion for play. In all of Capra's films, a character's capacity for playing – in all of its many verbal, social, and theatrical dimensions – is used as a way of expressing imaginative energies too powerful, mobile, or strange to be channeled into less creative forms of behavior. "Playing" with it is how we make life or art matter, for Capra. Just as Capra transforms a banal "establishing" scene at the beginning of his film into an occasion for delight and humor for his viewers, Molly and her brothers turn the drudgery of their taking a bath into an opportunity for revelry. Both the filmmaker and his characters are using their imaginations to "make a scene" – an interesting, witty, funny episode – out of these inauspicious materials. This capacity to play in life and in film represents more than mere playfulness; it is a sign of one's ability to make humanly important meanings and significances and entertainment where they would otherwise not exist. It is a sign of one's ability to remain undaunted by one's surroundings, however humble they might appear to be, and even to transform the ordinary into something rich and strange. Like Sargent's sitters or James's heroines, Molly "makes a scene" where none would otherwise exist. Her playing (in a theatrical sense of the word) does it. It is this ability that James described in a similar vein in his *Autobiography*:

> The great impression, however, the one that has brought me so far, was another matter .... the presence at my side of my young cousin Marie, youngest daughter of the house, exactly of my own age, and named in honor of her having been born in Paris, to the influence of which fact her shining black eyes, her small quickness and brownness, marking sharply her difference from her sisters, so oddly, so almost extravagantly testified. It had come home to me by some voice of the air that she was "spoiled," and it made her in the highest degree interesting; we ourselves had been so associated, at home, without being in the least spoiled (I think we rather missed it:) so that I knew about these subjects of invidious reflection only by literature – mainly, no doubt, that of the nursery – in which they formed, quite by themselves, a romantic class; and, the fond fancy always predominant, I prized even while a little dreading the chance to see the condition at work. This chance was given me, it was clear – though I risk in my record of it a final anticlimax – by a remark from my uncle Augustus to his daughter: seated duskily in our group, which included two or three dim dependent forms, he expressed the strong

opinion that Marie should go to bed . . . . It had been remarked but in the air, I feel sure, that Marie should seek her couch – a truth by the dark wing of which I ruefully felt myself brushed; and the words seemed therefore to fall with a certain ironic weight. What I have retained of their effect, at any rate, is the vague fact of some objection raised by my cousin and some sharper point to his sentence supplied by her father; promptly merged in a visible commotion, a flutter of my young companion across the gallery as for refuge in the maternal arms, a protest and an appeal in short which drew from my aunt the simple phrase that was from that moment so preposterously to "count" for me. "Come now, my dear; don't make a scene – I insist on your not making a scene!" That was all the witchcraft the occasion used, but the note was none the less epoch-making. The expression, so vivid, so portentous, was one I had never heard – it had never been addressed to us at home; and who should say now what a world one mightn't read into it? It seemed freighted to sail so far; it told me so much about life. Life at these intensities clearly became "scenes"; but the great thing, the immense illumination, was that we could make them or not as we chose. It was a long time of course before I began to distinguish between those within our compass more particularly as spoiled and those producible on a different basis and which should involve detachment, involve presence of mind; just the qualities in which Marie's possible output was apparently deficient. It didn't in the least matter accordingly whether or not a scene *was* then proceeded to – and I have lost all count of what immediately happened. The mark had been made for me and the door flung open; the passage, gathering up all the elements of the troubled time, had been itself quite a scene, quite enough of one, and I had become aware with it of a rich accession of possibilities. *

Molly's "scene-making" richness of consciousness and capacities of per-formance are the source of both her dramatic interest and most of her social and romantic problems. Though she is dutifully and dully courted by a streetcar motorman who lives in her apartment building, she impractically, idealistically, and playfully rebuffs all of his earnest advances. In the second scene, we see her at her job as a sales clerk at a cigar counter in the lobby of a posh hotel, typically gazing off into the distance, daydreaming about marrying a millionaire. Like the capacity to play, the capacity to dream – specifically, to disengage oneself meditatively from the workaday affairs of the world, becomes one of the key events in Capra's subsequent work. Scenes involving daydream-ing, gazing out of a window, looking up at the stars, literally or metaphorical-ly turning one's back on social responsibilities, are used almost formulaically to suggest that a character has unrealized resources of imagination.

The fairy-tale quality of Molly's life is underlined by the fact that her dreams come true almost immediately in a comically overliteral way. She leaves the cigar counter at the end of the day vowing to "bump into a millionaire," only to knock Andy Charles down on the street seconds later, as she runs for a bus. The two are married after a six-hour courtship almost as brief and unrealistic

---

* Henry James, *Autobiography*, ed. Frederick W. Dupee (New York: Criterion Books, 1956), pp. 106–7.

as Cinderella's. What most intrigues Capra in this Cinderella story is not his or Molly's ability to treat life as a fairy tale but all of the ways in which life alternately fulfills and resists our fairy-tale transformations of it. Molly is a glorious dreamer, and her absent-minded dreaming indeed results in her actually "bumping into" and marrying the millionaire of her dreams, but Capra is at the same time profoundly distrustful of Molly's facile imaginative transformations of reality. Dreams, however grand and gorgeous, can also be an evasion of harder truths, and play can be a form of irresponsibility and frivolousness.

In the first scene of the film, when Molly plays with her younger brothers in the tub by splashing them with water, Capra momentarily dissolves away from the scene while tracking downward to show that the splashed water has soaked through to the ceiling and floor of the apartment below. He turns it immediately into a cinematic joke by showing the woman downstairs accusing her dog of wetting on the rug, but there is a serious side to Capra's playfulness as a director at this moment that is lacking in Molly's use of play as a form of escapism. In that sly imaginative movement downward into the apartment below and in the seriocomic tone Capra instantly establishes concerning the puddle is just the bracing double-mindedness, the exhilarating ability to hold in one thought both the escapist joys of play and the serious consequences in reality, that Molly herself fails to display. To make an analogy with the quotation from James just used, if Molly's performance in this scene is a little like Marie's, a little irresponsible and self-centered, Capra's more resembles that of James himself and is in favor of what James calls "detachment" and "presence of mind" – "just those qualities in which Marie's [or Molly's] possible output was apparently deficient." Or to take another example, in the scene in which Capra shows us Molly musing dreamily at the cigar counter and subsequently knocking down Andy Charles on the sidewalk, he allows a viewer to appreciate both her dreaming and the fact that it is a form of absentmindedness that is not entirely admirable at work or safe for other pedestrians on the street. It is in the details of Molly's whirlwind courtship, however, that Capra most complexly explores the ways in which life is or is not livable as a game or fairy tale. Smitten by her daffy eccentricity but unaware of her impoverished background, Andy Charles asks Molly to go dancing that night, but Capra emphasizes that, unlike Cinderella, Molly has no fairy godmother to turn her work clothes into a ball gown. However grand and iconoclastic her imagination of herself, Molly is immediately forced to deal with practical worldly and social realities that resist her imaginative transformations. She needs to find something to wear if the crazy dream-come-true is not to end then and there. She begs and borrows accessories, shoes, and a dress to wear, but in the next scene Capra literalizes William James's metaphor of the "pinch" between ideals and realities or his own metaphor of their "rub" (in the epigraphs to this chapter) by showing that the hand-me-down shoes hurt her so much that she is forced to make awkward excuses to Andy all evening long about why she does not want to dance.

Cinderella did not have to scrounge about for jewelry or a gown to wear, and her slippers fit her so perfectly that the prince used one of them to discover her true identity (which is the wittiness of Capra's decision to make Molly's dancing slippers the one completely ill-fitting item in her wardrobe).

If there is one moment in the scene of her date with Andy that summarizes the complexity of Capra's presentation of Molly's efforts to live her dream in a world that everywhere resists and mocks the ideals of our dreams, it is the moment in which she first comes down to Andy's waiting car. He compliments her on her appearance – "You look marvellous!" – and she replies, "Oh, it's just a little costume I threw together." In that apparently casual but actually carefully rehearsed and postured reply is summarized the full complexity of her situation. She did "throw it together," not in the way he thinks, but in desperation. It is a "costume," but not in the sense of the word he understands. Her reply suspends in one phrase the feelings, ranging from fear to wonder, aroused by the scene in which it occurs: on the one hand, the radical, dangerous falseness of her position as an impostor, and her own felt inadequacy to live up to the part she has for so long dreamed of playing; and, on the other, the daring, the glamour, the theatrical adventurousness of her effort, and the possible success of her whole imaginative enterprise of self-creation. We feel her real vulnerability and weakness, and yet also her true imaginative power and poise. We are made aware of the impossibility, the audacity, of attempting to live life as if it were art, fairy tale, or theater, yet we also glimpse the exciting, frightening prospect that perhaps one can make up one's identity in this way and successfully improvise one's lines as one goes along. Capra emphasizes the theatrical possibilities in Molly's reply – the possibility that life can be lived as theater – not only by having his actress employ a dramatic tone and gesture as she says these words but also by deliberately "staging" the entire scene in the courtyard of the apartment complex in which she lives. The courtyard, with the tenants leaning out of the windows gawking at Molly and her rich suitor, forms a natural amphitheater, within which the entire scene between Molly and Andy is explicitly transformed into a "scene" taking place in front of an audience. The viewer is more than half convinced that life can be turned into theater, that ordinary daily experience can be transformed imaginatively into something this rich and stimulating.

Natural amphitheaters like this one are going to occur in film after film as the places in which the performances of Capra's characters are forced to take place. From the boxing ring of *So This Is Love* and the bank lobby of *American Madness* to the Senate chamber of *Smith* and the radio station and baseball field of *Doe*, Capra imagines his characters performing in front of audiences in their films in surroundings that remind one of the crowded soundstages on which the actors playing these characters themselves performed in a central cleared space surrounded by hordes of onlookers. If for Shakespeare all the world was a stage, it would not be far wrong to say that for Capra all of life was a soundstage. The complexities and difficulties of making scenes in life was always understood in terms of the complexities and difficulties of making scenes in the movies.

It is not accidental or unimportant that *That Certain Thing, Ladies of Leisure, The Miracle Woman, Bitter Tea, Forbidden, Lady for a Day, Deeds*, and *Doe* all take costuming as their explicit subject. The individual's choice of clothing is the easiest way for him or her to establish an instant personal style or identity, and the most convenient visual way for Capra to represent it. Similarly, the manipulation of a person's costuming by others – which happens with equal frequency in these films – is the easiest way to represent the distortions of personal identity facing an individual. Costuming is never a neutral event in the power-saturated world of a Capra film. It is always either an act of imaginative prowess and power (when the person is in control of his or her own costuming, as in most of the films starring Barbara Stanwyck) or an act of imaginative domination (when someone else steps in to manipulate a character's appearance, as happens most obviously in the two films starring Gary Cooper).

In either case, the audience is made aware of the fragility and vulnerability of the self underneath the costume changes. This is obvious when the individual is being tyrannized, but it is equally true when the individual chooses his or her own costume and identity, as in *That Certain Thing, The Miracle Woman, Ladies of Leisure, Forbidden*, and *Bitter Tea*. The question each of these films implicitly raises is whether the self can live up to the stylistic identity that it has chosen. The question is whether imagination can successfully change reality, whether the self can gain in possibilities of expression by such theatricality, or whether it will only become more lost than ever, buried or hidden under its own theatrical proliferations and projections.★

That is why it is important that these films call our attention to the costumes worn by the star *as costumes*. Style does not unproblematically make the man (or woman) in Capra's art, but rather raises disturbing questions about where the person may be underneath the style. The social or verbal *expression* of authentic imaginative identity is not a primary concern in European art but is a near obsession in American. Capra's films locate us and their central characters in the world that Emerson, Hawthorne, Adams, and James worried about, where individuals are threatened with erasure by their own and others' relentless stylistic proliferations. We are in the world that Isabel Archer puzzles over when she tells Madame Merle that her own clothes do not and never can express her, or the world of much of Eakins's and Hopper's and Sargent's work. In Eakins's case, it is one in which the clothing frequently does not seem to fit the character putatively defined by it, or in which the character's costume seems out of place or uncomfortable to the character, both physically and metaphysically. In Hopper's it is a world in which the character's authentic self seems to be visible only when she has stepped out of her clothes – as in the studies of women in their bedrooms, or when work clothes have been shed for

---

★ See, for comparison, the discussions of theatricality and costuming in John Cassavetes's *Killing of a Chinese Bookie, Opening Night, Gloria*, and *Love Streams*, in my *American Dreaming*. In these films, as in some of Capra's work, theatricality and costuming become metaphors for the modernist dispersion of the self into a disconnected succession of superficial styles, roles, and functions.

Sunday or evening casual dress, as in his studies of men and women outdoors on their days off or in their spare time. Even Sargent, who obviously believed passionately in the expressiveness of clothing and theatrical gesture, raises implicit questions about their expressive function. Although he never dispenses with them in his paintings, as Eakins and Hopper do, the willful posing and posturing in Sargent's work raise the same questions asked by the other two artists, questions about to what extent the self can authentically express itself in such conspicuously public stylistic display. The felt incommensurability between the energies of imagination and the practical forms of expression available to it in the world that is expressed by each of these very different artists takes us to the heart of Capra's work.

A further resonance of the courtyard scene, which links it with a dozen similar scenes in Capra's early work, is the sense it communicates that what we are witnessing is not only Molly Kelly's exploration of the possibilities of theatrically transforming life into art but Frank Capra's as well. Though Capra is often regarded as a strictly realistic director, and his work is therefore contrasted with that of a stylistically self-conscious or "artistic" director like Sternberg, in Capra's first five or six years with Columbia Pictures (from *That Certain Thing*, in 1928, to *Bitter Tea* and *Lady for a Day* in 1933), his work displays an unashamed fascination with all the ways in which life can be heightened, enriched and transformed, cinematically, by special lighting, photography, acting, costuming effects. Capra's interest in artistic special effects culminates in the out-and-out fantasy costume dramas of *Bitter Tea* and *Lady for a Day*, but, stretching the term, more than half of the fourteen surviving previous films that he made with Columbia are costume dramas, in the sense that they are, in one way or another, enchanted evocations of special or exotic imaginative worlds, evocations that are themselves more than half in love with the sheer glamour of artistic transformation. What makes Capra different from contemporary special effects specialists like Kubrick, Spielberg, and Lucas, in even the most fantastic or exotic of his films, is that he explores not the kinds of transformations unique to art, but the ways in which the transformations of life overlap with (or at times outdo) those of art. The special effects of his films do not bring into existence alternative worlds more exciting than our own but are used to communicate the magic and excitement of the world we already live in. As the courtyard scene suggests, Capra is fascinated with the way an attractive young woman can transform life into theater, with how her sense of costuming can be just as exciting as a costume designer's, with how her performance with a suitable lover can be as erotically exciting and imaginatively stimulating as that of a movie star in a film.

Capra's earliest films are studies of women with the ability to transform and creatively enrich reality, and his imagination was as productively stimulated by the beautiful young women in his films (both the characters and the actresses who played them) and the theatrical possibilities that they brought to life as Henry James's imagination was by the young heiresses in his novels. For both artists this ability to transform reality never quite lost its connotations of deceit and illicitness, however. For both, artistic arrangements were always, at least potentially, forms of falsehood and betrayal. Especially in the films that Capra made from 1936 on, art, costuming, and the theatrical packaging of personality in general become increasingly questionable activities.

If theatrical young women are the key figures in almost all of Capra's early work, one actress in particular stimulated his imagination more than any other. What Dietrich was to Sternberg, Barbara Stanwyck was to Capra. She was the woman who for him most consistently and successfully could imbue even the most pedestrian moments of life with the mystery and gorgeousness of art. Capra has confessed in his autobiography that he was in love with Stanwyck in these years, and the fondness of the creator for what he himself has half created shows not only in the plots of the screenplays that he wrote to permit her to play Galatea to his Pygmalion, but in the style of the scenes in which she appears. The glamorous photography and lighting is Capra's way of working off imaginative energies that can find no other form of expression within the sometimes pedestrian plots. Like Dietrich, Stanwyck became the fortunate recipient of all of her director's fantasies about the power of art and the enchantments of theatricality. The Stanwyck visible on-screen is a pure projection of Capra's imagination of feminine allure. It is telling that even in the films in which Stanwyck plays an openly wicked or deceitful character, one in which her costumes and performances are deliberately and explicitly hypocritical, as in *The Miracle Woman* and *Ladies of Leisure*, Capra is so fascinated by the imaginative possibilities she opens up that he allows the films to make excuses for her theatricality. He holds moral judgments of her character in abeyance and implies that the artifice she uses to deceive may be preferable to mere plodding morality.

In short, one can say that, like Pygmalion or Dr. Coppelius, and like many another director, artist, or choreographer, Capra fell in love with someone who was at least partly a product of his own artistic powers of transformation.* During the time when Capra was making *That Certain Thing* and many of his earliest films at Columbia, Harry Cohn's tightfisted policy that actors and actresses must provide their own wardrobes for their parts (since Columbia Pictures had no regular costume department) only further blurred putative distinctions between the effects of art and those of life. The "costume" a character "threw together" may indeed have been a costume that the actress herself "threw together" to get a part or impress a director.

Molly Kelly's and Barbara Stanwyck's transformations of reality into art, and their capacity to imbue ordinary daily life with the excitement of a cinematic adventure, were of more than theoretical interest to Capra. What they are doing both as characters and as actresses is what he is engaged in doing as a director. Director, actress, and character are conspiring to stimulate the

---

* This recognition is incorporated into the plot of *Ladies of Leisure*, where an artist falls in love with a call girl played by Stanwyck because he sees in her lovely and pure pictorial qualities that bear absolutely no resemblance to her true character in the film.

imagination, to open opportunities for scene making where none were previously present in the rush and confusion of life or of a soundstage. Molly Kelly is a Cinderella in her film, but that is the least of Capra's interest in the myth of Cinderella. Filmmaking itself was for him a way of enriching reality beyond even what a fairy godmother could do.

Yet Molly is a far from adequate Cinderella. Her error is to fall for her own apparently easy enchantments. She makes the mistake of thinking that the imaginative transformation of life can be as effortlessly magical as her effects make it seem. As the rest of *That Certain Thing* is devoted to showing, the dream, in this form, cannot last. One wakes up sooner or later, and at that point the real work begins. At first everything goes well in her adventure. Andy courts Molly; they are married; she moves into a new apartment with him, and he buys her a whole new wardrobe of "costumes" on the first day. Almost immediately, however, his father disinherits him, cuts off his credit, and forces him to return everything he has bought. One morning Molly literally and metaphorically "wakes up" to discover that she has nothing. Before her eyes (and our own) the tradesmen and merchants swarm in to confiscate the costumes and remove the props of her existence.★

In a scene of crisis and despair that anticipates similar moments in *Lady for a Day*, *Deeds*, *Smith*, *Doe*, *It's a Wonderful Life*, and *Pocketful of Miracles*, Capra dramatizes the vulnerability of the self-created identity. Everything Molly has achieved is shown to be what she (and the viewer) knew it to be all along – merely a creation of style. It has all been theater, with the utter insubstantiality of all theatrical special effects. Once the homemade self has been denuded of its stage props, gauze scrims, and satin gowns, it must face the fact that perhaps it has no other resources, discovering the truth of the old bromide about Hollywood, that underneath all the tinsel and glitter is only more tinsel and more glitter. There are no substantial social or moral values for the traumatized self to fall back on; no supports outside of itself to lean on. Its declaration of its independence of social, moral, and psychological fixities made its fairy-tale ascent possible, but it also makes the ensuing disintegration of the self total and devastating. The American dream of success has turned into an American nightmare of shame, public humiliation, and powerlessness – or rather, the dream and the nightmare have been revealed to be two sequential acts in one inexorable drama played out by the naked, vulnerable, infinitely fragile American ego. This was never recognized by Horatio Alger. Not since the novels of Edith Wharton and Theodore Dreiser has the connection between the two states – of self-composition and self-dissolution – been more powerfully demonstrated. The self that can make itself up as it goes along with such facility and quickness always runs the risk of coming unraveled with equal rapidity and completeness.

★ As they do their work, it is impossible not to be reminded of stagehands striking a set. Though he probably was not conscious of it, Capra implicitly equates the shattering of Molly's social and financial illusions with the shattering of a filmmaker's or viewer's cinematic illusions.

Molly sneaks out of the apartment alone, without her new husband's knowledge, ashamed of having ruined him, and catatonically makes her way back home in rags and tatters, walking through a pouring rain. The neighbors who gawked at her performance from their tenement windows in the earlier scene are again there as an audience as she returns in this one, but whereas earlier they had applauded, they now ridicule her. They have read in the newspapers about both her fairy-tale marriage and her subsequent disgrace. Capra explicitly figures Molly as a dreamer or sleepwalker as she makes her way up the stairs of the tenement, back to her family's shabby apartment, under the prying, voyeuristic gaze of the onlookers. Capra edited this film himself, as he did almost all of the films from this point in his career on – something virtually without parallel in standard studio assembly-line production practice. In a two- or three-minute director's and editor's sequence, he fades in and out on distorted shots of the neighbors' jeering faces, lighted so expressionistically and photographed so unnaturally with a short-focus lens in extreme close-up, that the distinct impression is that it is all a hallucination or nightmare dreamed by the sleepwalking Molly.

In Capra's relentless cutting from terrifying face to face around Molly, she is shown going to pieces both psychologically and cinematically. Her costumed, posed body no longer defines a coherent, unitary, theatrical presence in this orgy of cuts and sutures, as it did in the earlier scenes. Significantly, however, little has changed in the film at the deepest level. The very capacity for stylistically changing reality by means of theatrical artifice that allowed Molly to imagine an alternative to her surroundings has now generated this expressionistic nightmare-hallucination of shame and humiliation. As he will so often in his subsequent work, Capra shows the intimate connection between the American romantic-dream film and the American film noir nightmare movie. The same empowering of personal imagination that creates the one creates the other. To daringly rise above one's situation imaginatively, as Molly does earlier, is simultaneously to risk the disastrous imaginative alienation from life that she experiences now. To allow the distorting forces of imagination and desire radically to criticize one's social situation is potentially also to abandon oneself to an orgy of desire and imagination without any possible form of expression or control.★

In Capra's work the Cinderella story almost always brings a character to the verge of suicide. Molly is one of the few Cinderella figures in his movies who does not explicitly consider suicide, but she is implicitly suicidal when she returns home. Suicide is the natural complement of the Cinderella story in Capra's cinematic universe, since to unmoor the self from customary social structures is potentially to court self-disintegration. As the dramatists of the English Renaissance understood, the self that has been granted such enormous

★ This is the same point made in John Cassavetes's *Opening Night* and *Lovestreams*. See my discussion in *American Dreaming: The Films of John Cassavetes and the American Experience* (Berkeley: University of California Press, 1985), pp. 252–9.

powers of improvising and "playing" with its own identity must face the prospect of the whole project of self-fashioning coming apart. The disastrous disintegration of the self is the flip side of its being given such a large scope to make itself in the first place. *That Certain Thing* dramatizes the instability of the identity freed to be deformed by the pressure of desire. To empower idealism and illusion as forces of self-composition is, unfortunately, equally to empower disillusionment and despair as forces of self-destruction and decomposition.

Few directors though, have a more characteristically American optimism about the power of the individual to break away from the fetters of past selves and roles and successfully fashion a free and independent imaginative identity. Although the central characters in most of Capra's major films contemplate suicide at least momentarily, no suicides actually take place. (The title character's suicide in *The Bitter Tea of General Yen* is a special case, not an exception to this rule.) For all of his appreciation of the vulnerability of the self in self-creation, Capra almost always has a sublimely American faith that his characters are adequate to the challenges facing them. In this respect, as in so many others, he represents a sensibility the very opposite to the pessimism of European filmmakers like Bergman and Antonioni, whose characters not only frequently contemplate and occasionally commit suicide, but who even more tellingly frequently live their lives for the duration of their films in a state of catatonic near death that makes suicide seem almost superfluous. Few directors, even in the American tradition, had greater confidence in their characters' strength. ★

Following *That Certain Thing* (to which I will return shortly), Capra made several other films that implicitly or explicitly continue his exploration of the Cinderella story. *The Miracle Woman, Ladies of Leisure,* and *Bitter Tea* all star Barbara Stanwyck in versions of the Cinderella role, and *Platinum Blonde* performs a sex-change operation on the fairy tale and puts a man in the lead. In each of these films Capra plays fairy godmother to his central characters, and they willingly conspire with him in attempting to transform their otherwise ordinary identities into something socially and cinematically extraordinary. In none of them is the transformation more daring than in the sixth, and what might be called the culminating film in the Cinderella sequence, *Lady for a Day*. The title proclaims the Cinderella theme. †

After a series of films starring the young and beautiful Barbara Stanwyck in the role of Cinderella, perhaps it was the challenge of orchestrating the

---

★ Cassavetes and May come to mind as directors whose characters have a similar resiliance and self-reliance under the most extreme adversity, even as they perform on the boundaries of their own impending self-destruction.

† Capra's use of the word *lady* in the title of this film (as in his earlier *Ladies of Leisure*), like Henry James's use of it in the title of his *Portrait of a Lady*, is never entirely free from a distinctively American sense of irony about the word. Neither James nor Capra is entirely convinced that becoming a blue-blooded "lady" is necessarily more of a gain than a loss for a red-blooded American woman.

transformation of a seventy-five year-old stage actress that stimulated Capra. *Lady for a Day* stars the aging May Robson, who, if the truth be told, had been no raving beauty even fifty years earlier when she was Barbara Stanwyck's age, but never was Capra to play a more benevolent and inventive fairy godmother to his star. *Lady for a Day* is his most exuberant and joyous display of his powers of stylistic transformation. None of his films better communicates his love of dazzling metamorphoses, both by means of the transformations that take place within the plot (as the characters transform themselves into fictional "characters" and execute a far-fetched "plot" of their own to advance their personal interests) and through the transformations that Capra achieves as director through his skillful manipulation of acting, editing, lighting, and photography. *Lady for a Day* is one of Capra's happiest and most high-spirited achievements, a song of praise to the power of the human imagination at work both inside and outside of the film's narration.

The film is based on a Damon Runyon story, the preposterousness of which Capra does nothing to lessen, since the subject of his film is the vulnerable factitiousness of certain stylistic arrangements of reality, in both life and art. Robson plays Apple Annie, a shabby street beggar who barely keeps body and soul together by selling apples and shaking down other beggars and ruffians who intrude into her territory. Eighteen years earlier she had had an illegitimate daughter, who has been shipped off to be educated in a European convent. Louise does not remember her mother or know her own true identity. In corresponding with her, Annie has maintained the fiction that she herself is a wealthy heiress, Mrs. E. Worthington Manville, a pillar of New York society. As long as she can keep corresponding with her in Europe on stolen hotel stationery all is well, but as the film begins Annie learns that Louise has just become engaged to a young European nobleman and that he, she, and his family are about to arrive in New York to meet Annie and to arrange the preliminaries for the wedding. The chief interest in the story for Capra is that Apple Annie must now make her fiction pass for reality. She must become a "lady for a day" (or actually for closer to a week) by stylistically transforming herself and her entire world. Like Molly, she must dare to make the fiction life, attempt actually to live the dream she has up to now only been dreaming for her daughter.

Needless to say, she succeeds at the preposterous masquerade, after a comic series of close calls and last-minute escapes. Yet one notices that even here, in this movie that is so much lighter than *That Certain Thing*, Capra never allows the viewer to forget the precariousness of Annie's fiction, the marginality of all stylistic achievement, the susceptibility to breakdown of the self that dares to attempt to create itself and a world for it to live in out of nothing but its imagination and its powers of performance. It is the work, the sheer difficulty, the labor of stylistic performance (both for Apple Annie, masquerading as Mrs. E. Worthington Manville, and for the veteran stage actress May Robson as an actress performing this complex double role in a movie) that is felt at each moment. Capra builds into the film a recognition of a rock-hard reality that nearly succeeds in resisting both his own and Annie's imaginative redeployments. Annie's transformation is achieved at the cost of the most extraordinary stylistic labor and split-second timing of effects, and is always on the brink of unraveling and falling apart. If there is magic in the film, it is a magic very much like the magic of the syntax and rhyme scheme in Robert Frost's greatest poems involving comparably chastened imaginative trans-forming – a magic delicately yet muscularly labored into existence moment by moment in a series of precarious, braced, and never more than tentative meta-phorical choices and tonal movements. As Frost puts it in his sonnet "Mowing," it is the opposite of a "dream of the gift of idle hours./ Or easy gold at the hand of fay or elf." His tough-minded magic is a stern ceremony in which "Anything more than the truth would have seemed too weak." That is why in this poem Frost's labor of love – like Capra's and Apple Annie's in this film – fully earns the right to be called "earnest."

As comically ebullient as *Lady for a Day* is, reveling in a series of crazily comical transformations, the emotional power of the film (and of its slightly attenuated remake, *Pocketful of Miracles*) derives almost entirely from the precariousness of the self in transformation. The final half hour of both versions leaves the viewer breathless with anxiety and sympathy for Annie as, on the big night toward which the entire film has been building, the carefully orchestrated "plot" and "characters" all but unravel, and Annie is faced with the potential humiliation of having to admit to her daughter that her whole life has been a lie. There is a moving moment in *Pocketful of Miracles* that sums up the potential psychic bewilderment of Annie's stylistic daring as complexly as the remark about throwing together a costume sums up Molly's. Immediately following her initial cosmetic transformation into Mrs. E. Worthington Manville, Apple Annie stands alone before a full-length mirror and admits that even she does not recognize herself: "I don't know who that is in there," she mutters, not reassured but disoriented at having succeeded in passing her own fiction off even on herself. She picks up her old apple basket and confusedly tries to remind herself who she is, mumbling into the mirror, "Apples?" It is a recurrent vision of the divided self in crisis, attempting to believe in its powers of making itself up and holding itself together as it goes along, yet continuously on the brink either of losing control of its own fictions or of having the fictions divulged only as fictions and the self left exposed and alone that links films as different as *That Certain Thing*, *Lady for a Day*, and *Doe*. Precisely to the extent that the self dares to extend itself imaginatively, it is increasingly exposed and vulnerable. It is always in danger of playing itself out, in more than one sense of the phrase. With an awareness that Whitman all too seldom seems to show, Capra suggests that in this Whitmanesque plentitude of being, the self may be on the verge of being lost or dispersed in the roles it dares to play.

Throughout the final third of *Lady for a Day* Annie is under the threat of exposure that could destroy her masquerade as Princess Cinderella and transform her back into the char girl. Her identity is threatened until the final minutes of the film. Capra takes pity on Annie and saves her, as is his wont, with a typically miraculous wish-fulfillment ending, but since the outcome (just like the ending of *It's a Wonderful Life*) seems as miraculous to her as it does to the viewer, it does very little to erase the anxieties about the project of fashioning a self that the film has documented at such length.

With this observation, after such a lengthy excursus, I want to return to the end of *That Certain Thing*. Though all of his films demonstrate the challenges facing the creative individual who is estranged from society, Capra also wants to believe that the final integration of the creative individual into society is both possible and desirable. Most of his endings gesture toward a grand reintegration of the alienated figure into the social matrix. That is why Capra cannot leave Molly in the state of alienation in which she returns home. The first two-thirds of the film traces the trajectory of Molly's personal dream of easy riches, followed by her personal nightmare of shame and disgrace upon awakening from her dream. There is always a triple movement in Capra's work, however: the dream, the awakening, and the enforced return of the awakened dreamer to the world. Molly briefly lived her dream; she was rudely and unceremoniously awakened; and in the final fifteen or twenty minutes of *That Certain Thing* she is forced to function again in the real world. Not to be included as a member of a larger, waking society is, for Capra – no matter how imaginative and creative an individual is – axiomatically to have failed. For Capra, the movements of individual imagination and desire must ultimately be expressible within the social and institutional structures of life, and of film. The private, anarchic energies of Molly's dreaming (in the first section of the film) and of her nightmare (in the second) must be converted into public, social expression (in the final movement). Capra follows this pattern even if he has to do violence to his own film to accomplish it, and that is exactly what he does in this movie. The clumsiness of his attempt to "make something," socially, of Molly's state of hallucination and shame is eloquent testimony to the extreme importance Capra attached to the process of the conversion of personal imagination into socially profitable action.

A scene or two after Molly's return home, Capra abandons his own film and all the interests and energies it has generated up to that moment in order to make a fifteen-minute coda that suggests that Andy and Molly can convert their condition of shared imaginative alienation and social estrangement into concrete capitalistic gain. The effect is rather primitive and absurd, and it would be almost comical if the effort it represents, especially in the light of the analogous and much better films to come, was not so touchingly serious. Molly and the disinherited Andy are reunited, and the remaining minutes of the film are devoted to a very sketchy presentation of their rapid climb out of poverty. Molly founds a company that sells box lunches, which competes successfully with the A. B. Charles restaurant empire and seriously cuts into its business. By the final minutes, the young couple have earned both the respect and the financial backing of Andy's father.

One sort of American dreaming has been glibly transformed into another.

Molly's imagination, which previously had no means of satisfactory worldly expression for itself, suddenly finds perfect and satisfying expression in business success. We leave a film that explores the glorious irrelevance of dreams and enter the fantasy world of Herbert Hoover Republicanism in which Molly and Andy turn dreams into dollars. The result, needless to say, is the destruction of everything that was interesting in the movie. The abrupt breakdown, the clumsy switch of theme, and the shift of tone from drama to farce is interesting, however, for the clarity with which it reveals Capra's irreconcilable double purpose. He cannot bridge the gap between the first two-thirds of his movie and its conclusion. For forty or fifty minutes he brilliantly evokes the wildness, the strangeness, the gratuitousness of Molly's fantasies and desires, and then in the final ten or fifteen minutes of the film he suddenly turns everything upside down to show that they can find perfect expression in the Molly Box Lunch Company. We go from vague yearnings, irresponsible daydreaming, alluring theatricality and bewildering nightmare, to a chamber of commerce after-dinner skit on capitalistic productivity. The film falls into two ill-fitting, unbalanced, totally mismatched pieces (though Capra, it should be emphasized, shows no awareness of this asymmetry or incongruity).

Since the two movements of *That Certain Thing* will return to haunt Capra in almost all of his subsequent work, it is worth taking some time to spell out how they differ in more than subject matter or theme. The dream and the nightmare sections of the film are filmed in a highly expressionistic style, with many expressive close-ups, much low-key lighting, use of short lenses for special effects, and long scenes that involve solitary or unsocial figures or that rely on a character's silence (scenes in which glances or gestures largely replace words). The final capitalistic section of the film is done in an entirely different style, however. It is scripted and staged as a comedy of manners, with what is usually called realistic blocking and *le plan américain* photography (middle-distance camera setups, use of medium-length lenses, and neutrally descriptive or so-called objective fill lighting), a heavy reliance (even in this silent film) on scenes of dialogue and social interaction, and vigorous group activity involving intricately timed and paced interactions between two or more characters, all in the service of a generally comic series of events. Capra's subsequent work will frequently alternate between scenes of the one sort or of the other: between expressionistic scenes emphasizing the personal point of view of a tragically or idealistically isolated character, and objective scenes of group interaction in which the individual is merged into a community of others. These are two stylistic worlds, two narrative systems, two visions of life, that will reappear in film after film, and that Capra will be unable to harmonize or blend into each other.

It is clear that in this final section Capra is trying to "wake up" his dream film and dream character by forcing it and her into contact with the practicalities of life. Formally, he is interested in converting his dream sequences into dramatic and narrative realities. Molly is being educated to what Capra had had to learn in his own profession as a young filmmaker: that dreams count only insofar as they can be expressed institutionally, and that can happen in Hollywood only when they are transformed into something socially and narratively palpable and practical.

The most telling fact about this film, though, is that Capra cannot benefit from his own insight. The first section liberates energies for which the concluding section cannot find a place or expression. The ending just does not work – but that, after all, is testimony to the power of the initial dream sections of the film.

The schizophrenia of *That Certain Thing* is going to repeat itself in almost every one of Capra's subsequent films. Capra is profoundly torn between two contradictory allegiances in all of his work. On the one hand, he is committed to affirming the absolute power and sovereignty of the individual imagination, and on the other he believes with equal fervor in the requirement that the individual become integrated into a community of others and express him- or herself in society. If the first commitment represents Capra's faith in the autonomy and strength of the individual, the second demands that he engage himself ethically with others and stylistically with the forms of common expression. These are not always reconcilable interests, and film after film will demonstrate that both commitments cannot always be honored at the same time.

I believe that Capra never made up his mind about whether both could be satisfied. At times, in particular films, he argues on behalf of the translatability of an individual's ideals, desires, or dreams into the forms of ordinary social life. He attempts to convince a viewer (and perhaps himself as well) that nothing is lost in this translation. Yet at other times, in the same films or others, he seems to argue the opposite: that all public, social, and institutional systems of expression into which we might translate our imaginations are inevitably repressive of our finest, freest energies and feelings. In the following chapters much of my argument will be devoted to tracing the ebbs and flows of Capra's alternating faith or doubt about the possibilities of individual imaginative expression in the forms of language or social relationship. His films are energized not by his certainties, but by his ambivalences about the repressiveness of social and institutional forms of expression.

What can be said about all of his films is that expression is intrinsically and unavoidably problematic for Capra, for the same reason that it is in the work of the most ambitious and challenging nineteenth- and twentieth-century American writers. Insofar as Capra (like these earlier artists) imagines the individual to be suspended between, and to owe allegiance to, two distinct and incommensurate realms – one the realm of the pure vision or transcendental impulse, the other the realm of social structures and forms of understanding – and, futhermore, imagines the second realm to be at odds with the first, an expressive gap inevitably opens between them. Something is always in danger of being repressed or lost in the movement from the one to the other. It is revealing that expression is not problematic in this way in either the more purely pragmatic, socially organized work of Hawks and Sturges, or in the more purely idealistic work of Chaplin and Sternberg.* That is because none of these four is interested in the problem of translation from one realm to the other as Capra is, since each of them more or less confines his work to one realm or to the other. Capra's films are – for himself and for his characters – attempts to bridge that gap, to make the movement or act of translation from the one realm to the other; to "speak" personal ideals and emotions in the always potentially repressive forms of coherent, social, moral narrative expression.

It is in this respect that Capra can be said to be working in the distinctive tradition of American modernism defined in the writing of Emerson, Hawthorne, Melville, and James. This tradition deserves to be called post-Romantic, in that it represents an attempt to translate the lyrical effusions of Romanticism into the prose of everyday life, and simultaneously recognizes the difficulties of that attempt. The American post-Romantic artist is in this respect committed to a more complex project than the Wordsworthian Romantic poet was: expressing the imagination of freedom in the forms of narrative involving social dialogue and relationship from which Wordsworth himself (in his great early poetry) turned away to states of solitude and merely lyrical or individual expressions of imaginative power.

More than half of Capra's films were adaptations of highly conventional stage plays and many of the rest of them had their origins in the most pedestrian forms of *Saturday Evening Post*–type fiction, forms of literature least given over to expressions of transcendental or visionary impulses. Hence the very process of making visionary films out of these eminently unvisionary plays and stories already involved Capra in complex acts of translation from one form of expression to another. Where the dialogue or social situations in the plot do not fully communicate the vision that Capra wants to express, he does not hesitate to transform the source by adding effects of expressive lighting and framing, complex editorial practices, or emotionally powerful musical orchestration. The expressive gap I have described is thus mirrored in the hybridization of the two forms. The unique expressive qualities of theatrical form are put into competition with those of cinematic form. The stage spaces, stage lighting, stage plots, stage pacing, and stage dialogue of Capra's sources are juxtaposed with the pictorial, expressionistic, or visionary qualities of the films. The result is an exciting contest between the realism

---

* Note that this expressive gap is not so pressingly felt to be an issue that must be addressed in the work of European modernists like Beckett, Proust, Flaubert, Antonioni, or Fellini. It is precisely because American writers like James and Mailer (and filmmakers like Capra and Cassavetes and May) feel that the individual owes his allegiance to both realms – both the social and the imaginative – and that social forms of expression must be (and can be) made responsive to imaginative impulses that expressive problems become the subject of their work. The European artists I have named in most cases have given up on social expression and therefore do not feel the need to wrestle with its repressiveness in their work. Social forms of expression are simply assumed to be inadequate to the expression of the individual imagination and therefore are merely rejected (or satirized) in their work. See Margery Sabin's brilliant "The Community of Intelligence and the Avant–Garde," *Raritan Review* 4 (Winter 1985), 1–25.

of the assertively social events and dialogue of his sources and the visionary or idealistic qualities expressed by his lighting, photography, and editing.

The contrast with Hawks's practice is again instructive. Capra's work straddles the aesthetic worlds of the stage play and the visionary film with complex results; Hawks's films have both feet firmly planted in the world of social drama. The unique cinematic effects present in Capra's work are largely absent from Hawks's. Hawks's earliest silent films did contain expressionistic lighting and heightening camera effects (he was, by his own account, under the spell of Murnau when he made them). He repudiated such effects almost entirely in his later work, however. As he himself has admitted, he was uncomfortable with these visionary or expressionistic effects at the time, regarded the films in which they occurred as failures "having no relation to my [good] work,"* and deliberately avoided them in his sound films or, in their rare later occurrences, employed them only negatively to express states of derangement or failures of proper relationships. The stylistic austerity of *le plan américain* is a statement about the nature of reality. In *His Girl Friday* one notices that when Hawks does employ musical heightening, expressive framing, and low key-lighting (as in the scenes in which Hildy interviews Eugene in his cell or when Eugene is in the psychiatrist's office), he uses them to identify not a psychological or emotional realm richer and more important than the previous fill-lighted social events and dialogue photographed at medium distance but to indicate a state of aberration (whether comical or serious) that must be exorcized or corrected by the rest of the film.

In arguing that Capra is a transcendentalist in the line of Thoreau and Emerson, devoted to keeping alive the transcendental spirit in a world of narrative and social checks and limitations, giving it cinematic visibility and power and releasing the imagination of his viewers even while acknowledging all of the forces that resist it, I am also arguing that he is attempting something more difficult than what the nineteenth-century transcendentalists did in their writing. He is levering the transcendental impulse out of the essay or the poem and attempting to keep it alive in the hostile social and formal environment of narrative filmmaking. Similarly, he is doing something more difficult than painters like Homer, Hopper, and Eakins attempted. Their figures, like the figures on Keats's urn, can be pictorially arrested forever, in states of silent self-communion or reverie. A narrative filmmaker in the tradition in which Capra worked, however, must make a space for meditation within the continuously encroaching and compromising spatial, temporal, and social constraints of dramatic form, resistances from which a poet's reveries, essayist's excursions, or painter's scenes are partially or locally exempted – though the writer's efforts have more in common with Capra's than the painter's, since poet, essayist, and filmmaker all shoulder the common burden of the resistance of language and the limitations of logic and of sequential narrative presentation to the expression of the impulse.

* "Howard Hawks," Interview by Peter Bogdanovich, *Movie 5* (December 1962), 8.

Capra's films, indeed, as we will see in specific cases, frequently seem to aspire to turn themselves into paintings by stopping the plot and silencing the dialogue at a moment of epiphany or vision, but the stasis obviously cannot be maintained. The pressures of narrative presentation and the requirements of exposition through dialogue and social interaction cannot be suspended for more than a passing moment, as even Keats usually remembered, and as a Hollywood filmmaker would never be allowed to forget. There was a real struggle, though, at least as strong as that waged by Keats, on Capra's part. As in the late novels of Henry James, in Capra one repeatedly feels a war between the desire to arrest the dialogue and action, stopping the narrative and giving oneself over to visionary, visual appreciation of a static scene, and the need to go on, recognizing that narrative development and plot cannot be arrested in such ways.

Both James's and Capra's work is concerned with the struggle (for the creator as well as for the characters) between such different sorts of scenes – the static, pictorial scenes that one imagines or comes upon, appreciated outside of space and time, and the disruptive scenes of dialogue and human interaction that are made in social interaction between the characters. James's late novels take the difference between the two kinds of scene making as their subject. For both James and Capra the poignancy of the one sort of scene making is that it is always interrupted or corroded by the other. The static scenes one makes as a visionary are always at odds with the scenes that one makes in society in the other way. The imaginative scene maker must always negotiate the obstacle course of social forms and relationships and, if a writer or filmmaker, the complex resistances and repressions of sequential, chronological, narrative form.

Another way to think of this conflict of allegiance in Capra's work is to understand it as a tension between the structure-breaking impulses of individual fantasies, desires, and ideals, and the structure-making forms of socially and psychologically coherent narrative. It is a competition in which neither side can vanquish the other, since as much as Capra wants to bend or break social and narrative structures, he is thoroughly American in his insistence that, in order to count, imaginative energies must be expressed in the "real world" of realistic social forms. It is this paradox that energizes all of his work: the insistence that vision resist oppressive worldly structures, but that it also be translatable into practical, realistic forms of expression that enrich ordinary life.

Capra's commitment to narrative reality is arguably his most American quality, the feature that decisively separates his work from that of his avant-garde, European filmmaking contemporaries, who were always more ready than he was to suspend the confining conventions of realistic social narrative. Capra's films – and *That Certain Thing*, most obviously – want to let the dream erupt into daily life to trouble and stimulate it, but they also want to suggest that the dream can be incorporated into society enriching it in a thoroughly practical way.

This is also the important difference between Capra's variety of American Romanticism and the European Romanticism represented by filmmakers such as Antonioni or Dreyer. Like Capra, Antonioni and Dreyer focus on passionate dreams that are not easily expressible within the ordinary social world. Unlike Capra, though, they seem utterly resigned to the separateness of the two realms of experience. Capra wants to be the poet of both the passionate dream and of the actual expression of it in the real world. The dream of America for Capra was that the finest movements of desire and imagination can find expression in our lives.

4

Blindness and vision

The Way of the Strong

> There are always two things to be done by the novelist; first, the aspirations of the mind are to be revered, that is, Faith; and, secondly, the way things actually fall out, that is, Fate. Fate and Faith, these two; and it seems as if justice were done, if the Faith is vindicated in the sentiments of the heroes of the tale, and Fate in the course and issue of the events.... The novel still weakly uses the cheap resources of property married away instead of earned.... But the novel will find the way to our interiors one day, and will not always be novel of costume merely.
>
> – Ralph Waldo Emerson, Journal, 1848

That Certain Thing falls into two pieces as a movie, but the unreconcilable doubleness of its vision is significant. Each of Capra's subsequent films will attempt to overcome its structural crisis, but its doubleness implicitly frames the central and recurring question in Capra's oeuvre: To what extent can the individual imagination express itself in our work and relationships with others? *The Way of the Strong* demonstrates how far from resolving the question Capra was. It was made only a few months after *That Certain Thing*, in the spring of 1928, Capra's first year at Columbia, and as if in it he wanted to correct the tacked-on happy ending of the earlier film, Capra takes an unyieldingly darker view of his central character's expressive predicament. In *The Way of the Strong* (the point of the title is the way the physically strong wipe out the imaginatively sensitive), Capra argues, in effect, that the imagination is ultimately doomed to be cut off from adequate expression in the world and that the creative self finally stands alone, outside of satisfying forms of human relationship or communication. It is a moving, tragic meditation on the inability of the human spirit to live its grand dreams in the forms of the world, and because it does not in the end back away from its own insights as *That Certain Thing* did, it is ultimately a much greater and truer film.

For anyone making such large claims, however, *The Way of the Strong* begins as inauspiciously as possible: as a gangster picture. Even worse, it begins with that cliché of gangster pictures – a chase scene between the cops and the robbers. It is Prohibition, and the police are pursuing bootleggers who are themselves engaged in a mob war with other bootleggers for control of illegal liquor shipments to their speakeasies. It is the most hackneyed and overworked of openings, and one that was, cinematically speaking, already a cliché in the twenties. The police sirens blare. The bootlegger flees in an open car and shoots backward over his shoulder, and the members of the audience relax in their seats, prepared to settle into a fully predictable course of cinematic events. The first sign that Capra may be propelling us into something other than a standard gangster picture comes when the police apprehend the bootlegger – only to discover that the liquor truck that has been the object of the entire pursuit is empty, because it has already been hijacked by a rival gang of bootleggers, who have beaten the cops there. That is to say, almost as if to proclaim what a narrative dead end he felt gangster picture events like this chase scene to be, Capra trumpets the fact that it leads narratively nowhere. Just as the police are left with an empty truck, the audience is left with a sense of itself having been taken on a narrative wild goose chase.

It is thus not surprising that in the scenes that follow this one Capra simply abandons the gangster-picture genre for most of the rest of the film. In its place he develops a romantic drama involving the thug who is the leader of one of the two rival gangs of bootleggers – "Handsome" Williams by name (ironically nicknamed because of the knife scars and fight marks that grotesquely deform his face).★ The police opened up the liquor truck at the end of the chase scene and found nothing there, but Capra, in effect, opens up the inside of his gangster movie itself to show us the human drama that is potentially within it or any other genre film, if we only know where to look. To talk of Capra's opening up interior psychological and narrative spaces is not a mere playing with metaphors on my part. Capra moves into or opens to view the consciousness of Williams in this film in the metaphorical, the psychological, and the literal, spatial senses of the terms. Such "movements" and "openings" become the subject of the movie.

Williams is the proprietor of an illegal speakeasy (he intercepts the rival gang's liquor shipments in order to keep his own stock replenished), and Capra uses the various physical, interior spaces within the speakeasy as metaphoric figurations of various public or private, exterior or interior, narrative realms.† Capra defines Williams's speakeasy initially in terms of the

---

★ The mistranslation of his name as "Pretty Boy" Williams in the intertitles of the only extant print is a result of its Danish origin. In addition, a number of puns, jokes, and word games in the original English intertitles (Capra's intertitles are invaribly quite witty in all of his silent films) have also unfortunately been lost in the double process of translation from English to Danish and back again.

† In most of his films of the twenties and thirties, most notably this film, *American Madness*, *The Miracle Woman*, *Platinum Blonde*, and *Bitter Tea*, Capra and the Columbia set designers favored the use of one large, main set defining an extended public space that was bordered by a series of smaller, interior spaces around its periphery, in which private events took place. Capra's use of such a combination of interrelated public and private spaces was always narratively and psychologically complex in effect.

closed doors with peepholes that lead into it to create a definite sense of its representing a sacrosanct private realm distinct from the public world outside of it. Within the speakeasy itself, he defines a series of even more private interior spaces where various psychological events take place. In short, whether he was aware of it or not, Capra metaphorizes the movement of his own narrative away from the public spaces and external events of a gangster picture and into the spiritual, psychological, and imaginative spaces and events involving Williams, through a spatial movement within the film itself from the outdoors settings of the chase scene to the more or less private and interior spaces of "Handsome's Place," in which the central events of the subsequent film take place. In the openings of doors within doors (and of peepholes within those doors), and in the movements into those interior spaces (which are occasionally accomplished by a forward tracking movement of the camera, a camera movement that was fairly rare and difficult at the time this film was made), Capra, consciously or unconsciously, visually figures his own narrative project of moving inside the gangster-picture genre to explore a series of private dramatic and imaginative events within it. The process of actually, physically moving into interior spaces, through doorways, or across thresholds becomes the chief visual metaphor in the film for the psychological movement into the interior of his characters and their relationships that Capra is interested in enacting within the genre framework.

More generally, almost everything associated with movement into or out of the third dimension in *The Way of the Strong* will come to stand metaphorically for the process of imaginative and psychological movement inward that Capra favors inside of the genre-film frame. Interactions or events that are dramatically blockable or visually representable within the two-dimensional plane of the motion-picture screen are what Capra wants to move beyond. In the service of this goal, forward tracking movements of the camera, glances or movements of a character away from the public spaces of the film and into more interior spaces, or Williams's actual physical movements through interior hallways, corridors, or down stairways will accumulate enormous metaphoric importance in the course of the film. Imaginative depths are metaphorized in terms of visual depths. It seems hardly accidental that the third dimension should take on this special imaginative resonance for a young filmmaker. The presentation and mastery of movement into or out of the third dimension, and the deployment and photography of characters in situations characterized by arrangements in depth, are two of the respects in which the filmmaker's art is distinguishable from the stage dramatist's, whose events and interactions must more or less always be imagined and displayed within the two-dimensional plane defined by the proscenium arch.★

★ As we shall see, something very similar to this metaphoric use of third-dimensional movement to stand for a more general capacity of imaginative power and movement is going on in many of Capra's subsequent films also. Compare *American Madness*, *Platinum Blonde*, *Bitter Tea*, and *It Happened One Night*. Tom Dixon, Stew Smith, Yen, and Ellie Andrews, respectively, each

Yet it can also be maintained that film is, on the contrary, even more than stage drama, a matter of purely two-dimensional effects. Film is the preeminent art involving the arrangement of surfaces and the manipulation of surface effects of lighting, makeup, costuming, and scenery. Certain formal properties of the art seem actually to foster superficialities of expression and understanding (which is why, it might be argued, film is the supreme medium of pornography); but if film, in general, including Capra's, tends to employ superficial effects of lighting and setting, much of the specific visual drama of Capra's work might be said to be generated by his paradoxical attempt to use surface effects to gesture to an imagined realm beneath surfaces, to use admittedly superficial effects of light and shadow to suggest imaginative openings out of such superficialities. Note that this is not a characteristic of all film. If "idealistic" filmmakers like Sternberg and Capra might be said to be engaged in using surfaces to point to imaginative depths beyond social or physical surfaces, "socially pragmatic" filmmakers like Hawks, Renoir, Lubitsch, and Cukor – to name a range of contrasted achievements – might be said to be interested in remaining in the world of social or physical surfaces at all costs.

The most apt comparisons with the work of Capra in this respect are the examples of Carl Dreyer and Charlie Chaplin, as odd as the yoking together of these three names might sound. Capra's cinema, as much as Chaplin's or Dreyer's is essentially engaged in the expression of spiritual, emotional, and imaginative depths or openings out of physical or social surfaces, even though, to speak strictly, such a movement beyond surfaces can be performed cinematically only in terms of surfaces. The visual texts of all of Capra's films attempt to use surfaces to move beyond surfaces, to use the superficial forms of social and verbal interaction to gesture toward an imaginative realm beyond such forms. He uses the necessary superficiality and physicality of his own forms of visual expression to generate evocations of almost ineffable states of spirituality and psychological interiority.

Capra's favorite means of suggesting imaginative depths in terms of surface effects when he worked with the cameraman Joseph Walker, who would become his regular supervisor of photography and lighting during the thirties, was to use a variety of diffusion filters and high-key-lighting effects on a character's face and hair at special imaginative moments in a film. Walker was Capra's cameraman and lighting supervisor on *That Certain Thing* (it was the first of twenty films they would work on together), and, as one might expect, Walker uses a diffusion grating or gauze scrim and high key-lighting on her hair in many of Molly's scenes of dreaming early in the film and completely lets out all of the stops in the nightmare scene in which she returns home in

embody possibilities of movement into or out of the third dimension that are metaphorically associated in those films with important qualities of imaginative depth that distinguish them from other characters in the same films who are almost invariably representatives of two-dimensional blockings and right–left movements in the same films.

disgrace in the middle of the film, lighting and photographing it in a visually stylized way, with unusually short lenses, low key-lighting, and extensive diffusion effects, to represent her hallucinatory state of mind. The film is the first of many in which Capra and Walker would use these special visual effects to suggest to a viewer the presence of extreme states of imagination and passion in a character that would otherwise be invisible, but for such translation into visible effects of light and shadow.

There has been much debate over the years about the extent to which Capra's visual style was actually created by Walker and not by Capra, and in a close collaboration, expecially a long-term one like that between these two men, it is probably impossible ever to sort out who most influenced whom, or who originated certain techniques and inventions. *The Way of the Strong*, following *That Certain Thing* yet relying on the skills of another cameraman (Ben Reynolds), does let us draw some conclusions about Walker's distinctive contribution to Capra's work. The most obvious thing to notice is that *The Way of the Strong* pretty much lacks the visual qualities I have described in *That Certain Thing*. Even at extremely emotional or psychologically heightened moments in the film there is little use of the sort of romantic or atmospheric lighting and photography that Walker employed in the other film. Thus the particular photographic means of representing states of enriched imaginativeness that one encounters in *That Certain Thing* seem clearly to have been Walker's unique contribution to the earlier film.

But this is not at all to argue – as has been suggested at times – that Walker was therefore largely or partly responsible for the overall direction of Capra's films. If anything, Walker's absence from *The Way of the Strong* proves the opposite: that Capra could make the identical sorts of films without Walker's input into the photography, completely independent of his admittedly brilliant employment of lighting and diffusion effects. That is what Capra does in *The Way of the Strong*. Without any of Walker's photographic help, he makes a film that is just as unyieldingly idealistic, just as operatic, just as imaginatively exorbitant as the early sections of *That Certain Thing* or any of his greatest subsequent work. Though Walker's contribution to all of Capra's work in which they collaborated is wonderful and its effects not to be minimized, in making *The Way of the Strong* without employing Walker or any of his special photographic methods, Capra shows how little he needed Walker to express his vision of experience.

In place of Walker's particular bag of photographic tricks, Capra simply substitutes another sort of stylistic heightening to generate the same sort of imaginative and emotional effects at special moments. Instead of using expressionistic photography, as I have already suggested, he plays off two- and three-dimensional spaces and blockings within the film to suggest the possibilities of imaginative depths and emotional openings out of social confinements and physical surfaces. On these grounds it is safe to infer, I think, that even without ever having met Walker, Capra would have been capable of going on to make the same sorts of films as he made with him. The principal difference would be that another set of stylistic devices (like the uses of space and depths in this film) would have been employed to do the work of Walker's luminist photography in the later films.

Let me return, though, to *The Way of the Strong* in particular. As I have already argued, Capra's most general stylistic goal (in this film as well as in almost all of his other films, whether they were lighted by Walker or not) is to gesture, in whatever manner – by means of effects of light or by means of metaphoric uses of spaces and blockings in two and three dimensions – beyond physical representation itself. Walker's nimbuses of light in other films or Capra's use of shadowy inner spaces here are meant to take us beyond all physical realms to psychological and emotional states that cannot be seen. In Capra's cinema in general and this film in particular, a viewer's attention is, at certain absolutely crucial moments, forcibly redirected from a physical depiction of an object or situation to a consideration of its imaginative or spiritual resonances. Over and over again in Capra's work one is systematically moved from an attention to event to attention to psychology, from an awareness of social actions to an awareness of imaginative transactions. This redirection of attention from physical surfaces to spiritual depths occurs with such predictability in Capra's work that the distinctive shift of consciousness demanded by it might almost be christened the "Capra shift"; but since it also occurs as an event of equal importance in the work of Sternberg, Murnau, Chaplin, and Dreyer, it will probably be better simply to call it more generally the "meditative shift."

Since we are going to encounter it so frequently in other films, it is useful to notice how this so-called meditative shift takes place in a specific scene in *The Way of the Strong* and what some of the practical evidences of it are in almost all of Capra's work. Conveniently enough, it would be hard to find a better example of the occurrence of this sudden enforced shift in point of view or range of awareness to use as an illustration of the process in general and a definition of its specific qualities than in the sequence of shots immediately following the chase scene in this film.

Capra cuts from the chase-scene conclusion to a shot of "Handsome" Williams looking at his own face in the mirror in his speakeasy. In that fairly dramatic shift from the one kind of scene to the other can be found all of the earmarks of what I am calling the meditative shift in Capra's work. The action-heavy eventfulness of the cops and robbers scene gives way to a momentary narrative lull – a state of stasis or arrest of action. Noise or disturbance gives way to a moment of silence or stillness. A scene of physical agitation yields to one of imaginative contemplation. Rapid editing rhythms and shots of multiple, moving figures are succeeded by a static, fixed shot of an isolated, single, still figure. The medium- and long-shots of the liquor-truck sequence are replaced by a close-up of a single face.★

★ In the Capra films lighted and photographed by Walker, it would be at this precise moment that the film would also suddenly and dramatically shift from emotionally neutral fill lighting to

In short, the reason to call this typical change from one scene to another in Capra's work a meditative shift is that at such a moment Capra suddenly moves a viewer and his characters into a meditative relation to his own film and its events. The scenes (or characters) are dramatically shifted from the world of outer happenings to inner ones, from action to contemplation, from physical events to possibilities of imaginative eventfulness, from spatial movemets to movements of mind.

In this particular scene, though, as always in Capra's work, the meditative opening to purely imaginative eventfulness cannot last. In his rage at the image of physical deformity it gives back to him, Williams shatters the mirror into which he is looking. Although the mirror momentarily sponsors a meditative movement in him as a character and in us as viewers, it also, at the same time, ultimately limits him and us to the world of surfaces and physical objects that Capra is interested in our leaving behind. Mirrors and mirrored images will consistently be employed thematically throughout *The Way of the Strong* to represent the world of surfaces and superficial views beyond which Capra wants to move us cinematically. As I have already suggested, virtually everything associated with two-dimensional representation in the film is suspect or is meant to figure an inadequate representation of experience. No physical, two-dimensional representation is less adequate, Capra suggests, than that figured by the purely physical and superficial image reflected by a mirror. Like the limiting blockings of characters' interactions along a two-dimensional axis within the plane of the movie screen, the mirrored representations of Williams's face, and the silhouettes and shadows in terms of which many of the actions of the rival gangsters scheming against him are depicted, are all meant to represent forms of superficiality that Capra is interested in rejecting and moving beyond.

It is in this regard that "Handsome's" systematic breaking of the various mirrors he encounters throughout the film takes on a larger metaphoric resonance in the structure of Capra's movie. "Handsome," as a character, is trying to do the same thing as Capra is as a filmmaker – to move beyond physical representations, to call us and himself to a more spiritual and psychological understanding of experience and selfhood. "Handsome" fractures superficial physical representations of himself (as they occur in mirrors) in a way exactly analogous to the way Capra fractures the superficialities of the genre-film cartoon characters and interactions that his film begins with in order to probe for spiritual depths beneath or beyond them.

Such an abstract description of its visual structure, however, perhaps makes *The Way of the Strong* sound more esoteric than the experience of watching it actually is. What I am describing as an abstract metaphoric comparison of

---

emotionally charged or atmospheric key-lighting. Though Reynolds is not a virtuoso of lighting effects the way Walker is, even in this film there is a perceptible shift in the lighting as we move indoors from the outdoor chase scene that parallels the other sorts of shifts of narrative and visual interest in the scene.

representations of surfaces versus depths, of physical versus spiritual significations, is, in fact, something expressed directly in terms of the basic dramatic situations in the film itself. In short, the explicit dramatic subject of the film – in an entirely obvious and literal respect – is a comparison of superficial versus deep ways of understanding and relationship between characters. That is Capra's dramatic purpose in making his central figure a physically ugly man with sometimes spiritually "beautiful" impulses. The narrative explicitly forces us to consider the ways physical appearances do not reveal spiritual realities (as they are almost always assumed to do in a movie), and, more generally, encourages us to move beyond a superficial visual view of the characters to a deeper, imaginative and psychological appreciation of them.

In the first scene in which we see "Handsome" – the one that begins with his looking at himself in the mirror and then subsequently proceeding to smash it – Capra narratively makes a point of drawing our attention to the difference between the ugliness of "Handsome's" physical appearance and the true spiritual handsomeness of his feelings and intentions. He shows us, on the one hand, Williams being mocked and jeered at by the patrons of his club and, on the other, his participation in a subtle series of acts of kindness, consideration, and love. The interplay of these two ways of understanding Williams is so subtle at points that it might be lost on all but the best of viewers, but there is no doubt about what Capra is doing when, for example, at the same moment that "Handsome" is being ridiculed for his ugliness, he has him toss a coin to a jug-eared patron sitting alone at a table. In "Handsome's" act of generosity and sympathy, Capra momentarily opens to view an otherwise invisible spiritual and imaginative bond that links the two homely, forlorn men. They are connected not socially or practically – not by means of dialogue or social relationships – but imaginatively at this instant, and it is the purpose of Capra's entire film to make us aware of precisely such imaginative connections and relationships that exist not only in the absence of, but as full-fledged alternatives to, social relationships.

The comparison of physical and nonphysical ways of knowing is even more explicitly incorporated into the central dramatic events of the film by means of Capra's introduction of a blind character into the narrative. Driven out of his own club in shame and humiliation by the mockery of his patrons, "Handsome" spends part of each evening on a street corner listening to a blind musician named Nora, with whom he gradually falls in love (as she does with him). The very essence of "Handsome's" relationship with Nora is that her blindness to his physical deformity allows him to establish an imaginative relationship with her that is not defined in terms of his superficial physical appearance but emphatically as a spiritual or emotional opening out of all such ways of knowing and relating. "Handsome" can indeed be handsome to Nora, in a spiritual sense of the term, as he cannot be for those whose eyes limit them to functioning in the world of appearances.

One cannot help but be reminded of Chaplin's *City Lights*, which develops an almost identical dramatic situation (three years after Capra's film was released).* The similarities between the Capra and the Chaplin films run, however, much deeper than the mere fact that they both involve romances between sighted men and blind girls. Far more important than the mere fact that both films involve sightedness and blindness is that both use blindness as a means of generating creative misunderstandings (or as a means of allowing outright impostures, if one wants to put it less charitably), since in both films the blind girl takes the sighted man to be something decidedly other than he is, and the man deliberately fosters and furthers the girl's mistake. That points up the deepest similarity between Capra and Chaplin in these particular films as well as in their work in general: Both are interested in creating and encouraging deliberate and at times quite daring and unorthodox substitutions of fantasy in place of reality.

The blinding of a central character in *The Way of the Strong*, *City Lights*, and *The Miracle Woman* is simply the means of facilitating this process of forced imaginative substitution. A cinema like Capra's or Chaplin's (or Dreyer's or Sternberg's, for that matter), notwithstanding all of its visual complexity, is not really interested in its characters' or viewers' capacities of vision in a physical sense at all. Vision is only a metaphor for a visionary capacity that is usually at odds with physical seeing. Sight is only a means of cinematically representing insight, and one of the easiest ways of representing this state of nonvisual vision for a character within the film, or of moving a viewer from a state of sight to one of insight, is simply to feature a situation or relationship for which physical vision is not available.

This process of wooing a character or a member of the audience from sight to insight, which in this case involves featuring a state of physical blindness in order to sponsor a compensating condition of imaginative vision, might be said to be the central event in both Chaplin's and Capra's work. The introduction of a blind person into the film is therefore only a kind of narrative literalization of the basic artistic impulse of both filmmakers. As figured by a condition of blindness, imaginative or spiritual presence compensates for worldly or physical absence; imaginative enrichments and movements of mind substitute for social or practical impoverishments and immobilities. That is the central dramatic impulse at work in both *The Way of the Strong* and *City Lights*.

Having acknowledged the extensive similarities between the work of Capra and Chaplin, one is, however, obliged to argue that in some respects Capra's work seems more tough-minded than Chaplin's, insofar as Capra much more rigorously reminds both his viewers and his characters of all the ways that the world resists our passional and imaginative substitutions. Capra never lets us forget (as we frequently are actually encouraged to in Chaplin) all the ways in which the world relentlessly insists upon the reinstatement of its own external, superficial, social and physical standards of valuation in the place of our

---

* In *The Miracle Woman*, released in 1931, the same year as Chaplin's film, Capra went on to make yet another film about a blind lover. In that film he uses blindness in the same way he does here – to suggest a visionary opening out of physical and social realms. Visual blindness is a means of stimulating imaginative insight.

personal imaginative substitutions. In a word, the imagination is far more powerful and uncontested in its transformations of reality in a Chaplin film than a Capra one. To put it another way, Capra's work relentlessly and comprehensively keeps reminding us of a realm of social and physical forms and forces that are in direct competition with the transformations of the individual imagination; Chaplin's, on the contrary, frequently does its best to make us temporarily forget that such a realm exists.

Furthermore, and perhaps most important, the fundamental requirement in Capra's work is that the personal imagination express itself not (as in Chaplin's work) as an alternative to, but *in terms of* the practical forms of social intercourse by means of a continuous act of translation from the one realm to the other. This requirement that private states of feeling and imagination ultimately be expressed in terms of public forms of discourse and relationship is simply not present with the same rigorousness in Chaplin's work.★ The imagination of the tramp is not asked to express itself in practical social or linguistic forms. His private state of personal feeling and imagination is more or less an end in itself. Though he interacts socially with others, there is no stringent requirement that his desires be expressed socially or translated into practical forms of interaction, as there always is in Capra. In *The Gold Rush*, *City Lights*, and *Modern Times*, the relationship of the tramp's imagination to the alien social and political realities around him is summarized in the statement that, for Chaplin, the tramp's gorgeous romantic fantasies are simply meant to *displace* the disappointing worldly realities around him. He is not asked (as Capra's heroes invariably are) to come to grips with the hostile social realities, or, even more difficultly and hazardously, to express his imagination in terms of them. How different Capra's work is in this respect. In all of his films, Capra passes the romantic impulses of his central couple through the nearly infinite resistance of practical forms of social intercourse that everywhere work against them but by means of which they are absolutely required to express themselves. In a Chaplin film, on the other hand, the romantic fantasy is merely held onto as a sovereign, supreme fiction separate and protected from the incursions of a hostile reality (in *Modern Times*) or until the world magically comes into miraculous congruence with it (in *The Gold Rush*).†

Thus the chief difference between Chaplin and Capra emerges. Chaplin wants and believes a state of imaginative enrichment to be an end in itself, but

---

★ To put it this way is to see the ways in which Chaplin's work resembles Beckett's in its imaginative privacy, just as Capra's, in contrast, resembles Henry James's in its insistence that vision and desire always be mediated in social forms of expression.

† Chaplin's decision to keep his tramp silent even after the coming of sound to pictures seems an important one in this context. The absence (or avoidance) of the give-and-take of social dialogue is revealing. The tramp does not have to be answerable to anyone's expressive requirements but his own. He is freed to a state of insulated subjectivity. It is in this respect that it might be argued that Chaplin yields to his own and his character's fantasies and dreams, whereas Capra worries and resists his. If this is what hostile critics are alluding to when they call Chaplin sentimental, it is understandable, but, by the same standards, Capra's work is the opposite of sentimental.

precisely because Capra wants imagination to communicate with a world of alien forms and structures beyond itself, he is forced to acknowledge expressive conflicts, compromises, and repressions that result from the discrepancy between our personal ideals and feelings and actual expressive possibilities that are glossed over in a Chaplin film. To put it more specifically in the case of *City Lights*, Chaplin allows his tramp magically to live up to the role of the spiritual millionaire that he has invented for himself. Imagination has that kind of autonomy and power in Chaplin's work. When there is an unavoidable discrepancy between one's imaginative identity and one's physical or social identity in *City Lights* – as in the exquisitely painful ending sequence – Chaplin clearly encourages a viewer to conclude that the imaginative indentity takes precedence over the worldly or social one. He clearly wants a viewer of the film to go away convinced that Charlie's being a spiritual millionaire is the controlling reality and that his being a worldly pauper is something to be overlooked or forgotten. The spiritual or visionary identity does not have to express itself in terms of physical, social, and worldly actualities (as in Capra's work). It simply displaces or supersedes them. It does not express itself through them or engage itself in a competition with them; it merely substitutes its own alternative understandings and forms of relationship in place of them.

This is the decisive difference from Capra's work. Although fully as much as *City Lights* paying homage to the potentially enriching and transforming energies of the imagination, *The Way of the Strong* relentlessly reminds both its characters and its audience of all of the ways the world will not live up to their imaginative reconstructions of it, and of all the ways it will, in fact, positively resist them. The forms of social and physical interaction in Capra's film relentlessly repress or redirect individual imaginative energies (as they do not in *City Lights*). As does not happen with anything like this inexorability in the relationship between Chaplin's tramp and the blind flower girl, the world of physical realities and the requirements of public, social forms of expression keeps intruding into Capra's film radically and repeatedly to deidealize the imaginative relationship of "Handsome" and Nora.

In the first place, one has the visual image of "Handsome" present throughout the whole picture to remind a viewer of his actual physical grotesqueness and therefore of the unbridgeable discrepancy between his physical and spiritual identities. In contrast, Chaplin empowers his tramp, tatters and all, to some degree to be able to live up to the fiction of elegant gentility, charm, and refinement that he is passing on his blind girl. His balletic grace of movement, aplomb under pressure, delicacy, sensitivity, and generosity implicitly tell a viewer that there is real truth to the imaginative fiction of his being rich and gifted and well-bred. Even if he is a tramp, his bearing, manners, and attitudes are as aristocratic and refined as those of a duke or a gentleman. Chaplin makes it easy for us to accept the fiction that he is passing on the blind girl as an actual reality. His poverty and tatters are reduced to being almost minor and seemingly accidental details, and, of course, more than anything else, the comic tone of the Chaplin film makes the tramp's awkwardnesses seem positively endearing. Chaplin's comedy charms a viewer out of harsher moral or social judgments about the tramp figure or the imposture he stages.

The opposite is true of Capra's film and the situation of Williams, which situates him in a much tougher world and a more threatened expressive situation than that ever encountered by the tramp. Williams pretends to be handsome, but he really, and painfully, is the opposite of handsome and, furthermore, has no overwhelming Chaplin-like spiritual reservoir of comic charm, poise, or elegance to draw on in the course of the film. He is really only an aging thug, and an ugly and clumsy one at that, even if he is genuinely in love with Nora. "Handsome" is an imposter. *The Way of the Strong* keeps reminding us that a physical and social reality exists that is unswervingly at odds with the imaginative reality depicted.

One can summarize the differences by saying that whereas Capra's film keeps deidealizing its central relationship, Chaplin's does the opposite. Charlie's balletic poise and grace keep telling an audience that the imaginative image of him is, in fact, the correct view of him, whereas Capra's reminds us that the fiction is a lie. In Chaplin, our attention is wooed away from an awareness of the tramp's physical shabbiness and impoverishment by an appreciation of his pantomimic ingenuity and performative grace, whereas in Capra the hard realities just will not be wished away. That is to suggest how much tougher Capra's film is on the claims of the imagination than Chaplin's.

A second deidealizing factor in *The Way of the Strong* is Capra's decision to place his hero's romance at the center of a bona fide gangster film, complete with car chases and narrow escapes. The pressures of time and forces beyond their control keep interrupting his central couple's imaginative relationship and telling us how little power imagination has in this world. Capra does the same thing in many of his later films as well: The central "visionary" figures in *Mr. Deeds Goes to Town*, *Mr. Smith Goes to Washington*, and *It's a Wonderful Life* must come to grips with, and express themselves not only in terms of repressive social forms but in terms of repressive spatial and temporal aspects of their own narratives that sorely test the conditions in which the imagination may be expressed in a hostile formal (as well as a hostile social and political) environment. In contrast, how different is the situation of the little tramp, and, relatively speaking, how much more protected he is in a romance world of slapstick comedy, farce, fantasies, and virtually magical metamorphoses. Just as he is exonerated from expressing himself within social and verbal forms of expression, the tramp is more or less freed from realistic constraints on his behavior. The temporal and formal constraints of an action-hungry gangster-genre plot are something against which Charlie never has to pit himself.

The most concrete dramatic manifestation of the built-in resistance of Capra's film to the visionary or imaginative derealization that "Handsome" would enact on reality (in this sense, acting as an alter ego for Capra himself) is figured in Nora's repeated attempt to run her hands over his scarred and disfigured face. She is not content with her imagination of his appearance (as Chaplin's blind girl is) but positively demands that her imagination of his handsomeness be upheld by (or expressed within) an actual physical reality. One has only to imagine the extraordinary difference in tone if *City Lights* had included (and not merely as a passing joke in the yarn-balling scene) an earnest attempt on the part of the blind girl to feel Charlie's rags and tatters and had developed scenes involving the tramp's genuine pain and mortification at not being able to uphold the fantasy he has launched.*

One of the most excruciating and moving scenes in all of Capra's work is the moment at which Nora finally forces Williams to let her touch his face with her hands (in the good faith, of course, that his nickname is unironically descriptive of his actual handsomeness). She playfully pursues him across a room, while he fends off her advances, at first jokingly and then with increasing pain, humiliation, embarrassment, and fear of discovery. At the last second – in profound dread and shame that she will discover both the truth of his disfigurement and the implicit deceit he has practiced on her – Williams thrusts a close friend's face into her hands in place of his own. "Handsome" continues the fiction of his handsomeness; indeed, he upholds and extends it at all costs, but with how much more complexly horrifying results than one ever encounters in *City Lights*.

As always in Capra's work, as a result of this threat of discovery one is painfully, awkwardly, poignantly aware of "Handsome's" fiction *as a fiction*, and this scene makes it clear how complexly Capra himself feels about the passing of such a fiction. He admires it and dreads it at the same time. He sees it as both an enrichment of reality and as a lie and act of deceit. There is no subtle – or not so subtle – confusion of it with a higher, supervening spiritual or emotional reality, as one finds in Chaplin. (Note that this is not meant as a limiting judgment on Chaplin's work. It is simply an attempt to discriminate Chaplin's yielding to fictions from Capra's relentless worrying of them.) Like Chaplin, Capra is emphatically in favor of ennobling imaginative transformations of paltry realities. That fascination with the power of supreme fictions profoundly unites the two filmmakers; but the difference between the two artists is the precariousness, the fragility, the potential irrelevance of fictions in the face of oppressive actualities of which Capra makes one aware.† In Capra, as never in Chaplin, one feels the almost unbridgeable gap between the fiction and the reality (and "almost" is the crucial word in this formulation). As I have

---

* This is what does happen at the end of *City Lights*, and the fact that Chaplin prevents the jarring intrusion of an imaginatively resistant reality until the very end of the film makes my point. When untransformable reality does finally intrude into the film in the concluding recognition scene between the tramp and the flower girl, who has now had her sight restored, the fact that we are aware that it is clearly the final scene in the film we are watching makes us respond to it in a special way, and further allows us to believe that, notwithstanding the sudden visual disillusionment of the flower girl, she and Charlie can in any case still be united in a visionary community of shared feeling and imagination.

† One thinks of the work of both William James and Henry James as being similar to Capra's in this respect.

already mentioned, in both *That Certain Thing* and *Lady for a Day*, in a similarly tough-minded way Capra explores both the beauty and the limits of consciously fictional arrangements of relentlessly resistant spatial, temporal, and social realities. Other films that do this are *Dirigible*, *The Miracle Woman*, *Forbidden*, *The Bitter Tea of General Yen*, and *Meet John Doe*; all of them depend on acts of fictional imposture, deceit, or transformation which enrich reality but also come into conflict with it with various degrees of disastrous results. In the particular instance of *The Way of the Strong*, the falsity and deceitfulness of Williams's impersonation come back to haunt him again and again in the film, most notably in a final scene in which he is ultimately forced to give up Nora because of it. He finally loses Nora precisely as a consequence of the fiction that was designed to hold and keep her. Capra keeps insisting on the discrepancy between our imaginations and the practical realities they would enrich and transform and on how those realities work to undo our gorgeous stylistic and artistic arrangements of life, or, at the very least, to make them utterly irrelevant, as beautiful and inspiring as they may be.

Just as Nora's attempt to feel his face reminds him and us of the painful and embarrassing difference between imaginative dreams and practical realities in his life, so Williams's own clumsiness in translating his imagination of romantic possibilities into practical forms of social and physical expression with Nora reminds us of additional discrepancies between the ideals of our imaginative and emotional lives and the practical forms of expression available to an individual in society. The delicate comedy of errors and awkwardnesses that results from Williams's clumsiness in *The Way of the Strong* makes for some of the most touching romantic scenes in Capra's work. At one point, when Nora has fainted, Williams runs to get her a glass of his best whiskey to revive her, only suddenly to realize the utter inappropriateness of his offer. Whiskey would choke this innocent, frail girl, not revive her. She would be unable even to sip what Williams drinks like water, so he dumps out the whiskey and replaces it with a mere glass of water instead. In another scene, we see this clumsy, well-meaning man attempting surreptitiously to find out the size of Nora's ring finger while she is asleep so that he can buy an engagement ring for her as a surprise. He first holds his own, gargantuan ring next to her delicate hand and realizes that everything about himself is out of scale for her delicacy and diminutiveness. He then holds a pencil next to her finger and realizes that it is far too small. (That he should go from the one extreme of size to the other is Capra's tactful way of showing us how truly alien women, and the size of women's hands, are to Williams's life and consciousness.) He then tries a cigar for size and sees that it is still too fat. Finally, he pulls out his pistol, of all things, and discovers that its barrel is an exact match in diameter to her ring finger. The crudity, clumsiness, and romantic inappropriateness of this sequence of objects is the dramatic point. This is a man who cannot express his dreams of love except insofar as he repeatedly reminds himself and a viewer of the film of the discrepancy between those exalted dreams and the paltry realms of experience and forms of expression within which he exists and in terms of which those dreams must be enacted.

The Way of the Strong ends with a final, climactic act of worldly renunciation. If, as I believe is the case, Capra could never make up his mind about the relationship between the imagination and the world, then the unremittingly dark ending of this film represents one extreme position he entertained in movie after movie, and which he was never able to exorcise from even the most apparently light and optimistic of his films. This ending speaks movingly on behalf of the part of Capra that despaired of the possibility of the imagination's ever adequately expressing itself in the structures of ordinary life and relationships. It expresses a crisis of confidence that will surface in all of his major films but that was apparently completely overlooked by contemporary reviewers of his work (and many subsequent critics who have written on it), who, as I have already suggested, took the films to be simpleminded homilies in favor of the triumph of the little man in a democratic society. That is obviously not the Capra I am describing.

Williams finally gives up Nora to Dan, the handsome, young piano player in his bar and the friend who stood in for him when Nora wanted to touch his face. As Williams realizes, Dan himself has fallen in love with Nora, partly as a result of the intimacy that Williams, ironically, forced upon him in his own attempt to hold onto Nora, and Nora has, in some sense, also been in love with Dan all along, since it has been Dan's face, not Willams's, that she has been touching ever since then. When, at the end, she accidentally discovers the ruse and chooses Dan, Williams instantly gives up his own claim.★

It is an act of worldly renunciation or social dispossession that will occur over and over in the endings of Capra's subsequent work – in *Dirigible*, *Bitter Tea*, *Lady for a Day*, *Lost Horizon*, and *It's a Wonderful Life*, to name only the most obvious examples. How is one to understand it? In this group of films, Capra, like Henry James, finally, sadly tells us that the imagination must be satisfied with its own powers. After exploring the possibilities of converting visionary possession and enrichment into forms of worldly or social possession and enrichment, Capra, in *The Way of the Strong*, reverses what he did at the end of *That Certain Thing* and argues that the individual is irremediably alone and dispossessed. He tries to bring into existence an actual romantic community that will realize the visionary community he and his central characters imagine, only finally to withdraw from such a possibility at the end of the film.

The renunciation that concludes *The Way of the Strong* represents a virtually Jamesian forced choice between the riches of the romantic imagination and a

---

★ It should be obvious how entirely different the tone and meaning of this final revelation scene are from those of the one that Chaplin uses to conclude *City Lights*. Chaplin's flower girl does not flee from Charlie in disgust and revulsion into the arms of another man, nor does Chaplin argue that the tramp must renounce her.

felt sense of the paltriness and inadequacy of actual forms of social and sexual expression to live up to those imaginative enrichments. The middle sections of *The Way of the Strong* tentatively entertained the possibility that one might just succeed in expressing one's imaginative dreams in the practical forms of a worldly relationship (just as *City Lights* also implicitly proposes this) – and parts of all of Capra's films entertain this possibility, which he seems never to have given up on – but (unlike Chaplin in *City Lights*) Capra radically withdraws from the dream at the end of the film. As in James's work, he suggests that there is no expression for this dream in society. In the final scenes of their movies, Florence Fallon, Lulu Smith, Jack Bradon, Stew Smith, Jefferson Smith, and George Bailey, like "Handsome" Williams, will have to be content with the riches of an enriched consciousness, in place of social riches of personal expression and practical, worldly relationship. That is why the Capra films in which the characters just listed appear end with acts of repudiation of worldly forms of expression or relationship directly related to that at the conclusion of this one.

This is, as I have suggested, a forced choice between imagination and expressive realities that Chaplin's major romantic films significantly do not exact, ending as they do with the prospect that the little tramp's dreams – however exalted or apparently unrealistic and out of touch with the financial and social practicalities of life – can actually be expressed in the world, usually in the form of a relationship with at least one other person. That is why the Chaplin films I have mentioned invariably end with a romantic pairing. In contrast, in Capra's work – over and over again, from *The Way of the Strong* to *It's a Wonderful Life* almost twenty years later – the imaginative individual is left alone, silent, and estranged from social expression or participation. The character's dreams and desires may be intact though severely tested, but, almost always, there is no linguistic or practical form for their expression.

Even the apparent exceptions to this generalization are usually more apparent than real. It is undeniable that, as testified by the forced happy ending in *That Certain Thing* and other films, Capra usually wanted to affirm the reintegration of the imaginative loner into a harmonious and supportive society of interacting individuals, but, just as in *That Certain Thing*, I would argue that even when Capra thought that he was successfully doing this, the work of art often tells us otherwise. It manifests strains or fissures in its structure that give the lie to Capra's own intention. The specific interest of *The Way of the Strong* is that it displays in a particularly pure form the Jamesian renunciatory impulse at the heart of Capra's visionary enterprise even in his more optimistic works with happier conclusions. It is a renunciation of social expression and participation that Capra, as it were, struggles against in most of his subsequent work by continuing to attempt to reintegrate the individual into a larger society at the ends of the films but, as in *That Certain Thing*, one cannot help feeling that it is a reintegration (or a channeling of imaginative energies into social causes) that is more willed than achieved, more honored in the breach than the observance.

Williams gives up Nora to Dan, and in a final chase scene that emphatically returns us to the gangster-movie genre left behind for so long, he drives off down the road pursued by the police as a diversionary tactic in order to give the lovers time to escape. Careening down the highway, we and Williams are reminded one more time of the unavoidable physicality and superficiality of the world and its value systems (and therefore of its inevitable resistance to his imaginative transformations), as Capra shows him glimpsing his own image in the rearview mirror of his car. In one final assertion of spirit over flesh, of the sovereignty of the imaginative eye over the physical, of the importance of depths over the superficiality of surfaces, he smashes the mirror to pieces with his gun. Capra's dramatic point, however, is that there can be no destination for his desire, no worldly home for his imagination, no possible relationship to express what he feels. The passionately imaginative individual is left socially estranged, alone, silent, and on the run. That is Capra's tragic and moving message.

Williams shoots himself in the head, and his car plunges off the edge of a bridge into a river. As the vehicle sinks under the surface of the water, a single sheet of music floats up. Capra comes in on it in close-up for the final shot of his film. It is a score titled "Love's Dreams," a piece Nora played on her violin during their courtship near the beginning of the movie. Williams has apparently been carrying it around with him since then. It is an apt title with which to end, and indeed it could have served as the title for Capra's entire film, less because of the fairly minor significance of the piece of music in the narrative than because of the symbolic resonance of the title with every aspect of the preceding work.★ It effectively summarizes the film's underlying question: To what extent must dreams of love ultimately stay dreams, even though momentarily appearing to be translatable into actual relationships between individuals? In the act of worldly renunciation and dispossession, and, even more, in the concluding act of social self-erasure and physical self-annihilation that he forces on his protagonist at the end of the film, Capra (unlike Chaplin) tells us that, in effect, love's dreams are only dreams and that they will never quite bear translation into practical forms of relationship and expression. They will never be realized in the world but only in our consciousnesses and in our most daring and glorious works of art – but that, for Capra, is no reason to abandon love's dreams.

★ I note in passing that this title has to my knowledge never been used for a film, though John Cassavetes's *Lovestreams*, which is a film whose point might be summarized in almost exactly the same terms I employ to describe Capra's film in this paragraph, puns on it.

PART II

Social performances and imaginative residues

Submarine, 1928
Flight, 1929
Dirigible, 1931
Platinum Blonde, 1931
American Madness, 1932

5

Making scenes

Submarine
Flight
Dirigible

As the greatest lessons of Nature through the universe are perhaps variety and freedom, the same present the greatest lessons also in New World politics and progress. If a man were asked, for instance, the distinctive points contrasting modern European and American political and other life with the old Asiatic cultus... he might find the amount of them in ... two main constituents, or sub-strata, for a truly grand nationality – 1st, a large variety of character – and 2nd, full play for human nature to expand itself in numberless and even conflicting directions.

– Walt Whitman, *Democratic Vistas*

Both *That Certain Thing* and *The Way of the Strong*, in their different ways, illustrate a tension in Capra's work between potential imaginative enrichments of experience and the problematic social expression of them that will run throughout most of his subsequent films. Bringing the two realms together, or expressing imagination in society, becomes a problem as much for the filmmaker as for his characters. In short, Capra, like his characters, has a double agenda and has trouble maintaining his commitment to both parts of it. He, like his characters, has trouble expressing the energies of the personal imagination in the forms of social expression, or at least has recurring doubts about his own and his characters' abilities to do it successfully. In his work of the early thirties, with which the next two parts of my argument are concerned, it is as if, sensing this doubleness in his films, Capra decides to make two generally distinguishable sorts of films, the one favoring the social side of his agenda, the other favoring the imaginative. In the first sort of film (with which Chapters 5, 6, and 7 will deal) Capra explores the situation of social performers generally functioning as central figures in complex, extended societies; in the second (discussed in Chapters 8, 9, and 10) he features characters at the other remove – visionaries, artists, or dreamers who turn away from social expression or who exist on the extreme margins of social interaction.*

* There is, needless to say, a degree of overlap between the two kinds of films and characters that my argument will attempt to bring out. As I suggested previously, social scene making and acts of imaginative possession are intimately related in Capra's work (as in American art more generally). My consideration of them separately is an argumentative convenience.

To understand this first group of films about characters who, rather than turning away from social intercourse into states of vision, attempt to express their imaginations in the forms of practical interaction and relationship with other characters, there is no concept more useful than that of "playing" – in all of the social, theatrical, and imaginative senses of the word. Playing is a potentially rich and resonant metaphor for any dramatist, but for Capra in these social films in particular, playing – in all of these senses – is a way of momentarily creating and maintaining a space for free imaginative movement within even the most confining social (or dramatic) situations, without leaving the social situation behind. Play is a way of expressing imagination in society and through social interaction.

In the otherwise dismally economic conclusion to *That Certain Thing*, one spark of life left in Andy, Molly, and the movie itself is that the young couple vanquish Andy's father not in serious capitalistic competition but rather in a zany scene of playacting in which they trick him into giving them his money. When the father stops by their factory to look over the competition, Molly and Andy stage an outrageous charade of raking in money that makes him propose a merger of their two companies. With its battery of artificial props (a bag of washers is used to simulate a bag full of money) and stage devices that call attention to themselves (Andy feeds Molly her lines and cues and directs her every action), the scene flaunts, rather than conceals, its theatricality. It is a little like getting a peek backstage at what goes on in a movie studio. Andy and Molly are meant to remind us of a silent-movie director and an actress at work on the set. And the instructions Andy holds up to prompt her, which Capra photographs in close-up, remind us of the intertitles of the silent film we have been watching. The scene communicates, in brief, the sheer joy of theatrical improvisation and suggests how much pleasure Capra must have gotten out of working with an actress the way Andy works with Molly.

The extravagant theatricality of this scene leavens the otherwise dreary capitalism of the conclusion. It is as if, through the nuttiness of this comic improvisation, Capra were confessing that imaginative energies are still present that cannot be expressed in a dramatically more frugal way, energies that capitalism represses but theater releases. The official moral of the film is that Molly and Andy have by this point successfully channeled all of their energies into the operations of the Molly Box Lunch Company, but this scene tells us that is not really true. A flamboyantly dramatic scene like this is evidence of an imaginative residue that Molly, Andy, and Capra can work off only in the extravagance of playacting. It is testimony to energies that have not been sublimated into the economical production of box lunches (or of movie plots) but that break loose in the comic weirdness, excessiveness, and gratuitousness of this protraced scene of theatrical, social, and imaginative playing.

In addition to *That Certain Thing* and *The Way of the Strong*, Capra made four other silent films in his first nine months with Columbia, only one of which survives today, a not terribly interesting comedy called *So This Is Love*.

He was turning out movies at about the rate of one every six weeks and was well on his way to becoming the king of the "B's" at Columbia when, on the basis of the moderate financial and critical success of his previous work, Harry Cohn asked him on short notice to step in and rescue a $250,000 picture that was in trouble. Irvin Willat, an expert at underwater photography and a specialist in sea pictures, had begun it, but Cohn, dissatisfied with the rushes, had summarily fired him and asked Capra to take over. *Submarine* was the result. In some respects, like Capra's two sequels to it – *Flight* and *Dirigible* – it aspires simply to cash in on the action-centered, buddy-boy war films genre that William Wellman's *Wings* had inaugurated the previous year. But what separates *Submarine*, *Flight*, and most of all *Dirigible* from *Wings* and marks it distinctively as from the hand of Capra is the complexity of consciousness that he creates in the two buddy-boys who star in each of the three films (played in all three cases by the same pair of actors: Ralph Graves – the pretty boy who had played Andy Charles, Jr., in *That Certain Thing* – and Jack Holt, an aging former silent-picture cowboy). Capra hedged his bets, in all three films, so that each of them contains enough action footage to satiate the most un – battle-fatigued of audiences, but it is obvious that the action scenes are not really the focus of his interest. As spectacular as many of the action sequences are (and, especially in *Dirigible*, they are truly impressive), Capra's attention is firmly centered on the effects of such extraordinary circumstances on the consciousnesses of his two buddies. When Graves is entombed alive in the hull of a sunken submarine (in *Submarine*), stranded in the wilds of Central America after his airplane crashes (in *Flight*), or wanders snow-blind and half crazy across the frozen wastes of Antarctica (in *Dirigible*), Capra uses the scenes to explore the consciousness of an individual in a situation of danger and self-doubt.

Even the locations seem to subserve Capra's overall psychological purpose. As in the work of Sternberg and in Capra's own later much more sophisticated adventure films set in exotic lands, *The Bitter Tea of General Yen* and *Lost Horizon*, the exotic sets function less as particularized landscapes than as metaphors for the enlarged states of consciousness that the central characters experience. The jungles of Central America, the glaciers of Antarctica, and the bottom of the sea interest him not as gorgeous picture plates out of a geography book but as landscapes of the mind – places where states of disorientation and crisis can lead an individual to increased self-awareness.

The form that the expression of a character's consciousness most frequently takes in these buddy-boy films is scenes of playing between Capra's two actors. Long after one has forgotten the banal plots, predictable crises, and shallow characterizations, one remembers Holt's and Graves's relaxed, self-pleasuring, often outrageous performances together.

The two experienced actors seem to have almost the same relationship to each other as the buddy-boy characters they play, performing together like an old married couple at a dinner party or a veteran pair of troupers who have worked together for years. They know each other's whims, gestures, and favorite attention-getting looks and lines and can play along with or disrupt each other's performances at will. The interest is less in what they say – the fairly trite and conventional lines in the script – than in how they say it, their mugging, winks, nods, and eyebrow raising, their finishing or interrupting each other's lines, cueing in or deliberately upsetting each other's bits of stage business, teasing each other and toying with the rather predictable lines and situations. Especially in *Flight*, the second of the pictures, there seems to be virtually a party atmosphere to many of the scenes, as if the final film was pieced together from outtakes and footage from the kind of clowning around that goes on during rehearsals. The placement of lights and camera and the matched cuts, however, show that this is not film of a rehearsal but a real take. Capra must have succeeded in putting the actors so much at ease that they were able to retain some of the same dramatic playfulness under the lights that would have been present in a rehearsal.

Capra was famous for encouraging his actors to improvise additions to their roles in rehearsal, which he then incorporated into their filmed performances. In a sense he was only doing, in more serious dramatic work, what he had learned to do when he worked as an all-purpose gag man and sometimes assistant director on silent comedies for Hal Roach and Mack Sennett. The eccentric inventiveness and unpredictability of the performances which resulted is interesting to watch, but Capra was not infatuated with improvisation as an end in itself; he was interested in the ways such apparently or actually "improvised" moments capture imaginative energies not expressible in any other way – in how one establishes a margin for performance within a fixed role that, without violating the role, still allows for the expression of individuality. That is what Holt and Graves are doing in their apparent clowning around on camera. They, as they and Capra both realize, are typecast: in the adventure-picture genre to which they are confined; as buddy-boys (one – Holt – is older, fatherly, mature, and responsible; the other – Graves – is younger, callow, brash, impulsive, and boyish); and in their lives as military men with specific duties, responsibilities, and codes of conduct to live up to . The challenge is to find some room to maneuver. Capra is fascinated with the ways in which, again, like an old married couple or pair of vaudeville troupers, they can still make a space for imaginative freedom within the narrow confines of their fixed roles and tried-and-true parts.

The repressiveness of narrative form and characterization (since characters do not exist in life, all characterization is to some degree repressive) is something that Capra wrestles with in all of his early films. The conventions of well-made dramatic structure and the economical presentation and development of a character are necessarily at odds with the free movements of the imagination and performance that Capra sought to release. Ironically, in the thirties and forties it was just this innovative aspect of Capra's work that was censured by many critics. (Otis Ferguson was a notable exception.) Capra was criticized as being overindulgent with his actors and was rebuked for the eccentricity of the scenes of playing and "horsing around" in his films that seem extraneous to their plots. Such scenes are there, however, because his films constitute efforts to express energies that a more tightly organized narrative would repress. The visual busyness of his scenes, the gratuitous visual and verbal jokes, the eccentric bits of stage business, and the occasionally overextended routines are not only the director's way of working off his own excess inventiveness that can find no outlet in the occasionally trite plots but are also his characters' expressions of their otherwise unplaceable imaginative energies. That is why offbeat playfulness, busyness, unpredictability, quirkiness, and eccentricity are such unequivocal signs of psychological health and imaginative life in Capra's films.*

Characters who do not derail the inexorable progress of the plot and mess up the tidiness of the characterizations with such displays of idiosyncratic individuality bore Capra. They have mortgaged their imaginations for the possession of a fixed, stylistically predictable institutional or formal identity. Like almost all of the characters in his films who are associated with institutions – psychiatrists, ministers, lawyers, businessmen, and politicians – they have channeled desire into an all too predictable form of behavior and feeling. For Capra, these characters are the truly damned, much more so even than the ostensible villains, who sometimes, at least, display an appealing appetency, eccentric passionateness, and spunky power of improvisation that ally them with the heroes.

Capra's efforts to liberate his central figures from the formal and social constraints of a fixed character resulted in characters who do not act or develop like those in most other movies. Usually, characters behave throughout their films in ways that simply confirm our initial impressions of their motivations and personal ties. Capra's characters are willful, passionate, imaginative, and, at least initially, are committed to no particular agenda of expression. Whereas ordinary characters are given a few leading motives for their behavior and keep repeating themselves, displaying the same predictable qualities in scene after scene, Capra's figures perform more spontaneously and eccentrically because their roles, functions, and "characters" are unusually free to be deformed by their imaginations.

Their lives and performative expressions of themselves, unlike most movie characters', are disorganized, contradictory, even incoherent. Such characters

---

* Just as they are in the related contemporaneous work of Howard Hawks, Michael Curtiz, and Leo McCarey, and in the subsequent work of John Huston, Nicholas Ray, Elaine May, and John Cassavetes. Joe Cook's performance in *Rain or Shine* is the most extreme demonstration of Capra's willingness in this case completely to destroy his narrative in order to be faithful to the eccentricity, extravagance, and pointlessness of certain kinds of imaginative energies. With his overblown, overlong, overinventive vaudeville routines, Cook explodes the film he is in. Seldom has a viewer more powerfully been shown both the incredible repressiveness of narrative form and the nightmarish dangers of attempting to leave it behind: dangers to art, personality, and human relationships. Though it is a very unsatisfactory film, the questions it raises about the problematic representation of the self and its free imaginative energies in social and narrative forms are the same as those explored more complexly in the great trilogy of Capra's later work: *Smith*, *Doe*, and *It's a Wonderful Life*.

are figures of desire with no home for their feelings, no inheritable roles, automatic styles, or stable functions within which they can button down their energetically mobile identities. And that is why, subjected to this tug and pull of desire and imagination, they are distinguished by such performative obliquity and mobility. Capra's goal is to map that uncharted territory beyond socially inheritable styles of expression where individual imagination and desire are liberated in a quest for adequate forms of expression.

Needless to say, this quest is not always a happy or successful one. With their always shaky and provisional efforts of self-creation, these figures, like Molly Kelly, are potentially on the brink of self-destruction. The homemade identity is a fragile one. The improvised performance is always in danger of degenerating into confusion and nonsense. The American performer, from Capra to Cassavetes, inevitably courts existential as well as dramatic embarrassment. Much of the excitement of Capra's subsequent work resides in watching his characters walk this fine line between self-creation and self-destruction, between liberating their imaginations from confining social and narrative situations and becoming lost or bewildered by the results.

Having said all of this in favor of the interest of these scenes in general, one must finally insist that the three adventure films in particular do not realize most of these possibilities. In these films Capra and his characters, with only a few exceptions, imagine free performance in terms of the most primitive sorts of playing, goofing off, or horsing around; playing lacks the serious consequences that it will acquire in his later work. Only one or two years later, playing takes on all sorts of complex and creative dimensions that are absent here, where it is chiefly a series of childish pranks, jokes, and inanities that pass between Holt and Graves. Both as actors and as characters, Holt and Graves lark about on camera like schoolboys on vacation. That is the problem with the expression of freedom in these films: It is viewed as a vacation from life's duties and burdens, not as an act of finer, sterner engagement with them. Freedom is something that exists between serious moments, unfortunately, not within them.

The adventure trilogy is Capra's most Hawksian series of films, but that is just what makes it comparatively uninteresting in relation to Capra's later, more sophisticated work. As Capra does here, Hawks habitually dichotomizes life into alternating scenes of work and play, responsibility and freedom, dour dutifulness and holiday pranking. That dualism is present in all of Hawks's work, from *Scarface* and *Twentieth Century* to *His Girl Friday* and *Monkey Business*. It is sobersided Ralph Bellamy and his mother versus playboy Cary Grant and highjinks on the newspaper in *His Girl Friday*. It is youthful, irresponsible, fun-loving Cary Grant and Ginger Rogers versus adult, mature, serious, responsible Cary Grant and Ginger Rogers in *Monkey Business*. Within this series of alternatives, Hawks invariably prefers play over work, zaniness over dutifulness, and vacation over home, but the telling fact is the dichotomous nature of his vision. There is no way for Cary Grant, in *His Girl Friday*, to be halfway like family man Bellamy; there is no way for Grant and

Rogers, in *Monkey Business*, to keep the energy and passion of their younger, "animal" selves fully alive amid the responsibilities of their adult marriage. Hawks sees drama (and life) as offering two contrasted, mutually exclusive possibilities: on the one side is the creativeness of eccentricity, play, idiosyncracy, and theatricality; on the other are an individual's responsibilities to home, a peer or professional group, and society. That is either the truly upsetting and anarchic quality of Hawks's vision or its great imaginative deficiency, its evasion of a tougher task. In the first view of his work, his films are acts of bomb throwing at polite society; in the second, they embody a bank-holiday sense of creativity as something you do (or get away with) on your day off. Yet both views really come to the same thing insofar as they wall-off life into alternative water-tight compartments.

The Hawksian dichotomy is a recurring imaginative problem in American art that cannot be easily dismissed or ignored. It extends far beyond the films of Hawks. One could illustrate the same phenomenon with examples from the work of Nicholas Ray, Martin Scorsese, Mark Twain, Wallace Stevens, or Vladimir Nabokov. It is the reason American art and American characters so frequently have been dismissed out of hand by unsympathetic critics as being irresponsible and escapist. The question asked again and again by all of these artists is how one reconciles the putatively free movements of the imagination and the openness of personal identity with the claims of home, family, and social responsibility.

Although, as I have argued, Capra's earliest films fail egregiously in the attempt, in his later work he attempted to do what Hawks and these others apparently thought was impossible. For him, the disturbing energies of the wildest and most exciting kinds of playing, dreaming, and feeling must be allowed to trouble and enrich all of life. The energies of our most powerful desires must be expressible in our marriages, our adult friendships, and our social institutions, and not merely in escapes or vacations from them.

Only two scenes in the adventure trilogy even begin to use the playing of Graves and Holt in a less Hawksian and more complex way to explore the eruption of nonfrivolous imaginative energy into everyday life. The first is a sequence from *Flight*. Graves and Holt play Marine Corps buddies linked together by a complex network of personal allegiances and rivalries. Graves is "Lefty" Phelps, a well-meaning but nervous-in-the-service bungler who seems to do everything wrong. Holt is "Panama" Williams, senior to Lefty, poised, and mature, who as his superior officer, has interceded at several crucial junctures in the most humane and tactful way to keep him from losing faith in himself, with the result that Lefty loves and admires Panama. Meanwhile, unknown to each other, they have each fallen in love with the same girl, a nurse at the base hospital, but, ironically enough, in love their destinies in life are reversed. Clutzy Lefty has been successful with the girl, whereas his superior officer is shown to be a romantic bumbler whose advances she has discreetly rebuffed.

In the scene immediately preceding the one on which I want to focus, Lefty has just learned of the romantic rivalry (of which Panama is still unaware). In a touching moment, Panama, not knowing that Lefty is in love with her, confesses to him, his best friend, his affection for the girl and shows Lefty a picture of her. After a brief action sequence comes a scene in which we see Panama and Lefty horsing around together that night in a field tent they share. The first anomaly is that Graves muffs a line and Holt, like the veteran actor he is, comes back with a reply that picks up on Graves's mistake, and Capra includes the whole "bad take" in the film. What follows is even stranger and more interesting still. Holt and Graves wrestle with each other on their cots for two or three minutes. They begin on Graves's cot; then Holt carries Graves over to his own cot and pins him down there with his legs awkwardly in the air. The scene stands out for several reasons. In the first place, it is inordinately long. Capra allows it to go on at least a minute longer than any other director would have. It is clearly improvised, and just as clearly it is a scene that gets out of hand, becoming more passionate and more physical than could have been intended. At one point Graves calls attention to the excessiveness of the moment by vigorously protesting, "I don't want to be clowning around!", in what sounds more like the honestly annoyed tones of his own off-camera voice than something that was in the script. When Graves is not protesting his rough handling, both actors are laughing almost uncontrollably at the absurdity of their physical positions and the madcap quality of the scene.

The homosexual resonances of the scene (Lefty and Panama are, after all, deeply torn between allegiance to each other and allegiance to the girl) are only one aspect of a constellation of senses we have that this horseplay is putting us in touch with subterranean sexual confusions that it would otherwise be difficult to express. The wrestling match summarizes the playful – but not entirely playful – rivalry and conflict of feelings of the two men. Above all, the very primitivism, clumsiness, and inelegance of this wrestling match – the fact that the rivalry cannot be expressed in a higher, more refined form of competitive behavior, say in the nuances of a more sophisticated verbal or social competition – quite eloquently express the true confusion of these complexities of feeling.

Capra's two heroes are expressive bunglers. They are hopelessly, pathetically, comically inarticulate. Far from being a deficiency in their characterizations, however, that is what makes them interesting. Capra is exploring the situation of men in emotional deep water, in over their heads and their ability to verbalize, rationalize, or articulate their feelings for or about each other. This horseplay is their only form of expression, however primitive, and yet of course it is also a strategy not of expression but of concealment and avoidance of expression. One wrestles playfully, to avoid fighting seriously. One wrestles to avoid having to talk. One wrestles because the actors, the director, and the screenwriter have not found a way to express themselves and the complexities of this moment in the form of dialogue or plot. This last observation is encouraged by the Pirandellian aspects of the film, and of this scene in particular. Capra seems bent on repeatedly reminding us that these are *actors* with expressive problems, playing *characters* with expressive problems. This scene uses its actors' improvisatory embarrassments, muddlements, and confusions to emphasize its characters' expressive inadequacies and anxieties.

Immediately following this bizarre yet touching moment of expressive failure, Holt/Williams goes off to what we know will be an even more poignant scene of expressive inadequacy. He announces that he is on his way to propose to the nurse. Graves/Phelps is left alone in the tent on the cot. There is now no one for him to talk to or interact with. There is not even a token animal for him to soliloquize to – the bird or dog that another director would have inserted into the scene. Capra, however, uncannily stays with him in the tent instead of cutting away after Holt exits. Graves lies prone on the cot for a few seconds, then rises to walk to the door of the tent.* Lefty stands in the entrance of the tent and, with extremely confused feelings, since he knows the futility of his buddy's pathetic errand, stares out into the darkness, listening to a sentimental song, "My Gal Sal," being sung by homesick Marines in the distance. In terms of plot or narrative progress, nothing happens – but Capra still stays on him. The film has suddenly modulated from playful raucousness to poetic meditativeness, with a rapidity that indicates how closely allied these two moments are in Capra's mind. As different as they apparently are, violent, agitated physical action and silent visionary meditation are both ways of capturing a psychological state that cannot be translated into the ordinary events of plot, dialogue, or social interaction (just as in the boxing paintings of George Bellows, where violent activity and passive observation, boxers and spectators, are linked in one enchanted, visionary circle). Standing still and staring off into the distance is only the flip side of wrestling around on a cot in a tent. Each suggests a charged but inexpressible state of feeling that is not articulable in a less oblique, more social, or more cinematically visible form. If anyone asked Lefty himself to say what he was doing or thinking in listening to the camp song, just as if he were asked the same question about his wrestling on the cot with Panama, he could give no adequate answer. Capra has moved his film out of the realm of character development or narrative eventfulness and into a realm of trying to express the inexpressible and narrate the unnarratable.

There is an equally complex series of interrelated moments at the end of *Dirigible* with which I want to conclude my discussion of the action films. Holt and Graves again play pals, this time "Frisky" Pierce (Graves) and Jack Bradon (Holt). Frisky is the pilot of a racing plane, Holt the captain of a Navy dirigible, and the difference in their personalities and their roles is roughly summarized in the difference between their vehicles. Frisky is a flamboyant, handsome stunt flyer. Bradon is a serious, level-headed, mature senior naval

---

* In another Pirandellian touch that insists on reminding us of the actor behind the part – and of the expressive challenge that·being alone like this on camera presents to even the most talented actor – Capra shows Graves getting up from the cot with a blanket tangled around his legs and tipping the cot over, revealing a Columbia Pictures Properties stencil on the other side of it.

officer. They find themselves not only in competition to be the first man to get to the South Pole by air but, more important, in romantic competition for Pierce's lovely wife, Helen, who is attracted to Jack and frustrated by Frisky's emotional immaturity and neglect of her.

To make a long and rather farfetched story short, after falling in love with Jack, Helen, to revenge herself on Frisky, sends a declaration of her love for Jack and her intention of divorcing Frisky in a sealed note with Frisky on his expedition to the South Pole – to be opened by him in his moment of triumph. By a series of catastrophic accidents the letter goes unread. Frisky indeed makes it to the pole, but his plane crashes through his own daredevil negligence, and he and his crew wander for days, lost and without provisions on the Antarctic ice, dying gruesomely, one by one, of cold and starvation, until only Frisky is left alive. He too almost dies, but at the last minute is miraculously rescued, snow-blind and half-dead, by a search party led by Bradon in his dirigible.

The scenes I want only briefly to consider come following his rescue and in the last four or five minutes of the film. Flying back in Jack's dirigible, Frisky, on the brink of death from exhaustion and starvation, finds Helen's forgotten letter among his possessions and, snow-blind and too weak to read it himself, forces Jack to read it to him. It is an impossible situation. It was only with the greatest ambivalence that Jack rescued him in the first place, knowing how Frisky had neglected Helen in the past and that his return could only separate Jack, who really loves her, from her. Jack knows that if he reads the letter Frisky, in his weakened condition, will probably die from the shock of the note. He reads it out without a hitch, but changes it all. He turns it into a love letter from Helen to Frisky, and of course in the same gesture implicitly gives up Helen once and for all to Frisky.

The final minute or so of the film is devoted to the day of the two men's arrival back home. A grand ticker-tape parade has been scheduled for them, but just before it starts Frisky leaves to be with his wife instead. He embraces her, tells her he has seen how irresponsible he has been in the past, says how much her love letter meant to him at his moment of crisis and doubt, and tells her that he will not ever leave her again. She, realizing what Jack has done and touched by Frisky's ordeal and his new profession of love, plays along with the fiction Jack has created and sincerely, lovingly embraces him. The final shot returns to the figure of Jack Bradon in the parade limousine, surrounded and cheered by well-wishers, the saddest and loneliest man in the city. He has given up everything for the love of his friend, even the woman he passionately loved.

What interests me in this poignant ending is the extraordinarily rich sense that the concept of playing has taken on in these two penultimate scenes. Jack and Helen have in the end each played a fiction, a lie, for Frisky, but in playing it they have, in effect, made it true. The "play" they have staged has brought Helen and Frisky together in love again. Capra has again used playing (in a thoroughly theatrical sense of the word) to capture a richness of feeling that has no form of social expression. The complexity of consciousness felt by both Jack and Helen in these final minutes cannot be communicated in any way except in such a play. Each still loves the other, and yet each lies both to Frisky and (implicitly) to the other, in order to save the marriage of Frisky and Helen.★ The play of lies they act out in good faith says what cannot be said more directly. The play summarizes the plangent muddle of feelings they each have. The play says it all.

There is nothing Jack and Helen could say to Frisky or to each other that would more eloquently communicate their complexly charged awarenesses of how they feel at this moment. Capra concludes the film with a shot of Bradon alone in the parade procession, estranged from everyone else in his incommunicable state of heightened consciousness. He is photographed from above, sitting alone, silent, and half slumped over in the open car moving down the street. There is nothing for him to say and no one for him to say it to, to communicate what he and we have just lived through and now feel. The only expression of it has been in the elaborate dramatic charade he and Helen have staged.

These scenes are exceptional, in their complexity, in their respective films, and their appearance in these early movies points up the fact that Capra's development does not follow a linear progression. There are isolated moments in his very earliest work that are fully as complex as anything later. Molly's nightmarish ascent of the stairway in *That Certain Thing* is no less subtle a moment than George Bailey's dreamland experience in *It's a Wonderful Life*, almost twenty years later. Lefty and Panama's wrestling on the cot is in no respect simpler than the scenes of game playing in *Mr. Deeds Goes to Town* or *You Can't Take It with You*. Lefty's meditative staring out of the door of the tent anticipates some of the most interesting scenes in *Ladies of Leisure*, and *Bitter Tea*. Helen's and Jack's deep silence about their true relationship at the end of *Dirigible* is every bit as interesting as George Bailey's deep silence at the end of *It's a Wonderful Life*. In short, the best scenes in Capra's earliest work are just as complex as those that appear in his most sophisticated and mature later work. That is why, rather than trying to trace a simple line of artistic development in Capra's films, it is much more useful to think of the sequence of movies not as striking out away from past territory, but as repeatedly resurveying it. Capra is haunted by certain kinds of characters and situations, certain experiences and feelings that are already present full-fledged in his very earliest work.

Thus I will not hesitate to compare scenes from movies made a decade or more apart, ignoring the years that separate them, or to discuss films out of chronological order, where that makes the understanding of Capra's concerns easier. In the next two chapters of this section, on *Platinum Blonde* and *American*

★ Though it is tangential to my argument in this chapter, I note in passing that Jack Bradon's act of renunciation repeats the renunciation by "Handsome" Williams that concluded *The Way of the Strong*, and anticipates many of the renunciations at the ends of Capra's subsequent films. The Jamesian renunciation appealed powerfully to Capra throughout his career.

Madness, and in several of the following chapters, I treat one film as if it were a rewriting or revision of another, even when this ignores chronology. Such procedures would be illegitimate or do violence to the artistic work only if Capra's career gradually and systematically developed along some strict temporal trajectory that must be rigidly respected. Capra's work does not progress this way (one wonders if any artist's does). He frequently moves tentatively in two or three different directions in a film, returning in successive later works to reexplore each of the paths that was present already in an earlier film. The effect is not one of linear artistic progression but of continually doubling back on old paths to follow up new possibilities, choosing new forks in old roads, or exploring old paths and possibilities in a slightly different way. The superiority of some of the later work is not at all that Capra discovers new material or develops different artistic interests but that he explores the same old areas, the same old bewilderments and anxieties again in perhaps a little more detail, at greater length, and sometimes with greater perceptiveness than he did previously.

The limitation of some of Capra's earlier work is not that it lacks complex insights but that it sometimes does not know what to make of them. In these earliest films Capra is usually unable to make the truly interesting moments and scenes count toward the development of the larger contours of the plot and the characterizations. In the three adventure films, the scenes of horseplay and improvisation, as well as the two moments of meditative silence in the second and third films, stand out from the rest of the films in which they occur precisely because Capra cannot find a way to integrate them into the larger structures of their plots or their characters' personalities. They remain detached and isolated moments that Capra, like his buddy-boys, is unable to relate to the rest of life.

To make such imaginative moments count for more, in life and in narrative, will be the accomplishment of his subsequent work. To do that, though, Capra needs to make changes. His central characters need to be embedded in much more elaborate, extended societies than they are here and to be given the opportunity for more meaningful forms of playing. Capra must test his characters in more complex social environments than those in which Molly, "Handsome," and the buddy-boys exist. He must allow them more complex forms of imaginativeness than dreaming at a cigar counter or horsing around on a cot. He must imagine both the constraining contexts of life and the power of social, theatrical, and imaginative playing more daringly than he does in these early films.

6

Mastering ceremonies

American Madness

There's no such things as a "good actor." Acting is an extension of life. How you're capable of performing in your life, that's how you're capable of performing on the screen.

– John Cassavetes, Interview with Grover Lewis

The difference between the central figures in *That Certain Thing*, *The Way of the Strong*, and the adventure trilogy, and those that follow them in *The Miracle Woman*, *Platinum Blonde*, *American Madness*, and *The Bitter Tea of General Yen* (as well as many of the films subsequent to these) is that whereas the central figures in the earlier films were more or less solitaries (paired off with a friend or a lover only), the later ones are imagined to be members of complex, extended societies.* The performers are asked to become social masters of ceremonies, as they were not earlier in Capra's work.

In order to appreciate this change in the situation of Capra's central figures in these social films, it is important to notice how the spaces in which they function have changed. From around 1931 onward, Capra was increasingly attracted to physically large and socially (or theatrically) quite complex spaces. Probably the most famous is the full-scale mockup of the U.S. Senate chamber in which he set much of *Mr. Smith Goes to Washington*, but in many respects the

---

* A reminder and a point to notice: The reader is reminded, as I have already mentioned at the beginning of Chapter 5, that I am deliberately leaving out of my account in this section (and saving for extended consideration in the following section) the more visionary or transcendental works that Capra made during the early thirties. An unrelated point to notice is that *Rain or Shine*, which falls at a transitional moment in the sequence of films involving explicitly social performances with which I am dealing (that is to say, it was made after two of the adventure films and before *The Miracle Woman*, *Platium Blonde*, and *American Madness*), shows a social performer in transition between more or less private, self-satisfying performance (like those of the buddy-boys) and performance in front of a more demanding or hostile audience (like those staged by Florence Fallon, Stew Smith, and Tom Dixon). Smiley Johnson (Joe Cook) performs as crazily and self-indulgently as the buddy-boys and yet is forced to do it in front of audiences larger and more critical than any that Holt or Graves faced.

bank set in *American Madness* and the set of the Schuyler mansion in *Platinum Blonde* are equally or even more detailed and remarkable sound-stage fabrications. In the work he did with Robert Riskin as his cowriter (which includes all but four of the twelve films he made in the decade of the 1930s, after *Dirigible*), Capra usually imagined his central characters' crises as taking place within an extended bureaucratic or institutional context in which they are located for the duration of the film. Capra's preferred way of representing the characters' embeddedness was to photograph them on large sets that tower over and contain them and everywhere contextualize their movements.

Columbia was still considered a Poverty Row studio in the early thirties, but it is remarkable how well they concealed the fact. While Warner Brothers was economizing (and letting it show) by favoring small, casually thrown together sets, heavily shadowed to hide their flaws, Capra was economizing at Columbia by adopting the opposite strategy, constructing a few huge, detailed, complex sets for each film and confining the action as far as possible to them.* To think of any of the central characters in the films of the thirties (with the exception of *It Happened One Night*) is to remember them as living and acting within specific institutional or social spaces: Florence Fallon, in the Temple of Miracles, in *The Miracle Woman*; Megan Davis, in Yen's Palace, in *Bitter Tea*; Robert Conway, in the Valley of the Blue Moon, in *Lost Horizon*; the Vanderhof family in their home in *You Can't Take It with You*; and Jefferson Smith, in the U.S. Senate. The protagonists are always seen *in* something in these films, and involved with crowds of others as a result. Much as they may aspire to be on their own, they never are. They are never released into the state of insulated romantic subjectivity that is so common in Hollywood films of the thirties and forties. The paradox of Capra's work, and the predicament with which his central characters must cope, is that although they aspire to be the most independent, individualistic characters in all of film, they are seldom able to remove themselves from the extended social contexts that are figured in Capra's enormous sets. Like Henry James, Capra maximizes both individualism and social embeddedness.

Large sets also allowed Capra and his cameraman, Joe Walker, to employ the multiple-camera setups they liked to use. Most of the complex scenes in Capra's films of the thirties were shot with at least two cameras, usually three, and sometimes as many as four to eight going at once. A number of publicity stills survive showing a wide variety of different kinds of two-, three-, or even four-camera setups from the making of *Smith* and *Meet John Doe*, and Capra claims to have used between eight and twelve cameras in particular scenes in these films. He apparently began using multiple cameras in his early sound

---

* The Columbia set designers deserve a large measure of credit for the extraordinary sets in *Platinum Blonde, American Madness*, and many of Capra's subsequent films. The head of the set department and the man who was to be the artistic director for almost all of Capra's films of the thirties was the talented Stephen Goosson, who went on to design not only Yen's palace in 1933 and Shangri-La in 1937, but, equally memorably, the house of mirrors in Orson Welles's *Lady from Shanghai* in 1946.

pictures because of the difficulty that the technicians had in synchronizing the sound tracks from different takes. To minimize the problem, he tried recording important scenes with all of the angles in one take, and this quickly became his preferred method of filming. He felt that his actors gave fresher performances when the number of takes was reduced and that he himself had more liberty for creative tinkering with the assembling of a major scene in the editing room when he had more or less complete photographic versions of it from two or three different angles.* The use of large sets not only gave Capra and Walker more freedom in the placement of cameras and the choice of shots but also allowed them to employ a variety of longer shots with a generally greater depth of field than one encounters in the average thirties film.

The result is, again, socially and institutionally to contextualize a character's performance. Close-ups and shallow–depth-of-field photography inevitably elevate the individual star above the constellation of others with whom he or she nominally interacts, but by being able to pull the camera back five or ten feet farther than in the typical Hollywood set and take in more of the background, Capra and Walker subtly but decisively broke their compositions free from the star-system hierarchies. The central figure is no longer walled up in the tiny box of the close-up; instead, through long-shots and medium-length shots, the central actor is immersed in a social matrix of interacting others. Capra's films, needless to say, do not avoid tight close-ups, but in nearly every scene the occasional close-ups are intercut with contextualizing long-shots.

Gregg Toland and Orson Welles are often given credit for inaugurating the use of complex compositional depth in film, but it would be easy to argue that the set design and photography in *American Madness* and *Platinum Blonde* (not to mention the even more elaborate effects in *Bitter Tea* and *Lost Horizon*) create social spaces much larger and more complex than those that Welles and Toland create in *Citizen Kane*, for instance. There is a fundamental difference between Welles's and Capra's use of space. Capra's extended spaces function to bring the characters within them into social relationship with each other. Welles's spaces function in every way *but* a social one: They function abstractly to register ironic differences between characters and their backgrounds, to make us feel the gaps, separations, and failures of communication between people, to suggest intellectual or moral differences between characters, or to comment on a character's psychological situation or relationship with the

---

* Capra often admitted that many of his films' effects were discovered in the editing room. He has told many stories about editing completely different versions of scenes in order to arrive at the best one for the final print of the film. The hilarious "hat fumbling" sequence in *Smith* (in which Capra brilliantly and comically stays on a shot of Smith's hands and hat while Smith talks to Susan Paine) apparently occurred to Capra only in the process of editing the film. A camera had been assigned to "follow" Stewart's fumbling in order to intercut it with other shots of the rest of the scene, but in the process of assembling the footage for the scene, it occurred to Capra to use the footage from that camera exclusively. The availability of multiple, complete takes of a scene proved invaluable in this instance, and undoubtedly in many others as well.

environment. The one thing Welles's spaces almost never do is to bring into existence extended, complex, interdependent societies of individuals performing together, as rivals or as team members, in mutual awareness of or nuanced interaction with each other.

In the scenes in Welles's work that contain crowds of characters who might appear to constitute an extended society (the ballroom scene from *The Magnificent Ambersons*, the trial scene from *The Trial*, or the convention scene from *Citizen Kane*, for example) the crowd of characters is usually not really interacting in any socially complex way as individuals or with the principal character. The space is not a representation of a society of mutual influence and relationship. Instead, Welles's spaces function expressionistically or metaphorically: to indicate the psychological state of a character, to make an abstract point about his life, personality, or present situation.

Paradoxically, because Capra's spaces are so full of people interacting and never call attention to themselves in such metaphoric or metaphysical ways, his use of space has been largely ignored. Rather than noticing the abstract (and often empty) spaces, as one almost always does in a film by Welles, the viewer is so busy paying attention to the complicated relationships of the figures in the space that one forgets the space itself. Rather than being impressed with the complex visual and physical composition of a shot, one is drawn into engagement with the human events taking place within it.

The parallel with Capra's practice is not the expressionistic use of space that is Welles's or Hitchcock's dubious legacy to film appreciation and a succeeding generation of directors (such as Coppola, Kubrick, and Altman) but the "realistic" spaces of Jean Renoir's work in the thirties, which achieves its illusion of realism by being filled with people who, in effect, hide the space within which they exist. The closest parallel with *American Madness* specifically is Renoir's *The Crime of M. Lange*, which uses a small courtyard set and the apartments adjoining it much as Capra uses the bank in his film.

Capra's bank set looks, and functions socially, like a European close, a small, confined neighborhood in which several houses and apartments are nestled together, overlooking a common entrance way. The bank consists of a series of overlapped and interrelated spaces, the interlocking quality of which guarantees that the events taking place in one part either are visible somewhere else or intimately affect the events taking place in another part of the bank. At the center of everything is the bank lobby, like the entrance way of the close through which everyone passes. On one side of the lobby are the tellers' windows (like the windows of a concierge who can see everything going on in the building), and on the other side of it are the doors through which all of the customers pass (like the gateway from the close to the street). Around the periphery of the lobby and overlooking every foot of it is a mezzanine with the bank secretary, the various bank offices, and the telephone switchboard distributed along its length (like the apartments of first-floor tenants). Two other spaces mark the bank's interior and exterior limits: Behind the tellers' stations and below the lobby is the vault space where the money is kept and the tellers' days begin and end; and at the opposite end of the lobby are the front doors of the bank, its interface with the world. We see Dixon entering and leaving through these doors on the three mornings on which the story takes place, and for two scenes we leave these institutional spaces entirely, but with those exceptions, for the rest of the film – better than nine-tenths of it – we, like Tom Dixon, live and breathe the air of this particular institutional space and are psychologically, socially, and physically confined within it.

The group of characters assembled within this special space constitute an intimately interacting community. They have such intricate ties to each other that they might be thought of as a kind of extended family. Capra is the maker of family films, in more than one sense of the phrase. The bank building in *American Madness* can be viewed as an enormous two-story house, not very different from those in *Platinum Blonde* or *You Can't Take It with You*, with its employees as loosely but intimately connected as if they were relatives in one gargantuan, extended family of seniors and juniors, lovers and rivals, in-laws and outlaws. Everybody does not necessarily like everybody else, but they all know each other's business and look out for each other to the extent they are able. Most significantly, just as in a big family, the values most prized and in demand are less the grand public virtues of courage, intelligence, or heroism, and more small personal qualities like sensitivity, consideration, tact, and respect – the qualities that will allow individuals in a group like this to interact as kindly as they can. Capra's characters are often part of an extended family in this metaphoric sense, not out of some commitment on Capra's part to the family as a social actuality (the male protagonists in the films of the early thirties, with the exception of Tom Dixon, are bachelors, as Capra himself was at this time, and the female leads, also with only one exception – *Platinum Blonde's* Anne Schuyler – are all unmarried), but out of an imaginative commitment to what might be called the metaphysics of family life. Smith, Deeds, and Doe, in the later films also, like Stew Smith in *Platinum Blonde* or Tom Dixon in *American Madness*, are not family men in the literal sense of the term at all, but Capra forces them to be family men in an imaginative sense. They are forced to become participants in a complex social matrix of intimate relationships from which they can never extract themselves. There is no private space for them to inhabit where they can freely express their individuality. Tom Dixon, his tellers, and his secretaries have personal feelings and private lives in *American Madness*, but they are not separable from their public behavior in the social space to which the film is confined. Individuals in these films cannot shape an identity apart from their families, whether they are members of an actual extended family as prying and intrusive as that of the Vanderhofs, in *You Can't Take It with You*, or members of a merely institutional family like the Senate, in the case of Jefferson Smith, whose words and actions are scrutinized continuously by ninety-five senators, a dozen newspaper and radio reporters, and a few-score spectators.

When "Dude" Finney and two of his henchmen enter the bank near the beginning of *American Madness* and put pressure on the bank treasurer, Cyril

Cluett, a secretary observes their entrance and wonders out loud why they are in Cluett's office. That is one of the facts of life in the cinematic universe of these films. Performances are inevitably public. Perched on the mezzanine, this eagle-eyed secretary is a ubiquitous presence in all of Capra's work. She is the neighbor who watches and embarrassingly interrupts the awkward courtship of George Bailey and Mary Hatch on their way home from the high-school prom. She is Babe Bennet looking down on Smith on the floor of the Senate. She is one of the landladies or motel keepers who are always able to step forward and testify about the allegedly "private" lives and habits of their tenants, the protagonists in these films. Not only is there, in effect, no privacy in a Capra movie, but the desire for privacy or secrecy is itself usually suspect or potentially dangerous. To wish to be alone in a room, to sit and stare out of a window, to separate oneself from society or one's "family" becomes a moral or social crime, or at least an admission of personal failure. Capra is creating (and half endorsing, but only half) a universe in which social or "familial" expressive responsibilities are so unremitting that what cannot be sublimated into socially accepted forms of expression is forced into hiding.

In Part V this will be discussed as the "American way of repression." Freud saw in such a situation the seeds of psychic disaster, and Capra was far from complacent about its consequences. He and his protagonists, in fact, are extremely troubled about this state of affairs. Even as he has heaped unending social responsibilities on them, no director has mounted a more harrowing indictment of the psychic cost of the social contract, one at least as searching as Freud's in *Civilization and Its Discontents*. Capra's films are one long, sustained cri de coeur on behalf of the individual's need to be free from such compromising alliances and vitiating sublimations. Yet, notwithstanding his belief in the sovereignty of the individual ("The name above the title" and "One man, one film" were not idle phrases but principles by which he lived his life and took on all comers), Capra was unable to conceive of the value of individual experience apart from social expression, to affirm a life that transcends social pressures or rises above public responsibilities. He crosses a High Romantic sense of the power and sovereignty of the individual consciousness with a virtually Elizabethan conception of performance as something that takes place in public, experience as something that one has with others, never most meaningfully alone.

This is the great energizing ambivalence in Capra's work that he never resolved in his own mind, and it is the subject of most of his greatest films. His characters may try to avoid this problem, but they cannot. One of the recurring events in the films is the protagonists' effort to deny their relentless social involvement and Capra's attempt, in effect, to repudiate the social premises of his own work. From Tom Dixon and Stew Smith to Longfellow Deeds, Jefferson Smith, and George Bailey, at a crucial point in his film the main character does attempt to cancel his membership in the group. He attempts to withdraw from the "family" of which he is ostensibly a part, to cease to be a "performer" or "actor" in a public drama. As he tries to escape into absolute individualism, though, he invariably discovers that withdrawal is more painful than involvement. Like James's novels, which are torn between a faith in Emersonian self-reliance and a counterpointed sense of the expressive claims of society, Capra's films are powerfully energized by his inability to make up his mind about the rival claims of imagination and society.

The opening scene of *American Madness* establishes the social complexity of the story's setting. The first scene shows the opening of the vault on the first day.★ It is a scene that at the time of the film's release was praised for its realism, and it certainly appears to contain as detailed a depiction of a bank vault and of the actual procedures of opening it as Hollywood created up until the heist movies of more than thirty years later. The reviewers especially praised the massive, detailed substantiality of the vault door and vault space, either one of the most meticulous recreations of a bank vault ever constructed out of plywood and plaster by a set department or an actual vault photographed on location.

As impressive physically as is the vault itself, the much praised realism of the sequence is at least as attributable to Capra's blocking, photography, and editing of the scene as to Columbia's design department. His masterful control of cinematic space and time is the strength of all of *American Madness* and is what makes its physical settings seem so palpable. With a virtually neorealistic patience, Capra records each of the mechanical steps involved in opening the vault and then follows the interrelated activity of the five tellers and one supervisor as they enter it to pick up their cash drawers and wheel them out to begin the day at the bank. The visual effect is choreographic in its complexity, in its intricate tracing of the actions and complex interactions of the six men. A character will be measured in *American Madness* (and many of Capra's other films) precisely by his or her capacity to participate in this sort of intricate, dancelike process of social movements, adjustments, and corrections of position.

The social space that the characters inhabit and through which they move in this scene and many others in the bank is made especially real and tangible by Joseph Walker's lighting and photography. Walker's photography became as intimately connected with Capra's work in the thirties as Riskin's scripting and Goosson's set designing. As I mentioned in my discussion of *The Way of the Strong* , Walker originated many of the diffusion-filter and key-lighting effects in Capra's work, but his chief photographic contribution to these early films, and to *American Madness* in particular, is his pseudorealistic style of composing scenes in depth and lighting and photographing several planes of interrelated action at once, thus establishing the actors in a complex visual space that makes the social interdependence of the various characters visually meaningful.

In the first scene in the vault, for example, in one shot Walker lights five

---

★ The temporal span is as compressed as the physical and imaginative space described by the set – forty-eight hours, beginning one morning as the bank opens for business; taking in a robbery that night and a run on the bank the next day; and ending with the bank's reopening and the final restoration of order the following morning.

distinct spatial planes. In the plane closest to the camera, we see the grillwork of the barred cage surrounding the vault; in a second plane, the door and the passageway into the inside of the vault; in a third plane, another interior grillwork; in a fourth plane, the men inside counting out money; and in a fifth plane, a final further grillwork of bars surrounding the inner vault. The camera setups that Walker and Capra use in this scene are, interestingly, not the usual series of "angles" on the men inside – the standard alternation of point of view from forty-five or sixty degrees right of a perpendicular to the axis of events to forty-five or sixty degrees left of it – nor do Walker and Capra present a series of shot – reverse-shots of talking heads. Instead they choose to make a series of slices through space. Rather than maintaining a relatively constant distance and changing the angle of the shot, which is common Hollywood practice, they maintain a relatively constant angle and keep changing the distance of the shot. Thus the scene in the vault is photographed from more or less the central axis of the events but at a series of different distances (with occasional close-ups of faces at important moments, close-ups that also do not move far away from the central axis of the scene).

The shots used during the opening seconds in the vault scene run as follows: first, a long-shot from inside the vault, looking out through the opening as the tellers file in to pick up their cash drawers; then a reverse long-shot along the same axis, taken from outside the inner grillwork of bars surrounding the vault showing the tellers from behind as they file in; then a shot from outside the vault, still from the same angle but now taken from even farther back, so that now *two* layers of bars intervene between the camera and the vault opening. (Some of the tellers leaving the vault at this moment pass between the two rows of bars.) Next, Capra cuts to a medium-distance two-shot of two tellers, still taken from the same angle but now photographed from closer in than the two previous shots, from outside the vault entrance but inside both cages of bars. Then he cuts in on the two figures in a slightly closer shot. Finally, as these last two tellers make their way out of the vault and the sequence is concluded, Capra returns to the position of the third shot, the long-shot with two layers of bars visible between the camera and the vault in the background, between which the two tellers make their way.★

The result of this unorthodox series of unangled setups and editorial slices through space is to make the physical and social space within which the tellers perform highly tangible. The space is not abrogated by the movements of the camera or dissected by the cuts of the montage. It is respected and preserved whole, and its undeformed, uninterrupted depth and width are brought home to the viewer.

Welles, Wyler, Stevens, and Hitchcock, in Capra's day, and Kubrick and

---

★ It would be arguable that this avoidance of standard studio "angled" setups was forced on Capra and Walker by the use of an actual bank vault – if one was indeed used – if it were not for the fact that their studio work both before and after *American Madness* avoided standard shot – reverse-shot "angles" with equal assiduousness. One can only conclude that the decision to shoot this and many other scenes this way was chosen, not forced on them.

Altman, in our own, have used cinematic space in a fairly complex way, and I have already mentioned some of the differences between Capra and Welles. Another fundamental difference between all of these filmmakers and Capra is that Capra asks that his characters interact with and attempt to master the spaces in which he situates them in order to establish their worth. The space is not merely a metaphoric or metaphysical background against which the character exists. It does not simply define the objects that are part of the character's environment. It is not something the character merely exists *in*, or as an extension of. It is something he or she moves through, responds to, and tests his capacity for performance by negotiating. In an entirely unmetaphoric sense, *American Madness* is a study in choreography. For Capra, as for a ballet master, the human being is the center and source of all value and establishes his or her powers of performance through demonstrating the capacity for complex movement through space, around and in partnership with other human bodies. Capra's early films are studies in the choreography of everyday bureaucratic, institutional, and social life.

How differently the layering of space functions in the work of the group of filmmakers from Wyler to Altman. For them space expresses an abstract predicament by which a character is enclosed or oppressed. Space defines a static state of affairs. It is not something the character is encouraged to move through joyfully, to negotiate, and master. Wyler and Altman, as different as they are from each other, use complex visual, physical, and social spaces to trap, hedge round, or isolate their characters, not to stimulate them into social performance. For Capra, though, as for a choreographer, space is not something absolute, fixed, and dauntingly separate from or superior to the individuals who inhabit it and make it what it is. It is not made up of objects, facts, or realities to which they must subjugate themselves. It is, for fully alive performers, an extension of their spirit, and therefore it can be imaginatively valorized or remade at will. It can be bent, animated, leapt across, or transformed by their performance. They are contained and contextualized by it, but it is always at least theoretically possible for them to master it or to reshape it in the movements of their performances.

For Capra, the individual is always at least potentially capable of the task set before him (or her). Whereas for these other filmmakers, more often than not, the individual is weak, or dominated by his surroundings, for Capra he is up to the challenges he faces. Physical constraints and social contexts serve to stimulate the characters' choreographic performances, just as in the bank-vault scene they stimulate Capra into his own choreographic mastery of space and time in his direction of the actors, movements, the camera placements, and the editing. Like his actors and characters, Capra as a director asks to be measured in terms of his capacity to negotiate complex or constraining spaces confidently, deftly, and economically. In those visual slices through space Capra embraces the challenge of asserting the power of his directorial personality in and over these otherwise alien or inhuman spaces. In this apparently slight difference between the two kinds of filmmakers, in this difference in beliefs about the relation of the human figure and the social landscape, one encapsulates two radically opposed sets of belief about the potential power and role of the individual, the sources of value in the world, and the capacity to change so-called reality. Capra votes resoundingly for the power and centrality of the performer, and for the individual as the originator of meaning and value, which he must continuously create and affirm in the process of staging his performances in the world; the other filmmakers mentioned implicitly disagree.*

A few ingenious critics have offered metaphoric interpretations of the scenes in the vault that Capra uses to begin and end the film, describing the vault as "locking up the madness" or as the "heart of the machine of the bank." These interpretations are not exactly wrong, but they are fairly trivial and irrelevant. Focusing on the intellectual or abstract association of vaults with keys and locks, they are unresponsive to the far more compelling and immediate visual meanings of the vault scene. Its essential meaning is not verbal or metaphoric but spatial and choreographic, concerning the beauty and efficiency of perfectly coordinated, complex group activity (on the part of a director, the actors, and the film crew, as well as that staged by the characters). The scene speaks much more powerfully and eloquently in strictly visual terms about what it means to move freely and gracefully within the constraints of a confined physical and social space than it does abstractly about machines, locks, keys, or vaults.

Matt Brown is the head teller whose function in the vault scene is analogous to that of Tom Dixon in the whole bank: He is a ballet master. More than any of the other employees, he is at home in, and himself able to move nimbly through, the intricate spaces of the film. In the shot immediately following the one in which the last two tellers leave the vault, Capra cuts to a sustained traveling shot of them (Matt and a junior teller named Charlie) making their way back to their tellers' stations, wheeling their cash cabinets down the row of tellers' windows. As they walk, they keep up a humorous running conversation for at least fifty feet of continuous movement past different bank backgrounds and around many other figures. (The joke of the conversation is that Matt gave Charlie twenty-five thousand dollars to use for bank business that day but then politely turns down his request for a personal loan of ten dollars until payday, singing "I can't give you anything but love, baby.") It is a playfully amusing scene, with witty dialogue, but it is the breeziness of the physical movement that makes the breeziness of the talk especially enjoyable. Even today – long after the days of the heavy cameras and bulky microphones

---

* In their contrasting attitudes toward the power of the performer, the difference between Capra and Altman repeats the difference between William and Henry James, on the one hand, and Edith Wharton and Theodore Dreiser, on the other, which is a way of indicating the endurance of a fundamental ambivalence in American art. Altman's sense of democracy (like De Tocqueville's) is one in which individuals are leveled or reduced in the process of group interaction, whereas Capra's (like Emerson's) is one in which every man is potentially made into a creative artist of his own life and identity.

that Capra used – the scene is exhilarating in its energetic free movement through space (felt with special force because this tracking movement immediately follows the long static scene in the vault).★

In this tracking shot Matt, Charlie, and Capra and his crew speak volumes about the human capacity to negotiate complex institutional spaces. Matt's wit, tact, and humor, in this and the preceding scene, are the verbal and social equivalents of his physical dexterity, just as his boss's infectious high spirits are part and parcel of his capacity for controlled, lithe movement through space, as we shall see. To be able to move this way is to be able to negotiate complex social spaces in a poised and sensitive way, which is exactly what is asked of these figures.

It is not surprising that in these films Capra should want to free his camera and microphone to keep up with the energetic physical movements of his actors, to be able to communicate spatially some of their capacity for social and imaginative movement. He conducted some of the earliest experiments with extended, complex tracking movements and mobile miking in sound film. The long tracking scene that I have just described is an example of the mobility of his camera, and at the time of *American Madness* Capra was already concealing microphones on the bodies of some of his actors, running wires down their pants legs, out of sight of the camera. (One such wire is visible to a sharp eye for a fraction of a second in *American Madness*, running out of the pants leg of the guard during the bank robbery.) Such mobile and multiple miking not only allowed for the relatively free movement of the actors (though one can imagine the tangle of wires on the floor that had to be kept straight during the long tracking scene with Charlie and Matt) but also for the recording of several separate sound tracks simultaneously during one take, thus establishing the actors in an acoustic "space" that is the aural equivalent of the visual space articulated in the films.

Flight was the movie in which Capra discovered the expressive possibilities of this layered acoustic effect. Many of the outdoor scenes were shot at an airport, and the dialogue was recorded live. The result was a sound engineer's nightmare with the roar of airplanes revving up, taking off, and flying overhead cluttering up many of the dialogue passages. Capra, however, made a virtue out of necessity. Because of the unintentional layering, the film has a realism, a documentary feel, that more than compensates for the occasional lost word or phrase. The films following *Flight* are consequently more complex acoustically (especially *American Madness, Platinum Blonde, Bitter Tea,* and *It Happened One Night*) than anything to come out of the better-organized sound departments of the more affluent studios in the early thirties. By the end of the decade, as Capra and his regular sound engineer, Edward Bernds, worked on the effects for *Smith*, and the films that followed, the acoustic

---

★ While other cameramen were still relying on cumbersome fixed booths or the complete enclosure of the camera within a glass-windowed box for blimping in the late 1920s, Joseph Walker was the first in Hollywood to introduce a highly portable lightweight wood and rubber shock-absorber system on the camera that made the complete enclosure of it unnecessary.

density of Capra's work compared favorably with anything done in Holly-wood from Welles's *Citizen Kane* to Coppola's *The Conversation* and Altman's *Nashville*. *Doe*, in particular, is a sound engineer's tour de force, in which the densely layered sound track, mixing together four or more tracks in many of the crucial scenes, becomes the full acoustic equivalent of the force field of visual, social, psychological, and political pressures that the photography and editing register around the central figure.

The third sequence of *American Madness* introduces the principal character, Tom Dixon, and in case the point has not already been made sufficiently by his emphasis on the deft physical movements of his characters in the two pre-ceding scenes, Capra lavishes time documenting Dixon's physical progress into the bank, as he negotiates his way across the lobby and up into his office for his day's work. In a series of shots that will become a leitmotif in the film, marking Dixon's entrance on the three succeeding mornings, we see him skill-fully interacting with each of the characters around him. As he enters, he facetiously shines the doorman's badge with his sleeve and then sincerely inquires about the health of his sick wife. He takes a few more steps and calls across the lobby to a teller, asking him not to smoke on the job, then playfully throwing him a stick of gum. He then winks slyly at another teller about a secret they share and briskly strides over to the newly hired janitor and makes arrangements for him to get a free uniform to wear. Next he proceeds up the stairs and exchanges a few humorous comments with his secretary about the fact that the trustees, his institutional adversaries, are waiting for him in the board room. After that he politely but firmly directs a hovering, obsequious loan applicant, whose application he has turned down, to another bank, then enters his office and talks to his wife on the phone about something he forgot to tell her before he left home. Leaving his office, he shouts to the janitor on second thought to "make sure it's a blue uniform" and only now finally walks into the board room where the trustees are awaiting him.

Tom Dixon (or rather Walter Huston) gives a brilliant performance in this sequence of interactions, continuously adjusting his tone, stance, and move-ments depending on the dramatic requirements of the moment, without miss-ing a beat. The scene's point is just Dixon's capacity to do this – to navigate through this institutional tangle of friendships, hierarchies, priorities, and employer – employee relationships and to do it all so masterfully. He is alter-natively clowning and serious, facetious and firm, warm, humble, avuncular, or stern as the need arises, but in this fluid succession of roles and interactions he is always in control, poised and confident, the easy master of infinitely shifting spatial, social, and emotional adjustments and readjustments of position. If one is reluctant to call Dixon an ideal father in an extended family, it is only because to call him a father is to make the role he plays sound in-herited, unearned, unconscious, and easy when it is the opposite of these things. Dixon is not a father, and this is not a family. Rather, he *plays* being a father, and that makes all the difference. He is something harder to be than a father. He is an actor-director. He is an actor in that he can put on and take off a variety of different rolés depending on the part a particular scene requires him to play. He is a director, as many subsequent scenes demonstrate, in that he is able to deploy, educate, and lead large groups of people with confidence and ease – confronting them, challenging them, stimulating them, or giving them their head, as is appropriate to the particular scene he is managing. It is impossible not to compare Capra's own function as head of a film crew and cast with Tom Dixon's function directing and stage-managing the crew and cast around him at the bank.

American Madness is sometimes said to be a movie about depression-era economic anodynes, the importance of loaning money on character, having faith in the common man, or some other form of populist hokum, and Capra may even have thought that these were the chief subjects of his film. Even if he was not entirely aware of it as he made the film, though, he was obviously less interested in formulating an ideological statement than in simply exploring the capacity of a particular kind of individual to perform with grace under pressure. That is why *American Madness* is not, in the largest sense, about any cracker-barrel economic or political theory but is essentially an exploration of possibilities of theatrical and social performance, an exploration by a young film director of what it is to be an ideal actor or director.

I have already alluded to the fact that the sets of many of these films are built in a sort of amphitheater shape, with a central stage for public performance and surrounding tiers for spectators and commentators on the main action. Though the theatrical quality of his sets was probably unconscious on Capra's part, it reveals a lot about his conception of character and performance in public. In *American Madness* in particular there is a central area, or stage, in which most of the action takes place (the lobby and the tellers's stations); a balcony above and around it, for spectators and choric commentators on the action (the mezzanine); and changing, preparation, and rehearsal rooms behind or within it (the vault space). Capra became more and more explicit about the theatrical quality of his principal sets during the thirties, moving from *The Miracle Woman* and *Platinum Blonde* to *Smith* and *Doe*, but even the earliest films of the decade use these amphitheatrical spaces to encourage the viewer to see the central characters as actors or public performers in an at least implicitly theatrical sense of the world. Theater becomes life, and life becomes theater. Life in the film becomes a matter of managing a series of public entrances and exits, of responding to hostile or indifferent audiences, of interacting deftly and sensitively with casts of supporting characters arranged around one or two star performers. A capacity of public, theatrical performance is going to be required of most of Capra's central characters in the films of the thirties (with the important exception of the visionary characters played by Barbara Stanwyck which I will discuss in Part III). In these films an individual establishes and maintains his identity by means of public performance. He must negotiate demanding dramatic circumstances, play to groups of others (many of whom have alternative conceptions of the proper interpretation of his part), and generally hold together the theatrical ensemble of which he is a member by means of the unifying purpose and power of his performances. The buddy-boys of the adventure films were spared such complications, not only because they constituted their own self-contained and self-satisfied theatrical company but also because they acted, in effect, as both actors and audience to their own performances. Their self-pleasuring performances needed to please no one but themselves, and their script and interpretation of their roles were dictated by no alien bureaucracy or group of others around them.

Capra compares and contrasts three principal performers in the film – Tom Dixon, Matt Brown, and Cyril Cluett – the first two creative and engaging to different degrees, the third fundamentally flawed and inadequate. Though there is every reason to assume that Capra and Riskin intended the three to be of equal importance in the movie, Tom Dixon is the only one of them who is truly engaging. This is not only because, as head of the bank, he has the most complex series of roles and responsibilities in the film, and the position that is assaulted most powerfully, but also, probably, because he is played by Walter Huston. Huston, with his extensive experience in both vaudeville and legitimate theater, and his impressive dramatic talent, is far and away the most nuanced and daring performer of the three, able to play the most complex theatrical, social, and imaginative games.

His capacity to switch tones and styles – from benevolent big daddy (with the doorman), to sly romantic confidante (as in his wink at Matt), to a sternly practical banker (who turns down a loan applicant) – within seconds of each other in the first scene is only a hint of his powers. To his secretary (who is Matt's girlfriend) he plays matchmaker and romantic adviser; to his board of trustees he plays philosophical philanthropist and grand financial theorist (unfortunately, since it is the most abstract moment in the film, this one scene and function has become identified as the film's "theme"); to his tellers he plays genial supervisor and morale builder. Next to Huston's performance those of Pat O'Brien as Matt Brown and Gavin Gordon as Cyril Cluett are merely competent.

The near failure of the bank as its depositors panic after the robbery and withdraw their money, and the criminal investigation that follows (which treats the chief teller, Matt Brown, as the chief suspect) ultimately precipitate a crisis of confidence in himself on Dixon's part but also gives him the opportunity for his finest hour of performance. In a routine that has some of the controlled wildness of the Marx Brothers movies that were released in the years immediately preceding *American Madness* – *Coconuts*, *Animal Crackers*, and *Monkey Business* – Capra has Huston rapidly shuttling from office to office, raising cash over the telephone to pay the panicky customers, running out into the lobby and giving advice to the row of overworked tellers, then returning upstairs to keep his balky board of trustees at bay, in an almost crazed effort singlehandedly to hold together the institution falling into pieces around him.

However, whereas the Marx Brothers' manic performances were content with releasing anarchic and usually antisocial energies, Dixon's represents a much more complex achievement. Like a film director, he releases individual energies, but he also directs and organizes them to subserve a larger, coordinated purpose. As the social and institutional fabric of the bank begins to unravel before his eyes, Dixon tries to hold together and reweave all the fraying threads at once: fiscally, to manage the financial shortfall; emotionally, to placate his panicking depositors; bureaucratically, to resist the board, who see this as their opportunity to seize power and replace him; morally, to persuade the police of the integrity and honesty of Brown, a former convict struggling to make a new life for himself whom they automatically suspect of having engineered the robbery; and personally, to convince Brown not to lose faith in himself under the pressure of the police grilling.

A quotation from the dialogue can only begin to suggest the rapidity and density of events transpiring around Dixon and his ability to manage them, but the following selection can illustrate what interests Capra most about Dixon: his ability to deal with the pressure of competing influences without becoming intimidated, confused, or rigidly overbearing. At the beginning of the following rapid exchange of dialogue (the whole quotation takes up only about one minute of film time), Dixon is in his office attempting to persuade a police detective that Brown is innocent. There is no time to finish one "scene" here though, before beginning another. Dixon is no sooner launched on his defense of Brown than the manager of payments to the tellers rushes in and asks for his attention: The run has just begun, and it is rapidly depleting the bank's liquid reserves.

> *Dixon is interrupted in the middle of his defense of Brown to the police detective by a bank officer.*

OFFICER: (*Running into the office*) Mr. Dixon, can I see you for a minute?

DIXON: No, I'm busy. See me later.

OFFICER: But this is important, Mr. Dixon. (*Taking him outside to the mezzanine*) It looks like there is a run on the bank. Look.

DIXON: This is just a flurry that's all. They heard about the robbery and got panic stricken. Listen, get ahold of our available securities and have them turned into cash. (*Officer starts to leave*) Wait a minute. Get ahold of my personal stuff and have that turned into cash too. Tell the boys that anybody caught arguing with a depositor will be fired on the spot.

> *The officer leaves, and is immediately replaced by the Chairman of the Board of Trustees who jogs up to Dixon.*

CHAIRMAN: Dixon, we want to talk to you.

DIXON: What about?

CHAIRMAN: We'll discuss that in the board room.

> *The detective interrupts Dixon and the Chairman out on the mezzanine.*

DETECTIVE: Oh, I've got a check on Brown's alibi. You want to hear it?

DIXON: (*To the Chairman of the Board*) I'll be with you in a minute. (*Following the detective back into his office, and then turning to Brown*) No need to worry, son. All you have to do is answer the questions they ask you.

In this minute of film time Dixon deals with four different people, each of whom has an entirely different personal and professional relationship to him. Beset with conflicting loyalties and responsibilities, he remains in absolute control as the master of ceremonies, consoling and advising Brown; persuasively pleading Brown's innocence to the detective; clearheadedly giving useful instructions to the bank officer; dealing professionally but coolly with the chairman of the board, firmly putting him in his place and delaying him; acting humanely to respect even the foolish depositors who threaten to ruin him and wipe out the bank with their panicky withdrawals. For all the hecticness of the scene, all of the people coming and going around him, Dixon is the one person not confused or upset. Nothing he says or does seems hurried or sloppy. It is all poised and controlled. When film critics speak of "beauty" in a film, they usually intend to suggest that the photography or the sets or costumes are pretty in some way, but this scene shows us another meaning of the word. Dixon's performance as a bank manager, like Huston's performance as an actor, like Capra's performance as the writer-director-editor of the film can only be called beautiful, but in a sense having nothing to do with picture-postcard cinematography or locations.

Indeed, the only performance more remarkable than Dixon's here is Capra's performance as the manager of a soundstage that must have looked and functioned very much like Dixon's bank at this moment. In an interview Capra once described what it was like to work on one of the cramped, disorganized soundstages at Columbia in the lean early years. It was apparently not all that different from being a bank president during a panic:

> Filmmaking is decision making. That's all you do, make decisions, you make a thousand a day. You have got to make them fast and you have got to make them – not by logic, logic isn't connected with filmmaking – they're gut decisions. That's your creativity. You make a decision and you make it fast. And don't worry about it after you make it, because that's it.[*]

It seems hardly coincidental that in the same interview, Capra hardheadedly describes his function as a film director in the sort of financial terms that could be used to describe directing a bank. Capra, like Dixon, has no illusions that good faith or fine intentions can make up for a shortfall of hard cash. In an eminently practical sense, the filmmaker must be a manager of people, money, time, and bureaucratic realities, as well as being an artist – or rather, that is what it is to be an artist in this tradition of public, commercial performance:

> Film is a dichotomy of business and art and there's no other way you can figure it ... You've got to pay attention to both ... Your films have got to be successful. I know you don't think talking of commerce is very important. But don't lose sight of the fact that if you don't make money with your films

---

[*] This and the following two quotations are taken from "Frank Capra: One Man–One Film (Interview with Bruce Henstell)," in *Frank Capra: The Man and His Films*, ed. Richard Glatzer and John Raeburn (Ann Arbor: University of Michigan Press, 1975), pp. 20–2.

you're not going to make many films ... You must pay attention to the money side, the financial side. Writing a book, you know, you buy a typewriter and you buy some paper and that's it, that's the total expense and the rest of it is your time. Making a picture is hundreds of thousands of dollars, millions of dollars, tens of millions of dollars perhaps, and that's an enormous responsibility. Time is your great enemy, schedules, and budgeting and so forth, and I paid a great deal of attention to that.

It has got to be more than accidental that the chairman of the board of trustees with whom Dixon must deal not only performs as Harry Cohn did at Columbia but even bears a slight physical resemblance to him. In the same interview, Capra describes his relationship with his own chairman of the board:

> I worked for a very tough man called Harry Cohn. It was a constant battle, but he never won one single battle with me. I had to win every argument with him, because if you didn't, he lost confidence in you. He'd challenge you on everything ... He got results ... on the simple theory that an artist with courage and guts should know more about what he's doing than the sensitive ones who are unsure.

Between the lines of these three quotations is written a whole philosophy of artistic performance, one that, I would argue, is figured in Dixon's performance in the bank. It is a concept of the performer, not as one of those Capra dismissively calls the "sensitive ones who are unsure" but as a practical negotiator of schedules and budgets, a manager of groups of people and of dramatic pacings, a poised administrator and daring split-second decision maker. It is in this sense that Dixon is clearly an alter ego for Capra himself.

In a section of an interview in which he discussed *American Madness* specifically, Capra summarizes his own interest in the film and Tom Dixon's achievement within it as a matter of "timing." He implicitly equates Dixon's achievement as a character with Huston's as an actor and his own achievement as the director and editor. When he compares all three to generals, it becomes clear that he is talking about a conception of performance that is applicable not only within the special sanctified world of artistic achievement but within the world where we live our lives, as well. It is the essence of Capra's concept of performance that it does not cordon off a special place for art separate from life:

> I think [*American Madness*] was one of the best pictures I made. It had a lot of speed. It was one of the first pictures on the rough speedy side, where everything was just slam-bang, slam-bang. It came off, in a sense because of that technique of speed and tempo ... of course, timing is the same in everything. You have to have timing ... It's something you either have or you haven't got. It's when you do the right thing at the right time. Directors have it, actors have it, great generals have it.*

---

* Capra's lengthy interview for the Columbia University Oral History Project has, to my knowledge, never been published. It is available in typescript on microfilm in the Library of Congress.

Dixon is the dramatic embodiment of this practical ability to master the resistance of time, space, and a host of competing influences demonstrated by the ideal actor-director-producer, relaxed and in control even in the eye of a storm of distractions, calming and inspiring all around him.

Capra would never have accepted the late-Romantic dichotomy that separates the movements of the imagination from practical forms of expression in the world. His attitude is in this respect at odds with most British and European post-Romantic artistic practice and critical theory. The practical, economic, social mind is not split off from the artistic, creative consciousness. The one mind, as far as Capra is concerned, is an expression of the other. We are in this respect closer to the world of Marlowe, Shakespeare, and Kyd than that of Keats, Shelley, Tennyson, Beckett, and Antonioni. In his own life and work as a Hollywood director, after all, Capra made the identical wager that Dixon does, that imaginative vision can be translated into the form of practical, commercially bankable performance.

The similarity in appearance between a cashier's window at a bank and a ticket booth at a movie theater in both this film and (later) *It's a Wonderful Life* is quite striking evidence of Capra's probably unconscious linking of the two realms of performance. He, Dixon, and George Bailey (who is also a banker) are all in the job of the orderly processing of lines of money-clutching customers, giving them interest on their investment, and specifically in getting them to part cheerfully with their money and not suddenly ask for it back.

Similarly, although it is again probably unconscious on Capra's part, many of the films, including this one are set in spaces that, to some degree, mimic the dramatic situation of either a soundstage or a movie theater. This is not merely to repeat the observation I already made about the amphitheatrical shape of many of Capra's sets. More specifically, as I have already suggested in the case of this film, the films imagine the characters in their narratives to be performing in situations strikingly similar in their appearance or function to soundstage or movie-theater spaces, with a small group of intensely interacting and extremely visible characters at one end and a larger group of spectators distributed to one side of them.* The starring characters in such films must stage performances in structures like the U.S. Senate, a bank, a radio studio, or a courtroom, spaces that are almost the exact physical and imaginative equivalents of the Hollywood soundstage or movie-palace spaces within which Capra and his actors staged their own performances in front of comparable hordes of participants or spectators.

It represents an identification of the practical and usually financial, performances staged by his characters (and actors) and the artistic performances staged by himself as a director that is all the more compelling because Capra was apparently unconscious of the imaginative linkage he was making. The

---

* I am thinking of particular scenes in this film, *The Miracle Woman, Forbidden, Bitter Tea, Broadway Bill, You Can't Take It with You, It's a Wonderful Life, State of the Union,* and most emphatically, of course, the *Deeds–Smith–Doe* trilogy, in which almost all of the most important scenes are set in such spaces.

successful translation of imaginative insights into practical capital is difficult – as difficult as managing a soundstage or making a hit movie – as all the films recognize. That is what makes Dixon's (and Capra's) successes of timing and organization, when they do occur, so exhilarating.

At a lower dramatic and bureaucratic level, Matt Brown is Dixon's doppelgänger, and his scenes generally repeat or anticipate those in which Dixon appears. What Dixon is to the whole bank, Brown, as head teller, is to the tellers. He begins the film in the two scenes I have already described – the vault opening and the long tracking shot – as a poised, confident manager whose wit, good humor, and intelligent sensitivity make him the star of the scenes in which he is present, but (as is always required in Capra's work) one whose star quality is defined by his ability to make the other actors and bit players around him look good. The direct parallel to the scene in which Dixon exhibits grace under pressure is one a few minutes later in which Brown, having been cleared of suspicion, makes a series of telephone calls to the bank's largest borrowers to try to get them to repay their loans. In a series of simultaneous calls on a deskful of phones, Matt handles the individual telephones and the speakers at the other end as rapidly and cleverly as Dixon handled the importunities of the individuals around him (and much more proficiently than the bank's regular telephone operator – who precipitated the panic – did in previous scenes).

Capra establishes four explicit foils to Brown and Dixon, who make their powers of forging order out of confusion and sorting meaning out of chaos seem all the more impressive by contrast. The first is the lackadaisical, gum-chewing "dumb blonde" telephone operator who starts the whole panic by the carelessness of her comments at the switchboard. The second is Oscar, a bumbling young teller (played by the character actor Sterling Holloway), whose jokes and anecdotes are as leaden as Matt's and Tom's are nimble. (For example, he keeps repeating the tiresome line "You could have knocked me over with a pin" at the end of his anecdotes so many times that a viewer wants to scream.) He is a comic figure of awkwardness, confusion, and tediousness. The third is Mrs. Halligan. She is Matt's spinster landlady and a recurring type in Capra's films. In the courtroom of *Deeds*, four years later, the Faulkner sisters step forward virtually to repeat the testimony that Mrs. Halligan gives against Brown's alibi here. The detective quizzes her on Matt's return home on the night of the robbery:

DETECTIVE: What time was it?
MRS. HALLIGAN: I was up getting my hot mustard bath. For the rheumatism.
DETECTIVE: What time was it?
MRS. HALLIGAN: It was late I know. The Dooly sisters was already in. They work at the show you know. (*pause*)
DETECTIVE: What *time* was it?
MRS. HALLIGAN: Eh? (*pause*) Well let me see. Half an hour after the Dooly sisters. And the Dooly sisters . . .
DETECTIVE: I don't care about THE DOOLY SISTERS! What time did *he* get in?

MRS. HALLIGAN: That's what I'm trying to tell you. It was half an hour after the Dooly sisters.

There are several more, equally revealing exchanges before Mrs. Halligan gets to her main piece of information: "When my clock strikes four, it's one." She is as scatterbrained and easily ruffled as Matt and Tom are poised and focused.

   These three characters are comically placed (and dismissed) easily by the film. The fourth foil is the bank treasurer, Cyril Cluett, who arranged the robbery in order to pay off his gambling debts and get the mob off his back. He is a much more complicated and fascinating case, a dramatic equal to Tom and Matt, and a foil Capra is not able glibly to place or dismiss. Early in the film he is clearly established as a playboy, but when he is compared with Tom and Matt this is far from being a limiting judgment on him. Whether Capra intended it or not (and it seems unlikely that he did), he allows Cluett to be much more appealing in some ways than the prudent, conservative Brown, who is engaged but does not plan to get married until he gets a raise, or the married-to-his-work Dixon, who seems to have little or no sexual side to his identity at all. Dixon is nominally married, but with his numerous obligations to the bank he hardly has time for any more warmblooded mistress in his life. Cluett defines a sexual side of life that both Brown and Dixon have repressed. This philanderer, cad, and ladies' man therefore seems to be the only honestly and robustly sexual figure in the film.

   In other ways, though, he is a profoundly inadequate person, a superficial "playboy" in more than the sexual sense of the term. He thinks he can play any role he chooses and never be caught out. The point of the juxtaposition with master players like Dixon and Brown is the hollowness of all of Cluett's playing. He is insincere and cruel exactly where they are warm and humane. His poise and charm are shallow and false where theirs are profound. He plays at being calmly in control but breaks down completely in the two scenes in which he is placed under any real pressure: the initial scene in which the gangsters visit him in his office, and the scene in which the police, suspecting him at last, finally pay him a parallel visit. In the first instance he panics by agreeing to collaborate in the robbery, and in the second he panics by pulling a gun and futilely trying to escape. In a film that puts such a high premium on the talent for easy, graceful movement, it is significant that in the first scene Cluett is trapped in close-up, unable to move at all, pinned in the frame space between the shadowy bodies of gangsters on either side of him. In the second scene, the only motion he shows himself capable of is a wild, terrified, flight down a dead-end passage before he is recaptured by the police.

   Capra's artistic strategy in *American Madness*, like most of his other work, is simply to test each of the principal characters to the point of crisis and measure his response. The bank robbery and ensuing panic is, in effect, only a pretext, a means of creating a crisis in the life of each of these three performers that will test his powers of playing to the limit. Capra takes these three, each of whom has aspirations to competent, poised performance, and pushes them to the point of breakdown. All three panic as desperately as, if less publicly than the customers lined up in the lobby of the bank: Cluett in the scenes of hysteria I have just described; Brown, under the stigma of being publicly accused of the robbery and the further burden of the secret he believes he is in possession of that Dixon's wife has been romantically involved with Cluett; and finally Dixon too, in his crisis of confidence about his adequacy as a husband and his despair when he ultimately is convinced that his wife has been unfaithful to him.

The "American madness" of the film's title refers, obviously, to many things in it, from the craziness of the depositors who are so easily panicked to the crazy faith Dixon has in the innate goodness and worth of those same depositors. The central American madness in the film, however, which subsumes the others (without contradicting them), is the male ideal of control and the need for mastery and order. Cluett, Brown, and Dixon all share this madness. Each, in his different way, thinks that he can arrange his own life and orchestrate the lives of those around him into a series of smooth, professional performances that, beneath a calm exterior, will hide his own emotional confusion and eliminate his feelings of weakness and vulnerability. As the specific scenes of personal crisis reveal, all three have cordoned off important areas of their emotional lives in order to maintain their sense of control. Dixon's relationship with his wife is a shambles. Matt, as a former convict, has doubts about his own value and his future in his job that make him unable to propose to the girl he loves. Cluett's playboy image is a camouflage for his emotional vulnerability.

Capra suggests that there is a hollowness not only to Cluett's oily urbanity, but also to both Brown's and Dixon's more appealing charm – a madness at the heart of their sanity. There is a deep act of repression, a denial of fundamental human emotions that makes each man's performance false and inadequate. That is why each one panics under pressure, as completely as the bank's depositors do.*

If one has serious reservations about the ultimate value of *American Madness* it is because Capra does not truly plumb the depths of this American madness. He does not allow the moments of crisis and self-doubt at the secret center of his three principal characters' poise to emerge complexly or long enough. Even to dwell on them critically at this length is to make *American Madness* sound like a thoroughly different film from the one Capra made, because the crises are only hinted at before being magically erased and forgotten in the conclusion of the film. Capra creates the private crisis of Dixon's momentary contemplation of suicide, only to dismiss it almost immediately, as Dixon himself does. The weakness of the film is that the American madness in it – the effort to be a poised public performer who can freely and effortlessly

---

* The connection Capra makes between the personal panic of his protagonists and the public panic of the common man in the film suggests how pervasive he felt the hollowness at the center of American cultural confidence and optimism to be.

circulate through various styles and forms of relationships without paying a psychological price in terms of feelings of alienation and rootlessness – is not explored profoundly enough. That remains to be done in Capra's later work.★

Like the conclusion of *That Certain Thing*, the ending of *American Madness* finally papers over the potential psychic disturbances the earlier scenes momentarily brought into view and replaces them with a superficial set of social ceremonies and routines, repressing the disturbing energies it has released and denying its own previous insights. *American Madness* apparently gets Capra into much deeper water than he can navigate, and after only the briefest allusion to the madness at the center of these lives he turns away from his own dark awareness to end his film on a happier note. One cannot ask him to pitch his camp in the state of madness itself: to end *That Certain Thing* with the nightmare scene of Molly ascending the stairs, or to conclude *American Madness* with Dixon's suicide. One can ask, however, that the madness be explored more thoroughly and that its cultural roots be examined more carefully. If the madness must eventually be covered up again and buried out of sight, one can also ask that it be sealed up from view more tightly at the end than it is in this film.

Capra's inability to handle his chosen subject is clearly evidenced in the perfunctory way in which he exorcises the madness and restores order at the end of the film. All three psychic crises are quickly resolved from outside by dei ex machina. Brown is suddenly saved by the identification of Cluett as the prime suspect and by Dixon's then giving Brown a raise that will enable him to get married. Dixon has his faith restored by a visit from his wife and by the surprising generosity of a few of his depositors. Cluett, whose crisis was the most interesting of the three, since it was generated by no one's actions but his own, is eliminated as a problem by being spirited out of this movie entirely and into a melodramatic gangster-movie finale (accused and pursued by the police, he is apprehended in a shoot-out and taken off to jail) that simply erases all the personal questions his role posed.

Sanity is genially restored in the final scene as Dixon, once again the benevolent father of the extended family of bank employees, enters the bank for the third and final time on the morning following the run. He plays the part to the hilt, confidently joking with the same employees with whom we have seen him bantering in his two previous entrances. Again he moves easily and smoothly through both the cinematic space of the frame and the institutional space of the bank. He is once again the polished performer, right up to and including the little joke that ends the film. He jokingly orders Brown and Helen, his girlfriend, who is a secretary at the bank, to get married "or

---

★ Of the films made around the same time as *American Madness*, Stew Smith in *Platinum Blonde* and Florence Fallon in *The Miracle Woman* represent Capra's continuing exploration of this issue. In Capra's subsequent work, Ellie Andrews and Peter Warne in *It Happened One Night* will represent further investigations of the joys and hazards of stylistic virtuosity.

else," and then pretends to give them a cruise as a honeymoon present. It is Capra's joke, as well as Dixon's. As he was well aware, it was only in the movies that such an easy escape from life's difficulties could be plausible even as a joke.

It is a sentimental and superficial ending. Dixon is too poised, too affable and charming. The emotional difficulties between himself and his wife and the failures of communication that the film revealed in his personal life have been glossed over too easily. The honeymoon trip, as it turns out, is for himself and his wife, suggesting that he and she have magically worked out all of the differences that the film has documented for the previous hour. Is a honeymoon cruise an adequate response to the psychological problems the film has raised? Dixon too closely resembles those playful buddy-boys of the earlier films, and it is significant that just as at the ends of those films, in which the wives or lovers who have caused so many of their emotional complications are suddenly removed or disarmed of any emotional reality, so Dixon's wife is absent from this scene. If Dixon's final scene of "playing" is richer and more complex (that is to say, more theatrical and more imaginative) than the scenes of playing at the ends of the first two adventure films – not a matter of clowning around on camera and playing tricks with a hat (as at the end of *Submarine*) or inadvertently throwing a car into reverse instead of forward (as at the end of *Flight*) – it is still too superficial a sense of personal performance to be an adequate response to the problems exposed by the film as a whole.

In summary, although earlier he was ostensibly documenting the limitations of Dixon's and the two other main characters' fantasies of control, Capra himself, not only in the final scene but throughout the film, seems to be more than half in love with such performative virtuosity, such tidiness, such an illusion of the possibility of psychological law and order. Not only does he fail to detect the social evasiveness of Dixon's performance in the final scene but the tidy formal symmetry of Dixon's entrance on the third morning, exactly parallel to his entrance into the bank in the two previous scenes, meant to close the sequence and neatly cap the film, repeats in the narrative structure of the film the very problem with Dixon's performance within it. Capra's rage for narrative and cinematic order is too much like Dixon's rage for bureaucratic and emotional order. With its insistent double and triple parallelisms of corresponding scenes, characters, and leitmotifs, *American Madness* is one of Capra's most complexly organized narratives; that is not a virtue, though, but a problem. The film has a lust for control and arrangement that affiliates it more with Dixon's and Huston's brilliantly superficial capacities of performance than with any authentic exploration of emotional territory. *American Madness* is finally confused in its feelings about masterful performance. Capra wants to point out the potential limitations of Dixon's, Brown's, and, more obviously, Cluett's rage for mastery, at the same time as he seems enormously impressed by their performances (especially in the case of Tom Dixon/Walter Huston).

One is reminded of the inherent contradictions in Capra's own situation as a young filmmaker with very little experience, functioning under the dictatorial thumb of Harry Cohn. It is not accidental that in the excerpts of the interview from which I quoted earlier in this chapter, Capra places great emphasis on his own powers of control and organization. Not to be in absolute control, to have let down his guard for a moment, would have been to have his film taken away from him. As he himself acknowledges, working for a man like Cohn forced him to feign a certainty and self-assurance that he did not always feel. Just like his character Dixon, laboring under the constant hostile surveillance of a chairman of the board who was looking for a vulnerable spot in his armor or an excuse to fire him, Capra had no chance to let his hair down, to confess to merely human doubts and weaknesses. In the same interview, he admits to having moments of acute self-doubt like those Dixon has, terrifying midnight moments when all of his confidence evaporated:

> I've often gone back in after a picture started and the whole thing just evaporates, just goes off into the air. How can you possibly make anything out of this crap? You have these ups and downs and you go and hide in a room and read it and conceptually it's pure nothing. How did you get started in this thing ? You want to leave the country fast. And you can't do that. You have got to trust in that original, "Why did I pick it in the first place?" You have got to go back to the original decision making, that you thought it was pretty good at the time and stay with it. And it'll evaporate at times but you have to trust that first instinct. You have to discipline yourself to trust in those instincts ... You don't know what you've got until the very last minute. Until you've spent all the money and put the picture together, you don't really know what you've got and you worry. You worry because there goes hundreds of thousands of dollars of expense, millions of dollars of expense, and it's all in a few cans of film. It looks very, very cheap for the amount of money you spent on it and you don't know what you've got until you play it before an audience. You really do not know. There's no way of knowing.*

In the face of this pressure, the anxiety he felt throughout his career about his own talent and accomplishments, the sudden, recurring "evaporation" of confidence that beset him, and this deep not-knowing, Capra ambivalently maintained his own fantasy of control, calm, and poise, even as he acutely felt the hollowness at the center of it all. *American Madness* is the American master performer's ambivalent self-reflection on his own capacity for masterful performance.

* "Interview with Bruce Henstell," p. 22.

7

The play's the thing

Platinum Blonde

> For after the rest is said – after the time-honor'd and really true things for subordination, experience, rights of property, etc. have been listen'd to and acquiesced in – after the valuable and well-settled statement of our duties and relations in society is thoroughly conn'd over and exhausted – it remains to bring forward and modify everything else with the idea of that Something a man is...standing apart from all else, divine in his own right, and a woman in hers, sole and untouchable by any canons of authority, or any rule derived from precedent, state-safety, the acts of legislatures, or even from what is called religion, modesty, or art.
>
> – Walt Whitman, *Democratic Vistas*

As *That Certain Thing*, *The Way of the Strong*, and *American Madness* all suggest, endings present a special problem in Capra's work.★ It is not enough to say that Capra typically retreats into wish fulfillment or "happily-ever-after" endings. This is sometimes the case, but it is more important to note that the films are energized by such polarities of values, such conflicts of allegiance that Capra himself makes it almost impossible for the oppositions to be reconciled at the end. The weird, fantasy qualities of Capra's endings are an acknowledgment of this problem. The conflicts built into the films usually require a sudden, otherwise gratuitous mimetic shift to miracle or wish fulfillment in order to make any sort of conclusion possible. That mimetic shift is evidence of Capra's inability to reconcile the irreconcilable in any other way. It is neither good nor bad art in itself, but an aesthetic fact of life in works of art as divided in their consciousness as these are.†

Platinum Blonde is a more interesting work than *American Madness*, largely because of its willingness (both throughout the film and in its ending) to allow itself to be confusing and ambivalent where *American Madness* aspires to be orderly and clear. Whereas *American Madness* finally tries to suggest that there

---

★ They do so for similar reasons in American literature in general.
† Capra's use of jokes or elements of farce in the endings of his films – as in the endings of both *That Certain Thing* and *American Madness* – is another sign of his attempt to gloss over difficulties by inducing a kind of comic amnesia in his viewers.

is no conflict between the feelings and imagination of the individual and the expressive requirements of group life or to erase the conflict that occurs, *Platinum Blonde* is more ready to admit that these conflicts exist and must be dealt with at a deeper level of personal exploration. Problems very similar to those Capra generated around Dixon in *American Madness* are raised in *Platinum Blonde* around the central character, Stew Smith. The difference is that *Platinum Blonde* does not suggest that the ensuing crisis of identity and the issues of the relationship of the individual's imagination to the society of which he or she is nominally a member can be so easily or tidily resolved. In every respect, *Platinum Blonde* is a far less polished film than *American Madness*. It seems more hastily and sloppily made, and its narrative is not structured nearly so elegantly into the series of parallel "scenes" and "acts" distributed across the three days of the other film, but its comparative shagginess, its tentativeness, its structural inconclusiveness is the source of its interest.

The similarity of the two films is striking, but, since they were made in successive years, probably should not be surprising. Like *American Madness*, *Platinum Blonde* is organized around the central figure of a masterful, confident performer, played by another actor whose chief quality (both as an actor and as a character) is that he dominates (or, another actor would say, steals) virtually every scene in which he appears. Capra had no seasoned stage actor like Walter Huston for the central role, so he daringly chose a young vaudeville comedian named Robert Williams for the part. It was Williams's first and only important part (he died shortly after *Platinum Blonde* was completed), but he radiates – in a comic, wisecracking vein – exactly the same confidence and "I can do anything" aplomb that Huston did in the other film.

This character – the masterful, unflappable social performer – was the one that most fascinated Capra – the young, struggling Sicilian outsider – in his early years at Columbia. Joe Cook plays such a part in *Rain or Shine*. Ralph Graves plays the part in the adventure films. Clark Gable plays the part in *It Happened One Night*. The two major films Capra made prior to *Platinum Blonde* – *Ladies of Leisure* and *The Miracle Woman* – star Barbara Stanwyck in other similar roles. She plays a female paradigm of the confident, cocky, public performer. From all evidence it is the role Capra himself most aspired to play in his own life and his endless battles with Harry Cohn, and the role he in fact convinced almost all of his friends and coworkers he had mastered. (From his first days at Columbia he was always described as the most poised, relaxed, and volubly witty person on his sets). It is surely significant, though, that in all of the films of the 1930 to 1934 period, Capra creates such a performer only to reveal that there is a private inadequacy concealed by the flamboyant public performance, an anxiety gnawing at the heart of the poise, a feeling of hypocrisy or self-doubt underpinning the grand illusion of mastery. From *Ladies of Leisure* to *Lady for a Day*, each of the films proceeds to break down its central character's poise and control in the course of its narrative, to raise profound questions about the psychological adequacy of their performances, to reveal doubts that the performers had almost succeeded in hiding from themselves.

Platinum Blonde begins with Stew Smith, a newspaper reporter, being sent to interview the high-society Schuyler family about a breach-of-promise story. He is the only reporter his editor is sure will know how to gain access to and to handle himself within the imposing architectural and social spaces of the Schuyler mansion. To drive the point home, Capra has Bingy Baker, a reporter from a rival newspaper, accompany Smith to the mansion, wait with him in the drawing room, and be paired with him in several parallel scenes, to make the one reporter's powers of social performance seem all the more breathtaking in contrast with the clumsiness of the other's. While they wait together at the Schuylers', Smith settles easily into an overstuffed chair with a book, as if he had spent half his life in upper-class drawing rooms, while Bingy nervously paces back and forth and puts fingerprints on the silver plate.

As in *American Madness*, the specific evidence of Stew's imaginative and social powers is his choreographic mastery of movement through space, though as befits the differences between the expressive capacities of a Broadway actor (Huston) and those of a vaudeville comedian (Williams), the cocky reporter's spatial and social performances are even more eccentric and iconoclastic than those of the fairly straitlaced banker. It is rapidly established that Stew moves not only more entertainingly, but with even more grace and confidence than the Schuylers themselves. Capra cleverly uses a sequence of four matched dissolves, which comically match the nervous back-and-forth pacing of a third reporter outside the Schuyler gate, the walking in circles of a dog, the restless movements of a parrot in its cage, and the anxious fidgetings and pacings of the Schuyler family inside the house, to suggest how much they are prisoners in their own home. They lack the capacity for just the sort of free and creative spatial movements of which Stew shows himself to be the master.

Smith's achievement is, in brief, that he is able to avoid the ruts of life in which everyone around him is trapped. Capra works out every possible visual expression of this metaphor to communicate Stew's (and Williams's) powers of performance. When Smith is finally ushered into the living room for his interview, he clearly outmaneuvers the confused Schuylers as much as he had previously outclassed Bingy. The Schuylers stay seated, stand immobilized in one place, or move from one spot in the room to another in the crudest and simplest front-and-back blocking, while Smith lithely traces oblique diagonals and sinuous "S's" among them, around them, past them. As the film goes on, Smith's imaginative mobility is increasingly expressed in terms of movements in the third dimension, into and out of the plane of the screen. While the Schuylers, hemmed in by their family traditions, their pasts, and their stodgy sense of social propriety, are immobilized or nervously pace to screen right or screen left, confined within the plane of the picture, Smith runs circles around them, dancing in and out and between them in depth, outplaying them spatially and stylistically.

To put it in terms of Walker's camera movements, which astonishingly anticipate some of the extended, expressive experiments with systematically signifying camera movement in the work of Antonioni and Kubrick more than thirty years later, while the Schuyler family (with the significant exception of Anne, with whom Smith will become infatuated for just this reason) is photographed in setup after setup in a fixed focal plane, at almost a constant middle distance from the camera, seldom requiring more than a panning movement to keep them within the frame, Smith and Anne are repeatedly identified with forward and backward tracking movements in depth.* Walker and Capra imagine them as virtually unphotographable in fixed distance or panning shots. Their ability to move imaginatively, as it were, elicits sympathetic movements into and out of the picture plane on the part of the camera. Walker's camera must become as free and mobile as they are in order to search them out and hold them in view. In a world of two-dimensional relations, Anne and Stew are the only three-dimensional characters. It is this quality in Stew and Anne that marks them off from all of the other characters in the film, sparks her initial interest in him, precipitates his infatuation with her, and leads to their ill-fated marriage.

One might note in passing the similarities and the equally revealing differences between Capra's film and Jean Renoir's *Boudu Saved from Drowning.* (Since Renoir's film was released almost exactly one year after *Platinum Blonde*, there is even the possibility of a direct influence. Not only are the general narrative situations in the two films strikingly similar, but one particular shot of Boudu sprawled laterally across a table in the kitchen, explicitly recalls one of Smith sprawled on his bed.) Within Renoir's narrative, Boudu functions quite similarly to Smith in Capra's. Boudu creatively disrupts the bourgeois codes of acting, framing, blocking, staging, and behavior around him that attempt to repressively subdue him. Like Smith, he releases energies that cannot be expressed in a more conventional theatrical (Comédie Française) style of staging, acting, and photography.

If one wanted to trace the possible imaginative lineage of *Platinum Blonde* even further, one could leap from Renoir's film to Jacques Rivette's *Céline and Julie Go Boating*, which seems undeniably indebted to Renoir's film, and possibly to Capra's as well. The shenanigans of Rivette's two title characters in the Henry James house not only function like Smith's behavior at the 'Schuylers' to extol the virtues of spontaneity and improvisation as alternatives to the narrative, psychological and social overdeterminations of conventional drama but seem actually to repeat specific gestures and moments from the Capra film.

The differences between the Capra film and the French movies are equally telling too. The only response to the bourgeois codes of life that Rivette and

---

* Antonioni's *The Passenger* employs a similar system of signification by means of camera movement, in which objects or events that are confined to or photographable by slow panning or tracking movements within the plane of the screen are systematically used to suggest states of imaginative confinement or limitation, whereas movements into or out of the third dimension by the camera or a character are used to evoke contrasting possibilities of imaginative transcendence or visionary expansion. Also compare Capra's use of the third dimension to similar expressive purpose in *The Way of the Strong.*

Renoir imagine is a zany avoidance, a comic mockery, or a parodic deconstruction of them,* but Capra, in *Platinum Blonde*, wants to investigate the possibility of their transformation or rehabilitation. To put it another way, whereas Boudu and Céline and Julie offer only the option of an escapist disengagement, Capra, in the figure of Stew and in the two romantic partnerings that he undergoes in the course of the film, holds out the possibility that Stew's iconoclastic performance could become the basis for a new society of nonbourgeois, nonrepressive, imaginatively expressive relationships.

The connections between *Platinum Blonde* and Capra's own *American Madness* point up important similarities and equally important differences between the two films. Just as in the case of Tom Dixon, Smith's balletic movement and the answering camera movements are the metaphoric expression of his ability to make a free space for himself in even the most threatening or impersonal surroundings. Like Dixon, Smith humanizes institutional and familial spaces and even the most unpromising societies with his good humor, his wit, and his powers of improvised, spontaneous performance.

Even from the sketchy resumé that I have given, however, certain decisive differences between the two films should already be apparent. In the first place, Smith is in a far more marginal and less powerful position than Dixon was. In the second, the spaces within which Smith must operate are much more alien to him and complex than those through which Dixon genially glad-handed his way. For all of the temporary threats to his authority and sense of confidence, Dixon is unequivocally and indisputably the head, manager, and father figure of the world within which *American Madness* is set. He is the head of the bank, and he personally has hired the people around him. Even in his relationship with his wife, there was no doubt that he was ultimately the ruling figure. None of this is true in Smith's case. He is not a bank president but a young reporter who has no official authority or prerogatives. Neither in the newsroom in which he works, the Schuyler family into which he marries, nor in his relationship with his financially independent and strong-willed wife can Smith have, even for a moment, the sort of authority that Dixon takes for granted. If the bank constitutes a kind of extended family, with Dixon as its father, the extended family that Smith marries into already has a head in the powerful, matriarchal figure of Anne's mother or in Anne herself, neither of whom seeks to share power with anyone. Smith's marriage to Anne brings his authority in his own home (which is more her home than his) and in his most intimate relationship into question. In short, Smith is in what might be called a much more modern predicament. He is a latecomer, and a rather puny and relatively powerless one at that, to a system of power relations that he did not create and over which he has no institutional authority. Dixon, in his moment of crisis, was a temporarily deposed king or a king threatened with rebellion,

---

* For more on this point, see my articles on Rivette's *Céline and Julie Go Boating* and Carl Dreyer's *Day of Wrath*, in *Magill's Survey of Cinema, Foreign Language Films* (Englewood Cliffs, N.J.: Salem Press, 1986).

but he was a king in his palace none the less, who, in the final scene of *American Madness*, was restored to his throne and to his royal powers to give orders and dispense patronage. There is no possibility of Smith's being a king in the universe of *Platinum Blonde*. The nature of power and authority has changed decisively. Smith defines the possibilities of modern heroism, in a modernist work.

It is out of the marginality of his position, the poverty of his resources, and the absence of any mantle of institutional authority within which to warp himself that a performance more complex than Dixon's and more relevant to our own condition of marginality and disenfranchisement is generated, which is why the differences between the two films are all in favor of *Platinum Blonde*. Smith's assertions of personal power and mobility within a social space must be much more devious and fugitive than Dixon's. Smith becomes a master of indirect leverage as a substitute for institutional power. He is thrown back on his capacity for wit, play, and parody as a response to systems he cannot overthrow or act more directly against but by which he refuses to be oppressed. His response is the same as that of many other post-Romantic artists to the same unenviable predicament.

To locate him in the traditions of twentieth-century stage performance, Smith represents Capra's interest in an entirely different tradition of performance from that of Dixon. Whereas Walter Huston's acting style drew on the institutional and historical authority of the nineteenth-century stage tradition, Robert Williams offers a kind of performance that manages to make something out of its own marginality. It is the performance of the music hall and the vaudeville circuit. Our major twentieth-century playwrights, such as Beckett, Pinter, and Shepard, all affiliate themselves more with this tradition of improvised vaudevillian performance than with that of the legitimate theater. Smith/Williams looks ahead to the characters in the central texts of twentieth-century drama and Capra's future films; Dixon/Huston, as theatrically and socially polished as the figure he cuts may be, is essentially a nineteenth-century dramatic performer of a type that will drop out of Capra's work.

Dixon/Huston could never threaten the Schuyler family and their traditions as radically as Smith/Williams does. Huston's acting style would, in fact, not disrupt but dovetail with their style. Smith is a game player, a parodist, and a deeply serious prankster, something that Dixon never wanted or was required to be. The Schuylers snobbishly call this his "eccentricity," their word for anything at all different from themselves, anything that stretches their imaginations beyond their comfortably complacent assumptions about life, but Capra makes us appreciate Smith's eccentricity in a more creative sense of the word than the Schuylers intend. Smith's movements are literally "eccentric," whereas those of almost all of the characters around him are "concentric." Visually, socially, and stylistically, he propels himself away from the centers that the rest of them use to anchor their existence. He is an excitingly decentered performer in a sense of the word that strangely anticipates the work of Derrida: a postmodern personality playing with and against the reigning systems of signification, unmooring the fixities, and putting into question the unexamined assumptions of the lives of more conventional people, while those around him desperately scramble to reestablish the discredited centers for outworn systems of value.

Smith plays verbal and social games with his editor and the various members of the Schuyler family that are a delight to watch (and that only a vaudeville comedian with Williams's timing could have brought off). One game that runs throughout the film is the tried-and-true bowing ceremony that former vaudevillians like the Marx Brothers elevated into a fine art. It is another instance of Smith's ability to project his personality through space, while pinning his opponent to a fixed plane of action. Smith stands in the main drawing room in the foreground of the shot and parodically bows goodnight, across the whole length of the room and up the stairs to the balcony, as the various members of the family retire to their rooms, always refusing to be outbowed by his adversary. In Capra's and Walker's composition of the scene, Smith's puckish personality radiates outward in the third dimension, playfully controlling the whole depth of the shot, while his opponents are trapped, bowing absurdly against the back wall of the distant hallway, as boring, flat, and dimensionless as if they were back-projected onto it. This is a less direct but more interesting kind of power than Dixon's polished assertion of authority. Smith's artistic power is less the assertion of a paternalistic Godlike mastery and control, and more the oblique, parodic leverage of a fallible and fugitive human art.

There is a still more profound difference between Tom Dixon and Stew Smith. Smith's feelings and imaginations are not entirely expressible in social life, as Dixon's apparently are. Smith's kingdom, if kingdom it be, is not entirely of this world. The difference is made clearest by the contrast between the initial scenes in which we see Dixon and Smith. Dixon makes his "entrance" striding confidently across the bank lobby, bantering with each of the employees in turn, directing and acting the scene with all of the combined force of his personal, institutional and dramatic authority. In Dixon's universe, the arrangements of life are not essentially different from or inconsistent with those of art or theater. His "entrance" functions identically as a theatrical and a social event because the two realms dovetail, but there can be no such completely satisfying scene making, and no such theatrical entrances, for Smith.★

In the parallel scene at the beginning of *Platinum Blonde* Smith's physical and imaginative situation at the newspaper office is entirely different from Dixon's. Far from being a central figure in the newsroom, in fact, he initially cannot be seen at all. The news editor is at the center of things, behind his

★ Compare the discussion of the relationship between making scenes in art and in life in my introduction to Henry James, *What Maisie Knew* and *The Spoils of Paynton* (New York: New American Library, 1984).

desk, looking in vain for Smith in order to send him out on the Schuyler story, but Smith, significantly, is not there at the nexus of power but outside of it, on the margin of events. He does not stride into the newsroom but is discovered – by the first of the many exploratory, spatially appetitive camera movements to be associated with him in the film – off to one side, on the periphery of the newsroom, hiding behind a folding screen. He is not working on a story at all, but is playing one of those hand-held games that involve rolling ball bearings through a maze and into a series of holes in a board.

The game playing not only associates Smith with deft movement of the sort he will soon demonstrate verbally and socially in more significant ways, but to anyone who has seen *American Madness* it suggests the profound difference between him and Dixon. What does it mean for this so-called central character to be so completely on the edge of things, and to be playing a game, as opposed to some other activity? He is not working on a news story; he is not sleeping; he is not talking or just goofing off. He seems to be as indifferent to the attractive girl who is behind the screen with him, watching his progress at the game (his newspaper sidekick and sometimes girlfriend, Gallagher, played by Loretta Young) as he is to the newsroom around him whose various noises are registered on Capra's layered sound track. With his feet up on the desk, Stew Smith, the alleged newspaper man (who does not write a single story in the course of the film) is playing a game called Radio. (Radio had only come into its own in the preceding five or six years but was already perceived as a threat by both the newspapers and the movies.) It would be impossible to imagine Tom Dixon (or Matt Brown) hiding in a corner of the bank, playing a game of this sort, or playing any kind of actual game at all. Dixon was able to *live* his games in society. He could publicly enact them as he strode across the lobby of the bank every morning. Stew Smith has occasional opportunities of that kind, and when given the chance he can outmaneuver any of his verbal or social competitors with his wit and charm, but he is also a game player in an entirely different sense.

He does not have the luxury of having an institution like Dixon's bank through which he can express himself. He does not have a stable society to play to or on. He is able frequently to act socially, but, as the scene with the ball-bearing game suggests, he also has imaginative energies that cannot be expressed in social activity. He has public performative powers, but he also apparently has private imaginative states that are not expressed in his public behavior. Lacking social situations that can fully engage or express him, he must at times be satisfied with the free play of his imagination. That is why his most significant act of mastery over the Schuyler drawing room in which he and Bingy wait is ultimately not the social skill that I have described but the imaginative leverage that he displays over his environment by reading a Conrad novel that he finds there.

His powers of play and parody represent an entirely different kind of power from Dixon's social poise and institutional mastery. Smith's skill is not simply to maneuver in society but at times to render all social maneuvering, all social arrangements and values, irrelevant with movements of his mind. As the opening scene in the newsroom suggests, rather than mastering a social situation he is also able imaginatively to exempt himself from it, withdrawing beyond its claims into a realm of free imaginative and stylistic movement. In his relaxed, playful moments, Smith frequently engages in forms of social expression as Dixon did, but he also potentially represents an opening out of all social arrangements. His most radical leverage, as in American artistic expression more generally, is frequently one of style and consciousness, not of acts that engage themselves with social reality. Stew represents a power of meditation, of imagination, that may at times have only imaginative consequences. He frequently creates not a social but a free imaginative space. Given Capra's commitment to social expression and engagement, Smith functions as a criticism of the filmmaker's own assumptions; that is, he represents an expressive problem with which his creator will have to deal.

Just as Smith's position within and response to the space he inhabits is different from Dixon's, the spaces he moves through in *Platinum Blonde* are different from those in *American Madness* (though both films were designed by Stephen Goosson). Dixon moves within a well-lighted, practical, old-fashioned, nineteenth-century dramatic world, in a realistically detailed set out of a "well-made" drama.* There is a solidity to the oak wainscotting, steel vaulting, and brass fixtures of his world that is as publicly demonstrable, solid, and dependable as his own estimable powers of social and theatrical performance. *Platinum Blonde*, however, takes place in spaces that seem to have become strangely plastic. We have moved from the world of realistic social surfaces to a world of potentially surrealistic imaginative warpages. The sets of *American Madness* could have been built to stage a comedy of manners, but the sets of *Platinum Blonde* have the metaphoric resonance and expressionistic plasticity of a psychodrama, almost as if they had been dreamed by Smith himself.

The spaces are organized around two pervasive sorts of patternings: The first consists of images or instances of bars and cages; the second is an alternately elegant or oppressive black and white checkerboard pattern. The checkering extends from specific details in the sets (such as the black and white parquet tiles on the floors of the Schuyler mansion) or in the costumes (such as the black and white designs in Anne Schuyler's clothing) to more general cinematic contrasts of extreme colorations within particular shots: in the contrast between Harlow's brightly key-lighted bleached hair and pale complexion and the velvety blackness of her clothing and the backgrounds against which Capra photographs her, or in the high-chiaroscuro night-lighting effects in the outdoor scenes, involving the use of extremely bright key-lighting on particular objects and the minimizing of fill lighting in between

* I am speaking of the bank set in metaphoric terms. There is no question that, literally, Capra is attempting to depict a contemporary bank in the heart of a city, but my argument is that it is, imaginatively, a world of old-fashioned values and stable relationships and hierarchies of authority.

key spots.* The Schuyler mansion itself becomes a kind of giant checkerboard in which Smith can play games, Capra suggests at more than one point. This particular metaphor is less interesting, though, than the fact of the metaphoricity itself. Insofar as a house can be imagined to be a checkerboard, or a light and dark pattern can extend from the tiles on the floor to a character's clothing to the lighting of a scene, we are in a realm where imagination at least at certain times shapes reality, and not the other way around. Space has been sprung free of strictly realistic constraints and been made responsive to the pressures of imagination. We have moved from a world of neoclassical solidity and dependability (in *American Madness*) to one as infinitely responsive to the pressure of desire as a dream or an expressionistic work of art. Smith both creates and is forced to negotiate imaginative territory that Dixon never had to confront.

If Dixon is the happy inhabitant of a classical or Lockean universe of straightforward, Euclidean relationships, Smith inhabits the artistic equivalent of an Einsteinian universe, where space has become malleable. (Smith is actually compared to Einstein at two points in the film, the only two references to Einstein in all of Capra's work, but surely this is the sheerest of coincidences.) The character who shares with Smith the capacity to bend space through the power of imagination is Anne Schuyler. Einstein theorized about the gravitational warpage of space by stars and planets, but Anne Schuyler erotically warps the space around her with the sexual pull of another kind of stardom, the spatial distortions created by a very different kind of heavenly body. Smith can bend space to his playful purposes with the pull of his imagination (as in one scene when he turns a hallway floor into a colossal hopscotch/checkerboard upon which he plays), but Anne is in many respects much more powerful than he is, and her imaginative warpages and coercions are more threatening and less playful than his own.

The most vivid visual representation of Anne's ability to warp space imaginatively, to disort reality and social situations with her sheer bodily presence, is Capra's registration, in numerous close-ups, of how Jean Harlow's breasts and hips bend the checkered silk fabric of her dresses to attract and hold the eye of the camera, the eye of the film viewer, and the eye of Stew Smith, with an almost irresistible erotic pull. *Plantinum Blonde* is quite erotically charged, but to recognize that is to suggest how far we are from the standards of reason and decorum in *American Madness*.

The scene in which the full Lobachevskian plasticity of this space first becomes apparent occurs early in the film, on the morning following Smith's initial encounter with the Schuyler family. He revisits the mansion, ostensibly to return the purloined copy of Conrad but actually in order to have an excuse to meet Anne again. Waiting until her mother leaves the house, he deftly

---

* Use of this last technique flattens out and abstracts the already visually abstract space still further, so that three-dimensional space is given a virtually oriental, two-dimensional quality on the screen. Since the viewer is unable to establish depth relationships between the various lighted positions within the scene, the shot resolves itself into a black and white pattern defined within the plane of the screen.

weasels his way past the butler. Anne eventually invites him into an inner office in the mansion, leading him there herself. In one astonishing and uninterrupted half-minute tracking shot, Walker stays with Anne and Smith as they snake through the hall and through three intervening rooms on their way to her study. Anne walks in front, with Smith immediately behind her, and Joe Walker uncannily tracks backward, from a position in front of her, with the camera pointed back on her, as they walk through the house, across what must be one hundred feet of floor space. In a voyeur's fantasy come true, Walker holds Harlow's body (sheathed in a thin silk dress, as she is throughout the film) in full view at the center of the frame for the duration of the shot. Smith, who is walking only a foot or two behind her, is obviously enjoying the reverse-field view of everything we are seeing. He keeps up a patter that salaciously free-associates from observations about Indian-style walking to speculations about self-defense during "attacks from the rear" (launching the first in a succession of ass jokes that Capra and Riskin weave into the film). The locker-room jokes in which Smith and his friend Bingy occasionally indulge (the Production Code was on the books in 1931 but was not enforced very strictly until 1934) are something more than sexist ribaldry. They are evidence of how much more inclusive the imaginative world of *Platinum Blonde* is than that of *American Madness*. Among other things, *American Madness* completely ignored the imaginative pull of physical bodies, and that is one of the things that invalidates (or at least seriously limits) its analysis of the dynamics of human relationships.

A world everywhere susceptible to the distortions of liberated desire is a thrilling but dangerous place to live. For all of Smith's sexist double entendres and male sexual swagger in this scene, the consequences of inhabiting such a world are far from comfortable for him. If he is able to spring space and time free from their realistic determinants in order to play the sort of imaginative games which he likes to, Anne Schuyler shows that she can play too. She can bend space and time erotically. She, as well as he, can imaginatively valorize them with possibilities. Physical space is hers to curve with her curves, and she powerfully sucks in and holds Stew's gaze, a viewer's gaze, and the gaze of Walker's camera in this scene. Stew – in other circumstances so much the master of free, eccentric, self-generated, self-pleasuring, independent move-ment – began the film as a planet (in Greek "a wanderer"), but he is gradually pulled by the force of Anne's sexuality into a fixed orbit set by her and eventually into marriage with her on her terms. (The technical astronomical term for such a movement of a planet out of its own independent course is *perturbation*, and Smith gives an emotional meaning to the term.) He even-tually becomes "Mr. Schuyler." This cocky, fast-talking master parodist, game player, and storyteller loses his independence, his freedom of move-ment, and even a sense of his own identity. One of the most touching moments in the film is his proposal to Anne on the patio during one of her high-society parties at which he feels hopelessly out of place. He and she walk off together, and in a film that puts such a high premium on his freedom of movement we watch in horror as he kneels down in front of Anne. The master of easy banter can hardly put together coherent sentences as he stutters, "You know, Anne, I begin to get goofy ideas and they concern you. My name is Smith. That you seem to forget. I am white, male, and over twenty-one. I've never been in jail. I prefer scotch to bourbon. I make $75.00 a week. I have $847 in the bank." Up to this point, Smith has been a master of quick changes and multiple identities, but it is as if, in this meager inventory, we watch him going to pieces under the influence of Anne's attraction. All he can do to hold onto an identity is to itemize himself in this paltry and only half-facetious shopping list of details. Everything above this level has been pulled away from him.

I risk (as I did with *American Madness*) making the film sound more interesting and complex than it is. Much of the rest of *Platinum Blonde* is a fairly schematic elaboration of Smith's crisis of identity and of his ultimate reassertion of personal authority when he pulls himself back together near the end of the film. Despite this, *Platinum Blonde* probes disturbances of imagination and personal identity to which *American Madness* briefly alluded (in the scenes of Dixon's contemplated suicide and of Brown's deep dejection) but did not explore even this far.

In the scenes of Smith's married life that follow the proposal scene, Anne refuses to leave her family's home and go to live in his. He must move into the Schuyler mansion. She sees to it that he is costumed in proper Schuyler attire, established in one of the wings of the house, and incorporated into the family. We see him losing his former identity as literally as he loses his name. He becomes "Anne Schuyler's husband," "Mr. Schuyler," a "gigolo," "a bird in a gilded cage," "the Cinderella Man" – in short, anything but himself.

At the completion of the process, his only remaining expression of personal freedom lies in his eccentricity. He punches Bingy on the nose. (Longfellow Deeds and Jefferson Smith have recourse to the same childish, feeble assertion of freedom when they are most hard-pressed too.) He plays hopscotch on the floor. He teaches the butler how to make echoes in the cavernous hallway of the mansion (another gesture that Deeds will repeat). All of these actions (as Capra knows, though some of his critics assume that he is endorsing them) are trivial and immature assertions of independence. They show that a character's spirit has not been completely broken, but they fail to address the problem: finding a way of expressing one's free imagination in a socially more mature way.

Capra does not know exactly how to solve that problem at the end of *Platinum Blonde*, but one is glad that he does not take the easy way out that he used in *American Madness* which, after alluding to certain imaginative disturbances, chooses in its ending to suppress the problems of imaginative expression in society it raised. *Platinum Blonde* does the opposite. In its last fifteen minutes or so, the film moves into an exploration of Stew Smith's private consciousness, almost to the exclusion of paying adequate attention to social realities or the requirements of narrative plausibility. Even if all society should perish, Capra takes sides on behalf of the importance of the individual exercise of imagination.

Let me briefly summarize the movie's ending. One evening, while Anne is away, a group of Smith's old friends drops by the Schuyler mansion, and a wild party takes place. Meanwhile Smith and Gallagher, the newspaper woman who previously worked with him, retire to an upstairs bedroom together, not to do what General Yen, in a later film, will call the "conventional thing" but to work together on a play Stew is writing, based on his life in the Schuyler family. In the final flurry of scenes, Anne returns and is furious when she discovers the party downstairs and Smith and Gallagher upstairs. Smith moves out, going back to his own apartment with Gallagher, never to return.

What makes this sudden change of events especially bizarre is that during the entire sequence of scenes – the party, Anne's return, Smith's and Gallagher's flight together, and his concluding proposal of marriage to Gallagher in the final minute of the film – Smith and Gallagher keep reminding each other (and the viewers) that they are writing a play with the same scenes in it as the scenes that they are living and that we are watching. The effect is artificial and strange and makes for a very unsatisfactory ending, but it indicates how entirely different this film is from *American Madness*. Capra is so intent on staying with Smith's feelings and consciousness that he sacrifices narrative plausibility and realism. He makes no pretense that polished social "playing" of the sort Dixon indulged in can free Smith. The only playing that holds out any possibility at all for him is to function as a dramatist, making a "play." It is only in an act of consciousness, a capacity of playing purely imaginatively, that Capra sees any positive outcome for him.

Smith's final victory (at the expense of all narrative plausibility) is a victory for the embattled and oppressed consciousness in an act of pure consciousness, an act of meditative withdrawal from the frustrating societies and spaces of life (away from both the newsroom and the Schuyler mansion) into the possibility of making something out of that world in a work of art. At the end of *Platinum Blonde*, Smith has given up everything socially in order to gain something otherwise unobtainable imaginatively. He is levered out of the newsroom as thoroughly as he is levered out of the Schuyler mansion. He sits in his wall-papered, cold-water walk-up, in tattered clothing (he has discarded the Schuyler clothing down to the silver garters), with nothing to show for the whole experience but his enriched consciousness. He has even given up the mobility that made him so remarkable earlier in the film: He is confined visually, cramped spatially, and alienated socially in his tiny apartment, sitting at his typewriter. All worldly forms of power and movement have been sacrificed to those of the imagination. It is an ending profoundly opposed to the easy reestablishment of social order that concluded *American Madness*. Whereas Dixon ends as he began – as a confident master of social ceremonies – Smith represents the possibility of an imaginative opening out of all social solutions, all public forms of order and control. He has his origins in the playful playboy figures of the adventure films, but in becoming a playwright, in transferring their principally physical and social movements into movements of imagination, he has redefined play in terms of the play of consciousness.

To put it in another way, Stew Smith has seen through all social arrangements of experience as Tom Dixon never could have done. Smith began the film on the periphery of one social system, as a poorly paid reporter in the bureaucratic system of the newspaper; moved on, in the middle of the film, to the periphery of another system – a system that a reporter writes about – the historical-familial system of the Schuyler family and its traditions; and ends the film as a playwright, outside of both, analyzing both systems. In moving from one system to another and refusing to be trapped or held by any, he has become a kind of anthropologist of all systems. He has eliminated the possibility of ever having a home in any system. He has seen what Jacques Derrida calls the "structurality of structure" (which is, of course, to become for the first time capable of being a playwright – or a filmmaker). That is why it is absolutely crucial that Capra does not have Smith do what one might have expected at the end of *Platinum Blonde*: simply leave the Schuylers and return with Gallagher to his former identity as a reporter and his "proper place" in life, the newsroom. Smith has moved into a realm of meditation where there can never again be such simple, unexamined identities and functions. Dixon questioned his own ability but never, like this, had to question the whole social system of which he was part.

There is a significant act of repression – or evasion – at the end of the film that will come back to haunt Capra's subsequent work. Capra's film, like Smith, is finally unable to cope with the forces of Anne Schuyler's eroticism, which precipitated Smith's crisis in the first place. In this most erotic of films, in the final ten minutes the erotic is repressed almost entirely. To put it in terms of plot, Stew can only flee from the dangers of Anne's eroticism to a relationship with Gallagher that is the least erotic imaginable. Gallagher's name, her physical appearance, even Stew's proposal of marriage to her in the final minute of the film and the discreet kiss in which they indulge are all desexualized. His relationship with her is as little like his relationship with Anne as possible. Their final, chaste kiss is more like the business handshake of two collaborators agreeing to work together on a script than the imaginative vertigo he experienced in Anne's presence. One could conclude that Capra was simply a sexual prude in favor of repression as the moral of the film if it were not for the earlier evidence of his obvious erotic interest in Harlow's body. The fact that he later went on to make two more highly charged erotic dramas – *Forbidden* and *Bitter Tea* – demonstrates that he was not insensitive to the pleasures of the flesh but just did not know what to do with them at the end of this film. Exploring the relationship of the erotic imagination to the meditative, visionary, and artistic imagination is something Capra will have to do in subsequent films.

One cannot help feeling that Capra's use of Jean Harlow in the film exacerbated this problem. His early films (most notably *Bitter Tea* and *It Happened One Night*) resolve the tension set up in them between the rival claims of powerful sexual energies (as embodied in Harlow, in this film) and those of meditative withdrawal and imaginative transcendence (as embodied in Loretta Young) by arguing that the one sort of energy or relationship can be converted into the other. Thus an attraction between the principal male and female characters that is incipiently sexual is translated into an imaginative or idealistic bonding, without entirely losing its sexual dimension, as both of the films just mentioned demonstrate. The problem in *Platinum Blonde* is that neither Harlow's voluptuous appearance nor her acting ability (which is marginal) lend themselves to such sublimation. Therefore she, and the sexual energies she represents, must simply be exorcised from the film in the clumsy divorce scene. Harlow has to be jettisoned from the plot (appearing for no more than four or five minutes of screen time in the last twenty minutes of the film) and replaced by the figure of Young. That, however, is only to restate the final limitation of the film. The arbitrariness of the substitution of Young for Harlow simply shows that Capra has not worked out the interrelationship of the physical world and the imaginative. He must remove one in order to depict the other, and that is inadequate.

American Madness and *Platinum Blonde* mark, in effect, a fork in the road of development for Capra. Stew Smith represents the presence of an imaginative residue of feeling and energy that will not be completely or satisfyingly expressed in the forms of social interaction, an energy that in the plot of *Platinum Blonde* can only find release in jokes, play, and playwriting. He represents a disturbing self-criticism on Capra's part of his own faith that imaginative energies can and must be translated into practical worldly forms of expression. Much of the interest of Capra's later work is going to be his attempt to find a place for the imagination of Stew Smith in the world, and his difficulties in doing so. He will do everything in his power to resist the conclusion forced on him by the ending of *Platinum Blonde*, and to achieve the social expression of the imagination in the world that *American Madness* (all too glibly) suggests is possible.

In short, he will repeatedly try to make the one kind of film pass for the other. He will attempt to create a character with the independence and imagination of Stew Smith and yet suggest that he can happily live the well-integrated social life of a Tom Dixon. He will attempt to have things both ways: to document the wild, anarchic energies and disturbances of imagination that make a merely social solution to a character's expressive predicament apparently impossible, and yet simultaneously to suggest that the imagination can express itself in the world, its energies smoothly channeled into the routines of everyday social existence, with no pain or loss.

Fortunately, no matter how much Capra resisted some of the insights forced on him by his own works, the disturbances in his movies continue to haunt him and us after their happy endings. We remember the gun in Dixon's desk, even after he puts it away and resumes his joking with those around him, just as the memories of Harlow's curves are not erased by Smith's final demure embrace with the sticklike Loretta Young. Capra never stops trying to tame and control the genie of imagination and desire, to teach him to sublimate his energies into productive, socially useful expressions, but the pain and confusions of the films that follow *American Madness* is testimony to his honest ambivalence about the effort and his refusal ever again to take the easy way out that he did there. If "The play's the thing" for Stew Smith, perhaps it can be the answer for Capra as well.

PART III

Transcendental impulses

Ladies of Leisure, 1930
Forbidden, 1932
The Bitter Tea of General Yen, 1933

8

Living through the eye
Ladies of Leisure

> The visible world, and the invisible. Or rather, the audible and the inaudible. She had lived so long, and so completely, in the visible, audible world. She would not easily admit that other, inaudible. She always wanted to jeer as she approached the brink of it.
> – D. H. Lawrence, *St. Mawr*

Stew Smith ends up as neither a rich man nor a reporter but as a playwright writing a play about a character who, like himself, has been both. Since he gets the girl who has been in love with him throughout the film, it could be argued that Capra is orchestrating the most trite and conventional of "happily-ever-after" Hollywood endings, but there is a strange quality to the ending of *Platinum Blonde* that cannot be ignored. In the final scene of the play Smith is writing, his leading character proposes to the girl he finally realizes he loves, and Smith simultaneously acts it out in his own life in his relationship to Gallagher. Not only does the play-within-a-play structure formally abstract the viewer from the events taking place, but it bizarrely abstracts Smith from his own experience as he lives it. One might conclude that Capra simply miscalculated the distancing effect of this ending, if it were not for the fact that Smith's state of alienation from his own experience in the last few minutes of *Platinum Blonde* is of a piece with his earlier alienation from the life of the newsroom when he was a reporter and with his alienation from the family life of the Schuylers when he was married to Anne.

One is reminded of Whitman's propensity to stand outside himself:

> Apart from the pulling and hauling stands what I am,
> Stands amused, complacent, compassionate, idle, unitary,
> Looks down, is earnest, or bends an arm on an impalpable certain rest,
> Looking with side-curved head curious what will come next,
> Both in and out of the game and watching and wondering at it.★

Note that in this passage Whitman calls experience a "game," using the same metaphor that Capra uses throughout *Platinum Blonde* to describe Smith's

---

★ Walt Whitman, *Leaves of Grass*, "Song of Myself," section 4.

relationship to experience. The attraction to play and games in Capra's work is very Whitmanesque in spirit. Both Capra and Whitman use comedy and playfulness, artistic and social games, to clear a space for the free movements of the personal performer. The calculated absurdity, the comic outrageousness of Whitman's tone and imagery in this passage are as much a demonstration of that effort as Smith's deliberate silliness and calculated frivolousness.

Capra is closer to Emerson than to Whitman though, in his quite mixed feelings about this American alienation, this unavoidable "double consciousness," as Emerson called it. Whitman (at least in "Song of Myself") seems all too content endlessly to play imaginative games, to stand off to one side of his own experience, to navigate an eccentric comic and parodic course through complex forms of discourse and relationship, but Emerson sees a more troubling side to the Whitmanesque position. His essay "Experience," written ten years before "Song of Myself," can be read as his reply to the Whitman in himself. Notice in the following passage what a different sense he gives to the concept of "glancing" than Whitman did with his comical phrase "Looking with side-curved head curious":

> I take this evanescence and lubricity of all objects, which lets them slip through our fingers then when we clutch hardest, to be the most unhandsome part of our condition. Nature does not like to be observed, and likes that we should be her fools and playmates. We may have the sphere for our cricket-ball, but not a berry for our philosophy. Direct strokes she never gave us power to make; all our blows glance, all our hits are accidents. Our relations to each other are oblique and casual. Dream delivers us to dream, and there is no end of illusion.

About the "slippery, sliding surfaces" of Smith's and Whitman's performances, Emerson would have had un-Whitmanesque ambivalences, as does Capra, who ultimately comes to criticize Smith's game playing. What is Smith's final transformation at the end of *Platinum Blonde* but an almost desperate attempt to make his playing serious and engaged in a way that it has not been up to that moment? His sudden metamorphosis into a playwright is at once a criticism of the superficiality of the earlier forms of playing in which he indulged and an attempted translation of them into a form of expression in which his disengagement will be transformed into engagement with the world, without sacrificing his freedom of movement. The strangely alienating and almost affectless ending of *Platinum Blonde* testifies to how difficult is the modernist effort to make a virtue of the necessity of slippage, lubricity, and alienation.

In *Ladies of Leisure* Capra brings together two characters who, in their different ways, possess many of the qualities of imaginative mobility that Stew Smith did. The fact that there are two of them instead of one, and that they are a man and a woman romantically paired off in the course of the film, helps to explain why *Ladies of Leisure* is more interesting than *Platinum Blonde*.

The central couple in *Ladies of Leisure* is an artist and his model, Jerry Strong and Kay Arnold – but that is far from typing either of them, since Kay is a call girl who is very uncomfortable and out of her milieu serving as an artist's model, and Jerry is himself undergoing a crisis about the relationship of art to life, and about his ability as an artist. He is an unsuccessful and profoundly frustrated painter, who cannot paint well enough to satisfy himself or to express what he feels, yet he refuses to yield to the importunities of family and friends that he give up his art and go into business. His particular problem is that he wants to paint visionary works of art but has been driven to the verge of giving up on painting altogether by his failure to get the "soul" of his sitters on canvas. Capra thus imagines his situation explicitly as an expressive crisis involving the difficulty of making the translation from physical surfaces to spiritual depths in his art.

There are, then, a number of obvious parallels between Jerry's aspiration as an artist and Capra's as a filmmaker in this film and most of his other works as well. Not only are Jerry and Capra both artists working on "pictures" in "studios" (there is a running pun on these two words in the film that explicitly links the creation of the two sorts of pictures) but, more significantly, both artists embrace the same set of aesthetic principles: an extreme emotional, social, and physical realism – with a suspicion of makeup, fancy costumes, gauzed close-ups, and elaborate backgrounds or sets – employed in the service of expressing an equally extreme imaginative idealism. The Jerry Strong who insists on removing Kay's makeup is clearly a version of the Frank Capra who was one of the first Hollywood directors to remove his actors' and actresses' makeup. The Jerry Strong who, after this act of "realization," attempts to "derealize" his sitter by painting her as an allegorical figure of Hope is a version of the Frank Capra who, in *The Way of the Strong* and much of his other work, attempted to make films that would represent the spiritual depths underneath the physical surfaces. In short, Jerry's artistic project involving the expression of spirit in terms of flesh, of ideals in terms of realities, and of abstractions in terms of concrete events is Capra's as well, and there is every reason to regard this maker of pictures as an alter ego for his creator.

An important related issue in *Ladies of Leisure* that links Jerry and Capra is the question of the commodification of art and the human body. Jerry adamantly resists the commercialization of art or human relationships in a film in which call girls, readily selling their bodies and their emotions for a few dollars, abound. It is impossible not to see in Jerry's absolute rejection of commercial art and commercial relationships Capra's own statement on the general commercial premises of Hollywood filmmaking and specifically on the selling of the bodies of stars at the movies.*

We first meet Jerry at a crowded unruly party. He is brooding and unable to enjoy himself because of his doubts about his artistic ability to express himself in the ways he wants to. There are two expressive foils explicitly contrasted

---

* One can only speculate to what degree Capra's Roman Catholic background has anything to do with his relentless spiritualization of experience, but for whatever cause, this becomes the secret antimaterialist, anticapitalist, anticommodification subtext of this film and many of his others.

with him in the film who help to define his situation within it – his best friend Bill Standish, and Kay's roommate, Dot Lamarr. If it is difficult to express spirit in terms of flesh, they have solved the whole problem by simply despiritualizing their existences. It should be no surprise that whereas Jerry has trouble expressing himself (artistically, verbally, and interpersonally) during the film, is embarrassingly hesitant, awkward, and stumbling, these two are facile, confident, and voluble. They have none of the expressive problems he has because they have eliminated spirituality or deep feeling from their lives.

Dot treats the whole world as a source of food and drink. Almost every time she appears she is either eating, preparing to eat, or talking about eating. As Capra gently and comically satirizes her, she is what she eats. She has succeeded in corporealizing all of existence, turning it into a matter of calorie counting, "oodles" of rich desserts, and pinches of her ample behind. Her vocabulary is unmitigatedly physical and at times coarse, but like Molly Bloom's it is a model of perfect and complete self-expressiveness. The difficult expressive movement from flesh to spirit has been replaced by her comic determination to stay in the realm of the senses, so nothing is lost in translation.

Jerry's friend, Bill Standish, a seducer of young women, is similarly free from expressive problems. He is an artist of sorts, but his art has none of the problematically mediated status of Jerry's, since he is an artist of sexual seduction. In the opening scenes of the film, after several shots of the rowdy crowd at the penthouse party, Capra dramatically cuts to a sublime center of artistic stillness and concentrated composition in the center of the room. Bill, playing painter wearing an artist's smock and holding a brush and palette, is applying the final careful touches to a work that is offscreen. At the moment when he places his final stroke and steps back contentedly to admire his work, the camera dollies back to show that the "canvas" being painted is the back of a beautiful girl, and that, in short, for Bill, the "work of art" is only another way to play the game of sex. There is no problem of expression for him, and none of the gap between imagination and the articulation of it that Jerry feels. Painting the body of an obliging and attractive young woman represents the possibility of moving directly and unmediatedly from imaginative to worldly possession. Art becomes foreplay. Desire is directly and unproblematically translatable into forms of action and social expression. For him, too, nothing is lost in translation.

When, in the next shot, Jerry peevishly interrupts Bill's "painting," it is obvious that Bill regards him as merely churlish, but Capra is offering us a conception of a possible form of art that Bill could not understand. It is an art of romantic ideals nearly, or actually, inexpressible in the forms of the world. In fact, Jerry's art is not even expressible with paints on canvas, and is, in its own right, as unorthodox and unsalable as Bill's body painting. Jerry is a painter, but more than that he is a dreamer of dreams that he cannot express anywhere – on canvas, in his talk, or in his life and relationships with others. Capra is implicitly asking what can be the destiny of the personal dream in a society where the drunkenness and debauchery of a Hollywood party are the closest any of these people come to expressing themselves freely. After upbraiding Bill for ruining one of his best brushes, Jerry turns away and walks out onto a balcony of the apartment, outside of the group of partygoers.

It is an extremely significant movement for several reasons. In the first place it tells us something important about Capra's attitude toward crowds. The wild party is the kind of frenzied, visually busy group scene, with dozens of characters boxed into a confined space, all talking and moving energetically, for which Capra is famous and to which he was attracted again and again. The sheer energy of such scenes obviously fascinated him, but he had a love–hate relationship with crowds. Far from believing that the individual could easily or naturally interact with a group of others in a process of democratic give and take, Capra more often than not shows how difficult it is to establish an adequate relationship to a group. The individual is threatened with a frightening loss of identity in a crowd, and a crowd is always on the verge of turning into a mindless mob in his work. That is why the achievements of figures like Smith and Dixon are so significant to Capra. They have succeeded at an almost impossible task: establishing a complexly responsive and creative relationship to groups of others around them. Many more characters fail at this effort in Capra's work than succeed, and the successes always have to be earned with pain and difficulty. Thus Jerry's movement to the fringes of this group is an important assertion of independence from it.

In *Ladies of Leisure*, as in *Platinum Blonde*, a character's physical position at the center or the periphery of a group and his ability to move independently of the group itself is a principal expression of his or her imaginative relationship to it, but the difference between Jerry and Stew Smith is that Jerry is given a capacity for vision that Stew never had. Jerry not only moves physically to the edge of the party out onto the balcony, but he stands looking meditatively at the skyline of the city (which Capra presents with an intercut shot from Jerry's point of view). Jerry's capacity not only socially to turn his back on society, to move outside of it that way, but his ability to leave it imaginatively behind in such a moment is one of the crucial events in the film. To be able to move meditatively even a few steps outside the commotion of society in order to look away from it is to establish imaginative and social limits to its power, to recognize the artificiality and arbitrariness of its roles, structures, and institutions, to begin to "frame" it, or put it "in perspective," in a different meaning of the words than Bill would understand.

To be able to "turn" on one's own "premises" (physically, socially, and imaginatively) in such a way (to employ a Thoreauvian pun to describe a prototypically Thoreauvian activity) is one of the crucial movements in American art, as important there, and in Capra's films, as in the seventeenth-century British meditative poetry that so strongly influenced the major writers of the American Renaissance. There is no more significant moment in the work of Melville, Emerson, Thoreau, Whitman, or James than that in which the author or his character performs such an act of "turning" on himself and his own situation – when he, as it were, meditatively pivots in place, in order to reflect on his own life and actions. Just as it is in Capra's work, in the High Romantic tradition that descends to American fiction and film from the poetry of Wordsworth, such a meditative, imaginative turning away from past positions and roles is almost invariably mirrored in a physical movement away from the groups in which the individual would otherwise be absorbed or lost.* Such imaginative turnings – usually marked by bodily turnings or by actions such as looking out a window, moving out onto a balcony, looking through a doorway, gazing meditatively off a bridge, or simply moving to one side of a larger group – define some of the central events in Capra's greatest work, in films otherwise as different from each other as this one, *The Bitter Tea of General Yen*, *Mr. Deeds Goes to Town*, *Mr. Smith Goes to Washington*, and *It's a Wonderful Life*.

One might find numerous analogies with such moments in the rhetorical and social turnings in the work of Emerson, Hawthorne, Melville, Whitman, or James, but one is also struck by similarities between the visual representation of such meditative moments in Capra's films and paintings by Homer, Hopper, Tarbell, and Eakins, among others. The analogy between scenes in Capra's films and works of American painting is important insofar as particular moments within Capra's work deliberately aspire to approach the condition of paintings. As James does in a novel like *The Ambassadors*, in these moments Capra attempts to release his characters from certain narrative and temporal pressures so that they and the scenes in which they participate can assume more visionary proportions.

This is what I previously called the meditative shift in Capra's work. As I have already described happening (in a more primitive form) in certain shots of *The Way of the Strong*, at such moments the dialogue and plot are stopped for an instant, and the shot is almost always composed and framed as a static visual composition. One is irresistibly reminded of a painting at such moments, even though in a narrative film, unlike a painting, the effect cannot last. The momentarily achieved moment of "composition" quickly decomposes under the pressure of time. Plot and events intrude into and disrupt the purity of the meditative moment. The difficulty of achieving or maintaining a meditative or reflective relationship to the world becomes one of the implicit subjects of the film.

Capra himself seemed highly aware of the counterpoised double lineage of his work – its uneasy yoking of narrative and temporal traditions of literature and drama with the static visual qualities of painting and the other visual arts. It can hardly be a matter of chance that of the four principal artist figures in his early films, two work within the literary-dramatic tradition, and two within the traditions of the fine arts. In the first group are Stew Smith, journalist and dramatist, and Florence Fallon of *The Miracle Woman*, a speech maker and

---

* See my "Making the Most of a Mess," *Georgia Review*, 35 (Fall 1981), 631–42.

pulpit rhetorician; in the second are Jerry Strong, a painter, and Yen, the eponymous star of *The Bitter Tea of General Yen*, a combination of set designer and architect, among many other roles that he plays.

If one uses the concept of turnings in the broadest sense to describe meditative, social, and physical movements – to include physical turnings of characters away from participation in social groups; inward turnings of the bodies and minds of figures upon themselves; and, most important, turnings of moments of narrative action or eventfulness into moments of static, pictorial composition – the work of Thomas Eakins and that of Frank Capra are strikingly similar in many respects. Such turnings might be said to be the subject of all of Eakins's work – literally, in paintings like *Starting Out after Rail, The Biglin Brothers Turning the Stake*, and *Max Schmitt in a Single Scull*, and figuratively, in ones like the portraits of Professor Henry A. Rowland, Dr. John H. Brinton, and Maude Cook. Eakins was attracted to painting these instants of contemplation, stillness, or pause between moments of violent activity (in the sailing, boxing, shooting, and rowing paintings), and instances of inward-turning contemplation (in the great portraits) because, like Capra, he wanted to explore the point at which one sort of eventfulness is replaced by another, the point at which meditative movements of the mind interrupt or impinge on the world of action and event.

Such a meditative moment can take many different forms in Eakins's work, just as it does in Capra's. The block-building infant giant of *Baby at Play* is arrested at that precise moment at which action has been replaced by concentration, an absolute concentration of attention and effort in which one can feel the whole mind and spirit of the baby's truly monumental body poised and utterly concentrated on one square inch of building-block placement. The pyramidal composition of the painting combined with the effect of the mutually converging lines of the baby's arms, the pattern of bricks on the patio, the alignment of the toy horse-cart, and the downward concentration of the baby's attention indicated by the inclination of her head and the lighting on her face, absolutely focus the viewer's attention, like the baby's, on that arrested act of delicate, balanced placement. Everything in the painting is designed to communicate the complex, concentrated mindfulness of the baby at this moment and to contrast it with the slack prostration of the sawdust and rag doll thrown down casually behind her. The state of focused concentration embodied by the infant truly makes society (even the society of dolls) irrelevant.

The rowers, sailors, boatmen, and shooters who are the figures in Eakins's best-known paintings are caught at similar moments of concentrated, instantaneously arrested balance, but theirs is an even more complex act of mindfulness than the baby's, insofar as it usually involves the interaction of two or more figures in an event of mutual interaction, as when the Biglin brothers yaw their boat around a turning buoy, or a shooter and his boatman delicately balance an unstable flat-bottomed boat in position as a shot is fired.

Eakins's obvious fascination with rowing scenes is interesting for more than one reason. The rower is a figure in the landscape released to a specially

Thomas Eakins, *Baby at Play*. The National Gallery of Art, Washington, D.C.; John Hay Whitney Collection.

Thomas Eakins, *The Biglin Brothers Turning the Stake*. The Cleveland Museum of Art; purchase, Hirman B. Hurlbut Collection.

socially unencumbered relationship to experience. This is the visionary sense of rowing that the expanses of water communicate in these paintings. What makes the rower different from other visionaries and apparently interested Eakins is that rather than being passive or dreamy, the rower is active physically and mentally. Further, in the pair–oared shell scenes (like *The Biglin Brothers Turning the Stake*) his actions have to be finely coordinated with those of another individual. The stroke and the bow–rower must pull, feather, and move in a precise relationship as they work together, never more precisely focused and concentrated in their activity than when they turn a stake together, as the complex depiction of the two rowers' different but interrelated positions in this painting indicates: the stroke looking directly backward, sitting erect and holding his oar in place, the bow–rower leaning back and pulling back vigorously as he watches the position of the stroke oar. In their blue caps and blue-trimmed shirts, which associate them visually with the blue-flagged stake they have just completed turning so tightly and closely at the instant Eakins chooses to depict them, the Biglin brothers constitute an island of concentrated calm and cool poise in the heat of the race and against the busy background of the crowds of spectators on the shore and the overheated colors of the red-clad team. With his interest in moments of achieved poise and calm and mindfulness in the heat of action, it is entirely fitting that, in contrast to George Bellows, who was interested in painting club fights in all their brutal blur of movement, Eakins was attracted to the quite different moments in which a fighter leaving the ring paused momentarily to turn to the crowd and salute it (in *Salutat*) or paused within the ring between rounds to compose himself and gather his concentration (in *Between Rounds*).

The greatest of Eakins's paintings of this type, and the ones that most remind one of moments within Capra's work, are the portraits of Dr. Gross and Dr. Agnew at work in their clinics. These paintings imagine the social, meditative, and artistic act of turning in the most complex and extended worldly matrices. Disregarding the difference in the settings, *The Gross Clinic* and *The Agnew Clinic* imagine their central figures' acts of withdrawal and contemplation in almost exactly the same terms Capra uses for Jerry Strong at the penthouse party. Drs. Gross and Agnew move off to one side of the groups depicted and turn their bodies at a slight angle to them. The social and physical movements and turnings in both the film and the paintings are not the most important things, however. They are pictorial metaphors for far more important imaginative pivotings. Each of Eakins's surgeons is imagined to be at the center of an agitated, active, intense, indifferent, or restless group of people, and yet to be simultaneously meditatively released from the turbulence, to have imaginatively mastered the pain and risen above the disturbance without ceasing to be responsive to it. In the earlier, more powerful painting, especially, Dr. Gross demonstrates a capacity of imaginative self-possession that is the equivalent in painting of the imaginative self-reliance Emerson praised in his *Representative Men*. Eakins deliberately situates him half inside the circle of surgeons and half turned out of it, half active and half withdrawn

Thomas Eakins, *The Agnew Clinic*. University of Pennsylvania Medical School.

Thomas Eakins, *The Gross Clinic*. From the Jefferson Medical College of Thomas Jefferson University, Philadephia, Pennsylvania.

into his own thoughts and meditations, half a surgeon and half a teacher of surgery. It is significant that he is framed on one side by the writhing shape of a distraught relative of the patient – all discomposed pain and emotionality – and on the other by the disciplined, coordinated activity of a team of surgeons making an incision on a patient – all dispassionate, businesslike efficiency. Dr. Gross imaginatively mediates between these two realms – between science and humanity, between emotion and reason, between involvement and detachment.

That doubleness of stance is the import of his blood-stained, scalpel-holding hand, I believe. The blood on it tells us that it is the hand of a practicing surgeon actually at work at this minute, but the arrested gesture in which Eakins presents it tells us that this is also a professor of surgery turning to his students to make a dramatic point or to explain or ponder his next step. Elizabeth Johns's concept of modern heroism as applied to Dr. Gross is a useful one, but it must always be remembered that this is not a heroism of activity and accomplishment alone, but a kind of heroism that would have been appreciated by Emerson or Whitman in which one stands, in Whitman's words quoted near the beginning of this chapter, "Apart from the pulling and hauling.... Looking with side-curved head.... Both in and out of the game and watching and wondering at it." The visual match in color and shape and gesture and contiguity between the hand of Dr. Gross holding the scalpel and the hand of the recording secretary of the operating theater holding a red pencil tells us of the equivalence of the two hands that is being celebrated here. It is not the operation that Dr. Gross performs that is the central subject of this painting but the translation of that activity into a series of points and procedures in a ledger book, into a sequence of instructions and interpretations in a lecture at a college of surgeons that matters to Eakins. It is the meditative movement from action and event to interpretation, understanding, and imaginative mastery that he paints. To say that Dr. Gross operates in a theater is to remind oneself of the essentially theatrical quality of the painting, which is not about an event in itself, but about the act of imaginative mediation or translation that turns an event into a lesson in a public form of expression, in front of an audience of pointedly tired, indifferent, or only partially attentive spectators.

It is in this sense that the real turning, in both Capra's and Eakins's work is a process of imaginative conversion or mediation that is only visually hinted at by the actual physical turning of a figure or by his movement to one side of a social group. The important turning is always inward and meditative. Capra and Eakins, like all of the artists in the meditative tradition that I outlined in my first chapter, are attempting to define another relationship to experience beyond the physical, the public, the social, or the political. Both Eakins and Capra sometimes express such states of awareness negatively by indicating what they are not, as Eakins does by juxtaposing nonmeditative figures with meditative ones in his clinic paintings, but they aspire to express such ideal states positively, through the composition of a scene, the play of light and shadow on a face, the expression of that face, and the position and posture of the poised body of the figure.

The difference between Eakins's surgeons and Capra's painter, however, is that Jerry egregiously fails where they succeed. Though he aspires to the meditative composure that Agnew and Gross possess and goes through the motions of seeking it, he absolutely fails in his attempt. Even as he moves out onto the penthouse balcony, he is still upset and agitated by the party, the noise of which can still be heard in the background. His effort, and the drama of Capra's film, consists in his (and later, Kay's) attempt to move into the position occupied by Eakins's central figures – as if the writhing, slumped, agitated figure at the left of *The Gross Clinic* attempted before our eyes to transform herself into the monumentally reflective, composed, and erect Dr. Gross.

It should be noted that a meditative stance is never valuable for Capra if it results in solitude or solipsism. It must always at least potentially be convertible into expression or the forms of a human relationship. Simply, as an end in itself, to move out onto a balcony and to look at the stars, as Jerry does, may be a gain for consciousness, but it is to be no more of a successful artist than Standish is. Perhaps, indeed, it is to be less of one. Standish and his girl at least have a (probably rather smudged) body painting to show as an expression of their feelings at the end of the evening; Jerry has nothing whatever. Between the cramped frame that Standish paints on the girl's back and the unpaintable experience of looking at the stars, it is hard to say that either "artist" is to be preferred. If Standish sells out the possibility of vision in order to live his life entirely in the world of the senses, Strong, in refusing to be anything less than a transparent eyeball, exemplifies a perhaps equally impoverished life that, in declining to be anything less than metaphysical and unbounded, gives up all the joy of the merely physical and earthbound. How does one transform the liberating vision of the stars and the skyline, yearningly viewed from a penthouse balcony on the periphery of a wild party, into an expression that can constitute a basis of life even for a community of two? Can one make room for such a vision in any imaginable society, or is one doomed simply to go on staring off into the distance in loneliness and frustration? The task that Frank Capra sets for himself as a filmmaker is exactly the same one that confronts Jerry Strong as an artist. He too must find a way to express his ideals in other ways than by inserting shots of the stars and skyline in his film. He must translate them into the form of dialogue, social interaction, and temporally and spatially practical, dramatic interaction. His success or failure in the course of the film, like Strong's, will be measured by his ability or inability to speak the transcendental in the lingua franca of the Hollywood movie.

Capra and Eakins share this commitment to imaginative expression in the structures of the "real" world. In their work, both depicted figures who were highly creative and imaginative in their own right – performers, artists, and intellectuals of one sort or another – and yet who expressed their creativity not alone in a garret or to themselves only but in the practical world of men and affairs. A surgeon (like Drs. Gross, Agnew, and Brinton); a physicist (like Professor Henry Rowland); a singer (like Maud Cooke); an industrialist (like Louis Kenton); and a poet (like Whitman), similar to the central figures in Capra's work, represent richly creative and original people who chose to express themselves in useful, public forms of achievement. In this regard they are alter egos for the artists who render them, both of whom find visionary possibilities in the heart of everyday activity, not as an alternative to or escape

Thomas Eakins, *Professor Henry A. Rowland.* Addison Gallery of American Art, Andover, Massachusetts.

from ordinary life. Each clinic painting has its central figure posed like an artist in front of his students. Gross, Agnew, and Eakins himself are equally engaged in translating abstract purposes and ideals into practical, social forms of expression: painting, surgery, and teaching. It is that process of translation across realms that Eakins is painting and that a painter, a surgeon, or a teacher continuously enacts.

In the scene following the one I have just described, Jerry moves completely away from the party physically, as he already has imaginatively. He abruptly leaves it and is driving down the road alone in his automobile when he meets another refugee from party life. Kay Arnold is a comely party girl who, we would have every reason to believe, is the type who would have been having her body painted in the previous scene were it not for the fact that she is fleeing a party too. Jerry comes upon her rowing a dinghy to shore away from a brightly lighted yacht in the harbor where another party is going on, and ends up giving her a ride to New York and persuading her to sit for him the next day.

There is an immediate affinity between the two refugees from social life, but Capra is also intrigued by the differences between them. If Jerry's imaginative mobility is the consequence of his idealism, Kay's is the result of an absolutely equal but opposite cynicism or worldliness. He has left his party because it cannot live up to his ideals of expression. She has left hers, she says, because it is not wild enough. She is a party girl, a piece of meat for the sort of event Jerry has just fled, and is utterly cynical about life, love, and human relationships. She could not be more different from Jerry, except for the fact that her cynicism is as powerful a force for potential imaginative mobility as his dreamy idealism. As different as Jerry and Kay are from each other, the artist and the party girl are deeply similar in one way: They are both imaginative outlaws, outsiders temporarily sprung free from subscription to the rules of conventional social life.★

Jerry recruits Kay as his model and tries to transform her into a figure of Hope in an allegorical painting. The middle of *Ladies of Leisure* is devoted to a comparison of ways of seeing. Jerry wants Kay to embody (and the pun is built into the film itself) imagination, idealism, and spirituality; Kay resists his transformations and insists on the preeminence of her physicality, sexuality, and feminine reality. As a result they repeatedly puzzle, confuse, and comically frustrate each other. Jerry sees painting strictly as a spiritual process and refuses to let physicality sully it (or his relationship to his sitter). Kay, on the other hand, regards painting much more the way Bill Standish did, as a sort of excuse for high-toned hanky-panky between artist and model. Consequently he misunderstands her sexual overtures, and she is offended by the coolness of his "treatment" (in both senses of the word) of her.

With this opposition so firmly built into it, there are moments when *Ladies of Leisure* almost rigidifies itself into a wooden allegory of the opposition

---

★ This paradoxical pairing of cynics and idealists and the consequent subterranean equation of the two kinds of imaginative marginality (or mobility) is something that Capra continues to explore in his subsequent work, most notably in his romantic pairings of boyish, impractical, idealistic male dreamers – played by Jimmy Stewart and Gary Cooper – with shrewd, unillusioned female secretaries or reporters – played by Jean Arthur or Barbara Stanwyck – in the films he made in the second half of the thirties.

between flesh and spirit. Some of the scenes between Jerry and Kay are among the weakest and most mechanical in Capra's work, as when Jerry wants Kay to look up in her posing, but she inevitably forgets and looks down at the floor; or when he asks her to "see the stars" while she is sitting for him, but she insists that she cannot see anything but the ceiling. What keeps the film from becoming tritely schematic is that Capra's position is significantly different from both Jerry's and Kay's and also capacious enough to include and to gently criticize both of their positions. The delicate and underplayed humor of many of the scenes between Kay and Jerry is a way of suspending judgment about either of them, at the same time as it educates the viewer into tolerance for their extreme points of view. Furthermore, it is pretty clear that Capra himself cannot quite make up his mind about the relationship of spirituality and sexuality in life (or in this film). I have already noticed in my discussions of both *The Way of the Strong* and *Platinum Blonde* that Capra was given to the same sort of spiritualizing impulse as Jerry is, and yet in those films and in this one also he wants to argue that bodies must be taken account of too.

Ladies of Leisure thus becomes a fairly ambivalent exploration of the limitations of both absolute positions for Capra. It attempts, not entirely successfully, to mediate between flesh and spirit, between worldliness and unworldliness in life, in painting, and in Hollywood filmmaking. In many concrete details of event, characterization, and photography, Capra ambivalently attempts to honor both Jerry's and Kay's positions. Jerry attempts to spiritualize his relationship with Kay completely, to expunge all sexual and social ramifications from their relationship, or at least to sublimate such feelings into artistic abstractions, as if he could do to Kay what Carl Dreyer did to Marie Falconetti in transforming her into Joan of Arc. Capra's film keeps reminding us, however, that Kay will not be etherealized in this way. That is the point of his decision not only to define Kay as a call girl, but, more important, to cast the young, alluring Barbara Stanwyck in the role. The film, made before the stringent enforcement of the Production Code, goes to great lengths to emphasize Kay's physical attractiveness. Capra deliberately keeps giving us desublimating glimpses of her body throughout the film – as she takes a bath, changes her clothes, displays her legs when she sits down, and generally preens, primps, and postures – so that it is impossible for the viewer to enter into full complicity with Jerry's effort to dematerialize her into an abstract, allegorical figure of Hope.

Kay deliberately indulges in sexually suggestive behavior in front of Jerry and his friend Standish, because in her view an artist's model is only another kind of call girl. Just as Capra prevents Jerry's spiritualizing efforts from controlling the meaning of his scenes, though, he prevents Kay's sexual allure from distorting his film in the direction of the body. He works as hard to spiritualize her at some moments as he works to physicalize her at others. Backlighting, high key-lighting, and an occasional soft-focus close-up are used at times to give Kay a virtual halo of luminous spirituality.

The film is a tug of war between these two opposing tendencies: between an interest in Kay's sexuality that borders on being voyeuristic, and a tendency to treat Stanwyck as a sort of goddess. Capra seems unable to make up his mind about either his actress or his character. Instead of achieving an aesthetic balance between the corporeal and spiritual sides of his narrative, the actual effect is much more of a double vision: Barbara Stanwyck will not stay in focus for either type of appreciation of her, and the character she plays is, by the end of the film, thrown into a suicidal confusion about who or what she really is – about whether she can live up to Jerry's idealistic vision of her or must continue to play out the party-girl role in which she has originally cast herself. The result is the opposite of an easy combining of the physical and the spiritual, or a gradual transformation of Kay from one state to the other. The film proceeds by painful lurches and oscillations between the two positions, and Kay and Jerry themselves become progressively less sure of their own and each other's respective positions and more, rather than less, sexually and spiritually confused, as the film goes on.

An important scene occurs about halfway through on an evening during which Kay has stayed late at Jerry's studio for a sitting. They pause at one point, and Jerry walks out onto the balcony to smoke. As I have already suggested, the movement outside of the confines of a social space is always significant in Capra's work even if, as in this case, it involves a change only in a character's direction or angle of vision. Jerry sits and looks up at the night sky. Kay first puts a record on the gramophone and then joins him outdoors, sitting on the parapet, off to one side of him. When Jerry expresses concern for her safety, she answers, "I'm never dizzy," which says more than that she is not afraid of heights. This is a woman who has mastered her emotions so completely, up to this moment in the film, that she has succeeded in totally separating sex from love, and the game playing of social life from all of the unruly claims of the imagination. In the rather wooden iconography of the film, which fortunately proves inadequate to the complexities of experience and feeling within it, Capra has Jerry look up, while Kay looks down at the street. He silently stares at the stars, while she watches the lights and traffic of the city below, until he forces her to look up by delivering an idealistic peroration about escaping penthouse parties, cities, and society altogether. He expresses his desire for freedom in terms of "going to Arizona":

JERRY: Have you ever been to Arizona?
KAY: Furthest west I've been is Jersey City.
JERRY: Great place to live ... Arizona ... great place to paint. No skyscrapers to stake the horizon ... nothing but purple hills ... Even the stars seem closer. You can almost reach up and grasp the big dipper by the handle.

As the heightened language suggests, this is an unusually poetic expressive moment, even for an artist like Strong. (It is only in an especially important scene that Capra and cowriter Swerling would allow a character such a verbal indulgence as "stake the horizon" or risk the potential absurdity of the imaginative extravagance that concludes Jerry's speech. Capra was usually too afraid of his hardheaded audience's jeers to chance such direct expressions of

Social and meditative turns away from larger groups; also, the use of cinematic lighting to represent spiritual illumination.

exalted feeling. The comic reply to Jerry's first question that Kay is given suggests that he and Swerling may have hedged their bets a little, in their anxiety about the audience's tolerance of such flights of fancy.) What is most interesting about this scene, however, is how long it has taken the film to work up to it (*Ladies of Leisure* is approximately half over at this point), and how fleeting the moment proves to be.

Capra's work is replete with eruptions of personal idealism of this sort, but

just as here, they are invariably chastened by being located within dramatic narratives that always resist and delay, and frequently suppress their
expression altogether. What I left out of my account of the scene is that at
the very moment in which Jerry is delivering this speech to Kay, she is not
listening to him or even taking him seriously but only humoring him while
she ponders how she can seduce him. In putting a record on the gramophone, following Jerry out onto the balcony, and setting on the railing al-
luringly in front of him, she has been weaving a cunning web of entrapment,
which, other scenes in the film make clear, if successful, will culminate in
her blackmailing (or, in the slang of the day, "gold mining") this wealthy
young artist.

Not the least Emersonian (or Jamesian) aspect of *Ladies of Leisure* is its
refusal to cordon off Jerry's idealism from the deidealizing aspects of social and
sexual life. Jerry himself indeed attempts to maintain such a separation, but
Capra uses the figures of Kay and Jerry's railroad-magnate father (neither of
whom is satirized or dismissed in the least) to criticize Jerry's transcendentalism and to reimplicate him in just the sort of sexual and social relationships
from which he initially withdraws at the penthouse party. Capra cannot, in the
mode of Antonioni, Sternberg, or Fellini, responsibly imagine the transcendence of the pressures of society. This is the importance of the scene that
immediately follows Jerry's poetic speech. Because of the lateness of the hour
and a sudden rainstorm outside, Kay stays overnight in Jerry's apartment.
Capra forces Jerry into precisely the sort of potentially erotic relationship with
Kay that his holding her at a distance as his model and his abstract allegorical
painting of her as the figure of Hope would ignore. Following a very difficult
night, we next see them at breakfast together the following morning. What
follows is a scene that in its daytime, fill-lighted pedestrianism and emotional
awkwardness (Jerry burns his hand on a hot plate, drops his napkin, knocks
over a vase of flowers Kay has placed on the table, and, most important,
clumsily hurts her feelings with his inability to treat her more warmly and
lovingly) is the opposite of the key-lighted visionary scenes of her posing for
Jerry the night before.

It would be a misunderstanding of *Ladies of Leisure* to describe it exclusively
as a personal drama, however. It is about general expressive problems as much
as particular personal conflicts. For Capra the significant resistances to the
expression of our dreams are only marginally the result of the actions of other
people or of specific events in our lives. When Jerry's father threatens to dis-
inherit him and to have nothing more to do with him, Capra takes the threat
seriously but deals with it briefly in two scenes in which Jerry simply refuses to
yield to his father's demands that he break off with Kay. The threats to expression that most interest Capra are not external but are built into us, or built into
the nature of all society and all expression. That is to say, Jerry is prevented
from expressing his ideals artistically not by particular individuals but by
limiting constraints of all social and sexual forms of relationship, and nothing
can change that.

The chief shortcoming of the film is the inability of Ralph Graves, who plays Jerry, to express Jerry's complex feelings about his frustration, whereas Barbara Stanwyck is superbly able to express Kay's. That is perhaps why, in the second half of the movie, after the night they spend together in his studio, Stanwyck increasingly moves into the center of the film in her ability to communicate her confusion, her internal divisions of feeling about finally daring to love Jerry, to embrace his idealism, and to go off with him to live apart from family and friends in Arizona. In a series of nuanced scenes, Capra shows Kay, in her ambivalence, going to pieces.

Like "Handsome" Williams in *The Way of the Strong*, believing the world can never live up to her dream of a possible relationship, Kay renounces Jerry, while attempting to spare his feelings by keeping her renunciation secret from him (and preparing to run off to Havana with Bill Standish in order to turn Jerry against her once and for all). Capra shows her going to pieces dramatically by having her play a painful series of contradictory parts, to arrange her affairs properly before she goes: with Jerry's mother, secretly agreeing to give Jerry up; with her roommate, Dot, pretending she has only been gold digging Jerry and now just wants to get drunk and forget the whole experience; with Bill Standish, telling him that she would love to go to Havana with him, on a wild fling, after all; and with Jerry, pretending to be packing for their trip to Arizona.

Stanwyck's performance is a tour de force. As the whole preceding part of the film has documented and as she herself is fond of saying, "posing" has always been Kay's specialty. As long as one can remain sufficiently detached and cynical about the poses one assumes, there is no difference between being a girlfriend, a gold digger, or an artist's model. Kay's life has been an endless succession of playing roles, but this, significantly, is the first time that posing has become painfully difficult for her. In falling in love with Jerry, she has lost her performative freedom and imaginative mobility. In gaining a true identity for the first time by making a sincere emotional commitment, she has lost her chameleonlike capacity for quick changes. That is why this role playing, unlike all of the previous posing in which Kay earlier indulged, leads to her attempted suicide on the boat to Havana. To come into possession of a self for the first time is to have to face the harrowing prospect of self-disintegration for the first time, too. As he did in *The Way of the Strong*, Capra defines a forced choice between imaginative and worldly possession, but significantly, he cannot accept that as a final position and has Kay restored to Jerry after her suicide is unsuccessful.

Kay is rescued and, in the final scene of the film, reunited with Jerry in her hospital room. Jerry's final words in the film to her, as he bends over her body on the bed as she is just waking up, are "There's nothing to worry about," but both Capra and the viewer have their doubts. Jerry is optimistically suggesting that he and Kay are now finally free to be married and go off to live together in Arizona, but that is anything but obvious. Nothing has been resolved, and none of the questions that have been raised have been answered. Kay and Jerry are still imaginative outlaws from society and estranged from his family. Their dreams have destroyed their previous lives and alienated them from their friends and relatives but have provided nothing to replace them in the world. It may be possible for painters to turn away from the burdens of time, space, and society, at least in their art, but Capra has mounted a powerful argument in the final half hour of the film that it is not possible to escape these forces outside of a painting. As a narrative work of art, with its characters anchored in time and space and tangled up in social interactions, his film tells us the opposite of Jerry's palliative in every scene. Perhaps that is why one feels more than half exasperated with him by this point for his innocence about such complications, for still believing that he can live through his eye.

Jerry's optative escape into an unspecified, unformulated future in this final assurance that he and Kay can live in Arizona is a characteristic American imaginative movement. As Henry Adams suggests in "American Ideals," the sixth chapter of his great *History of the United States*, the Romantic "surmise" (as it appears in Keats and Shelley) has, in America, been domesticated. The American speculator and investor in futures turns away from the pure imaginative idealism of the second generation of English Romantic poets to entertain a much more practical relationship to time and space, not at all, Adams suggests, at odds with Wall Street or real estate practices. It is only natural that the British visitor (whose views Adams gleefully parodies in the following passage) should misunderstand all of this. He is the product of another, far less practical Romantic tradition and is unable to appreciate that the finest flowering of American idealism can be expressed in the desire to go West and possess the land in speculation against the future:

> Even on his practical and sordid side, the American might easily have been represented as a victim of illusion. If the Englishman had lived as the American speculator did – in the future – the hyperbole of enthusiasm would have seemed less monstrous. "Look at my wealth!" cried the American to his foreign visitor [in 1800]. "See these solid mountains of salt and iron, of lead, copper, silver, and gold! See these magnificent cities scattered broadcast to the Pacific! See my cornfields rustling and waving in the summer breeze from ocean to ocean, so fat that the sun itself is not high enough to mark where the distant mountains bound my golden seas! Look at this continent of mine, fairest of created worlds, as she lies turning up to the sun's never-failing caress her broad and exuberant breasts, overflowing with milk for her hundred million children! See how she glows with youth, health, and love!" Perhaps it was not altogether unnatural that the foreigner, on being asked to see what needed centuries to produce, should have looked about him with bewilderment and indignation. "Gold! cities! cornfields! continents! Nothing of the sort! I see nothing but tremendous wastes, where sickly men are dying of home-sickness or are scalped by savages! mountain-ranges a thousand miles long, with no means of getting to them, and nothing in them when you get there! swamps and forests choked with their own rotten ruins! nor hope of a better for a thousand years! Your story is a fraud, and you are a liar and a swindler!

It is just such categories of truth and falsehood, fairness and fraud that the American visionary attempts to leave behind. To live in the future, in ideals, dreams, and visions, to gesture always elsewhere, to suggest that Arizona is not a desert waste but a paradise for painting and that the dream is not only imaginable but actually livable in the world is to exempt oneself from the charge of being a liar, storyteller, or swindler. For a speculator, the possibilities are always open and unresolved, as they are in the speculative ending of this film.

Jerry's undaunted idealism and Kay's despair, in effect, leave us with two endings at the end of *Ladies of Leisure*, between which Capra, I believe, is unable to decide. The film ultimately leaves a viewer with more questions than answers. Can one escape the burdens of family, friends, history, and society? Can one live through the eye, as Jerry aspires to? Where can there be a home for a visionary, or is his or her only home in homelessness?* Can there be a society (even a society of two) that will not repress the visionary energy that aspires to "reach up and touch the stars"? In short, can there ever be an "I" that is able to express the imaginations and desires of the passional and visionary "eye"?

One can find Capra's awareness of how far he is from answering these questions in two aspects of the final scene between Jerry and Kay. First, Kay, previously a chatterbox, is strangely silent for the entire scene. It is as if Capra and Swerling (or Jerry and Kay) knew that one had to leave all social intercourse behind at this moment in order to make Jerry's visionary mumblings sound at all plausible. A single line of dialogue, a single minute of social interaction, would bring Jerry's dream of escape into too close contact with social realities that he wants and needs to wish away at this moment.

The second complicating aspect of the scene involves the fact that Kay is introduced in an unexpected tracking movement that moves slowly up her prone body from her bare feet to her face. Capra and Walker linger bizarrely on the soles of her feet for a beat or two longer than is necessary. It is the strangest tracking movement in all of Capra's work, but it is his attempt, in a film so devoted to urging the claims of the spirit, to remind us that the aspirations of the soul can never be separated from the reality of the sole. The physicality of Kay's exposed, uncostumed body reminds us how far we and she are from the transcendental condition of rising above physicality. As Capra knew as well as Eakins or Hopper, one can never, in a narrative film, a painting, or a life, express spirit except in terms of body, imagination except in terms of the necessarily restrictive forms of art, society, and biology.

* Kay expresses one form of Jerry's visionary impulse in leaping from the railing of the ship in her suicide attempt. Significantly, she looks at the stars just before she jumps. Suicide is one way to renounce her body, to become a perfect spirit.

9

Destinationless desire

Forbidden

Break off your association with your personality and identify yourself with the universe.

– Ralph Waldo Emerson, Journal, 1837

Only don't melt too much into the universe, but be as solid and dense and fixed as you can.

– Henry James, Letter to Grace Norton

Forbidden begins, as it were, where *Ladies of Leisure* left off, with Barbara Stanwyck attempting to escape her entire previous life and experience, with one impulsive trip to Havana, the land of romance. Stanwyck plays Lulu Smith, a mousy, frustrated, spinster who one day suddenly decides to change her life entirely and to dare to live her wildest dreams of romantic adventure. Lulu's act of self-transformation resembles that of the central characters in the two films immediately preceding *Forbidden* – Florence Fallon in *The Miracle Woman* and Stew Smith in *Platinum Blonde* – but it is more deliberate and daring than those of these others, since, unlike them, she herself is the sole author of her self-fashioning and in complete control of its effects.

She is a small-town librarian who one day decides to live what up until then she has only read about in books. She withdraws her life savings from the bank, reserves a passage on a luxury liner to Havana, costumes herself in furs and evening gowns, and scripts a stunning new role for herself in a play of her own creation. She will live the life of her imagination. She will make herself over as if she were a character in a film and transform life into art. In the first scene on the liner, Lulu is changed almost beyond recognition. Capra pointedly cuts from a fill-lighted shot of a frumpy librarian with wire-rimmed spectacles, severely drawn back hair, and plain clothing, to an elegantly key-lighted scene of a beautiful, gorgeously dressed woman making her entrance down a long, winding staircase to the ship's main dining room.

The theatrical quality of her transformation and of the scene that she is staging in this costume, making this elegant entrance, is deliberately played up, but Lulu Smith is no Lola Lola, and *Forbidden* is no Sternbergian fantasy. In the touchingly comic scene that follows, Capra shows how different life is from the movies. Lulu makes her grand entrance into the dining room, but then, like an actress on a difficult opening night or a leading lady insufficiently supported by the cast around her, her poise evaporates, as, seemingly under the scrutiny of every waiter and member of the band, she must undergo the embarrassment of being led to a table for one, to eat alone. (Capra turns the screw one more twist an instant later by having her suffer the embarrassment of thinking a handsome young gentleman is signaling to ask to join her when in fact he is gesturing to a group seated behind her.) Lulu is forced to realize that she cannot script a romantic drama with only one character in it.

She returns in shame to her stateroom, only to find another passenger, Robert Grover (Adolphe Menjou) asleep on her bed. It turns out that he has drunkenly mistaken her stateroom (Number 66) for his own (Number 99), but he is obviously as glad as she is to have this excuse to strike up an acquaintance, and the comical clumsiness of the initial mistake makes their friendship all the more charming. He is as hungry for love and romance as she, and they plunge headlong into a passionate, enchanted courtship.★

Almost as a literal fulfillment of Lulu's wish to erase her past life and identity and to live only in the fictions spun by her imagination, no names are exchanged. He is only "Number 99" and she "Number 66," as if all of history, biography, and the world outside their fictional reconstruction of it could be wished away. What neither of them knows is that the other is living a lie. Lulu is not the wealthy world traveler she pretends to be but someone who, Capra emphasizes in the rest of the film, will have to work every day of her life to scrape together every penny to pay for the smallest of her small pleasures. Bob is a married man, tied to an invalid wife he can never leave.

Havana cannot last forever, and in any case Capra never marks off a special, privileged space for love and imagination, at least not for a time longer than this enchanted, whirlwind courtship. The Sternbergian gauze shots, exotic settings, and romantic backlighting of the scenes on the beaches and in the nightclubs of Havana are joltingly superseded by a return to the States, and the confinement and dreary prosaicness of fill-lighted shots of the dingy, cluttered newspaper office where Lulu now works and of the high-pressure law office in which Bob Grover serves as city district attorney. Lulu has taken a job as a clerk for the newspaper in order to be near Bob, but neither is yet aware of the other's true identity. Lulu thinks Bob is a prosperous, unmarried attorney, and he believes that she is a well-off, independent woman. Capra creates a heart-rending series of pressures on both of them. Lulu is, unknown to Bob,

---

★ It is no accident that in this dream film and the one made in the following year, *Bitter Tea*, Capra chooses to have so many of the principal meetings and transactions between his central romantic couple take place while one or the other is lying down or just getting up from a sleeping position. *Forbidden*, like the subsequent *Lady for a Day* and *Bitter Tea*, might be thought of as one extended dream sequence, although it is the repeated waking up of the two lovers from their dreams that becomes the film's principal subject.

pregnant with his child and at the same time is being wooed by a reporter on her newspaper who knows nothing of her relationship with Bob. Bob is irrevocably married, not only because of his sense of responsibility to his invalid wife but also because he has large political ambitions that a divorce or even a hint of scandal would put an end to.

Capra jumps ahead to their meeting on a Halloween evening, in Lulu's apartment, a few months after their return from Havana. Each has independently decided that this night is to be a turning point in their relationship, a night on which they explain their real situations to each other, but it is typical of Capra that in this scene of highly charged emotions and powerful disclosures their mutual revelations emerge only indirectly. Howard Hawks has talked about Capra as the cinematic master of what he called the emotional "three-cushion shot" in which characters' feelings are expressed obliquely, through actions and words that are apparently unrelated to or, at times, in direct opposition to their true feelings.

Obliquity has gotten a bad name in a culture in which being "up front" has become a synonym for being honest and truthful. In Capra's universe, however, expression is always and necessarily mediated and therefore problematic; there can be no direct speaking of the emotional and imaginative states that he and his characters experience. Such states must always be mediated in various flawed, imperfect social forms. The ethic of frankness and directness denies the fundamental insight of all of his work – that social expression is always a rough, delayed, imperfect translation of something that cannot be expressed more immediately or directly. Thus when, in this scene, on Halloween night, he has both Bob and Lulu wearing Halloween masks when they meet and has them play games with them during most of their rendezvous, Capra is not attempting to score easy satiric points against them – say, by using the masks to symbolize the deceits and false identities in which each has indulged. He is telling us something about all communication, especially about all important, personal communication. It is always more or less a matter of masks, roles, and theatrical scenes that can betray us or hide us, even as they express us. Robert's and Lulu's ability to wear masks and to play creatively with them and their identities in general in this film is not a problem to be criticized; it is what makes them complex enough to interest Capra. To be unable or unwilling to wear a mask or play a role would be to lack the ability or the will to launch oneself on the adventure of performance that *Forbidden* takes as its subject.

Contemporary film criticism often elevates the psychological bluntness, "directness," and social "realism" of filmmakers like Ritt, Pakula, and Altman over the endless indirections in the films of Cassavetes, May, and Loden (or, to the extent that it accepts the work of the second group of filmmakers, it defines their characters' behavior as emotionally immature, false, evasive, or self-indulgent). The role playing in Capra's (or Cassavetes's) work, however, is not an evasion of something distinguishable from it that one might call "reality" or "life," which they are avoiding or covering up.

Their performances are not alternatives to life, reality, or truth, or evasions of them, any more than they are in the elliptical, litotic novels of Henry James or the multiple-voiced performances of the essays of Emerson or William James. Excesses and extravagances of performance, in art and in life, are the only way in which the fluxional movements of the creative imagination can be expressed. Not to perform in this way would be to have no imagination worth considering – in the sense that the characters of Ritt, Pakula, Allen, and most other "realistic" filmmakers for the most part have none. To have such an imagination is to be what I have called elsewhere a "figure of desire," who will not be expressed or comprehended by so-called realistic standards of consistency and coherence. These characters (whether they be Capra's, Cassavetes's, or Elaine May's in film, or Sam Shepard's on stage) are defined· not in terms of fixed qualities, goals, or motivations but as principles of movement and unregimented energy. To be a figure of desire, an identity liberated to an infinitely plastic responsiveness to the movements of the imagination, is to have no simpler or more direct way to express oneself, and certainly to be unable to confine one's expression to the forms of action and dialogue that fall within what is called realism.

That is why these characters so frequently resemble artists in their own right and their performances mimic the improvisatory inventiveness and spontaneity of actors acting or directors directing. The evening of Bob's visit, Capra shows Lulu bustling around her apartment precisely like an actor or stage manager on opening night, arranging the scene as deliberately as Capra himself did as the director or Stanwyck did as the actress. Bob makes his way down the street to Lulu's apartment exactly like a nervous leading man and at one point tries to find a prop that will help him "sell" his meaning (he buys flowers). Capra is not employing some facile metaphor, such as "Life is like the movies" or "All the world's a stage" – metaphors that implicitly elevate the structurings of art over those of life – but is, in fact, suggesting the opposite hierarchial relationship between art and life. Assertively theatrical performances in film, in all their intricacy and obliquity, are only representations of the imaginative mobility and expressive obliquity of our ordinary lives. They are not privileged ways of acting, not the special property of works of drama. The expressive complexities that make film or theater moving are continuous with the expressive complexities of everyday life.

The pantomime performance in Lulu's apartment is affecting not only because of what is unable to be spoken or otherwise communicated between these two people in love but even more for what their silence and evasions communicate all too well. Bob, wearing a Halloween mask, knocks at the door, announcing himself as a census taker. Lulu replies that she has lost her senses long ago. He hands her a mask he has bought for her, and they act out a brief pantomime of passionate love. Then Lulu escorts him into the kitchen and puts on a pantomime "magic" show of what a fine wife and homemaker she would make, by making food "appear" in the oven and on the stove. Bob matches her "trick" by making the flowers he has bought for her magically "appear" in the dumbwaiter. Then they return together to the living room and again pantomime their affection for each other. Even when they eventually remove their masks, Capra has them only slide them onto the tops of their heads, as if not to let them or us forget the ambiguity of their situations and their confused, mixed-up identities. The pantomime is brilliant enough to do any of Capra's silent films proud and eloquently communicates both the failure of intimacy between them, the unbridgeable gap that separates them, and the anxious effort on both sides to attempt to bridge it by exploring a way to "play" together some way or other.

There is a falling out that night, but after the birth of Lulu's daughter, whom she names Roberta, after Bob, he and Lulu are eventually reunited. To simplify what is perhaps Capra's most intricate plot, Roberta is adopted by Bob and his wife without his wife's discovering the child's true identity, and Lulu Smith lives her life alone, slinking from one shabby apartment to another, as the "other woman," in the shadow of Robert and his wife and her own daughter. The Jamesian principle of a central character's "having gained nothing from the entire affair" could never be more aptly illustrated. Over the twenty- or thirty-year period of the story, from her blooming youth to her haggard old age, Lulu is Bob's devoted mistress, confidante, counselor, and closest friend. Living in cheap apartments, able to see Robert only furtively and fugitively at night, Lulu lovingly follows his rise in politics from district attorney to governor of the state but is never able to stand in the limelight with him and never able to meet him in public for fear of wrecking his career. It is a sordid, sneaking life for her, and one of hypocrisy, guilt, and self-hatred for Bob, but what distinguishes *Forbidden* from a film like *Back Street* (which it resembles in plot) is that Capra does not want to condemn Bob, or, worse yet, elicit our sympathy for Lulu's suffering. He seems to suggest, especially in the case of Lulu, in the Jamesian sense, that to have gotten nothing at all may actually be to have gained everything.

One can imagine the automatic rejection a statement like this might provoke according to contemporary feminist standards of treatment. Here is a woman content to have become a virtual slave to a man, to have utterly renounced everything in the world – from possession of her own child to the merest public acknowledgment of her true status – and Capra is in some way (without in the least overlooking all of these deprivations, of which he repeatedly reminds us) endorsing her situation, even finding a possible redeeming value in it. As always, Capra refuses to confine his analysis of a relationship to the conventional "social" or "realistic" aspects, insisting that we recognize the equal reality of the imagination, a reality as substantial as the reality of economics, politics, or law.

In his first serious conversation with Lulu (on the Havana-bound ship) Bob tells of having "a worm" of desire and ambition eating away within him. He says he wants to make something grand of his life; he wants to live an adventure larger than anything he has found in "reality " up to that point. It is his worm that ultimately drives him into politics and propels him from one political office to another. It is his worm of unappeasable desire that drives him to want to possess Lulu as well, even though he is already, by conventional standards, a happily married man. *Forbidden*, in effect, takes as its subject the worm, the hunger, the desires that both he and Lulu feel within themselves. That defines a reality for them greater than any aggregation of nominally realistic facts or events.

Forbidden is a study of the reality created by desire and imagination and of their capacity to deform, enrich, or substitute themselves in place of what in another sort of film would be a fixed and immutable sociological or economic reality. The reality Capra cinematically validates is the reality of movements of imagination, the reality of stylistic transformations of space and time, reconstructions of the world and society in our dreams. This is not in the least to deny or overlook the outrageousness of this effort, nor does Capra for that matter. It is only to argue that it cannot be dismissed or criticized as a mere failure of cinematic "realism."

James and Welty work their comparable effects with language, but as a filmmaker Capra works with sounds and with images in the visual sense. *Forbidden* is one of Capra's (or Joseph Walker's) earliest full-fledged experiments with attempting to bring into existence this alternative reality of imagination and desire by means of special effects of lighting and photography.★ *Forbidden* attempts to create a stylistic environment that shows that despite the worldly impoverishment and deprivation in Lulu's and Bob's lives there is still an imaginative and emotional gain and enrichment. The achievement of the film is to balance one side of the ledger against the other, especially in the case of Lulu's life, which is detailed with more care than Grover's – to keep before us at one and the same time the poverty of her social and public life and the richness of her imaginative and emotional life.

The last half hour of *Forbidden* tallies Lulu's worldly and social losses as unblinkingly as it registers her imaginative profits. There is a kind of visual paradox in the final movement of the film: Precisely to the degree that Lulu's imaginative existence is increasingly felt, she becomes less and less socially and physically present in it. As her imaginative influence and power expands on screen, her image disappears from the screen. About halfway through the film, Lulu is promoted into being an advice-to-the-lovelorn columnist at her newspaper. She flourishes in the assignment, celebrating in her columns the possibility of a pure, transcendental love between man and woman, but Capra makes a point in his editing of this passage of the film to underline the fact that at this moment of imaginative glory not only does she cease to exist as Lulu Smith (to become "Mary Sunshine" in her column), but her image is replaced

---

★ *The Miracle Woman*, made six months earlier, is equally complex visually. Of Capra's other early work before *Forbidden* and *The Miracle Woman*, although *That Certain Thing*, *Ladies of Leisure*, and *Platinum Blonde* have an occasionally interesting effect, none of them uses light systematically to indicate states of imaginative heightening in the way those two films – and the later *Bitter Tea* and *It Happened One Night* – do.

on-screen by detail shots of her typed words on the page, as if she has ceased to have any physical identity at all.

At another point in the film, when Bob finally runs for the governorship, Capra makes it clear through his editing again that Lulu is, of all the people around him, the one most imaginatively intimate with Grover at this moment. She reads his speeches in advance and gives him advice on them, and probably even helps to type and write them in the first place – and yet she is absolutely socially or physically absent from all of the shots in which he appears on screen. She lives only through his speeches and ad lib comments, and has utterly no existence in his campaign in a more tangible way. As the final shots of the convention show, to be imaginatively closest to Grover is to be physically farthest from him: he sits on stage surrounded by family and friends, while Lulu sits watching him, almost invisible and lost in the crowd.

One of the most striking visual expressions of Capra's equation of spiritual presence and physical absence is in a shot very early in the film showing Lulu and Grover riding horses together on the beach in Havana. In a brilliantly lighted shot of the ocean and sand, photographed looking in the direction of the sun, Walker stops down his lens so that the dazzling light, water, and sand get adequate exposure but Lulu and the speeding horse she rides become only a dark blot on the screen. She is a galloping, passional presence who is a literal absence, a gaping, energetic, black hole in the picture, an opening out of society and what is realistically photographable.* That is what she will be throughout the film – an imaginative presence that is more powerful because of her "realistic" absence, self-abnegation, and willed self-removal. A photograph of Bob and Lulu together in Havana that Lulu carries with her everywhere to remind her of their enchanted time together is prominently displayed in each of the apartments in which she lives. It is, however, a photograph that, significantly, refers to *nothing whatever* that we saw her and Robert doing in the scenes in Havana. The snapshot has only an imaginative relationship to any reality we have encountered in the film. In Capra's commentary on photographic nostalgia, the event commemorated by the photograph exists for us and for Lulu only in the vision and memory of it, not in any worldly fact that it commemorates, since it commemorates none.

In the initial scenes in Havana, Lulu was splendidly costumed in evening gowns and furs. The splendor of her clothing represented the possibility that she could find concrete expression for her dreams in the form of worldly (and cinematic) glamour and theatricality. As *Forbidden* continues, however, that possibility recedes. All that Havana represents – romance, glamour, excitement, and adventure – eventually exists only in her imagination. There is no way in which she can express it or live it in the world. Lulu's achievement was always only a stylistic one, but initially it was enactable in the styles of society:

---

* Horse-shy Stanwyck was not, in fact, actually on horseback in any of these scenes, but since they are photographed in long-shot there would have been many other ways for Capra and Walker to conceal her absence. What they choose to do is not to conceal it but to celebrate it – to celebrate film's capacity to offer imaginative substitutions as replacements for worldly absences.

in ways of dressing and talking, in social and theatrical activities (like those on Halloween) involving others. As the film goes on, however, it becomes imaginable or attainable only as an achievement of pure consciousness. There finally is and can be nothing in the world to sustain or express Lulu's vision. That is the necessary tragedy of her situation as far as Capra is concerned (and his unconscious link with the work of Carl Dreyer, whose conception of Anne and Gertrud is strikingly similar to Capra's of Lulu).★

Lulu gradually disengages herself from the world, living increasingly in her imagination, her photographs, her books, her writing. The former librarian who had initially attempted to live the life expressed in writing, retreats back to become a writer and reader herself. She renounces worldly involvements and dresses more and more austerely and severely, changing from the sequined, satiny whites of the evening gowns of the Havana trip to the mournful plain black dresses she wears at the end. As her clothes become less and less cinematically present or splendidly representable in plays of light, her body as well begins to disappear from the screen as a sensuous presence. By the end of the film her hair is silvery, and her face is a pale, impassive, leathery mask. (She in effect becomes the Halloween mask she wore earlier.) Yet as she lives and expresses herself less and less in the world, less and less attracts the gaze of the camera and becomes more silent, she becomes more and more alive and energetic imaginatively.

That, I take it, is the only justification for what is certainly the weakest scene in the film, and one that Capra must have had powerful reasons for including, not only because it is so melodramatically bad but because it is so different from his normal cinematic practice. It is the scene near the end of *Forbidden* in which Lulu unexpectedly murders Al Holland (Ralph Bellamy), Bob Grover's nemesis and tormentor throughout the film, in order to save Bob from having his affair with Lulu revealed publicly. It is an overwrought, implausible, hysterical scene that is dramatically indefensible, except for one aspect of it. The lurid, expressionistic lighting on Lulu's face, the blood on her lip where Holland has struck her, the gunshots with which she replies to his threat to expose her relationship with Grover and ruin his career, and the bizarre camera angles with which Capra arranges the scene make explicit what was only more or less implicit in the previous scenes: We are in the world not of psychological, social, or any other form of realism, but of melodrama (in a nonpejorative sense of the word). I will have much more to say about Capra's use of melodrama in subsequent discussions of *Mr. Deeds Goes to Town, Mr. Smith Goes to Washington,* and *It's a Wonderful Life,* but suffice it to point out for now

---

★ We have encountered this inverse relationship between the imagination and the world already in the renunciations and forced choices of the endings of *The Way of the Strong* and *Ladies of Leisure. Dirigible* and *Platinum Blonde,* among the films preceding *Forbidden,* have a similar renunciatory impulse at work in them, and many of Capra's subsequent films, including even "comedies" like *It Happened One Night* and *Lady for a Day,* can be understood in similar terms. The renunciation of social expression and physical presence explicitly articulated in *Forbidden* haunted Capra's work.

that Capra uses melodramatic events and stagings in particular scenes like this one in order to attempt to represent states of consciousness for which no form of social or realistic expression is adequate. With the exception of the sound of the gunshots and of a radio playing in the background, like so many of the other crucial scenes in Capra's early films (compare some of the central scenes in *That Certain Thing*, *Ladies of Leisure*, and *The Younger Generation*), the murder scene is, significantly, silent. No language, no dialogue, no form of social exchange is capable of expressing the state of heightened consciousness Capra wishes to evoke and that Lulu finally represents in the film. Only the excess, the violence, the luridness of sheer melodrama will "speak" these meanings.

When Lulu does finally speak in the scene following the murder years later, following her release from prison for it, as Bob Grover is dying and she palely hovers over his deathbed like the dream specter she has become, it is, not surprisingly, only to lose herself in more memories of the long-past Havana vacation. Grover dies, and in the next scene, which concludes the film, as Lulu moves away down the street, alone with her memories, Capra has the camera dolly back from her, and she literally disappears before our eyes as she walks into a crowd. In gaining an imagination, she loses her self in any worldly or social sense of the word.

Near the end of *Ladies of Leisure*, when Kay asks Bill Standish what "living in Arizona" means to him, he replies, "Deserts," but of course to Jerry Strong living in Arizona is the opposite of that. New York society is the desert, but Arizona represents the richness and luxury of endless vision. *Forbidden*, in effect, lets Lulu Smith live her adult life in the imaginative Arizona to which Kay and Jerry were bound at the end of their film. Is it a desert waste and an arid emptiness, or is it a place of visionary richness, plenitude, and imaginative fertility? Is to live by the light of the stars to be chilly and homeless or to be inspired? We know how Jerry Strong would answer the question. We know how Lulu Smith would answer it. Capra, though, on the evidence of *Forbidden*, is still profoundly ambivalent.

10

Enrichments of consciousness

The Bitter Tea of General Yen

> Dream delivers us to dream, and there is no end to illusion. Life is a train of moods like
> a string of beads, and as we pass through them they prove to be many-colored lenses
> which paint the world their own hue, and each shows only what lies in its focus ... Of
> what use is genius, if the organ is too convex or too concave and cannot find a focal
> distance within the actual horizon of human life?
>
> – Ralph Waldo Emerson, "Experience"

Ladies of Leisure and *Forbidden* are, in an unpejorative sense of the term, films
about escapism. Like almost all of Capra's work of the early thirties, they are
set in stylistic and social environments that Capra and the central characters
(usually a man and a woman paired romantically) labor for virtually the entire
narrative to break free of imaginatively. Particular scenes within them document moments of success during which the harsher "realistic" social and
stylistic environment is briefly transcended or transformed· through the
character's imaginative efforts. They are, in this respect, largely negative or
decreative films that spend much of their energy anatomizing particular social
structurings of experience, prior to clearing a small space for the expansions of
consciousness of their central romantic pairs. Capra's next film, *The Bitter Tea
of General Yen,* simply leaves most such alien or hostile social arrangements
behind, after acknowledging them in its opening scenes, and becomes a study
of the would-be liberated consciousness of its central couple. The narrative
thus represents less an act of criticism of specific social structurings of experience, and more a wholesale rejection of them and an attempt to imagine an
alternative environment within which the imagination can be freely expressed.

Capra's films, as I have argued, usually begin with a rupture of some sort,
but *Bitter Tea*, significantly, goes farther than the films that immediately
preceded it. *Ladies of Leisure* began with a penthouse party that suggested a
society on the verge of chaos and breakdown.* *Forbidden* began with a small-

---

* As Capra does in *Doe* also, he literalizes the abstract rupture by representing it in terms of a
  series of actual breakages in the opening scene in which a group of girls smash champagne
  bottles by throwing them off the penthouse roof.

town librarian unsuccessfully attempting to repudiate her previous life. In *Bitter Tea*, complete social collapse has already occurred before the film even starts. It begins in a world in which social arrangements have, apparently, already disintegrated.* Through the flickering light and smoke of bonfires we can make out the outlines of a scene of civil war and anarchy. Sinkiang Province in China is in revolution. Buildings are burning. Peasants are looting. The entire opening sequence has the poor lighting, muddled compositions, and editorial disjunctions of newsreel footage. (Even the initial intertitles announcing the place and date are meant to remind a viewer of the experience of watching a newsreel.) We are denied not only the well-lighted sets and glamorous characters of a Hollywood feature film but even the implicit stability of feature-film framing, photography, and shot–reverse-shot editing patterns. The cinematic message is clear: This is a world of newsreel intensity and confusion, which tests both our emotional and our intellectual powers of grasping it.

As we gradually make out in the poor lighting, all is not chaos: Some of the movement in the darkness, rain, and tumult is apparently purposeful. A parade of rickshaws, carriages, and automobiles is stopping in front of a gate. A group of British missionaries and their wives are making their way into a bizarrely out-of-place English house in the middle of the riot-torn Chinese streets. They are being greeted at the front door by an eminently proper British hostess. We are suddenly and half comically projected into the entirely incongruous physical and imaginative world of wickets, tea and crumpets,

---

* It is tempting, though ultimately unproductive, I think, to generalize about the effect of the depression on Capra's mind and work. One could talk about the social ruptures in these films as being connected with the specific economic and social dislocations of American society at the time they were made. One could also relate Capra's skepticism of reigning systems of social value and meaning to the imaginatively alienating effects of the derailing of the American dream in the depression. The visionary aspects of the films could then be understood as a manifestation of a general desire to escape economic and social problems by projecting oneself into fantasy situations.

There are, however, two specific problems with such an approach as well as a more general conceptual fallacy. First, films like *That Certain Thing, The Way of the Strong,* and *The Younger Generation* indicate that Capra's basic attitudes antedate the economic and social collapses of the depression. Second, there is evidence throughout all of Capra's work that his concerns resonate with those of many other American artists who are completely unassociated with this particular historical event. This is not to argue that the depression did not influence Capra in any way, only that such an "explanation," actually begs the question to be answered, which is why the depression had *this particular influence* on Capra or other American artists of the period. That is the conceptual problem of invoking the depression as an explanation of anything. If the depression influenced Capra's or any other artist's work – as it undoubtedly did – the question of why it sponsored "American dreaming," "escapism," and "wish-fulfillment fantasies" is still unanswered, since comparable economic and social dislocations in Spain, Germany, France, Italy, and England at the same time did not result in the advent of a Capra in those countries or in the sorts of art produced in America in the thirties. One must always return to an understanding of the culture in question. The historical facts, as always, do not explain anything in themselves until we understand how those facts are interpreted by a particular artist in a particular culture.

and garden parties on the lawn. Every British missionary in Sinkiang, it seems, has turned out for the wedding of Robert Strike, one of their youngest but "most promising" colleagues. When, as the latest couple arrives, our hostess happily boasts, "Everybody in China is here, absolutely everybody!" nothing more need be said to make Capra's point. Her tone says it all. If this is a conception of "everybody" that excludes almost everybody (most notably the hordes of half-naked peasants we see running for their lives not one hundred feet away from her front door), it is all the more poised and secure because of its extraordinary selectivity. *Bitter Tea* is organized as a series of Chinese boxes or psychic compartments nestled one within the other. We have entered the first of them in the film, a secret island of order and stability in a sea of confusion. One builds such fences, walls, and boxes around oneself to control or contain the mess of the world. By giving us such a powerful glimpse of that other, alien world to start with, Capra makes us feel not the solidity but the lacquered thinness of these walls, their artificiality, and their fragility in the middle of this encroaching confusion.

Just as Joseph Walker's camera work in the newsreel footage conspired to render the chaos outside in a style that would do justice to it, by momentarily abrogating Academy principles of framing, lighting, and camera positioning, this scene of emotional placidity and intellectual insipidity is deliberately rendered with a vacant and neutral style of photography and lighting. In contrast to the documentary underexposure and alternately thrilling and threatening compositional confusion of the external shots, the house is lighted in the best and blandest British cinematic style (exemplified today in television's *Masterpiece Theater*). It is exactly the style that these dutiful subjects of the Queen would insist upon as their God-given right to be boring. In place of the flickering flames and shadows that we saw in the street, the rooms are illuminated with an evenly distributed light, feathered from the ceiling down, defining a homogenized world with no shadows and no depths, a well-lighted fishbowl for timid, tedious, colorless inhabitants. The rooms, decorated as if Picadilly Circus and not the Chinese civil war were just outside the lace-curtained windows (complete with grandfather clock, crystal chandeliers, and patterned wallpaper), are as superficially tasteful and pretty, as devoid of idiosyncrasy as a display in a furniture store. To be British is bad enough, Capra seems to say, but to be one of the expatriated British middle class, denied both the glamour and excesses of the true aristocracy, on the one hand, and the coarse vitality of the Dickensian underclass on the other, is to be one of the truly lost souls. David Lean and the Korda brothers knew that much more than Ronald Neame about the structural strengths and weaknesses of their own tradition and about the smug tiresomeness of the middle class.

In short, this is an interior in which everything possible has been done to wall out imaginative, emotional, and cultural disturbance. Of the vast range of experience that is being repressed from consciousness, there is only the faintest visible sign, in the presence of an oriental choir, two oriental houseboys, and the vaguely oriental tracery of the staircase bannister – or do these vestiges of the alien culture only all the more powerfully communicate how its energies have been tamed and domesticated? The tuxedoed Chinese choir singing "Onward Christian Soldiers" in the parlor, revealed in a subsequent shot, is more than an instance of Capra's wit. It is a succinct expression of the incorporation of even utterly alien energies into the comprehensive hygienic enterprise of making the world safe for the British Empire.

I emphasize the Britishness of the scene in order to put in its proper context the fact that the central character, Megan Davis (Barbara Stanwyck), the bride due to arrive any moment, is emphatically not an Old but a New Englander. She is, as one of the matrons breathlessly tells another, a daughter of the "finest old Puritan family in New England, my dear." To notice her alien background is to see that she takes her place alongside the central figures of *Ladies of Leisure* and *Forbidden* as an outsider to the group in which she finds herself, and is therefore at least potentially able to open herself to experiences beyond the confines of these four walls and the limits they so clearly demarcate.

Megan's capacity to move imaginatively is expressed throughout the film, as Stew Smith's was in *Platinum Blonde*, in her ability to move physically – across boundaries and walls – and tonally – beyond, for example, the limitations of habitual inflections like those of her hostess or the others who cluck over her in the Strike house. In the course of the film Megan will be associated with movements across walls and barriers (at first only physical in nature and then gradually psychological), even as, during the beginning and middle of the film, she is guilty of barricading herself behind emotional walls of her own construction. Her slow, painful progress will be measured by her ability to move beyond not just the physical, but all of the social and intellectual walls represented by the missionary house. After hearing about her from the staid, housebound missionaries, we significantly first meet Megan outside, and not standing still, as they are, but in motion. She is getting down from her rickshaw in the middle of a chaotic street. On her way to the wedding ceremony, her rickshaw boy has been hit by a car and, although her missionary escort advises her not to get involved and wants her not to stop, she chooses to thrust herself into contact with the world of the street. The man who has accidentally hit the boy, in the darkness and confusion of the mob scene, is the strange, enigmatic General Yen (Nils Asther), with whom Megan's destiny will be intertwined in the rest of the film. When she finally arrives at the Strike residence, Megan initially attempts to shut him out of her consciousness, just as those around her advise, but she does not succeed. While she is dressing upstairs, her hostess tries to expunge the encounter with a typically categorical dismissal: "They're all tricky, treacherous and immoral. They're all Chinamen to me. I can't tell one from the other." Megan, though, has lived through an opening night that will not be so easily repressed.

Her second movement outside protective walls occurs only minutes later. Robert Strike, her husband-to-be, arrives at the house only to announce that the wedding must be delayed for a few hours while he evacuates an orphange that civil strife has suddenly engulfed. Megan breaks a sexual role barrier by insisting that she go with him. When they arrive at the orphanage she performs under duress with a cool aplomb, but one gradually recognizes that her mechanical dutifulness and poise under pressure is itself only a psychological version of the barriers that the others at the Strike residence have erected. Puritanical stoicism and New England toughness, like the proverbial British stiff upper lip, are ways of coping with confusion by walling out emotional involvement. Her plea to the director of the orphanage, who does not want to risk carrying the children through the mobs outside – "Oh please, Miss Reed, we ought to do what Bob says" – like her other acts of mindless obedience, as her future husband directs their progress from the orphanage to the train station, epitomizes the unthinking subservience that Megan will have to unlearn.

Separated momentarily from her fiancé and struggling for a rickshaw at the mobbed train station, Megan is knocked unconscious in a scuffle, and the final step of her triple physical movement outside of the missionary world is taken. Even more explicitly than the earlier two, this third movement demonstrates Capra's metaphoric use of spatial movement in the film. Megan is rescued by General Yen, carried aboard his waiting train, and whisked out of the war-torn city, back to the secluded safety of his summer palace, but her real journey into the interior, Capra wants us to realize, is a psychological one. From this point on *Bitter Tea* becomes a dream movie that carries Megan and its viewers into a Sternbergian world of art and artifice, at the furthest remove from its gritty documentary beginning. The crucial "passages" in Megan's life, and the central scenes in the film from here on, will be, literally and metaphorically, passages from states of dreaming to states of waking, and back again. Megan may be capable of energetic and inventive physical and social movement early in the film, but she is still locked behind a series of psychological walls at this point. The rest of the movie is devoted to encouraging her to break down the mental and emotional barriers in her life, and one way to do this, Capra suggests, is for her to open herself up to the power of dreams. (It is the same metaphor he used in *That Certain Thing*.) Our dreams represent texts of desire in its most intense and unmediated form, and what Capra is telling us in this dream film is that Megan will have to find some way to let those dream energies into her waking life. In the metaphors of the film, she will have to learn to open doors that are normally kept closed and to move through secret passages between areas of feeling and experience that are normally walled off from each other and kept separate. She will have to open up and explore nestled Chinese boxes of experiences ordinarily closed off from each other. It is not accidental that Capra signals Megan's first major "trans-ition" in the film (literally: her "moving across") with her being knocked unconscious and experiencing a period of delirium. As each of the many subsequent scenes of dreaming, meditation, or reverie that punctuate the film suggests, Megan's passage occurs initially as a result of her having her conscious mind subdued and letting other forms of knowledge and experience into her life.

Capra uses a series of lap dissolves and a distorted musical sound track to represent her delirium as, disoriented and confused, she wakes up on General Yen's train a few minutes later. In those minutes, in both cinematic and psychological terms, we and Megan have already traveled worlds away from the bland, well-lighted universe of the Strike residence. She finds herself lying on an oriental divan, covered with a silk kimono, watched over by Yen and his concubine Mah-Li, in a space as opulently and exotically appointed as the Strike residence was barren and conventional. The train is speeding into the Chinese interior, away from Sinkiang, and Megan is speeding headlong into a brave new psychological world where all the certainties of her past experience no longer apply. She awakens (in both senses of the word) to a physical and tactile splendor and sensuality, communicated in a high-chiaroscuro lighting. Back at the Strike residence, even her reunion with her husband-to-be, after three years of separation from him, had none of this romantic aura. It took place in the same dull surroundings, lighted and photographed in the same flat way. The key lighting in this scene on the train, however, reminds us of the flickering lighting of the street scenes earlier. It incorporates some of the exotic, alien energy of those scenes, but the energies have been domesticated and brought indoors. The revolutionary excitement of those scenes has been transformed into the imaginative excitement of the state of emotional revolution into which Megan is plunged.

The scene on the train is brief. Few words are spoken between Yen and Megan before she falls back asleep on the couch, but the purpose of these few seconds is to make the viewer aware that this is a world in which the number of words spoken is much less important than another sort of event. Back in the Strike residence, hollow social chatter, gossip, and anecdote communicated all the meaning there was, but as Capra indicates in the passage of editing that concludes the train scene, Yen inhabits a world in which glances, stares, and silent looks carry meanings that words cannot. In a sequence of cuts whose effect can only be roughly suggested by verbal itemization, Megan looks at Yen; Yen looks at Mah-Li; Mah-Li looks at Megan; Megan looks at Mah-Li; Mah-Li looks at Yen; Yen looks at Mah-Li and then lets his eyes roll back as he falls asleep; Mah-Li looks back at Yen and then starts to fall asleep; and, finally, Megan looks back at Yen and Mah-Li and finally allows herself to fall back to sleep. No words are spoken in the entire series of eight counterpointed glances. Indeed, there is nothing to say that could communicate the mystery, intensity, and richness of meaning that these glances convey. In their silent emotionality we can measure the extraordinary distance we have traveled beyond the glib prolixity, polite verbal formulations, and social chitchat of the Strikes.

One is reminded of the immense importance of silent staring in Henry James's writing. Isabel Archer's one fleeting glance at Madame Merle and Gilbert Osmond together in a room significantly "says" volumes more to her than all the polished, brilliant, witty talk, talk, talk of the rest of *The Portrait of a Lady*. Maggie Verver's glances at Charlotte and the Prince "speak" to her and to them as no words ever could in *The Golden Bowl*. Strether's visions in *The Ambassadors* more than anything else communicate the utter impossibility and futility of ever translating them into the forms of social discourse. Or perhaps a comparison with Hawthorne is even more apt. In their climactic scenes stories like "The Wives of the Dead," "The Canterbury Pilgrims" and "Young Goodman Brown" turn on the possibilities of a glance or a look that cuts through all of the pretenses, falsities, gaps, and failures of communication so amply otherwise documented in their plots and passages of dialogue. The crucial moment in "The Canterbury Pilgrims" can stand for all of the others. It involves a married couple who have long ago lost the spark of life and feeling in their relationship, but Hawthorne suggests that a glance could still bring it back:

> As she ceased, the yeoman and his wife exchanged a glance, in which there was more and warmer affection than they had supposed to have escaped the frost of a wintry fate, in either of their breasts. At that moment, when they stood on the utmost verge of married life, one word fitly spoken, or perhaps one peculiar look had they had mutual confidence enough to reciprocate it, might have renewed all their old feelings, and sent them back, resolved to sustain each other amid the struggles of the world.

The glance opens up buried or lost imaginative possibilities that are expressible in no other way except in the fugitiveness of a look shared by an old married couple (in "The Canterbury Pilgrims"), in a glance and a shout exchanged at the last possible minute between Robin and his wife Faith (in "Young Goodman Brown"), or in a tender, silent gesture of sympathy between Mary and Margaret (in "The Wives of the Dead"), and, above all, expressible chiefly in the strange heightenings and intensifications of Hawthorne's prose that accompany all of these moments. His writing in these scenes, like the glance that did or did not but might have taken place, becomes as overcharged with otherwise inexpressible possibilities of meaning as the imagined, potential, silent, visionary, glancing look. Hawthorne himself as a writer is stimulated at these moments into generating and entertaining imaginative possibilities that have, literally, no other avenue of expression in terms of dialogue or event. That is why, in order to make an imaginative space for these possibilities in his paragraph, he has to suspend dialogue and plot. As the example from "The Canterbury Pilgrims" demonstrates, he has to stop the social and narrative progress of his story in order to register another entirely different form of possible imaginative progress within it.

As the immediate continuation of the passage I have quoted indicates, in Hawthorne such possibilities typically open only almost immediately to close down again with a finality that is utterly chilling in its inexorability:

> But the crisis passed and never came again. Just then, also, the children, roused by their mother's voice, looked up, and added their wailing accents to the testimony borne by all the Canterbury pilgrims against the world from which they fled.
> "We are tired and hungry!" cried they. "Is it far to the Shaker village?"

The doors of the prison house of society, and the burdens of biological and social responsibilities have closed down again, finally and harrowingly, around the couple for whom such marvellous and thrilling imaginative possibilities were momentarily entertained. The jolting return to direct quotation – to dialogue and narrative eventfulness – those staples of the "realistic," "social" story or novel, constitutes Hawthorne's own statement about the relentless repressiveness of narrative form itself. That return to direct quotation tells us that it is only by the greatest effort that a narrative, even one as tentative and self-conscious about its own potential formal repressiveness as his own, can be sprung away from the orthodox forms of narrative and social organization for even as long as he manages to do it in the first half of the passage.

The intensified editing rhythms that accompany the silent glances that take place between characters in Capra's films and the special effects of lighting and photography that he has recourse to at such otherwise "uneventful" moments are the exact equivalent of Hawthorne's prose heightenings at points of narrative stalling. In the series of silent glances in *Bitter Tea*, Megan, like the viewer, gazes into a world she apparently has never glimpsed before. She has an experience different from the dutiful busyness of rescuing needy orphans or bustling about converting "tricky, treacherous brutes." She and we are learning a lesson that is at the heart of Capra's film – a lesson in silent looking, in the potential power of the glance, the power of the picture. She and we are being educated to see, perhaps for the first time. The eight-cut editing sequence lasts less than a minute and generates no important action. (The three characters simply fall asleep at the end of the scene.) All that "happens" in the course of it is that Megan adjusts her dress and the kimono covering her on the divan to cover a little more of her legs, which were exposed in her sleep. That is not much in the way of action – but it is everything in terms of cinematic and worldly vision. It is an opening onto a world of sensual and sexual experience beyond what was present in any of the scenes at the Strike house.★

Yen and his domain are repeatedly associated with erotic possibilities. In the street scene in which we and Megan first meet him, he is riding in his car with a mysterious woman (Mah-Li). In the second scene in which we see him, Robert Strike comes to his headquarters to ask for safe-conduct through the city to the orphanage. Yen is watching dancing girls when Strike enters and immediately begins teasing the prudish missionary with a decidedly sexual offer to show the girls to him. However, if Yen represents sexual energies that the priggish missionary and the British community apparently exclude from their lives, he also represents a capacity for imaginative performance that is far more than merely sexual.

★ If Megan's pulling down her dress and the shawl that initially only half covers her exposed legs does not seem like much of an erotic event by today's standards, one has to remember that this is a woman who paused to put her hat on before she went downstairs to greet the fiancé she had not seen for three years. As Capra delicately orchestrates it, even the gradual loosening of Megan's hair becomes an important erotic event in the course of the film.

Yen is the character for whom Capra's cinema had been waiting – the culmination of all of the most imaginative performers in the previous films. When he teases Strike, asking him whether he is "curious about the sing-song girls," or later in the film when, after one of his advisers tells him not to flirt with Megan because she is a white woman, he replies that he is "not prejudiced about color," he displays an iconoclastic wit as playful as that of Stew Smith.* When, to make a point, Yen makes a superbly underplayed dramatic gesture (sticking his chopsticks upright in his bowl of rice at a dramatic moment in one scene or, without missing a beat or altering the expression on his face, removing his cigarette from his own mouth and deftly placing it in the mouth of one of his guards as he briskly strides into Megan's bedroom – there are, after all, no ashtrays nearby, and one does not smoke in the presence of a lady), he shows a confidently aristocratic mastery of timing and effect that rivals the best of Tom Dixon's performances. Just as Walter Huston and Robert Williams deserve full credit for their performances in their films, the character of Yen is made possible only by Asther's superb acting, but then in all of his films Capra seems to have been able to elicit such a level of performance from one or two of his actors. To think of any of his movies is almost automatically to think of a particular performer or performance within it. As in the work of John Cassavetes, the power of the individual actor-performer as the creator and controller of meaning and value is one of its essential assumptions.†

A difference between Yen and earlier figures like Dixon and Smith, however, is that Yen's character represents more than a power of socially visible and publicly enactable performance. As his name suggests, Yen embodies vaguer, less specifiable energies of desire and imagination. He is a general and a warlord, but he is also a man with an imagination and range of feeling too large to find expression in the rather petty feuding of the civil strife around him. Not only would he rather be doing almost anything but ruling a kingdom and leading an army, but he is, by all of the evidence, not even very good at doing that. His unimaginative, flat-footed financial adviser, the American, Jones (Walter Connolly), who plays an updated version of an

---

* According to Capra, this kind of wit got the film unofficially banned throughout the British empire, causing the cancellation of hundreds of bookings and the loss of hundreds of thousands of dollars in revenues. Charles Wolfe tells me that Capra is in error on this point and that only a few minor cuts of objectionable passages were made on the film when it was released in the British Commonwealth.

† If the force of this assertion is not obvious or if it seems merely rhetorical, I would add that there are quite few films or directors of which this could be said. To take Hitchcock as an example, I would argue that there is not one performance of a central character in all of his work to equal the typical starring performances Capra regularly elicits. It is not an accident that this should be so. Hitchcock does not believe in the individual as the ultimate creator and controller or meaning and significance. Meanings are created less personally and humanely in his work than in Capra's. They are generated by means of abstract systems of visual signification (by means of camera angles, lighting, editing patterns, and so forth). Capra's, in contrast, are created by performers in collaborative acts of social and imaginative interaction with other characters.

Aristabulus Bragg character – a shrewd, improvising, plastic man without principles who goes wherever the money is – would probably be a much better general and ruler than he. This again marks his difference from Dixon and Stew Smith, the first of whom is content to be a king, and the second a court jester, for most of their respective films.

It is the imaginative and emotional energies in excess of any social or worldly justification that Yen releases that cause him to be so frightening and mysterious to Megan.* With no conventional forms of speech or intercourse by which to express himself, like one of Henry James's young women in his early novels, Yen works off his imaginative energies in superfluities and ingenuities of performative stylization. The energies manifest themselves in his charged sexuality but also in the endless "scenes" he scripts and stages, in the extravagance of his costumes, and in the stylistic world of his summer palace, to which he carries Megan as if she were another exotic art object to add to his collection. To recognize how Yen has built himself a stylistic world is to see how much more complex his position is than that of Jerry Strong or Lulu Smith. If Jerry and Lulu have affinities with the world-forsaking heroes and heroines of Victorian and Edwardian poetry, the anemic, nostalgic sons and daughters of Tennyson, Yen's muscular creation of a homemade world is reminiscent of Emerson, conceiving of the world not as something we either take or leave but as continuously up for our imaginative appropriation and enrichment.

For Megan, as well as for the viewer, *Bitter Tea* becomes a lesson in entertaining the possibility of complex stylistic performances that carry us beyond the alternatives of living in Manhattan or fleeing to Arizona, and into the possibility of making a world of our own, both the enchanted stylistic world that Yen makes as a character, and the one Capra makes as a filmmaker. *Bitter Tea* does not simply pit its central characters against a fixed, external stylistic reality (like *Ladies of Leisure*'s New York high society or the stodginess of upper-crust life that Stew Smith parodies in *Platinum Blonde*). Instead it imagines its characters as being capable of bringing their own alternative reality into existence, through the power of personal style.† *Bitter Tea* teaches us to "see" stylistically and to make us aware of the ability of a particular consciousness to create the reality it sees, as no earlier Capra film did. Although both the Havana and the murder scenes in *Forbidden* briefly attempted this, the film as a whole recognized a supervening reality of the

---

* In pairing Megan with Yen as coequal stars of this film, Capra gives it a double agenda. Yen is a poised, masterful social performer; Megan is shy, quiet, and withdrawn (in part because of her situation as an alien in Yen's kingdom). Thus, in a sense, *Bitter Tea* knits together two previously somewhat separated strands in Capra's work – the social performer and the potential visionary – and further suggests that each shares qualities with the other that are, in fact, not mutually exclusive alternatives.

† The film following this one, *Lady for a Day*, is an even more outrageous, comic example of the same thing. In it, a group of New York street toughs and hoodlums creates an entirely fictional world of upper-class social life and then actually proceeds to inhabit it.

codes of bourgeois morality that was unresponsive to stylistic arrangement or the transformations of human consciousness. Nor, in *Ladies of Leisure*, were Jerry Strong and Kay Arnold given consciousnesses or powers of stylistic performance like Yen's. We looked up at the stars when Jerry or Kay saw them, but *Ladies of Leisure* did not attempt to display the independent consciousnesses of its central characters and to recreate all of reality in the style of their consciousnesses in the way this film does.

Megan falls asleep on the train after our and her first lesson in seeing and the power of style, and the next time we see her is in an extremely deep-focus shot in her bedroom in Yen's palace. The set and its furnishings are exotic, and the changing of the palace guard to the striking of bells holds our attention with its exoticism, but these things are minor. Capra's shot itself is what we notice more than anything in particular going on in it. The deep focus, the key lighting that accents specific artifacts in the room, the elegantly complex composition of the frame space are the subjects of the shot more than any object or activity in it. When Megan awakens to the sound of a firing squad in the courtyard outside her bedroom window, Capra sets up the camera at one end of the cavernous bedroom set and lets us see that her eyes are opening to the power of style at the same moment ours are. The shot itself is a lesson in seeing, in opening our eyes to purely stylistic possibilities that were not present earlier in the film. What we see is less a group of oriental objets d'art or a specific room in Yen's palace than a cinematically enriched style, a style entirely different from the BBC Third Programme style of the world of the Strikes. The lighting, photography, and frame composition (like the stylized furnishings and theatrical appointments of the room) in and of itself communicates energies that have no way of being expressed within plot or dialogue. They are energies literally beyond any narrative need or realistic point. That is their point. We (and Megan) are projected into a realm (very like that of Lee Garmes and Sternberg) in which the cinematic techniques exist not to subserve some realistic meaning but to replace it, to offer their own alternative kinds of energy as substitutes for absent or unimportant social meanings.

Much has been made of the fact that Megan awakes wearing a silk kimono and looking invitingly sensual, as if the point of the awakening scene were simply the awakening of sexuality and womanhood in this daughter of the Puritans. That omits a step in the argument that is perhaps more important than its conclusion. We notice things like Megan's kimono, her warm skin tones, or the moistness of her eyes in this scene only because Capra has ushered us into an entirely different aesthetic world from that of the initial scenes in the Strike residence. That change in our way of seeing changes our sense of Megan's potential erotic expressiveness, but that is because it also has changed everything else about Megan and the viewer's relation to her as well. The scenes on the street earlier, or those in the Strike home, were too busy with self-important movement and dutiful responsibility to encourage such possibilities of seeing between characters or between the viewer and the film. To convert one way of seeing into the other, as in the passage I quoted from

Megan's awakening to the pleasures of vision and style, Capra's awakening to a visionary style: other forms of the meditative shift.

Hawthorne earlier, social and physical action must, at least temporarily, stop. In order to learn to exercise their imaginations, characters must disengage themselves from forms of dialogue and plot. Like Hawthorne, Capra must still or stop his own work of art long enough to allow us to be able to exercise our imaginations. Capra's film will have to silence and immobilize itself and its central characters to allow a moment of vision to take place. From here on, *Bitter Tea* forces Megan to sit still, to submit to the enriching gaze of the camera in silence and solitude, in order that both we and she can learn to see in a new way.*

Notice the changes from the scene of Dixon's performance during the bank run (*American Madness* was made immediately before *Bitter Tea*). In that scene,

---

* As James Guetti has argued in *Word-Music: The Aesthetic Aspect of Narrative Fiction* (New Brunswick, N.J.: Rutgers University Press, 1982), in American visionary poetry and prose a similar movement may take place. The visual registration of events and physical details is frequently replaced by an aurality, or series of sound effects, in the text. The effect is the same in films as in literature, insofar as the nonmimetic textuality of the text (its pure "visuality" in the case of a film, or its pure "aurality" in the case of the text of a poem or novel) temporarily offers itself for our attention in place of whatever it is supposed to be representing or arguing. A condition of nonsocial stylistic or imaginative enrichment substitutes for unavailable social or interpersonal representation.

the viewer, like Dixon himself, is a busy, appetitive consumer and processor of a sequence of facts and fast-changing events. Here, the viewer, like Megan, has been encouraged to become a connoisseur of static visual effects. In deliberately retarding the pace of the narrative and minimizing the eventful-ness of these later moments, Capra has encouraged the viewer, like the central character, to assume a narratively less appetitive and imaginatively more speculative or meditative relationship to the scene.★ This does not represent a complete break from his previous work, for as my discussion of *American Madness* and *Platinum Blonde* suggested, even in these fast-paced and narratively more pressing worlds, the mastery of events and actions repre-sented by Dixon and Smith, in their different ways, represented a degree of willed removal from or rising above the situation one was in. The performa-tive superiority and poise that Capra advocated in those films is an incipient form of the meditative detachment from the sway of narrative eventfulness that he cultivates in this one.

How, specifically, does one see differently in the final two-thirds of the film than in the first third? How does Yen educate Megan, and the experience of *Bitter Tea* educate us, to see? Probably the best answer to that question, though one that will at first appear tautological, is to say that we and she learn to see the way we see *in movies*. Capra is, as a director, discovering that movies are potentially, in and of themselves, a way of seeing. Film does not simply represent a world outside of movies, which is then accepted or rejected as in *Ladies of Leisure*, but, as in *Forbidden* (a transitional work in this respect), the character's and director's consciousness can conspire to create and validate a world unto itself. Film can embody a world enriched by consciousness, as an alternative to the repressive or impoverished world of actual social relationships.

This idea seems so exciting to Capra that he appears to play with it in the film. It is surely not accidental that Yen's palace looks like one of the movie palaces of the thirties in which this film would have been shown. (This was the film, by the way, that was chosen to premiere at the biggest movie palace of them all – Radio City Music Hall, on January 11, 1933 – to inaugurate its new policy of screening first-run feature films full-time.) Like Yen's summer palace, the movie palaces were attempts to create a world of cinematic con-sciousness that could stand as an alternative to the world outside the film. Yen is a producer-director-stage designer in the practical senses of the terms, and his palace is as deliberate an extension of the principles of stage design into the real world as the picture palaces in which it was shown. His outer offices even

---

★ This is related to what Dreyer does in all of his work, and (although it may seem superficially unrelated) to what neorealists like Rossellini and De Sica do to woo a viewer from a narratively appetitive to a more imaginatively enriching relationship to their texts and characters. The retardation of the narrative pace and the diminution of social eventfulness encourages a compensating imaginative expansion on the part of both character and viewer. Dreyer's *Gertrud* and Rossellini's *Viaggio in Italia* are two of the supreme cinematic demonstrations of the rewards of narrative retardation or arrest.

look a little like the offices in a studio complex, peopled with the usual studio employees and hangers-on. Jones is the kind of financial manager that every studio has, who, neither caring nor knowing very much about the final artistic product that emerges, grudges every penny that it costs.* Visible in Yen's "front office," in addition to the financial manager, are various administrative types, miscellaneous "gofers," and, in the scene in which Strike visits Yen in the city, someone apparently engaged in something resembling set design, working with blueprints and drawings on a table off to one side.

The significance of the specially heightened experience provided by movies as a metaphor for experience in *this* movie is deeper than anything suggested by the presence of these fairly unimportant front-office figures around Yen, however. To explain how that can be, I want to discuss one of the most interesting scenes in all of Capra's work at some length. It takes place several days into Megan's enforced stay as Yen's reluctant guest. As if all of the earlier stylistic enrichments that I have sketched were, at least initially, wasted on her, it is only on the third night of her stay at Yen's palace that Megan's true "opening night" might be said to occur. One would never want to rigidify such a metaphorically tactful film into a mechanical symbolism, but surely it was deliberate, on the part of Capra and Edward Paramore, who collaborated with him on the script, that Megan (since no one in Sinkiang knows where she is) has been officially declared dead by the time she arrives at Yen's palace and three full days go by while she stays in bed, dead to the world around her, to arise on the third day. Her resurrection is different from anything that would be understood by the missionaries, however, insofar as it is clearly an awakening of her body and her senses, along with her soul. On the third day, Megan "comes to her senses" in more than one meaning of the phrase. A "yen" that had been dormant or suppressed earlier is awakened in her. She admits desire and the pleasures of taste, touch, and vision into her life, unlike Robert Strike, who, as Yen mockingly puts it, "prefers civil war to the loving arms of his bride."

While the missionaries emphasize the crucifixion as the central, determining event in Christian history and iconography – one smug old boy actually regaling the crowd at the Strike house, in the first scene, with a gruesomely humorous cocktail-party anecdote about it – Capra offers the experience of the resurrection as the central metaphoric emphasis in his film. We must not die to the body, he says in a revisionary reading of Christianity that has something in common with that of D. H. Lawrence, but be born again to it if we are to be saved. (One does not, however, want to exaggerate the Christian typology in this scene or any other in a film that is so critical of all – Christian or anti-Christian – abstract schemes of understanding.)

* Walter Connolly, who plays Jones, is another, and by far the most affectionately portrayed, of the Harry Cohn look-alikes. As Cohn aged and grew in power, so, interestingly enough, did the Cohn stand-ins in the films, and the bitterness and venom with which Capra depicted them increased as well. One wonders if Capra was aware of doing this; needless to say, Cohn was ignorant of it, or it would not have continued.

On that third evening Megan is drawn from her bed, almost as if she were sleepwalking. Wearing a silken kimono, she gets up and moves across the exotically furnished bedroom. Capra holds the entire room in a gorgeously detailed deep-focus shot as she rises from the bed, but, significantly, nothing really takes place in the shot. Megan simply seems to be seeing the space, as we, as viewers, are seeing it. That is to say, the effect is the opposite of the beginning of an action sequence. The shot calls attention to itself as a shot – as a carefully crafted artifact in a film – not as a transparent window on reality through which we watch events independent of the window itself. Or, to put it in perceptual terms, we are so busy relishing the visual pleasures of the shot itself that we are distracted from noticing or caring very much what Megan is doing in it. We are teased into an aesthetic contemplation of the shot itself that lulls our appetite for realistic details. Even if we do insist on looking "through" the composition to its "contents," what we see is not the world but an obvious stage set, equally in the sense of its being a soundstage at Columbia for Capra's film and a stage set in Yen's palace for the scenes he stages there: in either case, an emphatically artificial creation of the human imagination. Nature and Homer are the same, here. This is a world of artifacts, of spell-binding, enchanting human creations and arrangements.

Still in the same shot, Megan slowly walks to the back right of the frame space, where a large octagonal aperture is located. It is impossible to say immediately which it is – a window, a mirror, or a door; the ambiguity is deliberate, and important to the film. Capra locates three similar-looking octagonal or hexagonal openings against the back wall of Megan's bedroom, and the viewer has little or no way of deciding the respective functions of the three apertures. We only gradually make out that the one on the left is an arch or doorway into another room, the one in the middle a large mirror, and the one on the right an enormous walk-through window. As we shall see, the film works to confound even these discriminations. How do windows, doors, and mirrors differ from one another on a stage set, anyway? How do any of them differ from walls? Doorways are false or lead nowhere; windows are only more brightly illuminated or translucent sections of walls; and mirrors are not really mirrors, or are canted to reflect only other walls and surfaces.

At the very end of this scene, Stanwyck sits down and paints herself in front of a stage mirror (that probably is not really a mirror) and then uses it as a doorway through which to step, momentarily, into Yen's world. In the dream montage that precedes that moment, a shimmering mirror (which is actually a pool of mercury) suddenly turns into a door; the door turns into a wall; Yen breaks down the wall and turns it back into a door; and then a second Yen walks through a window as if it were a door and throws the first Yen through a wall as if it were a door. In the present scene, Megan walks up to what appears to be a window or mirror but suddenly turns into a sliding door and walks through it onto a balcony outside her bedroom. In Capra's cinematic world of passages into the interior, in which all true travel is psychological, it is natural that windows, walls, doors, and mirrors should turn themselves from one thing to another under the pressure of our powers of reflection on them and on ourselves.

As if to emphasize that something more than a physical movement is taking place when Megan moves through the window/door, Capra edits the passage so that she goes through it twice. In the first of three rapid cuts, in a shot taken from inside we see her from behind as she opens the sliding portal and takes a step through it, across the threshold and out onto the balcony. In the second shot, still taken from behind her, but from much closer, we look over her shoulder and away from the palace, as she stands completely out on the balcony, leaning on the rattan chair in which she will subsequently sit. Then, surprisingly, in the third shot of the sequence, a reverse shot taken from in front of her (from outside, shooting back into the bedroom), we see Megan standing in the opening of the sliding door and walking through it out onto the balcony *again*. The shots have been blatantly miscut. What I have called shots 1, 2, and 3 should, in normal editing, have been arranged in the order 1, 3, 2, or, for even more clarity and concision, the middle shot should have been eliminated altogether and shot 1 succeeded by 3.

The miscutting passes quickly enough not to disturb an audience and probably not to be noticed, but it is the sort of sequence that, even if Capra were not known to have personally supervised (and usually done) his own editing, would not have been mangled this way by even the most inexperienced editorial assistant. It is a standard "going through a doorway" sequence that is one of a trainee's first lessons in editing. Capra has not made a mistake, though. What he has succeeded in communicating, even to an audience perhaps unaware of the editing trick being played on them, is the strange portentousness – the length and the depth – of Megan's passage. This is not just any ordinary doorway, and if it takes Megan three separate shots and four or five seconds of film to take one short step through it, it is because it is a step into a new world, a world of experience that can change her entire life and way of feeling.

I have already discussed the metaphoric importance of such a movement outside of a building onto a balcony in *Ladies of Leisure*. As much as in the paintings of Eakins, Homer, or Hopper, or the novels of James, such a turning out of a space or society felt to be limiting had a powerful imaginative resonance for Capra, which is why, as here, it often defines a quietly climactic moment in a film.

Megan reclines in the chair on the balcony, and even this gesture is meaningful. This busybody, almost-wife of a missionary, this woman who interrupted her own wedding in order to accompany her fiancé on his dutiful mission of mercy, is at last learning how to sit still. She is learning much earlier in her film the lesson that Stew Smith – the peripatetic parodist and spatial game player – learned only at the end of his, in his final transformation into an artist: that in sitting still one may learn how to move imaginatively beyond any of the possibilities of movement in space or society. She sits and looks over the railing of the balcony into an enchanted garden that, at least as much as the shots of the palace room out of which she stepped, represents not nature but a world of art and cinematic artifice. The music of lutes and chimes swells on the sound track. (It is a very special moment, in Capra's films, when any sort of orchestration is used, and all the more special when, as in this scene, the music is not localized in source sound.) The chair that Megan occupies can be compared to a seat in a box high up in a theater, looking down on an elegant stage set, but the better comparison is that this daughter of the Puritans has wandered into a movie palace. She will be seduced into sitting down and watching, just as we in the theater sit still and watch her watch. What is going on in front of her is a kind of orgy in which Yen's soldiers pair off with geishas for a night of love (Yen subsequently tells Megan that it is called the Festival of the Cherry Blossom Moon), but the events themselves are vague and indistinct to her and to us, since all of the sexual resonances are denatured and transformed into artificial artistic arrangements. What matters most is the elaborate stylization of the scene: the pictorial arrangements and composition of the frame space, the orchestration on the sound track. They make us indifferent to mere eventfulness, plot, or characterization and instead encourage us, and her, to become aware of plastic possibilities of artistic presentation and arrangement that are different from the public "meanings" of an event. Everything Megan watches is turned into a scene, in the theatrical sense. As Capra presents and Megan views it, the otherwise tawdry sexual orgy is transformed into an artful pantomime or dance. A river separates Megan's balcony seat from the events on the opposite bank, like the apron of a stage. The river, sparkling with moonlight at the bottom of the frame, trees hung with paper lanterns on either side of her, and the cloud-streaked, moonlit sky above completely frame the scene within a proscenium arch. It is all theatrically lighted from the sides and back in low-key chiaroscuro, and it is as horizontally composed as a stage set or decorative landscape painting.

Who is the artist of the painterly effect, the author of this theatrical scene? Yen's palace and its gardens help to create it, and Megan's eye and personal point of view contribute the proper perspective on it, but the true master of these ceremonies is neither Yen nor Megan, but Capra. The artifice we admire here is only marginally the artifice communicated by Yen's garden and Megan's box-seat point of view. It is principally the artifice of Capra's cinematic arrangements: the proscenium framing of the scene; the use of glass-shots of trees, moon, clouds, and palace; the artful synchronization of music and editing rhythms.

Isolated moments in earlier and later films demonstrate a similar fascination with the possibilities of cinematic illusion: the conflagration aboard a crashing blimp, in *Dirigible*; the fire in the temple, in *The Miracle Woman*; the views of the travelers above the valley of the Blue Moon, in *Lost Horizon*; and the nighttown sequence, in *It's a Wonderful Life*. Here, though, the special effects become the subject of the film itself, as they never have been previously in Capra's work. It would be only a slight simplificaton to say that the subject of *Bitter Tea* is the glass-shot and all that it tells us about the power of film to transform and enrich reality. A glass-shot is a wall that film and the power of the gaze change into a window and that our imaginations can transform into a door through which we, like Megan, can move into another world.

Megan walks out onto the balcony, sits down, looks, and allows herself to be stimulated by her seeing, and it is not accidental that her first independent flight of imagination in the film immediately follows. She falls asleep and has a dream that is probably the most commented-upon section of the film. In it we see a grotesquely distorted Yen breaking down the door to Megan's bedroom, menacingly coming up to her in her bed, apparently about to rape her. However, at the very moment he is about to pounce on her, a masked savior comes in through the same opening through which she has walked to get onto the balcony. He vanquishes her assailant and steps forward to embrace her, revealing himself in the end, however, not to be Strike, as we had supposed, but Yen. The dream ends (happily or nightmarishly, depending on one's point of view) with Yen and Megan clutched in a passionate embrace.

This has probably been the most commented-upon scene because it is one of the most explicitly erotic scenes in Capra's work (or, for that matter, in all of thirties Hollywood film). It is a dream, in all metaphoric senses, of walls being broken down, of separations being bridged, of the most private and personal spaces being first forcibly penetrated and then swooningly yielded. These connotations are immediate and obvious. The dream is about violations of sexual barriers and social taboos, breakages of categories of understanding and surfacings of repressions of various kinds, and about the breakdown of a fantasy of male protection of the sort Megan had previously relied on, but is also a celebration of cinematic artifice. It is a carefully, imaginatively arranged event whose every detail is charged with the heightened intensity and over-determined meaningfulness we find not in life but in art, and specifically, in a movie. It constitutes an arrangement of experience as artificially enriched as the events in Yen's palace and garden, and as unlike the random noise and chatter in the Strike residence as possible.

The dream is, above all, stylistically crafted and an internalization or continuation of the intensive visual or visionary aesthetic of the film in which it occurs. Critical interpretations that stress its sexual content invariably slight the fact that, first and foremost, the dream sequence is a cinematic tour de force. It is a visual exercise in the expressive use of kick-lighting and shadow-ing, in the employment of extremely short-focus lenses (which artificially distort depths and elongate perspectives). It is a parody anthology of received cinematic styles, a camp send-up of melodramatic, silent-movie styles of acting and gesturing. The initial battering down of the door is shot and filmed in the style of a German expressionist film of the twenties. The "rape" moment is played as an exaggerated takeoff of Victorian (or D. W. Griffith) melodrama. The Strike rescue scene is shot, edited, and orchestrated as a parody of "Perils of Pauline" farce. The final romantic embrace is as comically exaggerated and self-consciously kitschy as a surrealistic scene from *Un Chien*

Andalou. Capra is playing with cinematic styles and effects★ and, in their parodically overblown and comically exaggerated quality, reminding us that they *are* artistic effects. They are arrangements of experience not found in the world but created by acts of human consciousness. The heavy-handed pseudo-Freudian symbolism is no less a part of Capra's playful calling attention to the dream's crafty construction than are his more purely cinematic jokes and allusions.

Moreover, notwithstanding the attempt to freight it with psychological or social meanings, the dream is in its essence an experience different from, and not reducible to, those sorts of meanings. It is silent (except for its heavy orchestration). There is no dialogue or nuanced social interplay of characters within it. That is the point. It is a stylized visual experience that communicates its meanings not through dialogue or the social interaction of characters, or narrative events enactable in a more public form, but through pure visual stylization (or, to be precise, through parodies of visual styles). The dream scene is allied with many other key scenes in *Bitter Tea* (and the films that follow), insofar as it renounces the attempt to communicate meanings narratively, verbally, or socially and substitutes a purely visionary, visual form of communication. The kinds of meanings and forms of relationship Capra is exploring at this point in his career simply cannot be expressed in realistic dramatic interaction. Melodramatic confrontations, parodic stylistic games, and silent gazing, vision, or reverie are used to generate meanings not otherwise expressible.

Megan the dreamer smiles at the conclusion of her dream as she embraces Yen. She might be smiling out of sexual and romantic pleasure in the final embrace and kiss, out of amusement with the parodic inventiveness and wittiness of the dream, or out of enjoyment of the consummate artifice of the whole thing. Most interpretations of the dream stop with the first possibility, but it is the heart of my argument that the second and third possibilities do not contradict the first but are in some ways more important to an understanding of the film than it is. Capra wants to carry us beyond (to use a phrase that Yen employs later) the "conventional thing." A door to Megan's sexuality is being opened in this scene, but so much more is being opened, both to Megan and the viewer, in the way of possibilities of new relationships to experience that the "conventional thing" seems almost paltry by comparison.

The dephysicalizing of sexual experience here – as in *Ladies of Leisure* and *Forbidden*, and indeed all of Capra's subsequent films – is an essential aspect of his larger imaginative project. The first Yen in the dream proposes what is obviously a physical sexual encounter, but the second Yen quickly intervenes to substitute an exaltedly romantic experience. As much as Capra exorcises various forms of social intercourse to make room for imaginative experience,

---

★ Capra, as a director, is doing what Stew Smith did, as a character, in *Platinum Blonde*: demonstrating his superiority to received forms of expression.

he defends his films against the desublimations of sexual intercourse and substitutes in their place abstract, romantic forms of imaginative intercourse between his characters. Megan is being awakened sexually in her dream, but only to an extraordinarily rarified and dephysicalized form of sexuality, a sexuality entirely consonant with the other "derealizing" imaginative substitutions in the film.

When Megan wakes up, she finds Yen looming over her out on the balcony. He apologizes for his intrusion into her bedroom by saying that after he knocked on her door and she did not answer, "I almost broke the door down, but you didn't hear me." The linkage of sleeping and waking states in the film is now complete. Like Adam, she awakens to find all true, and life – at least for the time being, in the enchanted realm of Yen's palace and Capra's film – continuous with art and imagination. The elegant, visual arrangements of "still life" will not stay still, however (to adopt a metaphor from *Ladies of Leisure*). Capra, like Hawthorne and James, those earlier American connoisseurs of scenic effects and the possibility of visionary intercourse not subject to the repressions and limitations of actual social or sexual intercourse, knows how hard it is to sustain visionary possibilities in the world, how difficult it is to keep them alive in the world of space, time, and society.

In the minutes that follow, Yen talks "love talk" to Megan. Leaning forward over her in her chair, tenderly, solicitously, almost whispering in her ear, he delivers an exquisite monologue about the possibility of life's becoming art, about the Festival of the Cherry Blossom Moon, and about paintings in which art and life are so merged that the "fruit trees look like women, and the women look like fruit trees." He speaks enchantingly and elegantly, and he seems on the verge of overcoming all of Megan's sexual and social resistance to him. There is, at the end of it, a sublime Hawthornean moment of suspense, exactly like the one I quoted from "The Canterbury Pilgrims," in which Megan leans forward, her guard down, momentarily seduced by Yen's poetic vision, and all of the imaginative possibilities that have been raised earlier astonishingly open up as perhaps enactable in the real world. Anything is possible in this enchanted kingdom for the imaginative viewer or for Megan, for a split second.

Just as in Hawthorne or James, however, the moment comes and goes. The exquisite moment of vision is not extendable or maintainable, nor is it really Megan's fault that this should be so. To focus on her Protestant prudishness at this moment, as she ultimately declines Yen's implicit sexual invitation, just as to focus on Lambert Strether's at comparable moments in *The Ambassadors*, would be to miss the point entirely. How, one wonders, could such glorious imaginative possibility be converted by a filmmaker, or by his or her characters, into dialogue or social event? How could what took such artistic effort to bring into being in the first place be translated into mere words and gestures? How could such imaginative stimulation be converted into the gropings of sexual intercourse in a bedroom without almost everything's being lost in the translation?

Yen interrupts his talk at one point, saying that he is reluctant to continue because he is afraid his words might "disturb" Megan. We realize, of course, that that is in fact the greatest service he could possibly render her. To be capable of being disturbed or jolted out of one's normal relationship to experience is the great test that each of Capra's central characters must pass – to be disturbed into a fresh relationship to life, to be disturbed into creativity and potential freedom. Megan is indeed disturbed by the boldness and imaginativeness of Yen's speech. The problem is not the disturbance but the fact that she is unable to make anything of her disturbance but embarrassment, vexation, and dismissiveness. At his use of the word *lovers*, she lowers her eyes. One is still not sure that something in her is not being deeply moved and opened to a new sense of possibility, but possibility suddenly gives way to impossibility. She tightens her jaw and curtly replies, "I think we ought to end this discussion."

Her imagination has closed down, and she has reverted to the tones of the Puritan schoolmarm. Her peculiar use of the word *discussion* tells us how far she has come, though, even as she shuts down imaginative and erotic possibilities. There has, strictly speaking, been no discussion at all in the scene. Yen has done almost all of the talking; after a few token replies, Megan has sat in rapt silence listening to him. (The camera stays on her face throughout Yen's monologue to express a communication more powerful than the verbal.) A discussion has been going on, however – one without words – inside herself. This is the sort of imaginative movement that Yen and his world represent the possibility of – a sense of "discussion" that would be unheard of and meaningless back at the Strike residence, where the only meaning of the word was the sort of vacuous social gossip and polite chitchat engaged in by the wedding guests. This is a sense of discussion as a movement of the imagination, turning upon itself to reflect upon its own premises and procedures, that the missionary at the wedding gathering who told the story of the pagans and the crucifixion, for one, never could have entertained. He can speak smugly from the pulpit or to the crowd gathered for the wedding, but to "discuss" something with himself or others in this way he would have to give up his verbal facility and confidence of tone. He would have to dare to move imaginatively around himself and his beliefs, as freely and deftly as Capra moves around him in the dramatic circular zip pan that concludes and comically comments on his scene.★

Notwithstanding her inability to rise fully to the occasion, the "passage" leaves its mark on Megan. Yen is rebuffed, and leaves. Megan stays out on the balcony and, a few minutes later, watches Mah-Li come out onto another part

---

★ If Capra, in his writing, directing, and editing, had not maintained a level of imaginative performance consistently higher than that of even the most creative performers in his films, one could not be so free critically to "place" and understand their efforts. Like a great novelist's narrative style, Capra's cinematic style represents a standard of stylistic awareness, meditative self-awareness, and generosity of response in comparison with which his characters must be judged.

of the balcony farther down, unaware of her presence. Mah-Li, on the balcony, and Yen's chauffeur, Captain Li, on the grass below, go through a strange, moonlit ceremony. He throws a knotted handkerchief up to Mah-Li; she throws her slipper down to him, and he kisses and embraces it. We see it all as Megan sees it, and what is most significant is that Megan smiles to herself at its conclusion, just as she smiled at the end of her dream. Even Mah-Li is astonished at Megan's attitude when she subsequently finds out that she has witnessed the entire mysterious rendezvous. She is afraid that Megan will inform Yen, but Megan assures her that her secret is safe. What is surprising is not only Megan's broadmindedness (since there is every suggestion that Mah-Li is still also Yen's lover) but her obvious enchantment with what she sees, the apparent pleasure she takes in having participated in the whole scene. (The slipper – handkerchief exchange is played as a comic pantomime, backed with the same lute and woodwind music as the Festival of the Cherry Blossom Moon, to suggest Megan's enchantment with it.)

She has just rejected Yen's advances, but without being aware of it Megan is being gradually converted by the fairy-tale atmosphere surrounding her. She is moving beyond her earlier stances of narrowly moral judgment and censure. She goes inside to her room and, after a brief conversation in which she assures Mah-Li that she will not tell what she has seen, decides to join Yen for supper for the first time. Even more significantly, she yields to Mah-Li's suggestion that she transform herself with makeup, perfumes, and new clothing. In a richly sensuous series of scenes that can also be read as a parable on the creation of a movie star such as Barbara Stanwyck in the studio makeup room and costume department, Megan sheds her Puritan weeds; bathes, powders, and perfumes her skin; makes up her face and eyes; and dons a mirror-inlaid oriental robe. The proper Bostonian of the initial scenes has been metamorphosed into a new woman.

The scenes of her bathing and dressing are some of the most erotic in all of Capra's work, and Megan's expanded sense of the possibilities of womanhood is paralleled by Capra's evocative use of light and shadow and the sexual suggestiveness of the framing and editing in these scenes. Doublings, mirror transformations, reflections (in both the meditative and the optical senses of the word), and watery shimmerings and sea changes were disturbing in her dream, but in Megan's bathing and costuming herself in her mirrored gown, as well as in the shimmering lap dissolves by which Capra represents them, they have become the stuff dreams are made on. The excitement of artistic transformation has been domesticated. Megan has brought the dream into her waking life and made it her own. Whereas the transformations in her dream had discomposed her, her makeup mirror becomes a way of recomposing herself. It becomes a door into a new world, and a window through which she can gaze on a newly created self. The mirror is a door and a window that turn her angle of vision not outward but inward and lead her farther into herself. Megan's journey out of herself, as a voyeur on the balcony, matters only because it ultimately carries her self-reflectively deeper into herself. Capra uses the same metaphor – of a woman's standing or sitting in front of a mirror and seeing herself for the first time – in crucial scenes in *Ladies of Leisure, The Miracle Woman, Lady for a Day, Here Comes the Groom*, and *Pocketful of Miracles*, to capture the same process of self-reflection that in his work is always a necessary prelude to a fresh appreciation of the possibilities of imaginative self-creation.

Megan still feels ambivalent about this access of possibilities. She runs away from her own insights. After entertaining such an enlargement of identity, like a character in a work by James or Hawthorne, she runs away from it. She suddenly recoils from her image in the mirror, wipes off her makeup, strips off her oriental gown, and goes down to supper in her drab missionary clothes. It is too simple to say that Capra is merely demonstrating her deep-seated conservatism and timidity. It is the strength of this film that the artist is almost as ambivalent about stylistic transformations of selfhood and artistic rearrangements of experience as Megan is. The set decorator's and costume designer's dreams of infinitely plastic reality do not extend much beyond the bedrooms, balconies, and dressing rooms of life, if they govern even there. Megan goes downstairs for supper, only to walk in on a tense scene of intrigue and espionage. The enchanted love scene between Mah-Li and Captain Li that she has just visionarily conspired in (and that we in the audience have been baited into seeing in the same way she does) is revealed to have been not a love scene at all but an act of treason. Mah-Li and Captain Li are spies and rebels within Yen's camp, plotting his overthrow. What Megan thought to be a fetishistic exchange of love tokens has actually been the passing of secret military documents out of the palace compound to waiting rebel bands.

This realization, which Capra divulges only gradually over the next ten or fifteen minutes of the film, comes with as great a shock as Lambert Strether's sudden discovery of Chad and Madame de Vionnet together on the river, and one is asked to condemn Megan's complete misunderstanding of the scene transacted before her no more than one is asked to condemn Strether's mistaken imagination of Chad's "virtuous" relationship. Even as one is made painfully aware of all the ways life does not live up to our imagination of its possibilities, one gives humble thanks for those imaginations.

As in the work of James, the achievements of style and consciousness are vulnerable to the predations of the world. Yen's gorgeous house of fictions, his palace of Midsummer Night's Dreams, is in fact, as we and Megan realize only now, crumbling around him. His soldiers are in rebellion, his treasury is almost empty, and his closest subordinates are defecting. His kingdom is a stage designer's dream of heaven, but, as a corollary of that, it is almost as insubstantial as the tricks of costuming, perspective, and arrangement that brought it into existence photographically.

Like Capra's other films, *Bitter Tea* oscillates between the hope that the movements of individual imagination can be directly and painlessly translated into practical, social forms of expression and the fear that such a hope is a delusion. Yen's practical power is finally revealed to have been an illusion, a glorious one, but an illusion nonetheless. As the end of the movie demonstrates (like the end of *Platinum Blonde*) the individual is finally compelled to renounce the hope of expressing his or her imagination in the languages of the world. Stew Smith, Florence Fallon, Kay Arnold, Jerry Strong, Yen, and Megan Davis are forced to sit or stand still at the conclusion of their films and be content with consciousness as an end in itself, with imagination as its own reward.

Contemporary reviewers criticized Winslow Homer's paintings of the late 1870s, invidiously contrasting his work with that of Monet, because the women in his pictures were not given clear social roles and statuses; because there frequently was an incongruity between their costumes and their facial expressions; because there was something imprecise and undefined about their activities and situations. In pointing out that Monet's or Renoir's women were seldom guilty of such vagueness of expression and activity, such mysteriousness and lack of social or psychological definition, they were only noticing the qualities that link Homer's central figures with most of Capra's and that make both of them distinctively American expressions. The vagueness, mysteriousness, and lack of definition, the strange staring off to one side, out of the (pictorial or cinematic) frame space at something undefined are registrations of the problematic expression in the world of individual consciousness for both artists, demonstrations of an awareness of what perhaps can never be expressed or rendered except through such mysterious vagueness.

It is at this point that any attempt to assimilate the major artists in the so-called American impressionist tradition (Sargent, Hawthorne, Homer, Tarbell, Chase, Wiley, Johnson, Beaux, and others) to the theories and practices of French impressionism breaks down. For all of the superficial similarities of attention to color, light, and tonal values, the two traditions operate out of entirely different value systems. In a Metropolitan Museum catalogue, Dianne H. Pilgrim summarizes the prevailing conflation of impressionist and realist traditions in arguing, about the work of John Singer Sargent, that the effect he strove for was the "transcription of what was before him, defined by light and color."* That could serve as a plausible beginning to an approach to the early French impressionists, but nothing could miss more of the essential quality of Sargent's work, which is, as I have already argued in Chapter 2, a study of the expression (or failure of expression) of individual consciousness in the forms of social life.

To turn to Winslow Homer's work, one need only compare his *Cotton Pickers* or *Girl with Laurel* with Monet's superficially similar *Women in a Garden*. (If there were space for it here, one might with equal aptness compare Homer's *Long Branch, New Jersey* etchings with Monet's *Terrace at Sainte-Adresse*.) The Monet painting might be taken as a literal illustration of Yen's

---

* Dianne H. Pilgrim, *American Impressionist Paintings and Drawings from the collection of Mr. and Mrs. Raymond J. Horowitz exhibited at the Metropolitan Museum of Art, 19 April–3 June, 1973* (New York: Metropolitan Museum of Art, 1973), p. 79.

Winslow Homer, *The Cotton Pickers*. The Los Angeles County Museum of Art.

Claude Monet, *Women in a Garden*. Giraudon/Lauros/Art Resource, New York.

vision of an art in which "The fruit trees look like women, and the women look like fruit trees" – that is to say, an art in which there are no awkward discontinuities between the human and the natural, no residue of consciousness that will not be completely translated into public, social, worldly action and expression. To reverse Isabel Archer's dictum, in Monet's painting, clothes – costumes, manners, gestures, and relationships – express the self perfectly (just as they do in paintings like *Terrace at Sainte-Adresse*). Monet and Madame Merle agree. Homer's work, on the other hand insistently calls our attention to the difference between flesh and spirit, the mismatching of physical or social and visionary occupations (literally in *Cotton Pickers*). Homer creates a gap between the specificity of the realistic details and the mysterious evocativeness of the expressions and oblique glances that makes the uneasy relationship of consciousness to ordinary life the subject of the painting. Monet, in effect, does the opposite, implying that there is no surplus of socially inexpressible consciousness, that everything that can be expressed is perfectly expressed by the costumes, poses, and manners of his figures.

Homer's figures invariably look out of the frame space, beyond the physical world defined by their paintings. The presence of the wind and the horizons in many of his works, though not here, does the same thing: It beckons a viewer to look beyond social valuations and depictions, moves the viewer to an appreciation of an intangible, gentle sublimity in which the individual consciousness participates, separated from the group or the social task at hand and not communicable in effects of light and color.

The result is a conception of the individual as in some sense "all dressed up with no place to go" – with a consciousness that potentially will not be expressed or translated into worldly roles, actions, or identities. Yen's vision of a Monet-like world where the women are fruit trees and the fruit trees are women is, after all, only a vision, an expression of a yen for a world that lives up to his imagination of it, which is precisely what the world finally fails to do. Like Yen and Megan at the end of *Bitter Tea*, the dreamer in Homer, Eakins, Sargent, and the others is ultimately compelled to turn outward or inward away from the social group and the realm of the senses to a state of meditation, reverie, or vision.

This turning away from social interaction skirts the edges of the pre-Raphaelite dream of world-weary disengagement from social and ethical concerns, and the resemblance between Yen's palace, Fredrick Church's Olana, and the artistic and worldly creations of William Morris and the Rossettis is telling. As I pointed out in Chapter 1, the American tradition shares some of the impulses of the pre-Raphaelites. What distinguishes it, however, is its simultaneous dissatisfaction with the art-for-art's-sake disengagment from the world to which the pre-Raphaelites resigned themselves. The fact that Yen's empire of beauty and art falls apart at the end of the film is Capra's commentary on its ultimate inadequacy, no matter how alluring it also is to him at other points in the movie.

The process of disintegration that interests Capra most, though, is not the social and political insurrection embodied in the figures of the rebels and the hostile forces around the palace, which is barely sketched in the film, but the potential personal and psychological disintegration within Yen himself. He starts to fall apart. That, I think, is the meaning of the deeply disturbing scene in which, having secretly resolved on suicide as the only course of action, Yen calls Megan into his chambers and talks to her about the portrait of himself that he has commissioned to be done after his death. It is a morbid oriental variation on paint-by-numbers, all to be done according to a catalogue of standard features. As he says, "The ear number 3, the mouth number 6, and the chin number 27 equals General Yen." He is going to pieces before our eyes.

Megan leaves, and one of the strangest and most haunting scenes in the film takes place, strange and haunting precisely to the degree that it is so delicately suspended between the energies of composition and decomposition. It dramatizes Yen's effort of reintegration and self-composure in the face of all of the disintegrations and decompositions that he and his empire are undergoing. His final artistic act will be the most stylistically marginal of them all – an act of ritual suicide – as if his only remaining power of self-composition is in framing the terms and course of his own final decomposition. It is a scene to compare with some of the tales of ghosts and the supernatural by Hawthorne and James in which individuals divided by conflicts of feeling fall into pieces of themselves and wrestle with ghostly alter egos and partial identities that they had previously repressed, trying to hold together a new self assembled out of all the poorly integrated and misfitting fragments of the old one. Deserted by all of his entourage, Yen goes wandering through the palace, calling for someone to help him with his suicide. More than calling others, what he seems to be doing as he walks, shouting, from room to room is to be calling up the ghost of his own past authority. He tries out different voices and tones from his past as if he could conjure the majesty of those past selves into existence by adopting the proper tone, but only his own echoes of his past selves answer him. (At one point, although the echoing sound track makes it difficult to be sure, I am convinced that he uncannily even calls out his own name, as if at least to call himself together when no one else responds to him.)

It is a nightmare vision of the loss of personal authority and identity, of the disintegration of the isolated, unsupported self that haunted Capra's imagination and that is dramatized in climactic scenes in almost all of his major films, from *That Certain Thing* and *The Younger Generation* through *It's a Wonderful Life* and *Pocketful of Miracles*. I have already discussed the scene of Molly Kelly's crisis in the first film. In the second, Morris Fish, having clawed his way to the top and cut himself off from his family and friends in the process, is left, in the final shot of the movie, in a *Citizen Kane*–like stupor, sitting alone before the fireplace in his palatial mansion. In the nighttown scene in *It's a Wonderful Life*, George Bailey's dream of ideal freedom turns into a nightmare of alienation and wandering, and the self, freed from both the compromises and the burdens of social expression and entanglement, discovers that it has no home to return to and no society within which it can express itself.

In this poverty of circumstances Yen attempts to create something in consciousness, even if the world utterly fails to support his effort. Nothing in his life is a greater artistic creation (for Yen or for Capra) than his ceremony of leaving life. It deserves to be called a ceremony because the achievement of the scene is to "make" something more of the events within it than a mere realistic narration of the actions. Capra began *Bitter Tea* with the preparations for one kind of ceremony – the wedding between Robert Strike and Megan Davis – and he deliberately ends it with the preparations for a contrasting one, the suicide of General Yen. To deepen the parallel, it is, furthermore, a ceremony that represents a spiritual marriage between Yen and Megan that asks to be compared with the very different sort of union Megan almost entered into at the beginning of the film. The photography and lighting of the two scenes contrast in every respect. Yen's world is one of mysterious, enriching styles and secret, alluring depths, and spaces within spaces, at the farthest remove from the spatial flatness, lack of shadow or style, and absence of true mystery of the Protestant wedding ceremony.

With a narrative retardation and visual attention to detail that imbue every object and action with a ritualistic resonance, Capra documents Yen's esoteric preparations for his suicide. In a series of long takes, the camera follows him through two inner chambers to a drawer from which he selects a poison. Then it follows him back, to watch his step–by–step prepartion of the tea. In a three- or four-minute silent sequence, we stay with Yen as he goes through the elaborate ceremony: lighting the samovar, heating the water, steeping the leaves, adding the poison, stirring the cup. The initial, sensuous, extended pans and elaborate tracking movements following Yen from space to space in his chambers at the beginning of the scene give way during the ceremony to a series of dissolves that detail the successive steps in the preparation of the tea. Of all of Capra's work, *Bitter Tea* is the film that uses dissolves most frequently, and they function, in this scene as in the previous ones, to call attention to the fact that we are watching not life but a movie. They situate us in a world where space and time are malleable, just as they suggest how Yen's palace itself suspends or stops worldly clock time and substitutes in its place an alternative kind of artistic and cinematic pacing that is the only kind that matters in its domain.

Yen has shored up his ruins with all that he has left – a ceremony, a mere creation of art and style and consciousness. As he is composing himself and his life in the only way that is left him in the final minutes before his ultimate dissolution, Megan, having fallen in love with Yen despite her best efforts to hold him at a distance, like a later incarnation of herself – Ellen Andrews in *It Happened One Night* – has returned to the mirror she repudiated earlier and is composing herself in an analogous ceremony. "Making herself up" (in more than one sense of the phrase) in front of her mirror, she puts back on the oriental gown that she had earlier removed. Megan, Yen, and Capra are collaborating in these effects, even as all three poignantly realize how small and fragile is the magic circle that they are able to inscribe and momentarily inhabit in one corner of Yen's palace in this country in the midst of civil war.

Yen seats himself in an ornate throne in front of a strange octagonal window (or is it a painting or decoration on the wall?) and looks across at a mantle covered with precious artifacts and a painting of one of his ancestors on the opposite wall. He has composed himself in this world of artifacts to incorporate himself as a figure in a kind of still life, and already, on the screen, he looks as much like a work of art as the paintings and sculptural objects around him. "At precisely the right moment," as Lambert Strether would say, Megan enters his bedroom, finally ready to give herself to him. As she comes through his door we are meant to be reminded not only of Yen's entry into her bedroom in her dream, with the roles this time reversed, but more generally of the possible conversion of all life into dream. The dream world of art and artifice is the last refuge of order and significance in a world that has no time or space for them. Capra slightly overcranks the scene of her entry and heavily orchestrates its silent, slowed-down pantomime to make this moment as unnatural, as dreamlike as he possibly can while still suggesting that this too is also life, not an escape from it or a special part of it that we experience only in our sleep. It is within our power to make this life, though to do it takes an expenditure of imaginative energy as enormous as that the entire film has documented up to now. Megan falls at Yen's feet and makes her profession of love for him: "I had to come back. I couldn't leave. I'll never leave you."

One parenthetical aside: The lines Megan speaks are strangely dubbed onto the shot of her with her face hidden in Yen's lap. They are the only obviously postsynchronized lines of dialogue in the film and are among the very few instances of the practice in all of Capra's work, which leads one to wonder why he did this at such a crucial moment in his film. The first possibility is that the scene as originally written, rehearsed, and filmed was entirely silent: As it now stands, these are the only words spoken in its three or four minutes of running time. If Capra had originally intended it to be an entirely silent scene, especially in an era when audiences were particularly sensitive to the presence or absence of sound in the "all-talking picture," then his decision to film it like a dream – and like Stanwyck's earlier (silent) dream – is emphatic. The second possibility is that it had originally been scripted to play exactly as it does now but that Stanwyck's voice was not picked up on the microphone during the take that Capra decided to use. The question then becomes why Capra did not use a portable microphone to reshoot the take, as he commonly did – why he deliberately chose to fix the scene with the much more artificial technique of dubbing. Under either conjecture, we have, I think, warrant to conclude that Capra intentionally made this passage between Megan and Yen as artificial as possible. He is at this point, making his sound track as mannered as his photography and lighting.

To judge from Megan's words, Yen, like Capra, understands the limits of artistic arrangements better than she does at this point. To argue that Capra is holding out the possibility of a retreat into supreme fictions and the gorgeousness of the visual composition of this scene (where reflections off the mirrors on Megan's gown, the highly polished silver tea urn, the jewel in

Yen's skull cap, his enameled fingernails, and the tears in Megan's eyes all compose the gauze-shot scene into one sparkling sea of light) would be a Sternbergian reading of it. Capra and Yen are painfully un-Sternbergian in their shared awareness of how marginal our aristic arrangements are and of all that inevitably frustrates them. Time and death undermine our magnificent houses of fiction and indeed make us all the more grateful for the momentary riches that ultimately evanescent artistic arrangements offer. Yen drinks the poison at precisely the moment at which Megan completes the visual composition of the scene. He knows there is absolutely no place for this supreme fiction in the world. It must be satisfied with itself.

Ladies of Leisure, Forbidden, and *Bitter Tea* are each in their different ways studies of the power and impotence of art and consciousness to transform reality. They are studies of the stimulations of artistic transformations but also of their potential falsifications and fragility. As Capra admitted in his autobiography, at this time in his life he stood in very much the same relationship to Barbara Stanwyck as Yen does to Megan Davis, endlessly stimulated by her, resisted by her, and working on her with the power of all of his art. Like Yen, Capra was a maker of houses of fiction, the master of ennobling tricks with light and glass and mirrors that could open up appreciations of new possibilities of experience. The Stanwyck who comes into Yen's bedchamber in this final scene never existed in the world; she is as much Capra's creation as Yen's. When Capra fell in love with his creation, he undoubtedly was falling half in love with his own powers of imagining such beauty. That creation of imaginative possibilities is what these films are ambivalently about, even as they acknowledge the expense, the waste, the irrelevance of artistic creation which has only the power of a flower (or that of an enchanted garden). Such a fictional creation cannot ultimately resist the erosions of time or even the slightest pressures of actual social or sexual intercourse. It is not accidental that to be plausible at all, the scene has to be absolutely chaste and nearly silent – the frictional nature of dialogue or of sexual interaction would be entirely too much for this vision to withstand. That is no reason, however, as Henry James and Wallace Stevens knew, to repudiate these creations but only cause to embrace them all the more fervently, even as we admit their limitations.

My discussion of *Bitter Tea* could end with that comment, just as the film could end with Stanwyck's final embrace of Yen at the moment of his death. There is one scene following Yen's death, however, that sums up its complex effect and forms a coda to the film as a whole (and the artifice of a coda is precisely suited to the film's other artifices). The scene takes place, oddly enough, between Megan and Yen's financial adviser, Jones – between the woman who has finally recognized the power of imagination, and the man most rooted in the philosophy of dollars and common sense, the character seemingly most immune to the blandishments of art and artifice. She and he are headed away from the wreckage of Yen's empire, sailing back home together on a tramp steamer. Capra chooses to situate them on a set as different as possible from the opulence and beauty of Yen's summer palace, not only insofar as a boat of this sort lacks the decorations and ornate appointments of a palace but, even more strikingly, insofar as this particular piece of film scenery is as unimaginatively constructed, uninteresting, and barren of detail as the set of Yen's palace was stunning. We have moved from an MGM or Paramount "A" picture to a Columbia or Warner Brothers "B" movie. The coda extracts the viewer from the mimetic world of the previous hour of film – a world of imaginatively stimulating illusionism, detailed trompe l'oeil, elaborate glass shots, expressive lighting, and luxurious and expensive sets – and plunks him or her down in the mimetic world of a high-school play, with stagey, two-dimensional flats, oilcloth backdrops, and board floors. Jones and Megan are on a boat that does not look at all like a boat, on a sea that does not roll or heave, speaking or listening to a set-piece concluding speech, in a coda that broadcasts itself as an arbitrary, artificial closure to everything that came before it.

If one had any doubts about Capra's awareness of the peculiarity of his ending, they would be dispelled by the way he chooses to edit the transition from the preceding scene to this one. It is done with a highly mannered editorial technique, not to make us forget the artifice of the transition from one moment to another but to call attention to the editing in its own right. In the only wipes of the film (and there are very few in all of Capra's work), Capra flaunts his editorial prowess. He first wipes diagonally from lower right to upper left on a medium shot of Megan kneeling at the feet of the dead Yen. Simultaneously with the wipe, he fades out on that scene and fades in on a shot of a sail drifting from right to left, which, as it moves across the screen, perfectly matches the diagonal of the wipe with the diagonal of the sail. He then fades out on that shot of the moving sail (which serves as a second diagonal wipe, continuing the motion of the first) and fades in on the figures of Jones and Megan in medium long-shot, sitting on the deck of a ship in an approximate match of the initial shot of Yen and Megan, and with a line hanging on the ship further matching the diagonal of the wipe and the intercut shot of the ship's sail. In short, for our cinematic delectation, in a matter of seconds Capra presents a virtuoso editor's sequence: a matched double wipe, quadruple fade, triple match cut (matching the wipe with the sail, the figures before and after the wipe with each other, and the wipe and the sail with the lines hanging on the deck of the final ship). One can play verbal games with how the boat trip seems to "wipe out" the memories of the palace or how the world erases art, but it is more to the point simply to say that the meaning of the shot is not in any verbal pun or reference outside of it, but in its own commanding stylistic presence. This sort of editing trick wipes out reality simply by being more intricately interesting than any possible reality it represents and in attracting our attention away from its putative realistic content to its own cinematic form. This series of shots ultimately directs a viewer's attention less to any meaning outside itself than to its power to make or unmake meaning – any meaning at all. It is a transition that, if it gets nowhere, calls attention to its power to move anywhere – to deploy meanings that are not available outside of art, to make moves that only artistic transitions can make.

In the brief scene that follows, Jones attempts to sum up the previous hour of film in a sophomoric and cliché-ridden homily about how death and life are interchangeable, but fortunately there is no evidence that Capra is taken in by the mystical mumbo jumbo.* Jones is obviously drunk (that is the only condition in which this hard-headed realist could be imagined to talk this way), flourishing a bottle as he speaks, and even Megan seems to pay no attention to him. She is seated facing away from him, staring impassively and silently into the distance, and says nothing in response to his rantings.

Her silence speaks Capra's position much more eloquently than any of Jones's hollow phrases. Megan's achievement is that she finally accepts the state of awareness that Capra has been urging on the viewer throughout the film, replacing words, movement, and action with states of vision and reverie. She sits still and stares beyond social interactions and understandings of experience. She has moved into a state of silent meditation, a world where vision is possible. She embodies a capacity for vision that, as much as Capra wants it to be, emphatically will not be inserted into the world of social or narrative discourse and relationship. In her silence and passivity she has indeed almost moved beyond the reach of Capra's cinematic narrative itself. In her silence and stillness, she has moved into a chilly, lonely region, beyond even Yen. All that she (and we) have lived through for this last hour of the film has no possible worldly expression. She has no summer palace to retreat to, no ancestors with whom to form even a visionary community. She has no place to go and no way to express her charged consciousness. She can neither go back to Yen and his palace, nor forward into her marriage with Robert Strike, converter of the heathen. All things have been unsettled and nothing put in their place. That is the inevitable trajectory of imagination and desire, for Capra: to disrupt our social routines and worldly activities but not to offer anything in their stead. The uncanny effect of this spartan, primitive, "B"-picture shipboard set is to make all of the previous settings – both the Strike residence and Yen's summer palace – seem equally unreal and dreamlike in comparison with this bareness and austerity. All of the world's systems have been rendered artificial, but nothing "natural" offered in their place. Megan has become a kind of Ishmael who is doomed to be always in transit between worlds, denied the possibility of finding a home port or even an anchorage in any.

One notes that she is also reduced to simple street clothes in place of the gorgeous, mirrored gown she wore in the previous scene with Yen. This is a

---

* Charles Wolfe assures me, on the basis of a conversation with Capra about Jones's speech, that Capra, far from regarding it as bosh, seemed to endorse it as a summary statement in the film. Even if we are intended to take Jones's ruminations more seriously than I do, it should be noted that Jones (at this moment, and out of character, sanctioned by his drunkenness) represents a position not very different from Megan's. His drunken ruminations represent another sort of turn away from dialogue and narrative eventfulness and into a realm of reverie and meditation.

characteristic stripping away of stylistic accoutrements and accomplishments that occurs at the ends of many of Capra's other early films. The final scenes of *Ladies of Leisure, The Miracle Woman,* and *Forbidden* all denude their heroines of the dazzling costumes they wore at points earlier in their films, just as in this film and the other three the heroines are stripped of their powers of social, stylistic, or verbal performance as well. Megan Davis, Kay Arnold, Florence Fallon, and Lulu Smith are left emphatically silent, alone, and passive in the final moments of their films: Kay, her posing ended, reduced to lying flat on her back in a hospital bed, denied the dramatic resource of her costume and covered only with a sheet; Florence, buttoned up in a drab black Salvation Army uniform in place of the gorgeous evening dresses she previously wore as a tent evangelist; Lulu, pale and black-frocked, wandering away to be lost in a crowd on the street; and, Megan, in a cloth coat, sitting silently on the deck of this ship.

One is reminded of the silent, naked women staring out windows and off into the distance from bare rooms in Hopper's late paintings. Like Hopper's women, Capra's heroines are stripped down to their uncostumed humanity. Everything Hopper and Capra view to be inessential to human identity has been taken away. Posing and acting, as they take place in society, have ceased. The figure and the viewer have been moved beyond an understanding of experience in terms of costumes, theatrical poses, and social definitions of behavior. Isabel Archer's feeling that clothes cannot express her and Madame Merle's reply asking why she doesn't then go without them have become a possible reality. This negative process of decreation – the stripping away of all of the trappings in which the individual previously camouflaged and hid him- or herself – Capra believes, may make possible the discovery of a truer, deeper self and a more profound relation to experience that is communicated by the quietness and oblique glances of these final scenes.

Near the end of Jones's blatherings, he speculates that Yen is still present with them on board the ship: "Maybe he's the wind that plays around your hair." The reference to wind and hair at this point in the movie is far from a casual one. Megan's whole pilgrim's progress can be traced in terms of the relationship of the wind and her hair, since in the course of the film Capra carefully maps her spiritual progress in the metaphor of her gradually becoming able to "let down her hair" literally and symbolically. I noted that she takes the time to put on her hat before she goes to meet the fiancé she has not seen for three years. The presence or absence of a hat on her head and her willingness or unwillingness, in particular, to let the wind play in her hair in important scenes – for example, the scene on the balcony and the scene in which she comes to Yen at the conclusion of the film – give these facts a powerful metaphoric resonance. To be able to remove her hat in front of a man, to let the wind play in her hair outdoors, and to be able to feel comfortable about either thing are some of the principal indices of Megan's awakening sexuality.

The weird thing, however, is that when Jones uses the metaphor in the final seconds of the film, with its clearly summarizing symbolic import, there is no

Edward Hopper, *Morning Sun*. Columbus Museum of Art, Ohio. Museum purchase, Howald Fund.

Edward Hopper, *Second-Story Sunlight*. Collection of Whitney Museum of American Art, New York. Purchased with funds from the Friends of the Whitney.

wind playing in Megan's hair. Even if Jones's reference to the wind were not here, it is bizarre in any case that there is no sea breeze on the deck of the ship – but maybe it is not strange. There is no wind at all throughout this stage-set coda, but there is no rolling or pitching of the boat, no salt spray over the taffrail, nor any convincing nautical gear either (and all this from a director who, when he made a movie four years earlier called *Submarine*, insisted on shooting it on location at real docks and harbors to ensure that nothing at all looked false). Everything is false here, deliberately and excessively so. In fact, at the moment when Jones utters the line about the wind playing in Megan's hair, Capra includes in the shot a view of a passenger smoking on deck in the background behind Megan and shows that the smoke is going straight up from his cigarette in the absolutely calm air of the absurdly unrealistic stage set.

Is this even conceivably an instance of cinematic sloppiness – as one could at least argue that the dubbing of Megan's voice in the preceding scene was? Was the maker of *Submarine, Flight,* and *Dirigible* unaware that it would be the easiest thing in the world to put a fan on Megan's hair at this moment? (Capra thought to use fans on her hair to make it blow in the wind in at least two previous scenes in Yen's palace, one of them the balcony scene of conversation between Yen and Megan.) Would a director who paid such attention to details elsewhere in his film, not to mention in his previous nautical films, forget such a detail here (or be reluctant to reshoot the scene if he did forget it), at the moment when it perhaps counted most? Then again, as I have argued, this whole coda is an affront to standards of representation that the entire previous film has educated us to expect. To have put Jones and Megan on location on a ship tied up to a pier in a harbor, or at least in a water tank on a sound stage, with stagehands gently rocking the boat and throwing a little spray up over the sides, with a fan blowing Megan's hair from off camera, would have been no trouble at all for Capra to have arranged – but he does the opposite. What he is gratefully, joyously, sadly paying homage to in this deliberately artificial, unrealistic, tacked-on coda is the sheer artificiality of his art. It is only in the assertive artifice of such art that meanings can be engendered to tally with our aspirations and desires.

The coda is a celebration of and a meditation on the deliberate manipulations of art, and on the powerlessness, the unworldliness, and the glory of a consciousness that has no way in which to express itself beyond the artifices of art, which are here so outrageously paraded, only to make us all the more consciously aware of them. The dream Megan finally awakens to in this final scene, as she pretends to be dreaming with her eyes open on that artificial set, is only, Capra is telling us, a dream. The coda is a celebration of the richness of that dream and yet is simultaneously acknowledgment of the falsity of it. What Yen's summer palace and Columbia's set designers supplied in the way of imaginative stimulation for the previous hour of film becomes the burden Megan and every viewer must finally shoulder for him- or herself. We have been taught the possibilities of seeing and imagining in a movie palace, just as Megan was taught in Yen's summer palace. We are also reminded that it is only in art and by human consciousness that life is lived in this enriched way.

It is all, as Jones puts it at the very end of his rambling, slurred speech, "a lot of hooey." Capra knows that is all the dream is, but when was that ever reason to abandon it? All that remains when the curtain goes down and we leave the picture palace in which we, like Megan, have learned to sit enchanted in silence, learning to see, is what Megan is left with in this final moment: an energy of vision, meditation, and memory that can celebrate its capacity to experience and remember this set as a ship at sea, just as it made the lath and plaster of Yen's summer palace something that satisfied our dreams. That is a sad recognition, but an ennobling one nonetheless, as we leave the theater and feel the irrelevance of all that we have seen.

Capra's films again and again dramatize the predicament of the individual who has made the move outside of the limitations of society's categories and ways of understanding and then has no way to express himself and his charged consciousness. He has all the ideals in the world but no place to put them. Like Shakespeare's Nick Bottom, he has a dream "past the wit of man to say what dream it was," just as Capra (like Shakespeare) has almost no way to represent it in his narrative or in the world of social events. The enriched consciousness may have to content itself with the waste, powerlessness, and uselessness of its own enrichment. This is the conclusion that Capra's work forced on him repeatedly, throughout his career, but this film is perhaps the only one in which he seems to accept it. There are finally a quietism and aestheticism in *Bitter Tea* that make it unlike any of his other work, and that, one feels, finally limit the film. Capra's other films, and especially the ones that follow this one, are energized by his rejection of this stance of detachment and powerlessness, even as the films themselves repeatedly forced it on him (and on his characters). Especially in the films from *Smith* on, there is something bordering on hysteria in Capra's desperate attempt to make the dream expressible in society and language, to make the dreamer a force to be reckoned with publicly. In those films, Capra fiercely fought and resisted the insights of his own work, the conclusions his own films frequently urged on him. If his later work is not nearly as gorgeously elegiac in tone, as placidly mellow, and as infinitely resigned to the uselessness of artistic consciousness as this film is – if it is, as a result, more confused and muddled in places – it is all to the good. It is the human ambivalences and uncertainties, the intellectual cracks and fissures, the passionate inconsistencies in their arguments that make a couple of them among the major twentieth-century art works of our culture.

PART IV

Figures of imagination and desire

Lady for a Day, 1933
It Happened One Night, 1934
Broadway Bill, 1934
Mr. Deeds Goes to Town, 1936
Lost Horizon, 1937
Mr. Smith Goes to Washington, 1939

11

A world elsewhere

Lady for a Day
It Happened One Night
Broadway Bill
Lost Horizon

Emersonian man, when truly liberated, must remove the walls that shelter him from the cosmic ether. He must raise the windows, pull down the balcony guard rails, dismiss the sentries, and welcome as his brothers and equals – ultimately as himself – the demon-like forces ... It is a bold plunge to make ... No individual can survive a world without walls, an ego without repressions, a society without sentries. The self requires mediation. It requires the fictions that hide the deeper alonenesses among men, the secret sins of their inner beings, and the fact of death, which ultimately isolates them from one another. Better the evasions of history and comedy, and the illusion of community, than to open Pandora's chest of truth.

– Bryan Jay Wolf, *Romantic Re-Vision: Culture and Consciousness in Nineteenth-Century American Painting and Literature*

"Good fences make good neighbors."

– Robert Frost, "Mending Wall"

Though it may seem perverse to turn back from a film as rarefied as *The Bitter Tea of General Yen* to the relatively crude adventure trilogy (*Submarine, Flight,* and *Dirigible*) that preceded it, one thing linking all four films is their common fascination with the possibilities of special effects. Admittedly, the effects in the adventure films are simulated explosions, crashes, and exotic locations, and those in *Bitter Tea* are predominantly matters of imaginatively evocative lighting, photography, and editing, but in either case Capra is interested in creating meanings that are in some sense inexpressible in terms of conventional theatrical dialogue and social interaction among the characters. Frisky Pierce's flight to the South Pole and stranding on the Antarctic icecap and Megan Davis's exotic voyage into the Chinese interior both represent not worldly and social but imaginative expeditions into an otherwise unvisualizable psychological interior.

Let me argue an even stronger position. Though an exotic costume drama like *Bitter Tea* (or *Lost Horizon*) is usually treated as an aberration in the Capra canon of "realistic" films like *It Happened One Night* or *Mr. Deeds Goes to Town*, I would urge that the dichotomy is a false one and that the films of the

225

second type can only be understood properly when the imaginative extravagance or inordinacy that profoundly links them with the "exotic" films is appreciated. In short, as I tried to suggest in Chapter 1 by juxtaposing Capra's work with that of Hawks, Lubitsch, Cukor, or Wyler, it is a fundamental misperception of any of Capra's work to regard it as part of the "realistic" or "pragmatic" tradition within which these other filmmakers are operating.

Capra's films are much more radically individualistic and imaginatively disruptive than theirs. Whereas their work, needless to say, criticizes particular social situations and relationships in various local manifestations, his work gestures far beyond to criticize, as it were, the very warp and woof of the social fabric itself, not merely the distorted forms it may take in specific instances. The radicalness of his social criticism manifests itself most obviously in the impulse to generate states of intense emotionality (frequently, but not exclusively, created by means of melodramatic confrontations) and imaginative heightening in his characters. (This is what his detractors call Capra's hysteria, bathos, and sentimentality.) Such emotional and imaginative intensities constitute fundamental criticisms of all public, social structurings of experience. Such states of feeling are intrinsically explosive of rules of social and verbal decorum and moderation.

The comparison really should be with the work of a director like Josef Von Sternberg, although I am not referring to the rather superficial and finally unimportant similarities between the situations in some of their films, such as the similar plots and settings of Capra's *Bitter Tea* and Sternberg's *Shanghai Express*, but to a much deeper imaginative affinity. *Forbidden* and *Bitter Tea* earn the right to be called Sternbergian (and probably are actually indebted to Sternberg's work insofar as Joseph Walker's camera work is imitative of Lee Garmes's in Sternberg's films), because they create worlds that acknowledge the individual imagination as the source of value. Sternberg's interest in artificial settings and lighting has frequently been commented upon, but that aspect of his films is only an extension into the style of the film of the stylistic power to change reality granted to the central characters in his work (most notably, the imaginative power granted to Marlene Dietrich in the five films they made together). The central character less inhabits a world of fixed or predetermined social realities and codes of behavior than she imaginatively improvises such things into existence through the power of style and freely revises them to accord with her desires. As Cleopatra was for Shakespeare, the Dietrich character is the culmination of this aesthetic for Sternberg. Everything about her is artificial, an assertively stylistic achievement: her gestures, her tones, her mannerisms, even her body itself – plucked, painted, made up, and lighted as it is in these films. She has no "character" in a fixed social, moral, or psychological sense, no predetermined biological, physical, or personal identity in any of the films, only an identity she stylistically creates for herself out of nothing and that she is able to revise and rework whenever the whim strikes her. Her identity is as changeable as the various outrageous costumes she puts on and takes off in the course of the film. And her "world" is as infinitely plastic under the distorting pressure of personal fantasy and erotic feeling as her personal identity or visual image is.

Sternberg's films, in this sense, ally themselves with Capra's as explorations of the possibility of improvising an identity that is freely responsive to movements of desire and imagination. Capra, however, in most of his films, is doing something more complex than Sternberg, for although they shared the same basic agenda, Capra was less confident than Sternberg of the ultimate ability of even the most imaginative performer to overcome the limitations of society and social intercourse. The absence of the social give-and-take of extended, complex passages of dialogue in Sternberg's work is a telling fact. Capra's characters must negotiate the obstacle course of practical relationships and extended verbal interactions with another character, whereas Dietrich turns all of life into a private theater in which it is always, more or less, a one-woman show. In brief, Von Sternberg yields to his characters' (and his own) fantasies and dreams, whereas Capra worries and resists his. Capra might be said to cross a Hawksian belief in the inexorable constraints imposed by social codes on personal behavior with a countervailing and paradoxical Sternbergian effort to liberate imaginative energies from these formal limitations.

The films following *Bitter Tea* can be viewed as Capra's attempt to up the ante and intensify both the Hawksian and the Sternbergian sides of his narrative: to increase the embeddedness of his central characters in a matrix of social and formal constraints, while simultaneously *not* decreasing their imaginative freedom, eccentricity, and power. The result of this hybridization is the virtually Manichaean drama of the later work, in which an individual with enormous imaginative energy and independence is put into competition with social forces and narrative forms that war relentlessly against his or her free expression.

One of the signs of the increasingly perilous situation of the individual in Capra's work is registered in an initially slight but progressively more important move backward of his camera and speeding up of the editing in the films following *Forbidden*. The heavy use of close-ups and the fairly slack editing rhythms in the earliest films of the thirties (for example, *Ladies of Leisure* and *Forbidden*), as well as the generally small casts, granted Capra's central pair a power to control both the visual and the dramatic spaces of those films in a relatively unchallenged way. Increasingly with the films following *Forbidden*, and most emphatically from *Broadway Bill* onward, culminating in his so-called populist work and his first two postwar films, Capra pulls his camera back from his central figures, enlarges the supporting casts, increases the complexity of the background and foreground action in his shots, accelerates his editing rhythms, and intensifies the amount of cutting away from a figure, even during the scenes in which that figure is nominally the star performer, to take in alien and usually hostile contexts invariably impinging on and constraining the performance of his stars, who are now no longer guaranteed stardom in their own films. The central figures cannot count on automatically dominating either the visual space of the frame, the temporal pacing of a scene, or the social space of the narrative environments in which Capra imagines them. Closeups, long takes on a dominant central figure, and scene-stopping "star turns," needless to say, do occur at crucial moments in the later films (though far less often, to the point of rarity in *Meet John Doe* and films that follow it), but they are not routine events. They must be earned and achieved. They define special and increasingly rare occurrences in a formal world of medium and long-shots and a dramatic and social world of power-fully encroaching others.

This shift parallels another in Capra's work, a shift from predominantly female protagonists to predominantly male, or, to put it more precisely, a shift from more or less passive, visionary central characters to more or less active, practical, worldly ones. One can see this shift as reflecting Capra's increasing willingness to explore biographical similarities between himself and his central figures – since he was himself not only a man but also more or less a man of the world, functioning practically in a complex, extended society – but it is more generally symptomatic of a much more profound change in the films. Whether they were male or female in actual biological identity, the lovers and artists in the earlier films were generally allowed to be fairly passive representatives of idealism, sentiment, and vision. Yen and Megan, Jerry and Kay, Lulu and Bob (to a lesser extent) were released into states of private, insulated subjectivity. They were intermittently allowed to indulge in private dreams, feelings, and relationships, apart from a larger society. The central figures in the later films, in contrast, have less chance to withdraw into cherished states of feeling and awareness, and to aspire to withdraw in such a way is in itself evidence of failure for them. (Tom Dixon anticipates this side of the later work.) They must act – vigorously, effectively, at times violently – in the world. They must express themselves publicly, in words and deeds. It is as if Capra dares and wants to test the men in the later films as he did not the women in the earlier ones, and, in particular, as he did not want to test Barbara Stanwyck. (*The Miracle Woman* is admittedly an exception to this generalization about Capra's development.)

One of the most intriguing aspects of Capra's so-called development is, as I have already suggested, that it proceeds less along a straight line of artistic "progress" than as a series of continuous self-corrections or repeated adjust-ments of course along previously taken paths. Capra revisits old works and alters them in slight but significant ways; he changes his mind about their central figures and explores new possibilities of expression for them; or he tests old characters in new, more demanding, more difficult expressive situations. Tom Dixon, though he lacks their visionary qualities, anticipates some of Capra's later protagonists in his social embeddedness. *The Miracle Woman* has affinities with *Doe*, and indeed almost all of the characters and situations from the earlier films are repeated in one form or another in the later ones. Perhaps most artists only imagine the same few characters and situations over and over again in their careers. All that changes may be a matter of tone or key, but of course in art as in life, such matters can be everything. It is from this perspective that the transitional films, *Lady for a Day* and *It Happened One Night*, neither of which is supremely interesting considered in isolation, take on considerable importance as revisionary "re-visionings" of earlier work. Each is an attempt to domesticate the experience of the American sublime that had been given somewhat freer and more exalted visionary expression in previous films. Apple Annie, in the first, is a version of Megan Davis, a Galatea or Cinderella being transformed in the palace of art, and Peter and Ellie, in the second, are an adaptation of artist and model Jerry Strong and Kay Arnold. In both cases what has changed is that the later characters are constrained and limited by the forces of "reality" from which the earlier figures were partially or occasionally liberated.

Capra attributed the commercial failure of *Bitter Tea* (following a string of box-office successes that were beginning to get his work noticed) to its exotic sets and its employment of special photographic effects that, in his words, were "liable to distract an audience [from the performance of the actors]." Thus it may have been at least partly to test his hypothesis that he made *Lady for a Day*, which partakes just as much of the fantastic as the preceding film but manages to bring it all back home, to downtown Manhattan, avoiding the exotic properties, settings, and photography of *Bitter Tea*, while holding onto a story with profound similarities to it. It is the old Cinderella story: the imaginative and physical transformation of a rather drab, ordinary woman into something rich and strange, with the suggestion that the beauty was already there, or could have been there, all along. The transformation that took place in Yen's summer palace under the Cherry Blossom Moon is forced to occur on the streets and docks of New York's Lower East Side. That makes Apple Annie's situation in some respects more dangerous and thrilling than Megan's was. Megan was transported to a "world elsewhere" for her process of enlightenment. Yen's summer palace was a special environment where the consciousness could be protected, not entirely but to some extent, from corrosive realities of space, time, and mundane social events. The imaginative and physical metamorphosis of Apple Annie into Mrs. E. Worthington Manville is more moving than Megan's because of the inauspicious and perilous conditions under which it takes place.

Consider, in particular, only the different attention to time in the two films (temporality of both the narrative and of the representational sort). How long does Megan's entire adventure in Yen's palace last? Days, weeks, or months? How long do crucial scenes (like that of Yen's preparations for his suicide or Megan's sitting on the balcony during the Festival of the Cherry Blossom Moon) take in worldly time or in screen time? To ask such questions is to realize how effectively Capra's meditative dissolves, elisions, and ellipses in the film succeed in suspending our awareness of clock time and in making judgments of it almost impossible. *Bitter Tea* suspends Megan (and the viewer) in a dream world that is deliberately protected from such temporal pressures and awarenesses (which is why the visionary scenes in the film can take on an importance out of all proportion to their quite brief running time on-screen).

All that has changed in *Lady for a Day*, "fantasy" though it may be. Time can never be wished or dreamed away, even for a moment, and temporality relentlessly conspires against luxuries of visionary expansion. Even the title emphasizes the galloping pace of time's chariot. Cuts have replaced *Bitter Tea's* languorous dissolves as the basic syntactic principle, and the narrative demands (of both its characters and its director-editor) the mastery of a clockwork precision of pacing that would do Tom Dixon proud. The central metamorphosis, the stunningly arranged artistic "composition" of Mrs. E. Worthington Manville, is put into competition with pressures of time and with events that everywhere threaten to corrode it.*

The final minutes of *Lady for a Day* summarize the effect. Only by means of a complex, second-by-second series of temporal revisions of strategy and adjustments of performance, as well as with the aid of a few nearly miraculous coincidences and accidents, does the central artistic creation of the film, the creation of the "character" of Mrs. E. Worthington Manville, playing her "role" in a previously scripted "scene" at home, actually come off. There is a pressure of ever-threatening temporal decomposition here that Sternberg, for one, never allows to threaten his film's artistic composition. What one senses in Capra's work is not so much the celebration of supreme fictions (à la Sternberg) but the fragility of all stylistic achievement.†

As if to make the point with the utmost emphasis, at the very end of *Lady for a Day* the dream startlingly evaporates altogether, rather than resonating in memory, as it does at the end of a Sternberg film. The coach turns back into a battered, bruised pumpkin, the princess back into a grimy Cinderella. Mrs. E. Worthington Manville harrowingly (if comically) reverts to the street tones, manners, and styles of Apple Annie. Like Megan Davis, Annie is finally left alone with her memories and her enriched consciousness; this is all she has to show for everything that she has lived through. At the ending of *Lady for a Day*, unlike the ending of *Bitter Tea*, we and Apple Annie have no opportunity to recline nostalgically into the glory and splendor of it all. This final visionary expansion is pulled out from under our feet by the flurry of feverish activity that concludes the film. Apple Annie, reconverted to street hustler, gives hurried instructions to her henchmen to start shaking down the crowd. The film concludes with her then giving instructions to another character for her final artistic effect – the staging of the death of Mrs. E. Worthington Manville. (May one compare it to Yen's suicide?) Her final artistic act, like Prospero's or Cleopatra's, is an act of self-dissolution, a final renunciation of the powers of artistic transformation expressed in a final consummate exercise of those powers, but one different in tone from Yen's.

---

* Needless to say, temporal pressures were important in the original Cinderella story, but Capra gives them powerful metaphoric resonance, so that they represent all of the forces that conspire against our visionary expansion.

† *Meet John Doe* will detail even further the work of creating a "character" and the difficulty of holding onto a free self.

In *Lady for a Day* and the following films, it is not so much that Capra has discovered the forces of time, space, and society as that he has, for the first time, brought together two strands that were normally separated in his earlier work. *That Certain Thing* kept the visionary dreaming and the pragmatic scheming so separate that, in effect, two films resulted, one after the other. In subsequent productions, Capra alternated between films that gave themselves over to one or the other contrasted side of his aesthetic: *American Madness*, *Platinum Blonde*, and *The Miracle Woman* detailing social, temporal, and spatial forces within which a character had to learn to perform in quite severely tested ways; *Forbidden*, *Ladies of Leisure*, and *Bitter Tea* exploring possibilities of reverie, vision, and meditation that allowed a character temporarily to escape or transcend those social and temporal restrictions.

Even within single films, Capra tended to keep verbal and social forms of experience and expression somewhat separate from imaginative forms. There is, admittedly and always in Capra's work, still a profound and unresolved tension between the two forms of knowing and feeling (what Emerson called the discrepancy between "the two lives, of the understanding and of the soul"), but the act of *translation* between the two kinds of experience matters more than before. No longer can Capra even imagine a Stevensian land of pure poetic vision and romance – call it Yen's palace, Havana, or Arizona – separate from the prosaic world of power politics, family obligations, temporal pressures, historical traditions, and social and institutional discourse. When Capra reimagines Yen's domain four years later in *Lost Horizon*, the "Megan Davis" figure, Robert Conway, is not only himself a man of the world but travels with a ghostly doppelgänger, a brother, who brings the vices and untidy passions of the world with him inside the palace compound. Capra's films still contain isolated moments of ecstatic (or despairing) visual and acoustic heightening, experiences available only for the eye and ear of the viewer and a solitary central character, but there is an increasing effort to express them within the entirely unvisionary occasions of everyday life. The transcendental impulse must be able to survive in a world not profoundly different from the world the filmgoer encounters outside of the movie palace.

If the imagination must acknowledge the pressures of the world in a new way, the corollary is that the world in these later films is newly forced to recognize the unappeasable pressures of the individual imagination. On being injected into society, the dreamer disrupts its routines as never before. Megan Davis, Jerry Strong, and Stew Smith politely stepped off to one side of their films' narrative and social events when they dreamed their dreams, but Jefferson Smith, George Bailey, and Grant Matthews are almost always still in the thick of them. There are no balconies or studios to which they can viably retreat.

Ellie Andrews (Claudette Colbert) and Peter Warne (Clark Gable) of *It Happened One Night* are transitional figures in most of these respects. They remind the knowledgeable viewer of most of Capra's earlier central performers and to some degree bridge the gap between the visionary and the social figures in the previous films. Like James's early heroines and many of Capra's earlier figures, they attempt to live their social lives not as if they were contrasted with the free movements of imagination and feeling imagined in works of art but as if they were naturally continuous with them. The effort is not easy or painless, and Peter and Ellie learn how difficult and confusing it can be. They learn the costs and difficulties of attempting to perform the same sort of scenes in life that one finds in a poem or novel, the psychological pains and social misunderstandings that such performance can cause, and the ways that it can also be less an act of creative self-exploration than a strategy of emotional evasiveness and personal self-protectiveness.

Probably a large reason for the charm they hold for an average audience is simply the well-meaning ineptness of their attempts. Stew Smith and Tom Dixon were performative geniuses compared to these two. Instead of the polished performances of professionals, theirs are the clumsy acts of the rankest amateur, all of which only make us love them the more insofar as they are so obviously in the service of such healthily good intentions of creative self-expression. It is undeniable, though, that they have a long way to go before they will be able to get their acts together, singly or jointly, in order to be able to play together with anything like the poise and mastery shown by Stew, Dixon, or Yen.

The first half of *It Happened One Night* is a comic anthology of their stupidities, miscues, mistimings, and extravagances, together and apart. In an attempt to assert her freedom from her wealthy father, Ellie impulsively marries a celebrity aviator, King Westley, who is a bigger stuffed shirt than anyone in her own fairly stuffy social circle. In the opening scene of the film, in which her father attempts to confine her to their yacht in order to prevent the consummation of the marriage, she first throws a childish tantrum and then jumps overboard and swims ashore, as if the expression of her independence were *that* easy, as if all it took to shape a performative "freestyle" were a stronger freestyle than one's father's. If Ellie's situation has something in common with that of a fairy-tale princess imprisoned by an ogre father, she makes the mistake of treating life as if it were as simple as a fairy tale, and a happy ending as unearned and automatic. Peter Warne is established in his initial scene as being almost as out of touch with reality as Ellie. When we meet him, he is in a telephone booth, drunkenly haranguing his newspaper-editor boss in front of a crowd of onlookers.

Capra's leading man and woman are thus both, in the opening minutes of the film, defined as high-spirited, willful, and cranky performers and would-be free spirits who throw scripts dictated by anyone but themselves to the wind in their determination to declare their independence from institutional or familial control. They are zanily gifted, if quite clumsy, self-centered, and headstrong improvisers. (Peter, in particular, seems to enjoy the sheer theatrical challenge of improvisation beyond any practical purpose, as when he continues his inspired monologue long after his editor has fired him and hung up.)

The dramatic metaphor is particularly appropriate to describe characters who are so self-consciously and deliberately aware of the possibilities of experimenting with stylistic inflections and acting strategies in life, as well as to a film and director so notorious for its (and his) improvisations. The creative results of dramatic improvisation, as we have seen, were fascinating to Capra whether it was of the scripted sort that creates the illusion of an actor's or a character's improvisation, or of the genuinely spontaneous sort in which an unplanned remark or gesture finds its way into the final print of the film. Capra was, after all, an old hand at managing and eliciting improvisations: The silent comedies that he directed at the beginning of his career were nothing more than extended exercises in improvisation by actors and directors, since usually little more than the writer's idea for a joke had been written down by the time filming began.

Improvisation has a venerable history in our art and culture, and Peter and Ellie take their places in a long line of American improvisers, from scoundrels and con men like Sut Lovingood, Tom Sawyer, and Flem Snopes to confused innocents like Huck Finn, Daisy Miller, and the Chaplin tramp, improvising their way through alien environments – all of whom are characterized by their ability to make the most of any situation they find themselves in. In a world in which no standard, agreed-upon code of behavior and social values exists, it is the resourceful social improviser who carries the day. The resourceful Yankee peddler, confidence man, and rip-off artist are, in this constellation of characters, only debased versions of Maggie Verver in *The Golden Bowl*, who learns in the course of the novel that even the most exalted forms of virtue are only brought into existence and expressible by means of spontaneously improvised performances. Dramatic improvisation is a fact of life on the American scene, in and of itself neither good nor evil. *The Golden Bowl* has an improviser for immorality named Charlotte Stant, as well as an improviser for morality in the figure of Maggie. Capra's *Lady for a Day*, in its gentle, fairy-tale-like way, comprehends both moral possibilities in the contrasted figures of Dave the Dude and Apple Annie. In the films that follow *It Happened One Night*, the characters that interest Capra most – the good and the evil – share a capacity to make up themselves and their agendas as they go along.

In fact, the chief respect in which Peter and Ellie differ from the other characters around them, and the reason they attract each other, against their better judgments (as Anne Schuyler and Stew Smith similarly attracted each other, notwithstanding their differences) is this shared capacity for improvisation. Indeed, the principal reason we are confident that Ellie cannot ultimately pair off with King Westley the autogyro ace, is that he is, in strictly performative terms, such a stiff. In each of the scenes in which we see him, Capra contrives that his acting be as wooden and rigid as Peter's and Ellie's is unpredictable and entertaining. Similarly, the hilarious scene in which Ellie sits down next to the traveling salesman, Oscar J. Shapely – "Shapely's the name, and that's the way I like 'em" – is basically another comparison of rival acting styles. Shapely is a "character" all right, of the sort that populates the entire cast of a Preston Sturges film, but that is how we recognize his comic inappropriateness as a partner for Ellie. His iterative line of patter and style of acting are as mechanical and repetitive as Ellie's or Peter's performances are inventive and eccentric. To be identifiable as a character, to have a tidy, psychologically well-defined bundle of attributes and a fixed verbal and theatrical style is by definition, in this film, to be inadequate.

Capra has a prototypically American suspicion of the stylistically portable, packageable, and categorizable. He has a distrust as great as Emerson's or Whitman's that even the thing we call the self is only a potential social and psychological dead end that must be avoided at all cost, a roadblock in the way of an otherwise endless development and imaginative movement. To be limited to any fixed style of performance is to limit the possibilities of free self-expression too much.

Thus even to the extent that Peter and Ellie are categorizable in terms of standard screwball designations like "the pampered, sheltered socialite" and "the smug, cynical reporter," they are uninteresting to Capra. Their performances begin with and repeatedly regress at moments to being as pre-fabricated and predictable as those of an Oscar Shapely or King Westley, but it is by virtue of their increasing awareness of the limitations and absurdity of all such fixed roles that they gradually become capable of more complex, self-critical, and eccentrically improvised performances.

Although one can find the seeds of it in Capra's interest in improvisation in some of the early adventure films and in Stew Smith's performance in *Platinum Blonde*, Peter and Ellie represent the beginning of a profound process of dramatic and cinematic exploration in Capra's work that will be of crucial importance to an understanding of the later films. They become figures in a cinematic parable about the expression of desire in the world that is couched in terms of the presentation of alternative and opposed kinds of acting within a single film. In *It Happened One Night* "fixed" characters like Shapley, the motel keepers and their wives, King Westley, Warne's editor, and Ellie's father represent one kind of acting. Representing the other are the sporadically "free" characters like Peter and Ellie. The first group comprises some of the most brilliant "character" performances in all of Hollywood filmmaking – but that is just the problem: These characters have "characters." They are examples of brilliant "technical" acting of the sort for which Preston Sturges's movies are famous. Capra differs from Sturges (whose entire cast, in *The Palm Beach Story*, *The Great McGinty*, or *The Miracle of Morgan's Creek*, possess such technical virtuosity) in his desire to offer an alternative to "character acting," which is what he does in the forms of expression represented by the central figures of his late films.

It is difficult, however, to label this other kind of acting. We have no term like "character acting" to describe it.★ It is a kind of acting that attempts to

---

★ In Chapters 12 and 13 I will relate this kind of acting to what has come to be called Method acting. As the example of Colbert's and Gable's acting in *It Happened One Night* illustrates, however, this range of acting and performance is clearly larger than what is normally meant by a term like *the Method*.

speak the language of desire instead of the language of society. It has more emotional interiority than the other kind of acting. It attempts to put the viewer in touch with private states of feeling that almost defy verbal or social expression. It is in these respects more mysterious and more imaginatively stimulating than the other sort of acting. It is, in brief, Capra's attempt at a transcendental acting style (if such an apparently bizarre entity can be admitted).

Ellie and Peter represent not merely more engaging and energetic social styles, roles, and tones than those of Shapley, Westley, and the others but a possibility of performance that moves completely beyond those things. The performances turned in by Jimmy Stewart and Gary Cooper in the later work are the imaginative extension of what Capra asks of Gable and Colbert here. Whereas the language and behavior of the fixed or character actors in *It Happened One Night* is socially overdetermined, psychologically overmotivated, verbally overpointed and dramatically overinflected, the language and behavior of the free characters, even more in the later films than this one, is excursive, centrifugal, extravagantly unfocused or unmotivated (in several senses of the word *extravagant*). The figures in the second group are representations of free-floating desire, of feeling unmoored from any specific practical point or purpose, undefined by social category or motivation. (Though it may subsequently become attached to some social or political goal or purpose, and usually does in Capra's later work, the desire is the central fact, and the particular application of it to some purpose or crusade is almost an afterthought.)

I am indebted to Richard Poirier for the terms "fixed" and "free" characters, which he uses to describe figures in the early novels of Henry James. It is especially useful to invoke the example of James, since he is so obviously a case of a nonpolitical artist who can help us to appreciate this nonideological aspect of Capra's work. In the medium of language, James is doing something similar to what Capra is doing theatrically in these films in eliciting alternatively fixed or free performances from his characters. Capra has too frequently been considered primarily an ideological filmmaker, but Ellie and Peter show that freedom does not have to be politically generated. As Capra and James both demonstrate, the most important freedoms in our lives may in fact be stylistic. The same idea is found in other stylistically daring American films – for example Nicholas Ray's *Rebel without a Cause* or John Cassavetes's *Faces* and *Woman under the Influence*. James Dean and Sal Mineo, in the first film, and Lynn Carlin and Gena Rowlands in the second and third, are not only aliens in the world in˙hich we imagine their characters to live and breathe; they are, perhaps even more significantly, nontechnical actors or non–character actors, in films populated by technical or character actors. That double alienation, or double freedom, is what Stewart and Cooper attempt to convert into transcendence. Acting in this nontechnical way, for directors of such sensitivity to alternative acting strategies, can itself be a powerful assertion of freedom.

Let me be as specific as I can about how Peter's and Ellie's performances differ from those of the other characters around them. Capra shows Ellie's and Peter's gradual attainment of a delicate, perilous, marginal freedom from narrow roles and limiting styles of behavior not by keeping such roles and styles out of their parts and the film in general but (in the method of American parodists from Melville to Gaddis) by allowing them into the text and their performances and then comically revealing their inadequacy to them and to us. *It Happened One Night* is initially an exercise in the comic testing and parodic exorcism of failed or inadequate styles. Peter and Ellie keep getting trapped and embarrassed by their stylistic choices throughout the film. They pick up and discard dozens of prefabricated roles in the course of the film, many of them inconsistent with each other, and most of them silly and childish. Ellie plays the roles of independent and liberated woman, the damsel in distress, the high-society princess, and the frightened little girl, breathlessly, one after another; Peter plays the romantic Romeo, the macho man, the male protector, the worldly-wise teacher, the cynical or disinterested reporter, and the irritated guardian, to name only the most obvious and mutually contradictory. Each role or style sooner or later comically disintegrates. Each time that they prematurely think they have gotten their respective acts together, their confidently assumed roles and postures break down under the pressure of emotional experiences too powerful and disturbing to be contained by them.

As in so many of Capra's films, the only thing that saves Peter and Ellie from their own misguided efforts at self-defense is the emotional confusion they generate in each other. It is only by virtue of their mutually induced bewilderment that the psychological, social, and stylistic barriers behind which they try to protectively immure themselves are undermined. The sexual "walls of Jericho" (in the form of a blanket that separates their beds in several motel rooms) do suddenly come tumbling down at the end of the film, but the far more important walls in the film are the stylistic walls that Peter and Ellie erect around themselves, which are comically chipped away at in the course of it. Both of them begin the film, as I have already argued, by deliberately fleeing from narrow, restrictive roles imposed upon them by others, Ellie fleeing from her father's authority, Peter from his editor's – only, in effect, to typecast themselves in a series of equally rigid and confining new roles as they board the bus to New York. It is by dint of bouncing off each other (literally and figuratively) on a three-day bus trip that they stimulate productive doubts and confusions in each other and in themselves and gradually learn to move away from their initial states of stylistic mastery and psychological complacency. They worry each other into creativity.

This is exactly where a Hawks screwball comedy would end: Unpredictability and eccentricity would have been allowed in to loosen up and lubricate otherwise rigid and confining social performances. This is also where most accounts of Capra's film stop. This, however, is where Capra's idealistic form of screwball comedy differs from the garden-variety Hollywood form. Capra suggests that even these new performances, however iconoclastic they may be, are themselves still potentially only further dead ends to development, traps for the free imagination, or if not dead ends and traps, then still only rather frivolous and trivial expressions of the self. His films stand as a radical critique of the aesthetic premises of the Hawks and Lubitsch comedies. One must move beyond these new social roles, but how does one move beyond the limitations of all social roles, beyond all technical acting performances?

It would be hard to tolerate the outrageousness of the imaginative project that Capra outlines for himself if it were not for the fact that other American artists make a similar effort. The strange adulation of the child, the primitive, and the atavistic throwback, in American fiction, is evidence of the same attempt to suggest that there is a reality somewhere, somehow beyond style, beyond social formulations, beyond all ordinary novelistic and artistic language that matters more than any of the things definable by them and articulable within them. One thinks of *The Sound and the Fury's* inarticulate, bovine Dilsey as a vivid example of Faulkner's attempt to evoke and cherish in his writing a realm almost beyond the verbal and novelistic. There is an unappeasability, a relentlessness, to the deconstruction of social styles and roles in *It Happened One Night* that affiliates the film with this tradition and that is at the same time potentially quite troubling and disturbing about it.

As in so many other aspects of the American expressive predicament, it was Emerson who most clearly articulated both the positive and the negative sides of this transcendental project, and the greatest of Capra's films and the central characters within them comprehend both the potential exhilarations and the lurking bewilderments and psychic disasters of this effort. In them we are not very far from the doubleness of feeling that Emerson displays in his "Circles," as he recognizes both the creative stimulation and the perilous uncertainty of a life led as an endless flight away from all destinations for development, away from the possibility of resting with security anywhere, at any time. An even more profound link with Emerson is the way Capra seems to need to hide, perhaps even from himself, the full radicalness of his own imaginative project, the depth of his criticism of social and dramatic forms. *It Happened One Night*, like most of his best later films, attempts to muffle the imaginative disturbances it creates in the innocuous laughter of romantic comedy. It attempts to deny its own strangeness, to (dare I say) blanket its own unappeasable imaginative aspirations, and pass its drama off as being merely comically conventional and commonsensical.*

Of course, one way of remaining free from limiting styles and confining roles is to adopt Peter's initial cynicism about all social relationships and commitments. As in so many of Capra's other films, from *Platinum Blonde* on, the reporter character is a representation of postmodern man in all his glory and despair. He is someone who, by virtue of his occupation, has become an ideal deconstructionist of all of the texts of his own society. In being able to circulate freely through his society's various social, political, and institutional

---

* Occasionally Henry James also conceals the radicalism of his own social criticism.

special-interest groups, as a reporter, he has recognized the arbitrariness and artificiality of their codes of behavior. Indeed, that truth has made him free. Yet however dazzling his freedom and mobility may seem, they, like that of all literary and cultural deconstructionists, are earned at the price of sacrificing moral and social involvement and belief, and with them the possibility of enduring personal or moral commitment. The postmodernist figure is, like Peter at the beginning of the film, the playful, detached, master of all roles and movements, except those that would compel him to sacrifice this mastery and movement – such as intimacy, commitment, or love of another human being.

In almost all of his early work Capra simultaneously admires and distrusts the consummate performer. Molly Kelly, Kay Arnold, Florence Fallon, and Stew Smith might each be seen as examples of performers who show a truly dazzling mastery of shifting tones, styles, and stances. They are, in their different ways, spectacularly able to stay on the move and uncommitted to any one limiting style or identity. They costume and dramatize themselves in a seemingly endless series of facile, polished performances, and yet each – like Peter and (to a lesser extent) Ellie here – uses his or her ability to play (in all senses of the word) as a mode of evasion, a way of avoiding authentic emotional or ethical involvements. Florence Fallon in *The Miracle Woman* is such a quick-change mistress of makeup, costuming, and role playing (she wears thirteen different outfits in the course of her film) that it is impossible to say where "she" is underneath them all or if there even is anyone underneath all of the different roles and appearances she assumes.

The ideal of leaving the shell of the old self behind, of making a new identity for oneself, strangely links the Hollywood starlet with the Puritans who came three centuries earlier. It is the ideal Hollywood has thrived upon, the dream of making a star out of a Midwestern teenager; the contemporary California dream of making up one's identity as one goes along. One can imagine how the director who had grown up in the Sicilian ghetto of Los Angeles, making his way in Hollywood in the roaring twenties and early thirties would have come to be interested in this situation. He would have had examples of it thrust on him at every turn. Hollywood's actors and actresses have always chosen to act out the furthest fantasies of the American dream of free self-creation and endless re-creation, just as they have suffered the depths of self-destruction when the dream turned into a nightmare.

The difference from the Puritans, however, is that the characters in these early films aspire to attain the rewards of self-creation without going through the pains of decreation, the analysis and understanding of their old selves. They avoid coming to grips with their deepest emotional needs and attachments. They try to break away from the past and make a new identity without first understanding the past or themselves. That is why their facile efforts of self-creation seem hollow and glib and invariably bring them to crises of identity.

In the largest sense, Capra forces his master performers in these films to acknowledge deeper emotional needs and commitments that bring their consummate mastery of performance, their brilliantly mercurial shifts of tones and styles, into question. They are compelled to realize that they have selves underneath all of the roles that may not be satisfied or expressed by them. Although Peter is not as extreme a case as Florence Fallon, Capra suggests that he too has ideals and feelings that are not being expressed by his virtuosic social and theatrical powers of performance. His capacities to "play" (socially and theatrically) make him wonderfully entertaining, but Capra wants to suggest that there is a self (or a set of beliefs and desires) underneath all of the play that is separate from it, and ultimately not satisfied by it.*

For all of these reasons, Stanley Cavell is only half right when he says, in the best essay yet written on the film, that the process of Ellie's and Peter's (and Colbert's and Gable's) learning to "play together" (in all senses of the phrase) is the subject of the movie and its great pleasure.† Learning how to play together, how to adjust and pace one's performance in terms of another's, as I have already emphasized, is immensely important in much of Capra's work and is an avenue of growth and maturation for Peter and Ellie. It is admittedly the kind of event in *It Happened One Night* in which audiences take the greatest pleasure. Capra is finally less concerned with Peter's and Ellie's ability to play together, however, than with their developing an intimacy, a romantic involvement, and a shared imaginative openness that is very different from, and practically opposed to, all that Derrida and other modern and postmodern critics and philosophers since Nietzsche have extolled in their elevation of dramatic, social, moral, and linguistic "free play."

The best way to explain a little more concretely what this means is simply to go through a few of the major scenes in the film. When Peter and Ellie play badgering husband and hurt wife in the first motel room in front of the detectives hired by her father, as any actors playing a role do, they certainly learn a lot about themselves and each other by being forced to pretend the emotional intimacy that each of them has been resisting up to that moment. (It is hard to imagine a more intimate and revealing relationship with a lover than an argument. It must be a close second to making love for the depth of involvement and emotional self-exposure it demands.) I would argue, however, that the real climax of the scene occurs after their joint-stock improvisation. When the detectives leave, as they hurriedly prepare to reboard the bus, Peter helps Ellie to straighten her hair and kneels down to button up the front of her dress, and each becomes momentarily aware of sexual feelings about the other that the polish of their madcap performance had kept contained.

The moment that passes between Peter and Ellie at the conclusion of this scene is analogous to the "epiphany" passages in the writing of James

---

* Compare my discussion, near the end of Chapter 1, of some of the differences between Capra's and Sturges's work.
† Stanley Cavell, *Pursuits of Happiness: The Hollywood Comedy of Remarriage* (Cambridge: Harvard University Press, 1981), pp. 71–109.

Joyce.* Although the Joycean epiphany is often mistakenly treated as if it re-presented a moment of revelation or sudden insight on the part of a character, it is typically the opposite of one. It represents an occasion of bewilderment, breakdown, or confusion of values and beliefs, or of an access of unorgani-zable and ungovernable feelings, when the social and verbal styles in which a character previously took refuge are suddenly discovered to be irrelevant or mistaken. It is not accidental that at such moments in *Dubliners* or *A Portrait of the Artist*, Joyce's conventional presentation of events in terms of dialogue, social interaction, and plot development also breaks down or gives way to another style of presentation. Joyce shifts at such moments to a poetic heightening of his prose – though some would call it (especially in *Dubliners*) a sentimental belaboring or adolescent flogging. However one judges it, the text switches out of one mimetic mode and into a distinctly different one. It changes from a novelistic presentation of events in terms of dialogue and plot to a poetic registering of strange, silent states of meditation or reflection. Evocations of states of private feeling and imagination are substituted in place of narrations of social and verbal events. Primarily aural and acoustic effects replace the previous registrations of visual and physical details. The writing changes from rather spare, usually short sentences to longer periodic construc-tions, with cadenced repetitions, and elaborate sequences of alliteration, assonance, and euphony. In short, the mimetic switch communicates how far Joyce (and his character) have moved from a conventional novelistic under-standing of events and how inexpressible such moments are in the social forms and structures of ordinary novelistic presentation.

Such literary effects are obviously unavailable to a filmmaker, but Capra, within the expressive resources of film, performs an almost identical mimetic shift at crucial "epiphanic" moments in his work. He too, at such moments, wants to move beyond what is "speakable" in terms of dialogue or social eventfulness, but not having Joyce's poetic language at his disposal he em-ploys gauze-shots, romantic backlighting on the hair of his heroine, or soft key lighting to model the expression on a character's face and eyes at an impor-tant moment in an otherwise fill-lighted scene. At other times he tries to transform the moment by charging it with the significance of some entirely private symbol (which may mean little or nothing to an uninitiated viewer) such as rain, which he always considered sexually suggestive.

Such moments are as different from the routine and hackneyed Hollywood stoking up of romantic interest (as seen in a Hitchcock, Lubitsch, or Cukor film) as Joyce's moments of epiphany are from the moments of revelation that

---

* Though this analogy may seem to take us very far afield from *It Happened One Night*, and although we must allow for the significant differences between the expressive resources of a fiction writer and those of a filmmaker, it can help to clarify Capra's artistic technique and goal. (I choose James Joyce as a point of comparison only because his work is probably more familiar to most readers than that of anyone else I could cite. D. H. Lawrence could be used as an example equally well, as could authors from virtually the entire American visionary tradition from Jonathan Edwards to Eudora Welty.)

Cinematic luminism: light speaking what characters cannot.

occur in a Fielding or Austen novel. Capra's epiphanies are moments of radical formal and social breakage, in which the very premises and operating procedures of the previous narrative are fractured or at least temporarily abrogated. Not built up out of or continuous with the public, social events preceding or following them, they represent ruptures in the narrative form itself. They are moments of emotional and psychological, as well as of formal and narrative breakage that will not be reintegrated into the social life around them, any more than they will allow themselves to be "spoken" in the artistic forms of that life. Rather than building upon and deepening the events that precede them, they swerve vigorously away from them and invalidate them. They move the film into an emotional realm that can only be fleetingly expressed, in such stylistic effects of light, shadow, or sound (I will have more to say later about the use of sound in Capra's work).

Consider the scene in the hayfield, which comes about twenty minutes after the one in the motel. Peter and Ellie have been forced off the bus by a breakdown and have been trekking cross-country, with Peter playing to the hilt the role of the cocky, wisecracking male protector to which he has repeatedly reverted. (He has been protecting himself from emotional vulnerability by hiding behind a series of wisecracks and sarcastic remarks, giving Ellie lessons in donut dunking and piggyback carrying, just as he will on the following morning give her one in hitchhiking.) Ellie is playing the role she habitually assumes of independent, liberated, unshockable woman. The point Capra is making is how far from being truly exploratory or creative this role playing is. (Though most audiences seem to find it hilarious, I must say that it is not even very funny, in my opinion, but increasingly tedious.) Their behavior is, in brief, only a form of social wall building and emotional self-protection.

Capra's photographic and acoustic additions to the mere script of the film – what is expressible in terms of the plot and dialogue – become his way of gesturing beneath the fairly superficial social and theatrical text, or even, at times, of indicating the irrelevance of everything we are watching being played out on the social surface of events. This passional stylistic subtext is brought into existence through Capra's use of effects of lighting and sound that are the rough equivalent of Joyce's mimetic shift to poetic language and aurality. There are, at important moments in Capra's work, in effect, two films superimposed one on top of another: the obvious one, which we can, for convenience, call the text of the dialogue and plot, and a quite different emotional subtext that is frequently covered up or hidden by the first text. The part of the film represented by the smart chat, comic routines, and games between Peter and Ellie is, we are made aware, all a dodge, an evasion of an emotional and imaginative subtext that neither character wants to be the first to disclose to the other. In the haystack scene, all the while Peter and Ellie are emoting about their toughness and independence, Capra's lighting on the haystacks and the cornfield and on Ellie's hair and face, the gauzed close-ups of her face, and, most of all, the registration on the sound track of all of the pregnant pauses and silences between the two of them communicate the opposite of their toughness, independence, and self-sufficiency.

The most important scenes in *It Happened One Night* redirect our attention *away from* the actions and social interactions taking place and *toward* something else that is apparently expressible only by the pauses between the words, the tones of voice used, the quality of the light on a character's face, the sounds in the background, or the musical orchestration on the sound track. At such emotionally charged moments the characters often are saying or doing nothing, or nothing very important – are silent, passive, or merely staring thoughtfully into the distance, in reverie or meditation – and we, too, shift into a meditative state.

It would be a mistake, however, to attempt to draw a hard-and-fast line separating Capra and Capra's preferred cinematic style of expression in this film, on the one hand, from his central characters and their preferred styles of verbal and social interaction on the other. In this particular case, the error would be to argue that Capra stands in a simply critical or clearly dismissive relationship to Peter's and Ellie's stylistic games and is offering an alternative cinematic style with the sole object of plumbing the private emotional depths underneath their evasive public performances. Rather, the movie suggests a much more vexed relationship between the creator and his creations, and one, incidentally, much more like the relationship of Joyce to Stephen Dedalus in *A*

Portrait of the Artist. Much of the fascination these characters have for their respective creators resides in their authors' inability to be merely dismissive of their characters, since they share so many of their vices and virtues. It is Stephen's quite Joycean ambivalence about his stylistic indebtednesses, and Joyce's quite Stephensian fascination with stylistic virtuosity and preciousness that makes *A Portrait of the Artist* such a complex and moving spiritual and artistic autobiography. Joyce is very like Stephen, even while dreading it a bit. Similarly, the fact that Capra, in his own potentially off-putting and self-defensive stylistic virtuosity, shows himself to be very much like Peter Warne, and the fact that Peter Warne, in his dissatisfaction with his own too cold-bloodedly skillful performance, shows himself to be a lot like Capra, make *It Happened One Night* a highly complex emotional and artistic exploration. Far from being simply set up for criticism, Warne is recognizably a portrait of a certain side of Capra's own cinematic personality in this film and others – the brash, smug, knowing, frequently cocky director who boasted, at about this point in his career, that he could film the phone book and make it interesting.

This is a side to Capra's personality that is inseparable from his simultaneous sense of self-doubt and anxiety about his accomplishments, as I mentioned in my discussion of *The Name above the Title.* The evidence of it in Capra's early work is his interest in and admiration of characters who are masterful social or verbal performers, even to the point of facileness. That is what fascinates Capra about Frisky Pierce, Stew Smith, and Kay – "I'm always posing" – Arnold and, one must conclude, that is probably why he was able to be taken in by the figure that Tom Dixon cuts in the final scene of *American Madness.* In short, the jokey evasiveness that runs through his autobiography was always something he was tempted to admire in his characters, and many of the films are themselves guilty of a kind of jokey evasiveness in their presentation of a character or scene. It was hard for Capra to avoid going for the easy laugh, as a way of avoiding the more difficult exploration. The comic and stylistic brilliance of the films is often used as a dodge.★ As a result, there are scenes and characters in all of the films that are too clever, too charming for their own good, a fault that Capra, unfortunately, does not always detect. As the same films demonstrate, though, Capra was generally aware of this tendency in himself and his characters and was disturbed by it. It is not for nothing that in his early work he features characters who get into trouble because of their performative virtuosity. Even as he sometimes yielded to it, Capra distrusted his facileness. What makes this most superficially brilliant of his comedies and this pairing of two of his most playfully witty performers so interesting is that

---

★ Particular sequences in *So This Is Love* might be cited as a case in point, if a specific illustration of the worst result of this aspect of Capra's work were needed. The film is so self-protectively cute and tiresomely humorous at moments that it ceases to be funny. In such scenes one watches it less as a movie and more as evidence of a pathology, an extreme need to disarm criticism by means of self-defensive cuteness. If such a state of affairs makes for screamingly bad scenes in some cases, though, it makes for fascinating emotional explorations in cases like this one when the filmmaker takes his own will to stylistic power as his subject.

it is as much about a love – hate relationship of a creator with his characters as it is about a love – hate relationship between the characters themselves.

The concrete manifestation of Capra's own Warne-like smartness of manner in *It Happened One Night* is the way the film picks up, parodies, and comically disposes of other films' styles. Capra works off all sorts of excess imaginative energy in gratuitous stylistic pyrotechnics. The positive way of looking at this is to say that, in the tradition of Melville, Whitman, Twain, West, and many others, he is as anxious to flaunt his stylistic independence of anything that would limit the frequently outrageous free play of his imagination as Peter is. To be a master parodist, though, as I have already suggested, has its potentially negative side. Though one admires the stylistic virtuosity of both Clark Gable's and Frank Capra's performances in these scenes, there is frequently something just a little too cute, and, worse yet, emotionally distant and coy about this aspect of the film. It is a danger that parody always runs, and one that has undone many promising American artistic careers, especially in the past forty years or so, from the writing of Nathanael West to that of John Barth, from the films of Preston Sturges to those of Robert Altman and Brian DePalma. The American master parodist always courts the danger of becoming such a consummate quick-change artist that he ends by giving up his own personal identity. He always runs the risk of protecting his freedom so dazzlingly, behind so many masks and postures, that his independence becomes anonymity and his freedom homelessness, and he himself ceases to be an emotionally involved participant in and contributor to the human community around him. Performative prowess can become not a means of more complete self-expression but a wall behind which the weak, vulnerable self hides in order to avoid self-disclosure. (The master performers in John Cassavetes's work inevitably come to mind as the most recent illustration of this American phenomenon.)

Notwithstanding these ontological dangers, it is undeniable that when Capra starts to show what he can do as a filmmaker by picking up and playing with styles, the result in strictly stylistic terms, is brilliant. One is glad for these moments, even as one is equally glad that Capra never showed quite this same self-pleasuring abandon in any other film. When Shapely guesses Ellie's real identity and Peter scares him off by pretending to be a gangster abducting her for a million-dollar ransom, Capra switches the lighting and photography and the intonations and pacings of Clark Gable's performance to a gangster-movie style that would do *Scarface* proud. When the publicity hound, King Westley, arrives for the wedding at the Andrews mansion in his absurd autogyro, Capra switches to "newsreel" style, which *Citizen Kane* was supposed to have been the first feature film to employ, with poorly framed, asymmetrically composed long-shots photographed past intervening objects and no close-ups. When Ellie, misunderstanding Peter's intentions, returns to her Long Island home near the end of the movie and prepares for a high-society wedding, Capra mimics the stagy tones, camera placements, theatrical entrances and exits, and Big White Sets of a Lubitsch film.

Like Warne, who sends free verse to his uncomprehending newspaper editor, Capra takes so much obvious pleasure in playing with styles and conventions that it perhaps does not matter that the stylistic commentaries in these scenes are thrown away on any but the most knowledgeable audience. Capra, the self-confident filmmaker who seems to have mastered all of the social codes and cinematic styles necessary to his craft, like Warne the veteran reporter, is left with the question of what to do with all of this knowledge. Once a character (or a filmmaker) has seen through the formal conventions and social styles that most societies or films are content to remain within, what is left for him or her? Is a kind of Wildean stylistic connoisseurship, characterized by social cynicism, aesthetic detachment, and imaginative alienation their doom, or can Capra and Warne find a way to affirm something beyond the superficial styles they have so completely mastered?

Capra's use of light and sound and special cinematic arrangements and effects in this film is his answer to this question. He attempts through such means to validate secret wells of personal feeling, moments of vision cut off from social expression. It is such moments that the film is endorsing when a backlighted Ellie is photographed in close-up on a bed in a motel room and Capra's camera holds on her face, while she says nothing. The function of Capra's use of light and shadow (and the sound of the rain on the roof here) is no different from its use in the scene in which we were introduced to Yen, shining and glimmering in the rain of the rickshaw-accident scene. The meaning of such scenes is definitely not comprehensible in terms of the dialogue, plot, or social interaction, but rather in visionary and acoustic effects of light and sound.

Capra's use of stunning visual and acoustic effects or non-source-sound musical orchestrations at crucial moments to communicate something that cannot be expressed through the characters' words or actions is obliquely related to the practice of nineteenth-century American luminist painting. The American luminists similarly used effects of light (or of imagined sound or silence) to communicate a spirituality that could not be expressed in social forms (through the interaction of characters or anecdotal narrative eventfulness in their paintings). Capra's cinematic effort, like their pictorial effort, is an attempt (in Peter Brooks's useful phrase) to "gesture toward [a] realm of true feeling and value" that is speakable only in such ways. The Jamesian novel, and much of the nineteenth-century melodramatic tradition in fiction (which is the subject of Brooks's *Melodramatic Imagination*,* from which the quotation is taken) employs various rhetorical devices to the same end. Its metaphoric insistences and purple passages are attempts to generate states of sublimity or emotional heightening that define a realm of values and feelings more intense, authentic, and important than our ordinary social organizations or forms of social expression can "speak." Films that function in this same tradition, as

---

* Peter Brooks, *The Melodramatic Imagination: Balzac, Henry James, Melodrama, and the Mode of Excess* (New Haven: Yale University Press, 1976), pp. 74–5.

Capra's do, substitute certain forms of visual, and acoustic intensification in place of the linguistic forms employed by the novelist.

One does not want to overlook the devices that the filmmaker shares with the novelist. Some film theorists argue that filmic expression must be treated as unique and assume that the more purely "filmic" an effect is, the better it is. In fact, however, visionary artists working in different forms of expression have a great deal in common. (That is also why an artist such as D. H. Lawrence can so readily move from one form of expression to another – from poetry to short stories to novels to essays – and still successfully express himself in each form.) For example, much of the luridness, violence, and confrontational drama in Capra's films subserves exactly the same expressive purpose that it does in melodramatic fiction. One has only to compare the function of the murder near the end of James's *The Other House* with the murder near the end of Capra's *Forbidden*, to compare the moments of silent, gasping, staring in James's *The Spoils of Poynton* with those in *Mr. Smith Goes to Washington*, or to notice the many comparable instances of charged moral and social confrontation between two opposed characters that run through both artists' work in order to see that the novelist and the filmmaker are working in the same expressive territory.

As I have already argued in the case of other Capra films, and as will be true of his subsequent work as well, although not compromising their commitment to the expression of operatic intensities of imagination and desire, Capra's works simultaneously recognize the force of realities from which the works and characters of Puccini or Verdi are relatively exempted. Consider, for example, the last scene in which Peter and Ellie are visible together in one physical space (in a motel room in which they stay overnight, still separated by a blanket hanging between their beds), a scene in which Peter delivers the most exalted and idealistic speech of the film. It is a vision so detached from any social reality or narrative relevance that Capra momentarily has to immobilize both Peter and Ellie flat on their backs in their separate beds in order to make sufficient cinematic time and space for its unimpeded expression. It is a speech that finally reveals this apparently hard-boiled reporter to be another one of Capra's dreamers or idealists, underneath it all. Peter tells of a dream that he would not have dared to express to Ellie any earlier in the film. It should be noted that Peter started off, in Capra's and Riskin's initial script, as a Greenwich Village painter before he was made over into an idealistic but wisecracking poet-reporter, and there are decided similarities between his dreams, as they are expressed in this speech, and those that Jerry expressed to Kay on the balcony in *Ladies of Leisure*. Not only does he imagine his dream world as one freed from the pressures of all social groups larger than himself and the woman he loves, but he explicitly imagines transforming himself into a kind of transparent eyeball, seeing all, nothing himself, letting the currents of the universe flow through him:

> I saw an island in the Pacific once ... Never been able to forget it ... That's
> where I'd like to take [the woman I'm in love with]. She'd have to be the kind

of girl who'd jump in the surf with me and love it as much as I did ... You know, the nights when you, the moon, and the water all become one. You feel you're a part of something big and marvellous. That's the only place to live. Why, the stars are so big and clear overhead you feel you could reach up and stir them around ... Boy, if I could ever find a girl who was hungry for those things.

After a long pause, Ellie responds by saying, "Take me with you, Peter." She is apparently romantic and innocent enough to believe that they can go off together and actually live such a dream of splendid isolation and visionary transparency, but it is significant that neither Capra nor Peter, however they reverence it, are taken in by Peter's dream. (When Peter and Ellie are finally romantically united at the end of the film, it will not be in the surf of Waikiki but in a shabby motel room in oceanless Michigan.)

Peter's description of his dream is the most operatic moment in the film, but life is not an Italian opera, after all, and Capra and Peter are as aware as Emerson of how hard it is to live through the eye, even an eye as passionately creative as Peter's is here. Peter, as we saw in the second scene of the film, has lost his job (since free verse, like a poetic reverie, is not readily translatable into cold cash), and he does not have a cent in his pocket. Capra ironically points out in the scene immediately following the one in which he tells his dream that this visionary voyager to a Pacific paradise cannot even afford gas for a thirty-mile trip to New York. Peter has to hock his hat and suitcase to a service-station attendant to get the money to go to the city, where he then must talk his former editor into rehiring him and giving him an advance of one thousand dollars on the strength of a story he writes, before he can even propose to Ellie. Enchanted poetic voyagers in Italian opera (or in the poetry of Walt Whitman and Wallace Stevens, for that matter) never had to haggle over the price of gasoline with a grease monkey. When Emerson called poetry "vehicular," even he conveniently glossed over the matter of cab fare.

Before following Peter into the city, I want to return to that scene in the motel room for a moment. The way Capra handles the sexual implications of the scene needs to be examined, especially insofar as this moment is symptomatic of a problem of sexual expression that runs throughout his work. Peter's ability to speak this way to Ellie is evidence that the psychological and social walls that have separated them throughout the film are effectively down by this point. The blanket remains hanging between their two beds, but after Peter meditates out loud, Ellie significantly crosses over to his bed, on the other side of the blanket, for the first time. She is in love with him and probably more than willing to sleep with him, too, at this moment. At the very least she is interested in translating some of the visionary communion they have just shared into some more practical form of physical and social communion. She moves to Peter's side, but he immediately sends her back. Why? In a world of pure vision, Peter would not need to resist her physical advances (since they would not be proffered physically); in a world of opera, imaginative communion is indistinguishable from physical communion, the blending of voices is the same as the coming together of bodies. Capra's world, though, is profoundly resistant to visionary mergings. Social mores, the codes of public decency (and the Production Code enforced by the Hays Office), the dictates of reasonable financial prudence and responsibility (in filmmaking and in life), and a dozen other repressive forces all resist the conversion of shared vision into shared physicality.

This repression of physical sexuality is perhaps the most vexing yet interesting aspect of Capra's work to the contemporary "sexually liberated" viewer, and something that surfaces in film after film. (I have already more obliquely noticed it in *Ladies of Leisure*, *Platinum Blonde*, and *Bitter Tea*.) Capra repeatedly resists translating the forms of imaginative and romantic dreaming that his couples come together to share into the physical form of a sexual relationship. As I pointed out in my discussion of *Platinum Blonde*, in that film Capra rigorously and systematically substitutes one form of intercourse – visionary and imaginative, for the other – sexual and physical, to the extent of suddenly substituting one actress (Loretta Young) in place of another (Jean Harlow) in the final minutes. He relentlessly idealizes sexual relationships and suppresses deidealizing forces in his own film.★

The result is that Capra and his male heroes have been charged with a kind of sexual cowardice and immaturity. Since his male dreamers are seldom able to translate their abstract visions of creative human relationships into practical sexual relationships, they have been called sexually deficient, emotionally immature, emasculated, or priggishly Boy Scoutish. (One wonders, for the sake of consistency, why the argument does not typically go on to indict the women in his films as well. The double standard seems to rule in criticism as in life, so that female sexual shyness is not as culpable as male.) The criticism is undoubtedly founded in a valid observation about his films, and Capra's autobiography provides suggestive material for speculations about his personal attitudes toward sexual relationships. This expressive problem in the films should be viewed less as Capra's personal problem, however, than as being profoundly representative of an expressive problem that crops up throughout American art and invariably involves the discovery of the problematic relationship of certain sorts of romantic ideals to concrete linguistic and social situations within which they can be expressed. Emerson, Hawthorne, Melville, Twain, and Whitman might be said to have been wrestling with the same expressive problem: the difficulty of the conversion

---

★ *Forbidden* is a possible exception to this rule, the one film in which his characters dare to express their romantic dreams physically and practically in the real world. The totally doomed results of their act of desublimation, however, make it an exception that resoundingly proves the rule. Even *Forbidden* hedges its bets by gradually derealizing or Neoplatonizing the relationship of its central couple. In the second half of the film, as Lulu becomes more and more a principle of abstracted emotionality and imagination estranged from social expression, and finally even starts to fade out visually, too, we realize that we are back in the desexualized imaginative world of the other films.

of romantic visions into eminently unvisionary sexual, social, and artistic forms of expression.

Capra's films, like the notoriously asexual essays of Emerson or the androgynous poetry of Whitman, are egregiously unable or unwilling to translate states of idealism into a practical form of action within a particular social situation. The work of Emerson and that of Henry James might be said to mark two extreme points of view along a spectrum of situations in this respect. James never shies away from – in fact, he plunges wholeheartedly into – explorations of the trajectory traced by the most extraordinary desires and imaginations as they are passed through the distortions and constraints of expression in a dense social and sexual matrix. Emerson, on the other hand, turned away from and declined this robust Jamesian engagement with the forms of ordinary life through which ideals are expressed. (This is indeed James's criticism of Emerson, in his essay on Cabot's life of Emerson.) Capra's work seems situated somewhere between that of Emerson and James in this respect (and as his work progresses in the decade of the thirties, he shifted slightly from the Emersonian side of the spectrum toward the Jamesian). Early and late, in sexual affairs at least, Capra never dares to go as far as James in exploring the practical expression of sexual feelings between consenting adults. In this particular area, though not so much in other aspects of adult social life, Capra remains an American transcendentalist, with all the complex evasions and inadequacies of expression that that implies.

Among the other forces working against the free expressive impulses of Ellie and Peter in *It Happened One Night*, time is one of the most important. As in *Lady for a Day* the pressure of time, especially in the last half of Capra's films, is almost always felt to be working against the desires of his characters to expand into states of vision or to relax into a visionary community. Cliff-hanger endings were common in thirties pictures and, as in Shakespeare's day, it was standard operating procedure to attempt to salvage an otherwise unexceptional drama by speeding up the pace of events in the final half hour or so. The picture that ended with a succession of whirlwind narrative reversals or narrow escapes, like the film that began with a surprise (like a train robbery or a car careening off a cliff), almost defined an action genre in itself. The logic seemed to be that if an audience was left sufficiently breathless, thrilled, or bewildered by the pace of events in the final ten minutes of a film, harder questions about the adequacy of characterization, motivation, and plot would not arise. (In the middle and late 1970s the movie that ended with a car chase, a big fight, a bicycle race, a climactic shoot-out, or another contest made the same assumption.) As early as *Submarine*, in which the audience is kept in suspense until the final minutes by the question of whether the crew of a sunken submarine will be rescued before their air supply runs out, Capra demonstrated his easy mastery of editorial pacing and cross-cutting in the service of manipulating temporal rhythms and audience response. It is a small step from the ending of *Submarine* to the endings of films like *Ladies of Leisure*, *Dirigible*, and *The Miracle Woman*, all of which hinge on split-second timing that threatens the central characters' imaginative achievements in the final minutes. If there were nothing more to these conclusions than their cliff-hanger qualities, Capra could justly be convicted of yielding to mere Hitchcockian manipulativeness of an audience's fears and anxieties. As the plots and themes of the films deepen beyond the relatively shallow emotional waters of *Submarine*, however, these otherwise formulaic suspense endings take on a new resonance and importance. Time is, in effect, being put in competition with atemporal vision. The most exalted ideals and aspirations of a character are forced to confront the tick-tock of the clock, the plot of the film, and the cut–countercut rhythms of the film's editing. In the final half hour or so, the imaginative compositions of the central characters in all of these films are tested against the powerfully de-composing pressures of time. The characters are forced to enact their visionary ideals in a world in which time cannot be wished or visionarily composed away (as it largely was in *Bitter Tea*).

Characters are not only exhaustingly pressured by time but are forced to learn to negotiate the resistance of a skeptical or hostile social milieu in order to earn an arduously achieved happy ending. Only to the extent that they prove themselves capable of such unvisionary negotiation of alien entanglements are they judged to be adequate. Longfellow Deeds, Long John Willoughby, Jefferson Smith, and George Bailey, in the later films, visionaries and dreamers though they be, are never able to escape the practical constraints of space, time, and society, and their dreams matter only to the extent that they are realizable or expressible in terms of these relentlessly resistant forms.*

In the conclusion of *It Happened One Night,* the romantic close-ups that Capra and Walker employ in the first two-thirds of the film to photograph Peter and Ellie in their most imaginative and idealistic moments are replaced in the final half hour of the film by medium or long-shots that situate them in the

---

* It is true that following this process of trying a character to the limit, Capra often has recourse to a sudden shift of events or reversal of destiny in the last four or five minutes of the film that releases many of the pressures that have been established up to that point. These "miracle" endings were criticized by reviewers in his own day and continue to be criticized by writers on his work in ours, arguing that they reveal the ultimate sentimentality of his vision. There are two replies to this, I think. In the first place the wish-fulfillment/fantasy quality of many of the endings is evidence of Capra's attempting to bring into existence last-minute imaginative communities that he was unable to represent earlier in the same films in terms of social or interpersonal interactions. Imagination or fantasy is made to do the work that plot and dialogue have proved unable to do. Thus these endings are, far from being happy, virtually tragic in implication.

In the second place, what gives these last-minute reversals their "miraculous" quality is precisely the vigorousness of Capra's depiction of the pain and difficulty of the central character's predicament up until that last-minute shift of events. The miracle endings, in this view, testify to the true arduousness of all that has gone before them, since even the quite mixed victories of the endings of the films take virtual miracles of coincidence and timing to pull off.

In any case, however one feels about Capra's determination to provide a happy ending, no matter how gratuitous, to his films, the "miracles" that take place in the last four or five minutes can never erase a viewer's memory of the pain and struggle that came before them.

middle of a series of changing events and intrusive social groupings. The earlier gauzed close-ups that ensconced and protected the lovers in their own private world of vision stop, and Peter and Ellie are separated and swept along different courses by a swirl of events largely out of their control. The earlier elegant, carefully composed backlighted or key-lighted "beauty shots" of Ellie (and sometimes of Peter) in a poetic mood give way to cluttered, fill-lighted, documentary-style middle-distance shots that include large groups of people around them and that, near the end of the film, narrate the inexorable progress of a series of spatial movements, hairbreadth escapes, and sudden shifts of action. The static frame space of the earlier shots of Ellie yields to a spatially and temporally anxious editing rhythm and an appetitive panning or tracking camera that, when it does stop to frame Ellie, includes a changing series of events taking place around her or an extended, complex social group of which she is now a member, for the first time in the film. Capra is using one formal aspect of his film to place or criticize the other. That, in formal terms, is why Peter and Ellie cannot fall in love once and for all and live on a Pacific island. The time-bound, event-hungry structures of the conclusion of Capra's narra-tive (like life itself) resist visionary releases from time and separations from society. To put it practically, there would be nothing for Capra's actors to say, no events to make scenes with, and nothing to photograph if Peter and Ellie transformed themselves into Pacific star-gazers and the narrative impulse were suspended. The structures of Capra's narrative correspond with the structures of life in the deepest sense. Both equally resist visionary appropriation. That is why negotiating the structures of narrative exposition, like negotiating the repressive and constraining forces of life, is so frictionally stimulating for the greatest artists, and why narrative form itself is the greatest and most enduring of artistic discoveries.

In the final section of Capra's film, while Peter is absent in New York, attempting to turn his romance into practical narrative and financial capital by writing a story for his newspaper so that he can pay the real cost of his vision and afford to elope with Ellie, the accumulated pressures of time, money, and physical and social arrangements all abundantly resist the translation of his and her shared dreams into the forms of waking life. Their expressive task, therefore, is not very different from that of a visionary filmmaker like Capra who himself could articulate his ideals only by negotiating and mastering the financial, social, and bureaucratic realities of a Hollywood film studio and by expressing himself within the narrative constraints of the films it produced. Like Peter, his alter ego, Capra makes his living in this process of conversion and translation. He must convert his inarticulate dreams into the forms of coherent, systematic narrative, in order to make the dreams count at all. Free verse cannot pay the rent.

The ending of *It Happened One Night* revises the final movement of most comedies of frustrated courtship from *A Midsummer Night's Dream* on. The orthodox comedy of this sort has a three-part structure that moves from an imprisoning or frustrating home, to a temporary escape from home into a relatively free space for personal exploration (whether to the woods outside Athens or a country estate in Connecticut), to a final return back home that reintegrates the previously alienated lovers into a world of extended social relations, under the doubly changed circumstances of increased self-knowledge on their part and increased tolerance and understanding on the part of the previously hostile parents or lawmakers. In *It Happened One Night*, though, Capra is significantly unable or unwilling to complete the third movement – to bring Peter and Ellie back together in a larger society and under the aegis of Ellie's father at the end of the film. Capra felt an overwhelming need to suggest that something like that takes place, and there is a kind of filmic sleight of hand by which he attempts to show that the lovers are reintegrated into society and returned to the authority of Ellie's father, but it is a sham, and even as Capra gestures toward it he confesses what every viewer feels: that there is no actual society in the film that can include his visionaries or within which their dreams can be expressed. There is no society larger, more substantial, or more enduring than the fugitive visionary community formed by the two of them, separated by a blanket in a motel room, sharing a dream about an imagined Pacific-island paradise for a few enchanted minutes, protected within the spell of Walker's low-key-lighted photography and the slackened pace of Capra's editing. Even to be magically transported to such a fictional Pacific island would not be adequate to Peter's and Ellie's dreams, since, as we have already seen, the problem is that their ideals cannot be converted into sexual realities. Life on an island would deidealize their relationship in ways that Peter and Capra are unwilling to accept.

Let me briefly turn from *It Happened One Night* to the film Capra made immediately following it, *Broadway Bill*. Its ending presents an even clearer example of Capra's inability to give his romantic dreamers a place and a way finally to express themselves in the world and can help us to understand the ending of *It Happened One Night*. In *Broadway Bill*, Capra incidentally uses a controlling metaphor almost identical to that which the use of the blanket establishes in the preceding work, a metaphor that judges the central characters in terms of their ability to move around or across walls or barriers that would limit their freedom. Dan Brooks is a restless, idealistic young man "boxed in" by a boring job in a cardboard-box factory and by marriage to a wife who is interested only in social climbing and obsequious subservience to her millionaire father, J. L. Higgins, and her family. Dan's one idiosyncracy, and the expression of his idealism, is his passion for horse racing (something that can never be boxed in). He owns a horse named Broadway Bill, and dreams of quitting his job and racing him professionally. Because of this he is regarded as a fool by everyone in the Higgins family except his sister-in-law, Alice, who is a horsewoman and, further, is clearly in love with him. To make a long story short, one day Dan finally leaves his home and runs off to race Broadway Bill in a major race, and Alice follows him to help him prepare for it. After a series of complications, Broadway Bill does, needless to say, win the big race, but the question Capra confronts at the end of the film that relates it to *It Happened One Night* is what to do with Dan and Alice. Alice is with Dan on the day of the big race, but it is unthinkable, within the terms of thirties morality (not to mention the dictates of the Hays Office), for the two of them suddenly to pair off together. Dan is still married to his boring wife. Alice is his wife's sister and will have to return home to father and family, now that she has no further excuse to legitimize her presence at his side. On his side, Dan himself cannot return home to the job at the box factory and to a slow death within the social circle of the Higgins family without repudiating everything he has stood for up to that point in the film.

One of the connections between the ending of *Broadway Bill* and that of *It Happened One Night* is the calculated complexity of Dan's and Alice's situation at the end of the film. It really would not have been difficult for Capra and Riskin to have arranged the plot so that Dan would be divorced from his first wife by this point, so that he would have been free to walk off into the sunset with Alice or, at the very least, for them to have created an initial situation in which Alice was not his wife's sister, so that a romantic relationship between Dan and Alice would have been more decorous. One can only conclude that Capra deliberately complicates the situation of his hero in *Broadway Bill* for some of the same reasons he complicates Peter's relationship with Ellie.

Dan and Alice are left frustrated and in a state of imaginative limbo after the race. Broadway Bill dies on the finish line, and Dan and Alice say goodbye after the funeral. It is Capra's ambivalence about this that is most interesting, and relevant to a consideration of *It Happened One Night*. On the one hand, he insists that the dreamer is left in the end with no social accommodation or worldly consolation, with nothing but his consciousness to show for his effort. In what announces itself as the final scene, Dan walks away alone across a field in a long-shot that pointedly tells us as much. On the other hand, and in complete contradiction to this sentiment, Capra wants to bring his hero back into society, to suggest that he can become a member of a community hospitable to creative eccentricity, iconoclastic idealism, and free self-expression. So, after this first ending, he inserts a second ending to *Broadway Bill*: a strange, brief "two years later" coda in which Dan returns to the Higgins house to win Alice. The intervening time presumably has allowed Dan to divorce his wife, Alice to grow up enough to marry Dan, and a decent interval to have elapsed between the two events so as not to violate any Hays Office dictates or offend matronly sensibilities in the audience.

Capra is ambivalently hedging his bets. This sort of narrative contrivance, with its conception of "decent intervals" and proper behavior, pays homage to the very social and temporal forces of repression against which the entire film has been gathering energy and of which Dan Brooks has from the beginning represented a wholesale rejection. An even more telling detail occurs in the scene of the coda itself. The Higgins family is sitting formally at the dinner table when a commotion is heard outside. A rock is hurled through a window; a car horn beeps. Dan has obviously returned, but he refuses to set foot inside the house. He sends a message to the table with the butler (whose hair has been rumpled and shirttail yanked out): "He says he came to rescue the princess from the dark tower." It is a quaint, fairy-tale way to propose to Alice in this quaintly implausible and fairy-tale-like, wish-fulfillment ending (and further, it works one final sea change on the metaphor of breaking out of formal and social enclosures that has been used so creatively in the preceding film).

What is even more interesting is a tiny gesture that follows the butler's announcement, a very small gesture, but one that is so important that it stays in the mind long after the film is over. Alice, needless to say, is overjoyed that Dan has come. She has not heard from him for two years, but now her dream has suddenly come true: He has proposed to her, albeit in a fashion as eccentric and iconoclastic as everything else he has done in the film. Before she rises from her chair to run outside to join him, though, she glances at her father and waits a split second for his nod of permission to leave the table. When she gets it, she trots to the head of the table, kisses him, and runs to join Dan. It is that glance at the father that is so significant. Capra, as I have already said, has ambivalently written two distinct and opposed endings for his film, but even within this second ending he attempts to have things both ways at once: to endorse Dan's, Alice's, and his narrative's iconoclasm and antinomianism but also, at the same time, to nod toward the token authority of the father and the value of obedience within the family. It is a cheat; he cannot have it two ways at once, but it is a cheat that haunts film after film. If there is any doubt at all about the sleight of hand built into the scene in this glance and nod between daughter and father, it is dispelled only seconds later when the father himself runs out after Alice to travel with the two lovers on the racetrack circuit, thus hopelessly compromising the basic dramatic opposition of Dan and the father around which the rest of the film has been organized. (There is another subtler if perhaps less offensive sleight of hand built into the script in the fact that Dan's rebellion against the Higgins family takes the form of thoroughbred horse racing, surely the most aristocratic of all forms of iconoclastic free expression.)

Note, in passing, that the importance of this reversal scene is not that there is a sudden and unjustified change of heart in the putative villain of the film. This is the standard criticism leveled against Capra's work, from this film through *You Can't Take It with You* and *Smith*. It is meaningless to talk about a psychological event, earned or unearned, as taking place at all, since we are given almost no insight into the father's character or any of the reasons for his decision to join Dan and Alice. No more than in *It Happened One Night* does Capra even bother to go through the motions of providing evidence for any such psychological change. J. L. Higgins's joining the lovers is not a psychological event, and Capra does not attempt to make it one. What this scene shows, in fact, is Capra's willingness to throw psychology, motivation, and character consistency to the winds, so powerful is his desire to form a community of appreciation around his hero, a community of feeling and sympathy so important to him that he thinks nothing of disregarding psychology and any other realistic standards of understanding and analysis in the scene.

Something very similar to this artistic sleight of hand involving Alice Higgins's simultaneous rebellion against and separation from her father and her inclusion of him in her life and obedience to his will is going on at the end of *It Happened One Night*. (Coincidentally, the same actor, Walter Connolly, plays the father in both films.) The first sign of the compromise is that although she is ostensibly running away from him in order to assert her independence, it is Ellie's father who suggests the idea of her eloping with Peter in the final minutes of the film. Something even more artistically complex ultimately takes place with the positioning of the father in the final minutes of *It Happened One Night* than did even in *Broadway Bill*. Rather than simply having the father run off with the young couple, as in the other film, Capra performs an extraordinarily subtle move that reconstitutes the repudiated family not socially but imaginatively. In the coda to *It Happened One Night* (which is roughly equivalent to the "two years after" coda to *Broadway Bill*), the father is present on-screen, while Ellie and Peter are absent, but he is receiving a telegram from them and dictating an answer to it. (They ask in their wire whether the annulment of the marriage to Westley has come through yet, and he wires an affirmative reply.) It is a blatant attempt to establish the family group that has been noticeably missing from the entire preceding film. (We have never in a single scene, set, or shot seen Peter, Ellie, and Mr. Andrews together.) By having Mr. Andrews send a sympathetic telegram to the two lovers waiting in their motel room in Michigan, it is as if he were spiritually present with them and as if all three were finally united in one sympathetic family group. That is, of course, the sleight of hand. The three enormously strong wills and powerful egos are no more physically or socially united in this scene than they were prior to it. To integrate all three into a real society of shared discourse and personal interrelations is just what Capra cannot do at this moment, even as it is the one thing he most wants us to believe he has done.

The scene with Mr. Andrews answering the telegram is the next-to-last of the film. The final scene presents an even more complex dramatic response to this imaginative problem of creating a society for his lovers to call home. Capra now shifts to the motel at which Ellie and Peter are staying, at the moment just after they have received Mr. Andrews's reply, secured a marriage license, and at last are about to let the walls of Jericho fall. In an ending that probably borrows from the final chapter of Faulkner's *Light in August* (published the previous year), Capra presents not Ellie and Peter but the motel owner and his wife, talking over the couple. It is a moment that, although it may be indebted to Faulkner, is profoundly true to the spirit of Capra's film.

WIFE: Funny couple, ain't they?
MAN: Yeah.
WIFE: If you ask me, I don't believe they're married.
MAN: They're married all right. I just seen the license.
WIFE: They made me get them a rope and a blanket, on a night like this.

MAN: Yeah?
WIFE: What do you reckon that's for?
MAN: Blamed if I know. I just brung them a trumpet.
WIFE: (*puzzled*) A trumpet?
MAN: Yeah. You know one of these toy things. They sent me to the store to get it.
WIFE: But what in the world do they want a trumpet for?
MAN: I dunno.

"Two look at two" in this scene (to adapt a line from Robert Frost), and what is most interesting is how the society that Ellie and Peter finally constitute exists in the film only virtually, in this interplay of dialogue between two other characters, and not actually, in their own exchange of conversation or presence on-screen. (Ellie and Peter are never seen together or even in the same scene together after the scene in the motel from which I previously quoted, which occurs almost twenty minutes earlier in the film.) Capra is, in effect, creating another family grouping, with the kind and solicitous motel keeper and his wife constituting a surrogate parental pair and a potential role model in marriage for Ellie and Peter, but it is a grouping as purely virtual as the one with Ellie's father (who has played a kind of father figure to Peter, as well) in the previous scene. Twice in a row, a purely imagined family group, whose relationships are supplied by the viewers of the film in their imaginations, is doing duty in place of the real family group or society that Capra is unable or unwilling to form around his lovers. This is exactly the sleight of hand that Faulkner's *Light in August* performs in its final chapter, which suggests a deeper similarity between the works. Faulkner has recourse to constituting an imaginary or rhetorical "family" or "society" of discourse around his central romantic characters, Lena Grove and Byron Bunch, for whom also – and for similar reasons – an actual family or extended society of personal relationships cannot be formed.

Like the union of Byron and Lena, the union of Peter and Ellie exists assertively as a fiction – as a story told by someone – in a triple sense. In the first place, Peter and Ellie are removed from actual society and the world and made over into fictional characters in the story another couple tells. They are removed a second time insofar as they make themselves over into characters in their own fictional narration involving heroic roles, blankets that are metaphorically transformed into the walls of Jericho, and a plastic toy that is transformed into a biblical trump. Finally, at a third fictional remove, they are further derealized in the sense that one cannot help feeling that these final scenes are merely Capra's process of tying up the film's fictional loose ends in a well-crafted ending, and that Peter and Ellie have become, by this point, mere semiotic functions in the film's formal process of closure.

Although there is a sense in which any well-made narrative work performs this final fictional tying up of metaphoric and narrative loose ends, this film is more emphatic about its fictionality than the average movie or novel, which usually attempts to do the opposite of what Capra is doing here. Whereas most works of art labor to make us forget the artificiality of their proceedings, *It*

Happened One Night calls attention to them. The coda structure of the ending itself, its emphasis on its own and its characters' process of fictional narrative closure and metaphor making, its foregrounding of its metaphors of opening and closing (involving blankets and sexual relationships) at such a point of narrative opening and closing, and the general demonstrativeness of the film's reminding us of the simultaneous, parallel, and interrelated processes of tying and untying knots that is taking place in its plot, its metaphoric structure, and its formal narrative acts of closure in these last three scenes make *It Happened One Night* unusually insistent about its own and its characters' distinctively fictional powers. Among Hollywood filmmakers, only Sternberg is more blatant than this. Just as in *Forbidden*, *Bitter Tea*, or *Lady for a Day*, in *It Happened One Night* Capra is deliberately treating assertively imaginative arrangements not as mere metaphoric enhancements or clarifications of some reality that stands above and beyond the fictions, but as autonomous, free-standing alternatives to so-called reality. He is insisting on the fact that characters can have something in their imaginative appropriation of life that they cannot have in their experience of it, just as Capra, the creator of *It Happened One Night*, can make an imaginary society substitute for the society that he cannot make and that does not exist in the plot in any more realistic way.

We are left at the end of the movie suspended, just as Peter and Ellie are, in an elaborately "made" world, a fictional realm that is an achievement of consciousness that has no necessary social correlative or worldly form of expression. Peter and Ellie leave social relationships and understandings behind in their flight to a secluded Michigan auto camp, but even more radically they leave all of the forms of cinematic dramatization behind in their retreat into a privacy and intimacy so deep that it not only cannot be photographed (they never appear in this final scene) but cannot even be spoken or scripted, except in the *oratio obliqua* of the other couple's dialogue and the jokey periphrasis of this self-referential, comically metaphoric ending. We hear the toy trumpet in the final seconds of the film, see the blanket fall to the floor, and hear on the sound track theme music that reminds us we have been watching a movie, and so we know that this is its clever, well-crafted ending, but there is no going beyond these fictional arrangements to realistic social ones. The elaborate fictional organization takes the place of an absent public or social organization.*

We are left appreciating moments in which the artistic devices of the film energetically "speak" and inventively fill in for the social silences and physical absences of the characters. Clever acts of narrative closure, complexly infolded metaphors, and what I have called formal sleights of hand create something that cannot be created or sustained in the world of the characteriza-

---

* The similarity to the coda endings of John Cassavetes's *Minnie and Moskowitz* and *Gloria* is worth noticing. As does Capra, Cassavetes attempts in the conclusion of each film to make an imaginative community substitute for an absent or unobtainable social one.

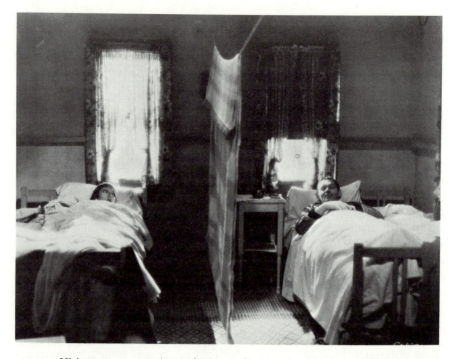

Visionary communion substitutes for social community: Peter and Ellie separated physically but joined imaginatively.

tions, the dialogue, and the plot or in the world outside of purely cinematic, stylistic effects. Typically for Capra, imaginative possession substitutes for worldly.

It Happened One Night attempts to substitute imaginative openings to discourse (between Peter and Ellie, between the motel keeper and his wife, between parallel artistic arrangements within the movie, and between the audience and the events in the film) for worldly failures of understanding and discourse. The ubiquitous blanket hung between Peter and Ellie captures exactly the doubleness of this process. On the one hand, it realistically separates them and prevents them from forming a romantic couple, but at the same time it imaginatively ties them together to form a special imaginative community of understanding.

The point is not merely that the blanket separates Peter and Ellie and that their imaginations link them. Capra is arguing a stronger case than that. He is arguing that it is the practical separation – the sexual frustration, the social gaps and physical walls between Peter and Ellie, symbolized by the blanket – that makes the imaginative communion possible and desirable. Though Capra's effort in the film is apparently directed to breaking down walls between Peter and Ellie, walls of stylistic virtuosity and smug self-confidence that they erect around themselves, he draws the line at this final wall and, in effect, does everything he possibly can to keep it up, to argue that it must be kept up. (The film has to end the second that the blanket comes down – not only according to the mandate of the Hays Office, but, more important, because there is nothing left to show on the screen as dialogue, action, and characterization after that point.) For the sake of Capra's drama, Peter and Ellie must be kept apart by that final wall, and what comes of it, Capra suggests, is, artistically and imaginatively, all to the good. What comes of this physical blockage are the stimulations of human imaginative compensation, whether in the form of Peter's pounding out the story of his life on a typewriter or of Ellie's inspired, improvised response to her own wedding ceremony.

Capra's argument is not very different from Freud's, for he implies that it is not in spite of but as a result of such frustrations and repressions that the imagination is ultimately released in its full creative glory. *It Happened One Night* is a film not only about the social necessity but about the potential imaginative desirability of sublimation. The blanket must be kept up for the sake of the film and our imaginations. It might even be argued that precisely to the extent that we in the audience also experience a blockage of our actual sight lines by the blanket, we too are stimulated to imaginative activity and potential insight. Capra was ambivalent about this recognition (as was Freud too). There is an imaginative imperative to break down walls and merge with the other in all of his films that is pitted against the opposite impulse: the recognition that the world, our own emotions, and our works of art will not allow their leveling. In fact, where walls do not already exist, they must be deliberately created, like the blanket hung between the lovers.

Music is one of Capra's chief expressive resources during scenes that attempt to move his viewers or his characters from sight to insight, from a physical community to an imaginative one. It is for this reason that although Capra generally avoids background orchestrations in his films, he has recourse to them during most of the emotional climaxes in his work, including the final minute of this one and the climactic scenes in *Broadway Bill*. The true emotional climax of that film occurs during the horse race. It is significant that in that race all Dan and Alice can do is silently gaze, and hope and pray. All the film itself can do to express their imaginative state is to cut rapidly from one face in the crowd to another, from those charged expressions to the progress of the race itself, and to underscore the visual passage with a musical orchestration. There are no words that can express the intensity of the emotions at that moment, no passages of dialogue or social forms of relationship that are relevant or appropriate to the expression of these dreams and ideals. We are at the boundaries of orthodox narrative filmmaking at such moments in which all of the standard events of ordinary narrative presentation become irrelevant or even distracting, and rapid editorial cutting and musical scoring pick up the expressive burden.

Consider the ending of *Lost Horizon*. In certain scenes of this film, Capra went as far as he ever would in attempting purely visionary filmmaking (with critical and commercial consequences that he regarded as less than satisfactory). If the central characters are silent and invisible at the end of *It Happened One Night*, and if they are immobilized in positions of inarticulate gesticulation and breathless gazing in the climactic moment of *Broadway Bill*, in *Lost Horizon* the human figure is even more radically removed from society and social forms of expression into a Wordsworthian realm of the sublime. At the powerful conclusion of the film, Robert Conway is visible only as a speck on the screen, fighting his way up the side of the snow-covered Himalayas to get back to Shangri-La. It might as well be an animal clawing for survival on a snowy mountaintop that we see. The viewer is momentarily forced to become as much a visionary to "see" the scene, as the figure of Conway himself has become one within it, renouncing all language and society. The meaning of the shot is not even potentially expressible in the forms of dialogue, human relationships, or anything at all with human dimensions or contours, but only by the light, the photography, the impressive scale of the mountains dwarfing the human figure, and the extraordinary Dimitri Tiomkin score (vaguely reminiscent of the music that Frank Harling wrote for *Bitter Tea*). The scene in a London club that precedes this one is there to underline the vapidity and irrelevance of *all* talk, *all* society, and *all* clubby relationships to the world of silent visionary awareness to which Conway and an ideal viewer have been transported in the course of the film.

Both of these visionary scenes have much in common with the scene that is certainly the most thrilling moment in *It Happened One Night* (one that Mike Nichols would imitate almost forty years later in *The Graduate*): Ellie's exhilarating flight from her own wedding ceremony. It is not enough to notice that Capra's middle- and long-distance photography, his editing and his layered sound track make us feel the oppressive pressures of the society from which Ellie flees. She flees from much more than the constraints of a particular kind of social ceremony at this point in the film. She is fleeing all social or verbal forms of expression and structures of understanding, not only those in her world but those in Capra's work of art as well.

When the time comes in the wedding ceremony for her "I do," Ellie does not give an angry or impassioned speech; she significantly does not say anything at all. She merely gives a strange shrug of her shoulders, a kind of shudder ripples through her body, and she turns away from the camera to run away across the lawn. That moment of turning away from scrutiny by the camera is reminiscent of many of the paintings of Winslow Homer, Edward Hopper, James Shannon, Charles Hawthorne, Edmund Tarbell, John White Alexander, Cecilia Beaux, Thomas Wilmer Dewing, and John Singer Sargent, in which the figure deliberately avoids eye contact with a viewer, looks away from him, or turns his body to look out of the frame space at an object or area beyond his view. Like Capra, these American painters were stimulated by the expressive potential of glances that assertively reject society and social forms of expression, in which a figure (like Kay Arnold in Jerry Strong's allegorical painting of Hope) deliberately declines a social stance in order to cultivate the possibility of a visionary stance.

Ellie's turn away from social and cinematic scrutiny and her speechless run away from the wedding ceremony, which substitutes gesture and action for verbal protest, dialogue, or reasoned argument is the crux of the passage. She runs along the lawn, almost out of the view of Capra's panning camera, and eventually disappears into a waiting car, never again to reappear in the film – just as Peter never reappears following his departure from the Andrews mansion. Neither of them will be cinematically photographable, acoustically audible, or socially interpretable again. From that point on, they exist only as principles of negativity, defined by what they are not, what they turn away from. They are imaginatively present only as figures of imagination – in the telegram to Ellie's father, in the conversation between the motel keeper and his wife, and in the Jericho metaphor – whose presence is made tangible, paradoxically, only by their absence offscreen somewhere when that blanket finally drops in the final shot. They have fled out of the narrative world of the film and out of all social expression and into some inscrutable, unphotographable, unscriptable other form of existence and relationship.

We are almost back in the world of the coda of *Bitter Tea*, with Megan sitting silent, alone, and off to one side of the scene, staring away from the camera and away from the society of Jones on the ship. Despite Capra's effort to transform such moments into apparent social events, we and the central pair are left in an incommunicable state of charged consciousness that is expressible only in terms of the whole preceding fiction and that can never be spoken in any more direct or public way. Capra's special cinematic arrangements and our own imaginations as viewers are being called upon to bring into existence a visionary community that has no social reality and cannot be rendered in the forms of dialogue and interpersonal interaction.

12

Deeds, words, gasps, and glances

Mr. Deeds Goes to Town

Real action is in silent moments.

– Ralph Waldo Emerson, "Spiritual Laws"

The true romance which the world exists to realize will be the transformation of genius into practical power.

– Ralph Waldo Emerson, "Experience"

Although *It Happened One Night* is in many respects a transitional work, the films before *Mr. Deeds Goes to Town* generally minimize the social pressures placed on the artist or dreamer. They deliberately reserve a relatively free, enchanted space for visionary expansion, whether it is the balcony of Yen's palace or Jerry's studio, Lulu Smith's apartment, the suite of hotel rooms within which Apple Annie can preserve the fiction that she is Mrs. E. Worthington Manville, or the secluded motel rooms where Ellie and Peter camp out. With the films that follow – *Mr. Deeds Goes to Town, You Can't Take It with You, Mr. Smith Goes to Washington, Meet John Doe, It's a Wonderful Life*, and *State of the Union* – Capra embeds the individual in a social matrix and denies him or her a place of retreat from the pressures of the world. There are no sanctuaries for consecrated vision. The central characters are involved in an extended network of relationships that they had been able to leave behind in key scenes in the earlier films.

The earlier films succeeded only to the extent that the central figures were ultimately removed from society. Their conclusions depend on a viewer's willingness not to ask embarrassing questions about the central characters' relationship to the larger world. What would it have been like if *Ladies of Leisure* had not concluded with the isolated figures of Kay and Jerry looking into each other's eyes? What if Jerry's father and Kay's roommate had been present in that final scene? In any case, what happens after the final scene? How do Jerry and Kay support themselves in Arizona, or, conversely, if they do not live in Arizona, how do they, as Capra has defined them, manage to live

262

anywhere else? In *The Bitter Tea of General Yen*, what happens to Megan Davis once she returns to the busy world of the Strike house, to which she is presumably bound in the final scene but which Capra has worked so hard to make her and the viewer forget? In *It Happened One Night*, what would it be like for Peter and Ellie to live their Pacific-paradise dream in a society more demanding and complex than that defined by a secluded auto camp in the woods of Michigan? These are questions that Capra does everything in his power to prevent us from asking. He protects his characters from them, and they need to be protected in order to allow communities of the imagination to form.

With the films that follow, vision, reverie, and idealism are forced to express themselves within a complex, extended society. When they cannot succeed at that task (as will inevitably happen, no matter how hard Capra resists it), it is felt as a real problelm or a failure in a way that it was not in *Ladies of Leisure*, *Bitter Tea*, or even *It Happened One Night*. As evidence of the change between the films of early thirties and the late thirties one notices the increasing distance of Capra's camera set-ups in particular scenes. His camera moves back from the frequent gauzed close-ups of *Ladies of Leisure*, *Forbidden*, and *Bitter Tea* to take in social surroundings relentlessly impinging on the central characters. *

Even a temporary visionary retreat from or transcendence of society is not possible, and certainly not desirable, in the films of the late thirties. Capra directly confronts the potentially tragic separation of imagination from social expression that keeps emerging in his work† by forcing the central characters in the films from *Deeds* on out of their palaces, motel rooms, studios, and apartments into institutional realms, to act publicly.

The most succinct notation of the completeness of this shift in Capra's work is in the change in the meaning of gazing off into the distance. To stare out a window (in *Deeds*), to stand on the edge of a balcony and look at the skyline (in *Doe*), or to look over the railing of a bridge (in *It's a Wonderful Life*) is now not evidence of a desirable state of imaginative elevation and meditative abstraction, as were comparable events in *That Certain Thing*, *Ladies of Leisure*, and *Bitter Tea*, but a sign of deepest despair or abject withdrawal from the world. To turn away from, or to disengage oneself (physically or imaginatively) from the social world in these later films has become evidence of impotence, cynicism, failure, or abandonment of hope.

For all of these reasons, the central characters in Capra's middle and late

---

* Note that in *Bitter Tea*, although Capra's camera had already begun to be withdrawn from the face and isolated consciousness of Megan Davis, it was withdrawn not to comprehend the moiling, shifting social forces around her but placidly to contemplate a series of artfully composed still-life effects and architectural arrangements.

† That Capra should feel this separation to be tragic and to be a problem needing to be dealt with is important in itself. It tells us much about his aspirations and beliefs. Proust, Beckett, Antonioni, or Fellini (to name as wide a range of achievement as possible) would not see the tragedy of this separation, since they would never have believed in the possibility of its being bridged in life or in art.

No visionary escapes possible: the barred window of Deeds's psychiatric cell.

films are in much more imperiled imaginative predicaments than those in the earlier ones. No longer can characters even aspire to flee from a repressive system of relationships to a more free one, as they did in *Ladies of Leisure* and *Bitter Tea*. At some point in their respective films, Longfellow Deeds, Jefferson Smith, Long John Willoughby, and George Bailey each attempt to run away from the systems in which they find themselves entangled, but Capra is clearly critical of their efforts to escape. There is nowhere to run to, no sacrosanct space where ideals may be even momentarily protected from institutional predation. Capra refuses to praise a fugitive and cloistered virtue in his heroes, and in fact to the extent that in these films a figure is fugitive and cloistered, he or she is utterly incapable of virtue. The result is a series of films in which it is required that the idealistic or visionary protagonists not rise above, but aggressively engage themselves with the social systems in place around them – with forces of personal manipulation, entrenched political systems, and diverse institutional styles of behavior ranging from law to banking.

A misunderstanding arose as a result of this change: Capra has the reputation in these later films of being committed to a specific political or social agenda – call it "populism," "ecumenicism," "humanism," or "messianism" – and his films were therefore dismissed by hardheaded critics (even critics as shrewd as Otis Ferguson and Graham Greene) as being politically naive, tendentious, moralistic, or homiletic. To reduce these films to such agendas is roughly equivalent to treating Shakespeare's history plays as attacks on or defenses of the Tudor dynasty. The presence of fairly schematic political or ideological content in a play or a film does not prevent it from having other kinds of more important content. Capra is not particularly concerned with making statements about the New Deal, the U.S. Senate, or the banking institutions of America, except insofar as an examination of the relationship of an individual to such public institutions allows him to explore the complexities of the expression of imagination and desire within the forms and structures of all institutional discourse. The fact that while he was making these "political" films Capra simultaneously went forward with plans to produce films based upon Cervantes's *Don Quixote*, Rostand's *Cyrano de Bergerac*, and the lives of Chopin and Shakespeare should help to convince his critics that the explicitly political settings and plots of *State of the Union*, *Smith*, *Doe*, and *Deeds* function chiefly as dramatic metaphors for explorations of certain expressive problems. Capra uses these public institutions as a means of testing his protagonists in ways in which his earlier figures were not tested, specifically to explore their difficulty in expressing their ideals and identities. It is not an anomaly that his late masterpiece, *It's a Wonderful Life*, has nothing explicitly political in its situation and theme. In that film Capra uses the societies constituted by an extended family and the claustrophobic world of an American small town for the same dramatic purpose as *Smith* uses the Senate.

On the other hand, it will not do to pretend that Capra was not interested at all in American political institutions. Such institutions may function in his work chiefly and most importantly as dramatic metaphors, but that is not their exclusive function. In four of the seven films from *Deeds* to *State of the Union*, Capra is engaging himself and his protagonists with recognizably real political, social, economic, and institutional issues, and only by acknowledging that fact can one account for the full radicalism of his position, as well as the reasons for critical reaction against it. (Shakespeare was doing no less in his history plays, although three centuries of intervening history and the past century of formalist criticism have worked to cleanse them of their originally radical political content.)

The reason Capra's mixture of politics and art meets with so much critical resistance is that it violates an unspoken taboo of the dominant tradition of twentieth-century Anglo-American criticism and art. As Frank Lentricchia has brilliantly argued,* one of the secret agendas of most advanced modern criticism and art is the willful divorcement of political and aesthetic issues. The reasoning runs that aesthetic concerns are, by their nature, inconsistent with practical political concerns. The pure "text," the "free play" of discourse in a work of art, the aesthetic state of suspended animation is offered as an explicit escape from the system of repressions, controls, and confinements of social understandings and relationships. Freedom may exist in the visionary and

---

* See, for example, Frank Lentricchia, "Reading Foucault: Punishment, Labor, Resistance," *Raritan Review* 2 (Summer 1982), 56–8.

artistic state in this definition of it, but it is a freedom not within but outside of repressive social forms. That is the contemporary critical and artistic legacy of the second generation of English Romantics, passed through what F. R. Leavis aptly called the world-losing, world-forsaking swoons and reveries of the pre-Raphaelite and Victorian writers and painters, the Aesthetic Movement of the turn of the century, and the final flowering of art for art's sake in the Georgian and Bloomsbury writers. (Any adequate history of this crucial era in England would, needless to say, have to focus specifically on the figures of Pater and Tennyson, who were the most powerfully representative and influential codifiers of this movement writing in English.)

If Capra participates in an alternative tradition of expression, it is one that passes from the early German idealists and the first (not the Shelleyan or Keatsian) generation of English Romantic poets, especially Blake and Wordsworth,★ through George Eliot and D. H. Lawrence in England, and Emerson and William and Henry James in this country (though I am not suggesting that Capra ever read a line of, or was even aware of, these illustrious predecessors). In this tradition the imagination is felt to have practical and potentially even radical consequences in the world of political and social structures.

Within American art specifically, the two traditions of expression can be divided as follows: the line of Thoreau, George Santayana, and Wallace Stevens (representing the self-satisfying activity of the imagination within the text and estranged from larger social expression); and the line of Emerson, William James, and Henry James (representing the socially engaged, practical position). Capra is in the second tradition and opposed to the first. To talk of two absolutely distinct traditions in American art is, however, to some extent misleading, since the greatest artists in the American idiom, and especially those in the second tradition, from Emerson and James to Capra and Cassavetes, have been torn by both tendencies: on the Stevensian side, feeling the isolated individual consciousness to be the last refuge of imaginative freedom, and the artistic text as the last space within which it can be enacted; on the Jamesian, feeling the effort to transcend the pressures and constraints of society to be problematic and believing freedom to be valuable only insofar as it practically engages itself with the concrete forms of ordinary language and everyday social life. If the first tendency reaches its apotheosis in the work of Hawthorne, Thoreau, Santayana, Stevens, and more recently Paul De Man, and the second in that of Emerson, Henry James, Capra, and Cassavetes it would be more accurate to say that in their finest and most complex expressions the second group is not so much opposed to the first as inclusive of it. Their work is troubled, torn, and ambivalent. Emerson, James, and Capra himself frequently aspire to visionary disengagement from the limiting and

---

★ I take the middle books of *The Prelude* and *The Songs of Innocence and Experience* to be the loci classici of this position, although both Wordsworth and Blake, in different ways, were unable to fulfill the poetic agendas they laid out for themselves in these works and even turned against them in later life.

arbitrary forms of social life, even as they regret the disengagement. They extol Coriolanus-like ideals of radical individualism, even as they simultaneously criticize this impulse and attempt to include complexities of social, sexual, and ethical involvement in their works that they feel can never be escaped.

For whatever complicated cultural reasons, however, most sophisticated literary and film criticism in Europe and America has affiliated itself with the first tradition and not the second. That is where Capra and his films court complete critical misunderstanding. In proposing to inject his characters' vaulting ideals into recognizably "real" social institutions – in deliberately failing to maintain a clear separation between the "pure" energies of imagination and desire and the practical forms by which such energies are expressed in the "real" world – Capra violated an entire culture's critical assumptions about how the free imagination must be – can only be – kept from pollution by being insulated from the actualities of social life. Capra not only refused to cordon off a special artistic or textual space within which freedom could be enacted but insisted on the at least theoretical possibility of a free imaginative performance being enacted in the real world in the expressive forms of ordinary experience.

The most egregious instance of his heresy of confusing realms in this way (which, needless to say, I am defining as one of the most profound aspects of his work) is *Smith*. Capra's recreation of exact dimensions and details of the Senate chamber, his insistence on strict fidelity within the film to the actual procedures and rules of Senate debate, his use of H. V. Kaltenborn (the thirties radio equivalent of Walter Cronkite) as the radio announcer reporting on Smith's filibuster, the presence of recognizable microphones from CBS, RKO, and NBC, and his attempts to use the Boy Scouts of America as Smith's organizational affiliation (only when he was denied permission to use the name did Capra fall back on the thinly disguised alternative of making Smith the leader of the Boy Rangers) are all instances of a deliberate aesthetic impurity in the film.

It was for just such reasons that political figures such as Senate majority leader Alben Barkley, Senator Burton K. Wheeler, Senator James F. Byrnes, the ambassador to Great Britain, Joseph P. Kennedy, and many members of the State Department and Congress put pressure on Capra and Columbia Pictures to suppress the film and Congress threatened to pass the Neely anti–block-booking bill as retaliation. Capra's heresy was that he refused to keep art sufficiently separate from life, a doctrine on which politicians and contemporary "advanced" critics of art, literature, and film can agree.* Capra's

---

* Ed Meese's or Ronald Reagan's implicit belief that whereas politics is serious business, art is a frivolous game played by sissies in which nothing is really at stake and in which nothing that matters is actually affirmed or denied, ironically meets contemporary deconstructionist efforts to insulate the text within the hermetic boundaries of its own margin of textuality and the attempts of formalist and most genre critics of film to treat the text as existing within a self-contained artistic realm of self-referential signification. See my "Criticism in the Dark," *The New Republic*, June 30, 1986.

radicalism, however, is that he wants to test the consequences of structure-breaking eruptions of imagination and desire on and within the "realistic" structures of society, not merely in the environment of artistic texts. Like Emerson and Henry James, Capra believes that the structures of a work of art are not alternative to the structures of society but are an extension or duplication of them, and that the work of art is not a turn away from them, but an act of finer, fiercer engagement with them. This is an attitude emphatically opposed to that of most twentieth-century metafictionists with their implicit social disengagement and connoisseurship of artistic effects that have no ramifications beyond the margins of the text.

Of course, such a belief in the potential responsiveness of the world to our imagination, such a refusal to keep the "text" separate from the messy "context" surrounding it, can be patronized as betraying a superficial American optimism, millenarianism, and historical innocence. Artists as different as Emerson, William James, and Capra have been accused of a similar innocence about so-called real life. The critics who implicitly separate the text from life will always resist texts that attempt to do what Capra's late films do, and will unconsciously probably prefer works that marginalize themselves. That is the only way I can understand why of all of Capra's works, the only film which is usually singled out for praise by the most advanced contemporary critics is *Bitter Tea*. What such critics find to praise about the movie is the pure, unsullied beauty of the shots and the state of aesthetic detachment they induce. *Bitter Tea* is, for them, about a willed act of escapism into the palace of art, safe from the mess of social life outside of it. It is admired insofar as it is different from the messy political and social engagement of Capra's later work. Needless to say, this is a film quite different from my account of it, which stresses the problematic aspects of Yen's kingdom of art and Megan's attempt to become a subject of it. To elevate to eminence one of Capra's more minor efforts in this way is finally to do an injustice to his whole career. In contrast, the life and experience that Capra chooses to explore in his middle and late films will never stand still long enough to be arranged into the elegant, placid frame compositions and lighting effects of *Bitter Tea*. It resists the arrangements of our imaginations and desires – but that is the true stimulation and challenge to the imaginative character, the imaginative viewer, and the imaginative maker of these films.

From its opening week at Radio City Musical Hall *Mr. Deeds Goes to Town* broke box-office records of all kinds and even threatened to eclipse the success of the greatest cinematic hit of the era, Chaplin's contemporaneous *Modern Times*. For whatever complex personal or political reasons, in the spring of 1936 both Chaplin and Capra, hitherto known more or less as directors of fantasies, farces, and romances, released films that emphatically engaged themselves with practical political and social events. *Modern Times* and *Deeds* both take as their explicit subject the expressive predicament of the individual almost lost in (or a semiotician might say "spoken by" or "inscribed within") the technologies and bureaucracies of the contemporary world. This represents a complication of the situation of the individual in both Capra's and Chaplin's work. He is embedded everywhere in a system of alien structures and pressures that make his individuality itself a questionable concept.

Deeds is one of Capra's warmest and most charming films, just as Longfellow Deeds himself is (along with Harry Carey in *Smith*) one of Capra's warmest and most charming characters, and the film and Gary Cooper's performance in the title role is a perennial favorite with audiences. I would argue, however, that we may have misjudged the film precisely because it does seem so merely pleasant and entertaining on a superficial acquaintance. Even if Capra wasn't completely aware of it, perhaps his film tells us that charm like Deeds's (or Cooper's) is not enough.

Early in the movie there is a scene that summarizes some of the darker aspects of the work. Having just inherited twenty million dollars from a distant relative and moved from Mandrake Falls, Vermont, to a mansion in New York, country mouse Deeds is being outfitted in new clothes by a group of tailors while his lawyer and executive secretary talk to him. Capra uses a series of medium-distance shots to take it all in: The tailors measure, pinch, prod, and gather him; Deeds's lawyer, sitting on one side of the room, offers him advice on his estate and the financial reponsibilities of his new position; and his personal secretary warns him about the press and public that will assault him. Meanwhile, a series of visitors and butlers come and go from adjacent rooms with requests for Deeds's opinion or claims on his time. There is nothing quite like it in any of Capra's early films. It is a scene that originates in *Lady for a Day*, but one that will be repeated in one form or another in all of the major films from *Deeds* on: *Smith*, *Doe*, *It's a Wonderful Life*, and *State of the Union*. Both visually and socially it succinctly figures the newly embattled and threatened predicament of the central characters in all of those films.

Longfellow is being warned about the predatory and invasive inclinations of the population of a big city by his lawyer, secretary, and butlers, but the warnings are themselves forms of predation and invasions of privacy . There is no escape from pressures for Deeds, not even in his own home. He will never be able to avoid being under public scrutiny. Even his "courtship" of Babe Bennett will have to take place in front of nosy reporters snapping photographs and writing stories about it, and in a courtroom, during a public hearing on his insanity. Similarly, Jefferson Smith's courtship will have to bloom under glass in the hothouse of the Senate, during a filibuster. One can perhaps see a reflection in this of Capra's own changed situation in the thirties, as he became a director who was, after the success of *It Happened One Night*, himself an increasingly sought-after, preyed-upon public figure.

The image of the tailors working on Deeds expresses another more specific and more sinister threat to the self as well. The individual is liable not only to be pressured bureaucratically and scrutinized socially but is actually threatened with being made over into something or someone else. When Molly Kelly dons her "costume"; when Yen changes from his military garb to his oriental

Gaining an identity or losing it? Self-fashioning or self-erasure in *Lady for a Day*, *Mr. Deeds Goes to Town*, and *Here Comes the Groom*.

kimonos or Megan changes from the funereal weeds of a minister's fiancée to a mirrored gown; when Kay Arnold tries a new frock to attempt to seduce Jerry Strong; when Florence Fallon costumes herself for her foray into theatricality as a faith healer; or even (in a more extreme transformation in the scene that comes closest to anticipating the one in these subsequent films) when Apple Annie transforms herself into Mrs. E. Worthington Manville, the change of identity is more or less initiated by, supervised by, and in the control of the character. The character chooses the particular costume, style, or tone as an expression of his or her deliberate expansion of identity, and the individuals around him or her cooperate and conspire with the character in the process of transformation. *Deeds* and the later films raise the harrowing prospect of losing control of one's own identity. A tailor (or, in *Smith*, a "Taylor") goes to work on the individual's identity, beyond either the explicit control, consent, or sometimes (in *Smith* and *Doe*) even the awareness of the character. It is a nightmare erasure of the self about which all of Henry Adams's or Sam Shepard's work might be said to be an extended meditation.* The individual comes perilously close to being refashioned (in two senses of the word) into someone else's image of him- or herself, or of being absorbed into the cultural styles around him. (*Doe*, most obviously, and *It's a Wonderful Life*, most subtly, are, in effect, feature-length nightmares about the consequences of such an event.)

It should not be surprising that Capra's dramatic metaphor for his characters changes to parallel this shift in the later films. The earlier films imagined the principal characters as being, explicitly or implicitly, the "artists" and authors of their own identities. Jerry and Kay, Yen and Megan, Ellie and Peter were masters and mistresses of self-improvisation: of postures and tones, stances and styles, which they tried out, manipulated, and discarded as audacious actor-directors of their own autonomous selfhood. If a dramatic metaphor were used to describe the figures in the later films, it would be that they have ceased to be authors and directors of their own destinies and have become characters acting in a script of someone else's authoring, directing, and producing. Rather than performing as self-pleasuring improvisors, they must perform pre-scripted (in both senses of the pun) roles within which they have only a narrow margin for free interpretation.

The earlier characters, of course, not only functioned metaphorically as artists, but often literally as well, either as painters like Jerry Strong, or as applied artists of theatrical effects like Kay Arnold or Yen. Even an apparent exception like Peter Warne not only began, in Capra's initial script, as a Greenwich Village painter, but, as a newspaperman in the final film, functions less in relation to any journalistic institution or larger society than as a kind of freelance creative writer, dreamer, and ad hoc dramatic improviser. That is what makes the change in the later films all the more striking. From *Deeds* to

---

* See my introduction to Henry Adams's *Mont Saint Michel and Chartres* (New York: Viking-Penguin, 1986) for an extended consideration of the ways the self is and is not erased in Adams's own work.

State of the Union, both the fine artists and the practical artists almost entirely disappear. Only George Bailey could possibly qualify as an artist in either way, and yet how different, more marginal and imperiled his artistic expressions are. He is, or aspires to be, an architect, but, significantly, has none of the opportunities to design or decorate buildings that Yen has. His architectural dreams are expressible only in matchstick models and unrealized blueprints on his hobby table at home. To the extent that he is a practical architect at all, it is only in the paltry form of building look-alike frame houses financed by the bank he manages. His artistic impulse, his architecture, is expressible only insofar as it is administered within and through the codes of conduct of a public institution like the bank, for the specific customers of the loan department, and severely circumscribed by the financial, physical, bureaucratic, and social constraints that the film so abundantly documents. That is what it means to say that Jefferson Smith, Doe, Deeds, and Grant Matthews are explicitly and implicitly actors in someone else's play, responding to cues and lines in a script that is not theirs to create or change, taking dictation rather than writing their own parts. Insofar as an actor or a politician is an artist at all (and Capra metaphorically equates politicians and actors in his later work to point up the similarities of the two occupations) he or she is one acting within entirely different notions of authorship and a definite sense of the limitations of imaginative and social performance from a painter of allegories about Hope, a visionary Chinese warlord, or a gold-digging call girl.

On the basis of *Deeds* and the films that follow it, there is every reason to believe that Capra's conception of his own situation as an artist has changed. The central figures in the films, as we have seen, often are alter egos for Capra himself and figure his conception of what it is to be a film director, and the later films are no different from the earlier in this respect. Jerry Strong, Stew Smith, and General Yen are stand-ins for Capra and function as scriptwriters, stage managers, directors, and producers of the experiences within their own films, just as Jefferson Smith, George Bailey, and Grant Matthews do in the later work. Whereas the earlier films frequently imagine creation to be an act of largely solitary, individualistic, and autonomous authorship, the later ones imagine the writer-director-producer to be much more like an admittedly idealistic but also extremely practical and pragmatic politician. The director in these films is a master of interpersonal relations, group decision making, and bureaucratic compromises. Capra's ideal of artistic achievement has changed. The artist-filmmaker is less a visionary-dreamer working cut off from the world in a "studio" (in the sense in which a painter or sculptor works in a "studio") than a man trapped in the confusion of the other sort of "studio" – in the middle of a crowd of people, down on the floor making endless snap decisions, expressing his dreams not outside of, or as an alternative to, but within and by means of resistant institutional and social structures.

Since the pure artists or more visionary figures like Jerry, Lulu, or Yen drop out of the later work, and Capra puts so much emphasis on a character's ability to maneuver bureaucratically and socially, it may seem as though he is merely reincarnating the figure of Tom Dixon at the center of most of these late films, but something more interesting than that is going on. Capra is imagining the possibility of hybridizing the social performers (the buddy-boys, Stew Smith, and Tom Dixon) and the visionaries (Jerry Strong, Lulu Smith, and Megan or Yen) in one character, with fairly complex results. Jefferson Smith and George Bailey will be Capra's two greatest achievements in this respect and their hybrid nature and task suggests the new complexity of the late films.*

Capra's earlier films esteemed states of reverie and idealism as positive ends in themselves, but his later work rejects such states of dreamy disengagement. George Bailey's, Jefferson Smith's, and Longfellow Deeds's idealistic dreams are imagined to be just dreams, worthy of being patronized by other characters or by viewers of their films, so long as they fail concretely to engage themselves with the brueaucratic and social realities of their worlds. It is imperative that they convert their dreams into practicalities. To be adequate as an artist in these later films is to be capable of expressing oneself in the practical forms and structures of institutional and social life. The *Deeds–Smith–Doe* trilogy is, in the largest sense, an extended study of a central character's capacities of performance in these changed circumstances: in public, in front of an invariably hostile or indifferent audience from which he is unable to turn away or to remove himself imaginatively, in a situation in which the authorship and interpretation of his particular role is largely out of his hands.

With his regular crew – cameraman Joseph Walker (for whom *Deeds* was his sixteenth collaboration with Capra), set designer Stephen Goosson, and sound engineer Edward Bernds – Capra skillfully uses the expressive resources of cinematic space and sound as ways of registering Deeds's social and bureaucratic embeddedness and of measuring his marginal capacity for performance, playing with the volume and resonance of his voice and the scale of his figure in the various vast institutional spaces through which he moves in the course of the film, contrasting his small, quirky movements against the static massiveness of the sets. No scenes more comically capture Longfellow's (and, by extension, Capra's) capacity to perform within, and therefore to humanize, an otherwise inhuman cinematic, social, or institutional space than the episodes set in the foyer of Deeds's New York mansion. The hall is impersonally enormous in scale, stone-cold and colorless in its marble appointments and neoclassical severity, and forbiddingly chilly in feeling, but, recalling a similar scene in *Platinum Blonde* in which Stew Smith plays hopscotch on the floor of the Schuyler mansion, Capra shows Deeds refusing to be daunted into frigidly decorous behavior within it. He slides down the banister, enters into a sexually suggestive relationship with a nude statue at the base of the stairs (perhaps half identifying with its conspicuous exposure and

---

* To appreciate the increased complexity of the later films over the earlier, as well as the eccentric path described by a phrase used as loosely and commonly as "artistic development," one has only to recognize that *Deeds*, *Smith*, and *Doe* are essentially remakes, respectively, of *Platinum Blonde*, *American Madness*, and *Miracle Woman*. Yet how entirely the situation of the central character has changed from the earlier films to the later.

vulnerability), and echoes his voice within the cavernous space of the hall. Before our eyes and ears, Capra demonstrates how to master and domesticate an otherwise overwhelming space, how to make it into a possible home for the human body, spirit, and voice. Deeds then forms an imaginative community with the hired help, whom he playfully coaches to experiment with making their voices echo in the hall.

His behavior is, in any possible interpretation of it, rather weird, but for Capra as we have seen, such eccentricity is always a healthy sign. When Deeds behaves childishly (by sliding down the banister or locking his would-be body guards in a closet); impulsively (by punching a poet who patronizes and insults him at an Algonquin-style gathering); or zanily (by running to the window when he hears the siren of a fire engine and declaring, "That's a pip!"), Capra is celebrating both the possibility of Deeds's making room with-in the structures of his personality and the social constraints on his behavior for such eccentricities, as well as his own directorial ability to break his scenes away from predictable narrative structures in the direction of the unforeseen and unsystematizable. The parallel between Deeds encouraging his butlers to experiment with their voices and Capra encouraging his actors to improvise is impossible to miss. Like a film director working with his actors, Deeds teases, taunts, and cajoles them into a freer, more spontaneous performance.

A realistic psychological analysis simply is not adequate for an understanding of such scenes. At certain crucial moments in his narrative, Capra wants to create scenes in which more is going on than can be reduced to structures of plot, motivation, or psychology. At one point in the movie, Deeds and Bennett perform a zany duet of "Swanee River" in the park, he pretending to play the tuba by making oom-pah-pah sounds with his mouth, and she beating on the lid of a trash can with two sticks. By all realistic standards this seems pointless, excessive, and to run on entirely too long beyond the expository needs of the scene. As proof that this was not merely an editorial lapse, Capra repeats the same scene almost verbatim in *You Can't Take It with You* (this time between Jimmy Stewart and Jean Arthur) and lets it run on even longer, with still more stage business. The pointlessness is the point. Such scenes express energies that have no place in the bureaucracies of everyday life, the technologies of economical, realistic, narrative exposition, or the critical parsings of a character's motivations and intentions.

Deeds is, in large part, a deliberate comparison of two contrasting styles of behavior, acting, theatrical blocking, and photography. Deeds, as I've just suggested, represents a series of stylistic choices involving personal, theatrical, and photographic decentering, eccentricity, and centrifugality, whereas his opponents in the film represent styles of personal, theatrical, and photographic overdetermination, concentricity, and centripetality. Capra explicitly contrasts the imaginative, social, and dramatic shagginess, pointlessness, and idiosyncracy of many of Deeds's scenes with the scenes at the law offices of Cedar, Cedar, Cedar, and Buddington, which are as overdetermined and overfocused as the scenes with Deeds are loose and baggy.

Capra initially ushers us into that other world with a complex fifteen second tracking shot showing John Cedar's entrance into his law offices. It is the sort of virtuoso set piece of camera movement – down a winding corridor and past and around a dozen different characters – for which a director like Hitchcock, De Palma, or Kubrick creates an entire scene as an end in itself. It is typical of Capra's suspicion of cinematic or verbal tendentiousness and of photographic or social overdetermination that he uses this passage of cinematic virtuosity as a summary expression of the inhumanity and insensitivity of Cedar's world. The calculated mechanicalness of the camera's movement communicates the calculated mechanicalness of human movements and relationships in the world in which Cedar exists. The angular, impersonal tracking movements of the camera dolly tell us how impersonal, rigid, and confined physical, social, and psychological movement is in these law offices.

Whereas Deeds represents an opening, Cedar and those allied with him in the film represent a narrowing of performative possibilities. They limit human movement to fixed, prescribed destinations that are mechanically blockable and trackable within such camera movements. They yoke imagination and desire to the expression of a prefabricated purpose. That is why their scenes can be blocked and photographed in this way. To the extent that human movement is expressible in this intricately mechanical way, Capra suggests that it cannot be free, entertaining, creative, or profoundly interesting. The middle-distance camera setup that Capra uses to photograph Longfellow's eccentric carryings-on in the foyer of his mansion is a recognition of the impossibility of understanding and photographing his unpredictable quirkiness in a similar way. The performance of a truly creative character, for Capra, is never regimented or restricted by the movements of the camera or followed or analyzed in such a rigid way. The camera and the director must learn simply to stand still and watch and make room for Deeds's (and Cooper's) inventions, just as a viewer must learn to sit still and watch the performance without preconceived notions that would define it in advance.

It would be hard to imagine a clearer contrast than that presented between the practices of Hitchcock and Capra. Hitchcock's subscription to his "actors are cattle" philosophy of directing, lighting, photography, and editing is totally of a piece with his reliance on cartoonish confrontations and characterizations, tendentious camera movements, and his subjugation of a character's (or an actor's) possibilities of performance to the inexorable eventfulness of the plot. Nothing could be further from Capra's aesthetic.*

Although it sounds deceptively simple, one of Capra's fundamental ways of cinematically empowering his performers and preventing the reduction of their behavior to a mechanical or abstract pattern was to do what he does here

---

* One has only to compare Capra's use of Jimmy Stewart with Hitchcock's for the difference to become obvious. Hitchcock's Stewart *is* cattle-weak, vulnerable, victimized, passive, reacting to events beyond his control. Capra's Stewart is a man threatened with being treated as cattle by everyone around him, whose very task is to resist what Hitchcock's Stewart is forced to accept by the visual tendentiousness and narrative coercions of Hitchcock's aesthetic.

in the early scenes with Deeds: simply to withdraw the camera far enough from his actor into the middle distance so as not to upstage or limit his or her capacity for innovation or draw the attention of the audience to the camera's presence by more required cutting. Capra's middle-distance setups (like Hawks's) additionally allowed his actors to use a full repertory of bodily postures and movements without being unduly constrained by the particular lighting or framing of a shot. For the same reason, as I have mentioned, Capra also preferred wherever possible to film long takes with multiple cameras that could pick up simultaneous events in different parts of the scene, thereby freeing up the blocking somewhat from what would be necessary if several things had to be registered in one take on one camera or if different takes from different angles had to be matched in the editing room.

Capra deliberately prefers keeping an event spatially and temporally whole in this way whenever possible by not dissecting it into a series of shorter takes – a series of shot–reverse-shots fragmenting dialogue passages or the usual sequence of cuts from long-shot to middle-distance shot to close-up and back. By holding the camera back and allowing shots to run on longer than is usual Hollywood practice, Capra creates a resonant social space around his characters within which they can visibly interact. The middle-distance placement allowed the actor to remain present within an extended social and physical context that he or she could be seen to react to and affect. Deeds and his butlers echoing their voices in the foyer; the Senators in the Senate chamber in *Smith*, and the Bailey family in *It's a Wonderful Life* thus exist as tangible, extended communities rather than as mere aggregates of individuals, because they are photographed whole, as communities of complexly interacting gestures, glances, and facial expressions simultaneously being exchanged from actor to actor in a larger unfragmented photographic (and acoustic) space.

A film that takes as its dramatic subject the subtle study of a character's attempt to master the social and physical spaces around him, and that consequently puts such a premium on the performative subtlety of the actor who plays him to express such complexly changing relations between himself and the spaces around him, asks at least as much sensitivity of its director, supervisor of photography, and editor. The performer must withstand the repressiveness of the technologies and bureaucracies of filmmaking as much as the repressiveness of the technologies and bureaucracies of society. The filmmakers must be aware of the constraints they place on a performer and the potentially repressive and frustrating effects of their institutional and discursive technologies of control. It would be a betrayal of the central character and leading actor even greater than Cedar's betrayal of Deeds within the film if they, in their technical decisions about lighting, blocking, camera placement, and editing, unconsciously worked against or defeated his efforts to act freely. Capra, Walker, Goosson, Bernds, and Gene Havlik (the editor) not only live up to the performative example Longfellow Deeds sets, but in some respects set an even higher standard for free and unsystematic performance than that he maintains. At moments they deinstitutionalize the visual space of the standard

Academy frame and the rhythms of Hollywood editing even more audacious-
ly than Deeds works to deinstitutionalize the mansion he lives in or Gary
Cooper works to deinstitutionalize (or de-Hollywoodize) the gestures and
tempos of his acting.

The photographic innovation frequently takes the form of opening up the
frame space in unexpected ways, allowing unorthodox bodily positions
within it, or tolerating surprising movements and unconventional bodily
repositionings during the course of a single shot or scene. There is a striking
moment in the scene that takes place in the park between Bennett and Deeds
that concludes with their musical timpani–tuba duet. They are sitting side by
side on a park bench talking, when at one point Jean Arthur pivots her body
ninety degrees away from the line of sight of the camera to turn to speak to
Cooper more intimately. Most directors would have yelled "Cut!" and taken
this opportunity to cut on motion to make a new camera setup at a right angle
to the first. Capra stays with the take, however, and the uncanny effect is of
the character's having momentarily freed herself from the confining grid of
the filmic gaze itself. Bennett demonstrates a surprising capacity to move
independently of the camera or the frame space, turning away from the potentially imprisoning technology of the well-composed shot to share, as it were, a
private moment with the other character in the scene. (This turn away from
the camera – and therefore from us in the audience – to, in effect, withdraw
from the shot into an unphotographable privacy recalls Ellie Andrews's comparable turn away from, and flight from, cinematic scrutiny in her final scene
in *It Happened One Night*.)

There is a slightly different effect in an even more unorthodox shot in an
earlier scene. Babe is sitting in the foreground of the shot to one side of and in
front of her newspaper editor's desk, talking to him about Deeds, whom she
has been following and writing stories about for the paper. Meanwhile, as is
her habit throughout the early scenes of the film, while she talks she performs
a series of meaningless little magic tricks to keep her hands busy. In the midst
of a trivial coin trick and in the middle of this fairly complex conversation with
her editor, Jean Arthur accidentally – (or deliberately? Could this have been
planned and rehearsed? It seems extremely unlikely) – drops the coin with
which she has been playing. While the dialogue continues and the camera
keeps running, she casually feels for the coin in her lap. (As an experienced
trouper, Arthur undoubtedly assumed she could pick it up, resume the trick,
and finish the take without a break.) This is where the scene gets really weird.
The coin is not in her lap, so still keeping up her scripted dialogue while she
rises from her seat a little, she discreetly glances down while she continues to
talk and looks for the coin in her chair. Still not finding it, she gets down on
her knees on the floor and searches under the chair. With this last movement
she not only drops entirely out of the editor's line of sight behind the desk but
almost lowers herself out of line of sight of the audience, almost but not quite
entirely out of the bottom of the frame space. The coin is not under the chair,
either. Searching around some more, she finally discovers that it has rolled

under the chair's seat cushion. She picks it up, sits back down, and completes the scene. It marks a moment in the history of Hollywood filmmaking. Long before the analogous late work of Antonioni, prior even to Renoir's *Rules of the Game*, the frame space is revealed as being the merest convention. It is an artificial grid that provides a necessarily partial and imperfect view of a reality that seamlessly extends beyond its range of comprehension. One can move around in it improvisatorily, spontaneously, eccentrically, almost at whim, even to the point of threatening to ignore it, to drop out of it in the pursuit of an impulse.

One more scene might be mentioned as yet another example of Capra's iconoclastic use of cinematic space. A little later in the film, Deeds, having fallen in love with Bennett, calls her on the phone from his bedroom. Capra photographs Cooper, lying on his back in bed, from the level of the bed, with the camera looking down the length of his body from his head to his sprawlingly crossed legs. There are few shots like it in film, unless one thinks back to a similar shot of Gallagher eating an apple in bed and talking on the phone flat on her back in *Platinum Blonde*, a film – not coincidentally – about the same subject – the capacity of a character and a director to establish a free and creative relationship to the spaces around them. The shot strikingly captures Deeds's vulnerability and false sense of security when talking to Bennett (who, he is unaware, has been using him as a pawn in a scheme to advance her journalistic career). Even more than that, it conveys the possibility of an eccentric and innovative relationship between an actor and the positioning of the lights and the camera. In a film concerned with the ways in which society straitjackets the individual (metaphorically and literally – as in the scene with the tailors) and limits free movement (in the first place with bodyguards, but then subsequently with even more insidious forms of psychological, social, and moral control), Capra is working as hard as his central character and the actor who plays him to explore possibilities of freedom. By deinstitutionalizing the space of the frame and the pacing of the acting in such scenes he, in effect, establishes a cinematic level of creative achievement that his central characters have to attempt to live up to.

These examples are all from the first hour or so of the film, since, although Deeds and Bennett begin with significant but admittedly marginal possibilities of free movement, as the movie proceeds they lose even that marginal mobility. They become increasingly trapped in a more and more confining visual matrix that corresponds to the increasingly confining social matrix working on and through them. The possibilities for creative movement become fewer as the increasing number of close-ups and the accelerated pace of Capra's editing progressively immobilize them in space or restrict their movements within the frame. That then becomes one possible definition of the essential dramatic situation that Deeds and Bennett must cope with in the final half hour of the film. They must find a way of expressing themselves in the changed visual and temporal suitation into which they are plunged by Capra's changed camera work and editing, just as they must find a way of asserting their freedom within the daunting bureaucratic structures of Deeds's insanity hearing.

Two crucial points remain to be made. First, in each of the scenes mentioned, freedom and creativity have become assertively public and interpersonal achievements. Deeds's or Bennett's positionings and repositionings within the spaces of these shots are exciting precisely because they are not solitary, individual acts of vision or imagination. They are social achievements shared with another character or characters, which must take into account the actions and feelings of those other characters. Deeds works to communicate his playfulness to his butlers; Bennett turns toward Deeds on the park bench to share an intimate revelation with him; Deeds lounges on his bed while talking love talk to Bennett on the phone. These are moments essentially different from, and more difficult to achieve than Megan Davis's or Jerry Strong's silent, visionary communings with the stars and the landscape.

Second, with *Deeds* Capra's work shifts from privileging predominantly visual structurings of experience to contrasting visual and verbal structurings. The films of the early thirties – most obviously *Ladies of Leisure*, *Forbidden*, and *Bitter Tea*, but also *The Miracle Woman*, *Platinum Blonde*, and *Lady for a Day* – concern themselves almost exclusively with acts of visionary possession and shared visionary communities, as expressed by predominantly visual strategies of scenic representation. The films of the middle and late thirties (and here again *It Happened One Night* is a transitional work) and the forties (Capra's final two important films, *It's a Wonderful Life* and *State of the Union*) juxtapose modes of verbal and social possession against modes of visual and visionary possession. The importance of this change cannot be overemphasized. It is as if Capra were engaging himself with and reenacting, in the very trajectory of his career, the split in the experience of film itself between the rival claims of the eye and those of the speaking voice, or more generally, as if he were fighting in himself and his films the war between the two ways of knowing that has been waged for two centuries in American literature and art.

The essays of Emerson and the poetry of Robert Frost represent perhaps the two most obvious examples of bodies of work that, like Capra's later films, have incorporated into their own nervous systems the dialectical conflict between the claims of the visionary eye and those of the social speaking voice. The final stanza of "Stopping by Woods on a Snowy Evening" might almost be read as an explicit reflection on this central tension in American art:

> The woods are lovely, dark and deep,
> But I have promises to keep,
> And miles to go before I sleep,
> And miles to go before I sleep.

The artist is tempted to lose himself entirely in his vision of loveliness, "dark and deep," but is simultaneously called back to himself and the world by the claims of society and all of its syntactic, metrical, social, and spoken "promises to keep." Frost, in his sly performance in this poem, recognizes the same thing that all of Emerson's essays might be considered to be an extended meditation upon: a situation of inevitable doubleness. To live in vision is necessarily to see through the claims of time, space, and society, to exempt oneself from social entanglements and responsibilities, whereas to become a vocal performer is inevitably to make the opposite movement – to reach beyond the self to recognize and honor one's enriching, troubling, stimulating connections with others. The distinctive achievement of both Frost's poetry and Emerson's essays is not merely to meditate on this split in the American consciousness but to embody it in the style and form of their writing. Both are visionary writers who in their most audacious work paradoxically attempt to express moments of transcendence and vision in the voice tones of ordinary speech. They attempt to speak the sublime in the forms of social intercourse. They, in their work, like Capra in these late films, embrace and embody the division of consciousness about which they are writing. They make it their own and live with it and through it in their style. If vision represents dreams and desires, dialogue is duty and responsibility. The true daring of Capra's work is its attempt to hold both realms in one thought, whereas I would argue, the comparative irresponsibility and insipidity of most avant-garde expression, from Maya Deren in film to Lee Bruer, Julian Beck, and Robert Wilson on stage is its failure to test desire against duty, vision against the claims of society, imagination against the repressions of language.*

In *Ladies of Leisure* and *Bitter Tea*, even in the scenes in which Kay and Jerry, or Megan and Yen are physically present together on their balconies, they are largely freed from the burden of establishing a practical social (or sexual) relationship, expressed in a verbal interaction. How different the romantic scenes are in *Deeds* or *You Can't Take It with You*. For lovers to be together in those films is not to look off in the same direction, to meditate together, or to share a vision or a dream but to *talk* together, and that makes all the difference. *Deeds*, *Smith*, and *Doe*, not to mention the two postwar films, powerfully argue that vision alone is not sufficient. Characters, however exalted their imaginations, however compelling their ideals and dreams, must learn to talk persuasively, passionately, and effectively to each other and to other characters around them. They frequently begin these films as if they were dreamers left over from the earlier work, but in the course of the films they must learn how to translate dreams into deeds and ideals into words, and relentlessly negotiate the space between the two realms. That, I take it, is the explicit subject of both *Deeds* and *Smith*. Characters must learn to convert their capacity for imagination and vision into practical worldly forms of verbal and social performance. Deeds's and Bennett's progress in the course of the film will be measured in their development of the capacity to use their voices socially, to talk, talk, talk, as social performers in front of public audiences.

One should not need to explain why film, of all twentieth-century art

---

* For a somewhat fuller discussion of the limitations of the avant-garde position, see my *American Dreaming: The Films of John Cassavetes and the American Experience* (Berkeley: University of California, 1985), pp. 3, 31–6, and 90–1, as well as my essay on John Ashbery in *American Poetry since World War II*, ed. Donald Greiner (Chicago: Gale, 1981), pp. 14–21.

forms, is perhaps uniquely suited to exploring the relationship between visual and verbal impulses. What Deeds and Smith have to do in the course of their films, in learning to translate back and forth from the one state of being to the other – from private vision to public expression, from intangible ideals to institutional embodiments of them – is what Capra had to do as a Hollywood filmmaker every time he made a movie. He had to negotiate the gap between his own unarticulated private vision and the assertively public forms of the film in which they might be expressed. Even more important, he had to stage the transaction between these realms in a medium that repeats this division of realms in its own formal division of allegiance between communicating through pictures and through words. To make a standard Hollywood narrative feature film is to be forced relentlessly to compare visions and words: to weigh the power of immediate, compelling, cinematic visions against the social responsibilities and obligations built into the time-bound, social forms of dramatic dialogue and narrative exposition.

It is precisely because of the overwhelming importance of social and verbal performance in the film that one finally has to judge the specific social and verbal performances presented for our inspection in the first hour or so of *Deeds* (including most of the scenes that I have already mentioned) to be of a trivial, if not downright irresponsible, sort. Longfellow's acoustic high jinks with his butlers, his "Swanee River" duet with Bennett, and her coin and rope tricks for her editor may be expressions of a generally desirable freedom, but they can hardly be the expressive basis for a mature relationship or an ultimate strategy of survival in the world in which Deeds and Bennett live. This man and woman must convert heavenly labials into worldly gutturals. They must translate their yearning but inarticulate echoes, hootings, and musical and poetic effusions into the forms of common syntactic speech.

Capra's cross-cutting from scenes of the romance growing up between Deeds and Bennett to scenes of plotting and scheming going on in the law offices of Cedar, Cedar, Cedar, and Buddington reminds us that the pair cannot live in the world of their imaginations. *Deeds, Smith, Doe, It's a Wonderful Life*, and *State of the Union* each rely on similar cross-cutting between scenes of play or idealistic dreaming involving the principal characters and scenes of Machiavellian scheming involving another set of characters, to implicitly criticize the irresponsibility of pure idealism. The dreamers are forced to confront the schemers, and more than that, they are forced to convert their private, impractical dreams into practical actions and words that can be expressed publicly. That process of conversion is the central drama of the late films.

Most discussions of the films of the *Deeds–Smith–Doe* trilogy present them as describing a simple movement of the central character from innocence to experience and from victimization to victory, as if the films were enactments of a ritualistic pilgrim's progress. As I have suggested, rather than treating them as simpleminded political bedtime stories or escapist romances, we need to approach these films as explorations of quite complex rhetorical strategies. Very much as Henry James is doing in a novel like *The Golden Bowl* (which has quite striking similarities with the narrative and rhetorical progress of both *Deeds* and *Smith*), Capra is exploring specific strategies of expression. The progress of Deeds and Bennett is not a mere optimistic leap of faith on Capra's part but a profound and distinctively American voyage of expressive exploration and discovery.

One can describe this change in psychological terms. In the course of the film Bennett moves from emotional detachment and self-interestedness to passionate involvement with Deeds and the cause he represents. She moves from a newspaper reporter's cool cynicism about all abstract values to a lover's idealism and passion. Deeds, on the other hand, moves from a boyish frivolousness and ingenuousness that is, in its own way, almost equally disengaged from the realities of mature emotional and social experience to a last-ditch self-defense of a few basic principles in which he believes. That, however, is a superficial and inadequate reading: The profound stylistic changes enacted within the individual films of the *Deeds–Smith–Doe* trilogy are much more radical than anything describable as mere psychological change in the characters. Deeds and Bennett (and later Smith and Saunders, and after them, Willoughby and Mitchell) are forced to leave behind the styles of gesturing, speaking, and consciousness with which they began their films and to invent other styles in their place. One style of acting breaks down and gives way to another; one cinematic style of representation is abandoned and replaced by another.

Capra obviously intended the viewer to think of Deeds and Bennett as a romantic couple whose individual destinies are intimately interrelated. I want to discuss the changes in their stylistic performances separately, though, since Capra's narrative strategy in all three "populist" films is to present the verbal and social maturation of the central male and female characters along quite distinct lines. There is every reason to conclude from these three films, and even more from *It's a Wonderful Life*, that Capra, like D. H. Lawrence and Freud, and unlike many contemporary theorists who attempt to erase or ignore sexual differences, conceived of there being fundamentally distinct and separate performative roles for men and women. Capra believed that the imaginative and social situation of women, and therefore the expressive possibilities available to them, was always and necessarily different from that of men. Let me consider Bennett first and then Deeds.

In a special, rhetorical sense of the term, Capra moves Bennett and specific scenes involving her into the realm of modern melodrama about halfway through the film. By melodrama, however, I do not mean the kind of dramatic settings, events, or character types that appeared most notoriously on the Victorian stage – scheming villains and innocent virgins, titanic combats between Good and Evil, deathbed confessions, thunder and lightning, and duels in the night – but a state of consciousness and an especially heightened and uniquely post-Romantic style of expression that sometimes, especially in its more popular or debased forms, has included such things. In his *The Melodramatic Imagination*, Peter Brooks has gone farther than any other contemporary critic to define the melodramatic utterance as a style in itself and to differentiate it from the lurid stage events and tawdry emotionality that are usually mistakenly regarded as the essence, and not the accident, of melo-dramatic expression:

> Melodramatic rhetoric, and the whole expressive enterprise of the genre, represents a victory over repression. We could conceive this repression as simultaneously social, psychological, historical, and conventional: what could not be said on an earlier stage, nor still on a "nobler" stage, nor within the codes of society. The melodramatic utterance breaks through everything that constitutes the "reality principle," all its censorships, accommodations, and tonings-down. Desire cries aloud its language in identification with full states of being. Melodrama partakes of the dream world, ... and this is in no wise more true than in the possibility it provides of saying what is in "real life" unsayable ... Desire triumphs over the world of substitute-formations and detours, it achieves plentitude of meaning.*

The triumph of desire over repression and the speaking of what cannot be said in the codes of society are, I think, the key concepts to keep in mind when one attempts to describe what happens to Bennett and to scenes involving her in this film in its second half. I have used the adjective "operatic" several times in the last few chapters to describe the intensities of feeling and imagination that erupt at certain moments in Capra's work, but those moments are only what Brooks would rightly call special instances of melodramatic expression. Insofar as social and narrative forms, manners, and language are repressive, in the sense in which Brooks uses the word, Capra's operatic and melodramatic moments are efforts to break through what is defined and bounded by social forms to release powerful moral, imaginative, and passional energies (in his characters and in his viewers). Capra attempts to liberate intensities and mobilities of feeling and imagination that are fundamentally opposed to all psychologically or socially normative forms.

That is why what happens to Bennett in the second half of *Deeds* is only quite trivially described by saying that she falls in love with Deeds. Rather (under the guise of the rather sketchily presented romantic development) in her character the film attempts to make a place for the expression of forces of desire that, in Brooks's phrase, "[break] through everything that constitutes the 'reality principle,' all its censorships, accommodations, and tonings-down." The style of the work is itself disrupted in an attempt to make room for the energies and movements of a desire that is at odds with *all* "realistic" or "classical" narrative representation, just as it is at odds with structures of social organization and expression. As Brooks and Capra define it (and, I would argue, as the great tradition of American transcendental aspiration defines it), desire and the style of expression in which it vents itself is, indeed, everything that such structures are felt to be inadequate to contain or express.

Brooks's description of the stylistic world of melodrama is an almost letter-

---

* Peter Brooks. *The Melodramatic Imagination* (New Haven: Yale University Press, 1976), p. 41.

perfect description of the change in Babe Bennett's (and Jean Arthur's) style of performance in the second half of *Deeds*:

> The desire to express all seems a fundamental characteristic of the melodramatic mode. Nothing is spared because nothing is left unsaid; the characters stand on stage and utter the unspeakable, give voice to their deepest feelings, dramatize through their heightened and polarized words and gestures the whole lesson of their relationship ... Life tends, in this fiction, towards ever more concentrated and totally expressive gestures and statements. (p.4)

To understand how Bennett's personal styles, Arthur's acting styles, and Capra's cinematic styles change, one needs only to compare the scenes I described earlier with those in the final hour of the film. In the first half of the film Arthur idly ties knots in a rope, does coin tricks (and looks for a dropped coin), and plays witty verbal games. There is an appreciation of the accidental, the unfocused, and the casual in life, acting, and film in these scenes that reminds one of the comparable relish for the random and the improvised in Renoir's *Boudu Saved from Drowning* or *The Rules of the Game* or much of Hawks's work. In the second half of the film, however, Capra moves in a direction Renoir never took and toward which Hawks could only fleetingly glance. Capra turns decisively away from these things to an entirely different sort of scene making for Bennett. Beginning with the unfinished telephone call between herself and Deeds about halfway into the film, she is transported into a stylistic world the opposite of the random, unfocused, and casual. It is a world of "totally expressive gestures," in Brooks's phrase, in which every facial expression, glance, and movement is freighted emotionally with an almost overwhelming "plentitude of meaning." Medium and long-shots are replaced by medium-close shots and close-ups. Her expressions and gestures are magnified into powerful significance on-screen, and her speech becomes as powerfully charged with passion as her gestures, so that, as never before, every word she speaks and, even more important, every pause or hesitation between words becomes fraught with emotional significance.

Brooks talks about the fullness or "plentitude" of significance in melodramatic expression, but as he well understands, this fullness is at the same time a profound emptiness in another respect. As gestures and words are increasingly burdened with significance and charged with emotion in one way, they simultaneously empty themselves of significance in other ways. That is to say, as Bennett's (and Capra's) style becomes more imaginatively and emotionally intense, more melodramatically meaningful, it becomes less expressive, coherent, or meaningful by realistic or social standards of narrative expression. Whereas earlier in the film she was coolly voluble, articulate, witty, and verbally poised to a fault, her speech now becomes hesitant, stuttering, and hysterical, or simply ceases altogether for long periods. The language of society becomes inadequate to express her overcharged feelings. In short, as her speech becomes imbued with a private, tonal richness of significance and depth of feeling, it becomes less and less publicly intelligible by the standards of realistic, classical codes of discourse. Tonal meaning displaces semantic meaning (which is why, the more passionately Bennett speaks in Deeds's defense during the hearing, the more the fair-minded judges – and not merely the shyster lawyers who oppose Deeds – fail to understand her). The movement into a world of melodramatic signification is a movement into an expressive realm that denies itself translation into institutional or social forms of expression. In the nightmare of the liberated consciousness enacted by Bennett during Deeds's hearing, to speak a language even partially answerable to the intensity and lability of imagination and desire is to cut oneself off irrevocably from the discourse of society. By all social or legal standards, she proves herself "insane" at his insanity hearing. Her language and performance is deranged.

Film, above all other narrative forms, has the capacity to offer an alternative, visual "text of muteness" to supplement (or at times even replace) the verbal or linguistic text of muteness represented by a character's spoken language. Film, unlike a novel, can offer us the experience of pictures in addition to the experience of words, pictures that have an impact and intensity that allows them to replace the words spoken and to substitute their fullness of visual meaning in place of the emptiness of verbal meaning of the newly impoverished or crazed language of the characters. This potential of film is not lost on a filmmaker who began his career with silent pictures. During the second half of *Deeds*, Capra's lighting, photography, and editing offer a visual spectacle of powerful pictorial silences and highly meaningful inarticulatenesses that in intensity and expressiveness frequently surpass Bennett's verbal melodramatics. The final half hour of *Deeds* is a visual extravaganza of briskly intercut close-ups of her agitated gestures, glances, facial expressions, and bodily movements that succeed in speaking more powerfully and poignantly than anything she did earlier in the film, in ways that dialogue and legal discourse cannot. Capra forces the viewer to remain simultaneously aware of both kinds of utterance – the melodramatic and the nonmelodramatic, the stunningly visual and the classically verbal, by choosing to have the switch to melodrama occur first over the telephone in a conversation with Deeds and then in a courtroom in his defense, two forums in which linguistic decorum and highly conventionalized codes of discourse reign. He wants the viewer to be able to hold in one glance both the stimulating private expressive power and the frightening public expressive limitations of melodramatic utterance.

In the love poem that Deeds reads to Bennett before he discovers her real identity, he has a line that might summarize the changed conditions of expression for Babe herself later in the film: "My heart longs to cry out, if it only could speak." Language in any public, conventional use of it proves inadequate to "speak" the feelings of her "heart." The intensity of Bennett's desire cannot be spoken in any more direct way than between the lines, in her pauses and stutterings, in the near hysteria of her tones, in the silence of her agitated gestures and looks. Capra's expressive lighting effects, photographic close-ups, and accelerated editing rhythms pick up the burden of signification that verbal language cannot bear. We and she have moved the maximal distance from the world of journalism in which she and the film itself began, where all human events are, by journalistic definition, verbally articulable in coolly coherent, emotionally neutral sentences, paragraphs, and narratives. For Capra, significant human experience and filmmaking begin where journalism, realism, or naturalism leave off.

Though it is, strictly speaking, an aside to my main argument, I cannot help noticing another, stranger aspect of Capra's melodramatic practice in the film, the bizarre scene with the crazed gunman who breaks into Deeds's mansion immediately following the unfinishable phone call that precipitates the melodramatic stylistic shift I have been describing. Almost everything about the scene is strange and jarring: not only its theatrical excessiveness and the overall hysteria and exaggeration of Capra's staging of it, but also its narrative implausibility and its complete tonal incongruity with the rest of the film. In the first place, it is not even necessary as a plot event. There would have been a dozen other ways to give Deeds the idea for his philanthropic homesteading scheme, all of them narratively more plausible and economical than having a poor farmer break into his home with a gun in his hand to threaten his life. In the second place, for the minute or two that the man threatens to shoot him, the scene momentarily plunges us into a gangster picture whose style and tone jar with everything else in the film, and then, as the man breaks down in tears, just as suddenly and clumsily it propels us into yet another kind of film – some sort of weird male-weepie picture.

One might simply overlook the whole episode and treat it as an aberration if it were not for the fact that this same sort of thing takes place in other Capra films at almost exactly the same point in their narrative development. Even more bizarrely, it almost always involves either the presence of a gun or the threat of sudden death, or both, as it does here. At a comparable moment in *Forbidden*, Lulu Smith pulls a gun on Al Holland and fills his body with lead. At a similar point in *American Madness*, Tom Dixon opens a drawer in his desk containing a gun, takes it out, and ominously contemplates suicide. Peter Warne pretends to have a gun in his pocket in *It Happened One Night* and threatens to shoot the terrified Shapely. George Conway pulls a gun on Yang and threatens to kill him, before he himself is wrestled to the ground, knocked unconscious, and disarmed in *Lost Horizon*. Joseph Paine suddenly grabs a gun and tries to shoot himself at a climactic moment in *Smith*. The police fire their guns at a half-crazy, fleeing George Bailey in the nighttown episode of *It's a Wonderful Life*. There are other gratuitous moments equally violent and disruptive but lacking guns that one might cite from *The Miracle Woman*, *Doe*, and *State of the Union*. It is an impressive cinematic record of threatened or actual violence, all the less expected from the filmmaker generally regarded as the one least capable of committing a gangster movie to celluloid. However, it is not merely the sheer presence of a gun or the sudden threat of violence that distinguishes these scenes. Virtually without exception they are each minimasterpieces of film noir stylistics, involving low-key-lighting effects, heavy background orchestration, point-of-view camera placements, oddly elevated or depressed angles and frame compositions, and violent, agitated editorial rhythms that make them stand out like sore thumbs from the rest of the films in which they are inserted. In short, these moments are not isolated aberrations but something Capra felt compelled to include again and again in work otherwise apparently so pacific, so domestic. Why?

The only conclusion one can come to is that in scenes like these Capra himself becomes a kind of Babe Bennett, working off intensities and excesses of feeling that are not expressible in more social narratives, or less deranged forms of dialogue and eventfulness. Such scenes usually occur in Capra's work immediately following a scene depicting a psychological or emotional crisis or breakdown, and it is as if in propelling his central characters into private, personal melodramatic intensities of feeling and awareness, in the elevated sense of melodramatic expression, Capra is unable to resist moving his characters and his whole film itself momentarily into melodrama in a more lurid, Gothic sense of the form – the sense in which murders, guns, conflagrations, violence, and tears are obligatory.

Another American master of melodrama in the high sense, Henry James, similarly switched repeatedly from high to low forms of it in this way, especially at climactic scenes and in the conclusions of his stories and novels. It is often forgotten that in addition to being the historian of fine consciousnesses, James was also frequently (both early and late in his work) the chronicler of Gothic thrills and chills, of flashes of lightning and rolls of thunder, of encounters with ghosts, and of midnight revelations and of charged glances and confrontations.* Both James and Capra are equally artists of what Brooks calls the "melodrama of consciousness," but the point I am making is that there are times in their work when the melodramatic energies that are definable in terms of the overcharged and socially inexpressible consciousnesses of their characters narratively overflow or are displaced, as it were, into these grotesque, lurid, or violent scenes. At these moments Capra's films go a little wild with their own otherwise unutterable intensities of significance that can, apparently, be expressed only in such bizarre and often gratuitous scenes of wildness or madness. The family drama turns itself into film noir and momentarily becomes almost as overwrought, hysterical and gesticulatory as the Babe Bennett character in the hearing.

One needs to emphasize that the excessiveness of these narrative moments, in both Capra and James, is never merely a cheap trick to titilate or mystify an audience, or to add camouflaging excitement to an otherwise trivial or silly story, as it is used in the lower forms of recent popular fiction and film, from the work of Daphne Du Maurier and Alfred Hitchcock to that of Stephen King and Brian De Palma. These moments count for so much in Capra's work only

---

* See the discussion of melodrama in the writing of Henry James in my introduction to *The Spoils of Poynton* and *What Maisie Knew* (New York: New American Library, 1984). Look at the end of *The Portrait of a Lady* as an example of what I am describing in James's writing.

because they correlate with and express otherwise inexpressible intensities of consciousness and feeling in the central characters on particular, complex dramatic occasions.

The implicit equation that I am making between Capra's (or James's) overfreighted consciousness and that of his principal character or characters at such moments is furthermore legitimized by the unspoken working assumption of their art (and of the greatest American drama and fiction in general) that the central character is a kind of artist of his or her own identity and experience. The melodrama can move inward into the consciousness of a character in James or Capra precisely because the character is granted an awareness potentially as complex, rich, and difficult to express as the consciousness of his or her creator. This seems fundamentally different from the European tradition. One can always tell Balzac or Flaubert from his characters. The author's awareness, his melodramatic utterances are necessarily more inclusive and interesting than the character's. James's and Capra's major characters, however, are uniquely American artists of their own identities and explorers of their own expressive strategies, with consciousnesses at times indistinguishable from, and almost never automatically inferior to, those of their creators. As Whitman and James both show us, America is the land where artistic effects and the creation of daring new stylistic identities are no longer the special province of artists. The Romantic dream has left the hills and garrets and come down to the streets, where everyone is potentially his or her own artist of experience and correlatively, as Deeds and Bennett demonstrate, with potentially the same expressive problems as a poet or a filmmaker.

Let me now switch from the figure of Bennett to that of Deeds. The voice that Longfellow Deeds arrives at by the end of the film is different both from the one he starts with and the one that Bennett ends with, and is at least as complex a stylistic achievement as hers. Like Bennett, Deeds is reduced to silence and inarticulateness, as a result of his confusion when she betrays him and the lawyers entrap him, but when he eventually emerges from his silence in the final fifteen minutes of the film, his voice is entirely different from hers. Most accounts describe this process of his regaining his voice in reductive psychological terms similar to those they apply to Bennett. For example, a recent synopsis of the movie describes his progress as follows: Deeds begins the film in a state of beatific innocence, undergoes a period of doubt and despair, and finally emerges from it when Babe professes her love for him during the hearing. At that point he regains the idealistic voice and vision he had temporarily lost and wins the court over with his country-boy reasonableness and down-home common sense. Such an approach is as inadequate for understanding Deeds's progress in the film as a description of Bennett as simply moving from journalistic cynicism to romantic infatuation would be. Both Bennett and Deeds lose the voices with which they began the film and eventually regain voices in the hearing room, but the voices they regain at the end are neither the ones they started out with nor merely voices of romantic innocence, idealism, naiveté, or common sense.

How are we to understand the stylistic possibility embodied by Longfellow Deeds? Most critics would answer by saying that Capra is (quite simple-mindedly) suggesting that the meek can and will inherit the earth, that inno-cence and gentleness will triumph over all opposition. In the best general discussion of Capra's films to date, Charles Maland argues this case and more or less summarizes the prevailing critical approach. He first asserts that Capra metaphorically compares Deeds with Christ, since both are the sons of parents named Joseph and Mary, and then describes Deeds's innocence as his most characteristic trait before, during, and after his period of temporary disillusionment:

> His innocence is stressed by his childish enthusiasm for fire trucks, his almost chivalric conception of love, . . . and his utter inability to fathom the manners and attitudes of the city vultures with whom he comes into contact. One of those vultures, the shyster lawyer Cedar who seeks to bilk Deeds of his fortune, explicitly sums it up. "He's as naive," he gleefully tells his colleagues early in the film, "as a child."*

I do not want to tackle the surprising and facile equation of Christ, Chris-tianity, and innocence implicit in this argument, except to notice in passing that one would have thought of all the world's major religions, the one built around the betrayal, torture, and crucifixion of its leader would have most embodied principles of Blakean experience and not innocence. Surely, though, when he found himself approvingly quoting and endorsing the view of Cedar, one of the most cynical and despicable characters in the film, Maland might have paused in his argument and wondered if he was being taken in.

I would argue that the contrary of innocence is being displayed by Deeds (and by Capra, who collaborates with him) in his final, climactic courtroom performance. His incontrovertible accomplishment is to shed every vestige of whatever innocence he might originally have had and to demonstrate one of the most stunning displays of verbal and intellectual sophistication on film. Deeds becomes a kind of literary-textual critic par excellence, a critic apparently subtler and more profound than any of the critics who have tried to understand him. When he rises to speak during the final minutes of the insanity hearing, Deeds is the opposite of Maland's innocent, with an "utter inability to fathom the manners and attitudes of the city vultures." He shows himself the master of all attitudes and manners, to the point of, in strict literary-critical parlance, wittily and playfully flaunting his ability to "decon-struct" their utterances at will. He systematically takes up each of the major pieces of testimony that have been used against him by the witnesses and lawyers in the hearing and (most brilliantly and exuberantly in the case of the testimony of the Faulkner sisters) reveals the essential textuality of the discourse, tracing and explaining to the court the particular set of arbitrary codes, assumptions, and consistencies that generate the text and attempt to

---

* Charles Maland, *Frank Capra* (Boston: Twayne Publishers, 1980), p. 95.

control and limit its interpretation. He explicitly treats each of the principal pieces of testimony as a system of rule-governed discourse, temporarily entering into and explaining each "author's" particular set of discursive assumptions and parodically adopting the author's vocabulary, prior to suggestively indicating the limitations of each discursive system.

To do this once is to liberate oneself from the expressive tyranny of a particular text, but to do it more than once, to realize that it can be done to every possible text, sooner or later, is to do much more. It is to recognize, in the phrase I have already quoted from Derrida, the structurality of structure. As every deconstructionist is aware, this process of "entering into" and sympathetically comparing a series of texts in such a way is potentially a strategy of escape from domination by *any* text. Deconstruction, that is to say, notwithstanding its suspiciously transatlantic origins, is thoroughly consistent with, and eminently convertible into an all-American assertion of freedom (which is why the Gallic theorists have received such a resounding welcome in Baltimore and New Haven). Deeds's activity of deconstruction is a proto-typically American way of levering himself outside of all texts, of asserting the artificiality of all systems, institutions, and codes of understanding. It is a form of mastery and an audacious assertion of the reader's/speaker's/critic's recognition of, and consequent ability to escape, the shackles of all linguistic entrapment.

It is not accidental that Deeds initiates the whole process with a brief, witty Derridean *jeu*. He prefaces his initial act of critical prowess over a specific text with a short exordium about the nature of all texts: He talks about *écriture* and the necessary gap between experience and verbal expression figured in a playful discussion of what he calls "doodling" and "o [or "oh!"?] filling" and other forms of extralinguistic "playing," like his playing the tuba to help him write. Deeds may be a country boy, but it is sometimes forgotten that he is also, like so many of Capra's other central figures, at least a part-time artist – a musician and a poet – one who, by all the evidence, has thought as long and hard about the nature of verbal, social, and artistic expression as his creator.

There is really no need to invoke fancy French pedigrees for Deeds's performance, though. Deeds is a performer in the mainstream native folk tradition of Mark Twain, Joel Chandler Harris, and George Washington Harris. He is teasing society and parodically playing with the rules, customs, and conventions of his own and others' speech in a thoroughly American way. As his elaborate digressions, witty asides, and playfully rustic illustrations and metaphors communicate, Deeds is toying with the rules and forms of testimony, stretching them, and testing their capaciousness (when I say Deeds, I mean Capra and Riskin, of course). As in all of Capra's films, one kind of playing is inseparable from another. Deeds is having fun, and he is poking fun, but, perhaps most important of all, he is playing in the dramatic sense of the word as well. He is turning the court into a stage for a consummately enter-taining, improvised performance that expresses his own unsystematized and unsystematizable imaginative energy. By the very eccentricity of his performance he escapes from those who would demand a more systematic form of behavior and style of testimony and self-defense from him.

As one watches and listens to his delightful and self-delighting performance in the courtroom, one remembers that Deeds is by avocation a performer on the tuba who plays with it in the same contrapuntal way in which he plays with tones and styles there, making his presence felt and heard not by blending into the melodic line but by virtue of his ability to trace an eccentric and innovative counterpoint to it, in the apparent comic clumsiness of his oom-pah-pahs. It seems hardly accidental that one of the most touching scenes in the first hour of the film explicitly celebrates this contrapuntal aspect of his playing. At the farewell party hastily thrown together for him at the Mandrake Falls train station, Deeds plays the sole tuba in the band that sees him off. As the train slowly pulls out of the station, the band breaks into the strains if "Auld Lang Syne" (a tune that was virtually a signature piece in Capra's later work). Deeds stands with his tuba on the rear platform of the train as it pulls away from the crowd in the station, and, in a directorial master stroke and a coup de theatre of sound engineering, Capra and his sound man, Edward Bernds, create the illusion that, in between passionate waves and shouts of farewell to the lifelong friends he is leaving behind, Deeds is still playing the counter-pointed tuba accompaniment to his own farewell party. That offbeat, eccentric performance on his own behalf (and yet also selflessly, for the benefit of his listeners), in its syncopated mixture of earnestness and quirkiness, is an affecting visual and acoustic anticipation of something very much like the eccentric, offbeat verbal and social performance he stages later in the courtroom.

In effect, Deeds's achievement in the courtroom is that he demonstrates his ability to play, in society, with linguistic tones, styles, and metaphors as creatively and wittily as he showed himself capable of playing for and to himself on the tuba all along. To be able to play this way in a courtroom, one has to recognize that a social institution like a court, and the discourse that is admissible or speakable within it, is as artificial and arbitrary yet as complex and potentially stimulating a creation of the human imagination as the theory of musical harmony and counterpoint. In the films of the early thirties, Capra's protagonists usually tried simply to rebel against society and its arbitrary rules and codes; here there can no longer be a question of taking or leaving them behind. Codes are everywhere, and everything is encoded. These is no nature, or reality, to run away to. Any momentary leverage over social discourse can and must be achieved from within the system. These styles and systems are what, if one is to survive, one must learn to play on, play with, and play against. This is the truly radical shift in awareness in Capra's work that is announced by *Deeds* (though it is a radicalism that, because of the nature of its insight, appears to be a new conservatism). Freedom is in the counterpoint.

If Capra's heroes no longer attempt to flee from the repressive forms of society into a world of romance or imagination, it is because for the first time they recognize that the society they flee from is itself an artificial, arbitrary creation of the human imagination and that any other society they would bring into existence outside of it would be no less artificial and arbitrary. If that sounds like something discovered by Wallace Stevens and elaborated by John Ashbery, it is in fact an American insight that can be traced from at least as far back as the writing of those deconstructionists before the fact, Jonathan Edwards, Nathaniel Hawthorne, and William James. There can be no escape from artificial relations. The fact that the outcome of *Deeds* turns not on solitary transactions between a transparent eyeball and a landscape, a shared vision, or a silent glance or embrace between lovers but on the result of public testimony in a hearing in a courtroom is Capra's insistence that there is nowhere to run to, no "world elsewhere," outside of artificial social or linguistic codes of expression.

Capra recognizes that the structuralist awakening can sanction several distinct kinds of response, as different from each other as the differences between European and American understandings of the deconstructionist enterprise. One possible response is the kind of affectless anomie or devil-may-care nihilism demonstrated by Babe Bennett at the beginning of the film. As a reporter, she has become aware of the structurality of verbal and social structures and of the artificiality of social codes, and she becomes indifferent to all of them. As she says at one despairing moment during the hearing, "It's all a game" – life, language, and all expression is all only a game with codes and rules like any other sufficiently inclusive game, and consequently one might as well abandon all beliefs and simply, indifferently, amorally play out one's "turn."

A second possible response to the recognition of the pervasiveness and artificiality of these structures might be called the Iago response, epitomized by the lawyers in the hearing room. They have seen the fictionality of the reigning fictions, and they respond with cynical opportunism and ruthless manipulation. If it is all an artificial game, then one plays to win, and any tactic that will succeed suffices.

A third response, represented by the crowd of despondent and disenfranchised farmers who attend the hearing, is another kind of alienation or despair different from Babe Bennett's, in which, even though one still has passionate beliefs, one feels oneself to be practically powerless, shut out from any capacity of authorship within the system within which one is inexorably inscribed and trapped. Since no one authors the systems that oppress us, no one can change or affect them, and all attempts at action are necessarily futile.

It is instructive and important that Capra incorporates these three distinct responses within the dramatic structure of the courtroom scene, because he is articulating a fourth view in the figure of Deeds himself. It is one that is so easily confused with these others, however, that we need their simultaneous presence in order to be entirely clear about how different it is. To what might be called these European responses to deconstruction, Longfellow Deeds might be said to offer a uniquely American vision, that, even as it recognizes the artificiality of these received forms of experience, offers the possibility of a performance that is neither nihilistic, opportunistic, nor despondently alienated. He offers the possibility of an optimistic aesthetic of parody, play, and artistic mastery that revels in its ability dramatically to tease fun out of old forms and to play meaning into new forms of its own imaginative creation. As a result of the utter and absolute decentering of his world, Deeds is finally released not to despair, opportunism, or nihilism (stages through which he passes) but to true creativity (at which he arrives in the courtroom in his final performance). He is able to toy with forms (the legal testimony in the courts, for example) as he never could if they were grounded on the bedrock of God, King, and Reality.

Deeds is progressively alienated from the social and moral structures in place around him and from his own experience in the course of the film, but his alienation is finally converted into a joyous principle of mastery and free movement as he finally rises to address the court. Alienation is discovered to be a mode of freedom. Life and expression do become a game of sorts, but it is a game not of anomie and cynicism but an adventure in the creation of a margin of free movement for one who can use and maneuver through the institutional and formal structures in place around him. It is interesting that William James's pragmatic philosophy, of which I take Deeds's courtroom performance to be the supreme dramatic example, was itself accused of being all of the other things that Deeds's performance comes so close to being mistaken for – a form of cynicism, opportunism, alienation, or valuelessness. In his writing James had to work as hard as Deeds and Capra do in this film to steer a free course among these shoals and was perhaps as unsuccessful in being generally understood as they are here.

This is a form of deadly serious play that dares to assert that we can create our margin of freedom as we go along. The capacity to play for these high stakes is exactly what Deeds's adversaries, formidable as they are, lack. To their artificial, decentered, ungrounded tones and styles Deeds and Capra do not oppose something more natural, centered, or grounded (since there can be nothing, and the search for it will lead one only to disillusionment or cynicism) but a mobility and quickness of movement among the various structures and forms that they lack. That is the point of Capra's parade of the eight witnesses who testify against Deeds. It is not that any of them are especially evil, deceitful, or even stupid, except insofar as to be locked into any one style or tone of speech and consciousness is to be all of these things. Each witness embodies a self-contained system of thought and relationships. That is each one's only limitation, but it is an enormous one, and in presenting their testimony in a series of quick vignettes, Capra makes us acutely aware of the structurality of each witness's structures.

The bodyguard gives a Mickey Spillane–like tough-guy version of events. The sentimental Irish pushcart owner tells his tenderhearted tale of man and horse. Madame Pomponi turns on her operatic inflections. Psychiatrist Emile Von Haller offers – what else? – a psychoanalytic analysis of Deeds's behavior. The lawyers raise their objections and cross-examine the witnesses within the rigid and repetitive codes of legal behavior. Capra's comic target is neither opera, psychoanalysis, nor the legal system, however – or rather it is all of these things insofar as they would systematize understanding and experience. The Freudian psychiatrist, for example, is not the butt of the usual string of heavy-handed Hollywood jokes about Viennese accents, men with goatees, or infantile psychosexual determinants of behavior. Capra's objection to him (as to any one of the others) is that he would squeeze the life out of a human being by making him or her accountable to the sort of abstract system of interpretation from which Capra labors so hard to free his most interesting characters and his entire film. When Deeds finally does rise to speak, he begins his response to all the testimony he has heard with a humorous discourse on "doodling," because it is just this sort of expressive eccentricity that these systematic understandings would either prohibit or (in the case of psycho-analysis) absorb into a systematic technology of knowledge.

Just as he does by about the halfway point in *It Happened One Night*, Capra makes socially defined styles of expression the problem in itself, not what the style speaks, but the mere existence of the fixed, predictable, verbal or social style itself. That is why in that earlier film, when, for example, Capra creates the "Lubitsch scene" at the Long Island wedding reception for Ellie, he does not have to have the butler tell the cook that there is something fishy about Ellie's forced gaiety or the entire scene itself. By that point in the film, Capra has made us so suspicious of all codified social styles that we do not need to be told. He and Peter, by merit of the virtuosity of their ability to pick up and discard them, have left us exasperated and impatient with all such forms of expression, or comically bemused beyond taking any of them seriously.

There is one final possible response to this awareness that needs to be mentioned, because it is one that Deeds (and later Smith, Doe, and Bailey) will flirt with, before finally rejecting. It is a last-ditch strategy of self-preservation in this state of affairs that is uncannily almost indistinguishable from an act of self-annihilation. One way of staying (or breaking) free from what Hawthorne called the "world's artificial systems" is to retreat into silence, stillness, and passivity – to attempt to withdraw from *all* expressive systems and insulate oneself in one's own privacy and inscrutability. That is in fact what Deeds initially does after he realizes he has been duped (and many of Hawthorne's own characters do). It is a prototypical American response that can be traced from Hawthorne to Cassavetes.★ Hawthorne's work in particular is a virtual anthology of ways in which the puny and beleaguered self, threatened with being absorbed into an alien system of relationships or understandings, can, in a last-gasp effort, assert its putative freedom by means of an act of self-defense that is almost equivalent to self-destruction. In danger of being "spoken by" an impersonal expressive system, it can, as its final free action,

★ See my discussions of Cassavetes's *Killing of a Chinese Bookie, Opening Night*, and *Gloria*, in *American Dreaming: The Films of John Cassavetes and the American Experience* (Berkeley: University of California, 1985).

Self-erasure as a strategy of self-defense: giving up on the possibility of representing the self in language or in society.

perform an act of self-erasure on itself. Rev. Hooper, Sylph Etheridge, Ilbrahim the "gentle boy," and Prudence Inglefield, like dozens of other Hawthorne characters, not only withdraw from the social communities of expression within which their narratives situate them, but ultimately withdraw themselves from the expressive environments of the works in which they appear. They become ghostly expressive presences in their own stories, with almost no social or linguistic form of self-expression available to them, or none in which they trust. They and their creators abandon self-representation.

In the scenes of his initial psychiatric confinement and his stony silence during the first part of his trial, Deeds momentarily figures that imaginative hazard. He would withdraw from the compromising systems of both the world and the work, into silence and passivity, as he (like Smith later) sits still and off to one side of the investigating group. Ironic detachment, social disengagement, and imaginative withdrawal represent recurring threats to Capra's characters (just as they do to Hawthorne's). Deeds, Smith, Doe, and Bailey (and Frank Capra himself) all wrestle with the ever-present temptation to beat the system by dropping out of it, to prevent the expressive erasure of the self by means of an act of self-erasure.

Deeds, I would emphasize, fortunately, finally arrives at another response. He shapes a performance out of a simultaneous engagement and detachment, out of shifting movements of susceptibility and withdrawal, of passionate involvement and slightly ironic removal, of alternating stylistic vulnerability and mastery – in the American tradition of the greatest imaginative performances of Hawthorne, James, or Whitman, which is why in the largest sense the voice he arrives at by the end of the hearing, like these other American voices, deliberately eludes all systematic understandings or descriptions of it. He begins in vulnerability and weakness and ends in a modest, humble, grateful, folksy mastery. In between he is alternately or simultaneously playful and preachy, puckish and moralistic, sternly logical and digressively anecdotal, warmly comical and morally indignant. Yet as he fashions a performance by means of parodically deconstructing the tones, styles, and forces that would otherwise oppress him, he is nothing fixed, systematic, or predictable. What William James would have called the "fluxional" qualities of his voice are its essence. As Deeds clears a small, free space for the movements of the self, one cannot forget that he is really only acting as a stand-in for his polymorphically performative creator. It is Capra's lovingly comical, ventriloquistic mastery of tones and styles, not only in the scripting and directing of the testimony against Deeds and of Deeds's final courtroom performance but in every scene of the film that precedes it that represents an American ideal of free and creative performance even greater than that Deeds embodies. It is Capra the filmmaker who is most free and powerful here, making others free with the exhilarating example of his own stylistic capaciousness.

The similarities between the characters and situations of Longfellow Deeds in *Mr. Deeds Goes to Town* and Tom Dixon in *American Madness* are too obvious to need elaborate explanation. Both men feel betrayed by the women they love and let down by the people around them. Both withdraw into despairing silence and passivity at crucial points, and both are, in some sense, reinstated as masters of social ceremonies at the ends of their films. One points out the analogy, however, only to argue for the essential difference between the two films. The significance of *Deeds* in Capra's oeuvre, and its difference from *American Madness*, reside in the kinds of performances the two central characters finally shape as a response to their crises. Dixon, as we saw, after a brief hiatus merely reasserts the unquestioned social and institutional authority he possessed at the start of the film. Father knew best. Deeds, on the other hand, learns to become a performer in an entirely more modern, marginal, and challenging sense (one closer to the vaudevillian marginality Stew Smith embodied). Kingship is dead. There is no possibility of simply reimposing order from on high as a kind of father, ruler, or god. That sort of authority is not available in the world he inhabits, and that is why Capra imagines Deeds, unlike Dixon, and unlike his opponents in the courtroom, first, last, and always as an outsider to the systems he negotiates. He has no inherent institutional authority, cachet, or constituency. He can never overcome his essential powerlessness, alienation, and marginality, and in fact the performance he shapes must not deny those realities of his existence but be shaped out of a profound acknowledgment of them.

Deeds is, in his essence, an exploration of what can be made of such performative marginality. That is why, in the first scene in which we meet him, he is lifted out of Mandrake Falls, taken away from family, friends, and all natural supports. He is a homeless alien, just as are Smith and Doe who follow him. Each is uprooted from his old world background and identity and suddenly set adrift in a new world of uncharted paths and relationships. Capra's argument is that, powerless and alienated and marginal as he is, the modern hero can perhaps shape a performance that is more than a match for anything he or she faces. Thrown back on his or her own resources, without any authority of the sort Dixon had, Deeds can stage a performance greater and more inspiring than that of the bank president. The power of a marginal, alienated performance is the only power available to him, and yet is enough. This is the profound performative metaphysic of *Deeds* and the reason an analysis of it either as a screwball comedy of manners or as a realistic court-room drama along the lines of *Inherit the Wind* is so inadequate. The working title of the film script was originally *A Gentleman Goes to Town*, but Capra and Cooper move Deeds's performance far beyond any definition of mere gentle-ness, gentility, or gentlemanliness. It is precisely as far as Babe Bennett is propelled from being a mere "lady" in distress, as she is referred to initially, to being the heroine of the most suggestive sort of melodrama, with a richness of consciousness and intensity of feeling that beggars language and social expression.

Bennett's presence and importance in the film indicates an even more pro-found difference from *American Madness*. Tom Dixon's momentary derange-ment in his movie was present only to be almost immediately swept under the rug, exorcised from Capra's narrative in its final minutes. Bennett, however, will not go away, and we remember her hysteria, her impassioned glances and screams long after the film is over, and arguably longer than we remember Deeds's performance in it.

In the melodramatics of Bennett and the performative playfulness of Deeds, *Mr. Deeds Goes to Town*, in effect, outlines two distinct and profoundly contrasting responses to the individual's radical loss of personal or institutional authority and power. One is a "happy" possibility (Deeds's charming per-formative puckishness), and one is sad (Bennett's stammering melodramatic anguish), but both accept as the fundamental state of affairs the marginality and alienation of the individual in a society that he is unable imaginatively to leave and within which he must therefore shape some sort of public expressive performance. In the *Deeds–Smith–Doe* trilogy and the two major films after the war, Capra seesaws uneasily between endorsing Bennett's melodramatic, doomed, stuttering inarticulateness and hysteria and Deeds's poised, confi-dent, performative volubility and mobility as the outcome of this marginality in which he most believed. There is no doubt which he preferred, or for that matter which outcome any of us would prefer to imagine our lives in terms of

– but the happy outcome is perhaps a whistling in the dark. In Capra's subsequent films, he will repeatedly explore the happy possibilities of verbal and social performative prowess of the sort Deeds displays in this film, as a response to institutional disenfranchisement, social powerlessness, and the absolute unavailability of possibilities of visionary transcendence, but he significantly will not be able to exorcise the convulsed ghost of Bennett from his work. In various transformation her character, her melodramatic gasps and stares, and her trembling voice will increasingly haunt the later work, gradually moving to the center of the films, inexorably displacing the spirit of Deeds from his confident position of eminence here. Bennett represents an imaginative unappeasibility and socially inexpressible ardency that Capra will, against his own will, increasingly come to be possessed by, as he loses faith in Deeds's possibilities of social and verbal performance in the world.

Longfellow Deeds manages in the courtroom scene to find an actual social voice and form of performance in which he can fully and completely express his originality, independence, and creativity, but most of the characters that follow Deeds will not be so lucky. Capra will find himself distrusting Deeds's perhaps too easy success and instead almost inadvertently substituting the figure of Bennett in his place, a figure with all the imagination and passion in the world but no way socially to express it, a figure forced to be content with stunned melodramatic gasps, glances, silences, and gestures in an artistic and social world where all happier, more public forms of linguistic power and social representation prove inadequate. Jefferson Smith, Clarissa Saunders, John Doe, and George Bailey, in all of their recurring expressive hysteria and anguish and pain and inability socially to speak their most vital dreams and desires, will follow in the footsteps of Bennett and not Deeds. Capra becomes a maker of American tragedies, in the most profound and exalted sense of the phrase.

13

Speaking the language
of the heart

Mr. Smith Goes to Washington

It is a mischievous notion that we are come late into nature; that the world was finished a long time ago. As the world was plastic and fluid in the hands of God, so is it ever to so much of his attributes as we bring to it ... In proportion as a man has anything in him divine, the firmament flows before him and takes his signet and form. Not he is great who can alter matter, but he who can alter my state of mind ... I believe man has been wronged; he has wronged himself. He has almost lost sight of the light that can lead him back to his prerogatives. Men are become of no account. Men in history, men in the world of to-day are bugs, are spawn, and are called "the mass" and "the herd."
  – Ralph Waldo Emerson, "The American Scholar"

Mr. Deeds Goes to Town in 1936, *Lost Horizon* in 1937, and *You Can't Take It with You* in 1938 marked the fifth, sixth, and seventh scripts to emerge from the screenwriting team of Capra and Riskin, the greatest director-writer collaboration in Hollywood in the thirties, and one unrivaled for more than twenty years until Billy Wilder and I. A. L. Diamond came together. When *Mr. Smith Goes to Washington* was in the planning stage as a sequel to *Deeds*, it was naturally expected that Capra and Riskin would continue their string of hits by working together on it. Riskin, though, like many another screenwriter after him, was determined to try his hand at directing, and, after completing the adaptation of *You Can't Take It with You*, he left Columbia for the chance to write and direct his own movie for Sam Goldwyn at MGM.

The result – *When You're in Love* – was a flop at the box office, but it gives the viewer an insight into the qualities Riskin brought to his half of the Riskin–Capra collaboration. The film is inventive and witty in the best tradition of smart, lightly cynical New York stage comedy. At its best (which is not that often), it combines the cinematic satire of Preston Sturges with the verbal play and knowingness of Dorothy Parker (that Algonquin roundtable scene in *Deeds*, one feels sure, was definitely Riskin's contribution to the script), but what it lacks is presumably what Capra brought to the collaboration: heart, sentiment, and soaring idealism. One can see why the Capra–Riskin marriage worked out so well in the thirties: Riskin's worldly-wise smartness and acid wit counterbalanced Capra's operatic idealism. The interplay of the two is the very pulse beat of the drama in *Lady for a Day, It Happened One Night,* and *Broadway Bill.*

Since Riskin was working as a producer at MGM when it was time to script *Smith* in the fall and winter of 1938, Capra turned to Sidney Buchman, an in-house Columbia writer who had already done extensive uncredited rewriting for him on *Broadway Bill* and *Lost Horizon.* Buchman was nominally Columbia's "other" specialist on sophisticated screwball comedy and had worked, or was to work, on such snappy numbers as *Theodora Goes Wild, Talk of the Town,* and *Here Comes Mr. Jordan,* but to *Smith* he brought an engagement with contemporary political and social ideas that one feels sure that Riskin and the set at the Algonquin would have scorned as being sweatily proletarian and tackily earnest – in short, declassé. Buchman was a member of the American Communist party during the thirties (and would be a victim of Joe McCarthy's disgraceful House Un-American Activities Committee hearings in 1951 and of Hollywood's cowardly blacklisting for ten years after that), and, as his party affiliations might suggest, was as much of an American dreamer as Capra. At the same time, he was in touch with the practicalities of where the dream had been derailed in American society. Thus it is not surprising that the film that emerged from Buchman's collaboration with Capra is both the most yearningly idealistic and the most shockingly topical and politically realistic of all of Capra's work.

It is important to emphasize the tonal difference between the work of Riskin and Buchman because although *Mr. Smith Goes to Washington* began as a sequel to the immensely popular earlier film (complete with plans for Gary Cooper again to play the lead role, and an initial working title of *Mr. Deeds Goes to Washington**) and is usually talked about as if it simply were a remake of the other movie, it in fact marks a deepening in Capra's work. If *Doe, It's a Wonderful Life,* and *State of the Union* go even farther in exploring the repressive forces of contemporary society and the psychic and social hazards of the American belief in the possibility of the creation of a free personal identity, it is not only because Capra was older and more experienced in the ways of the world when he made those films, or because of America's increasingly difficult and perilous situation in the pre- and postwar world, but also probably because of the education Buchman gave him in the writing and making of this film.

Mr. Deeds Goes to Town and *Mr. Smith Goes to Washington* may seem as similar as their titles and may appear to tell virtually identical stories, involving a country mouse's traveling to the city and confronting an institutionalized establishment, but the similarities are superficial. *Smith* and the two major films that follow it locate their central characters in worlds far more

---

* If I am not mistaken, Cooper's cartooned portrait is visible in the film on one of the billboards back in Smith's home state in a sequence that may have been prepared and shot before Stewart took the role.

threatening and oppressive than that which Deeds faced. The simplest way to understand the change in Capra's work is to note that the world over which Deeds scores a victory, however despicable at points, is one in which individual personality is the source of power, whereas the one Smith must learn to survive in has, in effect, unseated man as the center, source, or author of knowledge. (Buchman's Hegelian–Marxist understanding of the limits of the merely personal, as contrasted with Riskin's *New Yorker*-ish faith – or naive belief – that all of life can be understood in terms of a clash of powerful personal styles of thought and behavior is succinctly summarized in the difference between the two films.) In *Deeds*, man was at the center of the universe: Personal tones and styles – however potentially evil, hostile, petty, or avaricious the people might be – were the source of all values. In *Smith*, the individual has been "dethroned" (Marx would say "alienated") from the creation of value. That is the crisis the film examines. Capra has, in effect, moved from an eighteenth- or early nineteenth-century artistic world, in which the actions and confrontations of individual actors are dramatized, to a twentieth-century world where impersonal technologies, systems, and institutions have displaced individuals. Machines (in all senses of the word – political, journalistic, and industrial), bureaucracies of relationship, and impersonal networks of affiliation have replaced individuals as the authors of value and controllers of interpretation.★

In *Deeds*, as I have argued, Capra explores the conditions in which private, personal vision can be converted into public, social speech. In *Smith*, he goes a step farther to explore a situation in which the authority of individual speech itself becomes problematic. The film imagines a world in which, if not necessarily then at least conceivably, speakers are spoken by their texts, and not the other way around. In Derrida's and Foucault's sense, individuals are potentially reduced to being "semiotic functions" of discursive codes which "speak" *them*. Institutional sounds and voices threaten to drown out or erase merely personal ones.

Whatever happened, Longfellow Deeds could at least theoretically always offer his down-home personal styles and voice tones as an alternative to the institutional styles of expression at his fairly informal hearing. It was a forum in which individual voices could be clearly heard. Things have changed for Smith. One does not accomplish things in the Senate by being charmingly witty and anecdotal. Smith's voice only exists and counts for anything insofar as he can speak, not as an unbuttoned raconteur and village wit but through the rigid, formal discursive structures of that body. His voice cannot reach out directly to touch a live audience of judges, as Deeds's could, but must be projected beyond the walls of the Senate back to his home state. It can only be

---

★ If one did not have the work of Faulkner and West as contemporaneous examples of similar appreciations of the sheer vulnerability of the "simple separate person" to systematizing and institutionalizing styles and structures, one would have to leap ahead from Capra's work to that of Joseph McElroy, Rudolph Wurlitzer, and Thomas Pynchon to find sophisticated fictional instances of the same awareness.

heard to the extent that it is transmittable and amplifiable by the telephone lines, newspaper headlines, radio commentaries, and newsreels that package that institution in layer after layer of acoustic soundproofing.

Smith inhabits a modern world in which information is produced and disseminated in accordance with reigning rules and technologies. "Knowledge" does not exist except insofar as it is processed, packaged, and merchandised. Facts and raw data have gone the way of pastoral swains. There can be no unmediated experience or expression. Notice how the newspapers themselves have changed between *Deeds* and *Smith*. In the earlier film they were only personality writ large, directly translating the voices of individuals into sixteen-point type, but in the later one they represent a complete technology and bureaucracy of organizing and articulating knowledge that substitutes its own complex rules and structures in place of the mere expression of personality.

If one can detect Buchman's hand in this radical reformulation of the predicament of the Capra hero, Frank Capra's all-American analysis of the situation differs from Marx's or Hegel's or Foucault's in its doggedly untheoretical practicality and its dedication to tracing the specific feelings of particular individuals caught in this situation. The metaphor in terms of which Capra imagines the drama is not an abstract philosophical or sociological one but the social situation that he knows best and invokes most frequently as a metaphor in his other work: that of the casting, direction, and production of a film. Jim Taylor, the political boss who reluctantly approves Smith's appointment as Senator, is another of the Harry Cohn surrogates and occasional look-alikes in Capra's work. (D. B. Norton in *Doe*, Potter in *It's a Wonderful Life*, and Jim Conover in *State of the Union* will be other Cohn avatars.) The resemblance between the first fifteen minutes of *Smith* – during which Hopper, Paine, and Taylor agonize over a replacement for a Senator who has died in office – and the process of casting a film seems hardly accidental. Jim Taylor is a producer-director-writer. Horace Hopper and Joseph Paine are starring actors who are expected mindlessly to mouth the lines and play the parts they have been given. Jefferson Smith is a bit player inserted into the production as a last-minute substitute for another faceless bit player. Like actors in the elaborately articulated semiotic system called classic Hollywood filmmaking, Paine and Hopper have even sold out their real names to the public-relations symbol system. Paine has become the "White Knight," and Hopper has become "Happy" – the very things that both obviously are not – in deliberate erasures of their personal identities in the interest of creating and maintaining corporate identities.

Perhaps the most frightening aspect of Capra's vision is his recognition of how irrelevant personal relationships have become in this depersonalized, institutionalized universe. Taylor acts as a kind of father to both Hopper and Paine (and tries to become a father to adopted son Smith), giving them advice, helping them out, and rewarding them when they are good – yet he is a father with almost no personal or emotional involvement with his "sons." This political family is a bureaucracy of power relations, fundamentally indistinguishable from any other in the film. It is a series of institutional relationships in which feelings of loyalty or intimacy are worse than irrelevant; they would only get in the way of efficient action. Thus Taylor is a father who has no personal allegiance to his sons or emotional commitment to them. That is why at one point in the film he can suddenly threaten to drop Paine and ruin his career if Paine does not play along with the game plan. A few minutes later he can, equally precipitously and coolly, offer to help Smith become rich and successful if Smith will agree to play along with his schemes. There are no permanent enemies and no dependable friends in this impersonal world; there is only a network of shifting power relations to which one either conforms, to be swallowed up by them, or that one bucks, to be cast out from them. The emotions one feels are as completely scripted, rehearsed, and dictated by the semiotic system as are one's words and relationships.

As much as in Hegel or Foucault, the technologies of knowledge and the normative codes of discourse determine what constitutes knowledge and discourse. As Taylor recognizes in being so dispassionately ready to orphan Paine or to adopt Smith, individual speakers come and go, but the machine of speech (and political discourse) grinds on forever. The telephone becomes Capra's visual metaphor for that discursive network, a metaphor he will continue to employ in *Doe* and *State of the Union*. As Capra apparently realized long before the advent of video teleconferencing and corporate information processing, and nine years before George Orwell's *1984* (which *Smith* vastly outdoes in subtlety and complexity, even as it rejects Orwell's pessimistic conclusions), the telephone system represents a model of human interaction in which voices can be conveniently disembodied and stripped of all bothersome and superfluous personal and biological associations. Once they have been inscribed within such a network, individuals are no longer unique and irreplaceable but become interchangeable modular components within the larger, enduring, impersonal system. The individual is reduced to being merely a junction box, an interface, a synaptic node for the transfer and exertion of power. The network has replaced the person as the enduring, fundamental reality.

Capra drives home this changed state of affairs in the first few minutes of the film. In the series of opening shots he cuts briskly from one to another of four different characters: a political informant and newspaper reporter named "Nosey"; Senator Joseph Paine; political machine-boss Jim Taylor; and Governor Hubert ("Happy") Hopper. Each of them will become an important figure in the film, and it might therefore seem that Capra is employing a standard Hollywood opening devoted to succinctly introducing the basic characters and clearly defining the dramatic situation in which they find themselves in the film. The difference is that the four characters are kept almost anonymous. They are introduced not in a conventional manner – say, talking in a room together or engaged in some common activity – but making three rapid-fire telephone exchanges, one to another, in quick succession.

Nosey has been waiting in the hospital where Senator Jim Foley is on his deathbed, and calls to relay word of his death. A moment later Paine calls Taylor and informs him. Then Taylor calls Governor Hopper and gives him quick instructions on statements to the press and other matters concerning the appointment of a replacement. What Capra has done in these first few minutes, as even this summary may suggest, is the opposite of the standard Hollywood opening. The particular individuals and rapid-fire instructions hardly register. The dizzying cutting and panning from one almost anonymous speaker to another makes no one of them stand out as an actor or a person. That is the point. What is communicated here is not the presence of *people*, but the power and inclusiveness of an elaborately coded and hierarchical *system of relationships* (both the semiotic system of the film in which these actors appear, with its cinematic power to pan, and cut and suture, and move from one to another of them at will, and the semiotic system of the world they inhabit as characters, with its power, by means of lines of communication, to join or separate otherwise unrelated individuals). It is that network of inscribed relationships (telephonic, political, and cinematic – the opening of a Hollywood film is, after all, as complex a machine for establishing abstract hierarchies of connections as a political convention) that we take in: who phones whom and why; who talks and who listens; who gives orders, and who follows them. That hierarchical grid of relationships has a tangibility and reality greater than any of the almost interchangeable actors within it.

The various networks in the film, defined within it by telephone connections, radio networks, public-address systems, public-relations systems, newspaper syndicates, and political machines, all work to bring the practical existence of the individual into question by distributing power and meaning outward, away from the physical body, voice, and personality of individual speakers or actors and locating it in the technologies that amplify and disseminate their words and presence away from their bodies and selves. No single stylistic change in Capra's work communicates this changed situation more powerfully than his reliance on Slavko Vorkapich's montages (here and equally brilliantly in *Doe*). In the best Eisensteinian tradition of editing with which Vorkapich's work is closely affiliated, these montages imagine experience and events not as essentially unique and personal matters (these are distinctively western European and Anglo-American legal and moral assumptions) but as a function of membership in a social, political, or historical group. It is the group that speaks or acts, not a particular individual. It is the experience of the group that counts, not that of individual consciousnesses within it. In the sequence near the end of the film, showing the rallies for and against Smith back in his home state, the parades and marches, the speeches and billboards, and the headlines attacking or supporting him, Vorkapich is not interested in presenting solitary acts of principle or statements of conscience by particular men, women, and children who have decided to take difficult moral stands but (even in the minority supporting Smith) mechanical, programmatic, almost mindless expressions of mob behavior.

The scale of most of Vorkapich's montages dwarfs the human figure in the landscape so overpoweringly that the mere individual almost disappears and certainly seems not to matter very much. The monuments Smith gawks at during his initial day in Washington, the ringing Liberty Bell photographed in close-up so that it looks thirty feet tall, the gargantuan American flag that fills the length and breadth of the shot leave no room on the screen (or in the imagination) for the simple human figure, just as the swelling, heavily or-chestrated chords of Dimitri Tiomkin's patriotic scoring drown out the aural imagination of the sound of the mere individual human voice. Capra was a great admirer of the films of Sergei Eisenstein (he had met him in Holly-wood in the mid-thirties and had traveled to Stalinist Russia to see him again the year before he made *Smith*), and the montages in this film are the most powerfully Einsteinian sequences in all of his work, but that is to pinpoint exactly how these montages are alien to Capra's ordinary cinematic practice. They are the cinematic equivalent of Jim Taylor's political machine. They imagine a world in which mere individuals have ceased to exist or to count. Mere men and women have been levered out of the universe and replaced by a vast, elaborate network of depersonalized, overdetermined, figure-dwarfing symbolic significations.

Another way in which Capra indicates the complexity of the world of this film (and of *Doe*, *It's a Wonderful Life*, and *State of the Union* similarly) is by means of an almost baroque inversion of the conventional Hollywood estab-lishing sequence that is used to introduce the major characters at the beginning of a standard film. The basic Hollywood introduction of the star of a film seldom extends beyond an interlocked chain of three, four, or five shots or brief scenes. In an utterly banal but not untypical imaginary example, the first shot of the series and of the film might be a view of a car, seen in long-shot, driving down a road past a sign closer to the camera reading "Welcome to Smallville." A medium shot shows the vehicle stopping in front of the general store in the town. Another medium shot or medium close-up shows the driver getting out and walking into the store. Then a close-up of the central character's face finally appears as he or she goes in and asks for directions or strikes up a conversation with the owner. The Hitchcockian or virtuosic version of this opening sequence would probably differ only in inserting a few unexpected visual jokes or twists into this basic pattern: A traffic accident might nearly take place as the car pulls over to the curb; a bird might swoop down on the person as he or she walks into the store; the person might be revealed to be carrying an ominously gun-shaped package into the store; but notwithstanding the jokes or Maguffins, the general shot pattern would still be roughly the same. The shots proceed generally from distance to proximity, moving briskly from fairly general, unspecified actions to specific, pointed interactions, circling in on a central figure in an orderly, concentric trajectory, and arriving, at the conclusion of the sequence, at what is usually a one-on-one encounter in which at least one of the characters involved becomes a principal figure in the film we are watching.

Capra revises this process of succinctly establishing his central figure in the starring place at the center of the film's opening. He deliberately proceeds along a much more oblique, more Byzantine path of approach to his figure. Smith is glimpsed for the first time (with his back to the camera and no lines of dialogue to speak) in a scene eleven minutes into an extremely fast-paced and complicated film, after hundreds of shots involving the schemes, plots, and jockeyings for power of dozens of other characters. He finally "goes to Washington" and arrives at the Senate Office Building twenty-five minutes into the movie. We "meet" the eponymous star of *Meet John Doe* for the first time more than fifteen minutes into that film and first meet John Doe himself – the character into whom Long John Willoughby is transformed – more than twenty minutes into it. *It's a Wonderful Life* begins with two angels talking to each other up in heaven and then circles back thirty years prior to the central event of the film, to which it takes eighty-five minutes of narrative finally to return. It is probably the most rococo and circuitous sequence of "establishing" shots in the history of film, and an opening excursis and flashback that would do the author of "The Beast in the Jungle" or "The Altar of the Dead" proud. The effect in each of these films is the same. Never have characters, from the first second they appear on-screen, been already more hedged round, more "placed" in a system of spatial, temporal, social, and moral relationships; never have contents been more cinematically, narratively, and socially contained. Capra does to film what George Eliot and Henry James did to the novel. In their respective forms, all three might be called artists least capable of committing a truly short story.

Capra's cinematic creation of meaning and establishment of identity in these films is an imitation of the creation of meaning in the worlds that Jefferson Smith, John Doe, George Bailey, and Grant Matthews inhabit. He reverses the customary trajectory of the sequence of establishing shots or scenes. Instead of moving from the periphery of the circle to spiral rapidly in on a central protagonist in a series of focused, pointed centripetal movements, these films move in the opposite direction. After the presentation of one close-up event – a powerful politician dies, or a crisis in George Bailey's life is announced – the film circles out *away from* it in a series of ever-widening arcs, spiraling outward from the initial event. Centrifugality replaces centripetality. The result is to "establish" the central character, but in an entirely different and more elaborate way than in the other kind of film. These central characters are, by the time they make their belated entrance into the films, entangled in a complex, extended web of elaborated relationships, a reticulated network of pressures, influences, and significances already firmly in place and clearly articulated before they ever show their faces on camera or speak their first line.

One can refer to the "stars" of these late films, insofar as Cooper, Stanwyck, Arthur, Stewart, Tracy, and other principal actors in them have been accorded star status by Hollywood press agents and journalists, but Capra uses the late films to interrogate the machinery that makes or unmakes such stars. As his insistence on "the name above the title" in his own films indicates, Capra believes fervently in the importance of star leadership and star performances in art and in life, but he questions the actual ways stars are created. He emphasizes how hard it is to achieve stardom and to hold onto it when the machinery is not working in one's favor.★ He reminds us that stars are made and not born. (I take this to be one of the implicit subjects of *Smith* and the explicit theme of both *Doe* and *State of the Union*.)

Stardom is, in brief, not something automatic and unearned as it may appear to be to an outsider, but is the result of a complex interplay of forces and the expression of a highly articulated system of power relations. Stardom is made problematic in the late films. Their "stars" – Smith, Doe, Bailey, and Matthews, and the actors who play them – cannot count on star billing in their own lives or movies. They are stars who cannot automatically control a dramatic space within their own films. They are stars whose performances, from the first word to the last beat, are in danger of being wrested out of their hands by conspiracies, turns of events, and the likes of Jim Taylor and the pervasive systems of interpretation that he controls (just as squadrons of press agents and producers like Selznick or Thalberg or Mayer controlled the constellations of significances within which their stars shone.) In the case of Smith, he is a star whom Taylor casts, scripts, directs, and grooms to be only a bit player. Capra's insistence, as the release prints of *Smith* were being prepared, on listing the twelve principal characters in the film as coequal stars of it, indicates his own process of playing the game of making or unmaking stars in his own movie. Long before Altman's decision to treat the cast of *Nashville* as an ensemble of twenty-four coequal players, Capra was exploring the contradictions of the star system in a world of professed democratic values and equality of opportunity. Jim Taylor's conception of the universe is one in which he reigns unchallenged as studio head, producer, director, and writer over hordes of bit players, but Capra's credits to the film are an implicit reply to Taylor, even as they are to some degree an example of Capra himself playing Taylor in his own movie. They seem to offer a rival vision to Taylor's, a dream of a democratic community of mutual interrelationships, but it is a community selected and organized by Capra, as well as one that depends on a star like Smith (or Stewart) to galvanize it into action.

The excitement of *Smith* is that not only Stewart as an actor but Capra as a producer, director, and writer, pits himself against, and in direct competition with, Taylor, the producer, director, and writer of almost everything in the film. Capra pits his own value system against the elaborate technologies of

---

★ As Charles Wolfe pointed out to me, Capra's contract with Warners for *Doe* not only demanded a possessory credit, but insisted that the size of the credit be larger than Riskin's. This is evidence of Capra's anxieties about his position in the bureaucracy of his own film and an illustration of how hard he worked to assert his own auteurial "stardom," how hard he worked to maintain his starring place in the power systems of his own career. "The Name above the Title" was not a mere slogan for Capra but evidence of his ongoing struggle for self-preservation and self-assertion against all of the forces that would erase or neutralize the power of the self; it is a struggle on Capra's part that is paralleled by the struggles of the central characters in the late films as alter egos for their creator.

information processing in his movie. In effect, he attempts to unsay every-thing I have described as the "world" of the film. He depicts a Foucaultian universe, only to try to call it a lie. This "one-man–one-film" arguer for the crucial importance of individual authorship within the bureaucracies of the Hollywood studio system could never accept a view of things that denied au-thority to authors. Capra's goal is to rediscover the personl feelings and beliefs left out of Taylor's world, to reinstall the erased human figure at the center of the impersonal structures, to reground the abstract systems of institutional discourse on the bedrock of powerful individual expressions of personal emotion. Capra attempts to make a place for the mere naked expressive self in a world in which the individual has been written off (or more accurately, self-destructively written *into* a system of significances and relationships) before he or she even arrives on the scene.

The creation of the figure of Jefferson Smith is the crucial step in doing this. He has much in common with Longfellow Deeds before him, even as, in the extravagance and energy of his performance, he ultimately moves radically beyond him. Deeds, Smith, and, later, Doe represent Capra's revisiting of his own roots in silent comedy. He began, as a young writer, assistant director, and director, with the "Our Gang" and early Harry Langdon pictures, and Deeds, Smith, and Doe, in their different ways represent the troubled survival of the central figures of those films in a changed world. Stewart and Cooper both play variations on the Langdon role: They are somewhat childlike, sheltered, starry-eyed unsophisticates who represent a comic state of social disengagement or otherworldliness that separates them from, and elevates them above, the more practical and hard-headed characters around them.*

The mistake, though, would be to regard Deeds, Smith, and Doe as mere comic simpletons or innocents. That is, in fact, how they are sometimes treated critically and is, indeed, how their opponents in their films almost invariably evaluate them. Their marginality embodies a more radical and daring imaginative stance and attitude, however, one which is perhaps best described by Emerson in his essay, "The Comic." Emerson may have had Bronson Alcott or Henry Thoreau in mind, but his description of the imagina-tive effects of this form of comedy almost perfectly fits Longfellow Deeds, Jefferson Smith, or John Doe as well:

> There is no joke so true and deep in actual life, as when some pure idealist goes
> up and down among the institutions of society, attended by a man who

---

* The contrast between Capra and Hawks is again instructive. Hawks began as a maker of smart comedies and romantic dramas, and his subsequent work follows that trajectory. The typical Hawks leading man, far from representing idealistic dreaminess or disengagement from social codes, is clever, sophisticated, and resourceful. His range of skills is perfectly matched to the range of acting talents represented by actors like Cary Grant, Humphrey Bogart, and John Wayne. (The fact that the Cary Grant character in Hawks's comedies is subjected to a variety of pratfalls potentially injurious to his dignity only proves that he has a dignity to be injured.) The Hawks wise-cracking, fast-taking leading man or woman could never be confused with Capra's silent, saintly visionaries and idealists.

knows the world; and who, sympathizing with the philosopher's scrutiny, sympathizes also with the confusion and indignation of the detected skulking institutions. His perception of disparity, his eye wandering perpetually from the rule to the crooked, lying, thieving fact, makes the eyes run over with laughter.

This is the radical joke of life and then of literature. The presence of the ideal of right and truth in all action makes the yawning delinquencies of practice remorseful to the conscience, tragic to the interest, but droll to the intellect. The activity of our sympathies may for a time hinder our perceiving the fact intellectually, and so deriving mirth from it; but all falsehoods, all vices seen at sufficient distance, seen from the point where our moral sympathies do not interfere, become ludicrous. The comedy is in the intellect's perceptions of discrepancy. And whilst the presence of the ideal discovers the difference, the comedy is enhanced whenever that ideal is embodied visibly in a man.

This suggests, I think, the extent to which the comic disengagement from society of Deeds, Smith, and Doe represents not stupidity but a form of radical criticism, not naiveness but extreme idealism, and further suggests how their idealism is expressed *in* the comedy of their misunderstandings (as when Deeds deals with the Board of Trustees of the opera, when Smith gives his first interview to the Washington press corps, or when Doe arrives in his first hotel room), and not as an alternative to it. These mistakes and misunderstandings are not "comic relief" (to use that hateful phrase) in an otherwise serious film, they are essential expressions of the idealism that Capra wants to represent. As Emerson points out, and authors like Twain and West illustrated, comedy is a way of deconstructing the unexamined codes of social life.

Such an observation might suffice to comprehend Deeds; however, there is much more to Smith than is expressible in terms of comical incongruities and misunderstandings. If he were not anticipated by many of Capra's own previous figures, it would not be too much to describe him as a new kind of character in Hollywood film – a figure of transcendental desire and imagination who moves at moments beyond any realistic specifications or possible agendas. He crosses Babe Bennett's imaginative extremity and unappeasability with Longfellow Deeds's practicality. There are echoes of Molly Kelly, Jerry Strong, Lulu Smith, Megan Davis, and others in him. He is related to those earlier figures, even as he seems emotionally and imaginatively more extreme than any one of them.

Smith is easily misunderstood as some sort of political fanatic in favor of a particular piece of legislation (for example, a boy's camp), and this is indeed the way his adversaries in the film regard him. What is interesting is how different this is from Capra's actual presentation of him. At any one moment in the film, he may seem to have a particular political or expressive agenda, but it keeps shifting from scene to scene. When he is first discovered, he is content simply to be a leader of the Boy Rangers, expressing himself in the newspaper he edits; his next impulse, upon being appointed senator, is just to vote along with senior Senator Paine; he next wants to do something, anything, on his own; then arrives at the boy's camp legislation idea, almost accidentally, when it is suggested by Paine far into the film; and then, in his filibuster, actually seems to drop the defense of the camp and make fighting graft or the defense of democracy or some such abstraction his expressive subject. The point of rehearsing these events in the film is only to suggest that rather than thinking of Smith as a kind of Boy Ranger lobbyist, or an advocate for any other particular cause, it would be more accurate to call him a state of energy looking for an application; a principal of movement in search of a motivation, a free figure of imagination only partially or inadequately expressing itself in one specific act or another, and therefore continuously on the move to a new subject or issue that replaces the last.*

Smith is eccentric in more than his behavior and temperament. He lacks the "center" of fixed purpose or motivation that makes other film characters so comparatively staid and repetitious. Like his earlier namesakes Lulu Smith and (to a lesser extent) Stew Smith, he is a fugitive figure of desire in quest of a destination or point, which recedes as fast as it is attained. The vagueness or multiplicity or intangibility of Smith's goals or talk is the point. Chekhov's characters in drama, thirty years before Capra's work, John Cassavetes's and Elaine May's in film thirty years after, and Sam Shepard's recent stage work come to mind as exploring analogous dramatic possibilities. The metaphor Cassavetes uses in one of his films to describe this dramatic situation is of being "all dressed up with no place to go," and in a comment about another one of his films, he describes a character as "having all the values in the world but no place to put them." Character becomes a state of free-floating imaginative energy or appetitiveness in search of some outlet or expression in the world, and inevitably dissatisfied with all of those that present themselves. Any particular expression of himself is too much less than his ideal; too paltry, too limited in comparison with his conception of his possibilities. Character therefore endlessly proliferates itself outward away from particular motives or goals, distributes itself energetically outward away from each temporary stopping point at which one might attempt to fix the self in any more enduring or static social or expressive position. That is the situation of the transcendental self imagined by Capra. I think that suggests why Capra's (and Smith's)

---

* In my chapter on *Meet John Doe*, I will take up the larger issue of how the creation of character on the part of the writer-director in the process of making a film is increasingly represented in the events of Capra's films themselves in a character's effort to forge or hold onto a character for him- or herself. That is to say, Capra's and Buchman's task of finding something for Smith to say or do as an expression of the extreme idealism they have endowed him with is enacted within the film itself in Smith's own continuously shifting quest for something to do or say that will express or represent him and his imagination satisfactorily. Capra's and Buchman's problem of representation of Smith's imagination in worldly forms and activities within the film becomes Smith's own problem of attempting to represent himself in his life (without selling himself too short or being misrepresented by the press and others). This is what Emerson, in "Experience," calls the "transformation of genius into practical power," and it is one of the absolutely crucial issues in Capra's late work, about which I will have more to say. *Smith* (like *Deeds*) is a study of the limits of self-representation, in more than the legal and political senses of the term.

expressive project is fraught with immense peril both for the self launched on it and for the expressive systems that would attempt to get a fix on it or to lock it into any one position in an abstract system of signs and significations.*

The struggle articulated within *Smith* is waged between the elusive, mercurial figure of Jefferson Smith and the imposing semiotic machinery arrayed against him that would fix and systematize his position by locating him in an abstract system. Smith must define himself within and against these impersonal structures of signification (whethr they are the architectural structures of Capra's and Lionel Banks's sets, the ideological structures of Vorkapich's montages, or the political structures of Taylor's manipulations).

Capra uses a meeting between Smith and Paine in the latter's office, about halfway through the film, to summarize succinctly the semiotic difference between the two figures. Smith stands next to a doorway against a blank background, while Paine is framed in front of a wall papered from floor to ceiling with photographs, certificates of appreciation, and memorabilia of his years in politics. The one is embedded in a system of relationships and meanings as complex as the visual background behind him; the other is almost as unencumbered by historical commitments or institutional obligations as a newborn baby. Paine is fixed and placed; Smith is endlessly in transit.

As Capra argues in the film, such innocence is in itself a kind of culpability. Virtue can never be fugitive or cloistered. Smith cannot remain naked and unencumbered and still be maturely virtuous. He cannot avoid entanglements. In order to assert his freedom and independence from them, rather than leaving them, he must plunge deep into these systems and find a way to master them. The best way out, the only way out, is through. Smith is, in any case, rapidly encumbered by institutional meanings and understandings in the course of the film, whether he wants to be or not. The very point of Capra's extreme delay in introducing him at the start of the movie is to contextualize him, so that when he speaks his first word in the film he is already embedded in networks of extended, elaborate cinematic and bureaucratic signification. Even as he still feels himself to be his own man, innocent of political systems and free from compromises, he has already been unknowingly implicated in a series of arrangements and deals, so pervasive and all-controlling are the systems of interpretation and action around him.

What adds to the poignancy of his situation is not only that Smith cannot affect these systems already in place around him or extricate himself from them, but he cannot even be aware of them at this point. He would, in fact, have to have seen the movie we are watching in order even to begin to under-

---

* It is as opposed to the project of the critics who would incorporate Smith within their abstract systems of understanding as it is to the political project of Taylor. Criticism is at least as impersonal and potentially as repressive a system of discourse as any of those that Capra depicts in the film, which is why most of the critics who have written about Smith unconsciously play the part of Taylor in his efforts to pin Smith down to a particular position or goal. "What do you want?" Taylor asks Smith at one point, in an attempt to buy him off, but the point is that Smith wants nothing in particular. He is want itself; he is desire beyond any worldly satisfaction.

stand his own position in them. Even as he still feels himself to be innocent, he has already been interpreted, incorporated, and inscribed into the reigning *episteme*. One of the principal questions explored by Capra's five major late films (*Deeds*, *Smith*, *Doe*, *It's a Wonderful Life*, and *State of the Union*) is this issue of ontological belatedness. How can one possibly perform freely in a world in which performance is always already so entailed and predetermined, a world in which one is born into so many epistemological, social, and moral responsibilities beyond one's ability even to comprehend?

If the human figure has been dislodged from those systems of expression, as I argued earlier, one of the tasks before Smith (and Capra as well, who is in obvious partnership with Smith) is to attempt to reinsert the form of the individual body and the sounds of a personal voice back into systems that have expunged them. Specifically, Capra attempts to make a place for the willowy, frail, and faltering figure of Jefferson Smith amid the impersonality of Washington's stony symbols and vast architectural structures (or conversely, he attempts to expand and strengthen the figure of Smith, metaphorically and visually, until he is capable of holding his own, cinematically, within the outsize spaces and sets in which most of the film takes place). Jefferson Smith is related to his namesake in *Platinum Blonde* in this respect. He must learn to make his personality felt in Capra's and Banks's cavernous mock-up of the Senate chamber, just as his ancestor Stew had to learn how to make his personality felt and to move around in the Big White Set of the Schuyler mansion.

One notices, however, how much less daunting the large sets in the earlier films were than these are. The bank in *American Madness*, the palace in *The Bitter Tea of General Yen*, the Temple of Faith in *The Miracle Woman*, and the Schuyler mansion in *Platinum Blonde* were large and impressive structures, but they were without exception personal expressions of one strong individual who was at the center of each of them. However imposing or hostile, they were personal spaces, for all their sheer size, merely larger-than-usual houses or homes for the spirit; they were extensions, projections in space, as it were, of a performer's or group of performers' personal styles and personalities. The nightmare Smith faces is that the sets and systems of discourse within which he moves and in which he must learn to shape a human performance are the expression of no particular personality. They are abstractly, symbolically or technologically articulated. That is the expressive problem his film defines. Personality and personal style have been dislodged as the source of value. These enormous sets compete for dramatic attention with the actor who must learn how to master and perform within them. The power of the actor to stage a scene in such person-dwarfing institutional spaces becomes a representation of the power of personality to avoid being overwhelmed by inhuman discursive technologies and bureaucratic pressures.

As everything I have said up to this point would suggest, Capra, at this point in his career, argues that the individual is at least potentially powerful enough to stand up against any system in which he or she is enmeshed. *Smith*, like the part of *Deeds* involving Bennett, is a melodrama of absolute,

The self almost lost in a network of institutional relationships: the personal voice of desire resisting the abstract systems of life.

emotionally extreme, moral choices. This is not an aspect of the film that must be apologized for or overlooked, and both *It's a Wonderful Life* and *State of the Union* will see life in terms of similar possibilities of choosing between opposed and irreconcilable alternatives. It takes one to the heart of Capra's vision of life. Capra's melodrama of moral choice teaches a viewer, however unfashionably, that there are real and important alternatives in life that are within our power as moral agents to decide between. Life is not all gray. There are absolute sides and issues and causes to be defended.

Perhaps more important, it teaches us (or inspires us to believe in) the crucial importance of individual effort. The individual performer, however beleaguered and alone, can make a difference. In fact, it is the individual performer who creates the moral choices. They are not there until he comes on the scene and defines them. In a way that William James would have understood, the individual makes these differences; through his effort, his continuous exertion of intellect and will, he brings the alternatives into existence. Thus, as in James's philosophy (to quote James) we "engender truths":

> Lotze has in several places made a deep suggestion. We naively assume, he says, a relation between reality and our minds which may be just the opposite of the true one. Reality, we naturally think, stands ready-made and complete,

and our intellects supervene with the one simple duty of describing it as it is already. But may not our descriptions, Lotze asks, be themselves important additions to reality. And may not previous reality itself be there, far less for the purpose of reappearing unaltered in our knowledge, than for the very purpose of stimulating our minds to such additions as shall enhance the universe's total value ...

It is identically our pragmatistic conception. In our cognitive as well as in our active life we are creative. We *add*, both to the subject and to the predicate part of reality. The world stands readily malleable, waiting to receive its final touches at our hands. Like the kingdom of heaven, it suffers violence willingly. Man *engenders* truths upon it.*

That is, in effect, what Smith comes to realize, and what Capra's melodrama of choice demonstrates to us. Smith begins, in merely wanting to go along with Paine in the Senate, with a sense that moral "reality ... is ready made and complete" but gradually discovers that he can and must "*engender* truths upon it." Capra's late films, like James's philosophy, relentlessly define life in terms of real ethical alternatives and real possibilities of what James in the final chapter of his *Principles of Psychology* calls "heroism;" but it is a modern heroism in which the individual, through his unceasing effort, must make the differences that will make a difference. There are few filmmakers who more powerfully express the importance of endlessly renewed effort in the making of meaning and value against all of the forces of entropy and waste and indifference that work to erase him or to absorb his individual effort into a preexisting system of value.

Such meaning making, for Capra from this point on in his career, takes vigorous, at times violent action and decisiveness. States of passive dreaming or reverie are positively rejected. As I have already noticed, to slink off to the periphery of events or to go off to look out a window is no longer at all adequate. It is not "the sensitive ones who are unsure" (in Capra's contemptuous phrase) who are the heroes of these later films, but "men going places and doing things, not dropping off in corners." This was Capra's own conception of his role jousting with Harry Cohn as he made this picture, and subsequently, going off on his own to found his own production company to make the films following *Smith*, so that Capra could tell a group of directors even in 1971:

> If you're willing to take full responsibility, even right now, a director can go as far as he wants to, can have all the responsibility he wants to take. He has to say no; he has to argue; and he has to fight; but he can take it. And if he is willing to take the responsibility, and if the picture is bad, he has to take it ... All this is part of having enough confidence in yourself, enough courage in yourself, to go out and stick your neck out.†

Similarly, that is why he can interestingly brag that the strength of *It's a*

---

* William James, *The Writings of William James: A Comprehensive Edition*, ed. John J. McDermott (Chicago: University of Chicago Press, 1977), p. 456.
† "Dialogue on Film: Frank Capra," *American Film* (October 1978), 41.

Wonderful Life was that George Bailey did not rely on piety or prayer but concrete, practical action and wit:

> [In *It's a Wonderful Life*, the characters] reached for something they had inside, and they came up with a handful of courage and wit, and they beat their adversaries with it. *Not with prayer. Fighting* for a lost cause [my emphasis] . . . is the closest I can get to heaven.*

As Capra realizes, however, the individual can never just confront and overpower the machine of politics or language in some sort of primitive, direct combat – a sort of expressive shoot-out at the OK Corral. Smith's strategy of response to the systems around him (like James's pragmatic philosophy) demands a complex set of tactical responses. In inscribing themselves into symbol systems, networks of power relations, and systems of meaning, even the weakest and most ineffectual of his opponents accrue possibilities of power that would never be theirs acting alone as individuals (which is why bureaucracies can always find fresh and power-hungry recruits in any era in which the sheer possession of power is valued over the lonely, weak, difficult creations of the solitary imagination). Thus the question Smith faces, if he does not choose merely to give up his personal identity and become a faceless semiotic function in an impersonal system of discourse, is the prototypically American one of what sort of authority is available to the individual as an antinomian, an outsider on the margin of a social and linguistic system of discourse that he or she can neither directly overthrow nor is willing to succumb to. Smith rejects the chance to become a node in a semiotic system when Taylor offers it to him, but the question that the movie asks is what other kind of nonsystemic power is then available to the rebel outside the system. If the self is not plugged into the reigning network of relationships, within which a prefabricated identity and voice is automatically bequeathed it, what identity and voice can it have?

The Taylor syndicate has established as the lingua franca of political life a self-contained system of political rhetoric emptied of all personal values. The linguistic world Smith enters and attempts to speak within is a Saussurian utopia of deauthored *differances*. Ideals, principles, personal emotional commitments, and even the biological human body as a source of meaning have been levered out of the system, which reveals itself to be a Lévi-Straussian value-neutral, impersonal, self-perpetuating network of absolutely empty signifiers. This structuralist dream is obviously Capra's (and Smith's) nightmare. The task the film sets for both the filmmaker and his leading character is to find some way to recenter the decentered system of language, values, and institutions (and yet to do it without simply becoming another Taylor, another imperialist imposer of a system of self-serving, dehumanizing, arbitrary significations). Smith is Capra's attempt to restore the person to

---

* "Frank Capra: One Man–One Film (Interview with Bruce Henstell)," in *Frank Capra: The Man and His Films*, ed. Richard Glatzer and John Raeburn (Ann Arbor: University of Michigan Press, 1975), p. 20.

his or her rightful place as the center of value and author of significances.

It may seem perverse to apply such recent and fashionable terminology involving decentered systems, evacuated centers, and willful acts of recentering to a thirties Hollywood movie, but it is the implicit argument of this book that, in Gertrude Stein's phrase, America was the first culture to enter the twentieth-century and that such concepts are present in the native American tradition at least a century before they were "invented" by French linguists, philosophers, anthropologists, and historians. They can be found in such homespun, mainstream American writers as William James and Ralph Waldo Emerson, whose essays "Pragmatism and Humanism," "Circles," and "Experience" constitute at least as subtle an exploration of them as anything written a century later on the other side of the Atlantic. There is really no need to hark back to nineteenth-century American writers with whom, admittedly, one would be amazed to discover that Capra was familiar, to justify the language. These metaphors of decentering and recentering are in Capra's film itself; one does not need to import them into it from twentieth-century French or nineteenth-century American philosophy and criticism.

Capra's interest in literal and metaphoric fathers and in the concept of fatherhood in general has, in a practical sense, represented an exploration of the question of the origin and authorship of values and meanings in film after film long before this one. In Smith's loss of his father before the film begins, his adoption of Paine as his foster father when he arrives in Washington, and Taylor's patronizing subsequent attempt to adopt him as a son, Capra is quite explicit about his film's being an exploration of personal and institutional sources of authority. Paine is explicitly figured as little-boy Smith's fatherly guide and sponsor in the Senate and his paternally knowledgeable source of advice about legislation. (Paine even calls Smith "son" at one point.) Paine acts as a kind of fatherly matchmaker and would be father-in-law and counsellor in romantic and social matters concerning Smith and his daughter Susan. As a father figure, Paine would provide Smith with a ready-made set of inheritable values to embrace – but of course Capra's implicit argument in the film is that Smith's attempt to recenter his world in this way is a mistaken one. He must utterly abandon his attempt to replace his lost father with a new one. His foster father betrays him and lets him down. Smith must learn, in some sense, to become his own father, if he is to have a father at all.

Capra's clever use of the geography of the city of Washington demonstrates that he thought of his own film expressly in terms of an act of recentering performed on a system that has somehow "lost sight of" or "forgotten" its own center (both visual and historical metaphors are used at different points in the film). Capra's controlling metaphor is that of Smith's effort to put the Capitol dome back into its place (visually and historically) at the center of things. The Capitol dome is of course at the geographical center of Capitol Hill's radiating network of streets and buildings, but Smith suggests that though it is still physically where it always was, it has somehow ethically and imaginatively been lost sight of and disappeared from the systems of significations that are represented in the House and the Senate. Smith's self-appointed task specifically becomes that effort of moral and metaphysical recentering. The film is metaphorically quite explicit about this linkage of the geographical and metaphysical acts of centering that take place in the course of it. When he first arrives in Washington, Smith circles physically around the dome on a sightseeing tour, then gradually moves physically and imaginatively closer to it, but is still not in complete physical or imaginative possession of it as, about halfway through the film, he views it out of his office window and insists that "that" is what he wants to get "in" his bill. He eventually succeeds, to the extent that he does succeed, in his filibuster, by physically and imaginatively possessing the Capitol building itself, placing himself as a human figure at the center of it, as he stands under the dome and gestures upward to it in the final minutes of the film.

Notwithstanding his symbolic quest for authority in the figure of a father or his geographical spiral inward on the Capitol dome that his physical and imaginative travels in the film trace, obviously the most significant centering that Smith and Capra are engaged in is neither schematically geographical nor abstractly symbolic but personal and emotional, in an entirely practical sense. The metaphor of Smith's spatial centering is mechanical and superficial, both for a character to enact and for a filmmaker to use to generate meanings. It is relatively easy for a character to move geographically from the periphery of power and activity in Montana to trace an inward-spiraling trajectory around the Capitol, moving from the Lincoln Memorial, the Washington Monument, and Monticello to the Senate Office Building, finally to position himself under the dome itself in the Senate – and it is relatively easy for a filmmaker to depict such movements. That abstract or metaphoric centering is not difficult and might even be called facile. It is hard, though, to recenter a linguistic system of decentered values and significations, to put authentic, practical centers of meaning and emotion into words whose meanings have been centrifugally spun out of them, dispersed into hollow political rhetoric and empty institutional, bureaucratic, and public-relations networks. That task is the task Smith and Capra undertake.

An initial step in establishing personal meanings and values in a deauthored system involves reintroducing the human body itself. In resisting a semiotic system that makes mere bodies superfluous and interchangeable, that would reduce individuals to being virtual presences in a network in which only relationships are real, Capra's first goal is to restore the body to being a real physical presence in the world. As a second, related item on his agenda, Capra works to restore an awareness of the distinctive and unsystematizable sounds of an actual spoken human voice against the background of anonymous discourse. If Taylor represents the concept of the machine of politics and language throughout the film, Capra insists that the person is a ghost in the machine that can never be actually exorcised or erased. As Taylor attempts to disembody language and to remove the individual speaker from the system, Capra everywhere reminds us of the presence of distinctive, individual bodies and unique, human voices still present within the semiotic structures of the film. Cranky, ungeneralizable individuals are the saving remnant that will not be expunged.

The most brilliant comic summary of this standing war between Taylor's forces of disembodiment and Capra's efforts of reembodiment is the running gag involving Taylor's porcine henchman Chick McGann (played by the more than portly Eugene Pallette). The fat, frog-voiced McGann is prevented from becoming the cool, impersonal operative in the service of the Taylor machine that he aspires to be and that Taylor wants him to become – a perfectly frictionless and efficient and totally disembodied speaker (like that posited by many critics as the speaker of their ideal works of literary truth and beauty) – not only by the gravelly timbre and the gruff tones of his voice, for which he was legendary as a character actor, but by the fact that his enormous body gets stuck in a telephone booth every time he tries to make a quick call to Taylor.

Capra uses the character of Governor Hubert ("Happy") Hopper (and the brilliant comic performance of character actor Guy Kibbee) to make the same point. Even in the initial scene – the rapid-fire series of telephone conversations involving Paine, Taylor, and Hopper – Hopper's stuttering, bumbling, comic incompetence represents an unassimilable residue of eccentric, unique humanity that will not be absorbed into the abstract semiotic and discursive system. It is not for nothing that Capra was the great favorite of character actors. Kibbee's performance, like Pallette's, is deliberately played up to remind us of the quirky, eccentric, bodily individuality and personal, unsystematizable voice tone that will not be erased or neutralized by a high-tech system of semiotic arrangements (in art or in life). In terms of the two major figures of twentieth-century American poetry, Capra, in effect, chooses sides with Robert Frost and against Wallace Stevens in his determination to ground experience in an appreciation of the ungeneralizable tones of a fallible, error-prone, all too human speaker. Capra effectively refuses even to contemplate the possibility of a disembodied Stevensian experience of truth or sublimity.

Capra's insistence that "each actor brings his own clout" to a part (that is to say, his particular body type, vocal range, and facial expressiveness), as he put it in his 1978 American Film Institute seminar,* is his own acknowledgment that, like life, the experience in a film cannot be boiled down into the ideal text of the deconstructionists. The individual is what Henry James called a "value intrinsic," who cannot be reduced to being a semiotic function of the script (whether it is the script dictated by the director of a film or by the Cedars, Taylors, Nortons, and Potters of life). Tone, expression, emotion, and personality – the personal speaker, in short – cannot be eliminated. That is what some directors, critics, and semioticians forget, which is why one can read through volumes of criticism devoted to Hitchcock, Antonioni, or Dreyer with nary a reference to the fact that the films were acted and the characters performed into existence, separate from the scripting, lighting,

---

* "Dialogue on Film," p. 45.

camera work, and editing. Capra is offering an appreciation of scripting and directing in which the individual actor (in both the dramatic and worldly sense of the word) is not erased or ventriloquized out of his or her distinctive presence, not treated as cattle, but is brought into the fullest possible existence, particularity, and "clout."

From at least *American Madness* on, almost all of Capra's films are distinguished from the run-of-the-mill Hollywood movie by the sheer energy of the performances of the bit players in them. Dozens of these performances stand out over the years. In *It Happened One Night*, one remembers not only the performative virtuosity of Gable and Colbert (or of Peter and Ellie) but of Roscoe Karns as Oscar Shapley, Walter Connolly as Ellie's father, and Alan Hale as Peter's newspaper editor. In *Deeds*, one remembers not only the performances of Cooper and Arthur but of Raymond Walburn as the butler, Lionel Stander as the bodyguard, and Margaret McWade and Margaret Seddon as the Faulkner sisters. Capra's films always seem to have enough time and space to make room for these little people. Regular bit players like Clarence Muse, Walter Catlett, Halliwell Hobbes, Sterling Holloway, and George Meeker (as well as the actors and actresses I have already mentioned) gave their finest and most memorable performances in Capra's work. This is more than an example of Capra's famous "niceness" to actors with small parts. The energy and passionateness (however quirky and eccentric they are) he encourages these performers to express that makes their work with him so incredibly vivid and memorable is a vote, in effect, in favor of the power and not the weakness of the individual, no matter how minor his part in life or art. As in the work of John Cassavetes, there is a Mediterranean robustness and vivacity to Capra's conception of the expressive possibilities of life (at the opposite extreme from the withdrawal, quietism, or passivity that one finds in the work of Altman, Bergman, or Antonioni). The energy, intensity, and vividness of the performances in Capra's work is an expression of faith in the power and endurance of the individual actor, however flawed and fallible he might be, a vote of confidence in his semiotically unabsorbable, undeconstructable "clout."

What Capra does comically in the cases of Hopper and McGann, he does in earnest with the figure of Smith. Jimmy Stewart's reedy voice and wispy figure insist that he is a real human presence that will not be discursively erased, philosophically bracketed, or made a mere function of an abstract system of relationships. He is significantly taller, more angular and physically striking, and more adolescently ungainly than any of the other Senators, and his voice is noticeably more fallibly human even than those of the ten-year-old Senate pages with whom he speaks – boy actors all, whose voices have been polished to a fault by years of professional vocal coaching. The plangency and desperation of Smith's voice during his filibuster represent a vocal residue that will not be assimilated into any discursive system of analysis. Its timbres and tones – unmodulated, falsetto, pleading, pathetic, inspiring, weary, and hoarse by turns (Capra had a doctor swab Stewart's vocal cords with iodine for some of the concluding scenes, to add an additional raspiness) – cannot be absorbed into an abstract system.

Actual bodies, voice tones, and emotions are what the technologies of knowledge (like most literary and film criticism) are unequipped to take into account or transmit, Capra knows as well as Frost or Emerson. In a world in which language has been decentered and words unmoored from personal meanings, a world in which the corrupt Joseph Paine is the "White Knight," harried Governor Hopper is "Happy," and the Willett Creek Dam is a "beneficial piece of legislation," Smith's and Capra's task is to restore language to some intimate, practical, physical relationship with actual human desire and imagination. Their way to beat the system is to use the voice and body to remind their listeners and viewers that, as we might say today, Saussure, Derrida, and Foucault are all equally wrong in leaving out the individual voice and the human body. Language is not a "free play" of signifiers. It is not a merely arbitrary system of impersonal differences (or *differances*). It is an individual, eccentric, human expression of desire and imagination.

That is why its play of signification is not free, neutral, arbitrary, or, even, usually, a kind of play. As Emerson and William James, in the American individualistic tradition, were wise enough to know, language is not the abstract, impersonal semiotic system of the European theorists except in its most trivial or uninteresting forms – say, the language of advertising, of penology, or of fashion – the sorts of language these theorists are usually content to analyze. In its living, important, and vital manifestations – in great works of art, in passionate talk, or in the idealistic rantings of a young junior Senator – it is the opposite of the negotiation of an abstract, neutral system of codes. It is the registration of a unique, unsystematizable, individual trajectory of intense, idiosyncratic, and all too human movements of desire and imagination from which the particular speaker can never be written off. That is the truth of which Smith and Capra repeatedly remind us by the very eccentricity and imaginative energy of their respective performances.

Speaking with one's own voice may seem like a small enough accomplishment, but the very point of Smith is that one is not born with a voice or self apart from the systems in which one is embedded. One must create them. Individuality and an individual style must be achieved; they cannot be inherited, and *Smith* and *Doe* take their difficult creation (or threatened existence) as their subject. It is not enough simply to be abstractly idealistic or patriotic (the particular metaphors this film uses to stand for the individual energies of creative imagination and desire). Smith must gradually and painfully achieve a voice and physical presence that are capable of expressing his idealism. He does not begin with them at all, except insofar as they initially represent only a kind of expressive disability or handicap. Smith has to learn how to use his body and voice practically, in a series of difficult encounters. I will avoid rehearsing the sequence of scenes in which he exercises his fledgling voice in the first hour or so of the film, since this is the one aspect of the film that seems to have been fairly well appreciated by past criticism. The scenes of the young, inexperienced speaker's embarrassing stutterings, false starts, confused hesitations, and gradual fine tuning of his voice as he clumsily explores its expressive range and tentatively tests its power in public are among the most moving in the film. What has been overlooked, though, is that when he first arrives in Washington, Smith does not have a bodily presence either, in the sense in which he needs ultimately to achieve one.

Smith begins the film, and his stay in Washington, as a "transparent eyeball" in the authentic Emersonian sense. In Vorkapich's patriotic montage sequences and in the general situations and events of the first hour of the film, Smith virtually lives the Emersonian dream of perfect transparency, even to the extent of making himself a window to transparently pass along to the theater audience the various sights and sounds of his whirlwind tour of patriotic sites and monuments. "Seeing all, nothing [himself], the currents [not of the universe, but of his country] flow through [him.]" He is a transcendentalist of patriotic ideals and experiences. He is, in both the optical and the mystical senses of the word, a seer, and in scene after scene we see him seeing, gazing, or abstracted in silent raptures, touring Washington in a bus, looking up at the Lincoln Memorial, gesturing out of his office window at the Capitol dome, or gazing at it through the back window of a taxi.

These passages are a stirring tribute to Smith's capacity for imaginative transport, but the irony is that to lose oneself in this way, in this movie, is to lose oneself almost as thoroughly as if one were disembodied or dehumanized in Taylor's way. There is no practical difference between being lost in vision and being passive and neutralized as a semiotic cog in a political and rhetorical machine. In either case one gives up all practical, individual social or ethical existence. That is why Smith's initial patrotic transparency threatens none of Paine's or Taylor's schemes and can even indirectly serve their interests by keeping him usefully out of the Senate during the debate on the infamous Deficiency bill. That is why Hopper, Paine, and Taylor do not fear Smith's patriotic idealism but cynically chuckle over it. Things have altered since Capra showed us Kay Arnold or Megan Davis seeing, and let us briefly see through their eyes off the balconies on which they stood. A retreat into vision and transparency may be a way of escaping the technologization and bureaucratization of experience in the world, but as Emerson himself did not seem to realize when he wrote the passage I have adapted, and as Capra apparently did not realize in his earlier work, such a retreat is profoundly problematic. It escapes the threat of erasure by, in effect, beating it to the punch – by performing an act of self-erasure. It escapes the pressures besetting the self, but it fails to master or come to grips with them. To change the metaphor back to the one of semiotic decentering that runs through the film: To disperse the self in a centrifugal whirl of images, as Smith is initially dispersed (both visually and visionarily) in Vorkapich's first patriotic montage, is to render the self as disembodied and characterless as if it were dispersed into a sequence of discursive functions within an abstract semiotic system. One has only to notice what the newspaper reporters do to Smith's idealism in their morning editions to see what Capra thinks of his naive Emersonianism, what he thinks of ideals and dreams divorced from forms of practical expression in the world.

Needless to say, Capra is not repudiating these ideals, but as Emerson himself came to, he is acknowledging that they are insufficient or irrelevant as ends in themselves. They matter significantly only in the activity of translating them into the expressive structures of the ordinary world. They count for anything only insofar as they can be spoken (in the largest sense of the word) in the languages of everyday life. It is not with mere abstract ideals but with this practical translation of ideals into the cadences of ordinary speech that Capra and Smith propose to fill the metaphysical and epistemological absences in bureaucratic discourse.

Smith's career in the film is thus not merely a physical shift of position from an apparently full periphery of actually empty historical sites and shrines to occupying and eventually filling with value an apparently empty, but actually full, patriotic center of meaning under the Capitol dome. Nor is it a mere shift from being a disembodied, patriotic visionary to possessing and employing an actual body and voice on the floor of the Senate. Rather, it is an act of connecting the two realms: connecting ideals and visions with voices and bodies. Like an essay by Emerson, the film in general and Smith's personal career within it are, in the largest sense, acts of fallible, almost impossibly difficult translation from abstractions to practicalities, from ideals to linguistic expressions, and *Smith* is at least as complex an exploration of that process of translation as an essay by Emerson. (The only one of Capra's other films about which this could be said is *It's a Wonderful Life*, his other most complex expressive exploration.) To recognize that this activity of translation of ideals into language is almost insuperably difficult, frustrating, and incomplete, and that much, sometimes almost everything, is always and necessarily lost in the translation is to begin to define and perhaps to appreciate the marginal and extremely flawed performance that Smith eventually shapes in the Senate and in the film.

This is a linguistic situation quite different from that imagined in *Deeds*. Deeds could express himself and his creative iconoclasm through his playfully inventive style of testimony in a fairly direct way. Smith is a character who, like Capra and Emerson as artists, must muddle through the expressive limitations, constraints, and repressions of a complex system of discourse. Smith's personal voice and bodily presence can never escape these repressive mediations. His bureaucratic and institutional predicament is thus inseparable from a larger stylistic predicament that he confronts and that the film and Capra himself must confront. It is an expressive predicament that major American artists have repeatedly experienced, and one that has been explicitly theorized about by Edwards, Emerson, and William James in their own recognition of the inevitable and unbridgeable gap between ideal expressive intentions and practical, social possibilities. As *Smith* first recognizes and *Doe* and *It's a Wonderful Life* will take as their starting points, there can be no unmediated expression. There can be no idealistic vision that counts for anything apart from the forms and structures that always and everywhere contain, control, and work to repress it – repressive forces that are embodied not only obviously in Taylor's chain of newspapers and in the various institutional technologies of information processing in the film, but more subtly and pervasively in the routine forms of everyday social expression and action. From this point on in Capra's work, the energies of imagination and desire must endlessly negotiate the always inevitably repressive forms of institutional, social, familial, and domestic life. Smith's difficulties in speaking his romantic feelings to Susan Paine (in the comic scene in which he fumbles with his hat in her apartment) and later, to Saunders (on the steps in front of her house) are inseparable from his difficulties in speaking his ideals on the floor of the Senate. Feelings and ideals must be verbally and socially mediated or translated to count for anything at all.

Capra's daring effort is to remain faithful to both texts in this act of translation – the text of the forces of imagination and desire, as well as the text of the inevitably repressive forms and languages of everyday life. Smith and Capra attempt to speak one in terms of the other without compromising or softening either. That, and not any merely social, moral, or political struggle, is the central drama of this film and the unenviable task that Smith, like many an American figure before him, finds set for him.

To underline the audacity and difficulty of his effort of translation, Capra creates two foils to Smith's effort, both of whom function less as social and moral adversaries than as stylistic or linguistic alternatives within the film. They are two of the three father figures in the film (Taylor is the third), and the two to whom Smith initially looks for some linguistic authority before he discovers that neither of them can be of help to him in his hour of expressive need. Each represents a strategy of stylistic failure, because each in his own way has chosen to compromise the difficult struggle of translation in which Smith is engaged. Paine, Smith's would-be father in the Senate, is the more obvious failure; the president of the Senate (who is given no name, but is played by Harry Carey), Smith's spiritual father and support during his filibuster, represents the more subtle and insidious compromise.

To take up the clearer case first, Paine sold out his private passions, commitments, and dreams long ago for the sake of preserving institutional and social forms. The contrast between Paine and Smith is explicitly defined as a linguistic or stylistic one. Paine is the most consummately articulate and polished speaker, the most masterfully glib and unctuous performer, in all of Capra's work. It was a stroke of genius on Capra's part to cast Claude Rains in the role, not only because he is in general one of the suavest and most charming of thirties film actors, but more specifically because in this most American of films, with the most idealistically American of protagonists, engaged in a most prototypically American stylistic struggle, Rains is identifiably and emphatically British. Born in London and trained on the London stage since the age of eleven, Rains represents, in every cadence and inflection of his voice, in every gesture and stance, not only an essentially

British but an essentially British theatrical form of expression, opposed in its very essence to everything for which Smith stands (there is a pun in that last phrase since even the different ways the two figures stand is significant). Paine is the representative of a style of discourse and a tradition of theatrical performance opposed in every respect to Smith's. That is to say, the difference between Paine and Smith is only trivially one of good versus evil, idealism versus political realism, or honesty versus deceit. The important difference is the stylistic and linguistic one, the difference between the American filmic style and the British theatrical style.

Never was Capra more vindicated in his conviction that casting is nine-tenths of filmmaking. Claude Rains *is* Joseph Paine – not by virtue of any simplistic equation between the actor's and the character's ethical or political principles, but in something much deeper than those things: in their shared definition of possible (or conversely, of inadmissable) styles of expression, in their mutual understanding of the nature of language and discourse. Rains represents the acme of eighteenth- and nineteenth-century British theatrical expression; the absolute genius of its expressive resources and assumptions. (The chamber of the United States Senate in which he stages his eminently theatrical performance even looks a little like that species of British amphitheater that extends from the old Globe to the new Barbican, with its steeply tiered balconies on three sides of a central arena for performance.) He represents a masterful control of tone and gesture, a graceful, polished refinement of manners, and a sense of secure social hierarchies. He represents, in short, the authority of an institutionally and socially sanctioned system of oratorical and theatrical discourse. None of the confusions of personal feeling and inarticulable mess of ideals that continuously disrupt Smith's style and speaking voice disturb Paine's.

In this respect Paine, as played by Rains, represents not only the culmination of the acting tradition embodied by Walter Huston in *American Madness* and Nils Asther (a graduate of Stockholm's famed Royal Dramatic Theater) in *Bitter Tea*, but Capra's stunning final, emphatic rejection of it. In more than one scene of *Smith*, as Paine strides confidently down one of the aisles of the Senate, exchanging clubby nods and smiles of recognition with the other Senators, one cannot help but be reminded of Dixon's or Yen's almost identical performances as they move through the halls and corridors of their fiefdoms, but what Capra more than half admired in the earlier films, he decisively repudiates here. Paine's is a performance, for all its elegance and eloquence, to be shunned. To metaphorize it in terms of the two central figures of *Bitter Tea*, Capra is (as he did not in that film) forcing a choice between the polish and panache of Yen and the silence, stillness, and staring of Megan. Smith is Megan in this film, but whereas in the earlier film Capra saw no necessary or inevitable conflict between the styles of expression of Yen and Megan, here he argues for their utter opposition. In *Bitter Tea*, Megan's final imaginative richness of consciousness could ultimately be expressed in terms of a Yen-like elegance and opulence of costuming and mastery of movement and gesture. In *Smith*, Jeff's vision and idealism is cut off from all such Yen-like (or Paine-like) social expression. Capra rejects the possibility of social expressiveness previously represented in his work by Dixon and Yen (and Stew Smith and Peter Warne, to a lesser extent). The language of desire is irrevocably estranged from the language of poised, polished social speech and relationship, even as it relentlessly, desperately continues to attempt to speak itself in such public forms and relationships. Though he is dispossessed of a language like Paine's with which to express himself, Capra's argument, needless to say, is that Smith's inarticulatenesses, his gasps, and pauses – like Babe Bennett's in *Deeds* – are in touch with a reality from which Paine's theatrical polish and poise forever exlude him.

There is a larger dramatic context within which one can understand the difference between Smith's and Paine's (that is to say, Stewart's and Rains's) acting styles. The difference is repeated in Capra's five most important films of the period between 1936 and 1948. Deeds and Bennett (in *Mr. Deeds*), Doe and Norton (in *Meet John Doe*), Bailey and Potter (in *It's a Wonderful Life*), and Matthews and Conover (in *State of the Union*) each enact a parable about alternative styles of acting similar to that staged in *Smith*. Capra is engaged in a comparison and contrast of alternative acting strategies. It is only the slightest of simplifications to say that long before the parallel experiments of Uta Hagen, Lee Strasberg, Elia Kazan, or Robert Lewis at the Actors Studio (which was founded in 1947) and elsewhere, Capra was exploring and defining in his films the possibility of what has to be called a distinctively post-Romantic performative aesthetic. As they were encouraged to perform in Capra's work, Stewart, Cooper, Stanwyck, Arthur, and (to a lesser extent) Tracy and Gable were Method actors before the fact, and frequently with results at least as interesting as those Strasberg got on the stage.*

By (anachronistically) calling them Method actors, I certainly do not have in mind the fist-clenching, jaw-tightening, and mumbling to which the Method was reduced by its most mechanical practitioners. At its best, as the category might be applied to describe the performances of Stewart, Cooper, Arthur, and Stanwyck especially, the Method was intended to express ebbs and flows of emotion that are not fully expressed in an actor's scripted lines of dialogue, social interactions, or external blocking of movements. Capra uses the silences, the stutterings, the occasional hysteria, and the emotional inward-nesses of their performances (contrasting their acting styles with the technically polished style of stage veterans like Claude Rains, Adolphe Menjou, or Lionel Barrymore, or with the externalized styles of character actors like Douglass Dumbrille, Guy Kibbee, Edward Arnold, and Thomas Mitchell) as a way of validating the expression of nearly incommunicable

---

* Not that Capra is working alone in this respect: Jimmy Cagney, Humphrey Bogart, Edward G. Robinson, and John Wayne might be said to have been experimenting with acting strategies unconsciously similar to those of the Method in other directors' films. Lee Strasberg's article in the *New York Times*, September 2, 1956, actually invokes the examples of Cooper, Tracy, and Wayne as Method actors.

private states of feeling and imagination. The performances of these central figures (like the performances of the central figures in the work of Tennessee Williams, Sam Shepard, John Cassavetes, Elaine May, or Nicholas Ray) refer us to a state of feeling that is ineluctably personal and socially almost inexpressible, except in such agitated glances, gasps, and gestures.

If one puts these remarks next to those I made about Bennett's performance in *Deeds*, it will be seen that I am treating what I am calling Method acting in this chapter as being a special instance of what I called melodramatic expression in the previous chapter. I need to forestall the confusion that might arise from my use of the terms to refer to related expressive situations since, far from being synonymous, the two terms (*melodrama* and *the Method*) are usually taken to be opposites. In conventional theatrical parlance, it is said that Stanislavski and his actors were specifically reacting against the forms of stage melodrama that they inherited in the Moscow Art Theater and that, in general, Method-acting techniques are an emphatic repudiation of the melodramatic acting styles of nineteenth-century drama, which employed grand, histrionic gestures, lurid actions, and hysterical, overwrought performances. Method acting is at the opposite expressive pole, featuring small, naturalistic actions and gestures and nuanced, underplayed delivery (to the point of fumbling and mumbling).

It is a false antithesis, however, given the sense of the concepts as I am using them, especially the sense of the word *melodrama*, which I am using in an imaginative and nontheatrical connotation. Both melodrama and the kind of acting I am describing as Method acting are instances of marginal social expressiveness. Both, consequently, depend heavily on silence and imaginatively charged gestures, as well as emotionally freighted glances, pauses, gasps, or groans. Both are, in short, examples of the imperfect translation of the energies of imagination and desire into the forms of conventional social, verbal, or theatrical interchange. Although they may seem to be opposed forms of expression in their superficial qualities, they actually share much more in the way of common assumptions about the nature of human expression than either of them has in common with "technical" or "character" acting. They share what might be called a post-Romantic sense of the possibilities of expression, in film, on stage, and in fiction.

The link between the Method and the apparently so different melodramatic styles of acting and expression is revealed once one realizes that the Method is not essentially a "realistic" or "naturalistic" mode of expression, but, like the most complex forms of melodramatic expression, is essentially an acknowledgment of all that is emotionally and imaginatively ineffable, undefinable, and socially almost unspeakable for a character. Both sophisticated melodramatics and Method acting are ways of expressing intense states of passion, dreaming, or yearning that will not be mediated into more poised, controlled, or conventionally theatrical, social, and verbal formulations. Like melodrama, the Method is a strategy of expression that essentially expresses the inadequacy of the available social, verbal, or interpersonal forms of interaction. That, and not fundamentally for the sake of "realism" or "naturalism," is why it encouraged actors to fall back on mumbling, jaw-tightening, gestural fumbling, and brow-furrowing in place of the well-turned phrase and significant gesture of the well-made drawing room drama. Like melodrama, the Method essentially expresses precisely what cannot be expressed in such conventional theatrical forms.

Of course there are different forms of Method acting and different qualities to individual actors' performances. Stanwyck, Stewart, and Cooper represent quite distinguishable expressive styles in Capra's work, just as Dean, Brando, and Clift do in later films. Yet it is also true that they all have a lot in common. Stanwyck's passionateness bordering on the point of emotional breakdown and hysteria, Stewart's vulnerability, boyish nervousness, and shy intensity, and Cooper's inwardness, stoicism, and privacy – each, in its way, represents a common state of social alienation, expressive disenfranchisement, and verbal and gestural clumsiness combined with a feeling of emotional intensity and imaginative energy. This expressive predicament is figured in the inarticulate but powerfully charged gasps, grunts, glances, or silences of their acting. In their different ways, then, each actor embodies the fundamental assumption of the Method (and of American melodrama, as different as that might seem). To the extent that one is imaginatively full and passionally powerful, one is verbally empty and socially powerless. To the extent that one has something intense to express, one can find no words, stances, or social roles or relationships within which to express oneself.

It is not accidental that the great Method-related performances in Capra's films, like the major performances of Dean, Brando, and Clift in later movies, are all depictions of marginal figures – social outsiders, juvenile delinquents, or imaginative aliens – whose narrative predicaments emphatically mirror their psychological states of marginality and of verbal and social alienation as they are expressed in the acting performances themselves. Nor is it accidental that the Method is the acting style par excellence to attempt to leave behind language and social interaction in all of its rhetorically nuanced manifestations, and to offer in its place the concept of the primordial cave of the mouth and a sense of the body as an animal reality, beneath or outside of all social forms, understandings, and arrangements of experience. Silence, gutterals, or gestures replace poised or controlled verbal and social interactions. The individual offers private intensities of feeling and imagination in place of the codes of interaction legitimized by society, business, politics, or the family. Romanticism has left the lyric poem and found its way onto the performative stage of the world.

If, as I am arguing, these Method-related performances are manifestations of American Romanticism, it should not be surprising to find anticipations of these expressive stances in earlier American writing. I would argue that once the Romanticism of all of these Method-affiliated forms of acting is appreciated (as a corrective to the mistaken impression of the Method as a kind of naturalism) analogies with previously defined American expressive situations leap off the page at a reader. It is hard not to think of the performances turned in by Stewart in *Smith*, Arthur in *Deeds*, or Stewart again in *It's a Wonderful Life* (or of the later performances of Dean, Clift, or Brando in films like *A Place in the Sun*, *East of Eden*, *On the Waterfront*, and *Rebel Without a Cause*), when one reads Emerson's description of contemporary transcendentalists in 1841, in his essay "The Transcendentalist":

> It is a sign of our times, conspicuous to the coarsest observer, that many intelligent and religious persons withdraw themselves from the common labors and competitions of the market and the caucus, and betake themselves to a certain solitary and critical way of living, from which no solid fruit has yet appeared to justify their separation. They hold themselves aloof: they feel the disproportion between their faculties and the work offered them, and they prefer to ramble in the country and perish of ennui, to the degradation of such charities and such ambitions as the city can propose to them. They are striking work, and crying out for somewhat worthy to do! What they do is done only because they are overpowered by the humanities that speak on all sides; and they consent to such labor as is open to them, though to their lofty dream the writing of *Iliads* or *Hamlets*, or the building of cities or empires seems drudgery....
>
> They are lonely; the spirit of their writing and conversation is lonely; they repel influences; they shun general society; they incline to shut themselves in their chamber in the house, to live in the country rather than in the town, and to find their tasks and amusements in solitude. Society, to be sure, does not like this very well; it saith, Whoso goes to walk alone, accuses the whole world; he declares all to be unfit to be his companions; it is very uncivil, nay, insulting; Society will retaliate. Meantime, this retirement does not proceed from any whim on the part of these separators; but if any one will take pains to talk with them, he will find that this part is chosen both from temperament and from principle; with some unwillingness too, and as a choice of the less of two evils; for these persons are not by nature melancholy, sour, and unsocial, – they are not stockish or brute, – but joyous, susceptible, affectionate; they have even more than others a great wish to be loved. Like the young Mozart, they are rather ready to cry ten times a day, "But are you sure you love me?"....
>
> And yet, it seems as if this loneliness, and not this love, would prevail in their circumstances, because of the extravagant demand they make on human nature. That, indeed, constitutes a new feature in their portrait, that they are the most exacting and extortionate critics. Their quarrel with every man they meet is not with his kind, but with his degree. There is not enough of him, – that is the only fault. They prolong their privilege of childhood in this wise; of doing nothing, but making immense demands on all the gladiators in the lists of action and fame. They make us feel the strange disappointment which overcasts every human youth....
>
> With this passion for what is great and extraordinary, it cannot be wondered at that they are repelled by vulgarity and frivolity in people. They

say to themselves, It is better to be alone than in bad company. And it is really a wish to be met, – the wish to find society for their hope and religion, – which prompts them to shun what is called society.

In my particular sense of the term, then, Method acting is the practical theatrical expression on stage or in film of what in a novel by Henry James could be called the melodrama of consciousness. It is not at all accidental that the contrast of the two types of acting in Capra's films – "technical" and Method – is repeated, in a finer tone as it were, in the pairing in James's work that I have mentioned earlier of "fixed" and "free" characters. Figures like Henrietta Stackpole and Caspar Goodwood function as "technical" or "character" actors within *The Portrait of a Lady* in precisely the same sense in which they do in Capra's films, whereas Isabel Archer, if not obviously a Method actress, does certainly embody an imaginative inwardness, mysteriousness, and exorbitance resisting social expression that one has to associate with the Method. In *The Golden Bowl*, Maggie Verver is an actress of one type who is paired against two supreme "technical" actors in the figures of Charlotte and the Prince.

Both James and Capra, like many other American artists in the tradition I am describing, are exploring conditions of imaginative liberation which are accompanied by conditions of linguistic and social disenfranchisement. They are stimulated by characters who open themselves to excesses and extravagances of desire. They are interested in the expressive problems in which such a daring liberation of imagination and feeling results.

The comparison with James should also help one to understand why the zaniness and eccentricity of a performance in a Hawks or Sturges film falls outside this idealistic tradition. In the ensemble acting of a Sturges film, the performances, brilliant as they may be, are all technical. A character's expression of him- or herself can always be analyzed back into particular social or psychological determinants of behavior. The self expresses itself in terms of a publicly legible repertory of manners, tones, and movements. The performances in a Sturges film are not in any sense affirming the existence of energies disruptive of social forms of expression. Sturges's characters have no transcendental conception of freedom or free expression, in the sense that Isabel Archer or Jefferson Smith do. They neither need it nor want it. There is no gap between their felt sense of themselves and their expressive language. They are always perfectly expressed in their Dickensian tics and quirks and oddities of behavior. (This is Dickens, however, without the powerful Dickensian emotions or melodramatics, Dickens rendered entirely through technical or character acting.) In a Sturges or Hawks film we are in a world at odds with the forms of American melodrama, symbolism, and Romanticism as they are present in the line of expression defined by James, Chaplin, Capra, Williams, O'Neill, Shepard, Cassavetes, and May. It is a world in which the inner life of the human spirit and its expressive difficulties in society emphatically are not the central presence in the drama.

It is in this sense that Capra's work is closely, if unconsciously, related to that of avowed Method directors like Nicholas Ray and Elia Kazan. It is not that the work of any of these directors dispenses altogether with technical or character acting (any more than Henry James's work dispenses with fixed characters to give itself over to an exclusive depiction of free characters), but at crucial moments it gestures beyond what is depictable in that form of acting. Performances like those turned in by Barbara Stanwyck in even the earliest of Capra's films and Jean Arthur and Jimmy Stewart in the later ones have a passionateness and an imaginative intensity in search of an adequate form of social expression (which can never be quite attained) that directly anticipates the performances of Montgomery Clift, James Dean, and Marlon Brando in their best work of the fifties. Stanwyck, Stewart, and Arthur demonstrate that it did not take Lee Strasberg to bring the emotional inwardness, strangled intensity, and smothered hysteria of the Method to America. In fact, the reason Strasberg's seeds took such immediate and firm root in American soil was that it was already so well prepared to receive his doctrines. The Method is an interesting side path not opposed to, but parallel to, a vast highway of Romantic expression in American art that existed in this country long before the birth of Stanislavski in Russia and at least a century before Strasberg's creatively all-American misreadings of *An Actor Prepares*. If Strasberg had not come across Stanislavski, he could have gotten the same performative doctrines out of the pregnant silences, the charged glances, and the imaginative unappeasability of the characters in a novel by Henry James, characters like Isabel Archer or Lambert Strether, searching for, but never quite finding a way to speak their deepest, most authentic selves.

It is necessary to appreciate the specialness of Stewart's (and Arthur's) performances in *Smith* in order fully to understand the distinctive limitations in the performance of Harry Carey as president of the Senate. Based on the average audience's response to him, one would have to say that he presents an even more dangerously seductive and subtle foil to Smith's performance than Paine does. Carey is the almost universal favorite of audiences watching the film and represents the possibility of a folksy charm, common sense, and simplicity that most American audiences seem to find irresistible. With his relaxed sense of humor, his wry smile, and the perpetual twinkle in his eye, he reminds one a little of Deeds (in fact Carey even looks a bit like Coop), as he smiles, winks, and nods his way through Smith's twenty-three and a half hour filibuster. In a review of the film in the *New York Times* when it was first released, Frank Nugent summed up the customary appreciation of Carey, editorializing that, as humble and "just plain folks" as Carey was, he represented the very finest flowering of American democracy, insofar as the capacity to remain witty, playful, and flexible under the pull of rival factions was the prime requirement asked of its citizens. As I argued in Chapter 5, that appreciation for the ability of the human spirit to make room for a "play" of tones, attitudes, or styles of behavior under the most stressful and inauspicious circumstances is obviously central to Capra's practice as a director as well. He was, in fact, often described by his actors as himself frequently looking and acting very much like twinkle-eyed Carey, as he sat on a stepladder or camera crane looking down with amusement on the sets he was nominally presiding over, entertained by the scurryings of the assistant directors, cameramen, technicians, and actors around him. Carey is undeniably a stand-in for Capra, a playful, tolerant, always encouraging *spectator ab extra*, thoroughly involved in the dramatic situation and intimately part of it, but also imaginatively half removed from it, never allowing himself to become lost in it or to lose his ironic, comic distance and perspective.

Having said all this, it needs to be emphasized that although a capacity to play with a situation and to be able generously to encourage playing in others is necessary to a Capra hero (or director), it is not sufficient in itself, or Capra would never have gone beyond the buddy-boy films. For all of Carey's Capra-like geniality, good humor, and charm, he is virtually inarticulate and institutionally almost powerless. While Carey is nodding and mugging, winning the hearts of the crowd in the Senate as well as the one in the movie theater, Smith is dying on his feet and the Deficiency bill is moving hour by hour closer to passage. However charming, Carey is a man with neither principles nor a vision. He is not a leader but merely a bureaucratic functionary, just as equably tolerant of the corrupt opponents of Smith's filibuster as he is of Smith. A Senate chamber filled to the brim with such blandly encouraging, quietly charming old biddies, who believe that there are two equally valid sides to every question and (in what can only be called their moral, passional, and imaginative castration) always can find mitigating arguments all around every issue would be just Taylor's cup of tea.

Let me be clear why I am being so hard on everybody's favorite charmer. In another film, by a director with an entirely different sensibility (say, Jean Renoir's *The Rules of the Game*), Carey could be a mild-mannered, slightly bewildered, admirably modest modern hero. He could be Octave, with his conviction that everyone has his reasons. Even in an earlier film by Capra – say *American Madness* – much of what Capra is condemning in Carey's perform-ance here is presented favorably in the figure of Dixon. Capra, however, is no longer satisfied with the poised, well-meaning master of ceremonies, the Rotarian as hero. Carey, whatever his apparent virtues, must be judged in comparison with Smith, and Smith represents imaginative possibilities that begin precisely where Carey's stylistic reach ends (both as an actor and as a character). The similarity between Gary Cooper, in *Deeds*, and Carey in this film, and yet the difference between one's feelings about the two charact-ers is indicative of a significant change in Capra's work. Charm is just not enough. There are alien entanglements – repressive systems of understand-ing and expression – for personality to negotiate in this film that it did not have to face in the earlier one. Smith himself represents an imaginative intensity and passion that indicates the limitations of Carey's performance in his film as Deeds's performance was not similarly "placed" in his.*

If Carey's special imaginative limitation still seems obscure, perhaps an analogy with a character like Felix, in Henry James's *The Europeans*, is helpful, since Felix's personality (aptly summarized in the Latinate resonances of his name) is so strikingly similar to that of Carey's character and his imaginative function in James's narrative is almost identical to Carey's in Capra's narrative. In no sense is James simply condemning Felix, who epitomizes so much of his own creator's capacity for playful social expression and the large toleration of a wide range of experience. James, however, asks for more than social receptivity in his characters. He asks for an imaginative power that manifests itself as a capacity of absolute (virtually melodramatic) moral judgment and ethical discrimination, and Felix has nothing to offer in this respect. He is an imaginative lightweight, and we are made aware of it by James's contrasting him with his sister Eugenia. Like Carey, but operating more abstractly and in a higher sphere, Felix is an ethical dabbler, a social connoisseur and dilettante, and as such is ultimately the figuration not of the expanses but of the crippling expenses of a certain stylistic capaciousness and indiscriminateness of appreciation. His limitations become obvious when he is compared with Eugenia, just as Carey is an ideal of performance only for those who have failed to understand all the ways in which Smith (and eventually Saunders) move totally beyond him.

It is useful to turn to a work so apparently different from a thirties Hollywood film by Capra as a nineteenth-century novel by James to suggest once more the extent to which the types Capra creates keep appearing in the American consciousness. Carey, the social compromiser, Joseph Paine, the Tory of the imagination, and Jim Taylor, the con man and manipulator, have a venerable ancestry in Cooper, Hawthorne, Melville, and James. They are exemplary and archetypal because they summarize so many of the counter-currents of the American imaginative experience. Both as abstract styles and as fictional characters, they haunt the American imagination throughout nineteenth- and twentieth-century art.

Paine, Carey, and Taylor together stylistically triangulate the possibility of the existence of an imaginative position different from their own (and this spatial metaphor is built into this most spatially self-aware of all of Capra's films), a position Capra designates as "Smith," which is marked physically by the distinctive body and voice identified with the figure of Jimmy Stewart in the film. Paine and Carey (and the other characters in the film) have more or

---

* Bennett, as I have already argued, offered a performative and stylistic alternative to Deeds, but Capra worked hard to keep her in a firmly subordinate role – both sexually and narratively – in comparison with Deeds during the concluding trial scene. It is interesting, if somewhat fanciful, to think of Bennett and Deeds as being reincarnated in Smith but in significantly reversed positions. The hysterical, stuttering, imaginatively exorbitant Bennett becomes Smith; the laid-back, witty, relaxed Deeds becomes the president of the Senate. The leading and supporting characters trade places between the two films. What was earlier cordoned off in the wings of the drama steps into center stage; the narratively repressed returns with a wallop.

less fixed identities and styles that are quite easily described, but Smith's position is much harder to pin down; his identity is much more complex and elusive than theirs. I speak of his putative position being triangulated from theirs because at times he seems to have what Emerson would call a "referred" existence. He is, most succinctly, what is *not* Taylor, Paine, Carey, or the others. He is what is *not* speakable or formulatable in their styles – in the cadences of the stage, in mild-mannered toleration for all viewpoints, in radio bulletins or newspaper headlines, or in curt telephoned instructions to henchmen. He is what eludes such social or political categorization or psychological specification. His adversaries are often photographed in seated or sturdily fixed standing positions, but Smith is a principle of unbalanced movement, eccentric desire, or unpoised yearning that at times can only be understood as everything that is left out of *any system* of discourse. That is why "Smith" at times seems an almost anonymous, faceless, bodyless voice crying in the wilderness, without any distinct identity of its own (all the more so because during his filibuster he for the most part only reads the words of others, specifically the texts of the Declaration of Independence and the Constitution of the United States, letting those idealistic statements be transmitted through him, as it were, rather than authoring a distinctive statement of his own personal beliefs and feelings).

At times he seems almost to be an imaginative opening out of the film itself – an indication of the fundamental limits of realistic representation. His emotionally fugitive and imaginatively mercurial quality is not something to be explained away. To be reducible to a type, a character in the way Paine, Taylor, or Carey are characters, is to have repressively packaged the self in the very ways Capra uses Smith to avoid. The intense energies of desire and imagination associated with "Smith" in this film (and with Bennett earlier, and Bailey and Matthews in the subsequent works) are themselves as unorganizable within the tidy bundle of attributes critics call "character" or "self" as they are resistant to social and technological packaging by their adversaries within their films.

In contrast to Paine's polished language of the upper class and the nineteenth-century stage and Carey's folksy idiom, Smith's language (and that of Saunders, with whom he is linked in the second half of the film) is that of unsystematic, unformulateable feeling. More accurately, it is a language attempting to speak the energies of imagination and desire in the public expressive forms of the world, but that is to suggest what a complex and problematic linguistic task it sets itself. In one of the crucial scenes of the film, Capra summarizes Smith's expressive problem concisely. Smith and his secretary Saunders have stayed late one night in the Senate Office Building to draft a bill that Smith wants to propose in the Senate for a national boy's camp. The drafting is not going well. I quote from the shooting script of the film, which is slightly more complete than the released version:

SMITH: Did you ever have so much to say about something – you couldn't say it?
SAUNDERS: (*dryly*) Try sitting down.

SMITH: I did – and – and I got right up.

SAUNDERS: Now, let's get down to particulars. How big is this thing? Where is it to be? How many boys will it take care of? If they're going to buy it – how do they make their contributions? Your bill has to have all of that in it –

SMITH: And something else, too, Miss Saunders – the spirit of it – the idea – the –

In his walk he has come to the window. He points out suddenly.

SMITH: That's what's got to be in it.

She looks in that direction, and sees the lighted Capitol Dome, seen through the window – with Jefferson in the foreground.

SMITH: (*pointing*) That.

Saunders indicates that she sees the Dome, her eyebrows lifting a little.

SAUNDERS: (*quietly – with only a touch of sarcasm*) On paper?

SMITH: (*still looking out of the window, not conscious of her cynical question*) I want to make that come to life – yes, and lighted up like that, too – for every boy in the land. Boys forget what their country means – just reading "land of the free" in history books. And they get to be men – and forget even more. Liberty is too precious to get buried in books, Miss Saunders. Men ought to hold it up in front of them – every day of their lives and say: "I am free – to think – to speak. My ancestors couldn't. I can. My children will."

And we see a new Saunders looking at Jefferson with a new expression – listening rather raptly – then starting to make rapid notes.

SMITH: The boys ought to grow up *remembering* that.

He breaks off – turns from the window – collecting himself out of a daze – and a little embarrassed.

SMITH: Well – gosh – that – that isn't the "particulars," is it?

It would be hard for Capra to have been more explicit about the linguistic nature of Smith's predicament. His stuttering incoherence and inarticulateness, his embarrassing patriotic ramblings, his utter failure to write his bill in this way is the scene's dramatic point. How one can get "that" – the Capitol dome and a history lesson about freedom but, more important, the exalted yearnings, dreams, and ideals Smith's tone represents – "into" the world of the Senate and the film is the dramatic question Capra poses to himself. How does one get "that" into the codes of both legal and cinematic technologies that everywhere resist such imaginative afflatus and abstraction? Capra and Buchman were defining their own expressive predicament as they wrote the scene this way. Smith is an alter ego for them insofar as his problem getting "that . . . on paper" is their problem too writing a movie that attempts to get ideals and dreams embodied in events and words on paper.

Smith and Saunders, in their different ways, gradually find voices and learn to speak to an audience. The cleverness of Capra's pairing this tough, practical secretary, played by the husky-voiced Jean Arthur, with the tremulous, schoolgirlish, very junior senator is that Smith and Saunders are able gradually to hybridize their voices in the course of the film. Saunders's voice progressively becomes more loving, more committed, and more capable of register-

How to get "*that* . . . on paper": an expressive predicament for a senator or a scriptwriter.

ing the movements of desire and imagination in its increasingly passionate and idealistic cadences. Smith's voice becomes tougher, more practical, more logical and argumentative, as he is coached in the rules and learns the ropes of down-to-earth legislative practice. To go on from that, though, to argue that in this process of crossing their two voices Capra is endorsing a paradigmatic social, sexual, and vocal compromise of idealism and pragmatism is to be entirely false to the nearly hysterical tone and mood of the final film. In the second hour of the movie what Capra offers is less the experience of some vocal and imaginative middle ground in which reason and passion are brought together and blended, and in which they are allowed to neutralize each other, than the opposite of that. In place of stability he offers instability; in place of neutrality or neutralized stasis, he offers wild oscillations of feeling, vocal swerves between ideals and practicalities, and tonal excesses, imbalances, and dissonances.

The real language that Smith and Saunders finally employ, the important presence that they manifest ultimately in the film, is not conventionally linguistic or syntactic at all. It is not a verbal language of words and argument, but a visual and acoustic language of imaginatively charged gasps, pauses, glances, and gestures. The voice that Smith and Saunders offer as an alternative to the other voices in the film is at times indistinguishable from silence.

It is a melodramatic language of eruptions of desire, expressible in a cinematic language not of scripted speech but of high-key-lighting effects, extreme close-ups, violent actions, agitated gestures and movements, and powerful musical orchestrations. It is, to put it most briefly, a language opposed to everything Paine represents in the language of theatrical expression, everything Taylor represents in the language of bureaucracy, everything the newspapers and radio represent in the language of high-tech journalism, and everything the Senate and its members represent in the language of institutional legislative procedure and political scripting. Where Paine's voice is a complete, and completely verbal, speech in which there are no flaws, gaps, fissures, or failures of expression, Smith's is a speech that is more nonverbal than verbal and, where it is verbal, is almost nothing but hesitations, stuttering inarticulateness, elisions, and ellipses. Where Paine's speech (as in his scene of feigned moral outrage at Smith's conduct on the floor of the Senate) translates emotionality into consummately modulated eloquence and oratorical tones and cadences, Smith's speech – though ultimately enriched and authenticated by its emotionality – is broken up, disrupted, interrupted, and frequently completely arrested by his overcharge of feeling. His speech is a language of melodramatic silences, pauses, exclamations, gestures, and glances that emphatically is not reducible to anything that might appear in the script of a stage play.

Capra is suggesting that in a world devoted to the institutional control and normalization of desire and imagination, such articulate stillnesses, silences, gasps, and gestures may be the last remaining expression of personal imagination and desire. In concert with Saunders and Smith, he offers a new sort of language as an alternative to the social languages within the film. It is a photographic language of silent shrugs and glances, an aural language of music and sound effects, an editorial language of visual rhythms and juxtapositions.

If institutional and linguistic systems have been decentered, Capra attempts to offer a new center in the almost inexpressible intensities of feeling and idealism that are communicated in these photographic, acoustic, and editorial effects. The melodramatic glances, gestures, and visual and aural effects point (admittedly incoherently and gesturally) to a realm of pure feeling that has not been corrupted or leached out of life and around which a new order of values can be erected. Just as Smith's audience, the senators in the film, are asked to recenter their political and linguistic systems around an exalted patriotism, so the audience in the movie theater is asked to recenter its social and dramatic systems of value around the appreciation of intensities of imaginative energy that Capra generates in the melodramatic language of the film.

The essence of Smith's (and Capra's) expressive audacity is that both believe that these accesses of feeling can be brought into the real world to transform ordinary life and expression. In a novel or story by Proust, Conrad, Woolf, or Joyce, or in a film by Dreyer, Bergman, Antonioni, Fellini, or Fassbinder, such intensities of feeling and imagination are, in effect, openings out of the world of ordinary social and verbal life. They are escape hatches out of the traps and confinements of routine social structures and institutional systems of discourse. In *The Passion of Joan of Arc* or *Gertrud*, in *8½*, *Juliet of the Spirits*, or *Amarcord*, in *The Red Desert* or *The Passenger*, in *The Marriage of Maria Braun*, characters granted such momentary richness of consciousness stop participating practically in society and the world entirely and stare into the distance in silent rapture. During such scenes, these works themselves switch to an analogous rapturous style in which the progress of the plot momentarily stops, dialogue ceases, and narrative styles are replaced by special melodramatic or dreamlike cadences. Capra's characters' glances, gestures, and silences, their moments of passionate inarticulateness, and his visual and aural intensifications at such moments are indeed turns away from certain forms of social interaction and language, but the difference is that Capra does not regard this movement as a necessary repudiation of all society and all possible social intercourse. As in the old American Dream, the form of Romanticism that emerged in America, Capra and Smith attempt to create a new society in which such intensities of imagination and desire would be expressible. Simply to have the ideals and values and not to express them or make them count in any significant public way would be to remain a Boy Ranger leader back in Montana or to despair and go scurrying back there at the first evidence of the difficulty of such public expression in the Senate. In the filibuster, Capra summarizes the essentially public nature of Smith's expressive predicament. He must find a way to speak his dreams and aspirations in the most public forum imaginable. He must "stay on his feet" expressively; there is no opportunity, even for a moment, for him to recline back into a merely private imaginative realm. The language of desire must be translated into public forms and expressions.

Capra's faith in the possibility of this act of translation is increasingly shaken in these late works, however. That is why, as I suggested at the end of the previous chapter, he in effect becomes a maker of tragedies from *Smith* to *State of the Union*, notwithstanding the nominally "happy endings" of some of these works. They are films about the wastes of enriched consciousness, about the inability of their central characters to translate their ideals into practical forms of expression and human interaction, in life or in film. They are therefore films that increasingly have to rely on the melodramatic language of gasps, gestures, stares, and silences that emerges, in *Deeds* and this film, in place of the language of social relationships as the expression of a character's finest and richest insights.

The gap between the two realms of experience – between the language of the heart and the language of men – is just possibly unbridgeable. This widening expressive gap is at the center of Capra's major subsequent work, and I have mentioned it previously, but never again does he find such an eloquent cinematic representation of it as he does in this film. The necessity of that act of "trans-lation" or the "carrying over" of desire across a linguistic gap is brilliantly figured here in his use of the spatial and visual distance that separates Smith and Saunders and that must be bridged by them imaginatively and verbally in the second half of the film.* Seldom in film has there been such a long-distance courtship or one that depended so much on the translation or transmission of intense, private states of feeling across vast, public, institutional distances. For the entire second half of the film Smith and Saunders are separated physically by the width and height of the Senate chamber, and cinematically by the fact that they do not appear in a single shot together. (Note how even in the final seconds of the film Saunders is still up in the balcony and Smith still down on the floor, fifty or one hundred feet away.) There is no final embrace here, as there was at the end *Deeds*. Never in Capra's work have two characters been simultaneously more separated and more intimate, but the intimacy is all in this act of translation, of imaginatively reaching out across the distance to attempt to bridge it.

Saunders must attempt to translate her desire into a series of signs, gestures, and glances that will reach Smith. Smith must translate his imagination of that inarticulable "that" through his hoarseness, his falsetto, and his ramblings into something understandable in the Senate and the world outside of the Senate. If the spatial distance figures the Emersonian gap between the "two lives – of the understanding and the soul," Capra will compromise neither the importance of the "understanding" nor the "soul." Virtually every other institutional representative in the film has sold his soul in order to maintain the understanding of the world. I have already mentioned Paine and Taylor as examples of this, but even the radio networks and the newspaper syndicates, the nominal, official trustees of spatial and imaginative trans-lation from the one realm to the other, have utterly suppressed the text of imagination and feeling in the interest of maintaining, undisturbed and unperturbed, the text of institutional analysis and discourse.†

---

* As I have already pointed out, the insistent occurrence of this expressive gap is one of the most distinctive and familiar aspects of American art. That is why it appears in one form or another in so much American expression, in the work of Homer and Hopper, for example, in terms of almost exactly the same visual metaphor as it does in this film: an enormous physical space or distance that is looked across, gestured across, or visionarily traversed in an effort to reach across it or to bridge it. It is an expressive reach outward, metaphorically, through space that one significantly does not encounter in Degas's silent, inward-turning bathers or eccentrically poised ballerinas, in the dynamic solidity and staunch fixity of Cézanne's sitters, or in Renoir's or Monet's groups of café or bathhouse loungers and carousers, the individual figures of which find complete expression of themselves in their facial expressions, social relations, and costumes. Hopper's, Homer's, and Capra's figures, on the other hand, are not only denuded of social resources of expression but are propelled outward, visually and imaginatively, on journeys through space, beyond social forms, manners, and expressions, just as Smith and Saunders are here.

† This is no different from the practice of a television show like *60 Minutes* or almost all investigative journalism today. Articulating stories and situations in the language of bureaucratic and social codes and hierarchies, such an approach is unable to represent the energies of personal imagination and desire within the forms of its analysis and is therefore as unable to understand or report fairly on religious movements or personal beliefs as the press in this film is unable to understand or adequately represent Smith's actions. Capra's film is the only adequate representation of them. Its cinematic forms of representation contrast with those *in* the film.

It is up to Smith, in an alternative act of retranslation, to reestablish the relation of the lost or erased text of desire with the forms of public discourse. Private ideals must be spoken in institutional performances, however halting and imperfect. The aspirations of boyish "Jeff" must be linked up with the words and actions of mature "Senator Smith." Romantic "Clarissa" must be reconnected with practical "Saunders." The Capitol dome must be expressed in the coded legislative language of an appropriations bill, and even more vague and incoherent ideals concerning freedom, truth, and justice must be translated difficulty and imperfectly into general social and linguistic forms of discourse.★ Perhaps the most eloquent example of that process of reaching out and successfully carrying something across that gap between Smith and Saunders is figured in the written note that she passes down to him at a moment of crisis and doubt. Her act performs a double act of translation: in the first place translating her feelings for him into a handwritten piece of parliamentary advice in the body of the written text, and then, second, translating that text itself back into a statement of the desire that generated it in a postscript that follows it and professes her love for him.

We remain acutely aware, though, of the tentativeness and the inadequacy of this act of translation. We recognize all that is lost and almost unable to be spoken between Saunders and Smith, as well as between Smith and his constituents. The sheer obliquity of Saunders's profession of love is significant. It is buried in a periphrastic postscript to a note. Its irreducible textuality is its essence. Desire is textually mediated. It does not exist pure. The contents of messages are always contained. Capra makes us feel the difficulty of that task of translation not only in the cavernous physical spaces that surround Smith and Saunders and across which they must verbally reach, but also in the walls and offices that separate them from entry into the areas of information processing in print and radio, and in the geographical gap that separates them from Smith's constituents in his home state. Smith's tones, glances, and gestures, the catches in his voice that Capra represents visually and acoustically on film are not transmittable or translatable within the institutional structures of discourse in place around him (any more than such things are translatable into today's prevailing journalistic forms). The inadequacy of his voice to translate desire and imagination into public forms of discourse is registered in the melodramatic overfreighting of his words, gestures, and glances with a surcharge of inexpressible significance and in the gradual breakdown of his voice into hoarseness, pregnant pauses, and, finally, complete silence as, at the end of the film, he faints.

Smith's and Saunders's melodramatic language is doubled by the melodramatic turn that Capra's cinematic language takes in this film and those that follow it. In *Smith, Doe, It's a Wonderful Life,* and *State of the Union,* Capra's use

---

★ One has only to think back to *American Madness* to notice both the continuities and the discontinuities in Capra's work. Tom Dixon's situation resembled Smith's in some respects, but was never so complexly defined. Dixon's performance seems almost glib in comparison.

The difference between words and gestures: speaking through a silent glance more powerfully and eloquently than the written telegrams he holds in his hands.

of melodrama is his confession of his own expressive problems, which are parallel with, but different in nature from, the expressive problems he imagines to beset his characters. His films increasingly take on the stylistic earmarks of forties films noir and fifties melodramas. Just as Smith comes up against the limitations of publicly speakable language in his senatorial performance, Capra increasingly comes up against the inadequacy of scripted language and the irrelevance of manners, conversational interchanges, and domestic drama to speak the feelings that he wants to communicate to his audience, even as he remains firmly committed to making the sort of Hollywood feature-length, narrative films that require him to pass his aspirations through the expressive resistance of scripted social interactions and passages of dialogue between characters.

Capra's decision not to make a "purer" kind of film, that is to say, a film either more purely idealistic and imaginative or more purely social and political in its narrative form and content, like Cassavetes's similar decision two decades later not to embrace a more "visionary" cinema, is evidence of his determination that the most exalted energies of imagination and desire be formulatable and expressible in the forms and structures of ordinary social and personal life.

The late films dramatize the difficulty of this expressive effort both in the unenviable expressive predicaments of their protagonists – their hesitations and difficulties as actors and speakers within the films – and in their own expressive difficulties as films – their own comparable narrative hesitations, pauses, and silences. Just as Smith increasingly has to rely on silence or gesture to "speak" for him and ultimately has to swoon away into complete silence as his last and most powerful expression of all, the films themselves increasingly and disturbingly swoon away from passages of dialogue, the dramatic give-and-take of social interchanges between characters, and the play of manners, into their own emotionally and imaginatively charged silences. (By their silence, I mean only an absence of spoken words, since these "silent" passages are many of the most heavily orchestrated in all of Capra's work.) The "melo-drama" of these moments is not so much the use of music to intensify and emotionally editorialize about the social drama, as in most other films, but the use of music to take the place of social drama. The films faint (or feint) away from passages of dialogue and socially nuanced characterizations into emotionally intense musical orchestrations and sound effects, a series of violent or rapid actions, or effects of expressive lighting, framing, and editing.

Claude Rains's presence is brilliantly used to suggest a larger parable that Capra only now at this point in his career perceives about the relationship between the mimetic worlds of movies and the stage, in their most typical and representative forms. Just as in the figure of Smith Capra explores the possibility of a language entirely different from Paine's polished eloquence, so Capra explores the expressive resources of a filmic language that is made up of exactly what would not constitute "language" on the stage, a filmic language that could never be "spoken" in a theater by an actor like Rains. To the stage's traditional emphasis on the pacing and consummate expressiveness of the well-formed, cadenced, nuanced verbal expression, Capra offers the movies' exploitation of effects of expressive lighting and framing, violent, large-scale actions, and startling editorial juxtapositions. To the stage's privileging of verbal articulateness, he offers his film's pictorial pathos and emotionality, especially its ability to use silent (or musically orchestrated) shots and editorial cross-cutting as substitutes for the interplay of lines of dialogue between characters. To the stage's emphasis on publicly audible and articulable social interchange, Capra uses close-ups to communicate highly charged states of verbally inexpressible consciousness.*

The final half hour or so of *Smith* increasingly relies on Vorkapich's montage sequences, which are used not as in conventional filmic exposition to extend and explain the social narrative they accompany but rather to replace it with an alternative visual text that tells us what is left out of the rest of the

---

* Notice how Capra's shuttling between verbal and the visionary representations, between social and imaginative realms, is more bracing than the contemporary performance artist's general rejection of verbal, social, dialogic expression. Capra privileges neither the verbal nor the visionary text but instead puts the one into competition with the other.

narrative. In the final montage, Capra cross-cuts at a breathless pace between the Taylor machine's manipulation of public opinion and newspaper reports on Smith's filibuster, and the Boy Rangers' attempts to counter Taylor with the printing and distribution of a special issue of *Boys' Stuff*. It is a very powerful sequence, but it significantly lacks dialogue, distinguishably individualized characters, or any social interchange at all. In the final event of the montage sequence, a car full of young boys distributing newspapers is forced off the road by a truck manned by Taylor's hooligans. Capra cuts away on the sound of screaming and crashing as the accident takes place, but the unavoidable impression is that the children have been horrifyingly killed or maimed in the collision. There is no doubt that we are now in the world of melodrama, not only in the high-toned rhetorical sense but in the more lurid, Gothic sense as well.

The violence of imagery and action, however, does not subside with the car crash and the conclusion of Vorkapich's montage. The luridness carries over into the final scene in the Senate. Smith falls to the floor in a faint, after accusing Paine of betraying his ideals. Paine, stricken with remorse and grief, is apprehended with a gun in the vestibule, apparently on the verge of committing suicide. The gun is wrested out of his hand, and he makes an emotional public confession of his corruption.* The whole sequence of events is speeded up almost to the point of incomprehensibility. The important point is that even in a nonmontage scene, Capra has utterly abandoned anything that might be called linguistically orderly or theatrically modulated discourse. We have been propelled into a cinematic world in which the charged consciousness has no expression available to itself except in this expressive grotesquerie, luridness, and violence – in the violence of plot events and sudden reversals, in the violence of editorial juxtapositions and accelerated cutting rhythms, in violences of inexpressible feeling communicated in intercut close-ups.

It is fashionable in twentieth-century aesthetics to stigmatize art that uses such devices to generate extreme states of feeling in its viewers (or that represents it in its characters) as sentimental. In the critical cant of the last thirty years, it is good to be complexly balanced and poised, and bad to appeal blatantly to the emotions. One of the results is that the works of art most admired by advanced critics either do not offer powerful emotional experiences, or, if they do, the account of the emotional effect of the work has dropped out of the critical discussion of it. (Beyond that, we all know what

---

* The original script had a coda in which Smith and Paine were reunited as symbolic father and son as participants in a parade back in their home state. As I have indicated earlier, Capra repeatedly attempts to suggest, at the ends of his films, that the imaginatively alienated individual can be brought back into the social community from which he or she has previously been imaginatively estranged. Capra's decision not to use this ending (and instead to conclude with the figure of Smith still unconscious on the floor of the Senate, and with Saunders separated from him up in the balcony and Paine separated from him in the other direction) is evidence that even Capra has ceased to believe in the reconcilability of the free energies of the imagination and the formation of an actual (and not merely imaginative) community to which the individual can belong.

Monroe Beardsley's "The Affective Fallacy" had to say about focusing on the emotional effects of a work of art.) I would argue, however, that the emotions generated by Capra's works (and those of most other artists working in the same expressive tradition) are an essential aspect of their meaning. Capra's representation of intense states of emotionality in his characters, and his careful orchestration of such states of emotionality in his viewers, are ways of criticizing cooler, less personal forms of knowledge and relationship (implicitly including those that a detached critic adopts towards a work of art).

Powerful emotionality is not in and of itself either good or bad in a work of art. It is, like any other aspect of it, a way of creating a complexly meaningful experience and must be judged in terms of the intelligence and value of the particular experience it creates. Emotionality can be merely manipulative (as it is in, say, Hitchcock and De Palma), but the emotionality that Capra, like Dickens, James, or Balzac, generates and releases at certain moments in his films (most frequently in their whirlwind conclusions) is a way of placing and criticizing other cooler forms of experience in the same works, and must be judged as such. The intense emotionality at the end of *Smith*, as in many of Capra's other films, is a way of forcing a viewer beyond the abstract intellectual categories of journalism and politics, which the film attempts to explode. It is an attempt at validating the reality of states of imagination and feeling as alternatives to the "realities" defined by social and institutional systems of meaning and understanding.

In the final minutes of *Smith*, Capra's script indulges in brief comparisons of Smith to both Lincoln and Christ. It is the sort of symbolmongering about which Capra's critics typically argue, some claiming that the comparison is justified and (in the embarrassing jargon of literary criticism) gives a "mythopoetic" dimension to the film, others deriding Capra's clumsy and unearned effort at importing metaphoric or allegorical significance into his narrative. For my purposes, however, the relevant point to notice is that this symbolic or metaphoric gesture is part and parcel of Capra's other uses of melodramatic style. This symbolmongering (which becomes even more obtrusive in his next film, *Doe*) is yet another testimony to Capra's inability to find a social formulation of, or resolution for, his character's final situation. As a filmmaker, he is indulging in the same rhetorical technique that Smith uses in the Senate. Capra is retreating into the same sort of absolute expressions and symbolic stances and postures to which his characters have recourse in the absence of any other way to express themselves. The symbol is, as it were, a way Capra works off imaginative energies that are inexpressible in terms of narrative development and unplaceable in the forms of social dialogue or characterization.

The problem of finding a valid expression of imagination and desire is summarized in an unresolved oscillation in Capra's late work between what I have been calling verbal/social/theatrical forms of expression and pictorial/musical/filmic modes of expression. Again and again in *Smith*, *Doe*, *It's a Wonderful Life*, and *State of the Union* (and, in a more trivial way, in *Lost*

Horizon and *Arsenic and Old Lace*), the pictorial/musical/filmic aspects of Capra's films release energies through special cinematic effects of high-chiaroscuro lighting, violent editorial juxtapositions, expressive framing, and sentimental orchestrations that the verbal/social/theatrical sides of the films try to place or contain in terms of dialogue, characterization, and social and verbal interaction. The lurch of the late films from the styles of comedy or family drama to the melodrama of consciousness and what Peter Brooks usefully calls the aesthetics of astonishment is evidence of Capra's own expressive problem at this point in his career. Of course, it is not a defect in the films, any more than the analogous expressive problems (for both the creator and his characters) are in the novels of James.* It is a source of their unstable energy and the reason they have a lasting place in the history of the great American expressive experiment.

---

* To perhaps force a comparison, *Smith* could be profitably juxtaposed with *The Golden Bowl*. If Senator Paine, in his rhetorical capabilities, reminds one of no one so much as Prince Amerigo, with his consummate mastery of verbal and social forms, then Smith's imaginatively imperialistic filibuster finds its ghostly parallel in Maggie Verver's (and Henry James's) radical attempt to substitute the language of imagination and desire in place of those social forms and standards in the second half of the novel. James wants to move us expressively from early Jane Austen to late Balzac, and in doing so, in the second half of his novel moves Maggie and his own style into a realm of melodramatic possibilities that has similarities with what Capra does in the second half of his film.

PART V

The limits of self-representation

The Miracle Woman, 1931
Meet John Doe, 1941
It's a Wonderful Life, 1946

14

Crises of selfhood

Meet John Doe
The Miracle Woman

When Dick Gibson was a little boy he was not Dick Gibson...The private life. That
everybody has. Being loose in the world. On your own. On mine, Dick Gibson's.
– Stanley Elkin, *The Dick Gibson Show*

Meet John Doe goes much farther than *Mr. Smith Goes to Washington* or any of
Capra's previous films in its nightmare imagination of threats to the self and
the potential weakness of the self to withstand them. Amid all of the
compromising and constraining linguistic, bureaucratic, and cultural pressures
of *Mr. Deeds Goes to Town* and *Mr. Smith Goes to Washington*, there was still
room for one or two uncompromised figures, however small and imperiled
they were. The voices of Bennett and Saunders, of Deeds and Smith were
assertions of faith that in even the tightest social and stylistic quarters a space
could be cleared for free expressions of feeling. In *Doe*, however, the free self
has not survived. It has been erased or absorbed into the discursive system. It is
lost, on the run, or in hiding. Capra shows us that Foucault's vision of the
disappearance of man was anticipated by the Hollywood press agent's dream
(or nightmare) of a world in which there are no realities outside of media
events, advertising splashes, public relations blitzes, and image-building
appearances. Personalities have been replaced by "personalities." There is no
self separate from what has been planned, scripted, edited, and orchestrated (in
life or in film).

As I proceed, there will be much more to notice about the connections
Capra urges us to make between the technologies of experience and those of
film, but suffice it to say for now that he deliberately parallels the creation of
the figure of "John Doe," brought into existence by the bureaucracies within
the film, with the creation of the figure of the character played by Gary
Cooper, brought into existence by the narrative systems of the film itself. The
film becomes a meditation on the process by which a postmodern self is
created in life or in film. In implicitly equating the two kinds of figuration,
Capra makes the viewer acutely aware of how much the creation of an identity

347

is the result of an elaborate series of complex social, technological, and bureaucratic arrangements and compromises in both the narrative of a film and the course of a life.★

With the remarkably modern character of Long John Willoughby (or more accurately with his lack of "character," in several senses of the word), Capra in one bound moves beyond the aesthetic world of the previous films, with their assumption that there was, or could be such a thing as a simple, separate ego, existing and functioning apart from, and as an alternative to, the force field of relationships, codes, rules, and institutions around it. There is no self left except the self created, defined, and held in existence by such a force field. There is no self to insert into the system to recenter or humanize it. There is no unsullied identity, no pure state of desire or vision. Individuals (if such a word suffices) are all already inscribed in the system, speaking its discourse, heaped with history, relationships, and obligations.

Capra himself explained the shift of tone and the change in the principles of characterization in *Doe* in terms of his personal desire, in the face of criticisms that *Smith* and *Deeds* were sentimental and soft, to make a relentlessly tough, even "brutal" film.† Others have attributed the undeniable change in Capra's work to factors as different as the darkening situation in war-torn Europe or even to the fact that *Doe* was the first picture of Capra's to be produced not by Columbia but by Warner Brothers, a studio renowned for both the visual and the existential darkness of their stories. Undoubtedly these factors contributed to the quality of the film, but one might also think of the change as the result of Capra's personal experience as a filmmaker. He did not have to be influenced by events in Europe or by crews used to lighting low-budget gangster pictures to be aware of larger cultural forces and more ominous threats to the self than his earlier films had recognized. Over the course of the previous decade, Capra's films had themselves become media events, and the director, as a Hollywood filmmaker on the make, had himself newly become a press agent's idea of a "personality." (Is it accidental that at a comparable point in his career, after he had presumably become a kind of local celebrity and public figure, that Shakespeare wrote *Coriolanus* and some of his other great tragedies exploring comparable threats to the freedom and imaginative autonomy of the self?) In the four or five years immediately preceding the making of *Doe*, Capra had been discovered with a vengeance by the Academy, the Director's Guild, *Time*, *Newsweek*, and other pressure groups and packagers of public opinion in America. He was becoming a celebrity, with all of the mixed blessings that

---

★ This is an awareness that, as I have noted, appears in Capra's work as early as *Lady for a Day*, but in that film the narrative "figuring" of Apple Annie as Mrs. E. Worthington Manville, and Apple Annie's own strictly parallel and equivalent configuring of herself as Mrs. Manville, were entirely more personal and benign, principally because they were within the control and knowledge of the individual enacting the alteration, which is not at all the case in the high-tech, depersonalized narrative and social world imagined by *Doe*.

† *The Name above the Title* (New York: Bantam Books, 1972), pp. 331–5.

that status confers. He was getting a firsthand view of American mass merchandising and participating in the perilous adventure of creating and controlling a public image and self in ways that the young director-immigrant from Palermo would not have been able to imagine.

If no other experience had educated Capra about mass psychology, institutional behavior, and the threats to the free self in a free society, the imbroglio generated by the release of *Smith* would have. The film itself, as I have argued, alternates between deploring the pervasiveness of repressive bureaucratic systems and structures, and a belief in the power of the individual to leap outside such systems, but the response to the film was entirely undivided by such mixed feelings. Capra found out exactly how much power noble passions and patriotic ideals had against the U.S. Senate and the American press in the real world. Joseph P. Kennedy (then ambassador to Great Britain), several Senators, and a host of journalists, claiming that the film depicted the United States and its governmental institutions in an unfavorable light and would be bad for morale both at home and in Europe, launched a campaign that almost succeeded in suppressing it. It was a campaign ironically similar to, and orchestrated at least as well as, that against Smith in the movie, but Capra discovered that the real world left no place for a figure like Smith to fight it.

On the other hand, though *Doe* marks an undeniable darkening in his work, there is no reason to insist on Capra's sudden awakening to the pressures placed on free expression. As I have already argued, his earliest work understood the threats besetting the self. What has changed most markedly (increasingly in the sequence of films: *Deeds, Smith, Doe, It's a Wonderful Life*, and *State of the Union*) is that the threats to expression are progressively less personal and more cultural and institutional. It is increasingly the system that must be confronted and dealt with, not any one individual within it, and, especially for a director whose work has been so founded on a faith in the unquestioned power of the individual, that recognition that the system may be more important and dangerously threatening than any one person within it, is a potentially devastating one. Yet even this awareness obviously antedates *Doe*. In an interview published in *Esquire* in 1936, "A Sick Dog Tells Where It Hurts," Capra pulls no punches in his characterization of the threats not only to the freedom, but to the very existence of the individual posed by what he calls "pseudo-land" – the artificial environment of California society and Hollywood filmdom, where personalites, styles, and star careers are manufac-tured as synthetically and quickly as the pseudo-Spanish villas along Rodeo Drive in which the newly created self is housed. If no other evidence were available, the scene in *It Happened One Night*, in which Peter sees Ellie, back in her mansion, caught up in the phony Long Island social whirl and says to her, "Now you look natural," would serve to prove how completely and con-temptuously Capra had seen through the confusion of nature and culture on which Hollywood stars and star makers thrived.

The shift in the expressive function of montage sequences in Capra's work can summarize this gradual but significant shift in his point of view over the years. Montage sequences serve important expressive functions in Capra's work, and pseudo- or actual documentary montage sequences appear in every one of Capra's films from 1934 to 1948 (with the single exception of *Arsenic and Old Lace*), but with *Smith* and this film, Capra uses them in a new way. In several of his earliest sound films, Capra used montages the way most other directors have customarily employed them – merely as a means of indicating the passage of time in the story or as a shorthand way of rapidly summarizing a series of events. For example, when Kay Arnold attempts suicide in *Ladies of Leisure*, the brief montage of newspaper headlines following her leap succinctly conveys the fact of her attempt and her subsequent rescue.

Early in his work, however, Capra began to use montage sequences in more complex ways, to present a world of events, styles, and social and imaginative organizations of experience distinctly different from, and frequently in competition with, the forms of merely personal experience in the main plot. Thus, even in the simplest case, in the films of the early thirties, when Capra uses newspaper headlines to report Stew Smith's punching Bingy Baker in *Platinum Blonde*, or when he employs a montage of telephone conversations showing the spread of the bank panic in *American Madness*, he is doing more than concisely summarizing temporal or narrative events in simple visual forms. He is registering forces that are assertively beyond the personal control of the central characters and that therefore threaten their performative sovereignty. The montages in these particular films communicate how far Stew Smith and Dixon are from being masters of their lives and fates, notwithstanding the brave face each of them wears. The montages communicate a special category of public pressures or influences that each of them has overlooked and that he is not able to stage-manage as he does his personal affairs. They communicate forces and understandings that are intrinsically at odds with merely personal styles and forms of mastery.

Then Capra goes a step further. By the late thirties – incipiently in *Deeds* and *Lost Horizon*, and definitively and decisively in *Smith* and *Doe* – montages come to represent a self-contained, self-sufficient stylistic, bureaucratic, and technological system with its own self-perpetuating rules and codes entirely separate from, and in fierce competition with, the personal styles and tones of the chief characters in the films. The montages represent ways of organizing experience not only outside the control or understanding of the central characters as previously, but forces that are emphatically and violently at war, a war to the death as it were, with their merely personal forms of expression. In *Lost Horizon*, Robert Conway struggles not only against the scorn and indifference of his brother in Shangri-La but, perhaps even more significantly, against the inability of the newspapers, the radio, and all of the forms of communication that they represent outside of Shangri-La, as they are vividly represented in the montage sequences, to understand or express anything of his imaginative quest. Their very forms of knowing, like the clubby tones of the characters who uncomprehendingly "talk him over" in several scenes, are simply incapable of expressing or including the sorts of imaginative energies he and his quest represent. In summary, the montages in these movies offer not merely an accelerated narration of events but an alternative realm of experience in competition with them, one that would substitute its forms of social and cinematic knowledge for the very different styles of knowing that the other scenes in the film render.

By the time of *Smith*, the montage sequence has become a powerful threat to the actual existence of the protagonist. Jim Taylor is, in effect, only an epiphenomenal adversary to Smith. The problem Smith confronts is less that of the newspaper or political appointees personally controlled by Taylor than of the technologies of information processing represented by the mass media and the codes of political and legislative language in general. The movie is not so much a drama pitting two individuals against each other as a drama of two contrasted and irreconcilable styles or forms of expression: the form of expression within the montage sequences, and the form of expression in the nonmontage sequences.

Doe completes the technologization of experience by, as it were, expanding the individual montage sequences to the dimensions of an entire film. John Doe is forced to learn how to live in a world of montages, a world of pervasive packagings, processings, and merchandizings of identities as if they were no different from any other commodities. Things have grown even darker than they were in *Smith*. Smith could fight to break through, to break out of the muffling technologies of knowledge in place around him, but Doe does not have any identity apart from them. Smith at least had a personal body and a voice, however puny. Doe has neither. His broadcast body and amplified voice are, along with everything else about him, products of the technologies of knowledge, the packaging and processing of reality in the film.

The title is itself darkly ironic. "Meeting John Doe" is not only something that never happens – it is something that can never happen. There is no John Doe to meet. He is, like almost everything else in the movie, a creation of the media. Anne Mitchell, a newspaper columnist, publishes a letter from a character whom she has made up, who threatens to commit suicide on Christmas Eve to protest the state of the world, and signs it "John Doe." Faced with the potential embarrassment of her letter's being exposed as a fraud, her newspaper covertly interviews "John Does" willing to claim that they wrote it. "Long John" Willoughby (Gary Cooper), a down-in-the mouth, out-of-luck, former sandlot baseball pitcher is hired for the impersonation, and a second fiction is brought into existence to validate the first. "Long John" (it is significant in this movie of fictions within fictions without end that even his "real" name is only one more media construction, a nickname given him once by some sportswriter or pitching coach somewhere) is fed, shaved, costumed, and madeup like an actor playing a part (which is what he is), and, as "John Doe," is photographed, interviewed, and scheduled for a carefully orchestrated series of "personal appearances." (This particular phrase was invented within the past twenty years or so, but the technology of "meetings" that are really only calculated publicity blitzes, and of "personal" appearances that are really absolutely impersonal, staged media events, is something that Hollywood perfected decades before the era of Donahue, Carson, and Jack Kennedy.) With his popularity growing, John Doe is asked to make a radio broadcast, given scripted lines to mouth, and a series of John Doe Clubs spring up across the nation.*

One cannot help being reminded of Henry Adams's only half-facetious preface to his *Education*, in which he employs almost the identical metaphors Capra does involving the erasure of personal identity through costuming and scripting to describe the historical era after Jean Jacques Rousseau:

> As educator, Jean Jacques was, in one respect, easily first; he erected a monument of warning against the *Ego*. Since his time, and largely thanks to him, the *Ego* has steadily tended to efface itself, and for purposes of model, to become a manikin on which the toilet of education is to be draped in order to show the fit or misfit of the clothes. The object of study is the garment, not the figure. The tailor adapts the manikin as well as the clothes to his partron's wants.

One notes, however, how the very idiosyncrasy and eccentricity of Adams's tone, metaphors, and logic give the lie to the erasure of self that he is expounding. In a similar way, as I will explain later, throughout *Doe* Capra ultimately makes us feel the difference between the filmmaker who is the playful, quirky, artistic master of technological systems and the poor character who is the victim of them.

As the John Doe Show is being choreographed, coached, costumed, scripted, produced, and taken on the road, one thinks back to all of the earlier figures in Capra's work who anticipate Doe's situation, from Molly Kelly in *That Certain Thing*, Kay Arnold in *Ladies of Leisure*, Florence Fallon in *The Miracle Woman*, Stew Smith in *Platinum Blonde*, Apple Annie in *Lady for a Day*, to Longfellow Deeds and Jefferson Smith, of course. The lesson of these examples might be one of how untrustworthy a concept such as artistic development is – but there is a change as well. The crisis of identity documented was previously – in the films of the period from 1928 to 1933 – felt to be merely a personal or psychological problem, but in the late work it takes on the dimensions of a vast, pervasive, social predicament with cultural, political, and technological ramifications. That anxious enlargement of Capra's analysis

---

* Though I do not use quotation marks around his name to indicate its special status, much of the point of *Meet John Doe* arises from the conflation and confusion of the "Johns" in the film and the doubt about which John is being referred to at any one time. Every one of the dozens of times a character addresses Willoughby as John, neither he nor the viewer is quite sure whether he is being addressed as John Willoughby or John Doe. As the film goes on, John himself grows more and more confused about which John he "really" is: After all, his identity as a baseball pitcher named "Long John" is no less fictional than his identity as a public figure named "John Doe" – but then again, this entire film is an exploration of what "really" might mean in such an inquiry.

is necessary to make possible the achievement of these late films, and particularly of *It's a Wonderful Life*, which takes nothing less than the fundamental structural problems of American culture as its subject.

The difference between the John Doe Clubs and the Boy Ranger clubs of *Smith* illustrates the change from the personal to the institutional. The John Doe Clubs are not instances of unsullied small-town sentiment, offering an alternative form of affiliation to the dehumanizing systems of relationship of the big city or offering the possibility of recentering human affairs on individual ideals and personal emotions and commitments. They are, rather than being an escape from them, an extension of bureaucratic arrangements of experience into the fabric of everyday life. Not only are the John Doe Clubs created by the media, but they are cynically manipulated by D. B. Norton, the self-serving financial backer of the John Doe movement, in order to advance his political career and further his presidential aspirations.

One would be more surprised at the contemporaneousness of the film, and of its anticipation of our own era in which even "naturalness," "freedom," and "purity" are manufactured, packaged, marketed, and sold as special premiums by clothing, food, and cosmetics merchandisers, if Nathaniel Hawthorne had not anticipated Capra's observations by more than a century, writing, in "The New Adam and Eve,"

> We who are born into the world's artificial system can never adequately know how little in our present state and circumstances is natural, and how much is merely the interpolation of the perverted mind and heart of man. Art has become a second and stronger nature; she is a stepmother, whose crafty tenderness has taught us to despise the bountiful and wholesome ministrations of our true parent. It is only through the medium of the imagination that we can lessen those iron fetters, which we call truth and reality, and make ourselves even partially sensible what prisoners we are.

What is most interesting is that Hawthorne recognizes that even the "medium of the imagination" cannot allow us to escape the "fetters." It may "lessen," but not abolish them. It can make us, at best, only "partially sensible" of the extent of our imprisonment. That is the dark, harsh recognition Capra has come to in *Meet John Doe*. There can be no escape from systems, certainly no complete escape. The best we can achieve is only an improved (and always partial) awareness of our condition. As Hawthorne demonstrates in "Young Goodman Brown," "The Wives of the Dead," and *The Scarlet Letter*, even the creative imagination (both that of the author and that of his principal characters) is halfway already absorbed into the "world's [or fiction's] artificial systems," not a clear-cut alternative to such systems.

In *Doe* the self is never (or almost never) offstage. It is never able to lever itself away from the bureaucracies of understanding and experience that always contain it. There is no space left for a merely personal performance. *Deeds* and *Smith* had not gone this far. They both offered the sounds of their central characters' voices as absolute escapes from the repressive technologies of information processsing within them. In *Doe*, however, there can be no escape. There can be no appeal to the power of Doe's personality or his strength of character, since, like one of Stanley Elkin's fictional stand-up comedians to the world, he is only a "personality" and a "character," in the other meaning of the words.

Even the American dream of idealistic, passionate commitment to an abstract principle or belief, the stock-in-trade of Capra's previous films, becomes a commodity to be processed and sold to the public. It is as if Capra has seen through the commercial and ideological success of his own previous films and recognized that they in their own ways were only retellings of fashionable and extremely salable American mythology. (Again Hawthorne has anticipated him in a tale like "My Kinsman, Major Molineux," in which he showed that the American success story had already rigidified into the status of a portable mythology one hundred years earlier.) Capra sees that if his pet myth of personal freedom and independence from the mass market can be converted into a marketable commodity for sale to the mass market (in society or in film production), then none of our personal dreams and fantasies are safe from the threat of social, political, and institutional systematization and exploitation. The fiction of the rugged individualist and the self-made man can be turned into an inherited cultural style like any other. Just as the hippie movement and the putatively individualistic expressions of the sixties were able to be mass merchandised by boutiques and publishing empires under-written by corporate conglomerates, even our most private and personal imaginations of ourselves are in danger of being incorporated into the very networks of mechanical interpretation to which they were intended to be alternatives. Long John Willoughby and Grant Matthews (in *State of the Union*) are free spirits whose very iconoclasm and independence are subverted by being turned into the Horatio Alger clichés of newspaper headlines, media events, and political-campaign rhetoric.

In the course of the film, John has only three extended scenes in which he might be said to step offstage and to express himself in a merely personal, sincere, or human way, but each of these scenes raises more questions about the existence of such possibilities of expression than it answers. The only free expressions for the self possible for him in these scenes are so private, furtive, eccentric, or confused that they hardly count as assertions of freedom at all. We have come an enormous distance from Stew Smith's, Jerry Strong's, or Longfellow Deeds's capacity for imaginative movement within or outside of society, a long way from Bennett's, Saunders's, or Jefferson Smith's melo-dramatic vocal puncturings of polished institutional forms of discourse.

The first scene in which Doe could be said to be expressing himself in a free and unprogrammatic way is the pantomime baseball game he plays in his hotel room to pass the time. It is at least as bizarre as the pantomime tennis game that concludes Antonioni's *Blow Up*, but in many respects Capra's scene is more disturbing and complex than Antonioni's because of the difference between the two filmmakers. Antonioni's films so emphatically privilege private movements of the imagination over social or verbal forms of public expression (to which Antonioni is relatively indifferent) that the imaginary tennis game in his film is meant to represent an affirmation of the creativity of the imagination in and of itself. Capra, though, not satisfied with individual vision detached from significant public expression, has profoundly mixed feelings about John's imaginary baseball game. No one can gainsay its bizarre comic inventiveness, but it is also, for Capra, a waste of spirit. He wants his viewers to feel how pathetically confined and reduced John is, even in this imaginative moment of imaginary glory and stardom. To be capable only of imaginative movements, however inventive they may be, for Capra as not for Antonioni, is to be doomed to creative irrelevance. John's playing baseball here only has the value of childish playing in a world of hardball politics. If his adversary in the film, Norton, wanted to script an activity to keep John out of trouble and out of the way, he could not have done better.

The second, even more marginal free expression on John's part is his proposal of marriage to Anne. The problem, of course, is that it is not a proposal but a near proposal and that it is not to Anne but to her mother. The pathos of the scene, and the proof of John's complete entrapment within the fiction he has himself conspired in perpetuating, is that at one point he reproaches himself for not being as polished and articulate as the figure he impersonates: "He'd know what to say. . . . He'd know how to do it." His one clear opportunity in the film to break free of a script, to speak his own feelings in his own words with his own voice, is the moment he proves unable to speak for himself at all. He can only reproach himself and fumble, silent and embarrassed, in front of Anne's mother. He is much weaker than any of Capra's previous protagonists, both imaginatively and socially. That is why this film starring a baseball player, of all of Capra's work, is ironically the one with the least "play" in it. Eccentricity, wildness, and free play have been systematized out of existence and can erupt into the film only in such private, fugitive, and irrelevant expressions as the pantomime baseball game.

The final scene in which one might argue that John expresses himself freely is the scene two-thirds of the way through the film in which he tells Anne about a dream he had:

> You know I had a crazy dream last night. It was about you . . . It was crazy. I dreamt I was your father. There was something that I was trying to stop you from doing. So I got up out of my room and went through the wall here right straight into your room . . . you know how dreams are, and there you were in bed. You were a little girl about ten, and very pretty too. I shook you. You opened your eyes, hopped out of bed, and ran like the devil in your nightgown. You ran right out and over the tops of roofs and buildings for miles and I was chasing you. And all the time you were running you kept growing bigger and bigger and bigger, and pretty soon you were as big as you are now – grownup. And all the time I kept asking myself what am I chasing you for, and I didn't know. That's a hot one. Anyway you ran in someplace and I ran in after you, and when I got there you were getting married and the nightgown had changed into a beautiful wedding gown. You sure looked

pretty too. And then I knew what I was trying to stop you from doing. Dreams are sure crazy, aren't they? ... But here's the funniest part of all. I was the fellow up there doing the marrying – you know, the justice of the peace. [Anne: I thought you were chasing me.] Well, I was your father then. But the real me, John Doe, that is, Long John Willoughby, I was the fellow with the book, you know what I mean. Well I took you across my knee and I started spanking you. That is, I didn't do it. I mean, I did do it. But it wasn't me. I was your father then.

As the length of his monologue indicates, this is an extremely important moment in the film and one roughly equivalent in its narrative function to the moment of reverie on the balcony shared between Jerry and Kay in *Ladies of Leisure* in which they dream of going to live in Arizona, but the difference between the two moments is striking. Whereas Jerry's dream is one of a saving imaginative clarification and enrichment of life, John's is one of hopelessly muddled and confused identities. Whereas Kay's and Jerry's dream assumed that the dream of freedom could be enacted in the real world of space and time, John's dream takes what could be a real event (his marriage to Anne) and "de-realizes" it into a cryptic, confused, symbolic narrative. The social and emotional confusions of his public life have extended themselves into his dream life to become confusions of his deepest psychological nature. "Crazy" ideas and impulses have changed in meaning since the days of Stew Smith and the buddy-boy pictures. Doe's "crazy" dream is productive only of bewilderment and self-puzzled paralysis of will, not of redeeming creativity or iconoclasm.

With the exception of these three marginal and muddled expressions, John, like Hawthorne's Rev. Dimsdale or most of Edith Wharton's scoptophobic heroines, can never get offstage or away from the tyrannizing scrutiny and pressures of groups of others. Like Hawthorne or Wharton, Capra imagines a situation in which the self-made man or woman stands alone and vulnerable in the face of a crowd of intrusive, imposing, threatening others. Lacking the support of a more stable society or history of fixed or inheritable roles and relationships, the individual is especially vulnerable to the social and bureaucratic pressures deployed around him or her. Freedom leaks away in front of a crowd, when there is nothing more to maintain it but the force of personality. The simple, separate self that Whitman celebrated is dangerously susceptible to the distortions and perversions of demogogic manipulation and imaginative coercion.

No scene more brilliantly summarizes the contradictory pulls on the self or the difficulty of holding onto a free identity in this matrix of powerful pressures and influences than the scene of John's radio debut. He is to read a radio speech he has never seen before and has had no part in writing and yet that he comes half to believe expresses his real feelings by the time he is done with it. As he reads it, he is caught in a four-way tug of war: Connell, the editor of the newspaper sponsoring him, wants to use the speech to vindicate his newspaper's hoax and increase circulation; an editor from a rival newspaper who suspects the hoax has offered John a bribe to repudiate the speech onstage and to confess his actual identity during the broadcast; Anne, who has written the speech by culling thoughts from her dead father's diaries, is interested in it not as a media event at all but as a tribute to her father and as a public expression of his philosophy of life; and the "Colonel" (played by Walter Brennan), John's vagabond sidekick, wants him simply to run out on the whole event to avoid the inevitably accumulating responsibility and commitment.* And John, what does he want? It is impossible to say. Maybe he wants all of these contradictory and mutually exclusive things at once; maybe none of them. He is deformable and characterless. It is appropriate that we should not know where he stands, or if he stands anywhere, for anything.

Although when Capra began the scripting of *Doe* he thought of using Jimmy Stewart in the lead, the choice of Cooper for the part seems inspired, precisely because of the differences between the central characters in this film and *Smith*. Doe is not a character with the sort of breathless, bewildered innocence and emotionality that Smith represents and that Stewart captures in his acting. Doe represents not youth, innocence, or inexperience but a "doughiness," a plasticity, an availability for endless but impermanent deformation. He is a drifter without any particular convictions or beliefs, willing to take the path of least resistance. One could say that he is the perfect modern democrat, willing to obey the majority vote, the perfect unprincipled pragmatist, with no convictions apart from what opinion polls and advisers tell him. If this is where democracy has gotten us, needless to say, Capra is horrified by it.

The pressures on this American "dough-boy" are more powerful, and less personal, than the four lines I traced above. These personal conflicts are the least of his problems. Capra begins this crucial scene of John's transformation into a public personality with another stunning montage sequence by Slavko Vorkapich, documenting the advertising blitz that precedes his first radio speech. The publicity machine begins its job of processing, packaging, and selling John Doe. His photograph is blazoned on posters announcing his speech; ticket sellers and telephone operators answer questions about his appearance; the radio station goes into its high-tech preparations for the broadcast. As I suggested earlier, one of the points of such a montage sequence at this stage in Capra's work is that it creates a realm of experience that is not personal or humane. In this world of advertising copy, media campaigns, and market saturation strategies, John becomes symbolic, larger than life, heroic and mythological in stature, when in fact these are the very qualities lacking in him as a person. The fiction presented by the montage does not enrich or deepen our sense of his distinctive personal identity but utterly displaces it, substitutes its own alternative meanings in lieu of it.

Capra dissolves from Vorkapich's montages to the greenroom where pre-

---

* Capra is playing another name game with this character. He is given neither a name, a past history or occupation, nor any concrete ideological or personal identification. It is as if any more specific name and role than is described by the empty epithet the "Colonel" would commit him to too much, at the very least commit him to a kind of identity he has foresworn and that he wants John also to repudiate.

parations for John's speech are in full swing, only minutes before the speech is to begin, and the technologization of experience transpires before our eyes. It is a press agent's dream of an ideal media event, and a scene that would be comic if Doe were not so painfully trapped, so obviously in over his head, and subject to victimization by the whole grand process. He is mobbed with well-wishers, publicity groupies, ladies' club civic boosters, and a host of others whose careers directly or indirectly depend on his success or failure in the next half hour. Connell, the editor of the newspaper, stages last-minute photographs of Doe, first with a bathing beauty ("I want a Jane Doe ready to go on if this thing fails") and then holding two midgets in his arms ("symbols of little people"), and the scene would be ludicrous if it were not so ridiculously close to the sort of insane, news-fabricating publicity "parties" that Capra and his stars, like everyone else in Hollywood, had been forced to participate in dozens of times to publicize his films.

Anne finally succeeds in clearing the room in order to have a few seconds alone with John before he goes onstage. Far from taking pressure off him, however, she is only arranging a moment to stage a subtler form of emotional torture that supersedes the previous commercial or social coercions. She deliberately chooses this moment to reveal to John that she has composed the speech from quotations from her father's diaries and has fallen in love with it and with the "John Doe" of her creation. One thinks back to *Ladies of Leisure*, where Jerry Strong fell in love with a Kay Arnold who existed as a figure of Hope only in his imagination and on his canvas; to *The Miracle Woman*, where John Carson, a blind man, fell in love with a Florence Fallon of his imagination; or of the Frank Capra, who, by his own account, fell in love with the actress who played both of these roles, a Barbara Stanwyck whose identity was at least in part created in the process of scripting her lines and directing her scenes on the set.

The scene that takes place between John and Anne is one of excruciating emotional and imaginative blackmail. Nothing less than John's self is being held for ransom. Greater love hath no creator for his creation than Anne does in bribing John to lay down his life for her fiction:

ANNE: He turned out to be a swell fellow.
JOHN: Who?
ANNE: John. John Doe ... You won't let me down will you? If you'll just think of yourself as the real John Doe ... Now go out there and pitch.

That final reference to baseball is not only a reminder of how much out of his league John is at this moment but is itself another turn of the screw of torture on Anne's part. She is deliberately pitching her metaphor in a way that plays on his pride in his former identity, to coerce him into assuming this new one. "Just be sincere," "Be yourself," she tells him at another moment, but it is just what it means to "be yourself" that is being explored. What is Willoughby "as himself"? Does it mean anything, is it possible to have a "self" apart from these pressures and influences, these roles and parts? In his *America as a*

Civilization, Max Lerner has gone so far as to describe this problem as one of the central aspects of the American experience. (His metaphor of living up to someone else's "mirror image" of oneself captures some of the complexity of Capra's scene.) "The central problem of American personality is the quest for identity ... It is especially hard to find your identity in a society where the temptation to live in the mirror image that others have of you, where the patterns of group living are still unstable, and your role in the group is not clearly defined."* *Meet John Doe* is Capra's statement of how far from being mere philosophical or psychological rhetoric such questions of selfhood are in this destabilized world of unmoored identities and relationships. In a world like this one, to what extent can we claim to have a self, any self, other than the one we play under the influence of those around us? Where would that self be? Who would be left to play it?

The pressures of time will not allow John or Anne such reflections. In order to have the leisure to put such questions even momentarily to oneself or to others, one would have to be a gentleman or lady of leisure, to have the luxury of abstracting oneself from the world and retreating into Jerry Strong's studio and balcony or Yen's summer palace. To have such meditative inclinations (which John demonstrably lacks) would in and of itself be to bring into existence some marginal imaginative leverage over this situation. It would permit one to momentarily remove oneself from the situation in which one is trapped, to reflect on it and gain some distance from it, but such an opportunity of meditative movement or social withdrawal is unavailable in Doe's world. Even before Anne has finished pressuring him, they are interrupted by the stage manager, and Doe (or is it Willoughby? – but there is no possibility of keeping score from this point on; identities are already too compromised and confused for that) is presented onstage where a live audience and an orchestra await him in the studio.

He is plunged from the emotional pressures and confusions of the greenroom into a sea of technological arrangements. The contrast with *Smith* is again instructive. The viewer always had a double view of Jefferson Smith, a sense of him both as a distinct personal speaker and as the subject of the discursive systems within which he was inscribed. His success could be described as being precisely his ability to hold onto his individuality against the systematizing semiotic pressures. Capra visually cut from one way of viewing Smith to another, generally from close-ups and medium shots in the Senate that reminded us his eccentric individuality, to long-shots and montage sequences that reminded us of how the technologies of knowledge were at work to make him over into something else: the subject of "media campaign," a signifier in a political sign system, or whatever. Capra acoustically cut from direct-speech sound tracks featuring Smith's voice to canned and processed tracks featuring impersonal, institutional, unsynchronized sounds of masses of people: marching bands, political rallies, and machine and crowd noises. The

---

* Max Lerner, *America as a Civilization* (New York: Simon & Schuster, 1957), p. 695.

question of the film was which way of seeing and hearing, which kind of sound and presence, which political and cinematic way of knowing, would carry the day, and it was a live question, with two different but equally available answers during the film. That double vision has collapsed in *Doe*. John is embedded in layer after layer of technology, wrapping anything we might hypothetically denote to be the "individual, personal self" in packaging, to the point that there is no cinematic access to anything but the various layers of acoustic and visual processing.

I am using the metaphor of John's being packaged, wrapped, or processed, but strictly speaking, this metaphor is more appropriate to describe *Smith* than *Doe*, since in *Smith* one felt the presence of a personal self wrestling with or resisting the packaging encroaching on it and trying to muffle its voice, whereas in *Doe* it becomes bizarrely possible that there may be *no* John, *no* self at all underneath to break free. Capra's shots of Stewart standing tall and alone in the Senate made the individual self palpable to a viewer, but in the darker, more modern world of this movie the stage-managing, the packaging is all there is to see and hear. As he walks onstage to give his radio address, the orchestra plays a fanfare as an overture to the speech; an announcer introduces him; a stage manager positions him in relationship to the microphone and the studio audience; a prompter signals the audience when to applaud and when to hush; and the prepared text dictates what to say. Who is speaking here? Is anybody speaking? In a strange anticipation of the work of Foucault, it becomes a fallacy to assume, in the absence of concrete evidence to the contrary, that there is any self underneath the bureaucratic, technological, and cinematic presentation. In a conventional sense of the word, Cooper does no acting in this scene, or most of the other major scenes in the film (unlike Stewart in *Smith*). Rather, what he does might be called nonacting. He remains for the most part impassive, blank, and silent, except when he is reading a text someone else wrote. In this inversion of Emersonian self-reliance, there is no self to be self-reliant. The medium is the message. There is no product in the package; or rather, the product is the package. There is nobody at the center of this film, and Cooper's blank passivity is the perfect representation of it.

Capra's vision is even more bleakly modern than Orson Welles's contemporaneous *Citizen Kane*, which, with typical Wellesian (or Falstaffian) gusto and egocentricity, begins with a similar point of view but refuses to take the final, daring step and write off, or write out of the film, its own central, star presence, as Capra does here. That is why there are no star turns and no melodramatic gasps or gestures here. There is no one in the film capable of such rhetorical presence, excessive or hysterical or otherwise. The self is hidden, secret, and inscrutable, or gone altogether. Rather than revealing the self in all of its eccentricity and untamableness, public performance is now a way of hiding the self or even perhaps of concealing its total absence. The nightmare recognition is that perhaps these presentations and representations are doing the opposite of burying some hypothetical real self; perhaps they are expressing it all too perfectly – "expressing" it in the root sense of the word.

The packaging of the self and the voice in layers of bureaucracy parallels the visual layering of Capra's compositions.

They are broadcasting it outward (in more than a technological sense), frictionlessly, efficiently distributing it by cutting it into manageable, packageable pieces. (One has to look to the late work of John Cassavetes – *Woman under the Influence, Killing of a Chinese Bookie, Opening Night,* and *Gloria* – for a comparably complex exploration of the career of the postmodern personality.)

The "cutting" of Doe into pieces is more than a metaphor. *Doe* is Capra's most terrifyingly overcut film. As will happen in *State of the Union* also, Capra's photography and editing not only do not give us any way of knowing the central character that is an alternative to the packaging of his figure by the media within the film, but it actually extends that technology of arranging and processing experience into the editorial structure of the film itself. One has to lump Capra and his cinematic practices in with Norton and his bureaucratic practices in the film. In Capra's cinematic version of American cubism (extending the trajectory upon which Stuart Davis and Willem De Kooning launched themselves, that Kenneth Anger continued cinematically in *Scorpio Rising,* and that Sam Shepard and Stanley Elkin have explored in recent drama and fiction, respectively) the figure is fractured and proliferated outward into a series of dissociated images to the point that the self, in any unitary sense, disappears. Individuals have only a referred existence. They become conduits for cultural styles and energies beyond their power to organize or control. They are tuning circuits vibrating to the multiple frequencies impinging on them. The self is "expressed" away from any individual's personality or language. In an absolute reversal of the dramatic impulse of *Smith*, where the personal body and voice was reinserted into a system lacking them, the central character here is distributed outward, away from any coherent bodily or vocal presence into a series of fragmented poses, postures, stances, and "expressions" of itself.

Capra's film "works over" and processes John (acoustically, editorially, and photographically) in a way exactly analogous to the way the people and American institutions around him within the film technologically work over and process him. The movie is so overcut that, in the scene I have been discussing, for every shot of Doe there are at least two shots of others impinging on his performance, pressuring him, interpreting and understanding him. For the initial two or three minutes of Doe's appearance in the radio studio and onstage, in this era before television commercials, Capra cuts at the rate of a television commercial – once every three, four, or five seconds, manically slicing through and around the spaces surrounding Doe, onstage in the studio, the spaces reached by the broadcast, and across the time of the broadcast (condensing twenty minutes or so of speaking into three or four minutes of film time).

Not the least harrowing aspect of this cutting is that it represents no particular personal observer or group of observers in the film itself. The basis of Hollywood editing – the point-of-view editing convention that intercuts the respective points of view of one, two, or three ideal observers of the scene (who are also usually participants within it) – is stunningly abrogated. The different takes or cuts of John's radio speech do not cohere into one ideally complete personal view of it; rather, the opposite is true. Capra's cutting, like the technological and bureaucratic broadcasting and disseminating of John's image and voice within the film, tears him in pieces, broadcasts him outward in a series of mutually contradictory or irreconcilably different views. The reality presented by the film is impersonal, technological, and fundamentally inhumane. It is not a vision emanating from or even imaginatively unifiable by a personal center of consciousness. It coheres in the consciousness of a viewer of the film as little as it does in John's own consciousness. "John" cannot be brought into a personal, humane, living center of focus at the middle of all of these inhumanely mechanical and mutually inconsistent proliferations.

Just as in the best work of De Kooning, Davis, Shepard, or Elkin, there is at times a Whitmanesque glee about this process of broadcasting the self outward. It confers on the individual a superhuman multiplicity and mobility that is exciting and potentially creative. *Doe* is a celebration of the power of film itself to "broadcast" and multiply personality and presence by cutting and suturing it at will. Capra, however – like De Kooning and Elkin, but unlike Whitman – also has Edgar Allan Poe's view of the process: that what results from endless imaginative proliferations can be a series of ghosts or vampires. The postmodern self can, in the energy of its imagination, disperse itself out of existence. There is a fluidity and ethereality to Doe's existence, as his processed voice and presence are distributed outward away from his body, in which Capra almost rejoices, but there is also a frightening thinness of presence and a loss of identity that Capra dreads and from which he ultimately recoils. Doe's voice is distributed out away from his body, beyond his ability to maintain a personal presence anywhere or to control or even to understand the interpretations of his proliferated public images. Capra turns the star system on its head with his portrait of a reluctant, self-effacing, and self-dispersed star. In Capra's orgy of editing, Cooper represents less a star presence to be featured by the film (as Stewart was in *Smith*) than a virtual image, mysteriously silent and invisible, occupying the point of imaginative convergence of these rival interests. There is no one there, only a series of images or masks. Doe is an absence at the center of the events in which he nominally stars.

The change from the previous work should be obvious. In the earlier films exuberances and excesses of performance – from the clowning around of buddy-boys Holt and Graves to the shenanigans in the park of Arthur and Stewart – were expressions of surpluses of energy on the part of a character that interrupted or disrupted more parsimonious narrative exposition. Here, however, Doe is not originating these energetic acts of cutting and suturing, any more than he is originating the energetic merchandising of his identity. They are inflicted upon him (if there is a "him" for them to be inflicted upon); he passively submits himself to them. Capra has gone back on his own faith in the indisputable power and energy of the performer, an energy and power, however institutionally marginal, that even Smith had.

That should suggest why, between the attitudes of Whitman and Poe concerning self-distribution, it is Poe who is the presiding spirit of this film. Capra's vision is a nightmare inversion of his previous belief in the individual's ability to improvise an identity and to revise and adjust it as necessary in response to the pressure of the forces around him or her. The improvisation of an identity under pressure could be said to be the subject of all of Capra's films, but nowhere in film, outside of the work of Billy Wilder – most brilliantly in *Sunset Boulevard, One, Two, Three, The Fortune Cookie,* and *Fedora* – and the work by Cassavetes that I have mentioned have the dangers of the process's getting out of control and of the self's being left lost and alone in the house of mirrors of its own proliferated images been more frighteningly depicted. Where one looks for a presence, there is only an absence. Where one listens for a star, one hears only the resonant feedback of the star-making machinery of microphones, amplifiers, and speakers. Where one searches for a person, one finds a style, a technology, a person-creating linguistic, political, or filmic machine.*

---

* It is not accidental that Poe was also obsessed with the technologies of artistic expression. As his essays indicate, he was a structuralist before the fact and wrestled in all of his work with the relationship between technologies (in his case, discursive, stylistic, and narrative, rather than scientific, political, or bureaucratic) and persons, and, even more disturbingly, with the ways technologies can substitute for persons, which he often makes the subject of his own writing and criticism. One also finds this structuralist awareness and anxiety in James's Prefaces.

Not that John and Anne realize the complexity of their situations. Both central characters believe that *they*, and not Capra, Norton, or the technologies they command, are in control of their identities. Both would in fact define themselves preeminently as controllers: Doe is, in his own view, taking the newspapers for a ride, making a fast buck, playing out a charade; Anne is, initially, cynically and profitably milking her editor and D. B. Norton and, subsequently, finding a way to promote her father's philosophy of life. The controllers are not in control, though. They are not the masterful, poised, independent performers they fancy themselves to be but are actually puppets in Norton's scheme to advance his own political career. Furthermore, their emotions cannot be controlled. As even they realize, they increasingly become emotionally involved with each other and with others around them in ways that jeopardize their autonomy and freedom.

Doe is, in many respects, a remake of a film Capra had released nine years earlier, *The Miracle Woman*, with a man replacing a woman in the lead, but the differences between the two films are more interesting than the similarities, for they suggest the quite important changes in Capra's work in the intervening years. (The fact that Barbara Stanwyck plays a starring role in both films makes both the similarities and the differences more pointed.) Like Anne Mitchell, Florence Fallon of *The Miracle Woman* has her whole world shattered in the first scene of the film. She is the daughter of a small-town preacher who has given his life to the service of his congregation. His parishioners, however, rather than expressing their gratitude to him, have turned against him and dismissed him. At the point at which the film begins, he has just had a heart attack and died in his daughter's arms before giving his parting sermon to the congregation.★ She is left with nothing – no future, no happy memories of her father's accomplishments, and hardly anything at all to believe in, having had even her faith in the church and in the meaningfulness of her father's vocation undermined. Like both Anne and Willoughby in the later film, Florence, in her revulsion from all of the values of her past that she has seen suddenly shattered, embarks on a career of amoral opportunism and improvisation. With the backing of a cynical manager named Hornsby, she becomes a "John Doe" of the faith-healing business. Capra recognizes, as in *Doe*, that in a world in which religious, moral, and personal values have been shattered, the one value system ready to step into the breach is sheer Yankee opportunism and pluck.

With Hornsby's help, Florence builds a religious empire and acquires an enormous radio following by means of sham and fakery. Again as in *Doe*, Capra figures his central character's success in terms of metaphors of Hollywood stardom and Hollywood studio-publicity extravaganzas. Sister Florence's magnificent Temple of Faith looks exactly like one of those enormous sets on which the big production numbers in thirties musicals were

---

★ By this point in a study of Capra's work I should not have to emphasize the typicality of such an opening with an institutional rupture figured in the death of a male authority figure, or its imaginative importance to Capra.

staged and into which reality was never allowed to intrude. It is a space created exclusively to generate and sustain glittering, gaudy, crowd-pleasing Hollywood effects, complete with sequined costumes for the star (Florence), an elaborate light show, live orchestral accompaniment, death-defying stunts, and miraculous healings – all of which, needless to say, are totally scripted and rehearsed in advance. Capra gives us a view of life that is a cross between a soundstage and a circus, but then again a Columbia soundstage in many respects must have resembled a three-ring circus. (*Rain or Shine*, made the previous year, offered the same metaphor.)

The central drama of *The Miracle Woman* is generated when a blind man, John Carson, is completely taken in by her schemes and falls in love with Florence, and she becomes fond of him also, against her better judgment. Unable to confess the truth to him for fear of hurting and disillusioning him, in some part of her being she actually aspires to be able to live up to his glorious imagination of her. Finding herself in a hopelessly false position and confused about who she really is and what she believes, she is torn by conflicting emotions. (She is further torn because she feels a continuing allegiance to her manager, Hornsby, as another man in her life.) In brief, Florence, an imposter bewildered and troubled by her own impersonations, is very close to being in Doe's situation.

In all these layers of role playing it is impossible for her or for an audience to decide whether Florence really is the author of the deceits she conspires in producing or whether she is merely an unwitting victim of Hornsby's machinations. Capra himself pointed this out in his autobiography: "[Hornsby] cons Fallon into it. *He* gets wealthy. She becomes his flamboyant stooge. Did she or did she not believe those 'inspiring' sermons delivered in diaphanous robes, with live lions at her side? I didn't know, Stanwyck didn't know, and neither did the audience."* Capra, and various critics, have viewed this aspect of the film as a flaw, but far from being a flaw it is one of the most interesting aspects of the film, and one of the things that makes it most similar to *Doe*. Both films dramatize the predicaments of inadvertent stars, heroes strangely incapable of heroism, ventriloquism acts in which it is impossible to say definitely who is the master and who is the dummy. (*The Miracle Woman* actually makes a ventriloquist with a dummy one of the principal characters in the film, to literalize the metaphor of ventriloquism that is implicit in Florence's – and later Doe's – dramatic situaton.) Florence takes us partway to the universe John Doe will inhabit. She is so weak, vulnerable, and socially marginal that it is impossible to say whether she is in control of her actions and intentions or is being controlled. She takes us beyond the world of James and into that of Wharton or Dreiser where *Doe* will be set.

To change the metaphor, in the course of *The Miracle Woman* Florence becomes such a chameleon of self-protective social coloration, such a quick-change artist, that it is all but impossible to say whether there is any real

* *The Name above the Title*, p. 148.

Florence behind and separate from all of the disguises, tones, and roles she so consummately plays in the course of the film. Capra's creative characters always exhibit this sort of versatility, but *The Miracle Woman* implicitly asks whether such fluidity of selfhood is also the destruction of selfhood. We are in the same house of mirrors, with the self bewildered by its own powers of self-distributing performance, in which *Doe* situates its hero, and the result is so frightening and disorienting that it is not at all surprising that Capra avoided returning to it for nine years, and eleven intervening films.

Notwithstanding all of the nightmarish similarities between the two films, *The Miracle Woman* runs away from its own potential insights as *Doe* does not. Furthermore, it is neither able to put Florence deeply enough into a troubling predicament nor to reconcile itself to her remaining in it. In the first place, Florence is never as truly out of control as John is. If not the author, she is very much the star of her own scenes. She is a dazzling theatrical performer, a mistress of special effects, whereas, in contrast he is a nonperformer and nonstar who is overwhelmed by the roles he finds himself playing. Moreover, in order to guarantee Florence's ultimate safety in the film Capra offers an absolute escape hatch out of all of the imaginative bewilderments documented within it. He does the same thing he does in almost all of his early work, stylistically and thematically. He holds out the ultimate possibility of a visionary transcendence of all of the social and psychological problems the film otherwise so conscientiously documents. So, notwithstanding their deep similarities, *The Miracle Woman* and *Meet John Doe* finally offer entirely different filmic experiences that point to the profound change in Capra's angle of vision in the intervening nine years, for whatever complex personal or social reasons.

To put it another way, unlike *Doe*, but like so many of the other early films, *The Miracle Woman* cordons off a special, sacrosanct, private imaginative realm exempted from many of the confusions of the world in which Florence lives. As in almost all of Capra's early films, this private realm is figured in a series of key-lighted romantic scenes enacted between a man and a woman. Florence and John have a number of romantic rendezvous in his apartment. In a series of scenes in which the two of them sit together on a sofa in front of the fireplace, with only the fire for light, and with Florence wearing a different gorgeously sequined evening gown each time (the pretext is that she goes there immediately following her stage shows), Joseph Walker creates the most resplendently nimbused compositions in all of his work. John and Florence pulse and glow with light in a cinematic version of American luminism that moves us and them into a world of romantic sublimity separate from the confusion of the rest of their lives. Despite all of the deceits and hypocrisies of Florence's life, this silent light speaks a pure language of the heart that is meant to put the viewer and these two characters in touch with an absolute and unfalsifiable reality of honest emotion and romance. It is the same technique of switching his films into states of intense visuality in order to displace the social and verbal problems raised in them that Capra performs at one point or another in almost all of his early films, most notably, of the films I have discussed, in this film, *Forbidden*, *Bitter Tea*, and *It Happened One Night*. Florence and John, and Capra the filmmaker, escape from their social and institutional burdens by retreating into the pictorial gorgeousness of pure, silent vision. Voices may lie, roles and costumes may deceive, and social arrangements may distort reality, but the purity of romantic lighting provides an imaginative exemption from these bewilderments.

If there were any doubt about the luminist escape clause that Capra incorporates into the film as a special way out for his trapped characters, *The Miracle Woman* concludes with a nearly blinding blaze of light, through which Florence and John walk to escape from the traps and problems of the preceding scenes. There has been an accident, and Florence's temple has caught on fire. She is trapped in it as it burns down, but John enters amid the flames to carry her to safety and away from the corruptions of her past. It is the hokiest of happily-ever-after film endings, but what is most interesting about it is the way Capra explicitly uses light suddenly to resolve John's and Florence's predicament.

The dazzling light effects in all of these scenes are the outward and visible representation of the possibility of an inward and spiritual state of vision or purity. The scene in which the temple burns is not the final scene in the film. It is followed by a very brief epilogue, only a minute or two long, which jumps ahead a number of months or weeks in Florence and John's relationship. This scene, significantly, has no special lighting effects at all, no flames or fires. In this epilogue we see that Florence has given up her sequined evening costumes and returned to the monastic, black-garbed austerity of dress with which she began the film, and also that Capra has abandoned the glamorous photographic style that he had used for her earlier. The lighting on her has become as flat and dull as it was in the initial scene in the church when she announced her father's death. As in the final scenes of *Forbidden*, *Ladies of Leisure*, or *Bitter Tea*, external light effects are finally unnecessary, precisely because the spiritual light burns so brightly within the character. Florence has joined the Salvation Army and holds a telegram from John announcing that a new operation may restore his sight. It is all patently symbolic and deliberately carries us into a realm of imaginative meanings far removed from the pressing, bewildering, busyness of the world of show-biz hucksterism in which Florence had been a collaborator earlier.

This final scene is highly revealing, not only because (if there were any lingering doubt) it tells us how to interpret those flames and lighting effects used earlier but also because it, more generally, identifies Capra's cinematic enterprise in his early work as a deliberately derealizing or spiritualizing one. This epilogue, like the endings of almost all of the films from *Ladies of Leisure* to *Bitter Tea* (and of many of the films after that, most notably *It Happened One Night*) suddenly abandons social interaction, dialogue, and dramatic presentation altogether to move the viewer and the central character into a predominantly static, symbolic, meditative, or imaginative relationship to events. In the last shot, Florence stands silent and still, looking at the telegram, reflecting on all that she has lived through and all the imaginative possibilities that suddenly open before her, and the viewer is swept along by her silence and emotion at this moment into a comparable state of meditative reverie.

As I have pointed out previously and noticed in Capra's work as early as *The Way of the Strong*, at crucial scenes within the films as well as at their ends, Capra repeatedly transforms his characters and their situations in this way, out of the realm of social significance and into a realm of spiritual significance. Plot is arrested and dialogue stops; speech yields to silence; action or eventfulness is replaced by static, symbolic gesture (as in the purgatorial movement of John and Florence through the fire at the temple) or meditative stillness (as in Florence's final reading of the telegram in the final shot). In short, in these early films Capra habitually attempts to move his story, his characters, and his viewers from a physical relationship to the world to a metaphysical one. He moves his scenes from matters of sight to considerations of insight. He switches from action to meditation. The possibility of that meditative shift is what saves John and Florence at the end of *The Miracle Woman* and redeems the time, just as it is what redeems almost all of the central characters in Capra's early work.

Around the social and psychological confusions of *The Miracle Woman*, Capra draws a boundary and marks off a special meditative space shared by John and Florence, exempt from all those confusions and transcending them. After moving back and forth across it, into and out of the romantic scenes in the film, John and Florence in the end step across the boundary entirely, to run away from the psychological, theatrical, and social mess of the entire preceding film. A purely symbolic or visionary resolution offers itself in place of an unobtainable social or practical one, as happens so often in American art.

That is the difference from *Doe*. There can be no meditative shift out of the turmoil of the world for John or Capra's audience. The closest Capra comes to it is in the symbolmongering of the ending (in which, similar to what happens at the end of *Smith*, Doe is compared to Christ) and in the use of the sounds of Beethoven's "Ode to Joy" and ringing bells on the sound track (which, as happens so frequently in his work, indicates his inability to resolve his film in a more practical or social way). Unlike *The Miracle Woman*, however, visionary sublimity, silence, and meditative inwardness offer no avenues of escape in the course of the film from the repressive forces surrounding Doe, just as his very troubled romantic involvement with Anne offers no prospect of rising above his situation. To be silent in *Doe*, as John is during much of the film, is only to make oneself all the more available for manipulation by Norton. John's romantic infatuation with Anne becomes not only not a mode of transcendence but a further form of psychological and social enslavement. There is no free space exempt from Norton's control, and no possibility of imagining oneself beyond it. (One saw the beginnings of this in the change in Capra's attitude toward silence, dreaming, and looking out of windows in *Deeds* and *Smith*, in which social withdrawals and escapes into vision were similarly curtailed or criticized in his work.)

In this nightmare of a movie, perhaps there is, as I have suggested, no visionary dreamer to be sprung free from the forces around him or her, no pastoral self that is being repressed. The real horror of the film is thus not a vision of the repression, but of blankness and vacancy. John Doe all too completely expresses everything Willoughby stands for; there is no hidden, saving remnant. There is nothing under all of the speeches he reads, no repressed vision, no secret self struggling to make itself heard underneath all the scripted words. He is a cipher, a drifter willing to serve the highest bidder, to read anything that is given to him, and to play any part that is scripted for him, as long as it involves no profound emotional or social commitments. This film, is not, as *Deeds* and *Smith* were, a cri de coeur about the difficulty of translating the language of the heart into the language and social institutions of humanity, but a vision of an empty heart of darkness at the center of things. It is not about the repression of passionate imaginations by the forms of everyday life but a nightmare about a world in which there are perhaps no saving dreams and reveries possible, in which there is nothing but deals and packages.

The visionary American artist has always wrestled with this nightmare inversion of his or her dreams. Writers as different as Emerson, Melville, Twain, James, and Dreiser have at different points in their careers come close to arguing that the dream of the dream is a delusion, and that the world of surfaces is the only world. There is, however, a certain currently fashionable form of literary modernism that would actually extol the absence of depths in John; it would praise his characterlessness and his capacity to keep skating on the thin ice of the surface of reality as being desirable. In a recent review of Woody Allen's *Zelig*, Jay Cantor begins with Keats's remark about the characterlessness of the poet and approvingly uses it to celebrate modern characterlessness in life and in Allen's eponymous film figure. Cantor begins by quoting the familiar formula from Keats's letter to Richard Woodhouse and then proceeds to elevate it to a philosophy of life:

"As to the poetical Character itself . . . it is not itself – it has no self – it is everything and nothing – It has no character – it enjoys light and shade; it lives in gusto, be it foul or fair, high or low, rich or poor, mean or elevated – It has as much delight in conceiving an Iago as an Imogen. What shocks the virtuous philosopher delights the chameleon poet. A Poet is the most unpoetical of any thing in existence; because he has no identity – he is continually in for – and filling some other Body" . . . Nowdays we're all outsiders, all poets, and the unhappy consciousness of a sublime emptiness is our common property. The theory being this: each day capitalism reminds us that we're interchangeable integers, so much abstract labor power. Each night it reweaves the sense of personality that it has unwoven during the day, reversing Penelope's labors. We're offered new personalities for old, Calvin Klein jeans, a different style of life. Money is the universal solvent of personality, but it also allows us to dye ourselves any color at all – if we have the wherewithal. Our identities are so much cut and paste, picking up bits and pieces as we like . . . Pleasure [in Allen's films] isn't in the impossible dream of being a hero, having a single in-divisible voice, the gesture that reveals a soul. Pleasure is in the quick change.

> The most one is is an emptiness, a space between. There is a giddy sense of
> liberation to this, the pleasures of the modern – marrying a different woman
> every night because every night one is a different man. That is the joy of it.*

This is the perennially fashionable, if by now fairly tattered and shopworn,
line of goods that could be picked up at a discount in the bargain basement of
post-Romantic decadence any time in the last one hundred years. There is no
point in blaming Keats for the distortions and insincerities of his interpreters,
even if the mischief to both art and life done by this epicurean concept of
artistic "gusto" and "delight" and the philosophy of amoral connoisseurship,
voyeuristic detachment and social irresponsibility that has grown up around
Keats's concept of poetic chameleonism has been incalculable. To trace the
damage it has done (little of which is Keats's fault) would take my argument
too far afield. One would have to formulate an analysis that showed where
an entire culture and group of late-Victorian writers went wrong – where
Tennyson, Arnold, Pater, Wilde, Kipling, Katherine Mansfield, Virginia
Woolf, and John Fowles, to name only the most egregious examples, each
went astray.[†] Suffice it to say that there is no concept more alien to Capra's
work than this elevation of chameleonism, aesthetic detachment, and quick-
change artistry into a philosophy of life. What Barthes, Derrida, apparently
Cantor, and all self-proclaimed postmodernists revel in – the fluidity of the self
and what Emerson called the "most slippery sliding surfaces" of experience,
Capra has an Emersonian distrust of and feels to be a betrayal of the
fundamental responsibilities and continuities of our emotional and imaginative
involvements.

Endlessly succeeding in defying the gravity of one's social and psychological predicament, for Capra, only defines a character as a moral lightweight. The figure in *Doe* who comes closest to representing a postmodernist
aesthetic of emotional escapism and endless social mobility is, significantly,
the Colonel, whose geographical, ethical, and social vagabondage is devas-
tatingly criticized in the film. A world full of figures like the Colonel
would leave Norton undisturbed to continue his machinations. A world of
Colonels would be one in which there were no caring neighbors like those
shown at several points in the film, no families, no kindness or love at all,
except the self-love of absolute freedom and independence. A filmmaker as
passionately committed to the metaphysics and aesthetics of family relations (of
all others who come to mind, only John Cassavetes can even be compared to
Capra in this respect) can never see salvation in such self-centered irresponsibility and vagabondage. Life requires ethical and social intricacies of involve-

---

* Jay Cantor, "Review of Woody Allen's *Zelig*," *Boston Review* (December 1983), 7–8.
† See my introduction to Rudyard Kipling's *Kim* (New York: New American Library, 1984) for
  an analysis of this literary-critical phenomenon as it manifests itself in Kipling's writing and in
  his relationship to Emerson, or see my discussion of John Cassavetes's *Gloria*, in *American
  Dreaming: The Films of John Cassavetes and the American Experience* (Berkeley: University of
  California Press, 1985), for a brief analysis of a similar tendency in American art.

ment for Capra, just the sorts of things that Cantor's blithe chameleonism (and Allen's Zelig) avoids.

The three concluding scenes in *Doe* reverse everything I have indicated about the nature of what comes before them. Capra attempts to convert John – this absence, this hollow man – into a passional, imaginative, and epistemological center for his film. He in effect attempts to make him over into a Jefferson Smith in the three final scenes: his passionate peroration to Norton in which he declares that he refuses to allow himself to be used in his political movement; his attempt to address the convention of John Doe Clubs and explain the truth to them; and his ascent to the rooftop to kill himself, in the final scene of the film. However, John and Capra both equally fail. The speech at Norton's house is merely embarrassing and overwrought; his attempt to tell the truth to the convention is frustrated; and his final concluding gesture (in all of the five endings to the film that Capra prepared – whether Doe commits suicide, as he did in one ending, or, as in the ending of the film Capra finally decided on, he does not) is meaningless, wasted, and trivial. It is testimony to the tough-mindedness of Capra's approach that having begun filming without having decided upon any particular ending, he completely fails to do what he only barely and marginally succeeded in doing in the much less hostile and more humane worlds of *Deeds* and *Smith*. He simply cannot come up with a convincing biological or imaginative center for a world as relentlessly threatening to the individual imagination as this one is, a world in which a network of manipulative impersonal relationships and functions has completely replaced individual actors and actions.

In *The Name above the Title* Capra described his problems with the ending of the film in other terms: "Riskin and I had written ourselves into a corner. We had shown the rise of two powerful, opposing movements – one good, one evil. They clashed head on – and *destroyed each other*! St. George fought with the dragon, slew it, and was slain" (pp. 338–9). What is wrong with this formulation is revealed by Capra's switch midway through this statement from talking about the clash of "two powerful, opposing movements" to talking about the clash of "St. George and the dragon." Capra's very problem at the end of *Meet John Doe* is that he leaves no place for a St. George, for an individual or individual action, in this world of systems and arrangements. *Whatever* Doe does in the final scene, he is playing a part written for him by someone else – by the followers of the John Doe movement, by Norton, by Anne. He is not escaping the movement and becoming an individual.*

This world is one of such pervasive systems of control and interpretation that there is simply no way for John to break free into an assertion of mere

---

* Note that even for him to commit suicide at the end – *especially* to commit suicide (as he did in one of the test prints of the film) – is only to continue to play the part of a semiotic function in someone else's signifying system. He would, in that act, in fact, have been more than ever a merely symbolic entity, more the doughy, compliant dummy acting out the final act in the fiction generated by the text of the John Doe letter that Anne wrote at the very beginning of the film.

individuality in the final movement of the film, no matter what he intends or does. Personal intention counts for little or nothing in this world (perhaps as little as it counts for in a modern bureaucracy). The machine inscribes individuals within its own alternative "intentional" structure, independent of their will or wishes. It gives their acts meanings and values beyond their personal knowledge or control.* How radically and profoundly at odds this is with the traditional Hollywood film, grounded in its sentimental post-Romantic exaltation of the autonomous ego, needs no comment.

Capra's most powerful image of the pervasiveness of the systems of control and understanding around John is contained in the scene in which John attempts to tell the truth, to speak personally and as a mere individual to the John Doe Convention (though the utter impossibility and meaninglessness of merely personal and individual speech in this situation – in a convention, on a stage, in front of a crowd of thousands of people – is the point of the scene). Having just had Norton's effort to use the John Doe movement for his own political purposes revealed to him (and the passivity of his role in the discovery is relevant – he does not seek out the truth but simply has it disclosed to him by Connell), he leaves Norton's mansion and rushes to the field where thousands of his followers have assembled. His intention is to talk to them man-to-man, to tell them the truth candidly and personally, but Capra's narrative, photography, and editing tell us how radically displaced the individual presence or personal voice is in this institutional universe. One cannot talk to a convention man-to-man; one cannot talk to thousands of people personally and intimately. Capra's layered visual field reminds us one final time of all of the layers of technological and bureaucratic packaging that contain and control discourse in this world, from the radio announcers looking down on the stage from their sound booths above the crowd to the public-address system that strips the intimacy from the tones of one's voice. (The irony of this taking place in the first baseball field we have seen John actually present in in the film needs no underlining; but a baseball player, especially, should realize that self-expression on the diamond is possible only in terms of obedience to impersonal rules and regulations.) Capra's layered sound track and contrapuntal editing demonstrate that the technologies of knowledge and understanding are as completely in place in the field as they were during his speech in the radio studio earlier. The technology that allows Doe's voice potentially to reach thousands of individuals by the same virtue necessarily robs him of a personal

---

* This is, needless to say, what is beside the point in contemporary analyses of politicians', bureaucrats', or industrialists' "intentions." As Capra's film shows us, personal intentions have been replaced by structural and institutional ones in our world, but the High Romantic dream is slow to die, and we still futilely search for personal speakers where only codes of discourse are to be discovered. The semiotic universe of *Doe* absorbs and erases even the well-meaning intentions of the relatively innocent and unmalicious characters who enter into it. John does not have evil or especially venal intentions, and Anne Mitchell has almost noble ones by the halfway point in the film, but the system within which they operate, like any modern bureaucracy, works independently of the personal intentions of those who inscribe themselves within it. The discursive field, in a Foucaultian sense, writes itself and generates its own meanings.

The technologies of filmmaking mirror the technologies of experience in the stadium at which Doe unsuccessfully attempts·to make his voice heard.

presence. Every technology is precisely as repressive as it is expressive.

Doe makes his way through the crowd in the stadium to the stage, only minutes ahead of Norton's men, who are determined to stop him. Many of the shots of the convention are deliberately *not* direct shots of John or of the crowd but are shots of others – for example, radio announcers – looking at and describing John or the crowd to us and to their listeners. That is one of the things it means to say that experience is always repressively mediated in this world. The alternation of close-up shots with shots from the radio booth and the use of a layered sound track remind us that these contents are always contained. Both the visual and the acoustic effects are presented as layer after layer of packaging and merchandising. We are reminded of how the human figure and voice exist here only insofar as they are transmittable by a technology of information processing. In this study of visual and acoustic "perspectives" (in both the cinematic and the Nietzschean sense), events acquire significance only insofar as they are put "in perspective" by these technologies.

John is only a step ahead of Norton's henchmen, and every second counts, but even once he has pushed his way through the crowd and arrived on stage he cannot speak. He has to wait for the ovation greeting him to die down. Then a patriotic anthem has to be sung. Then a minister rises to offer the benediction and a silent prayer for "all of the John Does in the world."

Crowds of people, a national anthem, a prayer: The film metaphorically equates the hordes of ordinary citizens, the state, and the church as co-operating, interlocking forms of repression. All three are surrogates for and extensions of the moral, intellectual, and social repressiveness that Norton and his storm troopers represent. They keep John from speaking just as effectively as Norton does. Just as he is finally about to speak, Norton and his men arrive and move into action. They are at least as adept at the technologies of control as are society, the church, and the state. Newspapers denouncing him as an impostor have been printed up in advance, just in case of this eventuality. Cries are sent up by stooges in the audience to shout John down, and the instant he begins to speak and to accuse Norton from the stage, in the final coup de grâce, the wires to the amplifiers are cut.

This last event is one of the most powerful in all of Capra's work. Capra's close-up on the wire cutting makes it almost as tangible and painful as if we were watching John's vocal cords being cut before our eyes. Deeds and Smith were at least in control of their own voices. Whether or not anyone listened, they could at least hoarsely, hesitantly, passionately talk – to remind us that individual speakers were at least hypothetically still at the center of institutions, to restore an eccentric personal voice and tone to a system of discourse otherwise mechanically normalized and denuded of personality. That is what has changed in this film. This is a world in which even the individual human voice becomes inaudible except insofar as it can find a way to patch itself into the licensed networks of knowledge, to plug itself into the power system. With that almost surgically painful severing of John's vocal cords, the film might just as well have ended. The self is too small and weak to escape the systems (both cinematic and institutional) that create and regulate expression in this film.

This is the filmmaker who in his previous work was so much more attracted to zaniness, eccentricity, and spontaneity than to coherence and narrative systematization that he allowed his films to be sidetracked repeatedly by scenes of pointless improvisation, horsing around, and inarticulate dreaming. This is the director above all others committed to the power and interest of the individual. There is no room for creativity, eccentricity, or individualism in this film, which is why Doe is the only film in which there is almost none of the zaniness, horsing around between characters, or creative social or theatrical improvisation for which Capra's films were famous – except for a brief harmonica duet between John and the Colonel, and the imaginary baseball game, which in its privacy and peculiarity only proves how far in retreat from communication with the forms and forces of social life and meaningful human relationships the individual imagination is. The sort of social and imaginative movement within society represented by characters from Jerry Strong and Stew Smith to Longfellow Deeds and Jefferson Smith in Capra's previous work is impossible for Willoughby. Doe, in short, offers only the untenable choice between the cynical, irresponsible escapism of the Colonel and the embeddedness and enslavement to mechanical systems of meaning of everyone else in the film. There is no free margin between embeddedness and freedom, no way for a character to negotiate between entangling involvement and imaginative independence.

In effect, the self as a free and autonomous agent does not exist. The technology has done it in, erased or replaced it, as it will again, perhaps even more finally and definitively, in Capra's last important film, *State of the Union*. That is why every possible ending to *Doe* represents a form of suicide for John. Whether he literally kills himself by jumping from the top of a building or only symbolically erases himself by becoming part of Norton's network of faceless, personalityless puppets, or by becoming the symbolic head of the John Doe movement, the individual, eccentric, quirky, personal self has been written out of life and the film. Even suicide is superfluous or redundant insofar as "John Doe" has never lived, and "Long John" Willoughby has already committed suicide by an act of self-erasure long before.

The argument has been made that in *Doe* Capra is parodying the mythopoetic structures of his earlier work, playing with the filmic, as well as the social technologies of creating instant heroes. To talk about play or parody presumes a degree of detachment, control, and ironic bemusement that the film and Capra's account of the worried, anxious making of it nowhere communicates. Rather than being characterized by playful detachment, *Doe* is Capra's most disturbed work and the one most torn by conflicts of feeling. It is his most troubled and out-of-control work, and there is no reason to doubt his own account of his confusion about and dissatisfaction with the final film and with each of the five endings he made for it. It is possible, however, to feel that this confusion was a creative one. Capra brings all of the basic assumptions of the immediately preceding films into question. His form inadvertently overwhelms his characters' powers. The master of the depiction of individual imaginative energy and creative social performance, for the first time in his career, recognizes and is able to depict a system of social, institutional, and psychological controls that is fully as powerful as his individual performers and able to frustrate, absorb, or rechannel into its own repressive systems of relationship all of their free energies. *Doe* is a crisis film in which everything Capra had previously taken for granted is worried and puzzled, even the technologies of his own filmmaking, since, as I have already argued, the most pervasive of the systems "John Doe" is inscribed within, even more than the John Doe Club network and the political and journalistic systems, is the cinematic matrix of knowledge and interpretation that Capra's layered sound tracks, deep-focus photography, contextual editing, and complex narrative create around him. Out of that crisis of confidence in his own organizations of experience, as well as that new acknowledgment of the potential power and pervasiveness of the world's systems and arrangements, comes Capra's greatest film, *It's a Wonderful Life*.

In a more limited sense, *Doe* also marks an expansion of Capra's cinematic interests and an enlargement of narrative territory that he will draw on later. His layered sound tracks, his framing and editing to take in many multiple and competing planes of action and interpretation surrounding and impinging on his character, represent a movement beyond anything he attempted in the films before *Deeds* and *Smith*, and a movement beyond even those two films in his willingness to plunge into a world in which there are, or can be, no automatic stars or star performances. He has moved his film and his central character beyond the customary performances, editing techniques, frame compositions, and narrative of the Hollywood star system into a modern world of little people clamoring for cinematic recognition, person-dwarfing abstract systems of understanding, acoustic clutter, and inescapable visual and aural impingements on one's capacity to make a scene. We have moved into a world where all expression, including Capra's narrative itself, is felt to be potentially repressive and where there is no possible escape from, or transcendence of, the pervasive systematic mediations of society, bureaucracy, and narrative organization.

Capra is notoriously unable to see John through the difficult cinematic situation in which he imagines him. The star presence that Capra depended on to save the day even in *Deeds* and *Smith* is gone from the film, but Capra is unable to imagine anyone or anything to replace him. Capra will have to begin again from scratch in his effort to imagine an individual who is embedded in a matrix of pressures and influences and cannot ever escape from them into a state of imaginative transcendence or a style of unquestioned superiority and masterfulness, yet who is not lost or overwhelmed by that changed state of affairs, as John is here. The film documenting that effort to address the problems that *Doe* raises and fails to solve will not be made for five more years. The war intervenes and interrupts Capra's career, but the first film that he wrote, directed, and produced after his wartime service would do what *Doe* had failed to do. Its central character, George Bailey, is the character that all of Capra's cinema has been waiting for, and one who in his own person will internalize and dramatize the contradictions and ambivalence of feeling about the relationship of imagination and society that have haunted all of Capra's previous work.

15

American dreaming
It's a Wonderful Life

Where are the old idealists? ... Did the high idea die out of them?
                        – Ralph Waldo Emerson, "The Transcendentalist"
"I want to make her rich."
"What do you mean by rich?"
"I call people rich when they're able to meet the requirements of their imagination."
                        – Henry James, *The Portrait of a Lady*

As I have already observed, in *Mr. Deeds Goes to Town*, *Mr. Smith Goes to Washington*, and *Meet John Doe* Capra progressively broadens his analysis of the expressive problems facing the individual. One could make a limited case that in *Deeds* he was dramatizing an essentially personal conflict between Cedar and Deeds, a conflict that Deeds wins by using his voice to outmaneuver Cedar's and those of his witnesses. Such a line of argument becomes increasingly untenable, however, in the two subsequent films in the trilogy, where it is much less Taylor or Norton who frustrate the central figure than social, bureaucratic, and discursive systems that are identifiable with and authored by no particular individual.

In fact, even in *Deeds*, as I tried to show, the direct conflict between Longfellow Deeds and John Cedar was a fairly minor aspect of the film. The real drama was an expressive problem that faced both Deeds and Bennett, independent of the personal threat posed by Cedar. A viewer who came to any of the three films to see a personal confrontation between an antagonist and a protagonist (in the tradition that culminates in Clint Eastwood's work) would have become exasperated with the movie long before the episode ever took place. Capra treats such personal confrontations perfunctorily and far into his movies, and when such scenes finally occur they are frequently the weakest in their films. When Smith and Taylor finally face off in Paine's hotel room halfway through *Smith*, or when Willoughby confronts Norton man-to-man in Norton's mansion near the end of *Doe*, the consequences are anticlimactic and almost silly, and the scripting borders on being embarrassingly maudlin.

377

The important dramatic conflicts for Deeds, Smith, and Doe are not with other individuals, not with the Cedars, Taylors, and Nortons of the world, but with social systems, linguistic and discursive systems, and systems of belief that would repress or frustrate the expression of their ideals and desires. In short, these films are not conventional Hollywood dramas about conflicts of persons, although they do include token struggles of this kind in their plots, and consequently disguise their own originality. They are engaged in a much more radical and profound process of exploration: an exploration of the relationship of persons to cultural and linguistic systems of expression.*

That is also, incidentally, the reason the endings of these films are all more or less inconclusive and ambiguous. A villain can be decisively vanquished, but a system of expression cannot. Whether or not Cedar, Taylor, or Norton are revealed to the world as scoundrels and dispatched at the end of their respective films, the technologies of expression and the systems of manipulation and control that have threatened Deeds, Smith, and Doe are still necessarily, to a greater or lesser extent, in place at the films' conclusions. Consider *Smith*, in particular. Whether or not Taylor's political machine has been broken up and Taylor vanquished at the end of the film (and that in itself is far from obvious), ideals and principles of the sort Smith embodies will be just as difficult to express in the discursive codes of senatorial legislation, the journalistic technologies of information processing, and the forms of parliamentary debate in the future as they were in the past. Language itself resists such expressions of desire, *Smith* shows us, by comparing worldly languages and cinematic ones, by juxtaposing spoken, written, visual, and aural forms of expression.

Perhaps the reason Capra appears to be a much more conventional filmmaker of character conflicts than he is is that he so consistently provides his movies with personal villains who can be blamed for the hero's predicament, but, as I am arguing, neither Cedar nor Taylor nor Norton actually authors the systems their films depict. Especially in *Smith* and *Doe*, one has the sense that the villains have themselves become almost superfluous to the systems of power relations around them. That is why, as Capra's villains become progressively more powerful – from Cedar to Taylor to Norton – they become dramatically less important and interesting as individuals, and less present in their films. Norton, the most powerful of the three figures, appears on camera for only ten or fifteen minutes of screen time and does almost nothing to

---

* This is also the implicit subject of Capra's autobiography (but one that was ignored by almost all of its reviewers). In its very title, *The Name above the Title* embodies Capra's vision of the drama of life as being one enacted between particular individuals (names) and abstract systems of expression (embodied in titles, credit sequences, and studio policies that control and regulate the location of an individual name within a hierarchical arrangement of other names). The narrative of his book, like that of his film, is only in a superficial sense about personal conflicts, confrontations, and victories. Most centrally, it is an exploration of an individual's expressive relationship with studio bureaucracies, institutional codes and forms of behavior, and abstract social and artistic systems of expression.

forward the plot when he is on-screen. He does not need to. He is important and threatening not as a person but in terms of the immense system of relationships of which he is at the center and that renders his mere personal presence or absence on screen almost unimportant. That is to say, he as much as Doe has given up his personality to become a semiotic function in a chain of signifiers.

This is by way of preface to *It's a Wonderful Life*, Capra's most profound and searching analysis of the individual's relationship to the cultural, linguistic, and narrative systems by means of which he expresses himself. Just as in the preceding films Capra has almost invited the unwary to misunderstand his movie, by apparently organizing it around a personal conflict of two contrasted characters – an "innocent" named George Bailey and a "villain" named Potter. The first hint that Potter – like Cedar, Taylor, and Norton – is less a person than a mere narrative convenience, a way of representing a general principle of opposition, is that although we are once or twice told that his full name is Henry C. Potter, he is referred to for almost the entire film only by his last name. He has no more intimate personal identity – no family, friends, or relatives – than that single, stark, unadorned last name would suggest.

From James Agee, who reviewed the film during its original release in 1946, to Elliott Stein who wrote about it thirty-five years later, this aspect of the film has been misunderstood. Agee was the first in a long line of critics to compare it with Dickens's *A Christmas Carol*, and, more recently, Stein snidely argued that the point of *It's a Wonderful Life* was that the "only thing wrong with capitalism is Lionel Barrymore" – who plays Potter.★ The problem with either Agee's or Stein's approach is that it personalizes a dramatic predicament whose essential interest is its movement beyond personalities. It would be hard to think of a more profound misreading of the text Capra presents, and one that is especially unfair insofar as it trivializes and sentimentalizes the film by treating it this way and then proceeds to accuse Capra of the trivialization and sentimentalization the critic himself has perpetrated. Stein is inadvertently right in saying that *It's a Wonderful Life* is essentially about "what is wrong with capitalism" (though in saying this he only means to be sarcastic). What is wrong with capitalism, according to Capra, is, of course, nothing traceable to or localizable in any individual but rather its fundamental repression of our free imaginative energies, its demands that we relentlessly channel them into socially and ethically responsible careers of action.

The injustice of Agee's (and many subsequent critics') comparison of Capra's work with Dickens's *A Christmas Carol* is that it ignores the fact that in Capra's film the Bob Cratchett character is threatened less by Scrooge than by the frustrations of the social and linguistic arrangements of experience around him. There is all the difference in the world between the miraculous reformation of a bad man like Dickens's Scrooge and the crisis of expression and conscious-

★ James Agee, in a review in the *Nation*, December 28, 1946, reprinted in his book *Agee on Film: Reviews and Comments* (Boston: Beacon Press, 1958), pp. 233–4; Elliott Stein, "Capra Counts His Oscars," *Sight and Sound* 41, no. 3 (1972), 162.

ness that Capra analyzes in the character of George Bailey. (Furthermore, although this is not a crucial point, Capra's Potter does not reform, making the comparison doubly inappropriate.) To compare Capra's film with Dickens's story is to see the thoroughly American and quite un-British quality of Capra's effort. What Dickens analyzed as an ethical imbalance between two characters, to be rectified by an adjustment of social relationships and moral principles, Capra defines as an imbalance between imagination and desire, on the one hand, and the possibilities of their expression on the other. If one wants to force a comparison with Dickens, *It's a Wonderful Life* asks to be compared not with his early pieces like *A Christmas Carol* but with his work in the two decades following it – novels such as *Bleak House*, *Our Mutual Friend*, and *The Mystery of Edwin Drood*, which probe beneath the surface of social interaction to ask questions about our capacity to represent ourselves and our feelings and imaginations socially and linguistically at all.

Even more than in Capra's previous films, the frustrations that confront George Bailey are built into the expressive systems of the world he inhabits, and Capra's analysis of George's situation is closer to Emerson's understanding of the unavoidable war between Faith and Fate that I quoted in the epigraph to Chapter 4 than to being formulatable as a personal conflict between characters. As Emerson suggests, to depict this struggle the American work of art will have to move into "our interiors" in a way that in his view the eighteenth- and early nineteenth-century British novel had not done, and if there is one respect in which *It's a Wonderful Life* leaves even Capra's own previous work behind, it is in its movement into such an interior – in the depth of its exploration of the complex and troubled consciousness of its central character.

Deeds, *Smith*, and *Doe* explore the public systems of discourse by which we represent ourselves to each other, but without ignoring those systems or slighting their importance, *It's a Wonderful Life* goes farther than the earlier films in exploring the private symbolic systems by which we represent ourselves to ourselves. If Michel Foucault is the patron saint of the first kind of exploration, Sigmund Freud is the guiding spirit of the second and of this film. Neither system is authored in any personal sense, neither needs a personal agent to generate or perpetuate it, but whereas the systems of discourse in *Deeds*, *Smith*, and *Doe* are, for the most part, publicly visible and analyzable, many of those in *It's a Wonderful Life* are in some respects more pervasive and insidious because they are private and inscrutable. The repressive language, the compromising system is everywhere, because it is inside us. George Bailey and everyone he loves has internalized the system of repression that, in the previous films, was located somewhere outside the main characters. There can now be no escape from it and no leverage over it. There is no imaginative space apart from it.

It is no accident that in this changed situation even the function of the token villain has altered. *It's a Wonderful Life* really needs no villain, certainly no one like Cedar, Taylor, or Norton, to confront and attack the protagonist. Potter, in fact, hardly attacks or confronts George at all throughout the film. He only needs to remind him of his own doubts and internal conflicts. Potter, as the town miser and troublemaker, one of the leading stockholders in the Building and Loan run first by George's father and then by George, and the head of the powerful National Bank that is the competitive rival to the Bailey Brother's one-horse Building and Loan, is a recurring irritant in George's life, but he is really only a minor annoyance. He has little of the official clout and bureaucratic power of Cedar, Taylor, or Norton and no special power or control over George. Because the drama of the film has moved so profoundly inward, he needs none. The fault lines of American culture are inside George himself. Potter has only to disturb George along his own fault lines for him to come apart in the plate tectonics of this film.

Though Potter goes through the motions of being a stock figure of villainy (which has helped to mislead many ciritcs) – hoarding money, complaining about the Building and Loan, and harrassing George in various minor ways – he is less even a token personal adversary than Cedar, Taylor, or Norton and more a doppelgänger of George – a ghostly, distorted, fun-house mirror image of him. Capra emphasizes not the differences, but the similarities of their situations. They have, in effect, exactly the same job and function in the community. At certain moments in the film they even spookily trade lines of dialogue or personal identities back and forth, as when in the flashback sequence George discovers that Potter has completely filled the vacuum created by George's not having lived in Bedford Falls, or when, in a strictly parallel pair of scenes, George calls Potter early in the film a "warped, frustrated old man" and Potter calls George, late in the film, a "warped, frustrated young man." It is not accidental that halfway through the movie Potter's most threatening gesture to George is not an attempt to destroy him but an offer to merge with him – to hire George to work for the bank Potter owns and runs.

If George's problem is not caused by a personal antagonist, neither is it created by any particular abuse of normal institutional or bureaucratic arrangements of power and knowledge, as were some of the problems confronting Deeds, Smith, and Doe. *It's a Wonderful Life* is not even obliquely about an abuse of power or the perversion of a particular system of relationships. George's town, his occupation, and his daily routine are normal in every respect, but it is the potential frustrations and repressiveness of normal, ordinary life that Capra makes the subject of his film. It is the definition of normal life that is at fault, if anything, Capra suggests.

Each of the dramatic pressures or influences on George Bailey represents a deep internal division within himself, not merely an external institutional or social structure. The most fundamental way that Capra shows us this is by making *It's a Wonderful Life* a kind of psychodrama in which each of the major characters around George externalizes an imaginative contradiction or division of allegiance that already exists within him. Counting Potter, there are at least five partial or divided projections of George.

Each also represents a distinct stance towards capitalism – a personal position on the renunciation of instinctual drives that it asks of its participants, and on the promises that it offers (or betrays) as a result of the sublimation of desire into socially creative and beneficial forms of activity. I want to consider them individually.

Potter holds out the possibility of surviving (and even thriving) by repressing all merely human compassion, sexual impulses, and familial connections, all emotional, social, and biological intimacies and responsibilities. In the Calvinistic-acquisitive form of capitalism that he represents, Potter has cut his links not only with family, friends, and relatives (he has none) but even with his own body and the life of his senses. He dresses austerely in black; lives in a wheelchair, of which he is almost a mechanical extension; travels in a coach that looks like a hearse; and shows no interest in human pleasures, from sexual activity to mere entertainment. (He has apparently severed himself even from the biological processes of aging, appearing as shriveled and old in the first scenes of the film as in the last, thirty years later.) He has, in effect, given up his body and almost all practical bodily functions and biological impulses and gratifications for the sake of the denatured accumulation of capital.

As Capra shows us in the dreamland sequence, it is not that Potter is unaware of or indifferent to matters of sexuality and biology but that he is interested in them only in terms of their potential for being translated into capital. In the ordinary daylight world of Bedford Falls, that means that such realms must simply be suppressed or ignored, which is why Potter seems to have no sexual or biological existence for most of the film; but in the nightmare view of the world that Capra provides late in the film, in the dreamland sequence, Capra shows us that Potter's capitalism can handle those realms too, as long as they can be converted into abstract, capitalistic forms of accumulation. Pottersville, the town that Bedford Falls has been turned into in the dreamland episode, is Capra's 1940s version of today's Vegas, Forty-Second Street, and L. A. Strip, with their massage parlors, trashy bars, and expensive cheap thrills. Sex is merchandized in girlie shows, romance in dime-a-dance parlors; exoticism, ethnicity, and the lure of the strange or distant are marketed in sleazy "theme" nightclubs and bars; and even the excitement of raw human aggression is organized and made profitable through sports like boxing matches.

Pottersville includes in a perverted form all of the adventure, romance, and excitement that George dreams of living in the whole preceding film (and in which he is utterly unable to participate in the daylight world of Bedford Falls), but it has all been harnessed to the capitalistic project and cashed in on.*
Potter is interested in sex and violence and adventure, but only insofar as they

---

* One of the most horrifying capitalistic cashings-in is also one of the most unobtrusive. George's wild, passionate fantasy of lassoing the moon and bringing it down to earth for Mary to eat has been "realized" in the literal appearance of the Blue Moon Bar and Cafe in the nighttown scene. I do not have to emphasize, I am sure, that this detail shows again how fervently Capra is in favor of derealization, in favor of letting fantasies stay fantasies.

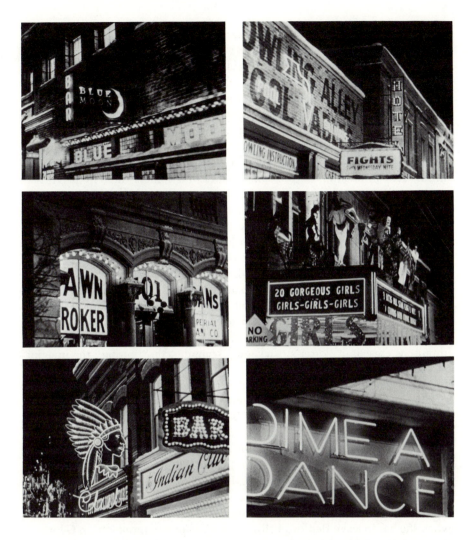

The commodification of life: selling out the previously free and eccentric imagination to the institutions of capitalism in Pottersville.

are convertible into marketable commodities. In this sense, it is impossible to miss the implicit parallel between Potter and the dream merchants of Hollywood. He is the perfect Hollywood producer or studio head, who, at least in the dreamland sequence, makes his living by selling the public's frustrated, repressed fantasies of adventure, romance, sex, and violence back to them in the commercially profitable projection of them on the movie screen. In short, he is the perfect capitalist, who has converted all of life into the currency of the abstract system of capital formation. Anything that can be converted, at whatever cost to the instincts or common good, is converted; anything that resists capitalistic denaturing and commodification – as do tender, loving, personal intimacies – is renounced and repudiated.

That should suggest why Potter, and Capra's other late villains, are so much more threatening than mere Dickensian bad guys. Potter represents a fairly trivial personal threat but a powerful stance toward the expression of basic needs, drives, and imaginations. He would regiment the imagination into specific worldly commodities and marketable transactions strictly articulated within the economic system he perpetuates. Whereas the Method-like stares, gasps, games, and improvisations of Bailey, Deeds, Bennett, Saunders, and Smith are stimulating expressions of destinationless desire, playful or pointless free movements of the healthy imagination that is temporariliy liberated from all practical goals, Potter, Norton, and Taylor function in the opposite expressive way. They are relentless expressive organizers and systematizers. Their actions and words, far from being even remotely free or freedom-inducing, are overmotivated, overdetermined, and overpointed socially, bureaucratically, economically, and narratively. They channel the otherwise free movements of imagination (and in so doing arrest them and destroy it) into always practical, pointed, purposeful expression: in Taylor's case, incorporating it into the "machine" of political organization; in Norton's, regimenting it into a fascistic police state in which the individual impulse is erased; in Potter's, packaging, canning, or "potting" the imagination into a marketable commodity.*

Diametrically opposed to Potter is Violet Bicks, who represents all of the sensuousness and physicality, the living thoroughly in the self-pleasuring realm of the body and the senses, that Potter has excluded or exorcized. Violet (played by Gloria Grahame, in her greatest film performance – but then this film represents the greatest performance of practically everybody in it) is the town flirt, coquette, and (subsequently) fallen woman who literally embodies the unrepressed sexual expressiveness that Potter removes from the body. (Her stunning success in this part was to launch her on a career as a film noir tramp and vamp in the fifties.) It is significant that near the end of the film, when she has to leave Bedford Falls, she has to borrow money from George to do it. To "spend" one's body and emotions as profligately as Violet does is necessarily not to have anything saved for contingencies, not to have any accumulated social or familial reserves on which to draw. Violet is almost as alone and cut off from the support of the larger community of Bedford Falls as Potter.

That is to suggest, finally, that Potter and Violet are less opposites than complementary and mutually dependent principles – as the symbiotic relationship of their names suggests.† It is not accidental that in the dreamland

---

* For a slightly different formulation of this theme, see my essay on Capra's work in *Magill's Cinema Annual, 1982*, ed. Frank N. Magill (Englewood Cliffs, N.J.: Salem Press, 1982), pp. 1–15.

† In the metaphoric dyad of Violet, the flower, and Potter, the restricter or container of growth, Bailey makes a metaphoric third. He is associated with water and rain throughout *It's a Wonderful Life*. Water has two conflicting metaphoric connotations in each appearance in the film. It can be life-giving, growth-stimulating, sexually arousing, and baptismally redemptive

sequence Potter's and Violet's visions of the possibilities of life momentarily coincide. In the form of late capitalism that our culture has inherited, the individual who has liberated sex from love and enduring emotional commitments and the financier who views love, sex, and emotions only as commodities to be bought, merchandised, and sold, work in an unconsciously intimate partnership. Violet is a profligate sexual spender, and Potter is a miserly sexual hoarder, but they perform frictionlessly together in the same capitalistic system, and in fact each needs the other to complete the cycle.

Potter and Violet, his mirror image, however, do not define the only possibilities within capitalism in the film. Sam Wainwright is a local playboy who combines Potter's financial success with Violet's eroticism and, in doing so, dramatizes the argument I have just made about their potential complementarity. Both Violet and Potter tempt George at specific moments, but each is recognizably crippled or incomplete in some way. In suggesting that there can be a reconciliation between the fulfillment of instinctual desires and the long-term financial and social accumulations of capitalism, Sam is for George far and away the most imaginatively disturbing of all of the characters in the film. He is a millionaire world-traveler and industrialist who lives the dreams of travel, glamour, romance, and wealth about which George only reads and dreams. He has made a fortune in plastics, manufacturing airplane windshields during the war, and yet he also has a blonde on his arm throughout the film (a different one each time we see him). His manufacturing windshields demonstrates his trick of turning other people's adversity into his own personal form of virtue. While George supervises scrap-rubber drives and plays airraid warden in Bedford Falls, Sam makes a killing on the murder and bloodshed of the war.

The fourth psychological presence in the film, first as a living character and then, after he has died, as an enduring memory, is George's father. He runs the Bailey Brothers Building and Loan in the first half of the film, and his photograph hangs on the wall of George's office and is the background of many of Capra's shots of George in the second half of the film. George's father's life is in complete contrast to Sam Wainwright's. He neither leaves Bedford Falls to travel nor achieves any financial success worth mentioning. He gives his life for duty and responsibility, sacrificing worldly success and the accumulation of capital on behalf of altruistically helping his family, his friends, and the depositors in his bank.

(as in George's saving his brother Harry from drowning, his plunge into the school swimming pool, or his rescue of Clarence from the river) – or life-threatening, spirit-dampening, suicidally enticing, and person-swallowing (in the same episodes, as in the pond that deprives George of his hearing and almost drowns his brother Harry; the rain that dampens George's honeymoon; the ocean that almost swallows the transport ship; and the river that would have taken George's body if Clarence has not intervened), but that doubleness seems central to all of Capra's work. The forces that threaten us with decomposition also sponsor our greatest potential achievements of imaginative enrichment and spiritual revival. For Capra, moments when we find ourselves socially helpless and, so to speak, in the deepest water, the most threatening imaginative predicaments, are the moments of potential vision and of imaginative growth and flowering.

The fifth important character situated psychologically with respect to George is his Uncle Billy, and subsequently Clarence, the angel who comes down to aid George near the end of the film and who replaces Billy in the narrative in the final section of the film.★ Billy and Clarence, as their names hint, represent decisions to remove themselves from the capitalistic systems of the film by remaining children all their lives. They represent qualities of childishness and innocence that Capra himself is sometimes mistakenly said to endorse, but the fact that Capra shows the incapacity of either character to get on without the help of grownups in the capitalist world should indicate how far he is from simply endorsing either of them as a mature possibility. A world made up of Clarences and Uncle Billys would be a world in which none of the houses that George's bank builds would be constructed. Both Clarence and Uncle Billy significantly depend on George to get them out of the trouble into which their naiveté keeps leading them.

Each of these characters represents an expressive stance or attitude that can be found in one or more of Capra's previous films, which suggests how far from arbitrary Capra's creation of these particular figures around George was. Uncle Billy and Clarence represent possibilities of innocence and childlike purity that both Jefferson Smith and Longfellow Deeds had within them and that the farmers in *Deeds*, the Boy Rangers in *Smith*, and the common folk in *Doe* embodied. Potter represents a worship of order and systematization, mechanical efficiency, and a suppression of the eccentric or free susceptibilities of the senses and emotions that was previously embodied in Taylor, Norton, and Cedar. Violet and Sam represent possibilities of sexual expression, sensual gratification, and living the life of romance that many of the earlier heroines (especially those played by Barbara Stanwyck) or a figure like Susan Paine in *Smith* embodied. Finally, George's father represents a sense of responsibility and obligation to the larger community and a belief in the value of self-sacrifice for the common good that almost all of the earlier films advocated.

Unlike the earlier films, from *That Certain Thing* on, which attempted to reconcile these different imaginative tendencies or, more frequently, to argue that there is no conflict at all among them, *It's a Wonderful Life* takes their counterpulls as its very subject. In the character of George, pulled in these different directions by the characters around him, Capra finds a way, for the first and only time in his work, to dramatize the conflicts of feeling and allegiance that he himself felt and that were present only more or less fugitively or covertly in his earlier work – the conflict between dreams of freedom,

---

★ The equivalence of the two is suggested by the fact that Clarence appears at the exact point in the narrative at which Billy disappears after having been repudiated by George, and Billy subsequently reappears as soon as Clarence is accepted by George and departs from the narrative. The actors who play the two parts, Henry Travers and Thomas Mitchell, look and act so much alike that were it not for the extreme demands placed on film to be realistic, the same person could have doubled in the two parts – if, for example, there had been a stage version of the movie.

romance, adventure, and visionary disencumberment from the toils and compromises of social life, and a powerful sense of moral responsbility to the
claims of family, society, social intercourse, and the limitations of action in
worldly space and time; the conflict between the life of the senses and the life of
the imagination. The conflicts about the expression of imagination and desire
in the forms of the world that are implicit in the earlier films are not exorcised
or gradually erased in the course of the film but are made the explicit subject of
it. They are embodied in the various characters surrounding George and pulling
on him and in the consequent confusions, self-division, and doubts he himself
feels in the course of the film. George is the closest Capra has ever come to
acknowledging his own divided impulses directly in his work, the torn and
uncertain imagination in conflict with itself that has been present as a subtext in
each of the preceding films. George, in this imaginative sense (though not
socially, economically, or ethnically) *is* Frank Capra.

The psychodrama quality of *It's a Wonderful Life* is its essence. Capra peoples
his film with his own unresolved and conflicting impulses in the various
figures arrayed around George, and shows, in the effect of those figures on
George Bailey, the consequences of these conflicting impulses on one imagination. The film that comes closest to *It's a Wonderful Life*, both in its
retrospective narrative structure★ and in this psychodrama quality, is *Lost
Horizon*, which clearly illustrates how Capra at times deliberately created
supporting characters to dramatize internal conflicts in his protagonist. In
adapting James Hilton's novel, Capra created a new major character who was
not present in the book. He was George Conway, the brother of the protagonist, Robert Conway, and a kind of doppelgänger to him who exists merely
to externalize a division in Robert's feelings about staying in Shangri-La that it
would otherwise be difficult to present dramatically in the film.

The characters around George in *It's a Wonderful Life* function just as does
the dark brother in *Lost Horizon* to dramatize George's (and indirectly,
Capra's) imaginative confusions and divisions of allegiance. George wants to
live up to the self-sacrificing ideal of conduct represented by his father, but he
also wants to live the life of his imagination and desires, as Violet Bicks and
Sam Wainwright apparently do. He is torn between his attempt to affirm the
simple, childlike values represented by his Uncle Billy (and, subsequently,
Clarence) and his recognition of necessary instinctual compromises in the adult
world, of repression and hoarding, of schemes and manipulations represented
by Potter. The characters around George need not confront or harass him;
they need only live with him to remind him of his own confusion concerning
values (and Sam Wainwright, Violet Bicks, and his Uncle Billy indeed, so far

---

★ In referring to its retrospective structure, I am describing *Lost Horizon* in its preview form. Only
weeks before its general release, Capra discarded the first two reels, which set up the flashback
situation, and decided to begin the film with the events themselves. An account of the earlier
version of the film is preserved in the Columbia final draft of the screenplay, a summary of
which is given in Rudy Behlmer, *Behind the Scenes: America's Favorite Movies* (New York:
Frederick Ungar, 1982).

from being antagonists, are George's closest friends). The drama has moved away from confrontation, coercion, and the attempted manipulation of a central character to become a psychodrama of contradictory imaginative tendencies within one figure.

The preceding films typically parceled out Capra's ambivalences into different characters representing more or less alternative and mutually exclusive careers for the self. The individual characters threatening the central figure were disposed of one by one, individually put in their places in the course of the narrative. The rival imaginative impulses were gradually sorted out in the course of the film to allow for the victory of the unified, monotonic self of the protagonist. That changes here. In *It's a Wonderful Life*, not only are the rival inclinations allowed to coexist simultaneously in the consciousness of the central character, as they presumably coexisted in Capra's consciousness, but they are not "placed" or gradually segregated in the course of the film. For the first time in his work, Capra imagines the possibility of a life that cannot escape or repress these conflicting imaginative tendencies but must live within their contradictions. George is Capra's attempt to imagine and represent a consciousness as richly vexed and inclusive of multiple impulses as his own. He is his attempt to imagine the possibility of a life larger and more capacious than any of the lives of the characters around George and that transcends their limitations, yet one that represses or sacrifices none of their diverse satisfactions. It will be a life of the senses and emotions that is at the same time more lasting and emotionally satisfying than the erotic dalliances of Violet Bicks; a life of responsibility to the community and concern for his fellow man that is not as confined as George's father's was; a life of childlike innocence and openness to experience like that of Uncle Billy that is not merely irresponsible and childish; a life of financial and worldly success and of the creative sublimation of desire that is not shriveled and frustrated like Potter's. It is not accidental that George's long-standing goal is to be an architect. An architect, like a filmmaker, is someone who reconciles the potentially contradictory claims of imagination and the requirements of worldly commercial enterprise, someone who finds a way to express the exorbitant, vaulting energies of desire in the public forms of the mature, adult experience.

Faced with similar expressive conflicts, *Deeds*, *Smith*, and *Doe* ultimately repressed one possiblity or another in the course of their narratives. To take only the simplest example, *Smith*, early in the film, opens up an alternative between the physicality and the eroticism of Susan Paine and the need to dutifully attend tedious but important hearings in the Senate and shows Smith initially wavering between them, only completely to foreclose the first alternative two-thirds of the way through the film. Susan is whisked offscreen, never to reappear on camera, and the orgy of Smith's exalted idealism in his filibuster is offered as an imaginative alternative to both the eroticism and the dutifulness, apparently combining the energies of both into one action but actually succeeding only to the extent that it represses both previous alternatives from Capra's narrative and erases them from a viewer's memory. Since they never have to grapple with the inherent contradictions and conflicts of fully adult behavior, Smith, Deeds, and Doe still seem limited and boyish at the end of their films, whereas George grows into the mess of adulthood, into acknowledging necessarily entangling conflicts of relationship and irreconcilable divisions of feeling in the course of his movie.

George is one of the supreme creations of American film: both the greatest and most idealistic dreamer in Capra's entire gallery of American dreamers and the figure in his work most unremittingly embedded in the structures of society and social discourse, most hedged round with responsibilities. He brings together in one performance all of the different manifestations from the earlier films of the ability of the imagination to avoid or break free of entrapping systems that would limit its free movements. At various moments he displays the quirky, eccentric, playful, improvisatory genius of Stew Smith, the social aplomb and mastery of timing of Tom Dixon and Longfellow Deeds, the melodramatic plangency and intensity of expression of Clarissa Saunders, Babe Bennett, or Jefferson Smith, the Method-acting inwardness and depth of feeling of Long John Willoughby, and the exoticism, imaginative allure, and romantic stimulation represented by Kay Arnold or General Yen.

From the earliest flashbacks in the film we see George dreaming of travel to exotic places, of touring the world, of studying art and architecture in foreign cities, of becoming an explorer, an artist, or an architect. He would be a figure of imagination to compare with one of the heroines of Carl Dreyer's work if it were not for the opposed aspect of the film: that George is never able to escape the pressures of society, space, and time. In Dreyer's work, the heroine's dreams and ideals – from those of Joan of Arc to Gertrud – ultimately constitute an escape hatch from the pains, pressures, and compromises of social action and speech, a cinematic release from the requirements of plot and dialogue into special effects of lighting and photography.★ The heroines could – admittedly with extreme difficulty and at the cost of great pain and self-sacrifice – ultimately escape from society into their exalted states of feeling and idealism. Joan of Arc's excruciating death at the stake is thus at the same time an act of beatific apotheosis and saintly transcendence. Gertrud's final act of renunciation and withdrawal into her hermitage is also a noble vindication of the free and independent life of the imagination as an absolute, self-sufficient alternative to the expressive compromises of all social intercourse. No such transcendence is possible for or available to George. His ideals and dreams must be, and can only be, expressed in social consequences and forms of expression. Whereas Dreyer's heroines are able to escape into an autonomous

---

★ See my discussions of Dreyer's *Day of Wrath*, *Ordet*, and *Gertrud* in *Magill's Survey of Cinema, Foreign Language Films*, ed. Frank Magill (Pasadena, Calif.: Salem Press, 1986). Although there is not space to go into it here, *Ladies of Leisure* may be profitably compared with *Day of Wrath*, and *Forbidden* with *Gertrud*. The central female figures in each pair are in strikingly similar situations in which imaginative movements are asked to substitute for worldly immobilities, and emotional enrichments are asked to compensate for social and verbal impoverishments.

imaginative realm, George can only express his dreams in the language of everyday life, if they are to be expressed at all. The wildest, most passionate fantasies must be translated into the ordinary language of social intercourse. Life ought to live up to such inspiring visions of its possibilities as those George represents to himself. It ought to allow us to live our dreams – but as Capra knows, and George painfully discovers, it everywhere resists them. It grounds such flights of imagination in the relentlessness of the ordinary.

It's a Wonderful Life encourages us to identify George's expressive predicament with Capra's all the more, insofar as the film is stylistically vexed and divided in a way that repeats George's social and imaginative vexation and division as a character. Dreyer's style protects visionary characters like Gertrud and Joan, while the social world preys on and eats away at them, sheltering them within an abstract, autonomous stylistic realm of cinematic expression that makes time and space for, and validates, the purely symbolic significances and unworldly states of imaginative awareness that he wishes to affirm. Capra's style cannot and will not do that. Grounded in the enforced "realism" of the structures of Hollywood studio film plotting, pacing, dialogue, and characterization, it can never offer an escape into a stylistic realm separate from the commonsensical structures and pacings of worldly experience. Capra openly flirted with such a possibility twice in his career, in the Sternbergianism of *Forbidden* and *The Bitter Tea of General Yen*, but both films were such financial disasters that they warned him never to attempt it again. It is rare that one can give thanks to the judgment of the American film-going public, but one would have to conclude in this instance that as a result of its condemnation of these two films, Capra was salutarily forced into a much more complex and ambivalent attitude toward cinematic stylization and the representation of specially protected states of consciousness, one that Sternberg, for example, never attained, and that ultimately made Capra a far superior filmmaker.*

Just as George must find a way to express his dreams in the common forms of intercourse available within the world of Bedford Falls, Capra must express his in the commonsensical dramatic and social forms of intercourse available within the codes of conventional "realistic" Hollywood feature filmmaking. If George is torn by his conflicting allegiances to the claims of imagination and society, Capra's film is divided by the identical stylistic conflicts of allegiance, oscillating from scenes in which the lighting and photography express the excitement of disencumbered visionary, visual possession, to scenes in which the plotting, characterization, and dialogue take pains to recognize the unavoidable constraints of the forms of social life within which most of Capra's narrative and Bailey's life is necessarily anchored.

---

* If there were space for it here, the analogy between Capra's commitment to making realistic, narrative films and Robert Frost's decision to write poetry in realistic, narrative poetic forms that committed him to sequentiality and metrical continuity, would be worth developing. Suffice it to say that both visionary artists embrace formal constraints on their expressions, for reasons that are more than formal. In contrast, Stevens's work is closer to Sternberg's.

The inevitable delays, deferrals, and frustrations brought on by the differences between the practical understandings of society and the dreams of the life of the soul (to adapt an Emersonian formulation) is the drama beneath the drama of *It's a Wonderful Life*. One of the most powerful means by which Capra indicates the gap between the two realms is by pitting certain forms of eccentricity, wildness, and quirkiness in George's performance against the most relentlessly inevitable plot progression of all of his work. *It's a Wonderful Life* has a dozen scenes of exuberant, experimental role playing, horsing around, and tonal swerves and shifts that testify as much to Capra's excitement at returning to feature filmmaking after the hiatus of the war as to his actors' enjoyment of having such richly playable parts. Yet counterpointed against this imaginative ebullience bordering on recklessness, in both the film's performances and in the events it depicts, is the greatest narrative, photographic, and social constraint to which Capra's characters and scenes have ever been subjected, a constraint that wars against their every imaginative indulgence and eccentricity. The film documents Capra's (and Bailey's) unresolved struggle between the desire to honor the importance of the wildest, most untamable impulses of free imaginative expression, and the opposed needs of consciousness and narrative for coherent form, moral shapeliness, and social responsibility, as poignantly as one finds the same drama enacted in the writing of Hawthorne, Emerson, and Henry James.

One way Capra does this is by making the first ninety minutes of the film a flashback. The climactic event – George's decision to commit suicide – is revealed in the first minute or so of the movie, and what follows is a chronological narration of a series of episodes from George's life leading up to that moment of despair. The result is that even during the most exuberant and joyous scenes early in the movie, the framing flashback organization itself, with its inexorably chronological presentation, its episodic structure, and its interrupting voice-over interpretations of the events we are witnessing keeps reminding us of George's formal and temporal imprisonment. As in film noir, the flashback communicates to us not only a nostalgic feeling of our own belatedness in encountering the events in the film (since we are reminded that everything we are seeing has already happened and concluded before we came on the scene) but also a practical sense of the central character's doom and of the inevitability of his fate (since he can do nothing to avoid or delay the catastrophic ending that has already been announced and preordained from the beginning). From *Lost Horizon*, *Doe*, and *Arsenic and Old Lace* to *It's a Wonderful Life* and the film that follows it, *State of the Union*, Capra's movies increasingly employ the expressive devices and narrative situations of film noir to suggest the increasing entrapment of the central characters and the growing perilousness of their situations. The director whose faith in the imaginative freedom and independence of his central characters was perhaps the greatest of all thirties filmmakers, increasingly imagines his characters trapped in networks of signification and affiliation that test their capacities of free expression to the limit. The director who initially seemed least capable of film noir becomes one of the greatest and strangest practitioners of it.

The flashback form creates a pervasive feeling of narrative burden and formal restriction that everywhere counterbalances the buoyancy of the performances in the film. The flashback style makes the characters – and this is opposed to everything Capra's films otherwise stand for – passive victims of a predetermined plot. Characters are always, to some extent, passive victims of a predetermined plot (certainly by the second and third viewing of a film one becomes aware of this, even if one was not in the first viewing), but what Capra has done is formally to acknowledge this felt constraint in the retrospective structure of the film itself. The coercions of plot and narrative form become representations of the expressive constraints and restrictions inevitably placed upon even the most imaginative and creative life. The result is that even if we are repeatedly carried away by the apparent spontaneity and freedom of the performances in the film, there is an unavoidable aura of impending doom and destruction surrounding each of them. There is a special poignancy to watching George fall in love or plan to do something when we already know that the film climaxes with his attempted suicide.

More important, and more continuously felt by the viewer than this intermittent and frequently forgettable formal constraint built into the film as a whole, are the social constraints established editorially and photographically in every scene. George Bailey is a dreamer out of a novel by Henry James, subjected to social scrutiny as relentlessly threatening and withering as that felt by the heroines of Edith Wharton's work. *Deeds* and *Smith* contained moments in which characters had to parade their most private feelings in public forums and translate them into public forms of discourse. Both of those films nonetheless demarcated certain private spaces for reverie and romance separate from the public spaces. That separation disappears in *Doe* and *It's a Wonderful Life*. As a member of a prominent if not especially prosperous family in a small town, George (like the media creation John Doe) can never get offstage. His experiences, his aspirations, and his private desires are made the subject of endless discussion among his friends. Every move he makes is scrutinized. His progress is continually watched and monitored by solicitous others.

In a recurring American nightmare vision of being robbed of one's mystery and privacy, of being known to the point of losing one's uninterpretable, independent selfhood, like one of James's, Hawthorne's, or Poe's vampirized ones, Bailey is virtually never not being interpretatively looked at, listened in on, or "understood." Mary Hatch's mother listens in on an extension telephone at the top of the stairs while George and Mary are talking downstairs. A neighbor watches their courtship from his back porch. A group of spectators gathers in the street to jeer at George when he talks with Violet Bicks. The bank examiner listens in and comments when a collect call from George's brother comes into the bank. The list could be extended, but what literally tops and subsumes these individual instances is that Capra uses the flashback frame to implicate even the angels themselves (and us, the viewers of the film) in this cosmic voyeurism. They (and we) become the ultimate connoisseurs of

George's misery under glass, served up scene by painful scene by the head angel, Joseph, the cosmic moviola operator, for Clarence's and our own delectation. As in James's *Turn of the Screw*, the frame itself implicitly implicates the viewer or listener in the same process of potentially vampiristic understanding and categorizing that the narration discovers and condemns in the characters. George is a "seer" who is trapped by being so relentlessly "seen." His imaginative vision would free him, if he were not so insistently made the subject of the witheringly unvisionary, gossipy, social vision of everyone around him. There is no private space left for merely personal or unencumbered "seeing" in this world where everything is "seen" or "see-able" in the other way. Every putatively free or unfettered self-expression is instantly absorbed into an alternative public system of narrative or social discourse.

The scene in which George and Mary walk home together from the high school prom summarizes the tug of war in the film between would-be free and unencumbered expression of imagination and feeling and a system of social, visual, acoustic, and narrative containment that works to frustrate it. George and Mary have accidentally fallen into the school swimming pool and are walking home in costumes hastily thrown together from the only dry clothes available. George is in a ridiculously overlarge football uniform purloined from the boy's locker room, and Mary is wearing a loose-fitting bathrobe borrowed from the swim team. (There are homemade identities here, but they comically fail to "fit" the individuals involved.) George and Mary engage in the sort of semicomic, indirect, and sublimated love play of which Capra is the cinematic master (even more than Hawks, who tends self-defensively to take refuge too frequently in scenes of low comedy and romantic absurdity between his lovers, as a way of getting an easy laugh from his audience and protecting himself and his characters from charges of sentimentality). George and Mary sing together, play little dramatic games and explore tones with each other, tell (or refuse to tell) their dreams and wishes, and spout bits of improvised poetry for effect.

Capra deliberately emphasizes the physicality of Mary's body in several of the shots of her legs, visible through the parted robe, and is not at all shy about recognizing the possibilities of an explicitly sexual liaison that present themselves in the scene. It is one of the most sensuous and erotic scenes in all of his work, and its point is to make us aware of the connection between our capacities of dreaming and of desiring. As the scene dramatizes, the most chaste and abstract idealism, poetry spouting, and visionary dreaming come out of the same well of displaced passional and libidinal energies that our most sexually arousing desires and fantasies do. As in *It Happened One Night*, Capra recognizes that it is only by being checked and displaced that our dreams and desires are forced into the stimulating sorts of expression found in this scene. Eroticism (as opposed to mere fornication), poetry, play, and theatricality are all expressions of otherwise frustrated imaginative or emotional energy. If the inevitable displacement of our dreams and desires into forms of performance is potentially frustrating to the dreamer, it is also potentially a gain for the world, insofar as it is out of that displacement that creativity is born.

George and Mary begin by singing an off-key duet of "Buffalo Gals." I have mentioned how music is used in Capra's films to capture feelings that cannot be expressed in more utilitarian or discursive ways. Music becomes progressively more important in Capra's work from *It Happened One Night* onward, climaxing in the powerfully emotional orchestration that runs through *State of the Union*. Songs become more common, too, up through this film. From Thomas Cole's *The Pic-Nic* and William Sidney Mount's *Banjo Player* to Thomas Eakins's *Amateur Musicians* and *The Concert Singer* music has been used in American art as Capra uses it here: to create and celebrate imaginative communities that substitute for missing or unobtainable social ones. That is why the songs in Capra's work are almost always subtly tinged with sadness (especially the recurring "Auld Lang Syne"). They celebrate something that has only an imaginary existence. In the case of "Auld Lang Syne" it is something that, like the golden age, must be retrospectively discovered in an archaic past or wished for in the future, since it is so patently unobtainable in the present.

This singing is different from the orchestration in the sound tracks of *Deeds*, *Smith*, *Doe*, or *State of the Union*, since, unlike those smoothly performed orchestrations, these imperfectly rendered songs anchor exalted feelings and unearthly ideals in the flawed particularity of personal voice tones, missed harmonies, and off-key melodies.* Moments of idealism in most of the earliest films – as in the scene of Megan's meditation on the balcony in *Bitter Tea*, accompanied with the celestial sound of lutes and harps – were allowed to be pure as this off-key duet is not. In Capra's later work, from approximately *It Happened One Night* on, but increasingly with the films immediately before and after the war, ideals are less and less able to escape the impurity of worldly infelicities and human disharmonies of expression. They are less and less able to exempt themselves from the inflections of a flawed voice (or the failed harmonizations of a pair of romantically mismatched voices). Ideals are always grounded in bodies, in what Robert Frost called the "cave of the mouth," in these films. Heavenly labials are spoken not as a Stevensian alternative to, but in the tones of, worldly gutterals.

Deeds and *Smith* mark Capra's turn away from the use of orchestrations to communicate disembodied and depersonalized states of imagination or idealism and his redefinition of ideals as existing only in the fallible performances of a particular human speaker. The narrative effort of both films is to humanize previously abstract, impersonal ideals by grounding them in the particular sounds of the principal characters' voices. Deeds and Smith must learn to speak their ideals in their own human voice tones and timbres for

---

* Another instance in the film is the ludicrous and touching duet sung by Bert and Ernie, standing outside in the rain, on the night of George and Mary's honeymoon.

those ideals to come into meaningful existence in the second halves of their films.★

Mary and George play theatrical games and try out formal stage voices at moments, but these received, institutional voices only indicate their inability to speak their true feelings. At one point, George plays a courtier and Mary a courtly lady, as he picks up the sash of her robe with the line, "My lady, your train," and she replies, "You may now kiss my hand." They throw stones at a deserted mansion and make wishes on its broken windows. They slyly and obliquely hint to each other about their secret dreams. In an unusually explicit poetic outburst George offers to "lasso the moon" and bring it down for Mary. It is one of the most delicately romantic scenes in Capra's work, and one of the major scenes in this film, but what is being accomplished narratively in the course of it? The scene literally goes nowhere, except to take us and them a few steps off the beaten path. It narratively beats around the bush, just as the two lovers do in the course of it, in more than one sense of the phrase – but that pointlessness is just its point. The theatricality, excessiveness, and obliquity of the scene communicate imaginative and emotional energies (George's, Mary's, and Capra's) that will not be translated into more purposeful, focused, and practical forms of expression (in George's and Mary's words and actions or in Capra's film). As in the buddy-boy films, such energies can be expressed only in the extravagances, abstractions, and occasional incoherences of play.

Notwithstanding all of the obvious allurements of this imaginative play, Capra feels so uncomfortable with it that, as he frequently does, he inserts a reactive character to bring the scene and his two lovers back to earth. A portly character actor makes an appearance as an anonymous neighbor watching their romantic shenanigans from his back porch. While George and Mary are carrying on, Capra intercuts seven comic shots of him grimacing and squirming as he watches them, until he has obviously worked himself into a state and cannot contain himself any longer. In exasperation, he bursts out to George, "Why don't you kiss her instead of talking her to death? ... Ah, youth is wasted on the wrong people." An instant later he storms inside, never to reappear in the film again, but the question he has asked lingers in the viewer's mind long after he has departed. It concisely frames the basic issue of

★ As I suggested in Chapter 13, *Smith* explicitly insists on the importance of anchoring ideals in the particular sounds of a fallible voice. The patriotic orchestrations on the sound track of the movie during some of the montage sequences early in the film indeed dally with the possibility of a pure, unmediated, abstract idealism; it is significant, however, that Smith's Senate filibuster is not backed by such orchestration. The authentic aural experience of idealism in the film resides in the strained sounds of Smith's voice, not in the strains of "America the Beautiful" heard during one of the patriotic montages. The film is, in effect, a celebration of the voice of Smith as the authentic voice of desire and imagination and a decisive choice of those sounds in preference to the neutralized and normalized (that is to say, institutionalized and depersonalized) modulations of the stage- and radio-trained voices of Joseph Paine, H. V. Kaltenborne, the other Senators, the radio announcers, and the page boys.

the scene and of the film. If George had desublimated his relationship with Mary to the point of kissing her (or, more radically, making love to her), needless to say we would have been denied all the gorgeous nonsense that preceded. It is in what the neighbor aptly calls the "waste" of the spirit that creation takes place, not in its hoarding or conservation. Notwithstanding the sentiments of the neighbor, Capra is loading the scene in favor of *not* kissing, but talking.

Only a minute or two later, George has a chance to desublimate the scene even more radically than that. In a zany bit of stage business, George inadvertently steps on Mary's bathrobe while they are walking, so that she accidentally sheds it and is forced to dive into a nearby hydrangea bush and hide. George is at first about to toss the robe back to her, but, on second thought, decides to mull over the possibilities. Capra milks the humor of the situation to the limit, as George circles around the bush, bathrobe in hand, talking to himself, speculating on the possibilities. Is he to throw the robe in to her, or is she to come out to get it, or he to go into the bush to give it to her? It is a comic moment, but as in all of Capra's scenes of comic courtship, the humor does not preclude a serious undercurrent of feeling; rather, it captures the awkward reality of it. (Comedy for Capra is almost never a means of mockery, but the opposite. It allows him – and a viewer – to suspend moral or social judgment and to entertain imaginative possibilities that a more serious stance toward a character or event would preclude.) Imaginative possibilities open before George. For the first time in this film of repressions and deferrals of instinctual and imaginative gratification, he is actually on the verge of living the sort of erotic possibilities that he has (in his own words) "only read about" up to now. The touching, comic difference here between George's sudden imagination of possible experience and the actual opportunities of his ordinary life summarizes the central drama of *It's a Wonderful Life*.

It is typical of the relentless social pressures on him and of the narrative constraints within the film that, comically puzzled and divided as he is, George is not allowed even to meditate on the possibilities before him for more than a few seconds. Just when the erotic fires have been stoked to their maximum, Capra has a car roar down the street toward the two lovers. We are suddenly stylistically transported into another film – perhaps a gangster picture, certainly not a romantic comedy. Over the sound of the screech of brakes and an ominous musical orchestration, Uncle Billy shouts that George's father has had a stroke and that George must come home with him immediately. *It's a Wonderful Life* is a roller coaster of such swerves of tones and styles and the clearest expression in all of Capra's work of the contest of Faith and Fate for the destiny of an individual soul.

The death of George's father not only short-circuits George's brief dream of erotic adventure but forces the cancellation of his summer plans to travel abroad before entering college in the fall. His subsequent plans to go to college to study architecture are then sidetracked by his inheritance of the responsibilities of running the bank, after the board votes him successor to his father.

Four years later, his attempt to get away by turning over the management of the Bailey Brothers Building and Loan to his brother Harry is frustrated when Harry unexpectedly marries and is offered a job in the family business of his new father-in-law. In a final ironic twist of the knife, Capra dooms George to live all his life in the very house in front of which we earlier saw him making his resolution to "shake the dust of this crummy town off my feet."

George's architectural fantasies never achieve any grander expressions than the row-house realities that the Building and Loan constructs for its customers. That is the central and recurrent crisis of imagination and expression in *It's a Wonderful Life*. The most exalted dreams can only be expressed in compromises of these worldly realities. The same energies that might have built skyscrapers in New York can only express themselves in the construction of four-room frame houses for immigrant families in Bailey Park and in George and Mary's renovation of the dilapidated, drafty old Granville place where they live. Ribbon-cutting ceremonies for the dedication of a new bridge are replaced by housewarming parties on the doorstep of the Martinis.

Capra is sometimes talked about as if he were the Norman Rockwell of filmmakers, but George Bailey's life in Bedford Falls would be more aptly compared with the vision of Western culture in Freud's *Civilization and Its Discontents* than to the genteel sentimentality of Rockwell's paintings. Bedford Falls represents a landscape of the imagination associated more with the repression of desire than with innocence and simplicity. George is relentlessly frustrated and trapped – formally, socially, and psychologically. A scene that summarizes his predicament is the one of him and Mary together in Mary's house, talking on the telephone to Sam Wainwright. In the scene before this one, George has just learned that his brother will not be taking over for him at the bank. A party celebrating Harry's wedding follows that night, but George, like Jerry Strong in *Ladies of Leisure*, wanders away in the middle of it. For George, however, unlike Jerry, there can be no escape into vision. There is no balcony where he can stare at the stars. He walks downtown and tentatively proposes a poetic flight from society into the mountains to Violet Bicks, but she does not understand, and he is laughed at and mocked by a crowd of townspeople who have gathered around him while he speaks to her. There is nowhere for George to run to avoid being observed. He then wanders to Mary's house, but a phone call from his mother to Mary has already alerted her to be on the lookout for him. In a far more subtle way than in either *Smith* or *Doe*, Capra shows what it is to be trapped in a semiotic and social system of understandings and relationships out of one's own control, what it feels like to be a character playing a part in a play scripted and directed by someone else. The tyranny of love is even more oppressive, and certainly more insidious, than that of hate. These are his friends and loved ones, truly so. George imagines himself to be making a freely improvised and unscripted "entrance" when he arrives at Mary's, but the phone call from his matchmaking mother has allowed Mary to costume herself (changing her dress and fixing her hair), to set out a stage prop (a piece of needlepoint she has done commemorating his

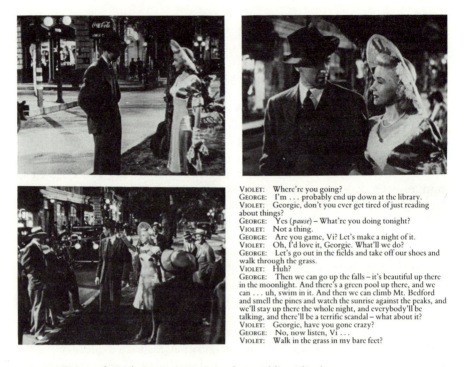

VIOLET: Where're you going?
GEORGE: I'm ... probably end up down at the library.
VIOLET: Georgie, don't you ever get tired of just reading
about things?
GEORGE: Yes (*pause*) – What're you doing tonight?
VIOLET: Not a thing.
GEORGE: Are you game, Vi? Let's make a night of it.
VIOLET: Oh, I'd love it, Georgie. What'll we do?
GEORGE: Let's go out in the fields and take off our shoes and
walk through the grass.
VIOLET: Huh?
GEORGE: Then we can go up the falls – it's beautiful up there
in the moonlight. And there's a green pool up there, and we
can ... uh, swim in it. And then we can climb Mt. Bedford
and smell the pines and watch the sunrise against the peaks, and
we'll stay up there the whole night, and everybody'll be
talking, and there'll be a terrific scandal – what about it?
VIOLET: Georgie, have you gone crazy?
GEORGE: No, now listen, Vi ...
VIOLET: Walk in the grass in my bare feet?

Private lyrical expressions opened to public ridicule.

statement that he would "lasso the moon" on their earlier walk), and to put on orchestral mood music (a recording of "Buffalo Gals" on the record player) in order to stage the scene that she, and not he, is obviously directing.

When Sam calls from New York and insists on talking to both George and Mary at once, Capra finds a visual image to summarize George's psychological and social situation. In one tight close-up, he frames the couple squeezed together, forced to listen and talk on the same telephone, George resisting the proximity to Mary and the enforced intimacy as much as he seems to try to break out of the tightness of the close-up itself. For all of his poetry, dreams, and plans to circumnavigate the world, he is trapped by the length of the telephone cord, pinned by the pull of sexual biology and romantic attraction, and caged by Capra's close-up. In the very scene in which George has attempted to assert his capacity to move freely, moving away from the party for his brother and making his way alone downtown, Capra shows us that there can be no free social, imaginative, or visual space or independent action of the sort he imagines. There is nowhere for him to go, nothing to do.

George's expressive opportunities are more limited and his situation more encumbered than that of Capra's previous central figures: Not only is there no Arizona to which he can flee or motel room in Michigan to which he can retreat, but there is no courtroom or Senate chamber within which he can make a passionate, idealistic speech. He is doomed to live (and die) in the

All dressed up but no place to go and nothing to say or do to express oneself.

narrow social and linguistic confines of the small town of Bedford Falls. He is a Jerry Strong forced to work for a living, who can only dream about becoming an artist; a Megan Davis who never gets to travel to Yen's palace but only reads about such things. He is a Longfellow Deeds with big plans but without an inheritance, and never given the chance to leave Mandrake Falls to take on the big city. He has the ideals of Jefferson Smith, without a *Boy's Stuff* to express them in, the Senate to give him a soapbox to stand on, or an abstract, patriotic cause for which to fight.

Even Deeds and Smith, puny as they were, had possibilities of actual heroic action that are denied George. They, in however faltering a way, could be heroes in their own films. It was possible in their worlds to make a big speech, to defend matters of abstract principle, to win a decisive victory or to lose valiantly. George, in effect, dreams of being a hero in the Jefferson Smith way, in a grand test of will and spirit, but that kind of heroism is utterly out of the question in his world. That is George's predicament for the rest of the film – to be able neither to abandon his dream of freedom nor to find any satisfying way to live or express it. He, in effect, crosses the personal weakness and entailment of Long John Willoughby with the visionary passion of Smith. He has no forum for a direct expression of his desires and dreams, no audience to whom he can appeal for justice, no clear-cut battle to fight or victory to win. His

nearly operatic imagination is forced to find secret, fugitive, and socially insignificant forms of expression. To spout poetry on a walk with a girl on the
way home from the prom, while dressed in a clownishly ill-fitting football
uniform, indulging in rhetorical extravagances about "lassoing the moon"
(however earnestly felt) is quite different from lecturing the Senate about
patriotism and graft. He must translate his transcendentalism into the forms of
small-town banking and building. He must trail his clouds of glory and feelings of something ever more about to be along the dust of the streets, shops,
and hallways of the dreary rounds of middle-class life.

George is, significantly, the first of Capra's protagonists not only to be
married but to be a family man and someone working to support himself at a
practical occupation.* For Dan Brooks in *Broadway Bill* or Stew Smith in
Platinum Blonde, the responsibilities of family life and a regular occupation are
something to be renounced or positively avoided. Capra's typical earlier
protagonists were loners, solitary artist-visionaries, political idealists, or social
millenarians who were freed by the very fact of their quirky individualism
from the compromises of social life or were at least allowed to oppose their
own impulses to such forms of experience.†

George is in a position betwixt and between more than any preceding Capra
protagonist. The unidealistic, unvisionary, familial, social, and occupational
entanglements of life are something from which he can never quite extricate
himself, and yet they are something from which he is also, always and continuously, at a critical distance. Never able to escape them, he is never able
quite to lose himself in them either. That this is an extremely complex (and
potentially creative – or self-destructive) situation to be in is one of the things
that Capra shows us during the course of *It's a Wonderful Life*.

In his writing on Hannah Arendt and American modernism, George Kateb
has provided a theoretical framework that can, I believe, help us to appreciate
George Bailey as a prototypical modernist figure. Kateb's fundamental insight
involves the recognition of the distinctive situation of the modernist self as
being (as I have described George Bailey and most of the protagonists of
Capra's late films, from *Deeds* on) simultaneously half inside and half outside
of society, half immersed in its codes and forms of understanding and half at a
distance from them. It is the "in betweenness" of the self's position – or what
Kateb calls its condition of "moderate alienation" – that gives it its special
status:

---

* The Dickensian "families" in *Arsenic and Old Lace* and *You Can't Take It with You* do not count,
  since they are only loose aggregations of more or less independent eccentrics – groups of people
  who live together in the same household but who sacrifice none of their individualism or
  independence to the claims of the community they constitute or the responsibilities of mutual
  interdependency.
† They were a little like Dreyer's heroines in this respect. It would be impossible to conceive of his
  Joan, Anne Petersen, or Gertrud's being tied down as mothers of children, devoted
  homemakers, or working for a living at an ordinary job and still being the visionaries they are.

The true beneficiary of all the dislocations and uncertainties of modernity is the democratic individual living in a culture of moderate alienation, and himself sharing in that alienation . . . The theory of democratic individuality . . . is the conversion of this distress and loss . . . into a great good . . . The key to [the individual's] stature is self-consciousness carried to the point of what Emerson calls, with mixed feelings, the "double consciousness" in "The Transcendentalist" and "Fate". . .One becomes all the more active because detached; all the more active because constantly enlarging one's passivities and receptivities; all the more active because one knows of certainties that underlie the futilities and imprecisions of action. There is no *social* identity worth holding on to. The self is loose-fitting. There is no chance that bad faith will substitute itself for reconciliation. There is restlessness, contradiction, bursting all confines. There is serious play, without winning or losing. Taste is put down, because everything is allowed in, everything can be poeticized . . . [The] idealism . . . of the American Romantics . . . aspires to the encouragement of a poetical or philosophical relation to reality on the part of all, to some significant degree. Democratic individuality is the doctrine of every person a poet or philosopher . . . One may say that the Romantic poetical or philosophical relation to reality is the democratically refined sense of wonder at and gratitude for Being.★

A few pages later in the same essay, Kateb continues his argument concerning the full-fledged emergence of a new form of modernist culture, based on a conception of the changed situation of the self:

The *vita activa* is not exhausted by labor, work, and political action; the sole alternative to the *vita activa* is not the *vita contemplativa*. There is the unstructured immensity in which people idle, observe, ruminate, imagine, move about, encounter, travel down the open road; in which, in short, they experience. For them, too, the world with its commitments must be kept "at a certain distance," if the unstructured immensity of possible experience is to be entered. The modern technologies of communication and travel, the modern technological media of art and entertainment, and the modern methods of reproducing and disseminating art and the works of culture all transform the very nature of experience, as well as its content. The achievements of modernity have made individuals more able to see, have given them more to see, have devised new ways of seeing. They have created utopia as vision. The key to the modern transformation of experience is to be found in the emancipation of sight more than in the emancipation of all of the other senses (to use Marx's early formulation). This is an unmeasurable advance.

Kateb is suggesting that modern culture at its most advanced, energetic, and interesting (and it is clear from the context in which this passage occurs that Kateb particularly has in mind life in modern America) takes place in this "visionary" middle kingdom between the immersions of mere activity and the

★ This and the following quotation are taken from George Kateb, "Hannah Arendt: Alienation and America," *Raritan Review* 3 (Summer 1983), 27–8, 31–2.

withdrawals of mere contemplation. As the reference to traveling "down the open road" suggests, Whitman's poetry is, for Kateb, a model of just such a half-in, half-out stance in which, by virtue of one's capacity to "idle, observe, ruminate, imagine, move about, encounter, [and] travel," one is able to enter the "unstructured immensity of possible experience."

Capra's late films to a large extent agree with Kateb (and Emerson and Whitman) in avoiding the tritely fashionable critical bemoaning of alienation. Whatever else it also is in Capra's work, alienation like George Bailey's or Jefferson Smith's is an avenue of enormous potential freedom and creative mobility. To be an alien is to gain perspective on a system denied one more relentlessly implicated in it. To be moderately alienated from a system in which one was previously caught, as Anne Mitchell and Clarissa Saunders prove, is potentially to be freed for the first time to a creative imaginative relationship to it. Deeds, Smith, Bailey, and Matthews (in the film that follows this one) are capable of savingly eclectic and eccentric acts precisely to the extent that they are imaginative outsiders or latecomers, castaways or fugitives. Their impracticality, idealism, or critical perspective is, in Kateb's phrase, a means of savingly keeping the "world with its commitments ... 'at a certain distance.'"

In summary, Kateb's argument is a brilliant application of Whitman's position and an elevation of it into a stirring phenomenology of contemporary experience. Yet one must insist that, on the evidence of these same films, Capra, while entertaining this position, also emphatically parts ways with Kateb and Whitman in several respects. Kateb's view of the effect of the "modern technologies of communication and travel, the modern technological media of art and entertainment, and the modern methods of reproducing and disseminating art and the works of culture" is much more benign than Capra's. Where Kateb sees merely an enriching, Whitmanesque expansion of the possibilities of experience in the technologies of contemporary information processing and dissemination, Capra – in *Deeds, Smith, Doe,* and *State of the Union* – sees an entirely more ominous and disturbing series of consequences. Moreover, where Kateb sees apparently only a "great good" in the self's condition of alienation, Capra recognizes from as early as *That Certain Thing, The Way of the Strong, The Younger Generation,* and *Ladies of Leisure,* through this film and the one that follows it, that the same alienation that confers potential freedom can also render one achingly homeless and alone. It guarantees independence and freedom of movement, but at the price of acute rootlessness. Neither Kateb nor Whitman, for that matter, seems to have taken into account the full personal and emotional consequences of "going down the open road" in this way. To become a stylistic eclectic or visionary is, as the sadder transcendentalists Hawthorne, Emerson, Melville, Henry James, and Capra realized, at least potentially to be estranged to the status of a voyeur. To be capable of such movements through space and society is perhaps to be doomed to ice skate across the "slippery surfaces" of life without being able to put down roots in any one community, intimate relationship, or system of belief.★ To revel in such quick changes of social identity and to have such chameleonic capacities of role playing is perhaps to give up the possibility of holding onto any self at all underneath the various roles and self-proliferations.

In glossing over these dangers, American modernism, in the form espoused by Kateb (and by many contemporary American metafictionists as well), comes perilously close to being indistinguishable from aesthetic dalliance and Pateresque connoisseurship. Though it is to be commended for escaping the dreary post-*Wasteland* thematics of anomie and angst in which most discussions of modernism are bogged down, Kateb's sense of the quintessence of modernism as being that it has "made individuals more able to see, ... given them more to see, ... devised new ways of seeing" has perhaps gone too far in the other direction of defining life as a form of epicureanism. Kateb is inadvertently embracing the world of Pater, Wilde, and Kipling (which admittedly at points does spookily border on that of Hawthorne, Emerson, Whitman, and James). He is celebrating an attitude toward experience that, in Kipling's work, turns all of life into "The Game." It is a view that Capra would have found disturbingly irresponsible. Although he was obviously attracted to such stylistic eclecticism (as witness *It Happened One Night*) and visual connoisseurship (as witness all of *Bitter Tea*, *Lost Horizon*, and *Arsenic and Old Lace*, and isolated sequences within almost all of his other work), the inherent conservatism of the Hollywood feature-film narrative form within which he worked placed and criticized such impulses (just as the expressive forms in which Emerson and James worked – the lyceum lecture and the novel of manners – did the same thing to their more radical imaginative impulses). Visionary moments and transcendental impulses exist in the impurity of Capra's work much as they do in the impurity of everyday life. They are put into formal competition with all of the unvisionary forms and forces of experience.

I would argue that in his braced and bracing depiction of the consequences of George Bailey's alienation, Capra in this film in effect outlines a fourth alternative to those Kateb invokes, an alternative markedly different from carefree, playful, visual eclecticism and visionary connoisseurship. If Thoreau and Whitman are the presiding spirits of Kateb's happy modernism, William James is the patron saint of Capra's somewhat sterner view. Capra's modernism has at the heart of it work – the work of making meaning and significance from our inevitable position of marginality and alienation – and George Bailey is Capra's exemplification of both the state of alienation and the consequent labor of significance that it asks of us in the world. Capra's modernism involves the practical realization of imaginative vision by means of unceasing effort in real time and space.

In our condition of alienation we are forced to bring imagination into expression in life by means of a perpetual labor of creation. We are as gods, but

---

★ D. H. Lawrence has written most eloquently about this situation in his *Studies in Classic American Literature*, a relevant excerpt from which is given as an epigraph to this book.

gods of particularly limited and marginal power, and for whom the universe is always about to subside again into chaos and confusion. In the epigraph to Chapter 12, I quote the stirring final sentence of Emerson's "Experience" in which he says that the "true romance which the world exists to realise [is] the transformation of genius into practical power," but *It's a Wonderful Life* tells us that Capra would never have used a word like "transformation" to describe this transaction. It suggests a process entirely too easy, instantaneous, and almost magical. *It's a Wonderful Life* documents a painful, slow, difficult, unending labor of wrestling the smallest impulse of personal genius into some marginal, minor, inevitably flawed and unsatisfactory practical representation.

Consider, for example, the narrative function of the old Granville place in the film. We first see it in the "Buffalo Gals" scene I have already described, in which George and Mary stand in front of it as a deserted, dilapidated mansion and make wishes about where they would like to live in the future by throwing stones at its windows. In this scene it is a purely imaginative home for their romantic wishes and dreams, but Capra forces George and Mary in subsequent scenes to become homemakers in the literal as well as the imaginative sense of the word. Work as well as imagination will be asked of them to give a local habitation and a name to what begins as a mere wish or dream. Significance is labored into existence. It is first a run-down mansion on which to make wishes. Then it is a drippy honeymoon hovel on a rainy night. It becomes a home, only gradually and with difficulty, as we encounter it in the course of the film at six distinct stages of imaginative and physical possession and rehabilitation, from its state of initial dilapidation to a final Christmas titivation near the end of the film. As if to drive home the fragility of the achievement, Capra also provides a seventh, harrowing glimpse of it during the nighttown sequence. We see a wreck even more decayed and fallen than its initial state in the film. Chaos comes again, to make us realize just how precious and difficult was the human creation of meaning and beauty in the first place. We watch the Granville place change physically in being cleaned up, painted, wallpapered, and lived in, and even verbally in being transformed into the Bailey home, but the most important transformation is imaginative, as objects and spaces within it accumulate meanings and cinematic resonances or lose them as we watch the film.

Capra's conception of imaginative creation has shifted from some of his earlier work. In *Bitter Tea*, Yen's creation of his summer palace and Megan's imaginative inhabitation of it were weightless, timeless acts of visionary possession, but the making of an imaginative home out of the Granville place is an entirely different matter. It is a painful, arduous, time-bound project, as unlike as possible the creation of an instant environment answerable to the dreams of the imagination by means of glass-shots. Imaginative activity takes place not as an alternative to or an escape from the confinements of the fabric of space and time, but within and as part of it. Never have both the pressures of time and the opportunities it presents as a potential creative resource been more felt in Capra's work than in the strictly chronological organization of this film (although, as I argued in previous chapters, Capra has used time both as a compositional resource and as a force of decomposition in his earlier work). So far from being temporarily erased or forgotten, as in a typical comedy by Hawks or Sturges, where it would be almost possible to lift a scene out of its position in one part in the film and put it down in another, time becomes integral to our experience of *It's a Wonderful Life*. Significance is slowly, laboriously worked into shape like the old Granville place itself, over time and within the severe limitations of a rigorously historical narrative progression, as we repeatedly visit and revisit a small number of places (or sets) and characters (or actors) over the course of a thirty- or forty-year span of time.★

George and Mary become surrogates for Capra himself in this respect. They laboriously create meanings during the time of this thirty-year narration, precisely as he does in the one hundred twenty-nine minutes of the film's running time. The detail and care of this labor of signification not only link them with him but make them stand apart from all of the other characters. They offer a vision of the process of imaginative creation not as an effortless transformation of dross to cash – what Robert Frost called the dream of "easy gold at hand of fay or elf" – as Sam Wainwright's plastics factory does, nor as a willed escape from historical and biological time in the oblivious hedonism, the eternal seizing of the day of pleasure of Violet Bicks, nor, least of all, as a matter of the miserly hoarding of bequeathable, inheritable riches, as Potter does, but as a process of continuous, expensive imaginative expenditure. The richness of significance is earned and paid for at great cost. The creation of significance in narrative or in life is something gradual, fragile, and temporal, something brought about slowly and arduously, always in danger of being lost again, forgotten, or eroded by the passage of time. The other characters, significantly, do not seem to have temporal dimensions to their situations as George and, to a lesser degree Mary, do. They do not seem to change physically or imaginatively. Potter, Violet, Sam, even George's Uncle Billy are what Foucault would call synchronic functions; they have no causal history or future. One must live in time to make meaning in this way. Furthermore, only Mary and George, of the principal characters in the film, extend their lives biologically. To have a child is not only to be entailed domestically, socially,

---

★ The similarities between Capra's sense of the labor of meaning making in terms of the Granville place and Wordsworth's in his poem "Michael" are profound. "Michael" is significantly organized in the same temporally relentless way as *It's a Wonderful Life*, not only as a strictly chronological narrative of the gradual accretion of meaning in otherwise meaningless objects and activities but also in the form of a vast flashback, quite similar in effect to the flashback structure of Capra's film. Wordsworth meticulously shows how meanings are created only slowly and arduously in the time and space of a life and a narration involved always and everywhere with the particularities of time and space. We or the characters are not given meanings as faits accomplis but only insofar as they gradually, tentatively emerge from a labor of signification. "The clipping tree," the one dog of "an inestimable worth," the couple which was "as a proverb in the vale/For endless industry," the sheepcote which Michael attempts to turn into a "covenant" are all made, not inherited. Meaning and value are precisely what cannot be bequeathed.

and financially; it is to choose to enact one's destiny *in time*. (Needless to say, to imagine an American transcendentalist with a wife, children, a mortgage, a job, and a home, temporally entailed as George is, is in and of itself to perform a powerful act of criticism on American transcendentalism.)

In William James's formulation (and I take *It's a Wonderful Life* to be one of the supreme expressions of this aspect of James's philosophy), "We build the flux out inevitably. The great question is: does it, with our additions, rise or fall in value?"* James's metaphors, especially his use of the word "build" here, suggest both the muscularity of the process and the tentativeness or impermanence of the result. The process of meaning making is far from being an effortless, frictionless, or perfect one, for James or for George Bailey. George spends his life's blood imaginatively "building" the Granville place, but can never be finished or really satisfied with the result. Our "buildings" are always to some degree sadly or tragically unsatisfactory and unfinished (a fact that is comically expressed in Capra's film in terms of the broken finial on the newel post that maddeningly comes off in George's hand everytime he goes upstairs in his own house).

Moreover, what is made in time can be lost in time. There are no guarantees in a universe from which temporality cannot be excluded. As James understood, virtue, beauty, order, and love, insofar as we must make possibilities of them in the first place, are incredibly open to disturbance and powerfully threatened with decomposition at any time. We and all of our creations (in James's phrase) continuously "breast nonentity" and therefore continuously risk falling back into nonentity. What James said of his pluralistic universe is equally true of Capra's artistic universe or of all of George Bailey's personal achievements of meaning and importance:

> Its world is always vulnerable, for some of it may go astray; and having no 'eternal' edition of it to draw comfort from, its partisans must always feel to some degree insecure ... The pragmatism or pluralism which I defend has to fall back on a certain ultimate hardihood, a certain willingness to live without assurances or guarantees.†

That hardihood is what Capra asks for in his greatest performers, a willingness to keep going in the face of this endless adversity and insecurity.

Capra has complex feelings about the practical results of this modernist project of making meanings, precisely because the meanings never can quite live up to the impulse that initially sponsored them and are never secure from decay or loss. Consider the career of one particular phrase as it moves through Capra's narrative. In the scene at the old Granville place, at one of the most exalted imaginative moments in the film George offers to "lasso the moon" and bring it down for Mary to eat: "You want the moon, [Mary]? Just say the

---

* William James, "Pragmatism and Humanism," in *The Writings of William James: A Comprehensive Edition*, ed. John J. Mc Dermott (Chicago: University of Chicago Press, 1977), pp. 455–6.
† William James, "The Absolute and the Strenuous Life," in *The Meaning of Truth: A Sequel to Pragmatism* (Ann Arbor: University of Michigan Press, 1970), pp. 228–9.

word and I'll throw a lasso around it and pull it down . . . That's a pretty good idea. I'll give you the moon, Mary . . . Then you could swallow it. And then it would all dissolve, and the moon beams would shoot out of your fingers and your toes and the ends of your hair." At the beginning of this poetic extravagance, Capra inserts a shot of the moon that recalls the similar shot of the moon during Megan's balcony reverie in *Bitter Tea*. The moments in the two films are parallel, but the difference between the two scenes tells us about the change in Capra's work during the intervening thirteen years. What in the earlier film was a solitary experience, with Megan sitting alone on Yen's balcony silently contemplating the moon, is here converted into a public, interpersonal, verbal expression. George is allowed to be neither alone, nor silent, nor merely contemplative. Ideals and imaginations must be translated into words and actions, and that makes all the difference in the world.

When one says that significance is made tentatively and imperfectly in time and space in *It's a Wonderful Life*, one of the things one means is that a phrase and scene like this will not stand still for exegesis. It cannot be symbolically fixed or locked into significance. Like everything else in the film, this imaginative expression accumulates personal meaning in time and changes its meaning in the course of the film. The lassoing-the-moon scene is referred to three more times in Capra's narrative, but each time it echoes with entirely different imaginative resonances, depending on its context. Several years later, on the night when George discovers that his brother has been secretly married and that he himself is trapped in Bedford Falls, he wanders over to Mary's house, in a scene I have already mentioned. There he discovers that she has completed a crude needlepoint titled "George Lassos the Moon," showing a cartoon stick figure throwing a cowboy lasso around the moon and pulling it down to earth. The phrase occurs twice more in the movie, ten or fifteen years later in George's life on the night Potter offers him a chance to work for him. George turns him down and returns home. He glances at Mary's needlepoint, now hanging on the wall of their bedroom, and the whole earlier scene comes back to him in a welling up of feelings of shame and self-reproach, as he suddenly realizes how far he is from living his youthful dreams of adventure and romance. The fourth occurrence of the phrase is only a few minutes later when Mary wakes up and (unintentionally adding insult to injury) comically uses a variation on the phrase ("George lassos stork") to announce the fact that she is pregnant with their first child.

It is a crucial phrase in the film, and one that might be said to epitomize all of George's unworldly idealism and unappeasable and otherwise inexpressible desire. It has traced a complex and twisting trajectory in these four occurrences, one that can summarize the complexity of George's situation and Capra's feelings about it. What began as a rhetorical extravagance punctuating a poetic and erotic reverie has been converted first into a needlepoint bromide, then into a jeer of self-reproach that George directs at himself because of his failure to realize his dreams, and concludes as a code phrase for the very burden of enslavement to home and family under which George staggers. The American sublime has been domesticated, but I do not need to dwell on the ironies of the conversion of George's dream first into the stuff of Mary's needlepoint and then into an announcement of her pregnancy. It is undeniable, though, even as Mary finally adapts it to her eminently homespun purposes, the phrase still trails some of the clouds of glory that George originally evoked. Even as a needlepoint aphorism hanging on the wall, it brings the memory of that youthful act of imaginative bravado alive in the present, and as a metaphor for Mary's pregnancy it refers to an event perhaps even more amazing than the one George conceived when he originally uttered it.

Another scene that summarizes some of the complexity of the activity of domesticating the sublime is the housewarming ceremony that takes place about halfway through the film. It may be unfamiliar to some recent viewers, since it has been cut from a number of prints of the rental version of the film, possibly because it seems unrelated to the crucial events of George's life and because cutting it and a few other scenes shortens the movie to almost exactly two hours' running time. It condenses into its few minutes almost all of the central issues in *It's a Wonderful Life* involving the expression of imagination and desire in George's life, the complex strategy of sublimation by which George works out his expressive problems, and Capra's quite mixed feelings about the results of his effort.

As head of the Building and Loan, George presides over a housewarming ceremony on the doorstep of a new home for the Martinis, an immigrant family who obviously would not have been able to afford a house at all if it were not for the generosity of the institution George runs. Before they occupy the house, George and Mary conduct a brief welcoming ceremony for them and their assembled neighbors with a symbolic presentation of a loaf of bread, a bottle of wine, and a box of salt:

GEORGE: Mr. and Mrs. Martini, welcome home ...
MARY: [Here is] bread – that this house may never know hunger. Salt – that life may always have flavor.
GEORGE: And wine – that joy and prosperity may reign forever. Enter the Martini castle.

It is a wonderful example of the literal domestication of imaginative energies otherwise inexpressible except in such touchingly mundane ceremonies as housewarming parties, the bedtime stories we tell our children, and the jokes we tell each other. There is nothing grand about the event. It is, after all, only a two-minute welcoming ceremony for an immigrant family moving into a four-room frame house in a crowded housing development, but as this immigrant director knows, it also represents a moving act of imaginative possession and domestication, a series of poetic phrases in its own way as important and freighted with meaning for the Martinis as any of George's grand poetic ejaculations earlier in the film were for him. Equally important, it is a way for George to convert the one sort of impractical energy into the other sort of practical expression. George was not able, in the earlier "Buffalo Gals" scene, to bring himself to convert his excess imaginative energies into the practical forms of making love, or even directly expressing his love, to Mary, but in this scene he is finding a way, however sublimated and oblique, to express his desires and imaginations in the social and linguistic forms of the world.

In a touch that reveals Capra's complete grasp of the larger imaginative significance of the scene, when George is halfway through the ceremony Capra has Sam ("Old Hee Haw") Wainwright drive up, chauffeured in a luxurious limousine, with one more of his ubiquitous honeys at his side. Sam tries to persuade George and Mary to go along with him on a spur-of-the-moment trip to Florida. He reminds George of everything George is not: Sam is a millionaire head of a corporation, an oversexed, overpaid, overconfident world traveler. He lives what George only dreams about. He travels around the world on his fortune in plastics, while George stays at home in Bedford Falls. He is part of ribbon-cutting ceremonies at factories and offices, while the high point of George's life is a small-potato housewarming ceremony like this one. The deeper point of Capra's comparison of the two men's lives in this scene, however, is Capra's obvious argument that George possesses something imaginatively that is closed to Sam, no matter how rich and successful Sam may be in worldly terms. Without for a moment losing sight of the pain and frustration of George's situation, *It's a Wonderful Life* suggests that something may come of all of it for George, something perhaps in some ways as great and moving as what would have come of the fulfillment of his dreams.

It's a Wonderful Life would be the supreme film of the American way of repression, however, if this were Capra's only point in this scene. Capra is indeed in favor of George's and Mary's acts of sublimation, but he also shows that such domestications of the sublime are not entirely satisfactory. Capra admires and endorses George's efforts to translate his passion and imagination into words and practical actions but knows that even so, it is a tragic expense of spirit. George's petty housewarming ceremony at the Martinis or his frustrated homemaking efforts in the old Granville place will neither express nor satisfy his deepest imaginative needs. George's dreams may be temporarily displaced into such paltry ceremonies, but they are not ultimately satisfying either for George or for a viewer.

In all of the examples I have cited, George's flawed, inadequate, threatened attempts to express his imagination in the forms of practical affairs – in Emerson's terms, to transform his genius into expressions of practical power – take us to the heart of Capra's artistic exploration in *It's a Wonderful Life*. The central questions of the film are ones that were implicit in *Deeds* and *Smith* also: How do we represent ourselves in the world? How can we convert our finest passional impulses into practical expressions? How can the free energies of the imagination be translated into the inevitably repressive structures of narrative and of life? Before I take up the ramifications of these questions in more detail, however, it is important to recognize how explicitly Capra frames them in this film.

I have been speaking of George's expressive problems, and not Mary's, because in the character of Mary Capra deliberately creates a foil to George who can perhaps help us better to understand the exact nature of his expressive predicament. Mary is able to channel her dreams into social, biological, and familial expressions of them, because her dreams were never as daring, socially disruptive, individualistic, or idealistic as George's. The mildness, biological rootedness, and natural attainability of Mary Hatch's dreams – in contrast to the dangerous exorbitance and exhilarating unnaturalness of George's – are emphasized by her last name, which Capra makes sure is recalled to our attention by having George pun on it in the stork scene, when he asks her if she is "on the nest." The pun summarizes much of their imaginative difference: Whereas George continually moves, physically and imaginatively, outward, conquering external spaces, Mary placidly possesses and fills interior spaces, in her pregnancy, her sitting still at home, and her thriving in the bosom of the family as she fixes up the Granville place. Even her initial wish on the windows of the Granville Place in the "Buffalo Gals" scene was only that she and George might one day live together in that house. She can get her wish in this instance, and in all of the others, because her wishes never radically threaten the worldly order of things and events.

There is reason to believe, not only on the basis of this movie and the one following it but from Capra's statements as well, that he intended George and Mary – and later Grant Matthews and his wife Mary in *State of the Union* – to summarize a fundamental difference between the male and female imaginations. However unfashionable the doctrine may be in so-called enlightened circles today, Capra takes his place in a long line of distinguished thinkers who have argued that there is an essential difference between male and female imaginative relationships to the world, men being more abstractly ideational, idealistic, and individualistic than women and suffering the unavoidable and frequent consequences of it in imaginative frustration, criminality, suicide, and sexual predation, as well as reaping the rare benefits of it in the creativity of certain kinds of philosophical, artistic, and scientific invention. (For someone who regards such a view as anathema, it can be said in defense of *It's a Wonderful Life* that the effect of the film does not overwhelmingly depend upon one's subscription to Capra's sense of a general biological difference in human imaginative tendencies.)

George represents an imaginative energy and mobility for which there can be no ultimately adequate expression in the world. Even to live the life of Sam Wainwright, the life of a millionaire playboy and world traveler, would not really satisfy George's dreams, which go beyond all worldly possibility of fulfillment. (That is also, incidentally, why George can resist the attractions of Sam's way of life so successfully in the scene I have just described.) For George, if not for Mary, the refurbishing of the Granville place and the housewarming ceremony on the steps of the Martinis' house can never express the intensity of his feelings and the grandeur of his imaginations, but neither could a ribbon-cutting ceremony in front of a skyscraper he had designed as an architect. His desire is and always will be in excess of any attainable destina-

Two scenes of girl watching: imaginative impulses that cannot be acted on socially or expressed verbally – evanescent narrative openings that close up almost as soon as they occur in the world of Bedford Falls.

tion. His feelings can never find words, causes, or an occupation adequate to express them. George is finally forced to repress his dreams, not because of the machinations of some evil opponent but because there *can be* no adequate expression for them in any actual world, just as Capra could find no direct expression of them in cinematic dialogue or narrative events. The dialogue and events in the film inevitably function only in a negative way to show us what George aspires to escape, to tell us what he does not want to be or do, to refer us to what cannot be said or lived within the structures of Capra's narrative, perhaps within the structures of any narrative. The most George can do is simply to hold onto his dreams and desires in silence and stillness, while the film's narrative takes place around him, almost independent of his deeper self and more profound impulses. Alternatively, he can sublimate such energies into the sorts of marginally useful and meaningful forms of expression I have just described, just as Capra himself had to obliquely and inadequately translate his own dreams and intensities of feeling into time-bound, socially responsible forms of conventional Hollywood feature-film narration.

In the largest sense, Capra's late figures (I am thinking of Bennett, Saunders, Smith, and Bailey) define a fundamental and unavoidable expressive problem that runs through American life and art. It is a problem of the representation of the self that, back in Chapter 2, I illustrated with examples from James's *Portrait of a Lady* and Sargent's *Madame X* and *Mrs. Fiske Warren*, but it is one that will not go away in Capra's work, and that I believe comes to the point of crisis in this film and *Smith*. Committed as they are to leaving behind confining, inherited structures of social interaction and expression, Bennett, Saunders, Smith, and Bailey (like Isabel Archer before them) make themselves close to "illegible" in their own narrative. They are figures of desire whose imaginative energy and emotional slipperiness cannot be contained or represented by any conceivable agenda or course of actions. They are principles of flux and movement that will not be articulated in the codes of narrative or of the world.

Their problems of self-representation are paralleled by their creator's problems in the representation of their selves. How does one represent a state of desire that in its essence is opposed to all codification, all limitation, all specification? The representation of each of these figures transports us (along with themselves) to the very limits of representation in art or in the world. How can one represent or express oneself as a figure of desire? That is why these characters are defined in Capra's narrative as radical openings out of narrative representation itself – in terms of what is not to be said or done, as absences or failures of language and social interaction. They represent themselves at their best and most interesting in terms of gasps, shouts, stares, silence, or stillness.

George Bailey is the culminating figure in this sequence. In the course of *It's a Wonderful Life*, he is, in effect, defined as a mere opening out of all of the social and narrative systems that would articulate him. In some of the ways I have already suggested, he embodies a principle of imaginative yearning that, no matter where he is or what he is doing, is always gesturing elsewhere, to a possibility that can never be realized in the practical forms of his expressive life. In this sense, he is defined more negatively than positively: as what Bedford Falls, the Building and Loan, capitalism, and every other representational possibility around him are *not*. If capitalism (at least in the form in which Potter embodies it, and as the dreamland episode demonstrates) figures a possibility of converting the entire world and all personal impulses in it into practical, pointed, purposeful representations in an all-inclusive system of capital accumulation, George figures the opposite possibility: an energy of imagination that will not be harnessed to any specific goal or object, a volatility and explosiveness of feeling that escapes all attempts to contain or represent it.

There is a new urgency, bordering on hysteria or desperation, in Capra's perception of the representational crisis confronting these late figures. In *Ladies of Leisure*, for example, the alternative to the commodification of beauty and sexuality was figured in a much more benign and less frantic form as a meditative turning away from society and its values that was fairly easy to perform for a character and never seriously objected to or resisted by others. As I described in the early films, characters were able to remove themselves at will from the eventfulness of their own narratives or to withdraw themselves from categories of social representation, just as Capra's film itself was, by means of what I called a "meditative shift." There was usually a fairly easily attainable state of calm and placidity in these films, but with the figure of Bennett in *Deeds* things change. In place of the easy, gentle, humane, meditative turnings of *Way of the Strong*, *Ladies of Leisure*, *Bitter Tea*, and *It Happened One Night*, Capra imagines a series of violent ruptures or puncturings of the representational surface of his film, openings out of the narrative representation of social interactions and dialogic exchanges in the form of a disruptive, disturbing sequence of melodramatically charged glances, gasps, or gestures.* One can continue to classify them as "meditative turnings," but they border on being states of hysteria and derangement.

George Bailey's most powerful and authentic expressions of himself are not in the narrative coherence and responsibility of housewarming parties, in fixing up the Granville place, or in building row houses for the multitudes, but in the moments when he, in effect, almost drops out of Capra's narrative, moments when he ceases utterly to be narratively or verbally active, purposeful, or responsible. They are moments when, like Bennett, Saunders, and Smith before him, he looks into the camera and says nothing; moments when an almost overwhelming passionateness comes into his voice or expression; moments when all he can do is to gasp or gulp or stare in stunned silence, pain, or astonishment. As registered in Capra's key-lighted close-ups of his face (often accompanied by a momentarily intense emotional strain of orchestration) at moments of crisis or frustration, such explosions of feeling threaten not only to disrupt the social ceremonies going on around him but to rupture the very narrative continuities and coherences of the work in which they occur. These eruptions† represent a residue of imagination and desire in George's life that cannot be sublimated into the forms of narrative or socially functional expression (any more than George's lyrical effusion that he will lasso the moon can be adequately represented in the form of Mary's homey needlepoint). They explode or subvert the structures designed to contain them – both the social and familial structures within which his life is organized, and the narrative and stylistic structures of the "family drama" film in which Capra situates him.

The contrast between *It's a Wonderful Life* and *That Certain Thing* can stand as a summary of the subtle shift in Capra's work in the two decades that separate the two films. The films are strikingly similar, with the equally striking difference that Capra reverses the narrative thrust of the earlier work in reformulating the situation in the later one. Molly's troubled consciousness

---

* To be strictly accurate, such violences of expression were intermittently present at moments in the earlier films as well, as I pointed out in my discussions of them, but they had nothing like the centrality and importance that they have in the films from *Deeds* to *State of the Union*.

† In my discussions of the early films I used this word in a fairly neutral sense to indicate any access of feeling in a scene, but in the later films I intend it in a much more violent, figurative sense. Emotion erupts into these films in a more powerfully disturbing, volcanic way.

Eruptions of imagination and desire into life figured as ruptures in the narrative: George suddenly learns that he has been named to head the Building and Loan.

is exorcised in the course of *That Certain Thing*, and its energies are sublimated into shrewd business practices and a scene of witty bargaining with her corporate rival. In 1928, Capra thoroughly endorsed *That Certain Thing's* course of narrative repression, but in 1946 things have changed. George's troubled consciousness is not exorcised or suppressed in the course of his film. His intensities of feeling and expression relentlessly continue to rupture the social surface of the narrative throughout the film, disrupting the harmonizations proffered by the narrative even more in the second half of the film than they did in the first half. Capra's film, in effect, resists its own inveterate acts of narrative arrangement and social organization to insist on a series of narrative arrests and imaginative ruptures.

That is why, unlike any previous Capra work, *It's a Wonderful Life* has to be presented in episodes. A more overarching narrative coherence and temporal continuity is beyond its grasp. It is structured episodically because it proceeds by means of epiphanic disjunctions and anecdotal discontinuities, a series of narrative breakages. There was one such moment of profound narrative and stylistic disruption in *That Certain Thing*, in the scene of Molly's stunned, silent return home after she woke up from the fairy-tale dream of her marriage, but the rest of the film consisted of Capra's effort to heal the wound that that brief scene had opened. *It's a Wonderful Life* is a series of such wounds with no final prospect of healing them, a series of narrative fractures that cannot be patched back together into a seamless plot line. Every ten or fifteen minutes in the film there is a crisis or a climax in which George (and the viewer) discovers that all of his plans, intentions, words, and actions in the previous segment have come to nothing or been negated. Capra's most common way of denoting such moments is typically to cut to a quick close-up of George's face (frequently key-lighted.) Nothing is said by him or by anyone around him at such a moment, because there is nothing to say socially or publicly, but the narrative has been disrupted socially, psychologically, and stylistically, to suggest an imaginative disturbance underneath or beyond all of the social and narrative forms of expression up to that moment. The hallucinatory dreamland sequence near the end of the film is only the most cataclysmic rupture in a film made up of a series of repeated narrative breakages.

It is only in artistic style – in the sense of the word that is equivalent to such special acoustic and photographic effects – that the imaginative energies Capra is interested in can be communicated, since they are for him by definition what cannot be communicated in the world of public, realistic, social, theatrical forms. Style or art for Capra, notwithstanding his mistaken reputation as the most unregenerate of realists, makes a space for the expression of energies that have no possibility of expression except in style or art.

What makes *It's a Wonderful Life* different from the previous films is that the narrative and psychological disturbances increase in severity as the film goes on. The initial ruptures are rapidly papered over. The moment of stillness or silence passes and is quickly filled up and almost erased by an ensuing stream of words and actions. The poignant glance or momentarily pained expression in George's eyes or voice is glossed over with the progress of the film's social dialogue and narrative. In the scene at the train station in which George discovers that his brother Harry has been secretly married and will not be replacing him at the bank, for a brief, stunned moment George stares into the camera in silent astonishment and profound disappointment. We are suddenly exposed to a depth of feeling that neither he nor Capra can find words for – here or in any subsequent scene, but the narrative arrest lasts no longer than a second or two. There is, as always in this world, an inexorable series of practical matters to be attended to, socially and narratively. There are suitcases to be picked up, formal congratulations to be paid, ceremonial celebrations for the newlyweds to be arranged, cinematic dialogue and movement to be resumed. The narrative wound opened by the glance is no sooner registered than it is quickly bandaged over, by both George and Capra.

Such narrative wall paperings do not last, however, and in fact the ruptures grow more serious in the course of the film. Instead of the narrative's subtly absorbing extraneous energies in its progress, repressing its own insights as it integrates the individual into a community photographed in fill-lighted, middle-distance group shots, such energies are allowed to increase in voltage in the course of the film, until, in a kind of cinematic capacitance, they flash

Closing the narrative wound: momentary narrative arrest reabsorbed by narrative appetitiveness and worldly eventfulness. On the train platform George realizes that his brother will not be replacing him at the Building and Loan.

out in one final discharge that short-circuits the realistic social narrative entirely, in the longest continuous sequence in the entire movie, a scene that is probably the most frightening nightmare sequence in all of Hollywood film: what I have been calling the nighttown or dreamland★ sequence – George's vision of himself as a displaced person, a being with no social identity, no home, no family, no social responsibilities or ties, and no form of communication with those around him. Whereas the expressively key-lighted imaginative

★ "Dreamland" is the name of the most conspicuous location on the transformed Main Street of Pottersville – the dime-a-dance hall in front of which Violet Bicks is arrested during the sequence. I sometimes also call it the "nighttown" episode, as an allusion to the uncannily similar episode in Joyce's *Ulysses* (though certainly the similarity between Joyce and Capra is entirely fortuitous).

disruptions, vocal quaverings, gasps, and stunned glances earlier in this film had been more or less isolated, momentary events, the dreamland sequence is one protracted series of stunning visual effects, social disruptions, gasps, stares, and tonal quaverings.

The nighttown episode makes explicit the issue that has been implicit in the whole preceding film: the consequences of the surfacing of energies that cannot be placed or represented in the forms of conventional life or Hollywood family-film lighting, photography, dialogue, dramatic progression, or narrative eventfulness. What was walled off into isolated moments in the preceding narrative and contained by the narrative and social ceremonies that surrounded it eventually bursts all social and formal walls erected to control it and emerges enlarged, deformed, and disastrous. Equally for Bailey as for Capra, nighttown represents a surfacing of the long repressed. George suddenly breaks free of the society that has hedged him round up to this point in the film, just as Capra breaks his own film free from the family drama organization of his preceding narrative. George momentarily becomes disencumbered from the constraints of social expression and the bondage of social relationships, in the same way as the film itself dramatically changes styles, from a family-drama commitment to gradual narrative progression through the social interaction of characters, to a film noir – related stylistics of sudden vision.

The visionary moments in Capra's earlier films were instances of his flirtation with such moments, but never before had he dared or been able to give himself and his film entirely over to such visionary stylistics. The dreamland sequence moves the viewer and George into a world of visionary ineffability and emotional intensity. Pictures and music replace words and dialogue. Operatic and melodramatic outbursts of intense feeling replace gradual chronological, sequential narrative exposition. Low-key-lighting effects, expressive close-ups, and emotionally powerful orchestrations communicate imaginative disturbances that have no social form of expression in the previous film or in George Bailey's ordinary life.

Jerry Strong and Kay Arnold, Megan Davis, and Lulu Smith each briefly experimented with the possibility of becoming all eye and spirit in this way – of living lives radically liberated from the limitations of ordinary social, temporal, and narrative existence. In jumping off a bridge one dark night, though, George plunges off the balcony, parapet, or railing that each of the others only dared to lean out across for a moment. He escapes utterly, as one can only in a dream or hallucination, from the ties of society, the limitations of social intercourse, and from the constraints of time itself. This figure who was previously so restricted in his movements (prevented from moving physically and imaginatively within the world of the film, as much as he was constrained and confined formally within the frame and sets of the film by Capra's fixed, middle-distance camera placements in most of the earlier scenes) is suddenly sprung free from space and time fictionally, formally, and imaginatively. It is not accidental that George's first significant action in dreamland is simply to

Dreamland: speaking a cinematic language of desire.

move freely and erratically through space and that Capra's first stylistic action is to move his camera with similar freedom. George runs down the main street of Bedford Falls, and Capra unmoors the camera for the first time in the film, in order to keep up with him.

In the largest sense, the dreamland sequence is Capra's attempt to conceive of and speak a language of pure desire. In his earlier films he and his characters glanced into such an imaginative abyss, but in this expressionistic sequence Capra attempts to move his film beyond the normalizing mediations of orthodox Hollywood studio form. He propels George and the film into the eternal, intense, unmediated present of a dream or a vision. This effort to break free of the formal repressiveness of the very film in which it occurs is, to my mind, the most moving and doomed expression of a filmmaker's own frustration with the formal restrictions of his chosen medium in all of Hollywood filmmaking.

The effort is doomed, however – not only because it cannot be sustained in its own film but because, as George, Capra, and the viewer all discover, it is an opening only into the prospect of incoherence and bewilderment (both formally and psychologically). To achieve such an intensity and purity of imaginative expressiveness, to be freed from the limitations of a stable personal or social identity, to be capable of bodily movements and self-expressions so fluidly responsive to the fluxional movements of feeling and desire may be, Capra suggests (in a mood much closer to that of Poe than to Whitman or Thoreau) not to gain a self but lose it. To break free of all merely ethical, personal, and social involvement may be not to achieve but to give up all that is most important in life or in narrative. From Molly Kelly's night-marish walk home and the wanderings of the snow-blind explorers lost on the Antarctic icecap in *Dirigible* to Doe's bewildered stumbling through the streets alone near the end of *Doe*, Capra has argued that to be daring enough to imagine oneself, in Robert Frost's phrase, an exception to all things – disencumbered from society's conventional definitions and customary cate-gories of selfhood and behavior – is, as in Poe, to court self-destruction, disorientation, and bewilderment. One part of Capra was powerfully attracted to this state of American exceptionalism and radical individualism, but another feared it equally as much. The nighttown scene represents Capra's revulsion from the visionary stylistics he most quests after. That way madness lies, he tells us. The radical liberation of the imagination may not free us so much as it dooms us to self-bewilderment and homelessness. The language of desire may be indistinguishable from social, verbal, and psychological incoherence and confusion. Freeing ourselves is equated with destroying everything that is valuable in experience.

It's a Wonderful Life leaves George Bailey and the viewer irreconcilably divided between untenable alternatives – between the repressive languages of society and the liberated language of desire, but with no way of mediating between the two realms, except in such paltry ceremonies as that at the Martinis' house. George returns to his family and home at the end of the film, but things are definitely not the same as before, for him or for us, precisely because we have lived through everything that has taken him away from those things and have been allowed to see through and beyond them. We have seen through the languages of society and seen the hazards of the language of desire. George is not (as is frequently asserted) simply reintegrated into society at the end of the film. He rejoins it physically and socially in the final grouping of the characters, but he and we are imaginatively, as a result of the nighttown scene, simultaneously somewhere outside of it too. We have achieved a crucial critical perspective on all of its languages and forms of relationship that was not available earlier. George is left in an essential doubleness, unavoidably involved with and surrounded by friends, relatives, neighbors, and the institutions of Bedford Falls, and yet at the same time somewhere off to one side of all of these things, inscrutable and silent, neither absorbed by that world and absorbed in it, nor outside of it or able to leave it behind. That is, as Kateb describes and Capra appreciates, the condition of American alienation – always understanding that to be alienated in this way is not to be lost and doomed beyond salvation but in some sense to be at least potentially in the most creative and stimulating situation possible. I am tempted to end my discussion of *It's a Wonderful Life* with that. The state of American alienation, as it is defined by the ending of this film is such a complex, rich, and vexed imaginative condition that one despairs of being able to say much more about it. It is so crucial to an understanding of Capra's work here and elsewhere, however, that, in the following pages, I want to continue my discussion, however hesitantly and tentatively from this point on.

Where does the ending leave George? Although he has been placed back in society, his social integration in that society has never been less perfect or his imaginative distance from it greater than at that moment. The harrowing effect of the twenty-five-minute dreamland sequence emphatically cannot be erased from George's (or the viewer's) consciousness in the four or five minutes of nominal "happy ending" that conclude the film. In any case, Capra does not want or allow George or the viewer to forget it. The unexplained appearance of Clarence's "gift" to George (his copy of *Tom Sawyer*) and the ringing of the bell on the Christmas tree (which reminds us of the cash–register bell in Nick's Place and Clarence's comments on it in the dreamland episode) in the final seconds of the film are deliberately calculated to bring back memories of the previous scene. The bell and the book remind us that George's understanding of them is necessarily and radically different from that of his wife Mary (who inquires about the book) and his daughter Zuzu (who dutifully recites what her teacher told her about the significance of a ringing bell). In short, at the moment when the movie most appears to be celebrating the possibility of a blandly homogeneous, small-town community of interest and shared understanding, Capra is driving a wedge between the consciousness of George, on the one side, and the putative community of sympathy and understanding rendered by the film, on the other.* The room is overflowing with George's closest friends, all apparently fused into an imaginative community by song, but the central objects and events in the scene and all of the summarizing feelings that George and a viewer have about the book and the bell, are completely incommunicable and incomprehensible to every other character there.

---

* This is, I believe, what is crucially left out of Robert B. Ray's reading of the film in *A Certain Tendency of the Hollywood Cinema* (Princeton: Princeton University Press, 1985), otherwise the best discussion of the film I have encountered. I should note that Ray's book was published after this manuscript was completed, or I would have taken up some of the strands of his interesting argument in more detail. See my review in *Art and Artists* (September 1986), p. 6.

There is nothing George can possibly say to represent his charged consciousness to the group around him at this moment, nor is there any passage of dialogue or action that Capra could have supplied to explain to them what George has experienced. George's enriched consciousness is all he has to show for it all. What George and we have lived through is an experience whose meaning *is* its unavailability to the forms of social representation and interaction in this scene. The nearest the final scene can come to expressing some of these energies is in the vague emotionality of the song being sung, in the imaginative resonances set vibrating by the sound of the bell ringing on the Christmas tree, and in George's silent glances and facial expressions. As in the dreamland sequence itself, Capra has to resort to using pure sounds and pictures to express what lines of dialogue or social interactions between characters cannot.

The closest equivalent to this sort of expression in the earlier films were Bennett's, Smith's, and Saunders's poignant, melodramatic pleas, gestures, and looks in the conclusions of their respective films, but George Bailey is denied such grandiosities of melodramatic expressiveness here and in the entire preceding film (with the exception of the nighttown interlude). Even melodrama has to be repressed here; the magnificently expressive gesture or look is forced underground. That is because melodrama presumes not a moderate state of alienation but a luxuriously, wonderfully grand alienation in the actor. The unrelenting moderateness of George's estrangement is what finally makes him, I believe, Capra's most interesting character.

The particular quality of his alienation may be most obvious in summary form in these final four or five minutes of the film, but it is something that Capra has established painstakingly in every minute of the preceding two hours. To appreciate the complexity of the presentation of his position throughout the film, one can begin with something apparently as slight as the way in which Capra's sound track functions. *It's a Wonderful Life* educates us and George to very complex kinds of multiple hearing. Consider the Christmas-tree bell that rings at the end of the film. One can hear it in terms of Zuzu's teacher's and Clarence's charmingly absurd saying, "Every time a bell rings an angel gets its wings." One can hear in it the cash-register bell at Nick's place, and therefore a more general echo of George's harrowing nighttown experiences. Or one can hear it in a third way that includes both ways at once and somehow moves beyond either. The point is not to have to choose between the Zolaesque and the Hans Christian Andersen interpretations but to be moved to the very special position of holding both at once in one thought.

Capra's film is an echo chamber in which George and the ideal viewer learn to hear (and see) in multiple ways denied the other characters in the film, and once one has been moved to this point, one no longer has the luxury of being free to recline into any simpler way of hearing (or seeing). When George, early in the film, in a moment of romantic idealism and pent-up, long-frustrated passion, proposes to Violet Bicks that they spend the night together on a mountain outside of town, she hears in his words only cold, dampness, and discomfort. The crowd of bystanders gathered around George and Violet hears only romantic fatuousness and comical impracticality, and laughs, but we and George hear the words in another way entirely. As the scene at the train station summarizes it, George hears an imaginative meaning for the "three most important sounds in the world" that is essentially different from Uncle Billy's description of them as "Breakfast is served; lunch is served; dinner is served."

Capra sensitizes the viewer to the importance of multiple hearing by giving George himself two distinct capacities for hearing: hearing ordinary sounds with one ear and only special or extraordinary sounds with the other, which is "deaf" to the routine sounds of life because of a childhood accident. The "deaf" ear is, in effect, the ear of childhood heroism, dreaming, and idealism, which has gone permanently deaf in all of the adults around George but intermittently functions for him to allow him to recapture the imaginative experiences of childhood. This endowment of a character with supersensory capacities as a compensation for a sensory handicap is anticipated in this film, as we have seen, by both *The Way of the Strong* and *The Miracle Woman*. In both earlier instances Capra makes a character blind in order to suggest the possession of a capacity of "insight" that goes beyond the reach of mere physical sight and that is, in fact, truer and more reliable than "sight" because it is more spiritual, and less liable to be misled by superficial or theatrical show.

George's situation is more complex than Nora's or John Carson's because his hearing functions not merely in an alternative way from that of other characters in his film but doubly: He hears in two ways at once, *both* with an "outer" realistic ear and with an "inner" imaginative one. Almost all of the romantic or revelatory moments in *It's a Wonderful Life* are associated with George's imaginative hearing (or failure to hear) through his otherwise "deaf" ear. He loses hearing in it in the first place by saving his brother's life; Mr. Gower slaps him on it when George saves the lives of a sick family by discovering the mistaken prescription sent to them; Mary professes love for him at the soda fountain by whispering into that ear; Joe presents the monogrammed suitcase from Mr. Gower with which George is to travel the world by announcing it into that ear; Mary admits on their honeymoon night that her secret wish had been to live in the Granville place one day with him by whispering it into that ear; and, of course, the entire dreamland sequence is heard through that ear, to which hearing is magically restored for that sequence only.

Capra's use of George's two kinds of hearing within the film is not a metaphoric gimmick. We, like George, undergo a profound education in hearing the crucial events throughout the film with two ears. Capra's complexly layered sound track, in the train-station scene and the ensuing wedding-party scene, for example, teaches a viewer to hear profound imaginative resonances and beckonings in the "sounds of trains, anchor chains, and boat whistles" (to quote George) that are mixed into the sound track during these and several other scenes in the film. George hears them in an imaginative way, as does a viewer who has been educated to appreciate their true imaginative significance

MARY: I don't like coconuts.
GEORGE: You don't *like* coconuts? . . . Don't you know where coconuts come from? . . . From Tahiti, the Fiji Islands, the Coral Sea . . . .
MARY: Is this the ear you can't hear in? George Bailey, I'll love you 'til the day I die.
GEORGE: I'm going out exploring some day – you watch. And I'm gonna have a couple of harems and maybe three or four wives. Wait and see.

Contrasted sounds of imagination: male and female, exotic and domestic, liveable and unliveable.

by Capra's sound track, but there is no evidence that anyone else in the movie hears them at all. We hear the ebullience, bordering on hysteria, of George's "Merry Christmas, Mr. Potter!" near the end of the film with the same outer ear, and in the same way, that Potter hears it, but we also hear it with an entirely different inner ear that has gone deaf in Potter, an imaginative ear that has been profoundly affected by our hearing of the dreamland experience of personal annihilation immediately preceding it. (Similarly, we "see" George's running down the street in the same scene doubly – both realistically and with an inner eye that remembers seeing the same event, photographed from the same angle, only minutes earlier in the dreamland scene.) We hear the Hawaiian music played during George's honeymoon in the leaky Granville place (which so strangely anticipates the exotic harmonies and rhythms of Tiomkin's orchestration of the dreamland episode) as coming from a scratchy record played on a tinny gramophone, but we also hear in it a half-mocking, half-exalting echo of George's dreams of travel to far off lands. We hear in George's congratulations to Harry's new wife on the train platform all the sincerity and good wishes she hears, but we also hear in them the dispairing cry of emotions too deeply frustrated and dreams too long deferred.

The double consciousness induced in George and the ideal viewer is much more than acoustic. Sometimes, as we have seen, the doubling takes the form of a comparison between two different "visions" or "hearings" of a scene. At other times, Capra in effect doubles his text by counterpointing the acoustic text against quite a different visual text. That sort of doubling takes place in the scene of Sam Wainwright's phone call to Mary Hatch. Sam's conversation about finances, plastics, and "getting in on the ground floor" of his new factory is counterpointed against a simultaneous rival, silent visual conversation of glances and facial expressions taking place between George and Mary.

The central achievement of *It's a Wonderful Life* is to keep two distinct texts of this sort going throughout almost every important scene: the one a realistic, publicly articulable social text, the other a private, ineffable subtext of desire and imagination. As the scene in Mary's house indicates, the two texts are in a potentially upsetting competition with each other. The second text is essentially untranslatable into the first, and finds its expression in alternative styles and forms of dramatic representation. The one text cannot be reconciled with the other or put into an easy relationship with it, and yet neither text is intended to be disregarded or demoted in importance. We and George are meant to live in both at once, irreconcilably, which is to say that Capra induces a state of alienation from either, even as he allows us to reject or ignore neither. We as viewers are suspended within and between incommensurable texts, just as George is in his own life.

It's a Wonderful Life is most usefully viewed, in the largest sense, as a profound modernist exercise in the consequences of such multiple vision (in the same sense in which Kateb argues that such visionary and re-visionary capacities are the "key to the modern transformation of experience," though without Kateb's privileging of sight over all of our other senses), consequences that, as Capra shows but Kateb does not fully acknowledge, can be equally liberating and bewildering. This suggests the most important difference between Kateb and Capra. For Kateb the result of the availability of multiple visions and perspectives is apparently always automatically happy, but for Capra such a state of affairs is potentially, but not necessarily, productive of confusion and anxiety. Kateb's different visions are apparently never in conflict or rivalry for our allegiances or beliefs, but Capra's George Bailey is, at times, painfully torn or divided by the doubleness of his perspectives and positions. George Bailey's (or Frank Capra's) task in *It's a Wonderful Life* will be to learn how to live satisfactorily in this situation, whereas Kateb seems to grant the satisfaction without cost or work on the visionary's part.

It's a Wonderful Life is about learning to live in one's multiple perspectives and visions, in a state of inevitable alienation from any one point of view and yet an inability to escape the multiplicity, in a way that might make the film's title unironic. In the course of the film George Bailey's task will be to learn to see, to hear, to feel, to experience in new ways, to move through the multiplicity and to learn to live with it. *It's a Wonderful Life* explores George Bailey's capacities of vision and re-vision, but, more than that, it is a film that treats film itself as one of our preeminent agents of modernist imaginative mobility and freedom. Film in itself, as Capra realizes, charts an endless adventure of vision and re-vision. In Kateb's sense, film and television have replaced fiction and painting as the chief means of enlarging the possibilities of experience in our century. As it did not take Godard to demonstrate, since one can find the awareness in native American art like *Sherlock, Jr.*, the movie house is the natural home of postmodern man, and the endlessly changing images on the screen are self-reflections of his own fluxional mind and figure. With its casually shifting intimacies, eclectic omniscience, and visionary voyeurism, the experience of film, virtually independent of whom or what is filmed, in and of itself involves a viewer in enacting the modernist project, of immersing oneself in a vast range of experiences while at the same time remaining imaginatively detached from them or at a critical distance from them.

Capra is surprisingly explicit about *It's a Wonderful Life's* being an experiment in modernist multiple vision in Kateb's sense. This aspect of the film is not, however, without parallel in his earlier work. His films, from the very beginning of his career, recognized the complex consequences of multiple visionary modes of perception in modern art and the modern world. *Ladies of Leisure, Forbidden, Bitter Tea*, and *It Happened One Night*, to name only the most obvious examples, explicitly compare and contrast alternative styles of personal and cinematic vision at the same time as they recognize that the sudden availability of a spectrum of alternative modes of perception can be both a blessing and a curse. The opening of new possibilities of artistic and personal vision in all of these films presents opportunities for fresh relationships and perceptions and enrichments of consciousness, but it can also chillingly cut one off from other, simpler pleasures and intimacies. It can be a liberation from confining social definitions and constraints, but it can also estrange one from desirable emotional involvements. Peter and Ellie are the paradigms of characters who are too stylistically eclectic and aware for their own good. In none of Capra's films, however, do the consequences of vision take on more complex resonances than in *It's a Wonderful Life*. Capra uses the film to reflect on the nature of cinematic vision itself, as well as on the career and function of vision in American life.

From its first seconds the entire experience of *It's a Wonderful Life* is couched as an assertively imaginative or visionary one. The credits sequence shows the credits displayed on the turning pages of an illustrated book, as if doubly to remind us that what we will be watching is a story. If that redundant emphasis on the fictionality of the film is not pointed enough, the first scene jolts us entirely out of anything that might be called realistic drama and into a purely visionary realm. Two glowing blobs of light come into view – two pulsating galaxies – that we are encouraged to see and hear imaginatively as two angels conversing in heaven. Capra originally filmed a more realistic opening scene, which is described in the shooting script of the film. It depicted actual heavenly bodies, in the nonastronomical sense of the word, talking together in a country garden setting, but he significantly discarded this Benjamin Franklinish conception of heaven as a rural theme park. In its place he put a radically different kind of representation, a conception of heaven as a state of consciousness that is brought into being by our powers of imagination. We have to work to see it.

More than the opening sequence of the film insists on the fictionality of what we are seeing. The daring ellipses and enjambments in the presentation of the principal events in George's life (as, for example, in the audacious juxtaposition of George and Mary's embrace during the telephone conversation with Sam Wainwright, in which George passionately protests that he does not want to get married, with the immediately following scene showing George and Mary leaving the church after their wedding, the discontinuous and anecdotal presentation of a series of episodes within George's life, and the repeated punctuations of the narration with the voice-over editorializing of the angels commenting on it keep reminding us that we are seeing something already seen, something made and imagined, something created by an observer somewhere, somehow outside of the events and more or less detached from them, continuously selecting and organizing them in terms of narrative relevance and coherence. We are reminded specifically that we are, in short, watching a movie, with a movie's unique power to collapse space and time into the flash of a cut, to leap years or miles ahead or backward with a rapidity beyond any other art.

It's a Wonderful Life is about the specific power of movie makers and moviegoers to imagine and reimagine events. Capra's heavenly spirit is not just any narrator or artist – he is a movie maker like Capra himself, and George Bailey is (at least in the dreamland episode) imagined to be a goggle-eyed moviegoer dreaming awake in the dark. Even more than *Bitter Tea*, which equated cinematic glass-shots with states of vision and taught its central character how to sit still and become a kind of moviegoer of her own experience, this film is an explicit and joyous celebration of the unique representational powers of film in all of its glory. The gods (or at least the saints and angels) of this modernist universe are imagined to be editors and directors of movies, movies at which ideal viewers like George (and the viewers in the movie theater, too, perhaps) learn to see.

This is much more than a fancy way to say that any work of art organized within a narrative frame and presented in an episodic flashback form calls attention to its own fictional presentation of reality. Capra insists upon the specifically filmic nature of events in this film. His god is not merely a god of art in general, but a god of the moviola in particular. When Joseph begins filling in Clarence on George's biography, in the first scene of the film, the experience is imagined explicitly as one of motion-picture projection. Experience is "screened," and it is impossible not to be reminded of someone's turning on a moviola or a projector, playing with the controls as he begins screening a movie. First there is sound without light, then there is unfocused light on the screen, and only finally, as it is focused before our eyes, can Clarence (and we) make out the figures within it clearly.

A few minutes later, as George is choosing a suitcase to take with him on a trip he ultimately never makes, Joseph (or Capra) actually stops the image on the screen to inspect it and comment on it, exactly as an editor or director putting a film together at a moviola might. It is an astonishing moment – a sudden and utter collapse of whatever illusion the movie has generated up to

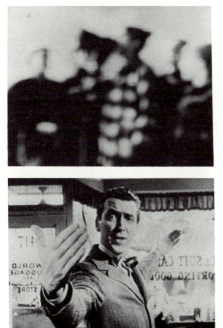

The god of the moviola:
focusing the action in one shot,
stopping it in another.

that moment, and a reminder that it is only an illusion.* It is rubbed in our faces that we are watching not life, but a movie, an artificial construction of human consciousness, something that has been photographed, lighted, and projected and that can be stopped or started at any time at the desire of the director, editor, or projectionist. It is a movie being edited and screened by and for angels, of course, but it is undeniably also a movie by Frank Capra that we are watching in a movie theater. At this exhilarating moment, it is hard not to enter sympathetically into Capra's equation of the two movies, not to feel his pleasure in and gratitude for his virtually godlike cinematic powers, his relishing of his own filmic effects as Clarence and Joseph comment on the attractiveness of the image of Jimmy Stewart stopped on-screen. *It's a Wonderful Life* is a celebration of such powers, a celebration of the power of movies to transport us, to give us new visions of life, to start or stop those visions, and to replace them with new ones, in an endless chain of imaginative substitutions, a chain of alternative visions, sights, and sounds with every shot and suture of the film.

The Capra I am describing as the celebrator of our powers of vision and revision is obviously a different figure from the one he is usually thought to be.

---

* Stop-action shots were not entirely unprecedented in previous Hollywood films. Sturges's *Palm Beach Story* (1942) starts with one, and Cukor's *Philadelphia Story* (1940) ends with one. There is, however, no other previous Hollywood film that employs one in midnarration, where the effect is entirely different from beginning or ending with one.

He is an artist reveling in our capacities of imaginative travel and meditative free movement, even as, in the tragic situation of George Bailey, he simultaneously acknowledges the impracticality of these forms of transport in the world's eyes. This is only once more to insist that Capra is closer to James than to, say, Steinbeck in his artistic aspirations. Whereas an artist like Steinbeck (in, for example, *The Grapes of Wrath*) describes the limitations of particular institutional and social forms of relationship, James and Capra are exploring the limitations all society places on the self. Whereas Steinbeck functions essentially as a journalist documenting the plight of the economically oppressed and politically disenfranchised, James and Capra are explorers of the potential repressiveness and impoverishment of all expressive systems – linguistic, social, and institutional – in comparison with the infinite richness of imagination and desire. This is a burden that rich and poor, the artistic genius and the average man on the street, successes and failures alike, labor under, and one that will not be lifted by governmental regulation or unionized solidarity. Capra and James are less interested in studying the legal and penal codes under which a few individuals unjustly suffer in American society than in exploring the invisible prison houses of society, language, thought, and action within which we are all condemned to serve life sentences.

No part of the film is more successful at reminding us that we are participating in an essentially stylistic experience, an experience of consciousness, than the dreamland scene, in which Capra deliberately switches the entire style of his film before our eyes. The fact that we are in the same film, seeing the same characters and the same settings but that everything is transformed stylistically makes the change all the more obvious and striking. It is as if one were watching two radically different directors make identical movies on different soundstages, in different studios, with different art departments and different sets of technicians. The acting styles, the lighting, the photography, the editing, and the sound track all suddenly and completely change, as does the physical style of the sets, actions, and events themselves.

Day gives way to night as decorous, modulated social interactions give way to nightmarishly exaggerated gestures and extreme expressions. Cinematic "realism" gives way to "expressionism," or, to put it more precisely, the fill-lighted styles of domestic, semicomic, Hollywood family drama give way to the low-key-lighted sensationalism and luridness of film noir. (Film noir was already a well-established Hollywood genre by 1946, with *Scarlet Street*, *Mildred Pierce*, *The Postman Always Rings Twice*, and *Double Indemnity*, to name only the most important examples, released in the three years preceding this film.)

Stable, fixed-tripod shots are superseded by kinetic tracking shots. Generally stationary and pictorially stable groupings of small numbers of characters are replaced by shots of disorganized, turbulent crowds, intercut with shots of solitary, frantic individuals violently and unpredictably lunging through the space around them or breaking the boundaries of the frame. The balanced, placid, well-lighted medium-shot compositions that dominated the earlier part of the film give way to disturbing, disorienting, poorly lighted long-shots of groups alternating with tight close-ups of individual faces. Shots of George politely and calmly interacting with small groups of people give way to shots of him in emotional anguish – running, gesticulating, shouting, crying, or staring into the camera – hysterical and isolated. "Objective," eye-level shots give way to "subjective" or point-of-view shots photographed from elevated or depressed angles. The use of source sounds and the spare musical accompaniment of the earlier film are superseded by Dimitri Tiomkin's eerie, melodramatic orchestrations that apply emotional pressure to every event.

The dreamland scene makes sense in terms of its film noir antecedents. In the same way that the genre of film noir itself functioned in the 1940s and early 1950s to express accesses of personal feeling and wildness of individual imagination that were summarily shut out of most other postwar Hollywood films, so this film noir episode serves as a sudden breaking loose of all of the hysteria, desperation, and imaginative frustration that George (and Capra) had kept bottled up in the entire preceding narrative. The repressed returns with a vengeance to flash out an explosion of emotional and cinematic intensity and violence, exactly in proportion to the intensity and violence of the initial act of cultural and narrative suppression that had contained it for so long.

That is an important aspect of the episode, but the dreamland sequence is more than the demonstration of a psychological and social truth. It is, first and foremost, a bravura cinematic performance, a tour de force of deliberately astonishing and sublime cinematic effects. It is a set piece in which Capra flaunts his own (and his set designer Emile Kuri's) dazzling cinematic ability to *reimagine everything we have already seen in the film in a new way*. To do this is not simply to expose the viewer (and George) to another particular style. To see something once in any one style is to seem to see reality, but to see it twice, in two different styles, is to see that there is only the seeing. We do not see just two styles; we see that everything we have seen or will see is style. Capra offers a practical cinematic lesson in the possibility of the re-vision of vision totally of a piece with the plot of the film itself. He shows us how he could have made another sort of movie all along – how consciously chosen, how artificial every aspect of the earlier part of the film was. Capra's analogue for George's capacity for revising his own point of view is a cinematic demonstration of his directorial capacity to reimagine the entire preceding part of the movie. Virtually every setting, every event, and every character we have seen and heard is reencountered, reseen, and reheard in a new way, a new light, a new style.

As Kateb persuasively argues, stylistic eclecticism, in the American experience as well as in modernism more generally, is a potential mode of freedom, but, as I have been suggesting at several points in my argument and as George's (or a viewer's) emotional state during the nighttown sequence makes clear, Capra has a much darker view of the modern condition than Kateb does. The state of buoyant emotional detachment and parodic playfulness that Kateb extols is unavailable to Bailey, who is entirely unable to achieve a state of ironic distance from his experiences.

Capra describes modern American experience in terms of a proliferation of imaginative possibilities and alternative visions. The self moves through a series of stylistic force fields without being committed to or expressed by any one in particular. Thus far he agrees with Kateb, but the difference is that, for Capra, far from being able to abstract himself from one after the other or to hold himself at a protective distance from all of them, the individual is disturbingly, disorientingly, warped, bent, manipulated, and worked on by each one in succession. In the figure of George Bailey, Capra implicitly replies to Kateb, saying that America is the land where the individual is freed from institutionalized supports and the shelter of unitary categories and beliefs, not to attain the imaginative detachment and mobility of a connoisseur for whom everything has become merely fictional but to be rendered all the more vulnerable to the coercions of the powerfully distorting force fields through which he moves, pressuring him in their competing ways. His rootlessness makes him all the more susceptible to being worked over by the successive, rival, contradictory forms of experience around him. Kateb, Whitman, and Thoreau describe a world of freedom and mobility, a world of "going down the open road," but nothing could be further from Capra's (or the viewer's) sense of things in these late films. George Bailey, Jefferson Smith, John Doe, Longfellow Deeds, and viewers of their films are almost torn apart by the competing, irreconcilable stylistic alternatives.

Kateb imagines a Whitmanesque world where free spirits and styles weightlessly meet, merge, or pass, but Capra, more like Henry James, defines a world of coercive pressures, unending, painful shifts of position, and wrenching distortions of vision. Like the powerfully beleaguered and put-upon central figures in Cassavetes's films, the torn and divided heroines in James's novels, the vulnerable ego pushed and pulled in various directions at the center of *The Education of Henry Adams,* or the unstably oscillating, self-critical consciousness in Emerson's journals, George Bailey lives in his affecting vulnerability and susceptibility to coercion and distortion. It is possible to mistake this continuously shifting stance for balance and detachment, but Maggie Verver and Isabel Archer, Mabel Longhetti and Minnie Moore, Suzanne Farrell and Patricia McBride, George Bailey and Jefferson Smith are figures of anxious, continuously adjusted imbalance. They live in these adjustments and imbalances, shifting between involvement and detachment, between susceptibility and withdrawal; but this represents a kind of poise too.

The dominant metaphors of *It's a Wonderful Life* involve comparisons of characters' capacity for physical and imaginative movement (or their lack of capacity for it); and the central progression in the film is the demonstration of George's ability to move imaginatively amid all these pressures with a freedom and openness to possible experience that beggars the mere physical movements of Sam Wainwright or the geographical travel offered to George by Potter. One can stay at home and still be a cosmic traveler in space and time, as George and an imaginative viewer of the film both learn. "Flying," or "getting one's wings" (in heaven, in Clarence's case, or in the Army Air Corps during the war, in the case of George's brother Harry), is one of the important metaphors in the film (as well as in *State of the Union*, Capra's next movie), but Capra makes us aware that true flight, on earth or in heaven, is not physical but visionary and imaginative, and that George has flown farther and faster through space, time, and landscapes of the mind than either Clarence or Harry. It is George's capacity to move and be moved, imaginatively and emotionally, and the film's capacity to move a viewer in similar ways that ultimately legitimize Capra's equation of his filmmaking capacities with the visionary powers of angels and gods.

Capra is not simply suggesting that imaginative movements can substitute for physical immobility. He is squarely in the radically Miltonic (or Romantic) tradition in arguing that such imaginative movements are a finer form of freedom than worldly movements, and one that becomes possible only with the renunciation of the other. If dreams and ideals are displaced desires and deeds, it is not until deeds are frustrated and desires are repressed that one acquires the full capacity to dream and imagine. That displacement defines the essential difference between George and all of the other characters in the film, most notably between him and Sam, Violet, and his wife Mary, each of whom does succeed in translating his or her desires more or less directly into practical, worldly expressions.

One of the most moving moments in the film in this respect is George's and Mary's improvised "honeymoon" on a rainy night in the leaky Granville place. George has just had to bail out the Building and Loan with his life savings to avert the closing of the bank, and as a result he and Mary are now unable to go to Bermuda for the honeymoon they had planned. It is a moment of utter desolation. This was to have been George's one chance to get out of Bedford Falls, however briefly; this was to have been the one successful adventure of his life, however tame a honeymoon may seem in the annals of adventure literature, but he cannot even have this. He ends up spending the time in a dilapidated, leaky house on the edge of town. To add insult to injury, it is the very house in front of which he had earlier vowed to "shake the dust of this crummy little town off my feet." Mary puts a record of Hawaiian music on the gramophone. She rigs up a primitive spit from the record player to the fireplace to simulate an outdoor barbecue, as if they were at a tropical luau. South Seas travel posters are plastered over the windows and on the walls. None of it, needless to say, erases a jot of the reality – that they are not in Bermuda, that George's dreams have been frustrated again, and that the drafty, drippy house is the last place in which he would have dreamed of spending his honeymoon. None of the reality is elided, and none of the frustration is denied, making this act of imaginative transformation different from the ceremony of the bread, wine, and salt in front of the Martinis' house, for example. In the housewarming ceremony, George, Mary, and Capra momentarily pretend that life can be made over by an act of consciousness.

Talking rather than kissing, reading rather than doing, imagining rather than traveling: going to the South Seas in the Granville place.

The scene pretended that George's exalted ideals could be domesticated, that his imaginative energies could be sublimated into and expressed by such paltry ceremonies, with nothing lost in translation, but the awful night, the scratchy record, and the leaky roof in this scene mock such aesthetic sleight of hand. The enormous incongruity between the dream and the world cannot be papered over with travel posters on the windows.

However, that is not to say that this scene is a mockery or travesty of George's ideals. On the contrary, Capra proposes an imaginative stance much more radical than the mild-mannered sublimation or domestication of imagination represented by the housewarming scene. To adapt the protest of the comically nosy neighbor who called down to George and Mary during the "Buffalo Gals" scene, "Why don't you kiss her instead of talking her to death?", Capra chooses talking instead of kissing. He asserts that in *not* kissing, in *not* going to Bermuda, in *not* leaving Bedford Falls, one may actually have more of what those things imaginatively represent than one could have in actually doing them. It is the apparently paradoxical Miltonic (or Jamesian) argument that, in James's (or Lambert Strether's) phrase, "in not having gotten anything out of it all" one may have gotten everything that was worth getting imaginatively. One only has the dream, in its true glory, in the moment of its displacement. What if George and Mary had gone to Bermuda instead of honeymooning in the Granville place? To have gone to Bermuda would have been not to have the honeymoon with the love, the passion, and the inventiveness of the scene as it stands (as they are evoked in Capra's shift to a point-of-view camera, mimicking George's loopy, exploratory glances at the touches Mary has creatively improvised on short notice in that truly wretched old house). What would have become of George's "lassoing the moon," his extravagant poetic spoutings, the wishes on windows, the ceremony of a lady and her courtier, if George had kissed Mary "instead of talking her to death"? What if Megan and Yen or Jerry and Kay had done the "conventional thing," and physically consummated their relationship? What would have become of the imaginative adventures in those films? Capra is arguing that these frustrations, repressions, and deferrals are not gaps to be bridged, obstacles to be overcome, but the origin of imagination and art. The frustration of desire and its resultant expression of itself in a displaced form is the beginning of creation. If this is what it means to be a socially conservative artist, then writers from Milton to James are equally guilty of the charge.

Capra's is finally a tragic sense of life. *It's a Wonderful Life* is a film of endless frustrations, deferrals of gratification, and of the complete impossibility of representing the most passionate impulses and imaginations of the self in the world – and yet the title is still entirely unironic. Capra wants us to know that George Bailey's life is wonderful – not because his neighbors bail him out with a charity sing-along, and certainly not because of the damnation of his life with the faint praise embodied in Clarence's slogan, "No man is a failure who has friends," but because he has seen and suffered more, and more deeply and wonderfully, than any other character in the film. This Cinderella, unlike the one in the fairy tale or *That Certain Thing*, is returned to the hearth, restored to being a char girl, with no future possibility of escape and with only the consciousness of what has just been lived through in the preceding dark night of the soul as consolation – but that, Capra argues, is enough. The adventure of consciousness that George has lived through in dreamland is greater than any of the romantic adventures he has talked about going on – but it is at the same time only an adventure of consciousness.

The final scene of the film enacts the same narrative movement we have seen previously in the final scenes of *The Way of the Strong, Ladies of Leisure, Dirigible, The Miracle Woman, Forbidden, Bitter Tea,* and *It Happened One Night.* In the last ten minutes or so, Capra does protractedly what he has done only briefly at crucial earlier moments. He retards or arrests the progress of the plot and silences the speech of the characters in order to move them and a viewer into a special meditative or imaginative relationship to experience. Capra briskly shifts from a scene involving vigorous physical movements and/or passionate talk to a scene of sudden stasis, stillness, and silence. In a kind of metaphoric transference, the physical, verbal, and social agitation of the previous scene is transferred into the following one as a psychological, emotional, or metaphysical agitation. The energy of the outward, public drama is suddenly redirected and released in the form of an intense inward, private drama of consciousness in a central character.

We move from eventfulness to meditation, from movements of plot to movements of imagination, from action to reaction. At the end of the terrifying dreamland experience, George is crying out loud and running for his life. Then, abruptly restored to his identity, he again runs, equally hysterical with joy, down the street, wishing Merry Christmas to everyone he meets, dashes into his house and up the stairs, crying over his wife and children and talking a blue streak. Then the shift occurs. Capra stops his tears, silences and immobilizes George, as we and he are suddenly moved into another realm. A crowd of friends, relatives, and neighbors pours into his house, surges around him, and comes forward, as they make their financial contributions one by one and he stands quiet and reflective at the eye of the storm. The whole of *It's a Wonderful Life* – and indeed most of Capra's work – might be said to exist simply to make possible and to legitimate this movement into the interior: In place of worldly movements, adventurous events, and public speeches, Capra substitutes possibilities of imaginative movement, adventures of consciousness, and silent revelations. George Bailey, like Jack Bradon, Megan Davis, Florence Fallon, or Kay Arnold at the end of their films, learns only to stand still, yet to make that standing still count for the most exciting movement of all.

In stilling ourselves in this way, in order to allow ourselves to become agitated in the other way, our consciousness can be enriched and complicated more than by a trip around the world. One can "gain one's wings" and make the most daring flights of imagination, without ever leaving home.

Whatever Capra may have thought he was doing, George, in his silent marginality and imaginative exile, is not merely integrated back into the society around him at the end of the film. He is irrevocably alienated from it, in both an exhilarating and an endlessly painful sense. The experiences he has had are untranslatable into its forms and incommunicable to its members. He is on the creative margin defining the modernist critical position, somewhere inside the text and yet outside it at the same time. He is on the margin of simultaneous susceptibility and detachment inhabited by modern heroes of American art and culture as different from one another as Hester Prynne, Huck Finn, Maisie Farange, Lambert Strether, Maggie Verver, the Chaplin tramp, Seymour Moskowitz, and Mabel Longhetti: living at home, but never able to feel simply at home; alienated and estranged to a critical distance from the society of which he is a part, but unable and unwilling to leave it, renounce it, or escape its powerful, threatening influences.

In the final seconds of the film, George's brother Harry arrives and toasts him as the "richest man in town." It is hard to know exactly what Harry intends by the remark. He is certainly wryly commenting on the nearly miraculous appearance of the money George needed to cover the bank loss, and he is probably also graciously alluding to George's social good fortune in having so many generous friends gathered around him in his house on this Christmas Eve. Yet the most important meaning of the phrase – the meaning that a viewer attaches to it and that George himself undoubtedly understands by it – is almost certainly unintended by Harry. George's true richness at this specific moment has nothing at all to do with either his social or his financial good fortune. It is utterly unrelated to the presence or absence of dollars and cents or of friends. It is imaginatively that George is rich beyond the wealth of kings, and it is not insignificant that even this fact can be communicated in Capra's film and in George's life only in the form of this private pun – a pun of which no one in the room except George is even aware.

With that silent pun (silent or inaudible to everyone but George and the viewer), as with the ringing of the bell on the Christmas tree or the sight of the copy of *Tom Sawyer*, we and George have left the group far behind. The significance of those events, like the significance of all of the crucial events in the film, is silent, inexpressible, and untranslatable into any terms that the society of Bedford Falls could understand. Their meaning exists only in the alienated richness of George's private consciousness and in the alienating enrichment of consciousness that the viewer undergoes in watching the film. George is inextricably embedded in the group, never to be released from its pressures or even able to want to turn his back on it, but with this imaginative movement he has also forevermore been propelled outside of it, at an infinite distance from it, reflecting on it.

George has traveled and, in his continuing imaginative movements, is still traveling at this instant, in what might be called the Keatsian realms of gold. Like Keats, or Keats's Cortez, a figure imaginatively wooed away from the pursuit of physical riches in the jungle to the possession of imaginative and visionary riches, as he stands silent on a peak in Darien, George has nothing to show for his truly excessive expenditure of imaginative capital but his visionary interest. Both imaginative travelers are left with nothing but a "wild surmise" to show for it all. George indeed is, in a sense Harry is utterly unaware of, the richest man in town – in a Miltonic, Keatsian, Emersonian, or Jamesian sense – not in spite of, but because of the absolute imaginative freedom his worldly bankruptcy has conferred on him. George – family man, burdened with debts, cares, children, and well-meaning but frequently inept friends – is the richest, most imaginative traveler in all of American film. In this film, he is second only to the god of the moviola who created, edited, and screened it for us – himself, like George, half within it, involved emotionally with it, and half outside of it, looking critically and dispassionately at it from an infinite and unbridgeable imaginative distance as the envisioner and reviser of the entire fictional text.

Awakening from the dream

16

The technologies of experience and of film

State of the Union

Human life is made up of the two elements, power and form, and the proportion must be invariably kept if we would have it sweet and sound. Each of these elements in excess makes a mischief as hurtful as its defect. Everything runs to excess.
– Ralph Waldo Emerson, "Experience"

[The war] burnt me out. The war was a terrible shock to me ... *What the hell is wrong with us?* I used to think. I thought that perhaps I had put too much faith in the human race – you know, in the pictures I made. Maybe they were too much as things should be. I began to think that maybe I really was a Pollyanna.
– Frank Capra, Interview with Walter Karp

Because ideals and desires cannot be expressed directly or forcefully in the forms of dialogue and social interaction in *It's a Wonderful Life*, Capra's mise-en-scène is called upon to pick up the expressive burden that they cannot bear. Particular stage props and symbolic aspects of the sets themselves are asked to "speak" imaginative meanings that cannot be spoken by the characters in a more direct way. The ringing of the Christmas-tree bell and the appearance of Clarence's edition of *Tom Sawyer* in the final scene, like the broken finial on the banister at the Granville place, the "George Lassos the Moon" needle-point, and the picture of George's father on the wall behind him in many of the earlier scenes, are used to communicate in ways that characters' words and actions cannot. The important point to notice is the essential *difference* between what can be expressed metaphorically, symbolically, or visually in the film by means of such devices and what can be spoken and acted upon more practically and directly in the forms of dialogue and plot. That difference is the funda-mental expressive reality recognized by the film, and it might be said to define the tragic gap between the enriched consciousness and the impoverished ex-pressive opportunities available to it.

Specific instances of Capra's use of objects hanging on walls – like Mary's needlepoint or the picture of George's father – remind one of the similar use of framed spaces in the paintings of Homer and Hopper. Such framed rectangular objects on walls or openings through walls function in

Winslow Homer, *New England Country School*. Addison Gallery of American Art, Andover, Massachusetts.

Winslow Homer, *The Noon Recess*. Courtesy of Hood Museum of Art, Dartmouth College, Hanover, N.H., Samuel H. Appleton Fund.

exactly the same way in their work as they do in Capra's. They represent imaginative openings out of the confined, cramped worlds inhabited by the central figures, even as they function only as imaginative, and not actual physical or social, openings. Consider the effect of the window on one side of the boy doing his homework in Homer's *Homework*, the windows on either side of the schoolmarm in his *New England Country School*, the map, the windows, and the chalkboard hanging on the wall in his *The Noon Recess*, or, more generally, the use of window frames, ledges, horizons, railings, or other strictly demarcated physical boundaries in Homer's or Hopper's other paintings. Such boundaries or demarcated limits are invariably juxtaposed against or are used to frame imaginative or visual openings that represent potential escapes from the physical confinements of the space defined. The worldly boundary in each case paradoxically outlines the possibility of an imaginative hole that ruptures it or offers a movement beyond it.★

In *The Noon Recess* and *New England Country School*, Homer's bored schoolmarms, oppressively shut in by the physical walls of their one-room schoolhouses and the tedium of their days (just as they are compositionally shut in by the oppressive symmetries, repeated parallels, barren rectangularity, and visual tedium of the artistic spaces in which Homer situates them) are offered visionary releases (just as in much of Hopper's work) through the windows on either side of them. In *The Noon Recess*, the more interesting of the two works, Homer attracts our eyes outward through the windows by calling attention to the activity outside. Inside is confinement and stasis and silence; outside is movement and noise and freedom, and the echoing of the diagonal posture of the boys in the window behind the teacher with the teacher's own diagonally presented figure suggests her imaginative yearning for their state of freedom, free movement, and free expression, even as her looking in the other direction implies her inability to participate in their freedom. However, the movement that interests Homer most is not physical but imaginative. By positioning the map on the wall just over the head and to one side of his figure (a device previously employed by Vermeer), he tells us, in effect, that the subject of the engraving is imaginative movement. His teacher's glance outward is actually evidence of a meditative turn inward. The actual state of the children playing outside is unavailable to her and ultimately unimportant. In looking outside she is meditatively entertaining possibilities of escaping westward, literally or metaphorically, beyond both the schoolroom and the children outside, beyond the physical, social, and expressive

★ There is a fascinating chapter in art history yet to be written about how particular American painters of the late nineteenth and early twentieth century creatively misread earlier European masters by viewing them through the eyes of Emersonian Romanticism. Specifically, much of the work of Homer and, later, Hopper, who is profoundly indebted to Homer in his methods and interests, is based upon that of Vermeer and Velásquez, and many of the same compositional and perspective techniques involving the use of imaginative openings out of confined physical and social spaces are found in all of their work; yet the result in Homer and Hopper is the creation of visionary effects that the Dutch and Spanish masters could never have anticipated or intended to be taken as the lesson of their works.

Winslow Homer, *Homework*. Canajoharie Library and Art Gallery, Canajoharie, N.Y.

confines of school life altogether, imaginatively beyond all of the surfaces and figures rendered in the work itself. The work indicates its own expressive limits.

Some of Homer's open-air compositions, such as *The Dinner Horn* and the *Long Branch* series of etchings and paintings, though they cannot use walls, windows, maps, or pictures in this way, complexly use the visual effect of juxtaposing a severely bounded foreground against an unbounded background space defined by a distant horizon to the same purpose. The eye is enticed into passing from socially costumed and encumbered figures, who are physically immobilized by a ledge or railing in the foreground of the painting (and formally immobilized by their placement within the composition, off to one side of it, or close to one edge of it) across and beyond these worldly and formal boundaries through the pictorial space to the sea or the unbounded horizon beyond. This is what might be called the transcendentalizing impulse in Capra's, Hopper's, and Homer's work. Figures physically, socially, and formally confined are offered imaginative releases from their entailment and immobility. The social body is (and must be) left behind in order to free the visionary eye to movement. All three are equally artists of the spirit whose spirituality involves spiriting the body away, dissolving the I into an eye. I emphasize that the common ground among the three is that the movements they are interested in are not social or physical but meditative and imaginative. One can look through a window or reach out visionarily toward the west or the horizon, but since one is not a transparent eyeball one cannot actually transport oneself (except in a visionary sense) outward along the line of sight or actually pursue one's own meditative path out of the world. George, on the edge of his group of friends, relatives, and neighbors, off to one side standing and listening to the ringing of the bell on the Christmas tree, is in the line of Homer's girl of *The Dinner Horn*, standing half within, half outside of the domestic space of her circumscribed existence and enticing our imaginations outward into the fields with the unheard sound of the horn she blows and to which she listens.★

Books are another rectangular opening out of the physical space of a painting that appear consistently in the work of Vermeer, Homer, and Hopper, and, even more obviously than windows or doors, they represent purely imaginative openings out of confined spaces. Homer's young girl reading, in *The New Novel*, like the boy looking into his book in *Homework*, and like the ubiquitous book readers in Hopper's paintings are momentarily released from the world, as much as if they were physically transported out of their bleak surroundings. George picking up Clarence's book from the collection basket and reading the inscription in it is directly in the line of these trapped visionaries and dreamers, enclosed as they are in confined and confining social and physical spaces, but moving beyond their walls in meditation and day dreaming.

★ This use of physical boundaries (walls, windows, and railings) and the suggestion of possible imaginative movements beyond them function similarly in Hopper's work (see pp. 18 and 220).

Winslow Homer, *Long Branch, New Jersey*. Charles Henry Hayden Fund; courtesy of the Museum of Fine Arts, Boston.

Winslow Homer, *The Dinner Horn*. Founders Society, Detroit Institute of Arts; gift of Dexter M. Ferry, Jr.

This does not put the case that Capra is making in *It's a Wonderful Life* and many of his earlier films (and the case that Homer and Hopper are implicitly making in their paintings as well) strongly enough. It is not merely that physical and social limitations allow visionary release or that the immobilization of the body is not inconsistent with meditative movement. The limitation makes the release possible; the immobilization in one way creates the very possibility of movement in the other. As at the ends of so many of Capra's films, from *Ladies of Leisure* and *Dirigible* and *The Bitter Tea of General Yen* to *It's a Wonderful Life*, it is in being silenced, stilled, and denuded of social resources and forms of expression that the imagination is born. It is in the prevention of seeing and moving in the world that another way of seeing and moving becomes possible. (To put it in terms of Homer's schoolmarm works, it is out of the social impoverishment of their scenes, the simplification of their settings, and the austerity of their tonality that the visionary richness, complexity, and powerful imaginative coloration emerges.)

The most eloquent example of this prior to *It's a Wonderful Life* is the sequence of blanket scenes in *It Happened One Night*. As I have already indicated in discussions of several early Capra films, just as in the schoolmarm paintings by Homer, two-dimensional modes of spatial representation are juxtaposed against three-dimensional ones to indicate states of imaginative limitation and release, respectively. What I am pointing out now is that, in both Capra and Homer, conditions of confinement and liberation are not opposites, but complements of each other. It is the confinements and immobilizations of the schoolmarm paintings that sponsor the meditative releases and movements, and the same thing is demonstrated by a work like *It Happened One Night*.

The blanket that separates Peter and Ellie in their various motel rooms is a two-dimensional plane of separation and limitation that functions essentially as an opening and a release to the possibility of a movement of erotic imagination and discourse in another dimension. It is a two-dimensional barrier, a plane blocking physical and social movement, which is also its own invitation to cross it, both verbally and imaginatively. Stanley Cavell has compared the blanket to a movie screen, a simile that seems to me merely fanciful and ingenious, except in one respect, which brilliantly vindicates it. Both the blanket and the movie screen are two-dimensional surfaces that, for Capra, exist in order to release the viewer into an imaginative space whose essential quality is that it is not definable or comprehensible in terms of two-dimensional surfaces and visual effects. This is not true of all film in the sense in which I intend it: Hawks, Cukor, and Lubitsch, for example, might be said to create worlds out of which there is no such available or tenable imaginative opening, worlds that are defined precisely as ones in which there are no such transcendental or visionary escape hatches.

Peter and Ellie cannot transgress the social boundary defined by the blanket (and the film has to reject Ellie's incipient move across it in the final motel, and actually to end, suddenly going black, the instant the blanket finally falls), but its presence is an imaginative stimulation to visionary movement that, Capra implicitly argues, would not come into being without the social, sexual, and physical prevention of movement that it represents. To get beyond the blanket, and the walls of reserve in the film, the blanket and the walls must be kept up, formally and personally. That is the deepest connection of the blanket and a movie screen – not in its size, shape, or color, all of which make Cavell's comparison seem farfetched – but in the fact that both of them force one to sit still, to cease one sort of involvement and intercourse in order to enter into another sort of imaginative involvement and intercourse. A movie screen, in all of Capra's films, is a barrier that is – because it is a barrier – an imaginative opening. It exists to transport us (and his central characters) out of one kind of society in order to allow us to enter another, visionary company.

I cannot leave the subject of the relationship of Winslow Homer's painting to Capra's work without noticing, parenthetically and in passing, one final uncanny and revealing connection with *It's a Wonderful Life*. Capra's use of the models of the bridges and buildings George aspires to build, which sit on his worktable at home (and which he destroys in the explosion of pent-up rage and frustration that precedes his suicide attempt) remind a viewer familiar with

Homer's work of the model boats built by the groups of boys in the series of paintings and etchings Homer did on the subject of boat building. Homer's work depicts boys making models of boats visually juxtaposed against the vessels actually built or manned by adults in real life, just as George's toothpick-and-glue models of bridges and buildings are imitations of those actually designed by architects and constructed by bridge builders.

The wrong way to approach the models in both the movie and the boat-building series is to view them as childish, amateurish, preparatory studies for more mature, sophisticated, realistic adult achievements. Homer and Capra are arguing something more radical, and less obvious, than that. Homer's boys in *The Boat Builders* represent a visionary or imaginative capacity for building that is intended absolutely to displace or replace the actual adult activity. It is not a poor worldly imitation of it, but an imaginatively rich substitution for it, a substitution more interesting than the so-called reality that stimulates it. *The Boat Builders* tells us as much by spatially displacing the adult activity with the boyish one and playing with the resulting distortions of scale. In both works I reproduce, the boys and their tiny models are allowed the full foreground expanse of the painting or etching, and the grown men building the actual ship are relegated to the background and shrunk by the perspective to the status of the real toys in the situation. *Ship Building, Gloucester Harbor,* with its emphasis on the sheer man-dwarfing labor entailed in building an actual boat, in contrast to the visionary composure and satisfaction of building a model and being able to hold it in one's hands and on one's lap, makes this clear. As the perspective of both works establishes, to be a boy model maker is to be an imaginative giant; to be an actual builder or sailor is to be only a kind of physical midget.

One is reminded by Homer's act of spatial and imaginative displacement that boats are themselves only rather ordinary vehicles of physical displacement that acquire their enormous pictorial value to artists as well as their powerful symbolic value to boy model makers only by means of acts of imaginative displacement. The model building in these works is not a preparation for the superior adult activity, or an inferior version of it, but an autonomous, full-scale imaginative alternative to it, just as the model making that is the painting of the painting or the making of a movie is a powerful imaginative enrichment and symbolic displacement of reality, not a weak or small-scale imitation of it. The boys in the foreground of the work form a visionary community of appreciation and value with which actual building cannot compete. Model making (of bridges, buildings, boats, paintings, and films) is the preeminent, grander activity. Actual boat or bridge building is a visionary comedown, by comparison.

That paradox is at the heart of *It's a Wonderful Life*. In his confinement, pain, and impotence, in his only being able to make models of the structures he would like to build in the world, in his only having visionary powers, George's frustration and achievement is summarized. George cannot express himself physically or socially, in buildings, words, or dramatic interactions,

Winslow Homer, *The Boat Builders*. Indianapolis Museum of Art, Martha Delzell Memorial Fund.

Winslow Homer, *Ship Building, Gloucester Harbor*. Courtesy of Hood Museum of Art, Dartmouth College, Hanover, N.H., Samuel H. Appleton Fund.

but he does, in Capra's use of images and props, have another, purely imaginative and visionary form of power. Those architectural models on George's worktable at home suggest ways in which he can possess imaginatively what he cannot really possess, ways in which he can imaginatively move beyond the social and physical walls that hem him in, modes of imaginative richness that beggar his worldly impoverishment.

State of the Union is, of his major works, Capra's bleakest film. In it he seems to lose faith in the possibility of sublimity or transcendence altogether. Where visionary stylistics do occur in this film they are increasingly associated with forces that do not liberate or elevate the individual but rather threaten only to confuse or annihilate him. The most concrete evidence of Capra's turn against states of vision or his loss of confidence in their redemptive power is the increasing importance of film noir stylistics in his work. (It is a tendency that began to trouble his work seriously and protractedly in *Mr. Smith Goes to Washington*, flourished briefly in the nighttown episode of *It's a Wonderful Life*, and culminates in this film.)

In the films from *Smith* to *State of the Union* Capra increasingly demonstrates what Byron did in his poetry; that the same imaginative energies that allow us joyously to transcend society's conventions (as in *English Bards and Scotch Reviewers* and the early cantos of *Childe Harold* and *Don Juan*) can turn on us to destroy us (as in *Manfred*, *Prometheus Unbound*, and *The Prisoner of Chillon*).* It is that awareness that makes the final cantos of *Childe Harold's Pilgrimage* and *Don Juan* such great and troubling expressions of the complex results of the liberation of imagination and desire, and two relevant landmarks in the exploration of emotional and imaginative territory surprisingly close to that which Capra is surveying in his late films. As they did for Byron, the states of heightened imagination and liberated feeling that Capra courted and teased into visual and acoustic expression in his earlier work, in the later work repeatedly threaten to turn against their creator and his characters. The energies of the dream generate more than passionate, idealistic speeches and patriotic dreams; they generate estranging hallucinations and private nightmares of homelessness and powerlessness. They energize frightening montage sequences and film noir scenes of unchecked appetancy, manipulation, and betrayal. In his late work, Capra is not only the great filmmaker of scenes both of film noir and of extreme idealism, but, more significantly, is the filmmaker who most powerfully demonstrates the profound connection between the two views of life. A world made responsive to the movements of desire in the form of idealism is a world of potentially nightmarish paranoid fantasies. The same mind that imagines the infinitely idealistic protagonists of these films imagines

---

* Although one could trace such an awareness back to *That Certain Thing* and the very beginning of Capra's work, the nightmarish energies momentarily released in the earlier films were generally able to be expunged from the films. This is no longer the case in the work from *Smith* on.

The imagination of possibility turns into the imagination of disaster: from romantic dreams to film noir nightmares.

infinitely compromising machineries of corruption and manipulation working against them and thwarting them.

Stylistic freightings, intensities of feeling, and violences of expression exist early and late in his work, but with *Smith* and the following films, Capra himself begins to fear and distrust such moments, feeling that he no longer knows how to control them. The imaginative derangements and extravagances of emotion seem to burgeon beyond the power of Capra's narratives or his characters to control or organize them. There were moments of expressive wildness and even occasional film noir–related stylistics in *That Certain Thing*, *Forbidden*, and *American Madness*, but Capra, as we saw, was always easily, and at times facilely, able to purge them from the films in the course of their narratives. They represented energies that could be creatively exorcised or converted into socially useful forms of experience. *Forbidden* already recognized some of what I have attributed to Capra's late work: namely, that there is only the slightest difference in one's angle of vision between the backlighting that beatifies Lulu Smith in the romantic scenes in Havana and the film noir kick-lighting in the scene in her apartment in which she murders Al Holland. The narrative is able to be purged of its momentary film noir overtones by having Lulu spend a year in jail for her crime and then be reunited with Bob Grover in a deathbed scene that sublimates the film noir stylistics of the earlier murder scene into a tender, imaginatively enriched reunion between the two lovers. In *That Certain Thing*, Frank Capra and Molly Kelly channel her earlier disruptive imaginative energies into a comedy of manners staged in her box-lunch factory in the final sequence. In *American Madness*, the narrative suppression or redirection of energies is more crude, but equally thorough. All of the film noir resonances are gathered around one character, Cyril Cluett, and near the end of the film he is apprehended by police, trundled off to jail, and totally expunged from the narrative, never to appear or be referred to again in the final ten or fifteen minutes of it.

State of the Union is never able to perform the act of narrative redirection or sublimation of the imaginative and stylistic disturbances that crop up in the course of the film that Capra's work depends on – which is one way of saying that it is ultimately a disappointing and confused film. It has the same position in Capra's canon, as a problem film, as *Meet John Doe* and in fact can be viewed as a remake and revision of that film.★ Both are films that imagine states of weakness rather than strength in their central characters, and both imagine vast networks of control and manipulation that the central figure is almost powerless to affect or evade. Both films are about individuals willing to make their identities and imaginations available for appropriation and redeployment by alien stylistic, narrative, political, and social machines. Although Long John Willoughby was more or less a drifter, a narrative cipher without a fixed identity of his own before the external manipulations begin, Grant Matthews is an idealist in the line of George Bailey and Jefferson Smith, who is, at the same time, disturbingly willing to make himself available for use by a consortium of political interests in order to obtain the presidential nomination of his party. In involving himself in a political race, Matthews steps into a world as power-saturated as that inhabited by Deeds or Smith, but the difference is that whereas Deeds and Smith were able to maintain a margin between an unsullied self and the systems that oppressed and affected it, so that at some point (or points) in their films they could break absolutely free, George Bailey and Grant Matthews, like Doe before them, in their different ways, have willingly compromised themselves by internalizing the repressive systems

---

★ Perhaps I should make explicit that in all of my account of *State of the Union* I take for granted that the one thing the film is *not* is what it is usually described as being: "A Tracy–Hepburn comedy." If one must force it into the Procrustean bed of a genre, it is hard-boiled film noir, if anything. As I explain farther on, the pairing of these two redoubtables in the film was a last-minute change forced on Capra when Claudette Colbert reneged on her contract just before principal shooting was scheduled to begin. The public's expectation, on the basis of the names of the film's two costars, of a dependable screwball encounter and its predictable feeling of being cheated when this did not materialize undoubtedly contributed to *State of the Union*'s poor box-office performance, but Grant Matthews's sermons on capitalism, hard to take no matter what one's expectations are, may also have been a factor.

around them.★ For Grant, as for George, there is no private, sacrosanct, free imaginative space to which he can retreat to escape from the systems around him. There is no passionate, idealistic self that is separate from the influences around it or that can be broken free from them. If George is forced to compromise his dreams in order to earn a living, Grant goes a step farther in the process of compromise by deliberately putting his dreams up for sale. He will be merchandised, with his full knowledge and consent, as a presidential candidate. He puts his own ideals on the auction block and adjusts them at several points in the film in order to ensure that they go to the highest possible bidder.

In the final scenes of State of the Union, Capra shows us that even the home and the family are not exempt from the bureaucratization and technologization of Grant Matthews's world. In the starkest possible scenic juxtaposition, Capra gives us a before and after. Immediately following a scene showing Grant's home life several weeks before he becomes a political candidate, Capra cuts to a scene at his home the day he announces his candidacy. The first scene shows us a typical Saturday afternoon in a home bustling with delightfully unorganized and stimulatingly unorganizable energies: family, friends, and children scurrying around in all directions, a colossal mess in the house and yard, and a more than slightly harried mother only half effectively presiding over it all. In the following scene a few weeks later we see the same rooms on the night when Grant announces his candidacy for the presidential nomination of his party in a "fireside chat" broadcast from his living room. We see the transformation of the earlier affectingly personal clutter into an entirely different sort of technological clutter embodying the mechanical inhumanity of a television broadcast studio. The array of lights, cameras, technicians, and electrical cables snaking across the floor make the set almost unrecognizable as being the same place we just saw in the previous scene. Even the children have been technologized out of their earlier idiosyncrasy. They have been costumed and uniformed for the big broadcast (the previous scene involved nutty and indecorous disrobings and confused mismatching of clothing as the children packed things in CARE packages to send to Europe). They have been made up, coached on how to act, and rehearsed on what to say and how to say it.

★ The similarities of the central characters' psychological and social situations in Capra's two postwar films and much of Cassavetes's work from Too Late Blues to Opening Night are extensive. Cassavetes's work begins where Capra's trajectory of development leaves off with It's a Wonderful Life and State of the Union. Cassavetes could not have made any of Capra's prewar films, with the possible exception of Doe, the only prewar film that anticipates the two later works. His sensibility is opposed to the visionary releases to which Capra repeatedly yielded, and the selves in his films are relentlessly embedded in society, compromised as only Capra's late figures are. Cassavetes's work, in short, picks up precisely where Capra abandoned the dream of visionary freedom and power and yet makes something appreciable of that unenviable situation for both the characters and their creator. Cassavetes never allows his characters the scope of visionary and imaginative expansion that Capra allows his earlier figures. His characters and films resist their own transcendental impulses much more relentlessly and effectively than Capra's earlier ones do.

This scene powerfully tells us that nothing, not even the mess and spontaneity of childhood behavior or the privacy of a person's home, is safe from the perils of bureaucratic organization, technological processing, and political scripting. Earlier in the film Capra has shown us that even an extra-marital affair that Grant has been having is not merely a personal matter. The other woman in Grant's life, Kay Thorndyke, is the influential publisher of a powerful chain of newspapers, and she and would-be political candidate Grant are necessarily unable to keep their relationship merely personal and romantic. There are inevitable not-so-secret agendas between them involving Grant's political aspirations, Kay's ability to help or hurt him with her newspapers, and the future of their relationship if Grant does make it to the White House. Even Grant's quite sincere and genuine, if frequently weak and faltering idealism and political naiveté is not an escape hatch out of the compromising system of power relationships in which he allows himself to be caught in the course of the film. As any politician knows, idealism, passion, and political innocence, real or feigned, are themselves eminently marketable commodities. Just as John Doe was all the more politically packageable because he appeared to be nonpolitical, Grant's "I'm no politician" stance is the most appealing political plank in his platform. He is packaged and sold to the public as an outsider, a nonpolitician, just as the scripted and timed-down-to-the-second political broadcast in his house is advertised and pre-sented to the public as being merely an impromptu visit with the candidate and his family at home.

One feels that this is a film that Capra could not have made ten years earlier. He has seen that the idealistic mythologies that his own earlier work uncriti-cally endorsed are potentially as packageable and salable as any other fictions. Further, in the travesty of family life in the final broadcast scene Capra recognizes that the forces he had earlier felt to be confined largely to the public world of politics and advertising do not stop there. The bureaucratization of experience does not end with the newspapers, radio, and the Senate. Cocktail parties, love affairs, and marriages are not necessarily escapes from a power-saturated society. It may extend itself into the most private recesses of our everyday lives, and our bedrooms may be as bureaucratized, and, certainly in the 1980s are as technologized, as our boardrooms.

Like *Miracle Woman, Mr. Deeds Goes to Town, Smith,* and *Doe, State of the Union* begins with the sudden creation of a momentary hole at the center of a previously fixed system of stable relationships and proceeds to demonstrate how abhorrent such a vacuum in a system is. The film starts with the suicide of a powerful political kingmaker, Sam Thorndyke, and the rest of it is, in effect, the documentation of the rippling shifts of relationship in the power networks that result from the sudden absence of this one placeholder. With Sam dead, his daughter Kay steps into his shoes as the publisher of his newspaper chain, and a mad scramble begins, as everyone around her jockeys for new positions and attempts to fill the successive openings that are created as a result of her father's death. In the scene near the beginning of the film in which we meet

Grant, he has been invited to the office of Jim Conover in Washington. Conover is a political power broker looking for someone to further his own interests in the Capitol and is one of many who see splendid opportunities for creative improvisation and a chance to improve his position in the melee of shifting relationships that ensues from Sam Thorndyke's death. If Conover has his way, Grant will help him win this round in the game of political musical chairs.

Grant is a self-made man, a millionaire industrialist who runs an aircraft company, and a public figure of the sort that Capra was in his own heyday, a type that pops up in American culture from Andrew Carnegie to Lee Iacocca today. (This film, though, implies that there is no such thing as a "self-made man." Grant is always subject to manipulation by vast networks of affiliation that are beyond any individual's control or cognizance.) He has just made the cover of *Time* magazine (as Capra himself had a decade earlier), and both Kay and Conover feel that he may consequently be useful to each of them in their quest for power. Grant, in short, has been invited to this meeting in Conover's office not because of any interest in his high-minded ideals – he has been delivering a series of idealistic lectures at his plants on the importance of cooperation between labor and management – but almost in spite of them, because Kay and Conover each see him as a potentially bankable investment. In their view, his idealism only makes him all the more available for their schemes, and at several points each of them cynically appeals to his idealism in order to manipulate him or cleverly win a point in an argument. As long as idealism plays into their schemes, they are as enthusiastic about it as Harry Cohn was about Capra's. Capra, usually thought of as politically naive, shows himself to have no illusions about the commitment of bureaucrats, politicians, or studio heads to abstract principles. When informed early in the film of Grant's relative innocence about practical politics, Conover, the professional politician down to his fingernails, snaps back that he is "never impressed by amateurs." Grant walks into a world as cynical and hard-nosed as a typical studio story conference. His political idealism is admired, as Capra's cinematic idealism was in Hollywood, not for itself, but because it is temporarily in fashion and makes an excellent selling point. If the people want a dreamer, a Pollyanna, an idealist, give them one, but just do not confuse ideals with political realities.

As early as *Smith*, Capra had mused about how the American mythology of idealism and innocence could be cynically manipulated by the press and politicians in a political campaign, but his tone has darkened significantly in the nine years that separates the prewar film from the postwar one. Capra could use the bumbling Governor "Happy" Hopper to make comedy of much of the manipulativeness and moral opportunism in the earlier film, which shows how far he was from feeling imaginatively daunted by it. His comedy in *Smith* was a form of mastery, a demonstration of his and his protagonists' superiority to the threatening or compromising situations and a display of his ultimate confidence in Smith's powers, but the comedy is gone here. *State of the Union* does not have one robustly comic scene in its entire length. It is the first of Capra's films of which that may be said (though *Doe* came close to it), and that in itself is an ominous shift in Capra's work. Capra's buoyancy is gone. His audacious, puckish tonal play with every cinematic situation is, for the first time, absent.

In addition to Grant, Kay, and Conover, Spike McManus, a reporter on Kay's staff who is subsequently assigned as a speech writer and press secretary to Grant, is present at the meeting in Conover's office among the three principals. At one point in the complex negotiations, Spike facetiously asks, "Shall we dance?", and the remark humorously sums up the complex movements and countermovements that are the interest of this scene and of nearly every scene in the film. Adapted from a stage play by Howard Lindsay and Russell Crouse (from which Capra does not hesitate to depart extensively), *State of the Union* would be intolerably talky for a movie if the verbal text were all that the viewer was paying attention to, but Capra supplements the verbal text with an intricately counterpointed visual text depicting the continuously adjusted power relationships among the main characters. Characters endlessly jockey for position and power among each other, and Capra captures a choreographic intricacy of shifting relationships and leverages in the complex theatrical blocking and contrapuntal editing, registering an almost symphonic interplay of continuously changing glances, facial expressions, and bodily positions of each of the characters with respect to each of the others. Capra edits the meeting in Conover's office, as he does most of the film, in alternating medium shots and close-ups, which complexly tease out this anxious dance of shifting relationships. The medium shots are used to register the general relationship of two or three figures together, and the close-ups are used to cut briskly from face to face around the room to register the ripple of reactions among the individual participants at crucial moments.

In adapting the Broadway play, Capra considerably toughens the characters of the political operatives around Grant, increases the pressures placed on him, and departs from the play entirely in several crucial scenes, but in one respect he sticks surprisingly close to the original stage production: in the stagy settings and the blocking of individual scenes. Just as in the play itself, and entirely unlike any of his earlier films except *Lady for a Day*, *Arsenic and Old Lace*, and *You Can't Take It with You*, nearly all of the major scenes in the movie involve the interaction of a very small group of characters (generally three or four at most, at any one time), situated in a confined central space (a hotel room or office), with entrances on one or two sides through which new characters enter or members of the central group depart. There are simply no outdoor scenes, no crowd scenes, and no large institutional spaces in the film. It would be hard to create a visual and narrative space apparently less similar to that in which *Smith* or *It's a Wonderful Life* took place. This stagy look and feeling may simply have been a vestige of the stage origins of his drama (as in *Arsenic and Old Lace* or *You Can't Take It with You*), but it is typical of a filmmaker of Capra's genius that rather than becoming an expressive liability, the staginess of the spaces and scenes in *State of the Union* and the intricately detailed, but spatially limited blocking of the characters' relative movements becomes a powerful and compelling expressive resource. Capra uses small, confined, cramped dramatic spaces and blockings succinctly to communicate the small, confined, cramped nature of this power-saturated world of shifting relationships, of continuous manipulations of one character by another, of promises relentlessly extorted and favors owed. Conover, meeting with a group of political henchmen or peers in his office (or Kay, meeting with a group of newspaper editors in hers) functions like a spider at the center of a complex, extended, invisible web of influences, pressures and connections. Characters move in and out of this central dramatic space with stagelike entrances and exits to obey instructions or execute plans, but what takes place outside of it is determined by the maneuverings of the small central group of characters.

A further stagy aspect of *State of the Union* is that it is a film almost devoid of lingering close-ups, romantic pauses in the action, balanced two-shots, intimate moments, or private encounters. The brisk cutting from face to face within a room, the unbalanced dances of power that take place between characters (registered in the predominantly middle-distance photography and the complex, asymmetrical, and shifting three-dimensional blocking of char-acters' movements relative to each other), and the intrusive, interrupting entrances and exits of characters moving into or out of the central "stage space" brilliantly capture the essence of the world into which Grant has moved, the world that Capra sets out to explore. In this realm of relentless public pressures and extended personal networks of relationship and influence, there is little or no private space left for the free movements of the individual imagination – for freely expressive, idiosyncratic, or unprogrammatic gestures or movements of the body, for the play of merely eccentric wit and humor, for idealistic, romantic, and meditative impulses, or for the delightful excesses and eccentricities of personal performance that were so important in the earlier films. (As I have already suggested, even Capra's own sense of improvisatorial playfulness and wit drops out of the film. This world of personal, political, spatial, temporal, and theatrical pressures leaves precious little space for his own directorial eccentricity and wildness.) As the long final scene in which Grant shamelessly uses his wife, children, and home as part of his election strategy tells us, no space or group is exempt from the warpages of these networks of public power. The world of Sam Shepard's *True West* has given way to that of Harold Pinter's *Homecoming* – or almost. No aspect of *State of the Union* is more expressive than the fact that at this point in Capra's career the individual actor seems virtually to have no imaginative existence outside of, or separate from, the group interaction and the public expression of experience as they are rendered in this film in the forms of orthodox theatrical drama. It is as if, as in stage drama (especially of the Pinteresque sort), individuals have no distinct identity or existence apart from the group and the sets within which their positions are relentlessly blocked and their words spoken. From a sense of the possibilities of personal performance that affiliates him with vaudeville improvisations, toppers, and turns, in which a premium is put on the ingenuity and resourcefulness of the individual to avoid getting trapped into any sort of predictable dramatic rhythm or convention, Capra moves into what one might call the aesthetic world of nineteenth- and twentieth-century British stage drama.

It is a dramatic world that prevents or firmly discourages tonal expressions of liberated desire and the occurrence of imaginative impulses unique to an individual. It is a cinematic world with few or no point-of-view shots, no looking at the stars or at the landscape, no sitting on balconies meditating (there are no windows or balconies in the film in any case, which is a revealing fact in itself), and not even the curse of private hallucinations, hysteria, or nightmares. This is a world in which there is virtually no cinematic or social space for the personal expression of the individual impulse (as there was occasionally even in the claustrophobic and confining social and cinematic worlds of *Doe* and *It's a Wonderful Life*). The so-called staginess of *State of the Union* (and the quintessential, Cukoresque staginess of the acting of the three troupers – Menjou, Tracy, and Hepburn – within it) is, far from being a defect, the most powerful evocation of the ominously changed expressive conditions in Capra's work.

While Grant is in Conover's office in that initial meeting, Kay reminds him that he has forgotten that it is his eldest son's birthday that day and that he should call to wish him well. She subtly insists on his making the call then and there on the office phone, in front of herself and Conover and McManus – two total strangers. In a series of shots briskly cutting from face to face around the room, while Grant talks to his wife and children and sings an embarrassed chorus of "Happy Birthday" at his son's request, Capra tells us that no action can be merely private. Like any presidential candidate, Grant needs the highly visible and enthusiastic support of his wife and family, and even a "private" call home is part of Kay's strategy of reassuring Conover that such support will be forthcoming and that Grant will be willing and able to use his relationship with his wife and children in all the appropriate ways. The quite subtle interchange of glances and facial expressions that takes place between Kay, Jim, and Spike while Grant makes a fool of himself on the phone tells us everything. Such a delicate social interplay has not been captured on film more authoritatively since the prewar dramas of Jean Renoir. (Yet how very strange to think of Capra's work now being related to Renoir's dramatic neoclassicism. It has taken an enormous shift in his sensibilities for him suddenly to resemble Renoir in even one respect.)

There is, however, one opportunity for Grant to escape the confinements of the forms of stage expression in the film. There is one form of relatively free expression available to him that could never be put on the stage and that does not force him either to knit himself bodily into a system of blocked positions and choreographed movements or to participate in a series of verbal parryings and thrusts. Grant is a flying buff, and his principal free expression of himself, as depicted in an early scene, and the only extended alternative to the confinement of the theatrical spaces in the film that Capra offers, is his flying. In a film that wholeheartedly endorses Grant's statement that "our planes have wings, but not our ideas" as well as his only half-facetious proposal that there "ought to be a law that every politician should spend one hundred hours in the air" (in order to get a true perspective on the country and, literally and metaphorically, to rise above small-minded sectional interests), it is not surprising that images of flight or grounding become controlling metaphors. For sheer exuberance and high-spiritedness, there is nothing in the rest of *State of the Union* to compare with the long scene of Grant's flight west prior to his first swing across the country on a speaking tour.

Grant pilots himself in his own plane, and when he is challenged in midair by two test pilots to an improvised acrobatic contest he indulges himself to the hilt in aerial pranks and stunts. Capra puts together an action sequence that recalls those in his adventure films nearly twenty years earlier and that in its visual outrageousness and playful inventiveness communicates some of the boyish energy of those films (as well as reminding us again that the physical action, adventure, and stunt sequences in the earlier work are completely of a piece with the depictions of visionary, imaginative, and expressive adventures in the later work). In actual stuntman sequences, the pilots playfully (and thrillingly) touch their planes' wing tips together and do daredevil acrobatics in attempts to outperform each other and win a bet. The conclusion of the long sequence involves an astonishing stunt that must be seen to be believed. In order to win a subsidiary wager that he can get to the ground ahead of the rival pilot, Grant jumps from his own plane and free-falls to an extremely low altitude. Capra thrills us with an uninterrupted twenty-second shot showing the unfaked stunt, filmed in the air from above (with an unusually daring stuntman standing in for Spencer Tracy, no doubt), as Grant falls from about ten thousand feet to just above the ground, opening his parachute only at the last possible second. It may be the only bona fide stunt sequence in all of Capra's work since *Dirigible*, but Capra uses the scene not, as so many filmmakers from Hitchcock to DePalma have done, to activate the reptilian brain in his audience but to communicate the sheer excitement and daring of Grant's imaginative performance when he has the rare opportunity to express himself in his own way.

In the air, Grant is able to be a free spirit, an eccentric and imaginative performer, as it is impossible for him to be when he is confined in the stagy space of Conover's office or that of a television studio. In his plane he is able to break away from the restrictions that confine him on the ground (as well as from the confinement of the stagy dramatic style of the rest of the film). In the air, like a reincarnation of Stew Smith, Grant (and Capra) shatter the two-dimensional plane of the theatrical presentation of previous scenes, and explode the choreographic patterns of polite stage blockings taking place in shallow spaces. They open up vast, deep three-dimensional outdoor spaces and new cinematic possibilities in this airborne scene. To observe this, though, is to notice how truly marginal and ultimately unimportant Grant's capacity for free movement really is, when his chief means of free self-expression is in an airplane two miles up. Such performative prowess, however momentarily inspiring and exciting, is worth nothing at all when he must flat-footedly play hardball politics down on the ground.

The network of unavoidable pressures and influences around Grant is more than political; in fact, the most interesting aspect of the film, which one wishes that Capra had developed in even more detail, involves not presidential but sexual politics. (Perhaps at least part of the film's frustrating obliquity about Grant's sexual life, though, is due to Capra's awareness of what the censors and the American public would not tolerate in 1948.) In any case, it is apparent only a few minutes into the film not only that Grant's marriage is on the rocks but that he is involved in some sort of illicit relationship with Kay. Kay (brilliantly acted by the twenty-three-year-old Angela Lansbury) plays a bitchy Lady Macbeth role, and it is clear from the first scene in which we see Grant and her together that she, and not his wife, is the driving force in his life. Like Lady Macbeth, Kay has channeled her domesticity, sexuality, and femininity into power brokering and king making, and not the least of her resemblances to Shakespeare's social-climbing, suburban-souled, dinner-party hostess is in her ability to use ostensibly private gatherings, intimate settings, and personal relationships in order to pursue ruthlessly ambitious public purposes. In this modern Jacobean universe, cocktail parties are tax-deductible business expenses, social relationships are indistinguishable from political relationships, and sexual and emotional involvements between consenting adults are not an escape from, or alternative to, office politics but are an extension of the political wranglings for position in the boardroom into positional jockeyings within the bedroom.

This is an understanding of sex that Capra's films are often thought to be entirely innocent of, but the sexual possibilities represented by Kay Thorndyke represent no fundamental change in Capra's work. They have always been present to his imagination. As early as *Say It with Sables*, *That Certain Thing*, and *Submarine*, sex was recognized as a potential form of power and control. The central female characters in *Platinum Blonde*, *Ladies of Leisure*, and *The Miracle Woman*, not to mention Babe Bennett in *Deeds*, Susan Paine in *Smith*, or Anne Mitchell in *Doe*, each use sex as a tool and use emotional involvement as a form of imaginative extortion. From the very beginning, Capra's films have anatomized American society in terms of power relationships among individuals and have clearly seen the strategies by which the weaker, institutionally disenfranchised sex converts its public weakness into private strength and its socially marginal position into an opportunity of imaginative and emotional leverage on the margins.

To reinforce our appreciation of Kay, Grant's wife Mary is set in the greatest possible contrast to her. Even as played by the fairly angular and brittle

Katharine Hepburn, she is quite kitteny and domestic, with much of the girl-next-door, corn-fed wholesomeness of Mary Hatch.* Mary represents the one possibility in the film of sexual relationships not as an extension of but as an absolute escape from codes of power and systems of institutional responsibility. Whereas sexual relationships are a serious business for Kay, for Mary they are essentially a form of play and recreation, a way of creating and maintaining an enchanted, free space within which the imagination can temporarily be liberated from the restrictive codes and conventions of most of the rest of adult social life. (The metaphoric linkage of Mary's sexuality with Grant's capacity for having fun and just playing around is made explicit by Capra's decision to name Grant's plane Mazie, his private nickname for his wife, and to show Mary present during – and thoroughly enjoying – the scene of aerial play that I have just described.)

However, Capra makes it abundantly clear in the first half hour or so of the film that in falling under Kay's spell Grant has lost touch with the possibilities that Mary represents of sexual relationships being a form of imaginative release and play, as surely as we will see him gradually lose his desire to pilot his own plane or clown around in the air in the course of the movie. Mary's way of expressing how the love has gone out of their marriage is explicitly to protest that Grant no longer plays with her, banters with her, or teases her. She tries to reinitiate the playing with him at several points in the film by teasing him affectionately and calling him by *her* pet nickname for him – Nappy (short for Napoleon) – when he gets a little too big for his britches, but the specific problem with their marriage, as Capra defines it, is that Grant cannot or will not "play" back. When Mary rallies him, he is merely defensive, insulted, or self-justifying. No matter how she taunts him, he no longer calls her Mazie, or, as she puts it, no longer affectionately "slaps her on the sitter" any more.

In the contrast between Kay and Mary, Capra is making a larger statement about the possible forms of human relationships that is integral to an understanding of all of his work. For two individuals to be able to "play together" – dramatically, socially, or maritally – in the way Mary intends, is one of the signs of an ideally free, loving, and unmanipulative human relationship for Capra. Such a capacity of "playing," in its full social and dramatic range of meanings – playing even in the heart of seriousness – is the margin of freedom the creative imagination makes for itself in even the most daunting or otherwise coercive social texts. As we saw in the buddy-boy films, to be able to play in this way is to keep alive the possibility of an unpredictable, unpremeditated, creative response to life and to keep oneself eccentrically beyond being too completely known or controlled by others, but this great filmmaker of

---

* She undoubtedly would have seemed even more dewy, vulnerable, and dependent if she had been played by the actress whom Capra originally cast in the role, the temperamental Claudette Colbert, who withdrew from the film only three days before principal photography began and for whom Hepburn was substituted at the very last minute.

narrative, social, and dramatic play and imaginative release is under no illusion about how difficult it is to keep the possibilities of play alive in this world of powerful influences, high pressures, and large ambitions. The opportunities of playfulness have contracted in Grant's life to escapist episodes of stunt flying and daredevil skydiving, just as they have been curtailed in Capra's narrative universe. Even Grant's flying by the seat of his pants eventually stops in the course of the narrative. The easy humor and wit that Grant sporadically if rarely shows in his initial scenes fairly quickly congeals into the fixity of boringly safe, vote-getting political stances by the middle of the movie.

Beyond the airplane sequence, there is only one other important, extended scene in the film in which Capra or his characters explore the possibility of a less socially constrained theatrical performance or less categorical relationship between human beings. There is only one other scene whose agenda has not been ideologically or politically prefabricated and in which tentative, awkward, free emotional exploration still appears to be marginally possible in this world of enclosure and social manipulation. It is the lovely and at times quite touching moment early in the film in which Grant is initially reunited with Mary, following what has obviously been a long and painful marital estrangement. Like the stunt flying scene, it functions as a narrative wild card: a gratuitous and unexpected moment of personal imaginative opening and exploration in Capra's otherwise clockwork theatrical narrative, a scene whose course or outcome can be predicted no more by the audience watching the film than by the characters participating in it. In the course of it, private feelings are revealed and confessions are made by both Grant and Mary, unexpected all the more in this world in which everyone is emotionally on guard against just such unprogrammed casualnesses and uncontrolled disclosures.

As a viewer educated by Capra's daring experiments with the expressive meaning of unconventional movement and nontheatrical blocking in *American Madness* and *Platinum Blonde* might expect, along with the stunt-flying scene this is the one other scene in the film that significantly breaks away from all of the theatrical and photographic conventions of middle-distance, eye-level camera placement, and that abrogates the side-to-side, shallow-depth dramatic blocking patterns and the stage lighting and patterned dialogue that organize most of the experience in the rest of *State of the Union*. As much as the flying scene used nontheatrical movement into or out of the plane of the screen to express free imaginative movement, this scene uses unorthodox, nontheatrical bodily positioning and non–eye-level camera placement to express possibilities of private, nondialogical, unconventionally theatrical relationships.

Grant and Mary awkwardly find themselves forced to share a bedroom immediately before he launches his political swing into the West. As the scene begins, Grant is at first totally caught up in the heady political whirl, but Capra uses Mary's practicality, domesticity, and at times quite sensuous physicality in the scene to bring him down to earth. At the start of the scene, while he, caught up in his own political rhetoric and grand ambitions, rants and raves about the "giants of political life," Mary notices a loose button on his vest and proceeds to sew it on. She literally and metaphorically encourages him to unbutton himself a little, to interrupt the political act in which he is getting a little too uncritically wrapped up. They banter briefly, playfully, and lovingly – she calling him Nappy at least once to mock his grandiosity in an entirely salutary way. Then, as she undresses for bed in an adjoining room and Grant (and the viewer) watch her shadow on the door, there is a sudden access of uncompromised and uncompromising sensuous and erotic possibilities, for the first and only time in the film. In these shots, and in the ones that follow, in which Mary, wearing only a nightgown and lighted in Capra's most romantically evocative manner, turns down the bed, sex is being removed from the network of impersonal power relationships within which Kay defined it and is being momentarily restored to the merely personal, physical reality of the body. (One can only speculate that Colbert might have made these gestures even more sensuous and erotic than Hepburn does.) Mary represents a warmly physical presence and personal sensuality entirely different from Kay's sexual power plays, however imaginatively seductive Kay's are in their own right. There is even a half-humorous moment in the scene (especially memorable in this otherwise so unhumorous and unplayful film) involving who will sleep where (since Grant and Mary are obviously too estranged to share the sole bed in the room). The conclusion of the scene is an extended series of backlighted shots of Grant and Mary talking in the dark before they fall asleep, separated physically but momentarily united, to their own surprise, in shared feeling, imagination, and erotic attraction. It is a moment that in its composition, lighting, and dramatic function recalls the similar bedtime moments shared between Gable and Colbert in *It Happened One Night* and it is almost as physically and imaginatively evocative as the ones in that film.

In this sea of pressures and constraints, Capra has momentarily moved his two central characters and, most important, Grant, away from the imperatives of action and eventfulness to a redeeming state of emotional vulnerability, personal disclosure, and reverie, but as lovely and imaginatively suggestive as this moment is, as Grant and Mary tentatively explore the possibility of readjusting their relationship to each other in strictly personal terms and then meditatively reflect on their lives in key-lighted intimacy and emotional exposure, it cannot last. Imaginative openings occur here for what turns out to be not only the last time in the film, but the last time in Capra's cinematic career.

Moreover, there are imbalances and tensions built into the scene that make it inherently less stable than I have indicated. Even in the culminating two-shot of Mary and Grant talking in the dark, Kay's disruptive presence is felt. She has extended her influence into this private moment by cunningly leaving her reading glasses on Grant's night table for Mary to find. Her intention is to compromise Grant and force Mary to retaliate by accompanying him on the speaking tour (thus unintentionally playing into Kay's larger game plan concerning Grant's future). Since Mary discovers the glasses during the course of the scene, indentifies them, and silently draws the obvious conclusion, Kay's stratagem has had the desired effect and considerably increases the tension between the couple, preventing them from ending up in the same bed.

Beyond that, several interruptions to the scene do not allow us to forget that however tender and merely personal it may seem to be, this meeting has been connived at strictly as a political expedient by Conover and serves his larger political purposes. Significantly, it takes place not in some neutral space (like one of the motels of *It Happened One Night*) but in Conover's Washington townhouse, a hostel for political has-beens and politicians temporarily down on their luck who can be of use to Conover in the future if they owe him a favor. Grant and Mary have been deliberately thrown together in the same bedroom for the night by Conover in order to test their compatability for a future campaign in which it would never do for a presidential candidate to sleep in a separate room from his wife.

I emphasize the "deliberately," since, as with so many other events in the film, it seems to have been by an accident (of overbooking) that Grant and Mary are required to share the same room – but Conover and Kay leave almost nothing to accident, and Capra gives an alert viewer unmistakable clues that most of the "accidents" of this sort throughout the film have in fact been carefully planned by someone in advance. (Early in the film, Spike McManus points out that Conover's name is easily mistaken for "conniver.") The effect is similar to that of a detective novel in which every event is made significant. Since apparently nothing, personally or narratively, is left to mere chance, the result in terms of the overall formal and narrative effect is to create an immensely complex and claustrophobic web of possible manipulations and coercions that makes one suspect that even more events have been arranged and connived at than already meet the eye.

Much of Capra's and his writer's energies obviously went into scripting and arranging these complex and interrelated events that admit of multiple interpretations and in which an individual intent on manipulating another is always able to cover his or her tracks by putting an innocent interpretation on what has happened. *State of the Union* is far and away Capra's most intricately organized and Byzantinely plotted film, not only possessing the intricacy of a detective novel in its plotting and in the multiple explanations available for each event at a given moment, but, even more important, possessing the intricacy of a well-made play in which no glance, gesture, line of dialogue, bodily positioning, or movement of a character is insignificant. Every detail bespeaks a subtextual meaning or purpose. Capra's previous films were complex, but in a different way from this one. The earlier films were complex not because they were complexly written, theatrically staged, blocked, and narratively structured as this film is, but because of the complexity and richness of feelings that they generated in their characters and induced in the audiences watching them. The early films were usually quite loosely plotted and structured, with an anecdotal sprawl and open-endedness to their scenes and interactions at many points. *State of the Union* is entirely different. No film is less shaggy, less loose, or less anecdotal. It is a machine for articulating and presenting complex social relationships. The characters and their attitudes are quite simple, even formulaic in quality, but every word, every glance, every beat, every adjustment of blocking is expressive of the subtly adjusted power struggle among them.

There is, in addition, an extraordinary formal intricacy to the overall narrative structure of the film, in its plotted succession of settings and groupings of characters in scenes. Nearly every scene, event, setting, or grouping within the film is compared and contrasted with another scene, event, setting, or grouping. The complexity has become a complexity of dramatic construction and scenic arrangement, in place of the relative indifference to these things in the earlier work for the sake of a complexity of individual feeling and characterization.

This is a highly significant change in Capra's work. *State of the Union* has the sort of complexity that is most prized by twentieth-century close-textual critics. Like complexly metaphoric poetry or complexly structured drama, it is relatively easy to discuss and explicate; scenes and groupings and lines of dialogue can be compared and contrasted, but for all the gain in narrative and theatrical complexity in these respects, there has been a fundamental and crucial loss in another respect. The earlier films and the relationships of characters were frequently shaggy, elusive and mysterious, with the opacity and density of experiences in life. This film is pellucid, tightly built, and complex, with the complexity, at moments, of a wind-up dramatic toy. A complexity of construction and arrangement has replaced a complexity of personal feeling and density of characterization.

The loose and baggy monsters of the previous work have been replaced by a sort of high-tolerance dramatic machinery in which each scene and shot meshes with or comments upon each other scene and shot. Capra has moved toward a structuralist cinema, but one cannot help feeling that as much as Grant allows himself to become lost in the technological maze of the modern mass media and the process of political selection by the middle of the film, Capra is allowing himself to become lost in the high technology of intricate dramatic construction. To put it another way, one could say that Grant Matthews (or Spencer Tracy) is imprisoned within the formal machine that is the film as much as he is imprisoned by the machinations of the politicians around him. In the final analysis, though, it is Frank Capra and his writers who might be said to be most trapped. They are so busy imagining intricacies within the plot and structure of the film that they forget that the only cinematic complexity that matters ultimately is the expressive complexity of the situation of the central character or characters and the creativity of his or her response to it. Then again, perhaps Capra does not forget this but simply gives up on the possibility of an interestingly creative response, for the first time in his work. (I want to take up this issue again at some length later on, in connection with the ending of the film.)

In any case, the intimacy between Grant and Mary in the bedroom scene, and Grant's aerial and imaginative hijinks in the airplane scene that immediately follows it, are the last true moments of imaginative daring or authentic emotional exploration in this dramatic machine of pressure and coercion. The political bureaucracy quickly and inexorably closes in around both of them to contain all such personal exploration, just as the technology of the film itself closes in around them as characters by explicitly paralleling these two scenes with the two that follow them. The first is a reprise of the bedroom scene, and the second parallels the flying scene, but in both everything has changed.

In the first, Capra picks up Grant and Mary midway through Grant's swing across the country in a speaking tour of his plants that is designed to test the level of his popularity and potential political support. They are in a hotel room in Detroit, and when Grant begins talking romantically to Mary about how beautiful she looked in the breeze of the propellers from the plane, the scene is just on the point of turning into the kind of emotionally open-ended meditation that had occurred in the earlier scene in the bedroom, but this time things are different. After only a few words, Grant breaks off his tender observation when a barber suddenly comes into the hotel room to shave him for a public appearance that night. Mary encourages him to continue talking, but Grant is dog-tired from campaigning all day and wants to take a nap. Then Spike, now his press agent, comes in to importune him with requests, questions, orders, and instructions. Cranks, lobbyists, and politically important delegations start to drop by. All of the cinematic timings are speeded up. Events are rushed. Pacings of lines, entrances, and exists are accelerated. This is a world of interruptions and pressures with no time for imaginative or emotional exploration. The press of events will not be stopped or retarded as Capra was able to do it in his earlier work in order to allow an imaginative opening to occur.

Grant occupies a central stage space with three doors, one on each side of the stage walls, through which bit players make quick entrances and exits around him. This is, in its essence, a space within which mere romantic love talk, rumination, or reflection cannot occur. One can only be a better or worse public speaker and performer in this theatrical world. There is no opportunity for Grant to whisper little nothings in his wife's ear and no way for Capra to register them in this brightly lighted and stagy theatrical space. Grant is now, as he will continue to be for the rest of the film, only a kind of puppet at the beck and call of dozens of different people. Pressed for time and energy, he is pointedly unable to complete even a ten-second scene of talking lovingly with his wife. All of the possibilities of emotional exploration opened up in the earlier scene have completely closed down. It is a scene that recalls the one of Longfellow Deeds being suited up and coached in his mansion, but Deeds could occasionally escape to a park bench with Bennett for romantic reverie. Here there are no parks and no park benches.

In the second parallel scene, having completed his speaking tour, Grant is flying back home in an episode that is designed to repeat almost every single detail of the earlier scene in the airplane. Grant and Mary are again up in Mazie. The same stunt pilots arrive as before and challenge Grant to the same trick flying, but this time he surlily declines to play and dismisses the flyers with a snarl. Playfulness is no longer allowable; Grant is too busy planning his political future and consulting with his advisers, McManus and Conover, who are along for the flight. We are expected to notice that even his physical position in the compartment of the plane has changed.

The shift in his position is a small one, and not really crucial to an understanding of the film, but the fact that meaning is communicated in this way is itself of immense importance to understanding it. The use of formulaic dramatic blockings within this film as one of the chief ways of communicating meaning is one of the most disturbing changes in Capra's work. (Partisans of the "well-made" work of dramatic art would regard this as a gain, but it is, rather, the greatest possible loss.) The earlier films celebrated their central characters' free, eccentric, and improvised movements, but in *State of the Union* it is virtually impossible for there to be any such movements. Not only are the physical spaces within which the drama is staged (like the interior of an airplane) more confined and the camera setups much more confining, but the use of parallel scenes and blockings to suggest changing relationships among characters prevents the characters (and the actors who play them) from expressing themselves the ways earlier characters did. This film is too tightly scripted, blocked, and photographed to allow them. The meanings of individual actors' (and characters') performances are dictated and affected by larger structures of narrative relationship as they never have been before in Capra's work. In both the narrative structure and the political world of the film, there is no longer room for improvised, unchoreographed dramatic or social movement. The dancer is not only becoming indistinguishable from the dance; he or she is sacrificing his or her identity to it. Spencer Tracy (or Grant Matthews) is erased into the choreography of the scenes in which he acts. Character, individuality, and personality are excess baggage that must be jettisoned. Idiosyncratic personal expression would only clog up the machine-like execution of this contemporary cinematic choreography.

We have left the romantic, individualistic world of Tchaikovsky and Balanchine and entered the deauthored, postmodernist universe of Wilson, Cage, and Glass. In the idiom of recent film, we have moved from the ragged aggregations of personal eccentricity and multiplicity in a May, Loden, or Cassavetes film to the cinematic technocracy of Altman, Hitchcock, or DePalma in which individual actors or characters effectively disappear because they have been absorbed into the overarching structures of the work.

The seat that Mary occupied next to grant in the earlier airplane scene has been given up to Conover, with Mary shunted off to a seat in the back of the plane. Conover and Spike, and not she, now sit closest to Grant and form a wall around him that excludes her physically, socially, and emotionally. Even the lighting of the scene has shifted. Capra uses the pretext of morning light streaming in through the windows of the aircraft to give a kick-lighted, low-key effect that contrasts with the lighting in the earlier scene, which was feathered and filled from ceiling to floor. Grant is being moved into the visual world of film noir, where much of the rest of the movie will take place – a world of pressures and compromises in which the actor exists, not, as Capra's earlier figures did, to prevent a scene from congealing into any systematic meaning or impersonal point by the force of his or her eccentric performance but to have his or her ability to act absorbed into an abstract system of spatial, visual, and institutional relationships. The rigid expressive codes of film noir presentation become surrogates for the repressive institutional codes of political and social expression in this world.

In the scenes that follow, Grant is rapidly enmeshed in a web of compromising political alliances with self-serving, single-issue fanatics, lobbyists, and power brokers. These scenes might serve as a final summary of all that has been gradually changing in Capra's work in the course of the three or four films leading up to *State of the Union*. In the first place, evil is no longer localizable in any one specific agent or traceable to any personal intention. In the earlier films evil resulted from predominantly personal actions and motives – opportunism, weakness, cupidity, self-aggrandizement – and was usually embodied in one character – Hornsby, Holland, Cluett, or (to a lesser extent) Cedar. Here there is no particular villain pulling the strings, least of all Kay Thorndyke or Jim Conover. They start Grant on his course, but it is quickly apparent that corruption is pervasive and systematic; they do not need to sponsor it personally. Compromises and deals are typical of the entire world of politics. Grant acquiesces entirely in this process of compromise. In order to win delegates, he agrees to pander to special-interest groups, to play on public fears, to soften his proposals. No one makes him do these things or fools him into misunderstanding what he is doing, and he resists them not at all, all of which measures how far we have fallen from the world of *Deeds* and *Smith*. Even during the bleakest moments of *Smith*, Capra had still believed in the power and purity of the individual self against the whole world, but *State of the Union* imagines a world in which there is no difference between the self and the world. Both are equally compromised, corrupted, and sold out.

Free and independent selves do not exist in this film in the way they did in the prewar films. Grant (and everyone else in the film) is no more than a pawn in a grand political (and narrative) game that no particular individual has corrupted or compromised. As Foucault would say, the individual has ceased to author the system. Grant is not being nominated for what he is in himself but for what he can be made to stand for – for the place in the system that he can fill. An interest in what a person is in him- or herself is alien to this whole movie. It is a conception of individualism that means nothing in a political and narrative world in which abstract structures of relationship communicate significances that individuals cannot. American exceptionalism and individualism has given way to a philosophy of the beehive.

There is nowhere to run to avoid the system. Grant has no identity except within that system, just as George Bailey, in the dreamland episode, discovered himself to have no identity outside of the system of personal relationships that he had spent the entire earlier part of the film attempting to escape.

The war between well-made dramatic form and the vagaries, excesses, and spontaneities of personal imaginative impulse and dramatic improvisation that previously animated all of Capra's work has been resolved in favor of complex, intricate, well-made dramatic form. In Emerson's terms, form has won out over power. None of Capra's works is more complexly put together, apparently more elaborately rehearsed and staged, and more intricately, self-referentially scripted, but that is just the problem. The competition between the wildness and unpredictability of individual impulse and social and dramatic form is over.

Perhaps the most frightening scene in the film is the brief and almost affect-less meeting that takes place between Grant, Conover, and Ed Lauterbach – a powerful Senator and a guaranteed deliverer of the farm delegations – in the back seat of a limousine moving down Pennsylvania Avenue in Washington. With the dome of the Capitol visible through the window behind them (only in this film is significance created in such depersonalizingly schematic and abstract ways),* Conover and the unctuous, despicable Lauterbach strike a sordid deal involving Lauterbach's control over farm policy and appointments in a future Matthews administration. The sordidness of the deal is not the most frightening aspect of the scene, however; this meeting is most terrifying because it points out how little emotional or personal contacts between in-dividuals matter in this world of deals and power brokering. Lauterback actually ignores the "candidate" throughout the scene, talking to Conover instead, closing the deal by shaking hands with him and only as an after-thought turning to Grant, at the last minute, and then momentarily forgetting his name as he goes through the formality of saying a few words to him. It is a vivid representation of how irrelevant the particular individual is, as is obvious even to Grant himself. The deal is all that matters, and anyone else could be substituted for Grant (and any other actor substituted for Tracy) in the scene with no difference. In that moment in which Lauterbach stumbles over the forgotten name, Capra shows the completion of the erasure of Grant's personal identity.

Grant, recognizing all of this, spends most of the scene staring out of the car window away from Lauterbach and Conover; but it is an indication of how far Capra has moved away from the imaginative worlds of *Ladies of Leisure* or *Bitter Tea* that such a meditative withdrawal, such an aversion of one's glance and shift of point of view, counts for so little here. In the films from *Deeds* on, as we have seen, to move off to one side of a group, to stare off into the distance or out of a window meditatively, is potentially to become all the more

---

* This shot recalls the similar one of Smith and Saunders together in a car with the Capitol dome visible through the rear window, but the dome did not function artistically in the same way in the earlier film. It was not an abstract, ironic, imposing symbol that indicated the absolute limits or powerlessness of merely personal performance (as it is in *State of the Union*). It was an encouragement and inspiration to personal performance. It was something that stimulated and sponsored Smith's idealistic crusade, both in the taxicab in which he first saw it and subsequently as he stood under it. Here it is an icon.

victimized by the power structures in place around the self. Capra turns on his own and his characters' turnings away from the world.

Grant walks out of several of the political meetings in which he is involved, in a revulsion of feeling, but we feel that he does not in the least escape from, or rise above, the political compromises of the world he lives in, any more than Smith can by skulking around the Lincoln Memorial, Deeds can by silently staring out of a window in the psychiatric ward, or Doe can by striding off into the darkness after the debacle of the convention. On the contrary: The passivity of a meditative stance makes one only all the more vulnerable to the schemes of the Ed Lauterbachs of this world. The dream of transcendence is dead. In the stagy, claustrophobic world of *State of the Union* there are no windows, balconies, or bridges to look out across. The sole exception is the scene in which Spike looks out of the doorway of Grant's plane, watching Grant's daring free-fall, and the viewer looks out with him, to watch Grant's descent through a shot that suddenly opens to view a ten-thousand-foot abyss. Otherwise there is no possibility of turning out of this enclosed world socially, imaginatively, or physically. After the first flight, speaking both literally and metaphorically, there is no opportunity of rising above it or of withdrawing from it, even in an airplane ride. The central imaginative possibility of the early work has died completely, which is another way of saying that Capra would make no more important films after it, and that this one is important only insofar as it constitutes a disturbing requiem for the earlier impulses.

Another ominous change is suggested by the observation that we get, in effect, only one important point-of-view shot (the one through Spike's eyes) in the entire film. In *Doe* and *State of the Union*, there are almost no individual points of view represented by the camera work and editing. The shots do not add up to provide a coherent personal overview of a scene; rather, the opposite takes place: The shots provide a series of disparate and often irreconcilable or conflicting points of view in the course of a scene. (To see the difference, compare the cutting in John Doe's first radio speech or in Grant Matthews's television address with the cutting in Florence Fallon's first performance in her Temple of Faith.) The editing of the film itself becomes inhumane in the same way that the technological systems in place around the central figure are. It is as if the world rendered by the film is now too complex to be comprehended by any ideal overview of it, however godlike. Reality is so complex and so technologically and bureaucratically subdivided that no one individual film viewer or filmmaker can hold all the different views of it together imaginatively, any more than the central characters themselves can in the scenes being depicted.

I want to conclude my discussion of *State of the Union* by considering in some detail the long final scene involving a nationally televised speech that Grant makes from his home, on the eve of his party's convention, as a final appeal for delegates and public support. It represents one of the most complex and extended spatial arrangements of characters and contiguous spaces in

Capra's work and neatly summarizes the changed situation of his protagonist, who has never before been so trapped by abstract, impersonal bureaucratic and dramatic systems. Not outside *Doe* has the system of technological and bureaucratic packaging and presentation been rendered with more authority, and even in *Doe* the technologization of experience did not extend this far into the familial and personal life of the protagonist (most of which was simply written out of the film).

The scene is staged on two large, contiguous sets. One is the living room of Grant's house, which serves as the broadcast studio. It has lost most of its appearance as a living room, since it is filled to overflowing with broadcasting equipment, technicians, announcers, and a host of variety-show acts – a brass band, a black singing group, and miscellaneous speakers and performers who are to provide entertainment.

The other set is the den, a glassed-in porch running along one side of the length of the living room, which has been forced into service as a combination greenroom and political cloakroom. Grant, Mary, and the politicians gather there to haggle and hobnob while waiting to go before the cameras. The two spaces are thus meant to be strictly equivalent and complementary to each other. Politicians and actors, studio technicians and political advance men, campaign managers and stage directors, scriptwriters for variety shows, and speech writers for political rallies are implicitly equated with each other. They are all in the same business, employing basically the same sorts of expressive resources. The genius of Capra's separating the two sets with only a glass divider is that through much of the scene parallel events going on in both spaces are visible at the same time. The point of the overlap and parallelism is the equivalence of the alternative packagings of experience provided by the technology of film and television, on the one hand, and the bureaucracy of political campaigns and personal relationships on the other. Capra creates the kind of overwhelming visual and aural complexity of overlapping, interrelated planes of action that Robert Altman is supposed to have invented in film, but with the immense difference that the bureaucratization of experience that Altman apparently accepts as a fundamental condition of life, Capra sadly bemoans as the greatest possible loss of individual freedom and independence.

There is one brief moment near the end of *State of the Union* in which Mary attempts to break absolutely away from the system of understanding and the roles scripted for her to perform, first privately, in the greenroom, among Grant's political managers and cronies (where she plays the part of the "gracious hostess" and "hard-headed, practical booster of her husband's candidacy") and then publicly, on the television broadcast (where she plays the part of the "devoted wife and loving mother"), but the results of her rebellion only go to show the indestructibility of the system in which she is involved. In a recoil of disgust at how Grant and she have allowed themselves to be used, she gets sloppy drunk, speaks her mind to the assembled politicians in the den, and then breaks down in tears and runs outside to the garden, only minutes before she is scheduled to appear before the cameras and read a speech

The loss of the individual in the technologies of expression and the bureaucracies of life: the broadcast from Grant's home.

on behalf of Grant's candidacy. She succeeds momentarily in making a unique, eccentric, personal scene, but Capra chillingly shows how this system is capable of absorbing any disturbance, no matter how emotionally affecting and disruptively personal. Mary makes her drunken, passionate speech and rushes outside, but even before she is through the door, Grant and Kay are busy formulating a substitute plan. Kay will go on in Mary's place and explain to the television audience that although Mary may be a candidate's wife, she is a mother first and foremost and is upstairs with a sick child and has asked Kay to speak in her place. There is no shock and no disruption. There is no eccentricity or intensity of personal expression that this technology of control cannot normalize or even turn to its advantage. As Kay smugly comments, her appearance in place of Mary, as a concerned and involved friend of the family, explaining Mary's absence in terms of her devotion to her children, will be an even better vote getter than Mary's appearance in person would have been. Kay, as she makes these decisions only split seconds before Mary is scheduled to go before the cameras, operates with the coolness under pressure of an experienced Hollywood writer or director making enormous changes at the last minute to a script only moments before the scene is to be acted and filmed. Is it a chilling insider's insight into show business as a mere matter of business, or an even more frightening insight into business as a matter of mere show?

Would it be entirely unfair to compare Kay's imperturbable sang froid at switching the star of her show at the last possible second with Capra's own cold-blooded switch from Claudette Colbert to Katharine Hepburn as the star of his show at five o'clock on a Friday afternoon, with principal photography on *State of the Union* scheduled to begin at nine the following Monday morning?

Kay's fallback plan is frustrated only seconds later – though she remains unflappable – when Spike goes out to the garden and persuades Mary to read her speech anyway. (He succeeds by suggesting to her that if Kay goes on in her place, Mary will have lost Grant to Kay once and for all – reminding us again of how inextricably even the most personal affairs of the heart are intermeshed with public, official networks of relationship in this film.) Mary nervously begins her television speech just as Kay is about to step in for her, but Capra cuts away from Mary to the faces of Kay and Jim as they watch her distraught, halting delivery. Gradually, almost imperceptibly, Kay begins to smile to herself, then turns to Conover and whispers, "She's perfect!' – with the heartlessness of a producer commenting on a screen test in which the embarrassment of an inexperienced actress only makes her more alluring. Like studio executives with both eyes cocked to the box office, Kay and Jim are utterly indifferent to Mary's suffering; all they care about is how her "scene" will "play," how it will be received by an audience, and what they see is that her unprofessional emotionality gives authenticity to the moment. This is not a scene of noble self-sacrifice and nearly hysterical breakdown by a candidate's wife almost torn apart by her own self-division but a scene in the other sense – a trained-animal act that is being cold-bloodedly evaluated for how it will play in Peoria – and it will play very well indeed. Their interpretations have remade it. They have completely contained the damage. The system can imperturbably channel even Mary's emotionality, pain, and tragedy into the material of box-office success. That's show business.*

There was something about this situation that haunted Capra's imagination, which is why one can find versions of it in several of his other films. To cite only one instance, it is an exact repetition of the moment in *Doe* when John Doe painfully, imperfectly, and nervously reads his first radio speech and D. B. Norton, listening to it at home on the radio and noticing the favorable response from his domestics, smiles smugly to himself and conceives his plan of using Doe for his own ends. Both instances represent a nightmarish blurring of the boundaries between acting and feeling, a confusion about what is scripted and acted and what is actually felt and experienced. Doe's or Mary's authentic emotionality is put under glass and served up to be coolly evaluated and used for a purpose by a connoisseur of stylistic effects. It is appraised for its bankability, its box-office potential, as if it were only a style among styles.

---

* Jefferson Smith's hoarse, faltering delivery represented a positive alternative to the stage-trained, oratorical systems of speech around him that attempted to normalize or control him, but here the system can absorb even Mary's hysteria. Nothing disrupts it or escapes from it.

Their states of profound emotional disturbance and pain are treated not as unique and humanly important experiences but as aesthetic, stylistic achievements. Their human actions are transformed into "scenes." Their emotionality only makes their "performances" more "powerful," "touching," or "persuasive" (and insert here any of the other terms that directors, producers, and critics use to distance themselves from life, until experience and value and truth drop away and everything becomes only a matter of the critical connoisseurship of alternative aesthetic strategies, styles, and performances). Capra made a career of using actors' and actresses' actual emotionality as a part of their performances – the acting of the young Barbara Stanwyck is only the best-known example of this – and it is impossible not to feel that he is reflecting on his own, or Hollywood's, ability to sell private emotions wholesale.

There is something else about this scene that seems to resonate with an enduring concern in Capra's work. Scenes of this sort depict moments in which the characters (and perhaps the actors playing them) have become unable to clearly distinguish what is scripted from what is freely felt and believed, or moments in which the scripted lines blend into felt and believed experiences. John Doe and Mary Matthews assert their free expression of themselves by reading lines written for them by someone else. Precisely at the moment they believe themselves to be putting their egos on the line, to be standing alone and acting out of the depth of their private feelings, their voices catching with emotion, they are living someone else's fantasy, playing into someone else's hands. Just when they believe themselves to be acting as free agents, they are discovered to be reading a script and performing in someone else's play, shackled into someone else's invisible chain of signifiers.

It is a frightening recognition of the complicated and subterranean ways our lives are scripted and controlled by individuals, institutions, and forces not only outside of our control but outside of our cognizance.* It is a nightmare hallucination about the absorption of individual utterances into institutional systems of discourse even when they believe themselves to have broken free of such systems – one that could probably only have come from a filmmaker both as battered and manipulated by the bureaucratic studio system as Frank Capra felt himself to have been by this point in his career, and yet as quixotically dedicated to affirming the power of the individual voice within it and committed to asserting his complete freedom from control by it. Capra's struggles with the Hollywood studio-system mass-production methods of making films were more than self-serving fictions of his own making. He had spent the four or five years before *State of the Union* unsuccessfully attempting to establish his own production company and had already been forced into bankruptcy once as a result of his efforts. Capra was in his own life discovering

* Compare Capra's own confusion over whether Florence Fallon in *The Miracle Woman* believed what she said or was only cynically playing a part of someone else's scripting. See *The Name above the Title* (New York: Bantam Books, 1972), p. 148.

exactly how weak the self is and hard it really is for individuals to express themselves freely in the bureaucratized, technologized, assembly-line world of Hollywood filmmaking, just as Grant and Mary, and John Doe, were discovering similar truths in their own lives.

This is, however, the last interesting scene in a flawed film. Following Mary's effort at speaking, Capra tacks on the limpest, most schematic, and most ineffective of all his endings. Grant, finally shamed by what he has put his wife through, rushes to the microphone and makes a public confession of the compromises he has yielded to in his quest for the nomination. It is an obvious attempt on Capra's part to have Grant finally break himself and Mary free from the systems of discourse that have silenced his true voice in the second half of the film, but (as Capra undoubtedly did not intend) Grant's "victory" is hollow and minor. It does nothing to overcome the system. Even in asserting himself at the end of the film, Grant can only make his presence felt and his voice heard through and by means of the technological systems that previously oppressed him. Deeds and Smith had distinctive bodies and unique voices apart from the media packaging, but Grant, even in his scene of rebellion, is only an image on a television screen, not an independent, ontological alternative to it. Moreover, given the actual process of delegate selection and the political machinery that the rest of the film has documented, Grant's campaign to win delegates as a mere individual or to be able to raise money to buy television air time to address voters directly (since, as much as in our contemporary political system, media packaging has made merely personal contacts with voters obsolete and useless) does not have a ghost of a chance unless he plugs himself into the system. In short, Grant has no body, voice, or presence apart from the systems of the film, a fact even this contrived, upbeat ending cannot deny or change. Capra's ending expresses only Grant's victory over his own base impulses to compromise his stands on issues, and not over any of the systems that have imprisoned him. That is why Grant Matthews's final success in his film, like George Bailey's in his, is indistinguishable from failure.

State of the Union is Capra's final important film. It is a deeply flawed and imperfect work of art, but its flaws are ultimately what make it interesting and important in Capra's oeuvre. Capra's expressive problems within the film are not merely matters of detail and emphasis; they are not mere technicalities involving aspects of its directing, scripting, or acting; rather, they are major problems of imagination and conception that take us deeply into Capra's always divided, confused consciousness and, I think, finally reveal a profound failure of confidence on his part in the postwar years.

The crisis that effectively concludes Capra's career is that he becomes unable to maintain his earlier belief in the expressive power of the individual, however beleaguered. One saw the seeds of this in *It's a Wonderful Life* and in *Doe* as well. In *Doe* Capra explored the situation of a nonperformer, an individual with virtually none of the emotional energy and imaginative creativity of even the most flawed of his previous figures. And the result was that the self was overwhelmed by the narrative and technological systems around it. In *It's a Wonderful Life*, Capra imagines another very vexed expressive predicament. He imagines a power of consciousness that is truly extraordinary, but that is almost inexpressible publicly. Following the depiction of his childhood and adolescence, George Bailey's free imagination is forced underground, below virtually any form of social or verbal expression, and almost below any form of cinematic expression, into a series of evanescent, fugitive glances and gestures, almost all of which are close to being invisible to those around him.

State of the Union, not content with the previous film's merely private states of awareness and emotionality, revisits the territory of *Smith* and *Deeds* and attempts to convert its central character's passionate beliefs into forms of public expression again, but Capra cannot do what he did in the earlier works. Capra cannot make Grant Matthews into a Longfellow Deeds or Jeff Smith. His free imagination is expressed in two principal ways in the film: in his stunt flying and in long, passionate, abstract, idealistic perorations to the characters around him that punctuate the film (and verge on putting an audience to sleep with their clichéd generality) at five or six points. Grant's expressive problem (or Capra's) is that in either form his flights of imagination are just too far up in the clouds and too far out of touch with the day-to-day realities of life to count for very much down on earth. Whether he is functioning as a pilot, a speech maker, or a general-purpose actor, his imagination does not express itself in terms of concrete, down-to-earth forms of social performance. What Grant's character tells us is that Capra himself as a writer and director, can no longer believe that exalted dreams and desires can be expressed as correctives to the deficiencies of worldly structures of understanding, or can no longer imagine meaningful ways for a character to do such a thing.

In the spatial metaphors of the film, both Grant and Capra are faced with the untenable choice between allowing the self to be grounded by the stagy spaces and the forms of expression of the corrupt politicians – shrinking the self and its capacities of performance to what can be theatrically blocked and staged in the cramped offices, smoke-filled conference rooms, and hotel rooms of the movie – or breaking it free in a flight of fancy up in the clouds, in a stratosphere of impossibly high ideals and noble feelings. The choice is untenable because it is the mediation between the two realms that needs to be achieved, not a shuttling between them. The problem is that Capra cannot imagine the possiblity of free, creative movement down on the ground *within* the practical forms of social expression and family-film drama.

All of Capra's films, from *Deeds* on, contain a certain number of set speeches in which one character or another holds forth in a longish monologue on one of Capra's pet ideas. *State of the Union* differs from *Deeds*, *Smith*, and *Doe* not only in increasing the number and length of these speeches but in altering their function within the narrative. Idealistic speeches in the earlier films (even as early as *Ladies of Leisure* or *American Madness*) were what Kenneth Burke would call a form of "symbolic action." They were calls to action, announcements of actions already taken, or verbal equivalents of action in which the word extended the reach of the deed across space and time. Grant's speeches are different. They are what has to be called "speeches in the air" – abstract, rhetorical, and metaphoric set pieces, delivered often for no particular reason, leading to or proposing no specific actions, and generally persuading or moving no one. His speeches are expressions of idealism that are nearly as abstract and general in their expression as the ideals themselves. They are not invigorating mediations or translations of the ideals into practical forms and actions, which is why the speeches in the earlier films were not nearly so annoying or boring as they are in this one. The changed quality of these expressions of himself tells us as much about Capra's expressive problems in imagining Grant and writing lines for him to speak as they do about Grant's expressive problems as a character. Capra can find no more practical or worldly expression of Grant's imaginative energies than in such grandiloquent abstractions, and he can imagine no more practical forum within which his speeches can make a real difference than these dinnertime rantings and ravings. If George Bailey's expressions of his idealism were forced underground (oc-casionally to surface in sublimated forms or to erupt after being long pent up in a nightmarish hallucination), Grant's energies are forced up into a rhetorical stratosphere.

Like his character, Capra has no other way of expressing his own lingering ideals and dreams than by giving Grant such speeches (and in the one scene of stunt flying and the one brief scene of romantic reflection between Mary and Grant that precedes it). As much as Grant's free physical movements have had to retreat to the sky above ten thousand feet, Capra's free imaginative movements have had to take refuge in such rarified verbal formulations. Capra and Grant can find no visual, social, spatial, or institutional forms of free expression because those forms are overwhelmingly controlled by the tech-nologies of information processing and the political bureaucracies of the film. The popular phrase has it that "talk is cheap," and the freedom to talk, talk, talk is the one opening to discourse that the political bureaucracy does not close, but it is one that also never seriously threatens the control of the bureau-cracy over all the rest of the life in the film. Tom Dixon gave somewhat similar speeches to his board of trustees in *American Madness* (though, significantly, there were fewer of them, and they were more specific in their content), but his speeches were doggedly practical, and, in addition, many other institutional and social expressions of his imaginative power and independence were available to him beyond his speeches that Grant totally lacks.

It is as if Jefferson Smith had been eliminated from his movie and the entire film made with Joseph Paine as the central figure, or as if Capra had ceased to believe in the possibility of a Jefferson Smith after that film. The best, or most, he can accept is the possibility of being a troubled, compromised, perhaps sooner-or-later-repentant Joseph Paine, which is what Grant Matthews is – but to make this single change is, needless to say, to alter absolutely every-thing. *Smith* without Jefferson Smith – with Paine instead at the center of the story – is a much bleaker and darker film. The power of personality has radically shrunk. There is no possibility of offering a clear alternative to the Taylor machine or of rising above it. Paine is too harried, surrounded, and embedded – too old, compromised, and used up to have stars in his eyes. The fire of Capra's belief in an absolute imaginative transcendence and spirituality flamed out, in a final burst of glory, at the moment of its extinction in *It's a Wonderful Life*. The dream was never more powerful than in that film, in the very instant of its being silenced, stilled, and forced underground into nostalgic memory in the final scene, but it has died here.

The problem with Grant's final peroration in the film, his pledge to go to both conventions and appeal for votes as an independent people's candidate, however differently it was intended, is that it is too reasonable, too decorous, too well-mannered, and bland. Grant dispassionately agrees to play squarely within the system, by the rules of the system, in order to reform the system. Smith's emotionality, his crazy one-man filibuster, his excessive, impractical rhetoric, and his final faint, and Bailey's excruciating silences, gasps, poetry spouting, and wild surmises were more disruptive and potentially more anarchic, than this. Grant is finally too sane, rational, and politically pragmatic. Even in willfully and arbitrarily attempting to assert its sudden eruption in the final seconds of the film, Capra's conclusion inadvertently confesses that the dream has been tamed and made safe for the world.

It is certainly not accidental that in the big broadcast scene Capra departs completely from the Lindsay–Crouse play, which concluded not in a cluttered, rigged-up television studio but at a fancy political dinner party. It would be tempting to try to treat this final scene in Capra's final major film, this journey behind the scenes showing what really goes on in the writing, timing, and rehearsal of a script and in the placement of lights, microphones, and cameras, as Capra's closing, calmly retrospective or nostalgic reflection on the methods of his own art. One could look for the sort of serene meditation about art and its arrangements that Shakespeare expressed through Prospero in the final scenes of *The Tempest* – but nothing would be more misleading or more false to the tone of this final scene. Capra does indeed draw a series of explicit parallels between the world he inhabits as a filmmaker and the forces surrounding Grant in this final scene. What the viewer is exposed to, though, is nothing like the calm, composed meditations on film in general and the expressions of gratitude for its healing or transforming powers that Bergman or Fellini have treated us to in their late work or that Shakespeare presents in *The Tempest*, but nearly the opposite. One feels not Capra's ease and calm but a sense of dissatisfaction, disturbance, and potential confusion about this art/technology/bureaucracy within which he is functioning. According to this final scene, filmmaking is a business and a technology, as well as a matter of poetic and artistic expression. It is a bureaucracy of codified and systematized relationships, as well as a means of expressing visions and dreams. Indeed, in the light of this final scene, it is safe to say that Capra uncomfortably feels filmmaking to have more in common with business, bureaucracy, and tech-

Alternative views of personal expression: the eccentric, inventive, spontaneous improvisations of individuals . . .

nology than it does with poetry, art, vision, and dreaming. It is at least as powerful a force for technological and bureaucratic repression as it is for imaginative expression and artistic release.

The representation of filmmaking that Capra creates in the cluttered and crowded Matthews living room is an entirely unglamorized, unillusioned image of the tangle of people and machinery in the rented MGM studio in which *State of the Union* was filmed. The petty power plays and ego contests taking place in the greenroom/den resemble nothing so much as a particularly unpleasant producer's meeting or story conference in which the various "creative people" involved in a film gather to primp and preen themselves, maneuver for position, and attempt to manipulate each other. There is even a vignette about that gadfly of sets, the still photographer taking the requisite publicity shot. A photographer comes into the greenroom for a photo opportunity and, quicker than the flash of his bulb, Spike, the unit publicist, has removed Mary's drink from her hand, Conover has concealed his bourbon behind him, and the "informal, unposed" group has smiled in unison.

This final scene reveals a different conception of artistic creation from that which the early films provided. It is instructive to remember, for contrast, the central figures in them, who were obviously alter egos for the director. In *American Madness* and *Platinum Blonde*, Capra clearly imagined himself in the

... and the technological and bureaucratic networks that invisibly mediate expression. A scene from *You Can't Take It with You*, and shooting the scene. Capra is seated to the right of the second camera.

figures of Tom Dixon and Stew Smith, who moved through their worlds with the aplomb and calm of masterful social masters of ceremonies. In *Bitter Tea* and *Ladies of Leisure*, Capra imagined himself either in terms of the practical sublimities of set design, elegant costuming, and special photographic effects (as Yen) or in terms of the pure art of creating a painting of the soul (as Jerry Strong) – but whether he was like Yen and Strong or like Smith and Dixon, whether he was an artist figure or a master of ceremonies, he was calm and superior, rising above or transcending common events and the confusions of ordinary everyday discourse. That is the figure Capra obviously aspired to be and apparently sometimes felt himself to have become.

In *Deeds*, *Smith*, and *Doe*, the central figures, and Capra's implicit alter egos, are no longer either artists of pure imaginative power and transcendence or poised, sophisticated, confident managers of groups of people. The film-maker, by extension, is no longer imagined to be a solitary, romantic artist working in his studio, forging his spiritual effects in the smithy of his soul, nor a puckish, creative social performer, parodically playing with social forms and structures. Just as Smith, Deeds, and Doe must arduously attempt to translate their ideals into the languages of alien social, temporal, and institutional structures, Capra must work to "speak" his ideals in what he now apparently felt to be the increasingly resistant expressive forms of Hollywood narrative feature filmmaking.

By the time he makes *State of the Union*, if the final scene is any indication, Capra conceives of filmmaking as being not even remotely like painting a picture, designing a palace, or deftly managing the personnel in a bank. Nor is it similar to finding one's authentic voice in order to speak out loud and clear as a unique, distinctive, individual presence amid a din of alien sounds, nor like translating the language of the heart into the public language of men, as it was in the films of the late thirties. Creation and expression, as this final scene tells us, have become tangled up with a confusion of cables and schedules, a crowd of technicians, and a snarl of personal, social, bureaucratic, and technological concerns that make an individual utterance as complicatedly entailed and circumscribed by forces outside of its control as a speech on television during a long and difficult political nomination campaign. In this world it is questionable whether any speaker can express pure ideals and principles, or whether an individual creative imagination can make any practical difference in the forms of the world. Being a Hollywood director is less like being a painter or a bank president, being an idealistic young Senator or a suddenly rich inheritor of great wealth, than it is like being the manager of a complex political campaign – striking deals, making compromises, negotiating for a position of power among rival interests. In that change in his conception of himself and of the possibilities of personal expression is all of the change implicit in *State of the Union*.

One of Capra's favorite metaphors can be used to describe the change that *State of the Union* seals. Capra was fond of talking of himself on the set in the thirties and forties as a kind of military general in charge of the deployment of an army and the establishment of a line of battle. In more than one of his interviews he uses the metaphor (in a playful sense, but also in a more than playful sense) to describe what it was like to supervise and coordinate the actions of a small army of technicians, actors, and stagehands. It is not surprising that a filmmaker who put such value on bringing order out of what he felt to be emotional, imaginative, and social chaos encroaching everywhere should think of his task this way or admire characters (like Yen – who is of course himself a general, though a failed one, or Tom Dixon, or Florence Fallon) who function as omnicompetent ringmasters in three-ring circuses of competing attractions. It helps one to understand why Capra has a much more than grudging admiration even for villains like Norton and Taylor, who are able deftly to marshal and deploy armies of men and to master complex social and bureaucratic maneuvers.

In these terms what happens in *State of the Union* is that Capra's blessed rage for order wins out over his allegiance to the registration of eccentric, individual imaginative impulse. As a result, Capra becomes an unconscious ally of Conover and Kay and their institutional arrangements of experience in the film. He becomes a technocratic general, almost a Norton or Taylor, in his

he text of desire

[*Lost Horizon* could have been made as] an opera perhaps – but not a musical comedy
... Every great novel, play, or film has always started from transcendental love.
                                        – Frank Capra, Interview at the Teheran Film Festival

ne observes that following *State of the Union* Capra in effect goes from
unsung opera to musical comedy, one has generally indicated the
of the falling off in his work. The energizing instability in his work
by the conflict between his virtually operatic commitment to the ex-
n of the individual imagination and his countervailing desire to honor
and social responsibilities and to integrate the individual into a
unity disappears or becomes trivialized. Good form, social harmony,
ecorous behavior win out over Capra's earlier rival allegiance to the
ration of the excesses, wildness, and unappeasability of the individual
nation. In the four final films – *Riding High, Here Comes the Groom, A*
in the Head, and *Pocketful of Miracles* (though these last two films have a
but too few, moments that weakly recall some of the greatest scenes in
arlier work) – the claims of narrative, social, and photographic responsi-
, the need to integrate the individual responsibly into a group vanquish
ntial wildnesses of photography, editing, and scene making.
hen he was asked in the seventies about a project that was under way to
ake *Lost Horizon* with a Burt Bacharach–Hal David light-musical accom-
ment and Capra responded, as quoted in the epigraph to this chapter, that
Horizon could probably be remade as an opera but never as a Hollywood
sical, he was making the same argument about the nature of his work that
n now. The difference between a Hollywood musical and an Italian opera
he difference between social comedy of manners and the form of high
alistic drama that Capra's films resemble. Even his lightest comedies
idate extremes of feeling, vision, and idealism. In the earlier work, our
ention is insistently directed to these realities of imagination and desire and
ay from the so–called realities of social forms, but in these final films, his

own work. The balance between structu
and unstable in his films, and the war b
exciting drama, as Capra explored how
extend themselves into and have consequer
and time, society and narrative, but now th
tipped decisively in favor of complex, orde
ringmaster (or general) previously involved
of large groups so as to maximize the rele
individual performers, it now dramatically
their distinctive individuality.

In these two postwar films Capra has mov
the power of the individual artist and idealistic
about whether they really can exist, ever expre
the world, or make a vital difference in this bu
they do. Social responsibilities and elaborate sy
family, the world, the studio, and the narrativ
threaten him or her with erasure, bringing the i
into question in the film as much as in the soci

Capra's masterpiece, *It's a Wonderful Life*, is the
is still alive, even though there it has been forced
all social expression. Its marginality gives th
poignancy and makes it the most tough-minded
State of the Union Capra has waked himself up. The
has been bureaucratized and technologized out of ex
society and drama; or it has been trivialized into Gra
high jinks; or, in the final seconds of the film, mos
been normalized and domesticated into a tame cou
activity. Capra's extravagant American dreaming,
posterity, ends in the final minute or two of this fil
lesson in civics.

cinematography becomes "realistic," his plots and characters "reasonable," and his social and psychological point of view "normative," in the blandest, most frightening, most nineteen-fiftyish sense of these words. There are no more truly crazy performances and scenes; no more wild, anarchic dreams and impossible ideals; no more passionate glances or stumbling speeches. Capra gives up on the power of personal style (which is to say, consciousness) to change reality. Reality is now something that all sane people can agree upon and agree to express themselves within, something fixed and immutable. The dream of the free and independent performer shaping an original performance answerable to the most exorbitant energies and mercurial movements of imagination and desire is gone.

It is either gone, or trivialized into mere silliness. The only kinds of personal eccentricity, performative independence, or imaginative wildness left in these films are embodied in instances of zaniness or nuttiness that are (alas) no different from what one might encounter in a contemporaneous Danny Kaye or Jerry Lewis movie, which is to suggest how little is now imaginatively or emotionally at stake in these scenes. Capra seems to confess his own embarrassment at these moments by adopting a tongue-in-cheek tone toward them, as if he wanted to protect them from the viewer's criticism of their superficiality by admitting that he is already aware of it. Consider the bedroom fight between Dave the Dude and Queenie Martin in *Pocketful of Miracles* (which may be usefully contrasted with one of the fights between Stew Smith and Anne Schuyler in *Platinum Blonde*). It is almost a parody of certain scenes in earlier Capra films. It goes through all the motions of being an improvised, exploratory, emotional, spontaneous interaction between two adults in love, but it lacks any important emotional content, which is why it only comes off as dramatic farce and silliness in the tradition of Danny Kaye, Jerry Lewis, or Doris Day.

At other times Capra's self-consciousness about the shallowness of the personal relationships in these films is revealed by his decision to treat the scene as if it were merely a theatrical exercise, an event taking place between two actors or an actor and a director, and not as an authentic emotional exploration at all. Life becomes nothing more than a theatrical game. Capra does this, for example, in the scene between Pete Garvey and Winifred Stanley in *Here Comes the Groom* in which Pete teaches Winifred how to be more sexually alluring (a scene that may be compared with the one that takes place between Anne Mitchell and Long John Willoughby before the first radio broadast in *Meet John Doe* to reveal the enormous differences between the previous and the final work). Nothing is really at stake in the later scene, because life and human interaction have been reduced to a choice of acting strategies. We have entered a comedy-of-manners world in the most cynical and superficial sense, the world almost of Conover and Thorndyke and Norton, in which tones and styles may be put on and taken off as easily as costumes or acting strategies. Profound feelings or beliefs are not at issue, and crises of conscience, of identity, or of the expression of the self in the world never get in the way, since there is nothing beyond equally superficial choices of alternative manners, tones, and styles of acting.

It seems hardly accidental that the central figures in the two films made from original screenplays during this period – *Here Comes the Groom* and *A Hole in the Head* (*Riding High* is a musical-comedy remake of *Broadway Bill*, and *Pocketful of Miracles* is a remake of *Lady for a Day*) – are imagined to be much older than Deeds, Smith, Doe, or any of the principal characters before them. With Grant Matthews, Capra's protagonists "grow up," but their gain in maturity and responsibility represents a sad loss of possibility. Note how in this way, as in so many others, George Bailey is again a transitional figure. We watch him growing up in the course of *It's a Wonderful Life*, growing from boyhood to be as old as Grant Matthews, but his glory is that he never *completely* leaves behind the imaginativeness and emotional sensitivity of his boyhood. His achievement in the film, the source of his imaginative grandeur as well as of his social and expressive pain, is that even as he ages biologically he keeps the boy in the man alive. The dream of childhood goes underground, but it does not die. It keeps erupting into his adult life.★

These final male figures are older, more conservative, more cautious, and their lives are necessarily more entailed with worldly commitments, responsibilities, and obligations, figured concretely in the form of families, wives, and children. The family, as we saw, came into existence in Capra's work as an important, coherent social entity only with *It's a Wonderful Life*,† but even there it was something to be struggled with and against. It was an essential part of the repressive expressive system in the film, a system with which Bailey had a powerful love–hate relationship. With *Here Comes the Groom* (the title tells it all) and *A Hole in the Head*, that has sadly changed. The films internalize the Eisenhower Era's unequivocal affirmation of the social integration and familial "placement" of the individual.

The whole plot and point of these films is, in the best musical-comedy tradition, only to get the central man and woman married to (or at least paired off with) each other by the time the curtain comes down. Many of Capra's earlier films, of course, concluded with the prospect of a marriage ceremony occurring at some point following their endings, but the final, putative marriage in those films was only a fairly minor and unimportant side effect of the central drama. The goal of the film was the creation of visionary community, and the actual, social marriage between the two visionaries or romantics was therefore unimportant and thrown in almost as an afterthought. As Capra's detractors are fond of pointing out (though they misunderstand its significance), the visionary communities in these earlier films almost always

---

★ That is one of the strokes of genius in Capra's use of such a temporally extended narrative and his refusal to use makeup to age his character during the course of it, so that viewers can never quite erase the image of the young George from their minds, no matter how old he subsequently becomes.

† I have already explained why *You Can't Take It with You* is not an exception to this statement.

make the establishment of actual sexual and social communities within them irrelevant, or even at times a positive hindrance. All of which is to suggest why *It Happened One Night* is less a comedy of marriage – or of remarriage, in Stanley Cavell's terms (as the concept applies to the work of Hawks, Lubitsch, Cukor, and Sturges) than a drama of romance, in the richest imaginative resonance of that word. It is the difference between *Every Man In His Humor* and *A Midsummer Night's Dream*. If the first is a comedy of marriage, the second is something else, a comedy of a possible form of relationship that changes the meaning of the word *marriage*, as it is used in the first case, to the point of making it irrelevant.

The heroes in the final films, however, are – like Grant Matthews – too tired, too worn down by events, too realistic and commonsensical to indulge or believe in the idealistic spiritual communities, the shared imaginative extravagances, or the romantic wildnesses of feeling subscribed to by the earlier films and characters. As a consequence, even their occasional expressions of freedom or play seem less like creative or inventive responses to their situations than irresponsible escapes from them, flights of fancy, imaginative vacations from reality. The result is that to the extent that they still do hold onto their extravagant dreams, as Tony Manetta of *A Hole in the Head* does in wanting to build a kind of Disneyland in Florida, even though he has no visible assets or capital, the characters seem not admirably idealistic but positively deluded or foolish. Moreover, the dream of building a theme park is in itself a radical change in the nature of dreaming from what was represented by Jefferson Smith or George Bailey. The dream has become not an alternative to the structures of capitalistic society but an extension of them.

Manetta's Disneyland project is representative of a more general change in the characters and in the kinds of visions and dreams that are allowed them in these films. The principal characters in Capra's earlier films were roughly categorizable into two contrasted types: the dreamers and the schemers. Dreamers like Jerry Strong, Robert Conway, Megan Davis, John Carson, Jefferson Smith, and George Bailey represented possibilities of human expression and relationship fundamentally opposed to the forms of experience subscribed to by schemers like Al Holland, Ralph Standish, Hornsby, Jones, George Conway, John Cedar, Jim Taylor, and Potter. Capra understood, however, that the difference between dreams and schemes was not absolute and unbridgeable. Latent or powerfully frustrated dreams could be sublimated into twisted schemes on occasion, and so once in a while a dreamer could be converted into a diabolical schemer or a schemer be converted back into a dreamer. Typically Capra imagined this – for whatever reason – as identified with the behavior of female characters like Florence Fallon, Kay Arnold, Babe Bennett, Clarissa Saunders, and Anne Mitchell. In any case, the two states of affairs – dreaming and scheming – were fundamentally separate and opposed to each other, and a character's transition from one to the other, when it occurred, was clearly demarcated. That is what eerily changes in his final work. The dreamers and the schemers become at crucial points disturbingly indistinguishable. It is as if, himself increasingly unable to believe in the direct and unsullied expression or enactment of ideals in the world, Capra himself becomes intellectually unable to maintain the clear-cut distinction between the two realms that the earlier films asserted. We have already seen the fuzzing of the boundaries between them in Grant Matthews. Tony Manetta, Apple Annie, Dave the Dude, Dan Brooks, and Pete Garvey (above all) scheme their dreams into existence (Garvey, especially, in quite underhanded and amoral ways). Capra is not, however, criticizing this aspect of their behavior or indicating their limitations; he just seems to have ceased to believe in dreams as absolute alternatives to schemes.

It is surely significant that in choosing to remake *Lady for a Day* and *Broadway Bill*, of all of his earlier films, Capra has chosen the two that most lend themselves to this blurring of motives. (Only *The Miracle Woman* or *Doe* could equally well have been used in a similar way.) In the world of these final films, the direct, passionate expression of personal imagination and desire simply stops. One must, like the opportunistic Pete Garvey or the more genial and likable Tony Manetta, become a schemer, a wheeler-dealer, in order even to attempt to realize one's dreams, but that is, of course, to be essentially different from Jefferson Smith, Jerry Strong, or George Bailey. The dream has not only become more utilitarian, more conservative, and less idealistic; the hero has ethically and socially compromised his expression of it from the start.

I have been concentrating on the male characters, but one can notice an ominous change in the female characters and in their dreams in the final films that parallels the change in the male characters. Again, the contrast between the female characters in the late films and those in Capra's previous work is revealing. In the earlier films, approximately corresponding to the male dreamers, there are female romantics or visionaries (or eventual romantics and visionaries) like Megan Davis, Lulu Smith, or Clarissa Saunders.* The opposing female group in the same films, approximately corresponding to the male schemers, manipulators, and bureaucrats, are the sirens, vamps, and gold diggers, ranging from the vulnerable and innocent (like Violet Bicks) to the more conniving and scheming (like Anne Schuyler, and Susan Paine), to the completely diabolical (like Kay Thorndyke). Whereas the male schemers in these films have public, institutional sources of power, these women have a perhaps more devastating erotic power at their disposal.

Notice how this changes in Capra's final work. Just as the powerful imaginative war in the early films between the male dreamers and the schemers is more or less eliminated in the final films by their being blended into one dreamer-schemer character, so the earlier dichotomy between the female

---

* In passing, one can note, in accordance with Capra's sense of the difference in male and female imaginative expression, that although the women are frequently romantically or socially paired off with the male dreamers in their films, they are almost always more practical and effective than their male counterparts – which is why they most commonly function in their films as secretaries, advisers, or assistants to the male characters.

visionaries and the vamps breaks down in the final work. The women in the last films – the putative mates for the male schemer-dreamers – represent neither imaginative extreme of the earlier work. They are neither vampires nor visionaries. They represent nothing more exciting, more imaginatively stimulating than happy marriageability, cozy domesticity, endless child rearing, and staying in one's place, snugly at home. In short, they almost perfectly embody the values of a housewife in a fifties television drama. They are apron-clad baby makers, meal cookers, and nose wipers, and the dismalness of domestic union with one of them is appalling – but it is a union that these films attempt to endorse.

One can, to force a point, perhaps see Mary Hatch in *It's a Wonderful Life* as predictive of this aspect of Capra's work. She is, unknown to herself or to Capra at this point in his work, the first in a series of figures embodying the joys of drearily safe domesticity that will lead through Mary Matthews to Emmadel Jones and culminate in the aptly named Mrs. Rogers (who would make a fittingly bland and sexless mate for television's Mr.). The crucial and redeeming difference between *It's a Wonderful Life* and the later films is that what Capra and George Bailey struggle against with every ounce of their imaginative energy, Capra and his male leads actually run to embrace in *Here Comes the Groom*.

On the other hand, to be fair to Capra, there are occasional small signs that show that he was not unaware of the imaginative compromises that he was urging in these films. In *Here Comes the Groom*, he attempts to introduce an element of destabilizing but rather limp zaniness into the relationship between his male and female lead, and in *A Hole in the Head* he suggests that Tony Manetta is as aware of the dangers of smothering domesticity as is his creator or a viewer of the film. In that film there is also a character who functions narratively in almost exactly the same way Violet Bicks did in *It's a Wonderful Life*, and with almost as much salutary complexity of result. Her name is Shirl, and she is played by the attractive Carolyn Jones. Her function in *A Hole in the Head*, precisely like Violet's in *It's a Wonderful Life*, is to embody dangerously exciting erotic energies that are squeezed out of the rest of the film. Violet is Capra's built-in criticism of Mary Hatch and all that she represents, just as Shirl is his built-in criticism of Mrs. Rogers (Eleanor Parker) in the other film. One admires Capra's toughness and daring in including Violet and Shirl in the films, but of course what one notices is how hard he then works to control and stage-manage the imaginative and erotic disruptiveness of both of them. Both Violet and Shirl are narratively expunged from their respective films precisely at the points when they become potentially most seriously threatening (which is to say, sexually appealing) to the male characters. (It is not narrative accident that Violet takes a trip out of town immediately before George's breakdown. George or Capra's narrative could not handle her physical availability at that point.) What is wonderful is that Violet *was* so powerfully present for so much of the previous film; Shirl is not allowed to trouble Capra's later narrative or his central character's life nearly so profoundly as Violet did George's.

All of these changes amount to the greatest possible imaginative sellout or compromise. All of the central premises of the earlier films are undermined or betrayed. How is one to explain it? The easiest course would be to blame all of the changes on factors outside of Capra's control. He was no longer a fairly independent producer-writer-director. The scripts were no longer his to write or even approve in advance. The actors were chosen strictly for their drawing power as stars, by producers who did not consult with the director. Musical comedy, the form of three of these final four films, as I have already noticed, is a genre opposed to everything Capra's earlier films imaginatively represent.★ Glenn Ford, Frank Sinatra, and Bing Crosby are actors who would have been incapable of playing the parts performed by Jimmy Stewart and Gary Cooper in the earlier films, even if Capra had had such parts for them to play. Ford and Crosby are too lazy, smug, cocky, and emotionally laid-back in their per-formances. Sinatra, a much greater artist (as a singer), seems simply mystified and embarrassed at his inability to express as an actor the intensity of imagination and feeling that he routinely communicates as a singer in front of a live audience. Furthermore, the obligatory song and dance interludes in the three films starring singers militate against the gradual, progressive creation of the sort of emotional intensity in which Capra specialized.

In another sense, all of these changes in the creative conditions in his work can be traced back to a change in Capra himself. In agreeing to work as a contract director for a large studio and turning over creative control of his films to others (as he had never before done), Capra was expressing in his own career his changed feelings about the expressive relationship of the individual to the forms of society, the filmmaking bureaucracy, and the constraints of narrative. When one searches for the root causes of such a profound spiritual change in a person's life (in this case, an outright failure of spirit), one can only speculate. Was it a matter of age, weariness, and conservatism setting in? Capra began his filmmaking career as a young maverick, an avowed outsider to American bureaucratic and social systems, acutely aware of and sensitive about his alienated position, and that undoubtedly energized his portraits of aliens like himself, the strength of whose marginal positions originated in their creative American alienation and skepticism about the forms and systems of the society of which they were nominally a part. By contrast, he was at this point in his career a grandfather, a Hollywood celebrity of sorts, and a venerable and welcome participant in most of the compromising systems on

---

★ Needless to say, I am not arguing that the mere presence of music (or singing) is at odds with the central energies of Capra's work. Musical orchestrations are crucial to the effects of many of the most imaginatively heightened passages in his early films, and songs are present in early films like *Broadway Bill* or *Deeds*, but there is all the difference in the world between the effect of an emotionally powerful orchestration on the sound track or a song sung in a duet in the early work and a musical-comedy song and dance number in the final films. The earlier music represents a turn away from society and social expression into a realm of powerful emotionality or lyrical reverie; the later use of music represents an assumption that the whole world can be knit together in a community of shared feeling.

the margins of which he had begun. It would be reasonable to surmise that at this point in his life he felt the claims of society and its institutions on behalf of social stability, harmony, and family as he had not previously. Such an explanation does not really suffice, though. Capra was not, after all, very old when he made *State of the Union* (only about fifty), and in any case he had been a father, a fairly wealthy man, and a pillar of the filmmaking community throughout much of the decade of the thirties, and yet the evidences of imaginative compromise are already there.

If a biographical explanation does not go far enough, one can attempt a sociological one. One could perhaps invoke the mood of the times. The Great Depression – certainly the most idealistic period in American life since the era immediately preceding the Civil War (ideals are always brought into service when practical, worldly results are difficult or impossible to attain) – ended with the Second World War. America was, by the time Capra made *Riding High*, as even the title suggests, headed full steam into the tranquilized, willfully optimistic fifties, and the era of mild good feeling of the Eisenhower years. A postwar society weary of the imaginative and social upheavals of the war longed for an extended period of rest. Americans wanted to be told what was right with their institutions and society. We were beginning the Baby Boom, and we wanted the values of the American family and American society affirmed, not questioned. This sociological explanation breaks down, however, when one realizes that the period of Capra's great compromise is almost exactly contemporaneous with some of the greatest, most uncompromisingly radical, and fiercely idealistic work of Norman Mailer, Allen Ginsberg, John Berryman, and Robert Lowell. Even within the constricting formal and intellectual confines of Hollywood feature filmmaking, this was the great era of film noir, certainly one of Hollywood's most imaginatively powerful forms and one that took as its explicit expressive subject precisely the accesses of socially unplaceable feeling and imagination away from which Capra's work emphatically turns in the same period.

Under Capra's own hypothesis of American imaginative individualism it is futile to try to blame some social or political change of climate for the decisive change in his work. One can only humbly conclude that for whatever unknown combination of private and public reasons, after *It's a Wonderful Life* and *State of the Union* Capra's spirit failed. The daring faith in his own powers and those of his protagonists that had animated the melodramatic conflicts in the previous work diminished or died. Since his work had all along tottered in such an uneasy, unstable balance of contradictory feelings and impulses, the slightest change in the mix of forces within it was apparently enough to do in its profound drama, to tip it away from individual impulse toward a resigned acceptance of bland cinematic good form, from the claims of the unappeasable imagination to the responsibilities of society.

The strength of the earlier work was the way it shuttled between powerful and usually conflicting imaginative extremes. The energies at war within it were embodied most visibly in the opposing camps of characters and the irreconcilable imaginative positions represented in the films. Wild-eyed dreamers were pitted against Machiavellian schemers. Exalted personal ideals confronted and had to negotiate Byzantine, repressive bureaucracies of expression. At the most extreme, good confronted evil. These conflicts, normally criticized as the melodramatic aspects of Capra's work, in the pejorative sense of the word, were actually their strength.

It is not that a melodramatist like Capra (or a melodramatist like Henry James or Norman Mailer, for that matter) actually believes in, or wants a viewer to believe in, the existence in the real world of heroes and villains walking the streets, of gods or devils manipulating or responding to our everyday actions, or of the possibility of absolute moral choices between saintly goodness and diabolical evil in ordinary life. To understand the characters and conflicts in the films in this way is to be entirely too literal-minded. These figures and principles of good and evil, of light and darkness, of extremes of individualistic emotion and idealism and of bureaucratic systematization and manipulativeness, and the titanic struggle between them in Capra's middle films are symbolic representations of the drama of our imaginative struggles of possession and our feelings of dispossession in the world. They are metaphoric expressions of the grand, glorious energies of the human imagination in conflict with itself or with the forms and forces of expression in society. Life admits the possibility of the existence not of such titanic conflicts of characters and events but of internal imaginative conflicts involving such extreme, excessive, irreconcilable energies and feelings. These melodramatic conflicts are Capra's way of representing in his film (and of generating in a viewer) a level of energy and conflict that is true to the actual drama and intensity of our inner lives, our exalted dreams, and passionate feelings when faced with the difficulty of their expression in the world. The Gothicism of some of the films' expressive styles is necessary to do justice to the exorbitance of desire and imagination at war with repressive forms of expression.

The final films leave melodrama behind. Extreme expressive styles and wild states of passion disappear. Life is lived in a middle ground of expressive compromise, mildness, and blandness (with occasional interludes of mere zaniness or silliness, the legacy of Grant Matthews's airplane tricks, the last sad remnants of the earlier flights of imagination). Life is imagined to be transacted, pathetically, by reasonable, moderate-minded family men and women who are willing to accept a state of middlebrow, middle-class domesticity as their definition of its most exalted possibility. There are no heroes or villains, no Manichean confrontations, few imaginative exorbitancies or violences of feeling or expression in the later work, because imagination and desire have been tamed. We have entered the heaven of Benjamin Franklin or of the local chamber of commerce. Imaginative wildnesses, excesses, and conflicts to the death are no longer possible or desirable. They are no longer necessary, metaphorically or stylistically, to evoke Capra's sense of life. There is no melodrama or Gothicism, because the passion has subsided, the faith in the individual's truly extraordinary and exceptional imaginative and emotional energies has failed.

Perhaps the clearest evidence of this imaginative shift is the change in the nature of the particular individual performances in the films. In the previous work, from *That Certain Thing* through parts of *State of the Union*, all of the major characters were at least potentially capable of turning in dazzlingly powerful, creatively inventive, and emotionally commanding cinematic performances – both the good characters and the bad; the male schemers and the dreamers; the female romantics and visionaries, and the vamps and gold diggers. Whether their power came from their diabolical, Iago-like capacities for evil improvisation (in the case of figures like Potter, Taylor, and Norton); from their extraordinary erotic energy and expressiveness, their sexual wiliness, and their beauty (in the case of Anne Schuyler or any of the characters played by Barbara Stanwyck in the early thirties); from their boyish emotionality and idealism (in the case of Deeds, Jefferson Smith, and Bailey); or from a combination of other things, Capra's principal characters (and usually even his bit players as well) were emotionally powerful and imaginatively stimulating. They were figures who embodied, in the very extravagance, audacity, and intensity of their dramatic performances (both as characters and as actors) Capra's affirmation of the enormous energy of the human spirit and imagination. They figured his faith in the power and potential autonomy of individual performers, whether for good or evil. That defines what has altered in the final work. Not only are there no extravagant, passionate idealists or dreamers like Smith or Bailey, but there are no evil geniuses like Taylor or Norton either, no black-frocked diabolical schemers like Potter, no dazzling sirens like Anne Schuyler or Kay Arnold, no erotic teases like Violet Bicks, no feisty, spunky, almost indomitable heroes or heroines like Dixon, Stew Smith, Saunders, or Bennett.

That is, Capra's critics would claim, a gain for realism, a moving of his work into a world like our own, a world without heroes and villains, a leveled world of mediocrity, and great, dim grayness. This alleged gain for realism, however, is in fact the greatest, saddest loss for the work's truth to the infinity of our souls and imaginations, or at least the truth of these things as they can be, at their best and noblest.

The only way that Capra might have saved his work after *State of the Union*, the direction implicit in it and the immediately preceding work that he could legitimately have followed, is by having become an out-and-out maker of the toughest of tough late-forties and fifties films noir. It is not accidental that Capra increasingly flirts with film noir modes of photography and narration in *Mr. Smith Goes to Washington*, *Doe*, *Arsenic and Old Lace*, *It's a Wonderful Life*, and *State of the Union*. As different as these individual films are from one another, that is one thing they have in common, and the film noir episodes inserted within them are the final gasp of imaginative energy, extravagance, and unappeasability in Capra's work. They represent anarchic, dangerous, disruptive energies that will not be controlled or expressed within the blander social forms of the societies rendered within the films or the dramatic interactions that are scripted into them.

It is as if Capra, aided and abetted by a string of movie reviewers, publicists, and producers who had always imperfectly understood his films, misread his own previous work. He convinced himself that his strength was his "up with people" populism and sentimentality and proceeded to accept scripts along these lines, when in fact his was, from the very start of his career, the opposite of such a sensibility. He was the supreme representative in American film of imagination that exceeds any available social expression or accommodation, and a cinematic explorer of crises of self-representation and self-definition. Capra, from the beginning of his career, plunged into the contradictions that have riddled the American expressive experiment in all of our greatest art, to worry the relationship between the would-be free imagination and a society that was felt everywhere to mediate, compromise, and threaten its freedom and expression. He is the greatest filmmaker after Chaplin and before Cassavetes of individuals functioning on the creative margins of social discourse and of the challenges and exhilarations of their attempts to find a social home and form of expression for imagination and desire.

The true American successors of his work in the forties are not Mary Poppinsish musical comedies or sentimental Andy Hardy–like paeans to the virtues of family and small-town community but the films that reacted most violently against these things: the films noir of the forties, the grand domestic melodramas or women's weepies of the forties and fifties, and the brooding Method-acting extravaganzas of emotion in search of an adequate form of expression of the fifties and sixties. It is films like *Written on the Wind*, *Giant*, *A Place in the Sun*, *East of Eden*, *A Streetcar Named Desire*, *On the Waterfront*, and *Rebel without a Cause* and performances like those turned in by Marlon Brando, James Dean, and Montgomery Clift in these films and others that would unconsciously continue the trajectory of Capra's work in American film. It was, I would suggest, with these sorts of projects and performers that Capra might conceivably have found himself and reestablished his filmmaking reputation, not with Crosby or Sinatra musicals.

The filmmaker of the fifties and early sixties with the most profound similarity of vision to Capra's in his greatest work was Nicholas Ray.* It was he and his characters, in their mixture of exalted, romantic idealism and doomed film noir brooding, who, after Capra betrayed his own genius to

---

* As a preparatory step in defining Capra's imaginative position in relation to Nicholas Ray, one might begin by comparing the narrative function of the deserted mansion in *It's a Wonderful Life* with the one in *Rebel without a Cause*. One notices that Ray does not seem to believe in the possibility of establishing a real family in a real social space in the way that Capra does. His "family" (with Natalie Wood and James Dean as mother and father and Sal Mineo as son) is only a fantasy one, a community of the imagination, just as their inhabitation of their "home" is only a matter of play-acting adult behavior. That represents a crucial shift from Capra's attitudes: Ray sees free and creative imaginative expressions possible only as alternatives to or escapes from actual social forms of organization and understanding.

make these final films, came closest to continuing Capra's operatic, melo-dramatic, grandly romantic representations of a world potentially responsive to and distorted by the forces of imagination and desire and yet everywhere working to frustrate the expression of them. The way Ray proceeded, especially in his great *Rebel without a Cause*, was finally, for Capra, the road not taken.

Edward Hopper, *New York Movie*. Collection, Museum of Modern Art, New York. This is a deliberate transformation of Homer's *Gargoyles of Nôtre Dame* (see pp. 15–16). The gaze outward becomes a withdrawal inward. The architectural energies of the thirteenth-century cathedral reappear in the forms of a twentieth-century movie palace. The cathedral and its gargoyles were a realization and externalization of communal fantasies; the movie palace is a temple to inner space, a cave in which public reality is punctured by private fantasies and derealized into the stuff of dreams. The cathedral is a grand, public expression of feelings; the movie palace opens to view secret dreams and wishes. Note that the presiding spirit of the one scene is masculine and of the other is feminine.

Filmography

1921

Fulta Fisher's Boarding House (Fireside Productions/Pathé). Producers: G. F. Harris, David Supple. Screenplay: Walter Montague, from the poem "The Ballad of Fisher's Boarding-House" by Rudyard Kipling. Camera: Roy Wiggins. With: Mildred Owens, Ethan Allen, Olaf Skavian, Gerald Griffin.

1926

The Strong Man (First National). Producer: Harry Langdon. Screenplay: Arthur Ripley, Capra, Hal Conklin, Robert Eddy. Camera: Elgin Lessley, Glenn Kershner. With: Harry Langdon, Priscilla Bonner, Gertrude Astor, William V. Mong.

1927

Long Pants (First National). Producer: Harry Langdon. Screenplay: Arthur Ripley, Robert Eddy. Camera: Elgin Lessley, Glenn Kershner. With: Harry Langdon, Priscilla Bonner, Alma Bennett, Betty Francisco.

For the Love of Mike (First National). Producer: Robert Kane. Screenplay: Leland Hayward, J. Clarkson Miller, from the story "Hell's Kitchen" by John Moroso. Camera: Ernest Haller. With: Ben Lyon, George Sidney, Ford Sterling, Claudette Colbert.

1928

That Certain Thing (Columbia). Producer: Harry Cohn. Screenplay: Elmer Harris. Camera: Joseph Walker. With: Viola Dana, Ralph Graves, Burr McIntosh, Aggie Herring.

So This Is Love (Columbia). Producer: Harry Cohn. Screenplay: Norman Springer, Elmer Harris, Rex Taylor. Camera: Ray June. With: Shirley Mason, Buster Collier, Johnnie Walker, Ernie Adams.

The Matinee Idol (Columbia). Producer: Harry Cohn. Screenplay: Elmer Harris, Peter Milne, from the story "Come Back to Aaron" by Robert Lord and Ernest S. Pagano. With: Bessie Love, Johnnie Walker, Lionel Belmore, Ernest Hilliard.

The Way of the Strong (Columbia). Producer: Harry Cohn. Screenplay: William Counselman, Peter Milne. Camera: Ben Reynolds. With: Mitchell Lewis, Alice Day, Margaret Livingston, Theodore von Eltz.

Say It with Sables (Columbia). Producers: Capra, Harry Cohn. Screenplay: Capra, Peter Milne, Dorothy Howell. Camera: Joseph Walker. With: Helene Chadwick, Francis X. Bushman, Margaret Livingston, Arthur Rankin.

The Power of the Press (Columbia). Producers: Capra, Jack Cohn. Screenplay: Frederick A. Thompson, Sonya Levien. Camera: Chet Lyons. With: Douglas Fairbanks, Jr., Jobyna Ralston, Mildred Harris, Philo McCullough.

Submarine (Columbia). Producers: Irvin Willat, Harry Cohn. Screenplay: Winifred Dunn. Camera: Joseph Walker. With: Jack Holt, Dorothy Revier, Ralph Graves, Clarence Burton.

1929

The Younger Generation (Columbia). Producers: Capra, Jack Cohn. Screenplay: Sonya Levien, Howard J. Green, from the play *It Is to Laugh* by Fannie Hurst. Camera: Ted Tetzlaff, Ben Reynolds. With: Jean Hersholt, Lina Basquette, Ricardo Cortez, Rex Lease.

The Donovan Affair (Columbia). Producers: Capra, Harry Cohn. Screenplay: Howard J. Green, Dorothy Howell, from the play by Owen Davis. Camera: Ted Tetzslaff. With: Jack Holt, Dorothy Revier, William Collier, Jr., Agnes Ayres.

Flight (Columbia). Producers: Capra, Harry Cohn. Screenplay: Capra, Ralph Graves. Camera: Joseph Walker. With: Jack Holt, Lila Lee, Ralph Graves, Alan Roscoe.

1930

Ladies of Leisure (Columbia). Producers: Capra, Harry Cohn. Screenplay: Jo Swerling, from the play *Ladies of the Evening* by Milton Herbert Gropper. Camera: Joseph Walker. With: Barbara Stanwyck, Lowell Sherman, Ralph Graves, Marie Prevost.

Rain or Shine (Columbia). Producers: Capra, Harry Cohn. Screenplay: Dorothy Howell, Jo Swerling, James Gleason, Maurice Marks, from the play by Gleason. Camera: Joseph Walker. With: Joe Cook, Louise Fazenda, Joan Peers, Dave Chasen.

1931

Dirigible (Columbia). Producers: Capra, Harry Cohn. Screenplay: Jo Swerling, Dorothy Howell, from a story by Frank Wead. Camera: Joseph Walker, Elmer Dyer. With: Jack Holt, Ralph Graves, Fay Wray, Hobart Bosworth.

The Miracle Woman (Columbia). Producers: Capra, Harry Cohn. Screenplay: Jo Swerling, Dorothy Howell, from the play *Bless You, Sister* by John Meehan and Robert Riskin. Camera: Joseph Walker. With: Barbara Stanwyck, David Manners, Sam Hardy, Beryl Mercer.

Platinum Blonde (Columbia). Producers: Capra, Harry Cohn. Screenplay: Robert Riskin, Jo Swerling, Dorothy Howell, from a story by Harry E. Chandler and Douglas

W. Churchill. Camera: Joseph Walker. With: Loretta Young, Robert Williams, Jean Harlow, Halliwell Hobbes.

1932

Forbidden (Columbia). Producers: Capra, Harry Cohn. Screenplay: Jo Swerling, from a story by Capra. Camera: Joseph Walker. With: Barbara Stanwyck, Adolphe Menjou, Ralph Bellamy, Dorothy Peterson.

American Madness (Columbia). Producers: Capra, Harry Cohn. Screenplay: Robert Riskin. Camera: Joseph Walker. With: Walter Huston, Pat O' Brien, Kay Johnson, Constance Cummings, Gavin Gordon.

1933

The Bitter Tea of General Yen (Columbia). Producers: Capra, Walter Wanger. Screenplay: Edward Paramore, from the novel by Grace Zaring Stone. Camera: Joseph Walker. With: Barbara Stanwyck, Nils Asther, Toshia Mori, Walter Connolly.

Lady for a Day (Columbia). Producer: Capra. Screenplay: Robert Riskin from the short story "Madame La Gimp" by Damon Runyon. Camera: Joseph Walker. With: Warren William, May Robson, Guy Kibbee, Glenda Farrell, Ned Sparks.

1934

It Happened One Night (Columbia). Producers: Capra, Harry Cohn. Screenplay: Robert Riskin, from the short story "Night Bus" by Samuel Hopkins Adams. Camera: Joseph Walker. With: Clark Gable, Claudette Colbert, Walter Connolly, Roscoe Karns.

Broadway Bill (Columbia). Producers: Capra, Harry Cohn. Screenplay: Robert Riskin, from a story by Mark Hellinger. Camera: Joseph Walker. With: Warner Baxter, Myrna Loy, Walter Connolly, Helen Vinson.

1936

Mr. Deeds Goes to Town (Columbia). Producer: Capra. Screenplay: Robert Riskin, from the story "Opera Hat" by Clarence Buddington Kelland. Camera: Joseph Walker. With: Gary Cooper, Jean Arthur, George Bancroft, Lionel Stander, Douglass Dumbrille.

1937

Lost Horizon (Columbia). Producer: Capra. Screenplay: Robert Riskin, from the novel by James Hilton. Camera: Joseph Walker. With: Ronald Colman, Jane Wyatt, John Howard, Thomas Mitchell, Sam Jaffe.

1938

You Can't Take It with You (Columbia). Producer: Capra. Screenplay: Robert Riskin, from the play by George S. Kaufman and Moss Hart. Camera: Joseph Walker. With: Jean Arthur, Lionel Barrymore, James Stewart, Edward Arnold, Ann Miller.

1939

Mr. Smith Goes to Washington (Columbia). Producer: Capra. Screenplay: Sidney Buchman, from the story "The Gentleman from Montana" by Lewis R. Foster. Camera: Joseph Walker. With: James Stewart, Jean Arthur, Claude Rains, Edward Arnold, Thomas Mitchell.

1941

Meet John Doe (Warner Bros.). Producer: Capra. Screenplay: Robert Riskin, from a story by Richard Connell and Robert Presnell. Camera: George Barnes. With: Gary Cooper, Barbara Stanwyck, Edward Arnold, Walter Brennan, James Gleason.

Arsenic and Old Lace (Warner Bros.). Producer: Capra. Screenplay: Julius J. Epstein, Philip G. Epstein, from the play by Joseph Kesselring. Camera: Sol Polito. With: Cary Grant, Priscilla Lane, Raymond Massey, Josephine Hull, Jean Adair. (Released in 1944)

1942

Why We Fight: Prelude to War (U.S. War Department). Producer: Capra. Screenplay: Anthony Veiller, Eric Knight. Narrator: Walter Huston.

1943

Why We Fight: The Nazis Strike (U.S. War Department). Producer: Capra. Codirector: Anatole Litvak. Screenplay: Eric Knight, Anthony Veiller, Robert Heller. Narrators: Walter Huston, Veiller.

Why We Fight: Divide and Conquer (U.S. War Department). Producer: Capra. Codirector: Anatole Litvak. Screenplay: Anthony Veiller, Robert Heller.

Know Your Ally: Britain (U.S. War Department). Producer: Capra. Director: Anthony Veiller. Screenplay: Eric Knight, Veiller, Jo Swerling. Narrators: Walter Huston, Veiller.

Why We Fight: The Battle of Britain (U.S. War Department). Producer: Capra. Director: Anthony Veiller. Screenplay: Veiller. Narrators: Walter Huston, Veiller.

1944

Why We Fight: The Battle of Russia (U.S. War Department). Producer: Capra. Director: Anatole Litvak. Screenplay: Litvak, Anthony Veiller, Robert Heller. Narrators: Walter Huston, Veiller.

Why We Fight: The Battle of China (U.S. War Department). Producer: Capra. Director: Anatole Litvak. Screenplay: Anthony Veiller, Robert Heller. Narrators: Walter Huston, Veiller.

The Negro Soldier (U.S. War Department). Producer: Capra. Codirector: Stuart Heisler. Screenplay: Carlton Moss, Jo Swerling, Ben Hecht. With: W. C. Handy.

Tunisian Victory (U.S. War Department). Producers: Capra, Hugh Stewart. Codirector: Stewart. Screenplay: J. L. Hodson, Anthony Veiller. Narrators: Leon Genn, Veiller, Bernard Miles, Burgess Meredith.

1945

Why We Fight: War Comes to America (U.S. War Department). Producer: Capra. Director: Anatole Litvak. Screenplay: Litvak, Anthony Veiller. Narrators: Walter Huston, Veiller.

Know Your Enemy: Germany (U.S. War Department). Producer: Capra. Director: Gottfried Reinhardt. Screenplay: Reinhardt, Anthony Veiller, Ernst Lubitsch, William L. Shirer. Narrators: Walter Huston, Veiller.

Know Your Enemy: Japan (U.S. War Department). Producer: Capra. Codirector: Joris Ivens. Screenplay: Ivens, Irving Wallace, Edgar Peterson, Carl Foreman, Theodore Geisel. Narrators: Walter Huston, Dana Andrews.

Your Job in Germany (U.S. War Department). Producer: Capra. Narrator: Dana Andrews.

Two Down and One to Go (U.S. War Department). Producer: Capra. Screenplay: Anthony Veiller. Narrators: Veiller, U.S. Chief of Staff Gen. George C. Marshall.

1946

It's a Wonderful Life (Liberty Films/RKO). Producer: Capra. Screenplay: Frances Goodrich, Albert Hackett, Capra, Jo Swerling, from the short story "The Greatest Gift" by Philip Van Doren Stern. Camera: Joseph Walker, Joseph Biroc. With: James Stewart, Donna Reed, Lionel Barrymore, Thomas Mitchell, Henry Travers.

1948

State of the Union (Liberty Films/MGM). Producer: Capra. Screenplay: Anthony Veiller, Myles Connolly, from the play by Howard Lindsay and Russel Crouse. Camera: George J. Folsey. With: Spencer Tracy, Katharine Hepburn, Van Johnson, Angela Lansbury, Adolphe Menjou.

1950

Riding High (Paramount). Producer: Capra. Screenplay: Robert Riskin, Melville Shavelson, Jack Rose, from the screenplay *Broadway Bill* by Riskin and a story by Mark Hellinger. Camera: George Barnes, Ernest Laszlo. With: Bing Crosby, Coleen Gray, Charles Bickford, Frances Gifford, William Demarest.

1951

Here Comes the Groom (Paramount). Producer: Capra. Screenplay: Virginia Van Upp. Liam O'Brien, Myles Connolly, from a story by Robert Riskin and O'Brien. Camera: George Barnes. With: Bing Crosby, Jane Wyman, Alexis Smith, Franchot Tone, James Barton.

1956

Our Mr. Sun (Bell Telephone). Producer: Capra. Screenplay: Capra. Camera: Harold Wellman. With: Dr. Frank Baxter, Eddie Albert, Sterling Holloway.

1957

Hemo the Magnificent (Bell Telephone). Producer: Capra. Screenplay: Capra. Camera: Harold Wellman. With: Dr. Frank Baxter, Richard Carlson, Sterling Holloway.

The Strange Case of the Cosmic Rays (Bell Telephone). Producer: Capra. Screenplay: Capra, Jonathon Latimer. Camera: Harold Wellman, Ellis Carter. With: Dr. Frank Baxter, Richard Carlson, Bill and Cora Baird's Marionettes.

1958

The Unchained Goddess (Bell Telephone). Producer: Capra. Director: Richard Carlson. Screenplay: Capra, Jonathon Latimer. Camera: Harold Wellman. With: Dr. Frank Baxter, Richard Carlson.

1959

A Hole in the Head (Sincap/United Artists). Producer: Capra. Screenplay: Arnold Schulman, from his play. Camera: William H. Daniels. With: Frank Sinatra, Edward G. Robinson, Eddie Hodges, Eleanor Parker, Thelma Ritter.

1961

Pocketful of Miracles (Franton/United Artists). Producer: Capra. Screenplay: Hal Kanter, Harry Tugend, from the screenplay *Lady for a Day* by Robert Riskin and the story "Madam La Gimp" by Damon Runyon. Camera: Robert Bronner. With: Glenn Ford, Bette Davis, Hope Lange, Peter Falk, Ann-Margret.

1964

Rendezvous in Space (Martin–Marietta Corp.). Producer: Capra. Screenplay: Capra. With: Danny Thomas, Tom Fadden, Benny Rubin.

Selected bibliography

By Frank Capra

"A Sick Dog Tells Where It Hurts," *Esquire* (January 1936), 87–8, 130.
"Breaking Hollywood's Pattern of Sameness," *New York Times Magazine* (May 5, 1946), 18, 57.
"The Cinematographer's Place in the Motion Picture Industry," *Cinematographic Annual* (1931), 13–14.
"Do I Make You Laugh?" *Films and Filming* (September 1962), 14–15.
"The Gag Man," in Charles Reed Jones (ed.), *Breaking Into Movies*. New York: The Unicorn Press, 1927, pp. 164–71.
"The Great Days of Hollywood Are Over," *U.S. News and World Report* (August 25, 1980), 66.
Introduction, to Bob Thomas, *Directors in Action*. New York: Bobbs Merrill and Co., 1973, pp. vii–x.
The Name above the Title. New York: Macmillan, 1971 (Capra's autobiography).
"Sacred Cows to the Slaughter," *Stage* (July 1936), 40–1.
"Unforgettable Jimmy Durante," *Reader's Digest* (November 1981), 115–20.

Interviews and profiles

Bailey, George, "Why We (Should Not) Fight," *Take One* (May–June 1974), 10–12.
Bishop, Harv, "Frank Capra Profile," *Classic Film Collector* (Winter 1976), 26–7.
Bressan, Arthur, and Moran, Michael, "Frank Capra Goes to College," *Andy Warhol's Interview* (June 1972), 25, 26, 30.
"Capra Corn," *Newsweek* (December 18, 1961), 97–8.
Childs, James, "Capra Today," *Film Comment* (November–December 1972), 22–3.
"Dialogue on Film," *American Film* (October 1978), 39–50.
Dougherty, Frank, "He Has the Common Touch," *The Christian Science Monitor* (November 9, 1938), 4–5.
"Frank Capra," American Film Institute Seminar, 1978 (videotape in the motion picture collection of the Library of Congress).
"Frank Capra Given American Film Institute's 10th Life Achievement Award," *New York Times* (March 6, 1982), 20.

501

"Frank Capra Interviewed at the Second Teheran International Film Festival," *American Cinematographer* (February 1974), 168–9.

"Frank Capra," *The Columbia Oral History Project*, 1960 (an unpublished interview manuscript available in the Library of Congress).

Glatzer, Richard, and Raeburn, John (eds.), *Frank Capra: The Man and His Films*. Ann Arbor: University of Michigan Press, 1975, pp. 16–39.

Hamman, Mary, "Meet Frank Capra Making a Picture," *Good Housekeeping* (March, 1941), 11, 74.

Hargrave, H. S., "Interview with Frank Capra," *Literature/Film Quarterly* IX (No. 3) (1981), 189–204.

Harriman, Margaret Case, "Mr. and Mrs. Frank Capra," *Ladies Home Journal* (April 1941), 35, 153–5.

Hellman, Geoffrey T., "Thinker in Hollywood," *New Yorker* (February 24, 1940), 23–8.

Henstell, Bruce, "Frank Capra: 'One Man–Film,'" *Discussion* (No. 3), Washington, D.C.: American Film Institute, 1971.

Jacobs, Lewis, "Capra at Work," *Theatre Arts* (January 1941), 43–8; reprinted in Glatzer and Raeburn (eds.), pp. 40–3.

Johnson, Alva, "Capra Shoots as He Pleases," *The Saturday Evening Post* (May 14, 1938), 9, 67–74.

Karp, Walter, "The Patriotism of Frank Capra," *Esquire* (February 1981), 33–5.

Minoff, Philip, "Frank Talk from Capra," *Cue* (November 24, 1956), 16.

Schickel, Richard, "Frank Capra," in *The Men Who Made the Movies*. New York: Atheneum, 1975, pp. 57–92.

Thompson, Howard, "Capra, 74, Looks Back at Film Career," *New York Times* (June 24, 1971), 32.

Wechsberg, Joseph, "Meet Frank Capra," *Reader's Digest* (October 1947), 80–3.

Critical studies and reviews of the films

Agee, James, *Agee on Film*. Boston: Beacon Press, 1958, pp. 40, 233–4.

Braudy, Leo, and Dickstein, Morris (eds.), *Great Film Directors*. New York: Oxford University Press, 1978, pp. 145–172.

Cavell, Stanley, *Pursuits of Happiness: The Hollywood Comedy of Remarriage*. Cambridge: Harvard University Press, 1981, pp. 71–109.

Dickstein, Morris, "It's a wonderful life, but . . .," *American Film* (May 1980), 42–7.

Ferguson, Otis, *The Film Criticism of Otis Ferguson*. Philadelphia: Temple University Press, pp. 58–9, 127–8, 236–9, 273–4, 349–51.

Glatzer, Richard, and Raeburn, John (eds.), *Frank Capra: The Man and His Work*. Ann Arbor: University of Michigan Press, 1975.

Greene, Graham, *The Pleasure-Dome: The Collected Film Criticism of Graham Greene*. London: Secker and Warburg, 1972, pp. 145–8, 203–4, 260–1.

Griffith, Richard, *Frank Capra*. London: British Film Institute, 1951.

Hochman, Stanley (ed.), *American Film Directors*. New York: Fredrick Ungar, 1974, pp. 29–37.

Maland, Charles J., *Frank Capra*. Boston: Twayne Publishers, 1980.

Pechter, William, *Twenty-Four Times a Second*. New York: Harper and Row, 1971, pp. 123–32.

Poague, Leland, *The Cinema of Frank Capra*. New York: Barnes, 1975.

Price, James, "Capra and the American Dream," *London Magazine* (January, 1964), 85–93.

Ray, Robert B., *A Certain Tendency of the Hollywood Cinema, 1930–1980*. Princeton: Princeton University Press, 1985, pp. 179–215.

Willis, Donald, *The Films of Frank Capra*. Metuchen, N. J.: The Scarecrow Press, 1974.

Wood, Robin, "Ideology, Genre, Auteur," *Film Comment* (January–February, 1977), 46–51.

Published screenplays

It Happened One Night, in John Gassner and Dudley Nichols (eds.), *Twenty Best Film Plays*. New York: Crown, 1943 (reprinted in 1977 by Garland Publishing, Inc.).

It's a Wonderful Life, in Jeanine Basinger (ed.), *The "It's a Wonderful Life" Book*. New York: Knopf, 1986.

Lady for a Day, in Lorraine Noble (ed.), *Four Star Scripts*. New York: Garland Publishing, Inc., 1978.

Mr. Smith Goes to Washington, in Jerry Wald and Richard Macaulay (eds.), *Best Pictures, 1939–1940*. New York: Dodd, 1940. Also in John Gassner and Dudley Nichols (eds.), *Twenty Best Film Plays*. New York: Crown, 1943 (reprinted in 1977 by Garland Publishing, Inc.).

You Can't Take It With You, in Frank Vreeland (ed.), *Foremost Films of 1938*. New York: Pitman Publishing Corporation, 1939.

General references

Scherle, Victor and Levy, William Turner, *The Films of Frank Capra*. Secaucus, N. J.: Citadel Press, 1977.

Thomas, Bob, *King Cohn: The Life and Times of Harry Cohn*. New York: G. P. Putnam, 1967.

Wolfe, Charles, *A Reference Guide to the Films of Frank Capra* (forthcoming from G. K. Hall in 1987).

Index